GATES TO THE OLD CITY

A Book of Jewish Legends

RAPHAEL PATAI

◆ AVON
PUBLISHERS OF BARD, CAMELOT AND DISCUS BOOKS

GATES TO THE OLD CITY is an original publication of Avon Books.
This work has never before appeared in book form.

AVON BOOKS
A division of
The Hearst Corporation
959 Eighth Avenue
New York, New York 10019

Copyright © 1980 by Raphael Patai
Cover illustration by John Swanson
Published by arrangement with the author
Library of Congress Catalog Card Number: 80-66154
ISBN: 0-380-76091-6

First Avon Printing, October, 1980

AVON TRADEMARK REG. U.S. PAT. OFF. AND IN
OTHER COUNTRIES, MARCA REGISTRADA, HECHO EN
U.S.A.

Printed in the U.S.A.

DR. RAPHAEL PATAI is a noted anthropologist, Biblical scholar, and author. He taught Hebrew at the Hebrew University of Jerusalem, and served as professor of anthropology at Dropsie University and at Fairleigh Dickinson University, and as visiting professor at the University of Pennsylvania and at Princeton, Columbia, Ohio State, and New York Universities. He was also consultant to the Department of Social Affairs of the United Nations Secretariat, director of the Syria-Lebanon-Jordan research project of the Human Relations Area Files, director of research at the Herzl Institute, and editor of the Herzl Press. Dr. Patai is the author of twenty-six books, including *Hebrew Myths* (with Robert Graves), *Man and Temple in Ancient Jewish Myth and Ritual, Golden River to Golden Road: Society, Culture and Change in the Middle East, Israel Between East and West, The Kingdom of Jordan, Tents of Jacob: The Diaspora Yesterday and Today, Myth and Modern Man, The Arab Mind, The Myth of the Jewish Race* (with Jennifer Patai-Wing), and *The Jewish Mind.* His two latest books, *The Hebrew Goddess* and *The Messiah Texts,* were published by Avon Books in 1978 and 1979 respectively.

CONTENTS

CONTENTS (continued)

PREFACE

This anthology is intended to serve as a guide and an introduction to the vast storehouses of the Agada (legend) literature accumulated by the Jews in the course of three thousand years. It contains selections from the seven major genres of Jewish literature that are, among other things, repositories of legends: the Bible, the Apocrypha, the Talmud, the Midrash, the Kabbala, folklore, and Hasidism. The background notes which precede each of these parts give essential information about the genre.

Only a very few legends about the Messiah have been included, since about a year ago I published all the material I could find on that subject in a separate volume entitled *The Messiah Texts* (New York: Avon Books, 1979, liii, 373 pp.).

In making the selections, preference was given to texts thus far not available in English. However, whether previously translated or not, all the selections contained in this volume were translated anew by me from the original Hebrew, Aramaic, Greek, Yiddish, or German sources, because I found the existing translations to be not quite satisfactory. An exception is the story "The Six Days and the Seven Gates" by Yitzhak Navon, which was translated by Misha Louvish, and which appears as prologue to the book. I wish to express here my thanks to President Navon for his permission to include his beautiful legend in this volume. In preparing my own translations I endeavored to retain, as far as possible, the flavor of the original texts, which reflect stylistic norms and ideals quite different from those one is used to in English.

My thanks are also due to Marc Bregman, Gedalyah Nigal, and Dov Noy of Jerusalem and Aliza Shenhar of Haifa, who supplied some of the material included in the sections of folklore and Hasidism.

R.P.

Forest Hills, N.Y.
April 1980

PROLOGUE

The Six Days and the Seven Gates

YITZHAK NAVON

On the day the king of Ammon went to Egypt the verdict was sealed. And the men of Jerusalem clapped their hands in woe and said:

"What will become of us now, for all the Arabs have encompassed us, from the River Euphrates even unto Egypt?"

There was a certain old man there; while they sat and grieved, he sat and laughed.

"Why are you laughing?" they asked him.

"Why do you grieve?" he asked in reply.

"Because war approaches," they replied, "and our enemies are cruel, and we do not know which of our sons will be killed, and what will happen to our little ones, and who will be the victor and who the vanquished."

He laughed and said: "Of you the sages said: No man recognizes his own miracle. Do you not see that it has all been brought about by the Holy One, blessed be He, to produce a miracle the like of which the world has never seen before?"

"And what will become of Jerusalem?" they asked.

He said to them: "He that does not love Jerusalem, what does he see in her? Stones and dust! And he that loves her, what does he see in her? Radiance and light! She is won only by suffering; she responds only to him who woos her with yearning and supplication, and gives his soul for her sake."

Before a few days had passed, the Land was on fire in every corner—North and South and East. And the children of Israel went forth to war and put their lives in jeopardy, and they were victorious everywhere until they reached Jerusalem.

Seven gates there were in the walls of Jerusalem, and they did not know by which gate they should enter, for every gate leapt forward, dancing before them, and said:

"Enter through me, for I deserve you more than any of them."

The Holy One, blessed be He, sat in the Heavenly Assembly, with the ministering angels on His right hand and His left.

"Which gate deserves to have the redemption come through it?" He asked them. "For two angels do not perform the same mission, nor two gates bring the same salvation."

And they did not know what to answer. Michael rose and said:

"Master of the World! All are beautiful, all are deserving. Summon the gates and let them present their pleas before Thee, and Thou shalt choose one of them."

Said the Holy One, blessed be He:

"As thou livest, so will I do!"

Then He beckoned with His finger and a kind of fiery tongue descended and struck the Jaffa Gate.

"Speak thou first," He said.

The Jaffa Gate leapt forward and said:

"Master of the World! I am the gate! Two roads go forth from me: one to Hebron, to the Tombs of the Patriarchs who founded Thy people, and one to Jaffa, where the Prophet Jonah suffered for Thy sake. May their virtues speak for me before Thee, that the redemption may be brought about through me. Let the young men of Israel enter through me, and I shall protect them; if all the winds in the world were to come and blow at me, they would not shift me from my place. And I shall make a covenant with the Tower of David, which is on my right hand, and we shall be of one counsel together."

As the Jaffa Gate spoke, Gabriel wrote down his plea, and the angels congregated together and said:

"True, it is deserving, it is deserving."

Then the Shechem Gate reared up on its pillars, higher than any part of the wall, and cried with a loud voice:

"I am the gate from which the road goes to Shechem, where stands Mount Gerizim, the Mount of the Benedictions, and Mount Eval, the Mount of the Maledictions. The maledictions have all been fulfilled. Now fulfill Thou the blessings. And if the sons of the tribes enter through me, Judah and Ephraim will become one band and one kingdom."

When leave was given, the Zion Gate leapt forward and said:

"Master of the World! I am the gate after which Thy Holy City was named Zion. Look down from Heaven and see, behold from Thy sacred habitation: I am all over wounds and bruises, fissures and fractures. All Thy calamities and tribulations have passed over me: Israel struck at me trying to enter, and the Arabs struck at me to stop them. And was it not I alone who opened myself in the War of Independence and let the young men of Israel enter Thy Holy City?"

As it spoke, the ministering angels wept and said:

"It is deserving, it is deserving!"

And they could not look upon its sorrow.

Then the Dung Gate trembled and said:

"Master of the World! See how I stand before Thee, poor and humble, shamed and degraded, half of me buried in the ground. Over me generation after generation has cast its refuse and I bowed myself, saying: Better the refuse of Jerusalem than the jewels of the whole world! And when, if not now, wilt Thou fulfill in me Thy promise: 'He that lifteth the needy out of the dunghill'? Nor is that all, for every day I gaze at the Western Wall, see it in its wretchedness, and soothe it with words of consolation."

And the Wall shook itself and said:

"It has spoken the truth!"

The the Holy One, blessed be He, said to Michael:

"Fine counsel thou gavest Us to summon the gates and listen to their pleas! Now that We hear, Our Heart is touched and Our Eyes burn with pain. See what counsel thou gavest!"

Then Michael replied:

"Sufferings cleanse the gates. Now that we have heard four gates, we cannot refrain from hearing the other three, for it might be said, Heaven forbid, that there is partiality in the Heavenly Assembly!"

Then the Flower Gate leapt forward and said:

"Heaven forbid that the young men of Israel should enter through the Dung Gate. On the contrary, let them go in through the Gate of Flowers, for if they enter through me, I shall pluck my flowers and crown the heads of our dear ones with them."

Hardly had it finished speaking, when a great cry was heard, and the angels saw the prophet Jeremiah tearing his garments and crying:

"Master of the World! How long will the Heavenly Assembly pile up words? Our sons are being killed there below, and you are debating by which gate they shall enter!"

Gabriel wished to rebuke him, but the Holy One, blessed be He, said to him:

"Let Jeremiah be, for he prophesied the Destruction, and the embers of his prophecy still glow and burn his tongue!"

Then the Holy One, blessed be He, gave leave, and the New Gate, in the West, shook and said:

"Master of the World! I am the least of the gates and I have no right of seniority, but I am lowly and humble, so that a tiny hillock seems to me a mighty mountain. And all the time my heart has been sore, for the legions of the sons of Ammon have been standing on my back and showering the Children of Israel with fire. How often have I tried to shake them off, but could not cast them down! Let me be credited with the virtue of my sorrow."

The angels said:

"It is humble, and small, and fitting for Israel!"

But the Court decreed:

"The gate is new, and is not numbered among the Seven Gates."

And the gate went aside into its corner and wept.

Before they could say anything more, a great wind came, and the voice of Moses the son of Amram thundered out from the banks of the Jordan and cried:

"How long will the Heavenly Assembly remain in session? You are a cruel court, for all night the Children of Israel are held down on Ammunition Hill and their blood flows to the Jordan, while you sit and debate!"

The ministering angels tried to silence him, but Moses protested and said:

"I will not obey you!"

"Moses, Moses," they said to him, "This is the Court and thou canst not disturb it."

Then Michael came forward to the Almighty and said:

"The night is over and done, but the sun does not wish to shine."

"For what reason?"

He said to Him:

"Because if it rises in the East it will blind the eyes of the Children of Israel, who come from the West," he replied.

Then the Holy One, blessed be He, said to him:

"Go and tell the sun that since the days of Gideon there is no changing the order of creation!"

Michael went out and came back, and said:

"It refuses to emerge from its sheath!"

"Scourge it until it emerges!" said the Holy One, blessed be He.

Then Michael scourged it with sixty rods of fire until the sun emerged from its sheath. And it wept as it shone, seeking a cloud to hide its face, but not finding one, for those were the days of Iyar.

Then the Holy One, blessed be He, gave a sign, and a spark of fire descended and struck the Mercy Gate. The Mercy Gate leapt from its place and began to cry. Its voice was indistinct, for it is blocked on both sides, one side for mercy and one side for repentance.

"Master of the World!" it said. "For many generations my mouth has been sealed with stones. All the other gates may be opened or may be closed, but my entrance is blocked and large stones are embedded in my throat. From here the Shekhina, the Divine Presence, went into exile, and from here She is destined to return. I look out upon the Mount of Olives, and to me men have come all through the years and wept upon my neck and pressed me, saying: 'Open thyself, open, that the Shekhina may enter in.' And I weep and say: 'Since the day the Temple was destroyed, an iron wall has risen between Israel and their Father in Heaven. Leave me alone, and go entreat your Father in Heaven.'"

Before it had finished speaking, a cry of agony was heard, rending the seven firmaments. The angels looked down and saw Rachel tearing her hair.

"Master of the World!" she cried. "How long wilt Thou lead my sons to the slaughter? Didst Thou not say to me, 'Refrain thy voice from weeping, and thine eyes from tears, and thy children shall come again to their own border'? Was it of living children Thou didst speak, or of the dead?"

And the ministering angels hid their faces in shame. Then the Holy One, blessed be He, said to her:

"Rachel, my daughter! What I have promised I shall fulfill, and thine eyes shall see it. We shall hear one more gate, and decide."

He stretched forth His hand and a flame descended upon the Lions' Gate.

Prologue

His voice thundered forth and He said to it:

"Speak!"

The Lions' Gate shrank, and did not say a word.

"Speak!" said the Holy One, blessed be He, but it still refused.

Then He scourged it with a rod of flame until it spoke:

"Master of the World! Every moment I can see from here, on the eastern side, soldiers of Israel on the hills and on Mount Scopus, and at the feet of the gates I see them falling, scorched by fire. Let them enter by any gate, so long as not another single one of them falls!"

When the Holy One, blessed be He, heard this, said He to it:

"Since thou hast belittled thyself, and held the lives of the young men dearer than thine own glory, I hereby decree that they shall enter through thee, and from thee shall salvation come to my Holy Mount. Let the young lions enter through the Lions' Gate!"

And before an hour passed, a flood of Israel's youth broke through the Lions' Gate in iron cars, and thence on to the Temple Mount and the sancties of Israel.

(Translated by Misha Louvish. Copyright © 1978, Shikmona Publishing Co., Ltd., Jerusalem. By permission.)

INTRODUCTION

I. Legend and Myth

The English term "legend" is derived, through Middle English, Old French, and Medieval Latin, from the Latin *legendus*, meaning "that which is, or has to be, read." Originally, a legend was something to be read at religious services or meals, a story supposed to provide spiritual uplift, such as a saint's or a martyr's life. In modern usage legend is a traditional narrative, handed down for generations among a group of people, and popularly believed to be true—that is, to have a historical basis. However, although legends often do include historical personages and facts, the stories they tell are not verifiable and cannot be considered historical records. Frequently the legends tell of wonderful or miraculous events, and their protagonists are kings, princes, heroes, saints, and pious individuals. Legends are often tied to a locality and explain some geographical feature, or a name, a custom, a tradition, by relating what a person did or experienced there in the past.

While in many cases it is not difficult to distinguish between legend and myth, frequently the line between the two is vague. Among the distinguishing features the following can be considered most important: The protagonists of the typical myth are not individuals who have actually lived in some past age, but divine beings or semidivine, superhuman heroes. The belief in the truth content of the myth is stricter, more profound and unshakable, more positive, imperative, and apodictic, and therefore more akin to a religious tenet. The myth lacks the legend's "uplift" character; it is raw, lusty, robust, often aggressive, occasionally vindictive—all features contrasting with the legendary hero's piety and moral rectitude. The myth, unlike the legend, is not concerned with local features and phenomena; its scope is general, its explanatory function worldwide, its concern universal, its subject matter—once properly understood—the great, eternal human problems of life and death, matters of cosmogonical and cosmological import, and issues between the human and divine realms. Yet, when all this is said, it still frequently remains difficult to decide whether a traditional story should be classified as myth or legend. The ancients who created these narratives shaped them as the spirit moved them, blissfully unaware of the taxonomical problems they would create for latter-day students of myth and legend.

If this blurring of the boundary between myth and legend characterizes the traditional corpus of narratives produced by polytheistic cultures, the difficulties become greater still when the stories to be classified were framed by the monotheistic culture of Judaism. In the Greek and other "pagan" stories, when we are told about the loves, jealousies, intrigues, competitions, wars, cannibalism, and other doings of the gods, the mythical character of the narratives is in most cases readily apparent. In the Hebrew stories, even if divinities other than God do appear, whatever they do in relation to Him, they cannot approach, let alone shake, His throne on high; His supremacy, even though occasionally, impudently, and temporarily challenged (especially in stories of very old provenance), is never really in jeopardy. His almighty serenity remains unaffected, His peerless power endures untouched. And as far as the relationship between men and gods is concerned, the typical polytheistic themes are those of a close, carnal, combative, competitive, or fraternizing involvement of gods with men, of men performing acts against the will of a god (often with the help or connivance of another god) and either actually or nearly getting away with it, of hybrid creatures who are half man and half god, or half animal and half man. As against this, the typical Hebrew mode of the human act which creates a narrative tension is man's disobedience to God, which is inevitably followed by swift divine retribution. The typical pagan human hero is a man who rises up against the gods, or at least acts independently of divine guidance; his Hebrew counterpart is a person who obeys God even if it costs him the greatest sacrifice. Therefore, the pagan hero is clearly mythical; the distance between him and the gods is small; the very natures of men and gods are conceived as being closely akin, and whatever distance does exist between them is bridged by demigods and demimen, the products of carnal unions between deities and humans.

No such proximity between man and God is conceivable within Hebrew tradition, which constitutes the mainstream of Biblical and later Jewish thinking. God is above and man is below; God is one and man is many; the distance between them is not merely great, it is absolute; the relation between them is that between the spiritual All and a speck of dust. The one and only feature of virtue with which the Jewish narrative can endow its hero is his extraordinary ability to understand what God wants of him, and his equally extraordinary readiness to obey every divine command. Typologically, almost all the Biblical and later Jewish heroes conform to this single pattern: they are heroes of piety, giants of belief, masters of obedience. Their one and only heroic feat is to perceive and obey God's command.

Thus the Biblical and later Jewish hero is only partly mythical; mostly he is legendary. In contrast to the great human and semihuman heroes of pagan polytheistic traditions who are totally and full-bloodedly mythical, the typical heroes of the Biblical and later Jewish narratives are of a pseudo-mythical character in which the legendary features predominate.

This being the case, one must recognize that pure myths are rare in the ancient Hebrew repertory. The brief Biblical reference to the Sons of God and the Daughters of Man is among the few; the story of the Tower of Babel is a less clear case in point. The vast majority of the Hebrew material is of an intermediary character: it is both myth and legend, or one can describe it as a mixture of mythical and legendary narrative features. As far as their charter character, their explanatory function clarifying great human problems, the identity of their protagonists— namely divine beings and heroes—and their sincerely accepted truth content are concerned, they are myths like the myths of any of the polytheistic religions. But because of the spirit of piety which is part of them, the moral imperative which they so often teach, and the inevitability of the just reward and punishment which they again and again illustrate, they are of one class with the pious legends of the Christian Middle Ages. In sum, the customary distinction between myth and legend, arrived at by students of religion and folklore on the basis of analyzing what can briefly be termed the Gentile material, and in the first place the popular narratives of cultures which were polytheistic to begin with and then, at a relatively late period, became monotheistic, can be applied only with considerable difficulty to the Hebrew storehouse of traditional stories of which selections are presented in this book.

II. *Agada and Halakha*

Since in traditional Hebrew usage no terms exist which would be equivalent to the English "myth" and "legend," at this point we must introduce the two-thousand-year-old *terminus technicus* under which not only these two categories but also all other types of oral folklore have been subsumed in Jewish literature ever since Talmudic times (ca. 100 B.C.E.– 500 C. E.). The term I am referring to is, of course

Introduction

"Agada" (also transliterated Aggada, Hagada, Haggada, or each with a final h). In fact, Agada is much more even than oral folklore. To explain what it comprises, one must begin with the traditional Talmudic distinction between Agada and Halakha.

As everything else in Jewish tradition, this distinction, too, has its roots in the Bible, the fountainhead of all Jewish religious, legal, and literary creativity. The Bible contains, very roughly speaking, two types of material: narratives and laws. (The narrative parts of the Bible will be discussed in section V below.) In Talmudic times, both the narrative and the legal parts of the Bible became the subject of painstaking study. By the beginning of the Talmudic era, every sentence, every word, contained in the Bible came to be considered true, sacred, and immutable. However, while nothing in it could be changed, everything in it called for— nay, demanded—explanation, amplification, refining, exegesis, commentaries, and supercommentaries, until the original meaning was often buried under huge, top-heavy, and complex superstructures. The efforts to define precisely the Biblical laws, to adopt them to the changing times, and to build protective "fences" around them gave rise to the rich Halakhic literature consisting of legal discussions and decisions, of law codes, and of scholarly rabbis' opinions (the so-called responsa). All of this, it was unswervingly maintained, went back to Moses on Mount Sinai. This, in a nutshell, is the Halakha, literally "walking" or "the Way."

The narrative parts of the Bible were scrutinized with almost the same close attention to the minutest details. They were expanded by the addition of further particulars and embellishments and became the basis of a literary creativity of great variety which formed the major component of what came to be termed Agada. Because of the amorphous character of the Agada, it has traditionally been defined by contrasting it with the Halakha: Agada, it has often been stated, is everything contained in the

Talmud which is not Halakha. Since the prime concentration of most rabbis, teachers, and sages was on the Halakha, it is not difficult to understand that they lumped together everything else contained in the Talmud under this generic catch-all term, Agada. For about twelve centuries, from the completion of the Talmud until the Jewish Enlightenment (the Haskala), which began in the late eighteenth century, no attempt was made to define or describe what the Agada comprised. Moreover, throughout that long period, the traditional attitude to the Agada was one of belittlement. The serious, important part of the Talmud, the part to which all yeshivot (Talmudic academies) devoted all their attention, was the Halakha. The Halakha had to be studied, one had to concentrate on it, to devote oneself to it, because only a knowledge of the Halakha, an understanding of how its decisions about the law were reached, enabled a Jew to observe all the minutiae of the *mitzvot* (the religious duties). Thus knowledge of the Halakha became the arena in which Talmudic scholars vied and sparred for excellence. Studying the Halakha day and night became the ideal way of life, and the one domain of Jewish intellectual activity in the major concentrations of the Diaspora, notably in Eastern Europe, until the Enlightenment.

While the Agada as a literary category still defies definition, one can enumerate the various genres subsumed under this term. In our modern terminology, some Agadot (plural of Agada) are myths, others legends. Still others are folktales, parables, allegories, idyllic tales, animal fables, etc. — all these in the narrative category. But the Agada can also be descriptive, can take the form of dialogue, of mystical allusion, or of didactic and moralistic advice. Topics such as astronomy and astrology, medicine and magic, theosophy and mysticism, angelology and demonology, are also parts of the Talmudic Agada. Brief Agadic pieces include terse maxims, plays on words, hyperboles, permutations and all kinds of ingenious utilizations of the letters of the Hebrew alphabet and their numerical values. Lyrics, dirges, satire, expressions of hope for future redemption, words of encouragement and comfort—all these fall under the overall designation of Agada. Since our intention in this volume is to present selections of Jewish *legends,* we can evidently not give a full complement of excerpts illustrative of all these manifold varieties of the Agada. However, we shall include, in addition to legends, also a few Agadic descriptions, or descriptive Agadot, such as those dealing with Paradise, Hell, the seven worlds, etc.

III. *The Sages as Agadists*

Although, as stated above, the main preoccupation of the Talmudic sages was with the Halakha, the law as they derived it from the Bible, through the Mishna and their rich oral tradition, they dealt with Agada as well and devoted much attention to legends, folktales, animal fables, Märchen, and other types of oral folklore. Of several of the sages it is stated in the Talmud itself that they were specialists in the Agada rather than the Halakha. Of others it is pointed out that their Agadic knowledge was extraordinary. Thus of Hillel the Elder (first century B.C.E.—first century C.E.) it is said that he knew "even the talk of mountains and hills and valleys, the talk of trees and grasses, the talk of animals and cattle, the talk of demons, and parables."[1] The Hebrew term *siḥa* here translated as "talk" can equally mean "lore," so that this piece of intelligence about Hillel, one of the greatest sages of the entire Talmudic period, presents him as the past master of nature lore and demonology. Of Hillel's disciple, Rabban Yoḥanan ben Zakkai, founder of the Yavne academy (in 70 C.E.), it was known that, in addition to his preeminence in Halakha, "he did not leave aside the lore of ministering angels, and the lore of demons, and the lore of date palms,

---

[1] Massekhet Sofrim 16:9.

launderers' parables, fox fables, great things, such as the Work of the Chariot, and little things, such as the discussions of Abbaye and Rava."[2]

In some cases the Talmudic sources quote impressive numbers of stories known to particular sages. Thus of R. Meir (second century C.E.) it is said that he knew three hundred "fox fables," that is, animal stories.[3] Of Bar Kappara (late second century C.E.) it is related that he regaled the guests at a banquet given for him by R. Y'huda haNasi with three hundred fox fables whenever a course of food was served, and the guests listened to him with such interest that all the dishes got cold and they ate nothing.[4] While these reports are anecdotal themselves, they attest to both the great folkloristic erudition of some sages and the equally great popularity of this kind of entertainment among the rabbis in general.

To be an Agadist in Talmudic times did not necessarily mean being a storyteller. Such, too, were of course found among the sages; e.g., Rabba bar Bar Ḥana (second half of the third century), a disciple of R. Yoḥanan, was famous for his fantastic sea lore, his tall tales about gigantic animals, and stories of miraculous adventures. His older contemporary, R. Y'hoshu'a ben Levi, was the author of bold imaginary descriptions of the future life of the righteous, of the punishment of the wicked, and of "conversations" with the Angel of Death, with Elijah, and with the Messiah. Others, however, expressed their Agadic proclivities by brief homilies and moralistic statements. To this latter type of Agadists belonged Abba bar Kahana and his friend R. Levi (both in the late third century), whom R. Zira (or Z'ira), a great Halakhist, chided by calling them "magician-scribes."[5] Although this designation indicates

---

[2] B. Sukka 28a.

[3] B. Sanh. 38b.

[4] Lev. Rab. 28:2; Eccles. Rab. ad 1:3.

[5] Y. Ma'as. 3:10, 51a.

that Abba bar Kahana and R. Levi were well known as outstanding Agadists, only brief Agadic epigrams, statements, and explanations of Biblical passages attributed to them found their way into the Talmudic text. Typical of Abba bar Kahana's Agada are sayings such as: "This is the way of the righteous: they speak little and do much."[6] In reference to the verse *If the serpent bite before it is charmed (laḥash,* Eccl. 10:11), Abba bar Kahana explained: "The serpent never bites unless he is whispered to (*nilḥash*) from Above; the lion does not tear apart unless he is whispered to from Above, and the authority does not persecute people unless it is whispered to from Above."[7]

R. Levi, and another outstanding Agadist, R. Y'huda bar Naḥman, were paid *darshanim* (preachers, expositors) in the academy of R. Yoḥanan. Their task was to entertain the public on alternate Sabbaths with their expositions until R. Yoḥanan himself arrived and began his own presentation, which was the major attraction.[8] Since R. Yoḥanan (early third century), who was a disciple of R. Y'huda haNasi and became the head of the largest Talmudic academy in Palestine, was himself a renowned Agadist, one can imagine the proceedings at his school every Sabbath: the doors were thrown open to the public; first either R. Y'huda bar Naḥman or R. Levi held forth with their Agadic expositions, then followed the main event, an Agadic lecture by the great R. Yoḥanan. This brief Talmudic reference gives us a rare insight into the intellectual amusements sought by the Jews in Palestine in the third century: while their Roman overlords thronged to the theaters and arenas, the Jews filled the benches of the Talmudic academies to listen to popular lectures by celebrated Agadists and to absorb their religious and moral

6 Deut. Rab. 1:11.

7 Eccles. Rab. *ad* 10:11.

8 Y. Sukka 5:1, 55a; Gen. Rab. 98:11.

teachings clad in the captivating and prepossessing garb of Agadic exposition.

Occasionally it happened that the assistant lecturer became involved in a contradiction with the master from which he had to struggle to extricate himself. Such an event is described about the three sages just mentioned. One Sabbath R. Levi stated in the course of his lecture: "This Jonah was of the tribe of Zebulun," and supported this view with Biblical quotations. Then R. Yoḥanan, who had not heard R. Levi's discourse, arrived and said: "This Jonah was of the tribe of Asher," and he, too, adduced Biblical references in support of his view. This put R. Levi in a delicate position. He said to his colleague, R. Y'huda bar Naḥman: "Although next Sabbath it is your turn to preach, take these two *sela's* (the fee for a lecture), and let me take your place." And in the course of his lecture he said: "Well did R. Yoḥanan teach us this past Sabbath that Jonah was of the tribe of Asher; but his father was of the tribe of Zebulun, and his mother of Asher." And he proceeded to present an ingenious way of supporting this view with a Biblical quote. This was reported back to R. Yoḥanan, who thereupon said to him: "You presented your exposition standing up; from now on you shall sit." This was tantamount to a promotion, for only the *Ḥakham* (in this context roughly corresponding to the rank of dean) preached sitting. "And R. Levi served as *Ḥakham,* or senior speaker, for twelve years."[9]

IV. The Value of the Agada

As a result of the disdain for the Agada by the post-Talmudic rabbinical scholars, the Agadic parts of the Talmud were (and still are) skimmed over in the yeshivot,

[9] Gen. Rab. 98:11.

the traditional Talmudic institutions of learning. "It is an Agadta" (Aramaic for Agada) was a frequently heard expression meaning that the passage referred to was not serious, not to be taken literally, not to be considered important. This attitude, too, persisted until the Enlightenment brought about a radical change in the Jewish view and an appreciation of the non-Halakhic parts of the Talmud, and of the Midrash literature in general.

The first to give full recognition to the Agada was no less a luminary than Leopold Zunz (1794–1886), celebrated father of the *Wissenschaft des Judentums*—that is, the scientific study of Judaism and Jewish literary sources—and the founder of the historical study of Jewish religion. In his seminal book *Die gottesdienstlichen Vortraege der Juden* (1832; the title means "The Synagogal Expositions of the Jews"), Zunz presented the Midrash literature in its historical evolution, and had this to say about the Agada:

> The eternal pole around which revolve the expositions of the Agadists is the splendid victory of the Jews and of Judaism over sufferings and tribulations, and over evil on earth. The Agada, whose purpose is to bring heaven down to the community, and, conversely, to raise man up to heaven, appears in this calling as the glorification of God on the one hand, and as Israel's consolation on the other. This is why the most important contents of the expositions are religious truths, moral teachings, discourses about just retribution, the inculcation of the laws which serve as authentication of Jewish nationhood, descriptions of the past and future glories of Israel, scenes and legends from Jewish history, parallels between the divine and the Israelite institutions, praises of the Holy Land, stories of uplift, and consolations of all kinds. With all the abstention from mystery doctrines, and despite the caution observed and recommended by prudent men in their homilies, they nevertheless permitted themselves, following the manner of the

Orient, to present powerful anthropomorphic images of the divine Being and Rule. In order to stir up a slumbering congregation, they did not disdain even colossal exaggerations; but many other things, about which modern idiots raise an outcry or a laughter, were but jokes and irony, momentary necessity and ecstasy, or hyperbole. . . .

The main ornaments of the lectures were the sayings, proverbs, similes, parables, and tales. The sources for them were either collections of Agadot and tales, or the speaker offered oral traditions or his own inventions.[10]

With these words of Zunz the Agada was not only recognized as a valued genre of millennial Jewish literature but became a subject of scholarly inquiry. Within a few decades, dozens of Jewish scholars were at work publishing critical annotated editions of the various Midrashim, which are collections of Agadic (and to a lesser extent also Halakhic) sources written or compiled from the fourth to the twelfth centuries. Many of these Midrashim, and especially the shorter ones, were until the nineteenth century available only in a few rare manuscript copies. Without the scientific Midrash editions published by Isaac Hirsch Weiss (1815–1905), Adolph Jellinek (1820–93), Solomon Buber (1827–1906), Meir Friedmann (1831–1908), Abraham Epstein (1841–1918), and their twentieth-century followers, no serious study of the Jewish legend literature would have been possible.

Simultaneously with this work began the compilation of the Agada in some systematic form. The pioneer in this field was Wilhelm Bacher (1850–1913), who gathered the Agadic teachings of all the *Tannaim* (the Talmudic sages who lived from the first century B.C.E. to the end of the second century C.E.), and the *Amoraim* (their successors from the 3rd to the 5th century). Bacher's great work

---

[10] Leopold Zunz, *Die gottesdienstlichen Vortraege der Juden,* pp. 349–51.

presented for the first time each of these sages as an individual, with ideas, approaches, and a personality of his own, and made their contributions to the Agada available in a systematic form. Bacher wrote in German; his Agada opus was subsequently translated into Hebrew, but, regrettably, it is still unavailable in English.

Among the twentieth-century masters of Agada research, Louis Ginzberg (1873–1953) must be mentioned in the first place. His seven-volume *The Legends of the Jews* (1909–38), which contains a chronological and topical presentation of the Talmudic, Midrashic, and early Kabbalistic legends woven around Biblical persons and events, is an exemplar of thoroughness and comprehensiveness. Ginzberg presents all the versions and variants of each legend subject in synoptic conflations, in which details contained in Midrashim separated by many centuries are merged into one. In his preoccupation with legends, Ginzberg was led to identify Agada with legend, and hence he offers this narrow definition of Agada:

> Folklore, fairy tales, legends, and all forms of story telling akin to these are comprehended, in the terminology of the post-Biblical literature of the Jews, under the inclusive description Haggadah (i.e., Agada), a name that can be explained by a circumlocution, but cannot be translated. Whatever it is applied to is thereby characterized first as being derived from the Holy Scriptures, and then as being of the nature of a story.[11]

The second sentence quoted does not stand up under objective scrutiny. In the Talmudic and Midrashic literature there are many Agadot which are not derived from the Bible but are the product of popular or individual fantasy. Rabba bar Bar Ḥana's tall tales about gigantic sea creatures, the stories about the Messianic banquet, about the punishment of the wicked in Gehenna, about the

---

[11] Louis Ginzberg, *The Legend of the Jews,* I:ix.

turning wheel of heaven, about the Messiah in the Bird's Nest, and many, many more belong to this category. Nor are all the Agadot in "the nature of a story." Many are purely descriptive of imaginary regions of the world, the heavenly halls, the various types of angels, the seven earths, the compartments of Gehenna, etc., which are not narratives, tell no story, speak not of sequential events, but are cataloguelike static enumerations of details and are devoid of all action. Nor are they, incidentally, derived from the Bible. We must, therefore, conclude that the broader view of Zunz about the nature of the Agada is closer to the actual variety of subject matter covered by the term.

V. Legends in the Bible

The Agadot, or, more narrowly, the narrative and descriptive pieces presented in this volume, are taken not only from the Talmud and the Midrash, the traditional sources of the Agada, but also from the Bible itself, which Jewish scholars of a bygone age would have considered too sacrosanct to come under the Agadic rubric. However, since in our view the literary, moral, and religious value of the Agada is even greater than the one accorded it by Zunz, we can see nothing wrong, let alone sacrilegious, in considering certain stories contained in the Bible and forming the basis for later Agadot as Agadot in themselves. Since the two major genres subsumed under Agada are myths and legends, both of which are, by definition, believed to be true within the culture whose product they are, one cannot fault the inclusion of Biblical stories in an Agada or legend collection. In fact, Louis Ginzberg himself, a religious Jew and a professor at the Conservative Jewish Theological Seminary of America, omitted Biblical narratives from his *Legends of the Jews* only "in consideration of lack of space," and felt called upon to explain and justify this omission by stating that this was "surely not a serious omission in a subject with which widespread acquaintance may be presupposed as a matter of course."[12] In the seventy years that have passed since Ginzberg wrote these words, the acquaintance with the Biblical stories has regrettably and considerably diminished. The inclusion of Biblical legends within the general purview of the present volume was therefore considered necessary from this point of view as well.

Most importantly, the Bible contains many narratives which formed the basis of Talmudic and Midrashic Agadot, and which themselves have a folktalelike quality. To this category belong the stories telling about the perils of the ancestress because of her beauty (Sarah, Rebekah), the victory of the weak over the strong (Joseph, Gideon, David), the perfect judgment of the wise king (Solomon), the miraculous birth of the hero (Moses), etc. The very fact that these motifs occur in literatures or folk traditions which could not have influenced one another points to their Märchen-like origin, that is to say, to their basis in a general, all-human tendency, akin to Bastian's *Völkergedanke.*

Most frequent in the Bible are legends of a historical content, that is, stories which developed around a historic kernel. Many legends about the fathers of Israel belong to this category. It is interesting to note that in these patriarchal legends the fantastic or miraculous element is practically absent—except for the occasional intervention of God. In this respect the central story cycle of Genesis, which tells of the Abrahamic family, is less akin to the Märchen (which is full of fantastic happenings) than to the saga (German *Sage*), whose story line hews close to reality. However, again, as in the case of the Agada as a whole, the Biblical stories resist classification according to categories established for other folk literatures.

Many Biblical stories are concerned with explaining the

[12] Ibid., p. xiv.

origin or the prime cause of something that exists in the world, that is, are etiological legends. Some of these explain such natural phenomena as the devastation of the Dead Sea area (Sodom and Gomorrah), the origin of a pillar of salt which resembled a woman (Gen. 19), or the origin of the big stones at the entrance to the Cave of Makkedah (Josh. 10:16ff.). A megalithic monument in Rabbat Ammon becomes the "iron" bed of the giant king Og (Deut. 3:11). In areas where water is scarce, legends attach themselves to the rare live springs (Exod. 15:22ff., 17:6ff.; Num. 21:16–18; etc.).

Another type of etiological legend explains the origins of religious rituals or cult objects. The origin of the important Hebrew rite of circumcision is attributed to no less than three events connected with three great Biblical heroes: Abraham (Gen. 17), Moses (Exod. 4), and Joshua (Josh. 5). The magnificent theophany on Mount Sinai explains the origin of the Two Tablets of the Law inscribed with the Ten Commandments, and of the building and ritual of the Tabernacle (Exod. 19–20; 24–31). The origin of the Brazen Serpent, which stood in the Temple of Jerusalem until late monarchic times, is explained in the legend about the infestation of the Israelite camp by snakes (Num. 21:4-9). The central sacred object of early Israel, the Ark of the Covenant, is the subject of several legends (1 Sam. 4-6; 2 Sam. 6).

The origin and interrelationship of various peoples and tribes are topics of special interest in ancient Near Eastern cultures. Hence numerous Biblical legends answer questions such as: Whence do the nomads come? They are the children of Cain, who was cursed by God to be a fugitive and a wanderer. Why do the Ishmaelites dwell in the desert? Because it is there that their ancestors, Hagar and Ishmael, fled. Why are the Hamites (Africans) slaves? Because their ancestor Ham sinned and was cursed by his father, Noah.

The Biblical legend comes nearest to myth when it

answers general, all-human questions, such as: Why must man work hard? Why is woman subordinated to man? Why must she suffer great pains at childbirth? Why is there an instinctive enmity ("hatred" is the Biblical expression) between man and snake? Why is there enmity between the nomads and the cultivators? These questions are answered satisfactorily, and to some extent reassuringly, by the legends in the first few chapters of Genesis.

Of the many more observations which can be made of the Biblical legend, let us confine ourselves to the most essential. In the Biblical legend the God of Israel is the central figure, the main person, to whom the whole world is subordinated. The Biblical legend affirms and validates the election, the chosenness, of the people of Israel, its genealogical and spiritual unity, and its central duty of being morally pure and God-fearing. The Biblical legend, despite its obvious ethnocentricity, is universal: its values are all-human values, its problems all-human problems, its solutions all-human solutions, its aspirations all-human aspirations, its protagonists all-human types, and its God the one and only almighty deity. These features in no small measure contributed to the acceptance of the Bible by a major part of humanity as the Book.

VI. *The Character of Jewish Legend:*
The Moral Order

Above, in section I, we touched upon some differences between the Jewish and Gentile traditional narratives in general. It is time now to focus on the features which distinguish Jewish legend from its Gentile counterpart.

If legends, by definition, are stories pervaded by a certain aura of piety, Jewish legends differ from their counterparts produced within other cultural contexts by their greater concentration on God and His works, on the inscrutability of His will and ways, on the subordination of man to God, on the moral duties of man to man, on the values of charity and family, and, last but not least, on the supreme value and duty of Tora study. Not in all periods do Jewish legends emphasize all these features in equal measure. The earliest legends, those included in the Bible, are, as we have just seen, strongly mythical in character, or, one could say, myth and legend are not clearly differentiated in them. Consequently, this early material is of a more robust, earthy flavor, even if its protagonists are God, the Sons of God, or other superhuman personages such as the Serpent, Lucifer (Helel ben Shahar), Leviathan, and the like. But with the passage of time, the rugged, lusty and muscular features of the stories diminish, and their place is taken by virtues of meekness: power pales into piety, prowess turns into prayerfulness, and physical strength is supplanted by devotion to study, to the fulfillment of divine command- ments. This metamorphosis was intuitively grasped by the great modern Hebrew poet Saul Tchernichovsky when, in his "Ode to the Statue of Apollo," he said of the God of the Hebrews: "He was the God of those who conquered Canaan in a stormwind, and they bound him with the straps of the phylacteries."

Such a transformation of the God concept to the point where Talmudic legend actually has God put on phylac- teries every day[13] is, of course, but a reflection of a commensurate change in the people's psyche. And not only the image of the deity, but the total corpus of Jewish legends mirrors the metamorphosis of the early Biblical Hebrews, a group of warlike Oriental tribes engaged in constant struggle against its neighbors, achieving and for centuries maintaining supremacy over them, into a de- feated, subdued, and exiled people able to hold its own under the tyrannical rule of powerful conquerors only by practicing the humble virtues of self-effacement, of turning inward, of finding solace in the spiritual values of piety, study, charity. In many of the later legends the portrait

[13] B. Ber. 7a.

emerging is that of downtrodden, persecuted Jewish groups who must have, from time to time, divine intervention in order to escape the cruel whims of despotic kings, counts, lords, and princes of the realm and of the Church. The most pitiful feature in all these legends, telling of last-minute, miraculous divine intervention, is that even in their flight of fancy, in the fantasy world which they create for themselves and in which they move, their scope is so narrow, so limited that the greatest miracle they have God perform for His people is to save a few of them from a death which they never deserved in the first place.

While the world which surrounds the Jews is thus shown in the legends as the cruel, inimical world of the *Galut* (exile), they at the same time paint a picture of totally different hues in their portraiture of life within the Jewish community itself. To use a Kabbalistic metaphor, the mundane order of the husks is overshadowed in the perspective of the legend by the glow of the sparks within. In the mundane order, which, of course, is confined to This World, the Jews both as individuals and as a people occupy the lowest of positions. They are ridiculed, abused, oppressed, persecuted, and martyred. Worst of all, they are treated with derision precisely because of their defiance of the mundane order, its values, its force of arms, its pleasures, its carnality and brutality, and because of their belief in, and self-subordination to, a moral order whose very existence is denied by the worldly powers that be. That moral order is not confined to This World, but embraces the World to Come. Of the two, This World is of minor importance: it is, as a Talmudic simile puts it, merely the *prozdor,* the antechamber, to the *traqlin,* the reception hall, the inner salon, which is the World to Come. Life in This World, therefore, is ideally but a preparation for the World to Come. The heavenly King observes how His servants behave in the antechamber, and accordingly allows or refuses them entrance to the *traqlin.* Hence the greatest value attaches to studying the Tora, to loving and serving one's neighbor, and to loving and serving God—for these are the only keys to the *traqlin.*

In this moral order death itself is reduced for the pious to a mere *rite de passage,* a transition one has to make, the passing through the doorway which leads from the *prozdor* of This World to the *traqlin* of the World to Come. As such it is important, it is fraught with forebodings and hopes, but in the totality of the moral order in which the Jew lived it was but a brief incident after which the Life Eternal began. Since it is human nature to fear death, to dread the suffering which so often goes with dying, to abhor the parting from loved ones, and to shrink from the uncertainty about what comes after, Jewish legend never tires of reiterating what amounts psychologically to a denial of death. Consciousness, fears and desires, pains and pleasures—in a word, life—continue after the brief interruption caused by the happening of dying, and the quality of that life after death is determined by one's conduct in This World, it is the fruit of the works performed while alive down here.

The story of the ten martyrs, contained in this volume (in part 4. Midrash, section "Warriors and Martyrs"), is perhaps the best example illustrating this general tendency of the Jewish legend. By mundane standards, the execution of the ten foremost sages of Israel during the Hadrianic persecutions (ca. 135 C.E.) was sheer tragedy. Saintly scholars who were guilty of no sin, let alone crime, were put to death at the whim of Caesar's men, some of them after unspeakable torture. In the course of the story several times the cry is heard: "Is this the Tora and is this her reward?" But this outcry, although put in the mouth of the sages' disciples, is the reaction of those who are imbued with the worldly values of the mundane order. For them, the supreme good is the good life in This World; the greatest evil is physical suffering; to be innocently tortured to death is the greatest, the starkest horror.

Not so for those who have all their lives bent their neck

into the yoke of the moral order. For them—and the story of the ten martyrs intends to propound and uphold their values—the essence of the events lies in what the sages did while they lived and what they were believed to do after their death. While they sojourned in This World, they fulfilled the greatest commandments in exemplary fashion. Their teaching, which was their life work, became part of the holy structure of the Tora. Their piety, which was of the very essence of their personality, helped sustain the world. After their death—this the story knows with the same realistic certainty with which it recounts their activities on earth—they continue their blessed work. Since they were great teachers on earth, they continue to teach in the Garden of Eden (as the Jewish legend refers to the heavenly Paradise), to expound the Tora, to expatiate on Halakha and Agada, and thus to delight God and themselves with that which was the greatest pleasure of their lives in This World.

In this overall perspective of the eternal moral order, the torture and the martyr's death suffered by the ten sages are reduced to insignificance. They are a brief incident, comparable perhaps to the pangs of childbirth a woman has to suffer before the joys of motherhood can commence for her. The very faithfulness of the martyrs to God, to the Tora, to the moral order is their triumphant defiance of the mundane order upheld by the temporal power. In presenting the fate of the ten martyrs in this metaphysical perspective, the legend achieves the supreme heights of myth: it establishes the prototype of piety, validates conduct, and points the way to facing, and surpassing, torture and death, which so often were visited upon the Jews in the dark night of their long exile.

The transformation in the Jewish psyche, referred to above, is further and most graphically illustrated by the changing attitude to sex as expressed in the Biblical legends on the one hand and in Jewish legends of later provenance on the other. In the earlier, more robust, atmosphere of the

Bible, irregular sexual activity or license is a theme figuring frequently in the legendary repertory without being necessarily execrated or condemned. Stories of this kind are those about the Sons of God and the Daughters of Man, Sarah and Pharaoh and its toned-down repetitions involving Sarah and Rebekah, the incest of Lot and his daughters, the rape of Dinah, Judah and Tamar, Joseph and Potiphar's wife, the harlotry of the sons of Israel with the daughters of Moab, Samson and the harlot of Gaza, Samson and Delilah, the mass rape of the concubine by the men of Gibeah which ended in her death, the adulterous cohabitation of David and Bath-sheba, the rape of Tamar by Amnon, Hosea and his harlot wives.[14] In these stories we hear only occasionally of punishment, and only once of the hero successfully resisting the temptress (Joseph). In general, extramarital cohabitation, if not precisely approved, is condoned, or at least presented as an inevitable part of life: men will be men, and women women, and there is little one can do about it.

In the post-Biblical era, and especially in the later Midrash, a much stricter view of sexual morality prevails. First of all, stories which have sexual affairs as their topic become rarer; and, secondly, if they do figure, they are told in strict adherence to the all-surpassing moral imperative. From Talmudic times on it was the inviolate law in Judaism that there were three cardinal sins which a man must not commit even in order to save his life. They are: idolatry, murder, and fornication. Several stories illustrating how sages and simple people (e.g., the seven sons of Miriam bat Tanhum) died martyrs' deaths rather than worship idols are contained in this volume. To commit murder was so unimaginable for Jews that stories about it are practically nonexistent. As for fornication, while Jewish legends tell about such occurrences, they are presented as temptations

---

[14] Source references in the order of the legends cited: Gen. 6:1–4, 12:10–20, 19:30–38, 20:1–28, 26:6–11, 34, 38, 39:7–20; Num. 25:1–9; Judg. 16:1, 4, 19; 2 Sam. 11:2–4, 13; Hos. 1:2–3, 3:1-2.

only, which the hero always resists, except when he cannot help himself because the temptress seduces him in his sleep. Thus of all the Biblical stories about sexual encounters only those about Lot and Joseph became prototypes for later legends.

The story about the pious R. Meir of whom the adulterous wife of his host takes advantage in his drunken sleep ("Touch Not a Married Woman") is, of course, based on the Biblical Lot story, but with a difference. While according to the Bible no punishment is visited on Lot, R. Meir, although as innocent of wrongdoing as the legendary ancestor of Ammon and Moab, not only feels that he committed a heinous sin, but seeks out his punishment, is condemned to die, and is saved only by a miracle.

Even more instructive is the story about Joshua and his parents. A comparison between this medieval Jewish Oedipus story and the classical myth of Freudian fame which it closely resembles throws light on typical features in the Jewish psyche. In the Greek myth, Oedipus kills his father, Laius, in the course of a chance encounter which degenerates into a fight. Although he does not know that his adversary is his father, he commits murder knowingly, impelled by his arrogance and quick temper. In the Jewish story, too, Joshua does not know that the man he beheads is his father, but the act itself is performed by him at the command of Pharaoh; he is merely the executioner who carries out what is a legally valid death sentence pronounced by the king. (In fact, in the Hebrew original of the story, the word I translated "guardsman" literally means "executioner.") The Greek myth goes on to tell of Oedipus actually marrying his mother, living with her for many years, and begetting children on her. In the Jewish version the incest about to be committed unknowingly by Joshua is prevented by a miraculous happening—the medieval Jewish mind cannot countenance one of the Biblical heroes committing incest, even if the sin is done unwittingly, and even if the account is a legend, a mere "Agada." In

Freudian terms, the moral superego does not loose its control over the Jewish psyche even when the latter moves into the fantasy world of legend. As we shall see in the Hasidic section, the sexual temptation of the pious occasionally crops up as a Hasidic legend theme, almost three thousand years after the Biblical Joseph story, but in it, too, we are never told of the Hasid or the Tzaddiq succumbing to the temptress: he is tempted, perhaps sorely tempted, but resists. The sexual temptation is there, the fantasy image of the beautiful woman in the nude appears and lures. Incidentally, how typical it is of the powerful hold ritualism exercises over the Jewish psyche that even in the moment when the naked seductress tries to entice the Hasid to committing the heinous sin of fornication, she is made to stress to him that she is in a state of ritual cleanliness, free of the taint of menstrual impurity: "I have just bathed," she says, "I am pure." This assurance is supposed to enhance the allure of the temptress. Presumably, were she not ritually pure, the Hasid would have no difficulty or less difficulty in resisting her. This feature, again, has its model in the Biblical David and Bath-sheba story, except that David does lie with Bath-sheba "for she was purified from her uncleanness" (2 Sam. 11:4). In the Hasidic temptation stories one cannot help feeling that the mere mental process of conjuring up the naked seductress in one's imagination must have in itself provided libidinous gratification. But the actual act does not take place (in the story, that is); it is blocked by the censorship exercised even on the world of imagination by the morality-suffused Jewish superego. This control of the superego over the id is, in fact, so strong in the Jewish psyche that whenever a Jewish legend does tell of a victory won by the id (in simple terms: of the commission of a sexual transgression), one can be sure that its purpose is to cast a protagonist in the role of the villain, to characterize him as a wicked person, an inveterate sinner, an apostate, a man in alliance with the forces of evil. The story of R. Joseph della Reina (or

Dolphina) tells of such a man, and does not fail to recount the supreme punishment which overtook him as a direct consequence of his sin.

Above, in section IV, we quoted what Zunz had to say about the intent and value of the Agada. We conclude this section with a brief characterization of the moral aspect of that component of the Agada which corresponds to the folktale given by one of the foremost students of Hebrew and Arabic Märchen. Prof. Bernhard Heller (1871–1943), whom I had the privilege to have as my teacher at the Rabbinical Seminary in Budapest, had this to say of the Hebrew Märchen in his essay included in the fourth volume of Bolte and Polivka's notes on the Grimm brothers' collection of folktales:

> We find that the specific character of the Hebrew Märchen consists in its having become the carrier of the Jewish conception of piety and morality which expresses itself also in attaching itself, wherever possible, to the words of the Scripture.[15]

VII. *Kabbala and Legend*

With Kabbalistic literature we are entering a world which is both similar to that of the Talmud and Midrash and yet fundamentally different from it. The similarity between the two is primarily due to the deeply religious outlook which dominates them. From the point of view of trust in God, reliance on God, self-subordination to God, deprecation of This World and glorification of the World to Come, and many more aspects expressive of an otherworldly orientation, as well as an all-pervasive morality, the same spirit permeates the Talmudic-Midrashic literature and the medieval Kabbalistic writings. This, of course, should not come as a surprise to anybody who knows the history of

---

[15] Bernhard Heller, "Das jüdische Märchen," in Bolte and Polivka, *Anmerkungen*, 4:364.

Jewish literature, which in every age and in almost all its manifestations expressed the same God-centered and morality-focused world view.

Where Kabbalistic literature differs from its Talmudic-Midrashic predecessors is in the extent to which mysticism is present in them. In the Talmuds and the Midrashim, mysticism, while unmistakably present, plays a limited and subordinated role. We do hear of sages who were attracted to the study of the "Work of the Chariot"—this term referring to mystical speculation about the form, structure, composition, and movements of that huge, awe-inspiring, half live—half mechanical combination of throne and chariot upon which God was believed to be seated in heaven. They were also intrigued by the question of what had existed prior to the six days of Creation, what were the forms of nothingness, of the Tohu vaBohu, which preceded the cosmic order, and they were inclined to assume the preexistence of an undifferentiated watery element which filled all space, and to fantasize about the relationship of the primordial waters to God. There was also a solid belief in angels, demons, and monsters, as there was in all ancient Near Eastern cultures. These were the central issues of mystical speculation in Talmudic times—thoughts about the present structure of the world belonged to cosmology rather than to mysticism—and even to them barely a few lines are devoted in the entire Talmud with its millions of words.

As against this, in Kabbalistic literature one cannot even speak of the role of mysticism, for the Kabbala in its entirety is mystical. In the Talmud and Midrash, while God is the Master of the World, the world is a corporeal entity subject to immutable physical laws, which are only rarely and momentarily interfered with by the will of God, if and when He chooses to perform a miracle. In the mystical view of the Kabbala, the divine spirit, often referred to as sparks from the Supernal Realm, ceaselessly intermingles with, or is entrapped by, the elements of the material world, the husks. Spirit and matter have a dynamic interrelationship, both are constantly influencing one another, always changing and moving, and the physical world itself, instead of being subject to fixed laws, is in a constant state of flux.

While the person of the deity is a subject from which the masters of the Talmudic and Midrashic Agada shied away, it is in the very center of Kabbalistic attention. His size is stated in fantastic, but still finite, numbers. His traditional Biblical, Talmudic, and medieval Jewish philosophical Oneness is exploded into ten Sefirot, emanations, each with a set of attributes of its own, and with interactions and tensions among them. The tenth of the Sefirot, identified with the Shekhina, God's immanence or presence in the physical world, and renamed Matronit, i.e., matron, is allowed to acquire a distinct personality of her own, and is made the spouse of God the King who becomes the personification of another Sefira. The relationship between the King and the Matronit, their passionate nightly unions in their sacred bedchamber which is none other than the Temple of Jerusalem, their separation and degradation resulting from the destruction of the Temple, the quasi-sexual relationship of the Matronit with outstanding men—all these are central, frequently recurring themes in Kabbalistic literature, which, as I have argued elsewhere, cannot be explained as the result of mystical speculation but bear all the hallmarks of genuine myth.[16]

It is because of the mystical, and often mythical, character of Kabbalistic literature as a whole, exemplified rather than described in the few points mentioned, that the legendary material embedded in it differs considerably from the typical Jewish legend of the pre-Kabbalistic period. Biblical, Apocryphal, Talmudic, and Midrashic legends tell mainly about flesh-and-blood creatures, whether human or monstrous, as they act, react, and interact among themselves, and as they are affected by rare

[16] Cf. R. Patai, *The Hebrew Goddess*, pp. 148–52.

and momentary interventions from On High, from demons, angels, the Shekhina, or God himself. They speak of people standing with both feet solidly on this earth, although casting frequent glances into the Above. In the Kabbalistic legend the main protagonists are souls who invisibly fill the entire palpable and tangible universe, and who are the true reality beyond and within the physical world. Kabbalistic legend operates with such metaphysical and transcendental concepts as the Good Inclination, the Right Side, the Pure Sparks, and their opposite numbers, the Evil Inclination, the Left (or Other) Side, the Impure Husks. The world of the Kabbala is full of mysterious fires, flames, lights, sparks, lamps, pillars of fire, lightnings, as well as voices, cries, weepings, sobbings, thunders, shakings, tremblings, rotations, ascents and descents, emanations, and expansions and contractions. Nothing in its world is solid or permanent: matter dissolves momentarily and changes, scenes are transformed, a heavenly city descends onto the earth only to soar up again into the firmament. Enormous movements take place, great comings and goings, often reminiscent of gigantic parades. Souls couple as if they were male and female beings, and produce other souls. Entities appear in astronomical numbers and dimensions. Time itself is fluid: past, present, and future warp, throb, palpitate, and merge. Everything is amorphous, indeterminate.

Reading these legends is like watching a masterly prestidigitator, nay, a true magician, at work. He stretches forth his right hand, and out of the air pulls down a bird; a motion of his left hand makes a rabbit, a jeweled crown, a complete human being materialize; at will he makes whatever he has just conjured up fly about him, dance at his bidding, metamorphose into something else, new, and unexpected. This is precisely how Kabbalistic authors proceed. In their writings they pull new concepts out of the air, transform them, and use them in surprising elaborations. A simple example will illustrate their method.

The author of the Zohar puts these words into the mouth of R. Ḥizqiya: "Every midnight, when the Holy One, blessed be He, awakens in the Garden of Eden..." Already we must stop. These opening words introduce us to several ideas which, although totally new, are presented as givens: (1) God dwells in the Garden of Eden. (2) He sleeps at night. (3) He awakens every midnight. R. Ḥizqiya continues and tells us that when this happens, "all the plants of the Garden are watered more abundantly from that stream which is called the Primeval Stream, the Stream of Delights, whose waters have never ceased to flow." Several more new ideas are conjured up here: (4) There is a perennial stream in the Garden. (5) Its names are Primeval Stream and Stream of Delights. (6) This stream waters all plants of the Garden constantly. (7) But every midnight, as a result of the awakening of God, the stream waters the plants more abundantly. The statement continues: "He who stands and studies the Tora, that stream, as it were, is poured over his head and waters him together with those plants." In this sentence the stream is magically metamorphosed into a spiritual image: it is no longer a stream of water, but (8) a spiritual emanation from heaven. And now we also learn that (9) this spiritual river pours down upon the midnight student who pores over the Tora.[17] This highly imaginative, unrestrained juggling with amorphous and indeterminate ("as it were") images is precisely the masterly feature characterizing Kabbalistic literature in general and its legends in particular.

Another example will perhaps better illustrate the fluidity, the transformational character, of the Kabbalistic legend. In the piece presented in the Kabbala section under the title "God Plays with the Righteous" we read that, paraphrased, (1) the river which went forth from Eden was the support on which the world stood; (2) it watered the Garden and made it bear fruit; (3) all the fruits blossom in

[17] Zohar 1:92a–b.

the world and are the maintenance of the world; (4) they are also the maintenance of the Tora; (5) these fruits are the souls of the righteous; (6) the souls of the righteous are the fruits of God's work (7) the souls of the righteous go forth every night; (8) every midnight God comes to the Garden of Eden to play with them.

And so it goes throughout the voluminous literature of the Kabbala.

The emergence of the Kabbala became the seed out of which, in the course of a few centuries, grew a sharp dichotomy in the Jewish world. Some, at the one extreme, turned away with revulsion from what they considered rantings and ravings of demented minds, suspect of heretical leanings; others, at the opposite extreme, saw in it the revelations of the greatest and deepest mysteries, the ultimate, ineffable truths of God, man, and the world. On both sides there were great scholars and deeply religious individuals, who nevertheless fought tooth and nail, to the extent of banning each other's books.[18] For the noncommitted reader, once he overcomes the obstacles presented by the initial strangeness of the Kabbalistic style and mode of delivery, these legends have a fascination which he will not find duplicated by any legend contained in nonmystical Jewish writings.

VIII. Legend and Environment

Considerations of space prevent us from making more than a few comments on the influences of the Gentile environment on the style, content, and quality of the Jewish legends. One of the most obvious of these, which the reader will certainly not fail noticing, is the difference between the legends of East European provenance on the one hand and those of Middle Eastern origin on the other. One cannot help being struck by the greater ruthlessness,

[18] Moshe Carmilly-Weinberger, *Censorship and Freedom of Expression in Jewish History,* pp. 51-59.

uncouthness, and coarseness, the lesser regard for the human personality and dignity, the more ready resort to violence, to verbal and physical abuse, which are features of the Middle Eastern Jewish legend as compared with its East European counterpart. In the East European Jewish legend, as typified by the Hasidic story, only the Gentiles are depicted—as they must needs have appeared in the eyes of the Jews—as cruel, ignorant barbarians, while the Jews themselves are shown to be pious, God-fearing, meek, and mild. In the Middle Eastern Jewish legend, by contrast, the cruel and barbarous features of the Gentiles often recur, albeit in a mitigated form, in the portraiture of its Jewish protagonists as well.

No East European Jewish folktale would, for instance, describe an ugly Jewish girl as "having the face of an animal," yet this precisely is the expression used in a Moroccan Jewish story. Nor would an East European Jewish folktale tell about its Jewish hero that he killed his adversaries "with an unnatural death," as does the Middle Eastern Jewish story "The Reward of Charity." Middle Eastern, too, is the gross act of the miser who swallows all his pearls and precious stones in an effort to take them along with him at his death. Less gross, but still strange to the East European Jewish mentality, is to threaten God as the Syrian story has the sexton do in "The Jar of Tears."

Since legends, as all folklore products, mirror the psyche of those who wrote them and liked to hear them, one cannot doubt that the differences between the tenor of the Middle Eastern and East European Jewish legends reflect a corresponding psychological difference between these two major divisions of the Jewish people whose genesis must be sought in local environmental influences.

The Jews who have lived for many centuries in the Middle Eastern environment of the Muslim North African, Turkish, Arab, Kurdish, Persian, and Afghan lands, even though they were almost invariably isolated in the *mellah, hara,* or whatever other name the ghetto had, nevertheless absorbed considerable influences from the culture of the Muslim majority and from the features of the Muslim modal personality. The Middle Eastern cultural configuration includes low literacy, low educational level, low income level, low housing standards, as well as widespread poverty, high fertility and mortality, and high incidence of disease. It is also characterized by patriarchal rule, extended families with strong familism, subordinated position of women, strict segregation of the sexes, fatalistic religious outlook and strong traditionalism, factional loyalties, and great emphasis on honor ("face"). Most of these features were present to some extent in the cultures of the Middle Eastern Jewish communities. Even as far as illiteracy is concerned, by no means were all Jewish men able to read and write, and almost all Jewish women were illiterate.

The Middle Eastern modal personality comprises exaggerated self-assertion and self-importance; flamboyant behavior and speech; the tendency to blame others for one's own shortcomings, weaknesses, and failures; a preference for quick and easy achievements (including instant, as against deferred, gratification); lack of correlation between thoughts and words on the one hand, and acts and the reality to which acts must conform, on the other; aggressiveness, quarrelsomeness, irascibility, and a vacillation between outbursts of uncontrolled temper and quiet resignation.[19] Because of their minority status, the Middle Eastern Jews could not absorb all these traits to an equal measure. E.g., flamboyant behavior and speech were patently impossible for them in their contacts with Muslims, and thus could not become a dominant behavior pattern in intra-Jewish relations either. In general it must be emphasized that the features of the Middle Eastern Jewish culture and personality appear as marked only when compared with corresponding features in the culture and personality of the East European Jews, and especially if

[19] R. Patai, *The Jewish Mind,* pp. 308–09, 426.

attention is focused on recent times, say, the first half of the twentieth century.

In any case, the specific conditions of the local Jewish culture and the specific traits of the local Jewish personality are easily recognizable in the legends of Middle Eastern and East European provenance presented in the folklore and Hasidic sections of this book. Nor must one overlook the internal differences among communities belonging to either one of the two great divisions of the Jewish people. A discussion of these differences would lead us too far afield, but at least passing mention should be made of the Dionysian, enthusiastic, warmhearted, emotional Hasid of Galicia as against the Apollonian, cool-headed, measured, sharp-witted Lithuanian *Mitnaged* (opponent of Hasidism) in the East European division, and of the patient, meek, self-effacing, humble Yemenite Jew as against the bellicose, quarrelsome, self-righteous, violence-prone Moroccan Jew in the Middle Eastern division. Each Jewish local group has, of course, many other features as well, of which the above were picked out only as illustrations of extreme variance.

The legends of Ashkenazi Jewish origin contained in the folklore section all come from East Europe, and are mostly products of a Hasidic environment. For this reason it was occasionally difficult to decide whether to assign them to that section or to the Hasidic section which follows it. The central hero in these legends is the Tzaddiq, the Hasidic rabbi. He is always represented as having an uncanny grasp of the true meaning of things, which, as a rule, eludes the eye of the simple Hasid. The Tzaddiq often has miraculous powers, which, of course, he uses most selectively and exclusively for the benefit of a deserving, believing Jew, of a group of such Jews, or, more rarely, of the Jewish people as a whole. Yet the greatest achievement of the Tzaddiq is not the performance of miracles, but his ability to reveal that which is unseen, to manifest the hidden, mysterious connections between human acts and their consequences, and to make his disciples understand the saintliness of very simple, seemingly totally insignificant individuals, such as a butcher, a wagoner, and even a drunkard. The Hasidic legend also points up the importance of the Tzaddiq as the psychological mainstay of Jewish life in East Europe. He was the saintly man, the man of God, to whom one could always turn for help, advice, encouragement, and reassurance, and from whose mouth one single word was enough to impart confidence in the future, however dire and dismal the present.

How utterly dire and dismal the present was comes through vividly and painfully in the stories included in the folklore and Hasidic sections. The environment and the period reflected in these legends were the worst Jews had experienced until that time, when the horrors of the Nazi holocaust were still hidden in the future. But every Jew was exposed to daily humiliations in his contact with Gentiles; frequently he was persecuted, beaten, abused, and robbed, and his womenfolk were violated. Whole communities were at the mercy of unfeeling, hostile overlords, of brutalized and brutal peasants. Attacks, expulsions, and other *g'zerot* (cruel decrees) could be expected any day and without any provocation, and the specter of pogrom and death was never far. All these experiences are amply illustrated in the legends of East European provenance, although calamities and arbitrary brutalities were no strangers to Middle Eastern Jewish life and legend either.

Nor is it surprising that in these circumstances of life in the Diaspora the very idea of opposing force with force, of defending oneself by fighting back, could not arise in Jewish life and is not described in Jewish legend. The one notable exception to this rule is the collection of heroic tales known as *Sefer haYashar,* which tells of the warlike exploits of the sons of Jacob, of Moses, and of other ancient Hebrew heroes. The *Sefer haYashar* was written in Spain, in the late eleventh century, when the memory of great Jewish warlords who commanded Muslim armies, such as Samuel haNagid (993-1055) of Granada, was still alive and inspired writers with the desire to extol Jewish heroism. However, even this one book of Jewish heroic folktales centering on Jewish exploits on the battlefield deals with the politically safe subject of the remote Biblical era when the enemies of the Children of Israel were nations long since extinct.

Following the destruction of Jerusalem by the Romans (70 C.E.), Jewish resort to force against Gentile opponents rapidly fell into desuetude. The typical Jewish social aggregate in the lands of the Diaspora was a small urban community, living in a quarter or quarters of its own, surrounded by a many times larger Gentile population. This lopsided power relationship sufficed to render any attempt at armed resistance utter folly: it would have been suicidal, and, in addition, would have brought disaster also upon those who for the moment were not involved in any Jewish-Gentile struggle. Thus the stereotypical, and soon instinctive, reaction to every *g'zera* was to offer no resistance, but instead to cry to God for help, to engage in soul-searching, to repent, to make vows of piety, and, from the eighteenth century on in East Europe, to turn to the Tzaddiq or, in the Middle East, to his much older prototype and counterpart, the miracle-working saint.

This is the background and the mentality reflected in many legends. What is remarkable is that, with all this, the Jewish psyche was still suffused with a loud note of undoubted self-esteem, with the solid conviction that the Jews were spiritually and morally superior to the Gentiles, that they were and remained God's own chosen people whom the Almighty loved and protected. This, too, is clearly reflected in the legends, which therefore present a curious mixture of self-pity and self-conceit, of full cognizance of the Jews' physical defenselessness and the unshakable conviction that their protection against the Gentiles and their onslaughts is the prime concern of God acting through His elect, the Tzaddiq or the saint.

I
BIBLE

The Bible is man's most revered, most influential, most widely read, and most thoroughly studied book. For a major part of mankind it is The Book. Yet as far as its authorship and provenance are concerned, millennia of study have not resulted in a general consensus.

Orthodox Jews (as well as fundamentalist Christians and Muslims) believe that the Bible is the word of God, revealed from On High, literally true, immutable, sacrosanct, and absolute. For Orthodox Jews, the laws contained in the Bible, as interpreted by the Talmudic sages and subsequent Halakhists, have a binding force for all times. They believe that the Five Books of Moses were written, at the behest of God, by Moses himself; that the other books were authored by those under whose names they appear (e.g., Joshua, Samuel, Isaiah); that when a book contains a reference to a future event—e.g., the mention of Cyrus, who lived in the sixth century B.C.E., by Isaiah, who lived two centuries earlier (44:28; 45:1)—this manifests divine prophecy; and that the present text of the Bible is identical with the one originally written by its inspired authors.

A different picture emerges from the painstaking studies of hundreds of Biblical scholars. Their textual and higher criticism of the Bible has satisfied them and modern readers of Scripture that behind the presently extant text lies a variety of sources and a long process of literary development, of oral and/or written tradition, and of careful, but occasionally not sufficiently careful, editorial work. While fully recognizing the unique ethical values, religious power, and literary quality of the Bible, they consider it not the verbatim record of the word of God, but the highest expression of inspired human thought about God, His will, His works.

According to this view, the Five Books of Moses (the Pentateuch, or Tora in the narrow sense of the word), which tell the story of mankind and of the Children of Israel from Creation to the death of Moses, and which contain several codes of law, are based on several oral traditions and written documents, some of which unquestionably go back to the times of Moses (thirteenth century B.C.E.). They were put in final shape probably by Ezra or in his days, that is, in the fifth century B.C.E. The historical books of Joshua, Judges, Samuel, Kings, Ezra, Nehemia, and Chronicles (the last mentioned dating from the first half of the third century B.C.E.) carry on the history of Israel until the fifth century B.C.E., that is, about a hundred years after the return of the Jews from the Babylonian Exile (586-538 B.C.E.), the rebuilding of Jerusalem and the Temple (517 B.C.E.).

The great prophets of Israel lived, worked, and wrote in the eighth century B.C.E. (Isaiah, Hosea, Joel, Amos, Micha); in the period shortly before and after the destruction of Jerusalem in 586 B.C.E. (Jeremiah, Ezekiel, Obadiah, Nahum. Habbakuk); at the time of the return in 538 B.C.E. (Deutero-Isaiah); in the fifth century B.C.E. (Haggai, Malachi); and in the fourth century B.C.E. (Zechariah) or even later (Jonah). The religious genius of the first five achieved the replacement of the old Israelite tribal Yahwist henotheism with the universal ethical monotheism which was destined to become the basis of Talmudic Judaism and all subsequent developments of the Jewish faith.

Of the remaining books of the Bible, the Psalms are attributed by tradition to King David. They are probably the greatest religious poetry to be written by man. While containing many ancient songs, the book as a whole was assembled in its present form not earlier than the second century B.C.E. The Book of Proverbs, attributed by tradition, together with the Song of Songs and Ecclesiastes, to King Solomon, consists of a number of divisions which were put together into the present book about 400 B.C.E. The Book of Job, probably of the same date, deals with the problem of human suffering, and has rightly been judged one of the greatest works of tragic literature. Of the so-called Five Scrolls, the Song of Songs (or Canticles) is actually a collection of love and wedding songs, some of which go back as far as the ninth century B.C.E., although its present form was given it as late as the third century B.C.E. It was saved from exclusion from the Biblical canon when the synod of Jabne (90-100 C.E.) accepted as valid its allegorical interpretation as symbolizing the relations between God (the bridegroom) and Israel (the bride). The Book of Ruth is a charming idyllic story, set in the early period of the Judges, probably drawing upon a very old tale, but put in final form between 450 and 250 B.C.E. Lamentations, attributed by Jewish tradition to Jeremiah, was written soon after the destruction of Jerusalem (586 B.C.E.) which it bewails. Ecclesiastes, a book of pessimistic philosophy upholding only the value of wisdom, was written in the early second century B.C.E. Esther is a harem story telling about the rescue of the Jews under the Persian king Ahasuerus (Xerxes, 485-465 B.C.E.); it was probably written in the early second century B.C.E.

Daniel, a partly legendary and partly apocalyptic book, appeared about 163 B.C.E. and is thus the latest book included in the Biblical canon.

The Bible thus comprises works dating from some

twelve centuries (thirteenth to second B.C.E.). It is written in Hebrew, except for parts of Ezra and most of Daniel, which are in Aramaic.

This part contains a selection of legends from the narrative parts of the Bible, from the Creation to Daniel.

Creation

In the beginning God created the heavens and the earth. And the earth was formless and void, and darkness was over the face of the abyss, and the spirit of God hovered over the face of the water. And God said, "Let there be light," and there was light. And God saw the light that it was good, and God divided the light from the darkness. And God called the light Day, and the darkness He called Night. And there was evening and there was morning, one day.

And God said, "Let there be a firmament in the midst of the waters, and let it divide the waters from the waters." And God made the firmament, and divided the waters which were under the firmament from the waters which were above the firmament. And it was so. And God called the firmament Heavens. And there was evening and there was morning, the second day.

And God said, "Let the waters gather under the heavens to one place, and let the dry land be seen." And it was so. And God called the dry land Earth, and the gathering of waters He called Seas. And God saw that it was good. And God said, "Let the earth bring forth grass, herb yielding seed, fruit-tree yielding fruit after its kind whose seed is in it upon the earth." And it was so. And the earth brought forth grass, herb yielding seed after its kind, and tree bearing fruit whose seed was in it after its kind. And God saw that it was good. And there was evening and there was morning, the third day.

And God said, "Let there be lights in the firmament of

the heavens, to divide the day from the night, and let them be for signs and season, and for days and years. And let them be for lights in the firmament of the heavens, to light up the earth." And it was so. And God made the two great lights, the great light to rule the day, and the small light to rule the night, and the stars. And God set them into the firmament of the heavens to light up the earth, and to rule in the day and in the night, and to divide the light from the darkness. And God saw that it was good. And there was evening and there was morning, the fourth day.

And God said, "Let the waters swarm with swarms of living beings, and let fowl fly above the earth upon the face of the firmament of the heavens." And God created the great dragons, and all the living beings which swarm, with which the waters swarmed after their kind, and all the winged for fowl after its kind. And God saw that it was good. And God blessed them, saying, "Be fruitful and multiply and fill the waters in the seas, and let the fowl multiply in the earth." And there was evening and there was morning, the fifth day.

And God said, "Let the earth bring forth living beings after their kind, cattle and creeping thing, and beast of the earth after its kind. And it was so. And God made the beast of the earth after its kind, and the cattle after its kind, and all the creeping things of the ground after their kind. And God saw that it was good.

And God said, "Let Us make man in Our image, after Our likeness, and let them rule over the fish of the sea, and over the fowl of the heavens and over the cattle, and over all the earth, and over every creeping thing that creepeth upon the earth." And God created the man in His image, in the image of God created He him, male and female created He them. And God blessed them and God said to them, "Be fruitful and multiply and fill the earth and subdue it, and rule over the fish of the sea and over the fowl of the heavens, and over every living thing that creepeth upon the earth."

And God said, "Behold, I have given you every herb yielding seed which is upon the face of the earth, and every tree in which there is tree-fruit yielding seed, to you shall it be to eat. And to every beast of the earth, and to every fowl of the heavens, and to every creeping thing upon the earth in which there is a living soul, shall be every green herb to eat." And it was so. And God saw every thing that He had made, and behold, it was very good. And there was evening and there was morning, the sixth day.

And the heavens and the earth were finished, and all their host. And God finished on the seventh day His work which He had made, and He rested on the seventh day from all His work which He had made. And God blessed the seventh day and sanctified it, for on it He rested from all His work which God had created.

(Gen. 1:1-2:3)

Eve

And the Lord God commanded the man saying, "Of every tree of the Garden thou shalt eat, but of the tree of knowledge of good and evil thou shalt not eat of it, for on the day on which thou eatest of it thou shalt surely die."

And the Lord God said, "It is not good for the man to be alone; I will make him a help-meet for him." And the Lord God fashioned out of the ground every beast of the field and every fowl of the heaven, and brought them to the man to see what he would call them; and by whatever the man called a living being that was its name. And the man gave names to every cattle, and to the fowl of the heaven, and to every beast of the field, but for the man he found no help-meet for him.

And the Lord God caused a deep sleep to fall upon the man, and he slept. And He took one of his ribs, and filled in flesh in its stead. And the Lord God built the rib which He had taken from the man into a woman, and brought her to the man. And the man said, "This now is bone of my bones and flesh of my flesh; this one shall be called woman, for out of man was this one taken."

Therefore shall a man leave his father and his mother, and cleave unto his wife, and they become one flesh. And they were both naked, the man and his wife, and they were not ashamed.

(Gen. 2:16-25)

The Fall

And the serpent was more cunning than all the beasts of the field which the Lord God had made, and he said to the woman, "Is it that God hath said 'Ye shall not eat of any tree of the Garden'?" And the woman said to the serpent, "We may eat of the fruit of the trees of the Garden, but of the fruit of the tree which is in the middle of the Garden God said, 'Ye shall not eat of it, and ye shall not touch it, lest ye die.' " And the serpent said to the woman, "Ye shall surely not die. For God knoweth that on the day on which ye eat thereof your eyes shall be opened and ye shall be like unto God, knowing good and evil."

And the woman saw that the tree was good for eating, and that it was delicious to the eyes, and that the tree was desirable to make one wise, and she took of its fruit and ate, and gave also unto her husband with her, and he ate. And the eyes of them both were opened and they knew that they were naked, and they sewed fig leaves and made themselves aprons.

And they heard the voice of the Lord God walking about in the Garden in the breeze of the day, and the man and his wife hid themselves before the Lord God in the trees of the Garden. And the Lord God called the man and said to him, "Where art thou?" And he said, "I heard Thy voice in the Garden and I was afraid, for I am naked, and I hid."

And He said, "Who told thee that thou art naked? Hast thou eaten of the tree whereof I commanded thee that thou shouldest not eat?" And the man said, "The woman whom

Thou gavest to be with me, she gave me of the tree, and I did eat."

And the Lord God said unto the woman, "What is this thou hast done?" And the woman said, "The serpent beguiled me and I did eat."

And the Lord God said to the serpent, "Because thou hast done this, cursed art thou from among all cattle and all beasts of the field! Upon thy belly shalt thou go, and dust shalt thou eat all the days of thy life. And I will put enmity between thee and the woman, and between thy seed and her seed, he shall bruise thy head and thou shalt bruise his heel."

Unto the woman He said, "I will greatly multiply thy pain and thy pregnancy, in pain shalt thou bear children, and thy desire shall be to thy husband, and he shall rule over thee."

And unto Adam He said, "Because thou hast hearkened unto the voice of thy wife, and hast eaten of the tree of which I commanded thee saying, Thou shalt not eat of it, cursed is the ground for thy sake, and thorns and thistles shall it bring forth to thee, and thou shalt eat the herb of the field. In the sweat of thy face shalt thou eat bread, till thou return unto the ground, for out of it wast thou taken; for dust thou art and unto dust shalt thou return."

And the man called his wife's name Eve (*Hawa*), for she was the mother of all living (*hay*). And the Lord God made for Adam and for his wife skin garments and clothed them.

And the Lord God said, "Behold, the man is become as one of Us, to know good and evil. And now, lest he put forth his hand and take also of the tree of life and eat and live for ever." Therefore the Lord God sent him forth from the Garden of Eden to till the ground from whence he was taken. So He drove out the man, and He placed the Cherubim at the east of the Garden of Eden, and the flame of the revolving sword, to guard the way of the tree of life.

(Gen. 3:1-24)

The Fratricide

And the man knew Eve his wife and she conceived and bore Cain (*Qayin*), and she said, "I obtained (*qanite*) a man from the Lord." And again she bore his brother Abel (*Hevel*), and Abel became a keeper of sheep and Cain was a tiller of the ground. And it came to pass at the end of days that Cain brought an offering to the Lord from the fruit of the ground; and Abel, he also brought of the firstlings of his flock and its fat. And the Lord turned unto Abel and his offering, but unto Cain and his offering He turned not, and Cain was very wroth and his face fell.

And the Lord said to Cain, "Why art thou wroth and why is thy face fallen? If thou doest well, shall it not be lifted up? And if thou doest not well, sin coucheth at the door, and its desire is to thee but thou canst rule over it."

And Cain spoke to his brother Abel, and it came to pass when they were in the field that Cain rose up against Abel his brother and slew him.

And the Lord said to Cain, "Where is Abel thy brother?" And he said, "I know not; am I my brother's keeper?"

And He said, "What hast thou done? The voice of thy brother's blood crieth unto Me from the earth! And now, cursed art thou from the earth which opened her mouth to receive thy brother's blood from thy hand! When thou tillest the earth, she shall no longer give thee her strength, a fugitive and a wanderer shalt thou be in the land."

And Cain said to the Lord, "My sin is too great to bear. Behold, Thou hast driven me this day from off the face of the earth, and from Thy face shall I be hid, and I will be a fugitive and a wanderer in the land, and it shall come to pass that whosoever findeth me shall slay me."

And the Lord said to him, "Therefore he who slayeth Cain shall suffer sevenfold vengeance!" And the Lord set a sign for Cain lest any finding him smite him. And Cain went out from before the Lord, and dwelt in the land of Nod, east of Eden.

(Gen. 4:1-17)

The Sons of God and the Daughters of Man

And it came to pass when man began to multiply on the face of the earth, and daughters were born unto them, that the Sons of God saw the daughters of man that they were fair, and they took them wives, of anyone they chose.

And the Lord said, "Let My spirit not strive with man for ever, for he is but flesh. Therefore let his days be a hundred and twenty years."

The Giants (*Nefilim*) were in the earth in those days, and also thereafter, when the Sons of God came in unto the daughters of man, and they bore children to them: the same were the mighty ones that were of yore the men of renown.

(Gen. 6:1-4)

The Deluge

And the Lord saw that the wickedness of man was great in the earth, and all the inclinations of the thoughts of his heart were only evil all the days, and it repented the Lord that He had made man on earth, and He grieved in His heart. And the Lord said, "I will blot out man whom I have created from the face of the earth, from man to beast, to creeping things and to the birds of the heavens, for it repenteth Me that I have made them!" But Noah found favor in the eyes of the Lord.

And God said unto Noah, "The end of all flesh is come before Me, for the earth is filled with violence through them, and behold, I will destroy them from the earth. Make thee an ark of gopher wood, make cabins in the ark, and pitch it within and without with pitch. And this is how thou shalt make it: three hundred cubits the length of the ark, fifty cubits its width, and thirty cubits its height. A light shalt thou make to the ark, and to a cubit shalt thou finish it upward, and the door of the ark shalt thou set in its side, and make it with a lowest, a second, and a third deck. And I, behold, I bring a deluge of water upon the earth to destroy all flesh wherein is the breath of life, from under the heaven; everything that is on earth shall perish. But I will establish My covenant with thee, and thou shalt enter the ark, thou, and thy sons, and thy wife, and the wives of thy sons with thee. And of all that is alive, of all flesh, two of each shalt thou bring into the ark, to keep them alive with thee; they shall be male and female. Of the birds after their kind, of the cattle after their kind, of every creeping thing of the ground after their kind, let two of each come unto thee to keep them alive. And thou take unto thee of all the food that is eaten and gather it to thee, and it shall serve as food for thee and for them."

And Noah did according to all that God commanded him, so did he....

And Noah and his sons and his wife and his sons' wives with him entered the ark because of the waters of the deluge. Of the clean beasts and of the beasts that are not clean , and of the birds and every thing that creepeth upon the ground, two and two went in unto Noah into the ark, male and female, as God had commanded Noah. And it came to pass after the seven days, that the waters of the deluge were upon the earth. In the six hundredth year of Noah's life, in the second month, in the seventeenth day of the month, on this day all the fountains of the great abyss burst, and the windows of heaven opened. And the rain was upon the earth forty days and forty nights.... And the waters became mighty, and increased greatly upon the earth, and the ark went upon the face of the water. And the water became very, very mighty upon the earth, and all the high mountains under the whole sky were covered. Fifteen cubits above them did the waters rise, and the mountains were covered. And all flesh that stirred upon the earth perished, the birds and the cattle and the beasts and all that which creepeth upon the earth, and all men. All those in whose nostrils was the breath of life, of all that was in the dry land, died. And He blotted out all the creatures which were upon the face of the earth, from man to beast, to the creeping things, and to the birds of heaven, and they were blotted out from the earth. And there remained only Noah and they that were with him in the ark. And the waters rose upon the earth a fifty and hundred days.

And God remembered Noah and all the beasts and the cattle which were with him in the ark, and God made a wind to pass over the earth, and the waters subsided. And the fountains of the abyss were stopped, and the windows of heaven, and the rain ceased from heaven. And the waters gradually returned from the earth, and the waters diminished after the end of a fifty and hundred days. And the ark came to rest in the seventh month, on the seventeenth day of the month, upon the mountains of Ararat. And the water continued to decrease until the tenth month; on the first day of the tenth month the heads of the mountains were seen.

And it came to pass after the end of forty days that Noah opened the window of the ark which he had made. And he sent forth the raven, and it went out, coming and going, until the waters dried up from off the earth. And he sent forth the dove from him to see whether the waters had abated from off the face of the earth. And the dove found no rest for her foot and returned to him to the ark, for waters were upon the face of the whole earth, and he stretched forth his hand and took her, and brought her to him into the ark. And he waited yet another seven days and again sent forth the dove from the ark. And the dove came back to him at eventide, and behold, a plucked olive-leaf in her mouth. And Noah knew that the waters had abated from the earth. And he waited yet another seven days, and sent forth the dove, and she did no longer return to him.

And it came to pass in the six hundred and first year, on the first day of the first month, that the waters were dried up from off the earth, and Noah removed the cover of the ark and saw that, behold, the face of the earth was dried. And in the second month, on the twenty-seventh day of the month, the earth was dry.

And God spoke unto Noah saying, "Go forth from the ark, thou and thy wife and thy sons and thy sons' wives with thee. Bring out with thee all the animals which are with thee of all flesh, the birds and the beasts and all that which creepeth upon the earth, that they may swarm in the earth and be fruitful and multiply upon the earth."

And Noah went forth, and his sons and his wife and his sons' wives with him. And all the animals, all the creeping things, and all the birds, all that swarms upon the earth, according to their families, went forth from the ark.

And Noah built an altar unto the Lord, and took of all the clean cattle and all the clean birds, and offered up burnt offerings on the altar. And the Lord smelled the sweet savor, and the Lord said in His heart, "I will not again curse the earth because of man, for the inclination of the heart of man is evil from his youth; and I will not again smite all the living as I have done. All the days of the earth seed and harvest, cold and heat, summer and winter, day and night shall not cease."

(Gen. 6:5-8, 13-22; 7:7-12, 18-24; 8:1-22)

The Rainbow

And God spoke to Noah and his sons saying, "And I, behold, I establish My covenant with you and with your seed after you. And with every living being that is with you, of the birds and the cattle and all the beasts of the earth with you, of all those that came forth from the ark, even every beast of the earth. And I will establish My covenant with you: no flesh shall again be cut off by waters of the deluge, and there shall be no more a deluge to destroy the earth."

And God said, "This is the sign of the covenant which I set between Me and you and all the living creatures which are with you, for all generation for ever: I set my bow in the cloud, and it shall be a sign of the covenant between Me and the earth. And it shall come to pass when I cover the earth with cloud, the bow will be seen in the cloud. And I will remember My covenant which is between Me and you and all living creatures in all flesh, and the water will become no more a deluge to destroy all flesh. And the bow will be in the cloud, and I will see it, to remember the everlasting covenant between God and all living souls in all flesh which is upon the earth." And God said to Noah, "This is the sign of the covenant which I have established between Me and all flesh which is upon the earth."

(Gen. 9:8-17)

Noah's Drunkenness

And Noah began to be a man of the soil, and he planted a vineyard. And he drank of the vine and became drunken, and he uncovered himself in his tent. And Ham, the father of Canaan, saw the nakedness of his father and told his two brothers outside. And Shem and Japheth took the garment and put it on the shoulders of both of them, and walked backward and covered the nakedness of their father, while their faces were backward so that they saw not their father's nakedness.

And Noah awoke from his wine, and knew what his youngest son had done him. And he said,

> *"Cursed be Canaan,*
> *A servant of servants be he to his brothers."*

And he said,

> *"Blessed be the Lord, the God of Shem,*
> *And let Canaan be a servant to them.*
> *Enlarge, O God, Japheth,*
> *And may he dwell in Shem's tents,*
> *And let Canaan be a servant to them."*

(Gen. 9:20-27)

The Tower of Babel

And the whole earth was one tongue and one speech. And it came to pass as they journeyed eastward that they found a plain in the Land of Shinar, and they settled there. And they said one to another, "Come, let us make bricks and burn them in fire." And the brick served them as stone, and the slime was for them the mortar. And they said, "Come, let us build ourselves a city and a tower, and its top in heaven, and let us make us a name, lest we be scattered upon the face of the whole earth."

And the Lord descended to see the city and the tower which the sons of man built. And the Lord said, "Behold, one people, and they all have one language, and this is what they have begun to do, and now nothing which they purpose to do will be withholden from them. Come, let us descend and confound (*navla*) there their languages so that one understand not the speech of the other." And the Lord dispersed them from thence upon the face of the whole earth, and they ceased building the city. Therefore is its name called Babel (*Bavel*) for there the Lord confounded (*balal*) the speech of the whole earth and from thence the Lord dispersed them upon the face of the whole earth.

(Gen. 11:1-9)

Abraham in Egypt

And there was famine in the land and Abram went down to Egypt to dwell there, for the famine was heavy in the land. And it came to pass as he approached Egypt that he said to Sarai his wife, "Behold, I pray thee, I know that thou art a woman of beautiful countenance. And it shall come to pass when the Egyptians see thee that they shall say, 'This is his wife,' and they shall slay me and thee they shall let live. Say, I pray thee, that thou art my sister, that it may be well with me for thy sake, and that my soul live because of thee."

And it came to pass when Abram was come to Egypt that

the Egyptians saw the woman that she was very beautiful, and the princes of Pharaoh saw her and praised her to Pharaoh, and the woman was taken into the house of Pharaoh. And he dealt well with Abram for her sake, and he had flocks and cattle and asses and slaves and slave girls, and she-asses and camels. But the Lord smote Pharaoh and his house with great plagues because of the matter of Sarai the wife of Abram. And Pharaoh summoned Abram and said, "What is this thou hast done to me? Why didst thou not tell me that she was thy wife? Why didst thou say, 'She is my sister,' so that I took her to be my wife? And now, behold thy wife, take her and go!" And Pharaoh gave him in charge of men, and they sent off him and his wife and all that he had.

(Gen. 12:10-20)

The Three Visitors

And the Lord appeared unto him by the terebinths of Mamre, and he was seated at the door of the tent in the heat of the day. And he lifted up his eyes and saw, and behold, three men were standing above him, and he saw, and he ran to them from the door of the tent, and bowed himself to the earth, and said, "My lords, if, I pray thee, I have found favor in thy eyes, pray do not pass by your servant. Let, I pray thee, a little water be fetched, and let them wash your feet, and rest yourselves under the tree. And I will fetch a piece of bread, and ye strengthen your heart; after that ye shall pass on, for ye have passed by your servant."

And they said, "Do as thou hast spoken."

And Abraham hastened into the tent to Sarah and said: "Hurry, knead three measures of fine flour, and make cakes." And Abraham ran to the herd and took a calf, tender and good, and gave it to the youth, and he hastened and put it before them, and he stood over them under the tree, and they ate.

And they said to him, "Where is Sarah thy wife?"

And he said, "Behold, in the tent."

And he[1] said, "I will surely return unto thee at the time of life,[2] and, behold, Sarah thy wife shall have a son."

And Sarah heard it at the tent door which was behind him. And Abraham and Sarah were old, well stricken in age; the way of women had ceased for Sarah. And Sarah laughed to herself, saying, "After I am grown old, can I have pleasure? And my lord is old."

And the Lord said to Abraham, "Why did Sarah laugh saying, 'Can I, in fact, bear when I am waxed old'? Is any thing too hard for the Lord? In due time I will return to thee, at the time of life, and Sarah shall have a son!"

And Sarah denied, saying, "I laughed not." For she was afraid. And He said, "Nay, but thou didst laugh."

And the men arose from thence, and looked toward Sodom, and Abraham went with them to send them off.

(Gen. 18:1-16)

The Destruction of Sodom

And the Lord said: "Because the cry of Sodom and Gomorrah is great, and their sin is very grievous, I will go down now and see whether they have done according to her cry which is come unto Me, and if not, I will know...."

And the two angels came to Sodom in the evening, and Lot sat in the gate of Sodom. And Lot saw and rose to meet them, and he bowed down, his face to the earth. And he said: "Behold, now, my lords, pray turn in into the house of your servant, and stay overnight, and wash your feet, and then get up in the morning and be on your way." And they said: "Nay, but we will spend the night in the street."

And he urged them greatly, and they turned in to him and came into his house. And he made them a meal, and baked unleavened bread (*matzot*), and they ate.

---

[1] One of the three men.
[2] An extremely difficult phrase in Hebrew.

But before they lay down, the men of the city, the men of Sodom, converged upon the house, from young to old, all the people from the outskirts. And they called unto Lot and said to him, "Where are the men who came unto thee tonight, bring them out to us so that we may know them!"

And Lot went out to them to the door, and shut the door after him, and said, "I pray you, my brothers, do not act wickedly. Behold, I have two daughters who have not known man, I will bring them out to you, and do unto them as is good in your eyes. Only do nothing unto these men since they are come under the shadow of my beam."

But they said, "Move aside!" And they said: "This one has come to dwell here, and he wants to be a judge! Now we will do worse unto thee than unto them!" And they pressed sore upon the man, upon Lot, and drew near to break the door.

And the men stretched forth their hand, and brought Lot back into the house unto them, and shut the door. And they smote the men who were at the door of the house with blindness, from the small to the great, and they wearied themselves trying to find the door.

And the men said to Lot, "Whom else dost thou have here? Son-in-law, and thy sons and daughters, and all those thou hast in the city, bring them out of the place. For we will destroy this place, for their cry is waxed great before the Lord, and the Lord sent us to destroy it."

And Lot went out and spoke to his sons-in-law who had taken his daughters, and said, "Arise, go out from this place for the Lord shall destroy the city." And he was as one who jesteth in the eyes of his sons-in-law.

And as the dawn rose the angels hastened Lot saying: "Up, take thy wife and thy two daughters who are found here, lest thou perish because of the iniquity of the city." But he hesitated, whereupon the men took hold of his hand and the hand of his wife and the hand of his two daughters, with the Lord's mercy unto him, and led him out and set him outside the city. And it came to pass as they were leading him outside, that He said, "Flee for thy life, look not behind thee and stop not in all the plain, but flee to the mountain lest thou perish."

And Lot said to them, "O, not so, my lords! Behold now Thy servant hath found favor in Thy eyes, and Thou hast shown great mercy in saving my life, but I cannot flee to the mountain lest the evil overtake me and I die! Behold, I pray thee, this city is near to flee to it, and it is small (*mitz'ar*); let me flee there—is it not small?—and my soul shall live."

And He said to him, "Behold, I will honor thy face in this matter as well, in that I will not overthrow the city of which thou hast spoken. But hurry, flee there, for I cannot do a thing until thou gettest there." Therefore was the name of that city called Zoar (*Tzo'ar*). The sun rose upon the earth, and Lot came to Zoar.

And the Lord caused brimstone and fire to rain upon Sodom and Gomorrah, from the Lord, from heaven. And He overthrew those cities, and the whole plain, and all the dwellers of the cities and the growth of the earth. And his wife looked back from behind him, and became a pillar of salt.

(Gen. 18:20-21; 19:1-26)

The Akeda

And it came to pass after these things that God tested Abraham and said to him, "Abraham!" And he said, "Here I am!" And He said, "Take now thy son, thy only one, whom thou lovest, even Isaac, and betake thyself to the Land of Moriah and offer him there as a burnt offering upon one of the mountains which I will tell thee."

And Abraham rose early in the morning, and saddled up his ass, and took his two young men with him, and Isaac his son, and he cleaved wood for the burnt offering, and arose and went to the place which God had told him.

On the third day Abraham lifted up his eyes and saw the

place from afar. And Abraham said to his young men: "Stay here with the ass, and I and the boy will go yonder, and we will worship and return to you." And Abraham took the wood of the burnt offering and laid it upon Isaac his son, and he took the fire and the knife in his hand, and the two of them went together.

And Isaac said to Abraham his father and said, "My father!" And he said, "Here I am, my son!" And he said, "Behold the fire and the wood, but where is the lamb for the burnt offering?" And Abraham said, "God Himself shall see to the lamb for a burnt offering, my son." And the two went together.

And they came to the place which God had told him, and Abraham built the altar there and arranged the wood, and he tied Isaac his son, and put him upon the altar on top of the wood. And Abraham stretched forth his hand and took the knife to slay his son.

And the angel of God called to him from heaven and said, "Abraham!" And he said, "Here am I." And He said, "Stretch not forth thy hand to the boy, and do nothing to him, for now I know that thou art God-fearing, and hast not withheld thy son, thy only one, from Me."

And Abraham lifted up his eyes and saw, and behold a ram, caught in the thicket by his horn. And Abraham went and took the ram, and offered him as a burnt offering in place of his son. And Abraham called the name of that place, "The Lord seeth," as it is said to this day, "In the mountain where the Lord is seen."

And the angel of the Lord called unto Abraham a second time from heaven, and said, "By Myself I do swear, saith the Lord, because thou hast done this thing, and hast not withheld thy son, thy only one, therefore I shall surely bless thee, and I shall surely multiply thy seed as the stars of heaven and as the sand which is on the shore of the sea, and thy seed shall possess the gate of his enemies. And all nations of the earth shall be blessed in thy seed, because thou hast hearkened to My voice."

And Abraham returned to his young men, and they arose and went together to Beer-Sheba, and Abraham dwelt in Beer-Sheba.

(Gen. 22:1-19)

The Stolen Blessing

And it came to pass when Isaac grew old that his eyes became dim and he could not see. And he called Esau his elder son and said to him, "My son!" And he said to him, "Here am I!" And he said, "Behold, I have grown old, and I know not the day of my death. And now, take, I pray thee, thy weapons, thy quiver and thy bow, and go out to the field, and go hunt a game for me, and prepare for me a tasty dish as I like it, and bring it to me that I may eat so that my soul bless thee before I die."

And Rebekah heard as Isaac spoke to Esau his son. And Esau went off to the field to hunt for a game and to bring it back. And Rebekah spoke to Jacob her son saying, "Behold, I heard thy father speak to Esau thy brother saying, 'Bring me venison and prepare for me savory food so that I may eat and bless thee before the Lord, before my death.' Now, my son, hearken to my voice as to what I command thee. Go, I pray thee, to the flock and bring me from thence two goodly goat kids, and I will prepare them as a tasty dish for thy father as he liketh it. And thou shalt take it to thy father, and he shall eat, so that he bless thee before his death."

And Jacob said to Rebekah his mother, "But Esau my brother is a hairy man, and I am a smooth man. Perhaps my father will touch me, and I shall be in his eyes as a deceiver, and I shall bring a curse upon me and not a blessing!"

And his mother said to him, "Upon me be thy curse, my son! Only hearken to my voice, and go fetch me!"

And Rebekah took the fine garments of Esau her elder son, which were with her in the house, and she put them upon Jacob her younger son. And the skins of the goat kids she put on his hands and on the smooth of his neck. And she gave the tasty dish and the bread which she had made into the hands of Jacob her son.

And Jacob said to his father, "I am Esau thy firstborn. I have done as thou hast spoken to me. Rise, I pray thee, sit and eat of my game so that thy soul may bless me."

And Isaac said to his son, "How is it that thou hast found so quickly, my son?" And he said, "Because the Lord, thy God, made me chance upon it."

And Isaac said to Jacob, "Pray come nearer, so that I may touch thee, my son, whether thou art indeed my son Esau or not."

And Jacob went near unto Isaac his father, and he touched him and said, "The voice is the voice of Jacob, but the hands are the hands of Esau." And he did not recognize him, for his hands were as the hands of Esau his brother, hairy; and he blessed him, and said, "Art thou my son Esau?" And he said, "I am." And he said, "Hand it to me that I may eat of the venison of my son, so that my soul may bless thee." And he handed it to him, and he ate, and he brought him wine, and he drank. And his father Isaac said to him: "Pray come near, and kiss me, my son." And he came near and kissed him, and he smelled the smell of his garments, and he blessed him and said

> "See, the smell of my son
> As the smell of the field
> Which the Lord hath blessed!
> God give thee of the dew of heaven
> And of the fat parts of the earth
> And plenty of corn and wine!
> Let peoples serve thee
> And nations to thee bow,
> Be Lord over thy brethren
> And let thy mother's sons
> Bow down to thee!
> Accursed is thy curser
> And thy blessers blessed."

And it came to pass when Isaac finished blessing Jacob, no sooner hath Jacob gone out from the face of Isaac his father, that Esau came in from his hunt. And he, too, prepared a tasty dish and brought it to his father, and said to him, "Let my father rise and eat of his son's venison, so that thy soul may bless me." And Isaac his father said to him, "Who art thou?" And he said, "I am thy son, thy firstborn, Esau."

And Isaac was seized by a very great trembling and said, "Who, then, was he who hunted a game and brought it to me, and I ate of all of it before thou camest, and I blessed him, and, yea, blessed shall he be."

When Esau heard the words of his father, he let forth a very great and bitter cry, and said to his father, "Bless me, too, my father!"

And he said: "Thy brother hath come in deceit and taken thy blessing!"

And he said: "Is he not rightly named Jacob (*Ya'aqov*)? He made me stumble (*ya'qveni*) twice: he took away my birthright, and behold, now he took my blessing!" And he said, "Hast thou not kept any blessing for me?"

And Isaac answered and said to Esau, "Behold, I have made him lord over thee, and all his brethren I have given him as servants, and with corn and grapejuice have I sustained him, and to thee, therefore, what can I do, my son?"

And Esau said to his father, "Dost thou have only one blessing, my father? Bless me, too, my father!" And Esau lifted up his voice and wept.

And Isaac his father answered and said to him,

> *"Behold, far from the fat of the earth*
> *Shall be thy dwelling place,*
> *And far from the dew of heaven above,*
> *But by thy sword shalt thou live.*
> *Thou shalt serve thy brother,*
> *But it shall come to pass*

When thou shalt break loose
That thou shalt shake his yoke
From off thy neck."

And Esau hated Jacob because of the blessing wherewith his father blessed him. And Esau said in his heart, "The days of mourning for my father will draw nigh, and then I will slay Jacob my brother."

And the words of Esau her elder son were told to Rebekah, and she sent and called Jacob her younger son, and said to him, "Behold, Esau thy brother findeth comfort in planning to kill thee. Now, my son, hearken to my voice, and rise, flee to Laban my brother in Haran. And dwell with him a few days, until the wrath of thy brother subsideth, until the anger of thy brother turneth from thee and he forget what thou hast done him. Then I shall send for thee and bring thee back from thence. Why should I be bereaved of both of you in one day?"

And Rebekah said to Isaac, "I am wearied of my life because of the daughters of Heth. If Jacob take a wife from among the daughters of Heth, such as these, from among the daughters of the land, what is the purpose in my life?"

And Isaac called Jacob, and blessed him and commanded him and said, "Thou shalt not take a wife from among the daughters of Canaan. Arise, go to Paddan-Aram, to the house Bethuel the father of thy mother, and take for thyself a wife from thence, from among the daughters of Laban, the brother of thy mother. And God Almighty bless thee and make thee fruitful, and multiply thee, that thou become a congregation of peoples, and give thee the blessing of Abraham, thee and thy seed with thee, that thou mayest inherit the land of thy sojournings which God gave to Abraham." And Isaac sent off Jacob, and he went to Paddan-Aram, to Laban son of Bethuel the Aramaean, the brother of Rebekah, the mother of Jacob and Esau.

(Gen. 27:1-28:5)

The Vision of Beth-El

And Jacob set out from Beer-Sheba to go to Haran. And he lighted upon a place and stayed there overnight, for the sun had set, and he took one of the stones of the place and put it under his head, and lay down in that place. And he dreamt, and behold, a ladder set upon the earth and its head reached heaven, and behold, the angels of God went up and down on it. And behold, the Lord stood upon it, and He said:

"I am the Lord, the God of Abraham thy father and the God of Isaac. The land on which thou liest, to thee will I give it and to thy seed. And thy seed shall be as the dust of the earth, and thou shalt spread to the west and to the east and to the north and to the south, and in thee will be blessed all the families of the earth and in thy seed. And behold, I am with thee, and I will keep thee everywhere thou goest, and I will bring thee back to this land, for I will not abandon thee until I have done that which I have spoken to thee."

And Jacob awoke from his sleep and said, "Surely, the Lord is in this place, and I knew it not!" And he was sore afraid and said, "How awesome is this place! This is none other than the house of God, and this is the gate of heaven!" And Jacob arose early in the morning, and took the stone which he had put under his head, and set it up as a pillar, and poured oil on top of it. And he called the name of the place Beth-El ("House of God"), but the name of the city was Luz at first. And Jacob made a vow saying,

"If God will be with me, and will keep me on this journey on which I go, and will give me bread to eat and clothes to wear; and if I return in peace to the house of my father, then the Lord shall be my God, and this stone which I set up as a pillar shall be God's house, and of all that Thou shalt give me I will surely give Thee a tithe."

(Gen. 28:10-22)

Jacob and Rachel

And Jacob lifted up his feet and went to the land of the children of the east. And he saw and behold, a well in the field, and behold, three flocks of sheep lying about it, for from that well they watered the flocks. And the stone upon the mouth of the well was big. And all the flocks would gather there, and they would roll away the stone from the mouth of the well and water the sheep, and then return the stone upon the mouth of the well to its place.

And Jacob said to them, "My brothers, from whence are ye?" And they said, "We are from Haran." And he said to them, "Do ye know Laban the son of Nahor?" And they said, "We know him." And he said to them, "Is it well with him?" And they said, "It is well, and behold, Rachel his daughter is coming with the sheep."

And he said, "Lo, the day is still great, it is not time yet to gather the flocks. Water the sheep, and go, graze." And they said, "We cannot, until all the flocks gather, and then they roll away the stone from the mouth of the well, and we water the sheep."

While he was still talking to them, Rachel came with the sheep which belonged to her father, for she was a shepherdess. And it came to pass that when Jacob saw Rachel the daughter of Laban his mother's brother, and the sheep of Laban his mother's brother, that Jacob stepped up and rolled away the stone from the mouth of the well, and he watered the sheep of Laban his mother's brother. And Jacob kissed Rachel, and lifted up his voice and wept. And Jacob told Rachel that he was her father's kinsman, and that he was Rebekah's son, and she ran and told her father.

And it came to pass when Laban heard the tidings of Jacob, his sister's son, that he ran to meet him, and embraced him and kissed him, and brought him to his house. And he related to Laban all these things. And Laban said to him: "Surely thou art my bone and flesh." And he dwelt with him a month's time.

And Laban said to Jacob: "Even though thou art my kinsman, shouldest thou serve me for naught? Tell me what should be thy wages."

And Laban had two daughters: the name of the elder was Leah, and the name of the younger, Rachel. And the eyes of Leah were weak, but Rachel was beautiful of form and beautiful of countenance. And Jacob loved Rachel and said: "I will serve thee seven years for Rachel thy younger daughter." And Laban said, "It is better that I give her to thee than to another man. Dwell with me." And Jacob served for Rachel seven years, and they were in his eyes as a few days so much did he love her.

And Jacob said to Laban, "Give me my wife for my days are filled, that I may go in unto her." And Laban gathered all the people of the place, and made a feast. And it came to pass in the evening that Laban took Leah his daughter, and brought her to him, and he went in unto her. And Laban gave her Zilpah his handmaid, to Leah his daughter for a handmaid. And it came to pass in the morning, and behold, she was Leah! And he said to Laban, "What is this thou hast done to me? Is it not for Rachel that I served thee? Why didst thou deceive me?" And Laban said, "It is not done thusly in our place, to give the younger before the elder. Fulfill the week of this one, and we will give thee that one too for service which thou shalt serve with me for another seven years." And Jacob did so, and fulfilled the week of this one, and Laban gave him Rachel his daughter to wife. And Laban gave to Rachel his daughter Bilhah his handmaid to be her handmaid. And he went in unto Rachel also, and he loved Rachel more than Leah, and he served with him another seven years.

(Gen. 29:1-30)

Jacob and the Angel

And he [Jacob] arose in the night, and took his two wives and his two handmaids and his eleven children, and crossed the ford of Jabbok. And he took them and brought them

across the stream, and he took across what he had. And
Jacob remained alone, and a man wrestled with him until
the rising of the dawn. And he saw that he could not
prevail against him, and he touched the hollow of his thigh,
and the hollow of Jacob's thigh became strained as he
wrestled with him. And he said, "Let me go, for the dawn is
risen!" And he said, "I will not let thee go, unless thou bless
me!" And he said to him, "What is thy name?" And he
said, "Jacob." And he said, "Not Jacob shall thy name be
called any more, but Israel, for thou has struggled with God
and man and hast prevailed." And Jacob asked and said,
"Tell me thy name!" And he said, "Why askest thou my
name?" And he blessed him there. And Jacob called the
name of the place Peniel ("Face of God"), "For I have seen
God face to face and my soul was saved." And the sun rose
upon him as he was crossing Penuel, and he limped upon
his thigh. Therefore the Children of Israel eat not the sinew
of the thigh vein which is upon the hollow of the thigh,
unto this day, because he touched the hollow of Jacob's
thigh, in the sinew of the thigh vein.

(Gen. 32:23-33)

The Rape of Dinah

And Dinah, the daugher of Leah whom she bore unto
Jacob, went forth to see the daughters of the land. And
Shechem the son of Hamor the Hivite, prince of the land,
saw her, and took her, and lay with her, and violated her.
And his soul cleaved to Dinah the daughter of Jacob, and
he loved the maiden, and spoke kindly to the maiden. And
Shechem spoke to Hamor his father saying, "Get me this
girl to wife!"

And Jacob heard that he had defiled Dinah his daughter,
and his sons were with his flock in the field, and Israel kept
silent until their return. And Hamor the father of Shechem
went out to Jacob to speak to him. And the sons of Jacob
came from the field when they heard it, and the men were

grieved, and they became very wroth, because he had committed a vile deed in Israel, to lie with the daughter of Jacob, for this is not done. And Hamor spoke to them saying, "Shechem, my son, his soul conceived a desire for your daughter; give her, I pray you, unto him to wife. And intermarry with us, give your daughters to us, and our daughters take for yourselves. And dwell with us, and let the land be before you, dwell and trade in it and take possession of it."

And Shechem said to her father and brothers, "May I find favor in your eyes: whatever ye will tell me I shall give. Put upon me the greatest amount of bride price and dowry, and I shall give it as ye tell me, and give me the girl to wife!"

And the sons of Jacob answered Shechem and Hamor his father in guile and spoke, because he had defiled Dinah their sister. And they said to them, "We cannot do this thing, to give our sister to a man who has a foreskin, for that would be a disgrace to us. But thus will we consent to you: if ye will be like unto us, to have all your males circumcised. Then we will give our daughters to you, and your daughters we will take for ourselves, and we will dwell with you and become one people. And if ye will not hearken unto us to become circumcised, we shall take our daughter and go."

And their words seemed good in the eyes of Hamor and in the eyes of Shechem ben Hamor. And the youth did not delay to do the thing for he desired the daughter of Jacob, and he was honored and respected above the whole house of his father. . . .

And all who passed through the gate of his city hearkened unto Hamor and Shechem his son, and every male was circumcised, all who passed through the gate of his city. And it came to pass on the third day when they were in pain that two sons of Jacob, Simeon and Levi, the brothers of Dinah, took each his sword and came to the city safely, and slew all the males. And they slew also Hamor and Shechem his son with the edge of the sword, and they took Dinah from the house of Shechem, and left. Then the sons of Jacob came upon the slain and looted the city because they had defiled their sister. They took their sheep and their cattle and their asses, and what was in the city and what was in the field. And all their wealth and all their children and wives they took captive, and spoiled all that was in the house.

And Jacob said to Simeon and Levi, "Ye have troubled me, making me loathsome to the inhabitants of the land, the Canaanite and Perizzite, and I am few in number, and they will gather against me and smite me, and I shall be destroyed, I and my house." And they said, "Shall our sister be treated as a harlot?"

(Gen. 34:1-19, 24-31)

Joseph and His Brethren

Joseph, seventeen years old, was a shepherd with his brethren, of the flock, and he was a youth, with the sons of Bilhah and the sons of Zilpah, his father's wives. And Joseph brought evil reports of them to their father. And Israel loved Joseph best of all his sons, for he was the son of his old age, and he made him a striped coat. And his brethren saw that their father loved him best of all his brethren, and they hated him and could not speak peaceably to him.

And Joseph dreamt a dream and told his brethren, and they hated him even more. And he said to them, "Hearken, I pray you, to this dream which I have dreamt. Behold, we were binding sheaves in the field, and behold, my sheaf arose and even stood, and behold, your sheaves surrounded it and bowed down to my sheaf."

And his brethren said to him, "Shalt thou indeed reign over us, or shalt thou indeed rule over us?" And they hated him even more because of his dreams and his words.

And he dreamt another dream and related it to his

brethren and said, "Behold, I dreamt yet another dream, and behold, the sun and the moon and eleven stars bowed down to me." And he related it to his father and to his brethren, and his father rebuked him and said, "What is this dream which thou hast dreamt, shall indeed I and thy mother and thy brethren come to bow down to thee to the earth?" And his brethren were jealous of him, and his father kept the matter in his mind.

And his brethren went to pasture the flock of their father in Shechem. And Israel said to Joseph, "Do not thy brethren pasture in Shechem? Come, I will send thee to them." And he said to him, "Here am I." And he said to him, "Go, I pray thee, and see whether it is well with thy brethren, and whether it is well with the flock, and bring word back to me." And he sent him off from the valley of Hebron, and he came to Shechem. And a man met him as he, behold, was about in the field, and the man asked him saying, "What seekest thou?" And he said, "I seek my brethren. Tell me, I pray thee, where do they pasture?" And the man said, "They departed hence, for I heard them say, 'Let us go to Dothan.'" And Joseph went after his brethren, and found them in Dothan.

And they saw him from afar, and before he came near them, and they conspired against him to kill him. And they spoke to one another, "Behold, this master of dreams cometh! And now, let us go and slay him and cast him into one of the pits, and we will say, an evil beast ate him, and we shall see what cometh of his dreams."

And Reuben heard, and saved him from their hand, and said, "Let us not smite his soul!" And Reuben said, "Do not shed blood, cast him into this pit which is in the desert, and stretch no hand forth against him," in order to save him from their hand, to bring him back to his father.

And it came to pass when Joseph came to his brethren that they stripped Joseph of his coat, the striped coat which he had on. And they took him and cast him into the pit, and the pit was empty, there was no water in it. And they sat down to eat bread, and they lifted up their eyes, and behold, a caravan of Ishmaelites was approaching from Gilead, and their camels were bearing spices and balm and myrrh, carrying it down to Egypt. And Judah said to his brethren, "What profit is it if we slay our brother and cover up his blood? Let us go and sell him to the Ishmaelites, and let our hand not be against him, for he is our brother, our flesh." And his brothers hearkened to him.

And Midianite men, merchants, passed by, and they pulled Joseph up and raised him from the pit, and they sold Joseph to the Ishmaelites for twenty silvers. And they took Joseph to Egypt.

And Reuben returned to the pit, and behold, Joseph was not in the pit, and he rent his garments. And he returned to his brethren and said, "The child is gone, and I, whither shall I go?"

And they took the coat of Joseph, and they slaughtered a he-goat, and dipped the coat in the blood. And they sent the striped coat and brought it to their father and said, "This we found. Dost thou recognize it? Is it the coat of thy son or not?"

And he recognized it and said, "The coat of my son! An evil beast ate him! Torn, rent in pieces is Joseph!"

And Jacob rent his clothes and put sackcloth upon his loins, and mourned for his son many days. And all his sons and all his daughters arose to comfort him, but he refused to be comforted, and said, "For I will go down mourning into Sheol [the netherworld] to my son." And his father wept for him.

And the Medanites sold him to Egypt to Potiphar, Pharaoh's officer, captain of the guard.

(Gen. 37:2-36)

Joseph and Potiphar's Wife

And Joseph was taken down to Egypt, and Potiphar, Pharaoh's officer, captain of the guard, an Egyptian man, bought him from the Ishmaelites who had taken him down there. And the Lord was with Joseph, and he became a prosperous man, and he was in the house of his Egyptian master. And his master saw that the Lord was with him, and that everything he did the Lord made to prosper at his hand. And Joseph found favor in his eyes, and he served him, and he appointed him over his house, and placed in his hand everything he had. And it came to pass from the time that he had appointed him in his house and over everything he had that the Lord blessed the house of the Egyptian for the sake of Joseph, and the blessing of the Lord in everything he had in the house and in the field. And he left everything he had in the hand of Joseph, and he knew of nothing save the meals he ate. And Joseph was beautiful of form and beautiful of countenance.

And it came to pass after these things that the wife of his master lifted up her eyes at Joseph and said, "Lie with me!" But he refused and said to the wife of his master, "Behold, my master knoweth of nothing in the house, and everything he hath he gave into my hand. He is not greater in this house than I, and he withheld nothing from me save thee, inasmuch as thou art his wife. How could I do this great evil, and sin to God?"

And it came to pass as she spoke to Joseph day after day, and he did not hearken to her to lie by her, to be with her, that one day as he entered the house to do his work, and nobody of the people of the house was there in the house, she grabbed him by his clothes saying, "Lie with me!" And he left his garment in her hand and fled outside.

And it came to pass when she saw that he had left his garment in her hand and fled outside that she called the people of her house and spoke to them saying, "See, he brought us a Hebrew man to mock us! He came to me to lie with me, and I cried in a loud voice, and when he heard that I raised my voice and cried out, he left his garment with me and fled, and went outside." And she kept his garment with her until his master returned to his house.

And she spoke to him these words saying, "The Hebrew slave whom thou hast brought us came to me to mock me. And when I raised my voice and cried out, he left his garment with me and fled outside."

And when his master heard the words of his wife which she had spoken to him saying, "Thus did thy slave to me," his wrath was kindled. And the master of Joseph took him and put him into the jail-house, the place where the king's prisoners were bound, and he was there in the jail-house. And the Lord was with Joseph, and showed him kindness, and gave him favor in the eyes of the warden of the jail-house. And the warden of the jail put into Joseph's hand all the prisoners who were in the jail, and everything they did there he was doing. The warden of the jail looked at nothing in his hand, for the Lord was with him, and whatever he did the Lord made it prosper.

(Gen. 39:1-23)

Pharaoh's Dreams

And it came to pass after two years that Pharaoh dreamt, and behold, he stood by the river. And behold, seven cows, fair to look at and healthy of flesh, rose up from the river, and they grazed in the reeds. And behold, seven other cows arose after them from the river, evil to look at and thin of flesh, and they stood by the other cows on the river bank. And the evil-looking and thin-fleshed cows ate the seven fair-looking and healthy cows. And Pharaoh awoke. And he fell asleep and dreamt a second time, and behold, seven ears of corn came up upon one stalk, healthy and good. And behold, seven thin ears of corn, blighted by the east wind, grew after them. And the thin ears of corn swallowed the seven healthy and full ears of corn. And Pharaoh awoke, and behold, a dream.

And it came to pass in the morning that his spirit was troubled, and he sent for all the soothsayers of Egypt and all her wise men, and Pharaoh related to them his dreams, and none could interpret them to Pharaoh. And the chief butler spoke to Pharaoh saying, "I must mention my sins today: Pharaoh was wroth with his servants and placed me under arrest in the house of the captain of the guard, me and the chief baker. And we dreamt a dream in one night, I and he, each of us dreamt according to the interpretation of his dream. And there was with us a Hebrew youth, a slave of the captain of the guard, and we related to him our dreams and he interpreted for us, to each according to his dream did he interpret. And as he interpreted it so it came to pass: me he [Pharaoh] restored to my position, and him he hanged."

And Pharaoh sent for Joseph, and they rushed him out of the pit, and he shaved, and changed his clothes, and came to Pharaoh. And Pharaoh said to Joseph, "I dreamt a dream, and none can interpret it, and I heard of you saying, you hear a dream and interpret it." And Joseph answered Pharaoh saying, "Not I, God will answer the peace of Pharaoh!" ...

And Joseph said to Pharaoh, "Pharaoh's dream is one: what God is about to do He hath shown to Pharaoh. The seven good cows are seven years, and the seven good ears of corn are seven years. Behold, it is one dream. And the seven lean and evil cows which rose up after them are seven years, and the seven empty ears of corn, blighted with the east wind, will be seven years of famine. It is as I said to Pharaoh, what God doeth He hath shown to Pharaoh. Behold, seven years will come, great plenty in all the land of Egypt. And seven years of famine will come after them and all the plenty will be forgotten in the land of Egypt, and the famine will consume the land. And no trace of the plenty will be left in the land because of that famine after it, for it will be very grievous. And that the dream was repeated unto Pharaoh twice, it is because the thing is established from God, and God will hasten to do it. And now let Pharaoh seek out a man, understanding and wise, and set him over the land of Egypt. Let Pharaoh do this, and appoint officers over the land, and impose a tax of one fifth upon the land of Egypt in the seven years of plenty. And let them gather all the food of the seven good years which will come, and amass grain under the hand of Pharaoh, food in the cities, and keep it. And let the food be a deposit for the land for the seven years of famine which will be in the land of Egypt, so that the land be not cut off in the famine."

And the thing was good in the eyes of Pharaoh and in the eyes of all his servants. And Pharaoh said to his servants, "Can we find such a one, a man in whom is the spirit of God?" And Pharaoh said to Joseph, "Since God let thee know all this, there is none so understanding and wise as thou. Thou shalt be over my house, and by thy mouth shall all my people be ruled. Only in the throne will I be greater than thou."

(Gen. 41:1-16,25-40)

The Egyptian Slavery

And a new king arose over Egypt who did not know Joseph. And he said to his people, "Behold, the people of the Children of Israel are more numerous and mightier than we. Come, let us outwit them, lest they become still more numerous, and it come to pass that when a war befalleth us, they will join our enemies and fight against us, and go up out of the land." And they set over them taskmasters to afflict them with their burdens, and they built storage cities for Pharaoh, Pithom and Raamses. But the more they afflicted them the more they multiplied and spread about, and they loathed the Children of Israel. And Egypt made the Children of Israel work cruelly. And they embittered their lives with hard labor, with clay and bricks and all kinds of work in the field, all their work which they forced them with cruelty to perform.

And the king of Egypt spoke to the Hebrew midwives, of whom the name of one was Shiphrah and the name of the other Puah. And he said, "When ye act as midwives to the Hebrew women, look at the birth-stool: if it is a boy, kill him, and if a girl, let her live." But the midwives feared God and did not as the king of Egypt had spoken to them, and they let the boys live. And the king of Egypt called the midwives and said to them, "Why did ye do this thing to let the boys live?" And the midwives said to Pharaoh, "Because the Hebrew women are not like the Egyptians, for they are lively, and even before the midwife cometh to them they give birth." And God dealt well with the midwives, and the people multiplied and became very mighty. And since the midwives feared God, He made them houses. And Pharaoh commanded all his people saying, "Throw every son born into the river, and let every girl live."

(Exod. 1:8-22)

The Birth and Youth of Moses

And a man of the house of Levi went and took a daughter of Levi. And the woman conceived and bore a son, and she saw that he was goodly, and hid him three months. And she could no longer hide him, and she took herself an ark of bulrushes and daubed it with slime and pitch, and put the child into it, and laid it in the reeds on the river's edge. And his sister stayed at a distance to know what would happen to him.

And the daughter of Pharaoh went down to bathe in the river, and her maidens walked along the riverbank, and she saw the ark in the reeds, and sent her handmaid and fetched it. And she opened it and saw the child, and behold, a weeping babe. And she had compassion on him and said, "This is one of the Hebrews' children."

And his sister said to Pharaoh's daughter, "Shall I go and call thee a wetnurse from among the Hebrew women, that she may nurse the child for thee?" And Pharaoh's daughter said to her, "Go," and the maiden went and called the

child's mother. And Pharaoh's daughter said to her, "Take
this child and suckle it for me, and I shall give thee thy
wages." And the woman took the child and suckled it.

And the child grew, and she brought it to Pharaoh's
daughter, and he became a son to her. And she called his
name Moses (Moshe), for she said, "For I drew (*mashiti*)
him out of the water."

And it came to pass in those days that Moses grew up and
went out to his brethren, and saw their suffering. And he
saw an Egyptian smite a Hebrew, one of his brethren. And
he turned this way and that, and saw that there was
nobody, and he smote the Egyptian, and hid him in the
sand.

And he went out on the second day, and behold, two
Hebrew men strove together, and he said to the wicked
one, "Why smitest thou thy fellow?" And he said, "Who
made thee a prince and a judge over us? Dost thou want to
kill me as thou didst kill the Egyptian?" And Moses was
afraid and said, "Indeed, the thing hath become known."

And Pharaoh heard of this thing, and sought to kill
Moses. And Moses fled from before Pharaoh, and dwelt in
the land of Midian, and sat down at the well.

(Exod. 2:1-15)

The Burning Bush

And Moses was a shepherd of the flock of Jethro his father-
in-law, the priest of Midian, and he led the flock beyond
the desert, and came to the mountain of God, to Horeb.
And the angel of the Lord appeared unto him in the flame
of fire from the midst of the bush. And he looked, and
behold, the bush burned in fire, but the bush was not
consumed. And Moses said, "I will turn aside and see this
great sight, why is the bush not burnt?"

And the Lord saw that he turned aside to see, and God
called him from the bush and said, "Moses, Moses!" And he
said, "Here am I." And He said, "Come not near hither,

take off thy shoes from thy feet, for the place upon which thou standest is holy ground." And He said: "I am the God your father, the God of Abraham, the God of Isaac, and the God of Jacob." And Moses hid his face, for he was afraid to look at God.

And the Lord said, "I have seen the affliction of My people which is in Egypt and I heard its cry because of its oppressors, for I know its pain. And I shall go down to succor it from the hand of Egypt, to bring it up out of that country to a good and broad land, to a land flowing with milk and honey, to the place of the Canaanite, and the Hittite, and the Amorite, and the Perizzite, and the Hivite, and the Jebusite. And now, behold, the cry of the Children of Israel is come to Me, and I also saw the oppression with which Egypt oppresses them. And now go, and I shall send thee to Pharaoh, and bring My people, the Children of Israel, out of Egypt."

(Exod. 3:1-10)

The Bridegroom of Blood

And it came to pass on the way, in the lodging place, that the Lord encountered him and wanted to kill him. And Zipporah took a flint, and cut off the foreskin of her son and touched it to his feet, and said, "Surely a bridegroom of blood art thou to me." So He let off from him. Then she said, "A bridegroom of blood because of the circumcision."

(Exod. 4:24-26)

Moses Before Pharaoh

And the Lord spoke to Moses and Aaron saying, "If Pharaoh speak to you saying, 'Show for you a miracle,' then say to Aaron, 'Take thy rod and cast it down before Pharaoh!' It will become a dragon."

And Moses and Aaron came before Pharaoh, and they did as the Lord had commanded, and Aaron cast down his rod before Pharaoh and before his servants, and it became a dragon. And Pharaoh too called the sages and the sorcerers, and they, too, the magicians of Egypt, did so with their witchcraft. And each of them cast down his rod, and they became dragons, and the rod of Aaron swallowed their rods. But Pharaoh's heart was hardened, and he hearkened not unto them, as the Lord had spoken.

(Exod. 7:8-13)

The First Plague

And the Lord said to Moses, "Pharaoh's heart is hard, he refuseth to let the people go. Go to Pharaoh in the morning, when he goeth out to the water, and stand by to encounter him at the riverbank, and take the rod which turned into a serpent in thy hand. And say to him, 'The Lord, the God of the Hebrews, sent me to thee saying, "Let My people go that they may serve Me in the desert, and behold, thou hast not hearkened until now." Thus saith the Lord, "In this shalt thou know that I am the Lord: Behold I will strike with this rod which is in my hand the water which is in the river and it will turn into blood. And the fish which is in the river shall die, and the river shall stink, and Egypt will weary itself trying to drink water from the river!"' "

And the Lord said to Moses, "Speak to Aaron, 'Take thy rod and stretch forth thy hand upon the waters of Egypt, upon its streams, its rivers, and it lakes, and upon all its pools of water, and they shall become blood, and there shall be blood in all the land of Egypt and in the trees and the stones.' " And Moses and Aaron did so, as the Lord hath commanded, and he lifted up the rod and smote the water which is in the river, before the eyes of Pharaoh and the eyes of his servants, and all the water in the river turned into blood. And the fish which is in the river died, and the river stank, and Egypt could not drink water from the river, and there was blood in all the land of Egypt. And the magicians of Egypt did likewise with their sorcery, and

Pharaoh's heart was hardened and he hearkened not to them, as the Lord had spoken. And Pharaoh turned and entered his house and had no regard even for this. And all Egypt dug around the river for water to drink, for they could not drink of the water of the river. And seven days were fulfilled after the Lord had smitten the river.

(Exod. 7:14-25)

The Passage Through the Red Sea

And the Lord spoke to Moses saying, "Speak to the Children of Israel that they turn and camp before Pi-Hahiroth, between Migdol and the sea, before Baal-Zephon, facing which ye shall camp by the sea. And Pharaoh will say of the Children of Israel, 'They are confused in the land, the desert hath closed in upon them.' And I will harden the heart of Pharaoh, and he shall pursue after them, and I will be honored through Pharaoh and all his army, and Egypt shall know that I am the Lord." And they did so.

And it was told to the king of Egypt that the people had fled, and the heart of Pharaoh and of his servants turned against the people, and they said, "What is this we have done that we let Israel go from serving us?" And he hitched up his chariot, and took his people with him. And he took six hundred select chariots, as well as all the chariots of Egypt and captains over all of them. And the Lord hardened the heart of Pharaoh king of Egypt, and he pursued after the Children of Israel, and the Children of Israel went forth with a high hand. And Egypt pursued after them, and overtook them camped by the sea, all the horses, the chariots of Pharaoh and his horsemen and army, at Pi-Hahiroth before Baal-Zephon. And Pharaoh approached, and the Children of Israel lifted up their eyes, and behold, Egypt marching after them, and they were sore afraid, and the Children of Israel cried unto the Lord. And they said to Moses, "Is it for lack of tombs in Egypt that thou hast taken us to die in the desert? What is this thou hast done to us to bring us out of Egypt? Have we not spoken to thee in Egypt saying, 'Leave us alone, and let us serve Egypt, for it is better for us to serve Egypt than to die in the desert'?"

And Moses said to the people, "Fear not, stand fast, and see the salvation of the Lord which He will work for you today, for as ye have seen Egypt today ye will not again see them forever. The Lord will fight for you, and ye be silent!"

And the Lord said to Moses, "Wherefore criest thou unto Me? Speak to the Children of Israel that they march on. And thou, lift up thy rod and stretch forth thy hand over the sea and divide it, and the Children of Israel will go through the sea on dry ground. And I shall harden the heart of Egypt, and they will go after them, and I shall be honored through Pharaoh and all his army, his chariots and his horsemen. And Egypt will know that I am the Lord when I will be honored through Pharaoh, his chariots and horsemen."

And the angel of the Lord who went in front of the camp of Israel removed and went to their rear, and the pillar of cloud removed from their front and stood at their rear. And it came between the camp of Egypt and the camp of Israel, and there was the cloud and the darkness, and it lighted up the night, and they did not approach each other all the night. And Moses stretched forth his hand over the sea, and the Lord drove the sea back with a strong east wind all the night, and He made the sea into dry ground, and the waters divided. And the Children of Israel went through the sea on dry ground, and the water was for them a wall to their right and to their left.

And Egypt pursued them and went after them, all the horses of Pharaoh, his chariots and his horsemen, in the midst of the sea. And it came to pass in the morning watch that the Lord looked down at the camp of Egypt from the pillar of fire and cloud, and He confused the camp of Egypt. And He removed the wheels of its chariots, and made it drive heavily, and Egypt said, "Let me flee from the face of Israel, for the Lord fights for them against Egypt!"

And the Lord said to Moses, "Stretch forth thy hand over the sea, and let the water return upon Egypt, its chariots and its horsemen!" And Moses stretched forth his hand over the sea, and the sea returned towards morning to its place, and Egypt fled from it, and the Lord shattered Egypt in the sea. And the water returned and covered the chariots and the horsemen of all the army of Pharaoh which had gone after them in the sea, not a single one was left of them. And the Children of Israel went on dry ground in the sea, and the water was a wall for them to their right and to their left. And the Lord saved Israel on that day from the hand of Egypt, and Israel saw Egypt dead on the shore of the sea. And Israel saw the great hand which the Lord hath wrought in Egypt, and the people feared the Lord, and they believed in the Lord and in Moses His servant.

(Exod. 14:1-31)

The Manna and the Quails

And they journeyed from Elim, and all the community of the Children of Israel came to the wilderness of Sin which is between Elim and Sinai, on the fifteenth day of the second month after their departure from the land of Egypt. And the whole community of the Children of Israel murmured against Moses and Aaron in the wilderness. And the Children of Israel said to them, "Would that we had died through the hand of the Lord in the land of Egypt when we sat by the flesh pot, when we ate bread to our fill, for ye have brought us out to this wilderness to kill this whole community with hunger." ...

And the Lord spoke to Moses saying, "I heard the complaints of the Children of Israel. Speak unto them saying, 'Toward evening ye shall eat flesh, and in the morning ye shall be sated with bread, and ye shall know that I am the Lord your God.' " And it came to pass in the evening that the quails came up and covered the camp, and in the morning there was a layer of dew about the camp. And the layer of dew rose, and behold, upon the face of the wilderness something thin, scaley, thin like hoar-frost on the ground. And the Children of Israel saw it, and said to one another, "What (*man*) is it?" For they knew not what it was.

And Moses said to them, "This is the bread which the Lord gave you to eat. This is the word which the Lord commanded: Gather of it, each man according to what he eateth, an omer to a head, according to the number of your souls, each man take for those in his tent." And the Children of Israel did so, and they gathered, one more, the other less. And they measured it by the omer, and he who gathered more had no excess and he who gathered less had no lack, each man gathered according to what he ate.

And Moses said to them, "Let no man leave of it until the morning." But they hearkened not to Moses, and some men left of it until the morning, and it raised worms and stank. And Moses was wroth with them. And they gathered it every morning, each man according to what he ate, and when the sun became hot it melted. And it came to pass that on the sixth day they gathered double, two omers for each, and all the princes of the community came and told Moses.

And he said to them, "It is as the Lord hath spoken: tomorrow is a day of rest, a holy Sabbath to the Lord. Whatever ye wish to bake, bake, and what ye wish to cook, cook, and set aside for you the excess to kept until the morning." And they kept it until the morning as Moses had commanded, and it did not stink and there was no worm in it. And Moses said, "Eat it today, for today is the Sabbath of the Lord, ye will not find it in the field. Ye shall gather six days, and the seventh day is the Sabbath, there shall be none in it."

(Exod. 16:1-4,11-26)

The Revelation on Mount Sinai

And the Lord said to Moses, "Go to the people and sanctify them today and tomorrow, and let them wash their garments. And let them be ready on the third day, for on the third day the Lord will go down in the sight of all the people upon Mount Sinai. And fence off the people all around saying, 'Take heed not to go up the mountain, nor to touch its edge; whosoever toucheth the mountain shall surely be put to death. No hand shall touch him, but he shall be stoned or shot, whether a beast or a man, it shall not live. When the ram's horn soundeth long they shall go up to the mountain.' "

And Moses went down from the mountain to the people, and sanctified the people and they washed their garments. And he said to the people, "Prepare yourselves during the three days; come not near a woman."

And it came to pass on the third day, when it was morning, that there was thunder and lightning, and a heavy cloud upon the mountain, and the voice of the shofar was very strong, and all the people who were in the camp trembled. And Moses brought forth the people from the camp to God, and they took their places at the bottom of the mountain. And Mount Sinai was all smoke because the Lord descended upon it in fire, and its smoke rose like the smoke of a furnace, and the whole mountain quaked greatly. And the voice of the shofar became exceedingly strong. Moses would speak and the Lord would answer him aloud. And the Lord descended upon Mount Sinai, upon the head of the mountain, and the Lord called Moses to the head of the mountain, and Moses went up.

And the Lord said to Moses, "Go down, warn the people lest they break through to the Lord to gaze and many of them fall. And also the priests who approach the Lord should sanctify themselves, lest the Lord wreak havoc among them."

And Moses said to the Lord, "The people cannot go up

Mount Sinai, for Thou hast warned us saying, 'Fence around the mountain and sanctify it!' "

And the Lord said to him, "Go, descend, and come up, thou and Aaron with thee, and the priests and the people should not break through to go up to the Lord, lest He wreak havoc among them."

And Moses went down to the people, and told them.

(Exod. 19:10-25)

The Golden Calf

And the people saw that Moses delayed to come down from the mountain, and the people gathered around Aaron and said to him, "Rise, make us gods who shall go before us, for this man Moses who brought us up from the land of Egypt, we know not what hath happened to him."

And Aaron said to them, "Take off the golden rings which are in the ears of your wives, sons, and daughters, and bring them to me."

And all the people took off the golden rings which were in their ears, and brought them to Aaron. And he took it from their hand, and fashioned it with a stylus, and made it into a molten calf. And they said, "These are thy gods, Israel, who brought thee up from the land of Egypt."

And Aaron saw it, and built an altar before it, and Aaron announced and said, "A feast to the Lord is tomorrow!"

And they rose early next morning, and offered up burnt offerings, and presented peace offerings, and the people sat down to eat, and they drank, and they rose to make merry.

And the Lord spoke to Moses, "Go, descend, for thy people which thou hast brought up from the land of Egypt became corrupt. They have turned aside quickly from the way which I have commanded them, they made themselves a molten calf and worshiped it and sacrificed unto it, and said, 'These are thy gods, Israel, who brought thee up from the land of Egypt.' " And the Lord said to Moses, "I have seen this people, and behold, it is a stiff-necked people. And now, let Me be, for My wrath is kindled against them, and I will consume them, and I will make thee into a great nation."

And Moses besought the face of the Lord his God and said, "Why, O Lord, should Thy wrath be kindled against Thy people whom Thou hast brought out of the land of Egypt with great power and with a strong hand? Why should Egypt speak saying, 'For evil did He bring them out, to kill them in the mountains and to destroy them from off the face of the earth'? Turn from Thy fierce wrath, and repent of the evil against Thy people! Remember Abraham, Isaac, and Israel Thy servants to whom Thou hast sworn by Thyself and to whom Thou hast spoken, 'I will multiply your seed as the stars of heaven, and all this land which I have said I will give to your seed and they shall inherit it for ever.'"

And the Lord repented of the evil which he had spoken to do to His people.

And Moses turned and descended from the mountain, and the two tablets of testimony in his hand, tablets written on both their sides, on this side and on that were they written. And the tablets were the work of God, and the writing was the writing of God, graven upon the tablets. And Joshua heard the sound of the people shouting, and said to Moses, "The sound of war is in the camp!" And he said, "It is not the sound of victory, nor the sound of defeat; but the sound of singing do I hear!" And it came to pass when he came near the camp, and saw the calf and the dances, that the wrath of Moses was kindled, and he cast the tablets from his hands, and broke them under the mountain. And he took the calf which they had made and burnt it in fire and ground it to powder, and strewed it upon the water and made the Children of Israel drink it.

(Exod. 32:1-20)

The Brazen Serpent

And they journeyed from Hor the mountain by way of the Red Sea, to compass the land of Edom, and the soul of the people grew impatient on the way. And the people spoke against God and against Moses, "Why have ye brought us up from Egypt? To die in the desert? For there is no bread and no water, and our soul loatheth this mean food!" And the Lord sent fiery serpents among the people, and they bit the people, and many of Israel died. And the people came to Moses and said, "We have sinned in that we have spoken against the Lord and against thee! Pray to the Lord that He remove the serpents from us." And Moses prayed for the people.

And the Lord said to Moses, "Make thyself a fiery serpent, and raise it on a standard, and it shall come to pass that all those bitten when they look at it shall live." And Moses made a brazen serpent and raised it on a standard, and it came to pass when the serpents bit a man that he looked at the brazen serpent and lived.

(Num. 21:4-9)

Hezekiah the son of Ahaz...removed the high places, and broke up the pillars, and cut down the Asherah, and broke in pieces the brazen serpent which Moses had made, for to those days the Children of Israel did burn incense to it and called it Nehushtan ("A thing of brass").

(2 Kings 18:4)

The Death of Moses

And Moses went up from the plains of Moab to Mount Nebo, to the top of Pisgah which is over against Jericho. And the Lord showed him the whole land, the Gilead as far as Dan. And all of Naphtali and the land of Ephraim and Manasseh, and all the land of Judah as far as the farthest sea. And the Negev, and the plain, the valley of Jericho the palm-city, as far as Zoar.

And the Lord said to him, "This is the land which I swore unto Abraham, Isaac, and Jacob, saying, 'To thy seed shall I give it!' I have showed it to thee, to thy eyes, but thou shalt not go over thither."

And Moses the servant of the Lord died there in the land of Moab, by the mouth of the Lord. And He buried him in the valley, in the land of Moab, over against Beth-Peor, and no man knew his sepulchre unto this day.

And Moses was a hundred and twenty years old when he died. His eye was not dim nor his sap abated. And the Children of Israel wept for Moses in the plains of Moab thirty days, and the days of the mournful weeping over Moses ended.

(Deut. 34:1-8)

Joshua Stops the Sun

Then Joshua spoke to the Lord, on the day when the Lord delivered the Amorite to the Children of Israel and said,

> *"Sun in Gibeon stop,*
> *And Moon in the Valley of Aijalon!"*

And the sun stopped and the moon stood still until the nation had avenged itself on its enemies—is this not written in the Book of Yashar? And the sun stood still in the middle of heaven, and hasted not to set about a whole day. And there was no day like that before it and after it, that the Lord should hearken to the voice of a man, for the Lord fought for Israel. And Joshua and all Israel with him returned to the camp in Gilgal.

(Josh. 10:12-15)

Gideon and the Angel

And the angel of the Lord came and sat under the terebinth which was in Ophrah, which belonged to Joash the Abiezrite; and Gideon his son was threshing wheat in the winepress to save it from the Midianites. And the angel of the Lord appeared to him and said to him, "The Lord is with thee, thou mighty man of arms!" And Gideon said to him, "I pray thee, my lord, is the Lord with us? Why then hath all this befallen us? And where are all His miracles about which our fathers related to us saying, 'Is it not that the Lord brought us up from Egypt?' And now the Lord hath forsaken us and delivered us into the hand of Midian."

And the Lord turned to him and said, "Go, in this thy might, and save Israel from the hand of Midian, for I am sending thee!" And he said to Him, "I pray thee, my Lord, wherewith will I save Israel? Behold, my kindred is the poorest in Manasseh, and I am the youngest in my father's house."

And the Lord said to him, "But I will be with thee, and thou shalt smite Midian as if it were one man." And he said to Him, "If, I pray Thee, I found favor in Thy eyes, make me a sign that it is Thou who speakest to me. Move not from hence until I come back to Thee and bring out my offering and place it before Thee." And He said, "I will sit until thy return."

And Gideon sent and prepared a kid of goats, and an ephah of flour as unleavened bread, the meat he put in a basket and the broth he put in a pot, and brought it out to Him under the terebinth, and presented it.

And the angel of God said to him, "Take the meat and the unleavened bread and put it upon yonder rock, and the broth pour out." And he did so. And the angel of the Lord stretched forth the end of the staff which was in his hand, and touched the meat and the unleavened bread, and fire rose from the rock and consumed the meat and the bread. And the angel of the Lord departed from his eyes. And Gideon saw that it was the angel of the Lord, and Gideon said, "Alas, my Lord God, for I have indeed seen the angel of the Lord face to face."

And the Lord said to him, "Peace be unto thee. Fear not for thou shalt not die." And Gideon built an altar there to the Lord, and called it Adonai Shalom ("The Lord is peace"); unto this day it is in Ophrah of the Abiezrites.

And it came to pass in that night that the Lord said to him, "Take the bullock of thy father and the second bullock of seven years, and demolish the Baal altar of thy father, and cut down the Asherah which is by it. And build an altar to the Lord thy God on the top of this stronghold in the ordered place, and take the second bullock and sacrifice it as a burnt-offering with the wood of the Asherah which thou shalt cut down."

And Gideon took ten men of his servants, and did as the Lord hath spoken to him. But since he feared the house of his father and the men of the city he did not do it in the daytime, but did it in the night. And the men of the city rose early in the morning, and behold, the altar of the Baal is demolished and the Asherah which was by it is cut down, and the second bullock was offered up upon the newly built altar. And they said to one another, "Who did this thing?" And they sought and searched and said, "Gideon the son of Joash did this thing." And the men of the city said to Joash, "Bring out thy son, that he may die, for he demolished the altar of the Baal and cut down the Asherah which was by it."

And Joash said to all those who stood about him, "Will ye contend for the Baal? Will ye save him? He that contendeth for him shall be put to death before the morning. If he is god, he shall contend for himself because he hath demolished his altar." And he called him on that day Jerubbaal ("Let Baal contend") saying, "Let the Baal contend against him because he hath demolished his altar."

(Judges 6:11-32)

Gideon and His Three Hundred Men

And Jerubbaal, he is Gideon, rose early in the morning, and all the people who were with him, and he camped by En-Harod, and the camp of Midian was to the north of him, near Gibeath Moreh in the valley. And the Lord said to Gideon, "Too many are the people who are with thee for Me to give Midian into their hand, lest Israel vaunt itself against Me saying, 'My hand saved me.' And now proclaim in the ears of the people saying, 'Who is afraid and trembling? Let him return and depart early from Mount Gilead.' " And twenty-two thousand of the people departed, and ten thousand remained.

And the Lord said to Gideon, "The people are still too many. Take them down to the water, and I will clear them out for thee there. And he of whom I will tell thee, 'This should go with thee,' he should go with thee, and everyone of whom I will tell thee, 'This should not go with thee,' should not go." And he took down the people to the water, and the Lord said to Gideon, "All those who lap up the water with their tongue as the dog lappeth, make them stand apart, and all those who kneel down upon their knees to drink [make them stand apart]. And the number of those who lapped up the water putting their hand to their mouth[3] was three hundred men, and all the rest of the people went down on their knees to drink water.

And the Lord said to Gideon, "With these three hundred men who lapped up the water with their hand will I save you, and will I give Midian into thy hand, and all the people should go each to his place." And they took the provision of the people in their hand, and their horns. And he dismissed all the men of Israel, each man to his tents, and he retained the three hundred men. And the camp of Midian was below him in the valley.

And it came to pass in that night that the Lord said to him, "Rise, go down to the camp for I have delivered it into thy hand! And if thou art afraid to go down, go down thou and Purah thy young man to the camp. And listen to what they say, and thereafter thy hand shall become strong and thou shalt go down into the camp." And he and Purah his young man went down to the edge of the armed men in the camp. . . . And as Gideon came, behold a man was telling a

---

[3] The water flowed down in a cascade. The three hundred men did not kneel down, but stood next to it, and directed the flow with their hand to their mouth. This showed great alertness which was the basis for their selection.

dream to his fellow and saying, "Behold, I dreamt a dream, and behold, a loaf of barley bread was rolling about in the camp of Midian, and it came to the tent and struck it and fell and turned it over from above, and the tent collapsed." And his fellow answered and said, "This is nothing else but the sword of Gideon son of Joash, the man of Israel; God hath delivered into his hand Midian and the whole camp."

And it came to pass when Gideon heard the tale of the dream and its interpretation, that he bowed down, and returned to the camp of Israel and said, "Arise, for the Lord hath delivered unto your hand the camp of Midian." And he divided the three hundred men into three groups and he gave horns into the hand of all of them, and empty jars and torches in the jars. And he said to them, "Watch me and do likewise. For behold, I will go to the edge of the camp, and as I do so do ye. And I will blow the horn, I and all those with me, and ye too blow the horns round about the whole camp, and shout, 'For the Lord and for Gideon!'"

And Gideon and a hundred men with him came to the edge of the camp at the beginning of the middle watch, when they had but newly set the guards, and they blew the horns, and shattered the jars which were in their hand. And the three companies blew the horns, and broke the jars, and held up the torches in their left hand, and in their right the horns to blow, and shouted, "A sword for the Lord and for Gideon!" And they positioned themselves all about the camp, and the whole camp ran and shouted, and fled. And they blew the three hundred horns, and the Lord set the sword of one man against the other, in the whole camp, and the camp fled as far as Beth-Hashittah, until the border of Abel-Meholah, by Tabbath.

(Judg. 7:1-22)

Jotham's Fable

And all the lords of Shechem and all Beth-Millo assembled, and they went and made Abimelech king by the terebinth of the pillar that was in Shechem. And they told Jotham and he went and stood on top of Mount Gerizim, and he lifted up his voice and cried and said to them, "Hearken unto me, lords of Shechem, and may God hearken unto you! The trees went forth to anoint a king over them, and they said to the olive tree, 'Reign over us!' But the olive tree said to them, 'Should I give up my oil which God and men honor in me, and go to lead the trees?' Then the trees said to the fig tree, 'Come thou and reign over us!' but the fig tree said to them, 'Should I give up my sweetness and my good fruit, and go to lead the trees?' Then the trees said to the vine, 'Come thou, reign over us!' But the vine said to them, 'Should I give up my juice which gladdeneth God and men, and go to lead the trees?' And the trees said to the bramble, 'Come thou, reign over us!' And the bramble said to the trees, 'If truly ye anoint me king over you, come and shelter in my shadow; and if not, let fire go forth from the bramble and consume the cedars of Lebanon!' Likewise, if ye have done it truly and sincerely, and have made Abimelech king, and if ye have dealt well with Jerubbaal and his house, and if ye have done to him according to the deserts of his hand—for my father fought for you and risked his life to deliver you from the hand of Midian, and ye have risen up today against my father's hand and have slain his sons, seventy men upon one stone, and have made Abimelech, the son of his handmaid, king over the lords of Shechem for he is your brother—and if ye have done today truly and sincerely with Jerubbaal and his house, rejoice in Abimelech, and let him, too, rejoice in you. But if not, let fire come forth from Abimelech and consume the lords of Shechem and Beth-Millo, and let fire come forth from the lord of Shechem and from Beth-Millo and consume Abimelech."

And Jotham fled, and escaped and went to Beer, and dwelt there because of Abimelech his brother.

(Judg. 9:6-21)

Jephthah and His Daughter

And Jephthah made a vow to the Lord, and said, "If indeed Thou wilt deliver the Children of Ammon into my hand, then that which cometh forth from the doors of my house to meet me when I return in peace from the Children of Ammon, shall belong to the Lord and I will sacrifice him as a burnt offering."

And Jephthah crossed over to the Children of Ammon to fight against them, and the Lord delivered them into his hand. And he smote them from Aroer until thou come to Minnith, twenty cities, and as far as Abel-Keramim, a very great smiting, and the Children of Ammon were subdued before the Children of Israel.

And Jephthah returned to Mizpeh, unto his house, and behold, his daughter came out to meet him with tambourines and dancers, and she was his only child, he had no other son or daughter. And it came to pass when he saw her that he rent his garments and said, "Alas, my daughter, thou hast surely cast me down and thou art become of those who cause me anguish, for I have opened my mouth unto the Lord, and I cannot go back!"

And she said to him, "My father, thou hast opened thy mouth to the Lord, do unto me as it hath come forth from thy mouth, since the Lord hath taken vengeance for thee upon thy enemies, the Children of Ammon." And she said to her father, "Let this thing be done unto me: leave me be for two months that I may withdraw and descend upon the mountains and bewail my virginity, I and my girl companions."

And he said to her, "Go." And he sent her off for two months, and she went with her girl companions and bewailed her virginity upon the mountains. And it came to pass after the end of two months that she returned to her father, and he did to her his vow which he had vowed. And she knew no man. And it became a custom in Israel ever since olden times that the daughters of Israel went out to lament Jephthah's daughter four days a year.

(Judg. 11:30-40)

Samuel Anoints David

And the Lord said to Samuel, "How long wilt thou mourn for Saul seeing that I have rejected him from reigning over Israel? Fill thy horn with oil and go: I will send thee to Jesse the Bethlehemite, for I have found Myself a king among his sons."

And Samuel said, "How can I go? If Saul hear it he will kill me!"

And the Lord said, "Take a heifer into thy hand and say, 'I am come to sacrifice to the Lord.' And call Jesse to the sacrifice, and I will let thee know that which thou shouldst do, and anoint unto Me him whom I will tell thee."

And Samuel did what the Lord spoke, and went to Bethlehem, and the elders of the city met him atrembling and said, "Is thy coming in peace?" and he said, "Peace. I am come to sacrifice to the Lord. Sanctify yourselves and come with me to the sacrifice." And he sanctified Jesse and his sons and called them to the sacrifice. And it came to pass when they came that he saw Eliab and thought, "Lo, before the Lord is His anointed."

But the Lord said to Samuel, "Regard not his appearance, nor the height of his stature, for I have rejected him. For not as a man looks, for a man looks at the eyes, but the Lord looks at the heart."

And Jesse called Abinadab and made him pass before Samuel, and he said, "Neither this hath the Lord chosen." And Jesse made Shammah pass, and he said, "Neither this hath the Lord chosen." And Jesse made his seven sons pass before Samuel, and Samuel said to Jesse, "The Lord hath not chosen these."

And Samuel said to Jesse, "Are these all the children?" And he said, "There is only the smallest left, and behold, he is a shepherd of the flock." And Samuel said to Jesse, "Send for him and fetch him, for we will not sit down till he come hither." And he sent and fetched him, and he was ruddy, with beauty of eyes and good in appearance. And the Lord said, "Rise, anoint him, for this is he." And Samuel took the horn of oil and anointed him in the midst of his brothers. And the spirit of the Lord rushed down upon David from that day forward. And Samuel arose and went to Ramah.

(1 Sam. 16:1-13)

David and Goliath

And the Philistines gathered their armies for battle and they gathered at Socoh of Judah, and they camped between Socoh and Azekah, in Ephes-Dammim. And Saul and the men of Israel gathered and camped in the valley of Elah, and they prepared to fight the Philistines. And the Philistines stood on the mountain on one side, and Israel stood on the mountain on the other side, and the valley was between them.

And a champion went out from the Philistine camp, Goliath by name, from Gath, his height six cubits and one span. And a brass helmet was on his head, and he was clad in a coat of mail, and the weight of the coat was five thousand brass shekels. And he had brass leg armor on his legs, and a brass javelin upon his shoulder. And the shaft of his spear was like the weavers' beam, and the blade of his spear six hundred iron shekels, and the shieldbearer went before him. And he stood and called to the lines of Israel and said to them, "Why do ye come forth to wage war? Here am I, the Philistine, and ye, servants to Saul! Choose a man for you and let him come down to me! If he can fight me and smite me, we will be servants to you, and if I prevail over him and smite him, ye shall be servants to us and shall serve us!" And the Philistine said, "I taunt this day the armies of Israel: give me a man, and let us fight together!"

And when Saul and all Israel heard the words of the Philistine they were dismayed and were sore afraid. . . .

And Jesse said to David his son, "Take, I pray thee, this

ephah of roasted corn, and these ten breads, and hasten to
the camp, to thy brothers. . . . And David rose early in the
morning and left the flock with a watchman, and took and
went as Jesse had commanded him. . . . and he came and
greeted his brothers. And as he spoke with them, and
behold, the champion came up, Goliath the Philistine his
name, of Gath, from the Philistine army, and spoke like
words, and David heard them. And all the men of Israel
when they saw the man fled from his face and were sore
afraid. And the men of Israel said, "Do ye see this man
coming up, for he cometh up to taunt Israel, and it shall
come to pass that the man who smiteth him, the king will
enrich him with great riches and will give him his
daughter, and will make his father's house free in Israel."

And David said to the men that stood by him saying,
"What shall be done to the man who smiteth this Philistine
and removeth the shame from Israel? For who is this
uncircumcised Philistine that he should revile the armies of
the living God?" And the people told him this thing
saying, "Thus will be done to the man who smiteth him."

And when Eliab his eldest brother heard him speak to the
men, the wrath of Eliab was kindled against David and he
said, "Why didst thou come down here? And with whom
didst thou leave those few sheep in the wilderness? Well do
I know thy willfulness and the evil of thy heart, for thou
hast come down only to see the war." And David said,
"What have I done now? It was only words." And he
turned away from him towards another and spoke like
words, and the people returned him words like the first
words.

And the words David spoke were heard, and they told
them to Saul and he fetched him. And David said to Saul,
"Let no man's heart fail because of him. Thy servant will go
and fight this Philistine."

And Saul said to David, "Thou canst not go to this
Philistine to fight him, for thou art a lad, and he is a man of
war since his youth."

And David said to Saul, "Thy servant has been a shepherd of his father's flock, and the lion came, and the bear, and carried off a lamb from the flock, and I went after him and smote him and saved it from his mouth, and he rose up against me but I seized his beard and smote him and killed him. Thy servant killed both the lion and the bear, and let this Philistine be as one of them, for he reviled the armies of the living God." And David said, "The Lord who saved me from the paw of the lion and from the paw of the bear shall save me from the hand of this Philistine."

And Saul said to David, "Go, and the Lord be with thee!"

And Saul clad David in his suit, and put a brass helmet on his head, and clad him in a coat of mail. And David girded on his sword upon his armor, but could not walk for he was not used to it. And David said to Saul, "I cannot walk in these, for I am not used to them." And David took them off. And he took his staff in his hand, and chose five smooth stones from the brook and put them in the shepherd's bag which he had, into the pouch, and his sling in his hand, and went to the Philistine.

And the Philistine came nearer and nearer to David, and the shieldbearer before him. And the Philistine looked, and saw David, and despised him for he was but a lad, and ruddy, with a fair countenance. And the Philistine said to David, "Am I a dog that thou comest to me with sticks?" And the Philistine cursed David with his God. And the Philistine said to David, "Come to me and I will give thy flesh to the birds of heaven and to the beasts of the field."

And David said to the Philistine, "Thou comest to me with sword and javelin and spear, and I come to thee with the name of the Lord of Hosts, the God of the armies of Israel whom thou hast reviled. This day the Lord will deliver thee into my hand, and I shall smite thee and remove thy head from thee, and I shall give this day the carcass of the Philistine camp to the birds of heaven and the beasts of the field, and all the land will know that there is God in Israel. And all this congregation will know that the

Lord delivereth not with sword and javelin, for the war is the Lord's, and He will give you into our hand."

And it came to pass when the Philistine rose and went and came near David that David hastened and ran from the line towards the Philistine. And David stretched forth his hand to the pouch and took from it a stone and slung it, and he smote the Philistine in his forehead, and the stone sank into his forehead, and he fell upon his face to the earth. And David defeated the Philistine with the sling and the stone, and smote the Philistine and killed him, and there was no sword in David's hand. And David ran to and stood over the Philistine and took his sword and drew it out of its sheath, and put him to death, and cut off his head with it.

And the Philistines saw that their hero died, and they fled. And the men of Israel and Judah arose, and shouted, and pursued the Philistines until thou comest to Gai and until the gates of Ekron. And the slain of the Philistines fell on the way to Shaaraim, and as far as Gath and Ekron. And the Children of Israel returned from pursuing after the Philistines, and looted their camps. And David took the head of the Philistine and brought it to Jerusalem, and his weapons he put in his tent.

(1 Sam. 17:1-11, 17, 20, 22-54)

Saul and The Witch of En-Dor

And Samuel died and all Israel mourned him, and buried him in Ramah, in his own city. And Saul had put away out of the land the necromancers and soothsayers.

And the Philistines gathered and came and camped in Shunem, and Saul gathered all Israel and they camped in Gilboa. And Saul saw the Philistine camp, and was afraid, and his heart trembled greatly. And Saul inquired of the Lord, but the Lord answered him not, neither in dreams, nor by the Urim, nor through prophets. And Saul said to his servants, "Find for me a woman necromancer that I may go to her and inquire of her." And his servants said to him, "Behold, there is a woman necromancer in En-Dor."

And Saul disguised himself, and put on other clothes, and he went with two men, and they came to the woman at night. And he said, "Pray, conjure up for me a ghost, and call up him whom I will tell thee." And the woman said to him, "Thou knowest what Saul hath done, that he hath cut off the necromancers and the soothsayers from the land! Why then dost thou ensnare me to cause me to die?" And Saul swore to her by the Lord saying, "As the Lord liveth, no evil shall befall thee for this thing!" And the woman said, "Whom will I call up for thee? And he said, "Call up Samuel for me."

And the woman saw Samuel, and cried in a loud voice and said to Saul saying, "Why hast thou deceived me? Thou art Saul!" And the king said, "Fear not! What dost thou see?" And the woman said to Saul, "I see gods rising up from the earth." And he said to her, "What is his shape?" And she said, "An old man rising, and he wrappeth a mantle." And Saul knew that it was Samuel, and bowed down to earth and prostrated himself.

And Samuel said to Saul, "Why hast thou disturbed me, to call me up?" And Saul said, "I am greatly distressed, for the Philistines fight against me, and God is departed from me and hath answered me no more, neither through the prophets, nor in dreams. Therefore I called thee to let me know what I should do."

And Samuel said, "And why dost thou ask me, since the Lord hath turned away from thee and is become thy adversary? And the Lord hath done as He spoke through me, and the Lord hath torn the kingdom out of thy hand and hath given it to thy neighbor, to David. Because thou hast not hearkened to the voice of the Lord, and hast not executed His fierce wrath upon Amalek, therefore did the Lord do unto thee this thing on this day. And the Lord hath delivered also Israel with thee into the hand of the Philistines, and tomorrow thou and thy sons will be with me. Also the army of Israel the Lord will deliver unto the hand of the Philistines."

And Saul hastened and threw himself full length upon the earth, and he was sore afraid of the words of Samuel. Nor was there any strength in him for he had eaten no bread all the day and all the night.

And the women came to Saul and saw that he was terrified, and said to him, "Behold, thy handmaid hath hearkened to thy voice, and I have put my soul into my hand, and hearkened to thy words which thou hast spoken to me. And now thou also hearken to the voice of thy handmaid, and let me put before thee some bread, and eat, that thou may have strength when thou goest thy way." But he refused and said, "I will not eat." And his servants urged him, and also the woman, and he hearkened to their voice, and rose up from the earth and sat on the couch.

And the woman had a fatted calf in the house, and she hastened and slaughtered it, and took flour and kneaded it and made unleavened bread. And she brought it before Saul and before his servants, and they ate, and then they rose up and went away that night.

(1 Sam. 28:3-25)

David Dances Before God

And the ark of the Lord dwelt in the house of Obed-Edom the Gittite three months, and the Lord blessed Obed-Edom and all his house.

And it was told King David saying, "The Lord blessed the house of Obed-Edom and everything he hath because of the ark of God." And David went and brought up the ark of God from the house of Obed-Edom to the city of David with gladness. And each time the carriers of the ark of God made six steps, he sacrificed an ox and a fatling.

And David danced before the Lord with all his strength, and David was girded with a linen ephod. And David and the whole house of Israel brought up the ark of the Lord with shouting and the sound of shofars. And as the ark of the Lord entered the city of David, Michal the daughter of Saul looked out at the window, and saw King David leap and dance before the Lord, and she despised him in her heart. . . .

And when David returned to bless his house, Michal the daughter of Saul went out to receive David, and said, "How honored this day is the king of Israel who uncovered himself this day before the eyes of the handmaids of his servants, as will one of the worthless shamelessly uncover himself!"

And David said to Michal, "Before the Lord, who chose me above thy father and all his house to appoint me ruler over the people of the Lord, over Israel! I will make merry before the Lord, and let me be yet more worthless than this, and let me be base in my own eyes, and with the handmaids whom thou hast mentioned, with them will I honor myself!"

And Michal the daughter of Saul had no child unto the day of her death.

(2 Sam. 6:11-16, 20-23)

David and Bathsheba

And it came to pass at eventide that David arose from his couch to walk about on the roof of the king's house, and from the roof he saw a woman wash herself, and the woman was very beautiful to behold. And David sent and inquired about the woman, and they said, "Is she not Bathsheba the daughter of Eliam, the wife of Uriah the Hittite?" And David sent messengers and took her, and she came to him, and she was purifying herself from her uncleanness. And then she returned to her house.

And the woman conceived, and she sent and told David, and said, "I am pregnant." And David sent to Joab, "Send me Uriah the Hittite!" And Joab sent Uriah to David. And Uriah came to him, and David inquired after the peace of

Joab, and the peace of the people, and the peace of the war. And David said to Uriah, "Go down to thy house, and wash thy feet." And Uriah went out from the house of the king, and the king's gift went after him. And Uriah slept at the door of the king's house with all the servants of his lord, and went not down to his own house.

And they told David saying, "Uriah went not down to his house." And David said to Uriah, "Is it not that thou comest from the road, why didst thou not go down to thy house?" And Uriah said to David, "The Ark and Israel and Judah dwell in tents, and my lord Joab and the king's servants camp in the field, and I should go to my house to eat and drink and lie with my wife? By thy life and the life of thy soul, I will not do such a thing!" And David said to Uriah, "Remain here today as well, and tomorrow I shall send thee off." And Uriah remained in Jerusalem that day. And the next day David called him and he ate before him and drank, and made him drunk. And he went out in the evening to lie on his bed with the servants of his lord, but he went not down to his own house.

And it came to pass in the morning that David wrote a letter to Joab and sent it by the hand of Uriah. And he wrote in the letter saying, "Make Uriah face the fiercest fighting, and then ye shall withdraw from behind him, so that he be smitten and die."

And it came to pass when Joab watched the city, that he put Uriah into the place of which he knew that men of valor were there. And the men of the city came out and fought against Joab, and several of the people, of the servants of David, fell, and Uriah the Hittite also died.

And Joab sent and told David all the things of the war. And he commanded the messenger saying, "When thou hast finished to tell all the things of the war to the king, and if the wrath of the king ariseth and he will say to you, 'Why did ye go near the city to fight it, did ye not know that they would shoot from the wall? Who smote Abimelech son of Jerubbesheth? Was it not that a woman threw a millstone upon him from the wall and he died at Thebez? Why did ye go near the wall?' Then sayest thou, 'Also thy servant Uriah the Hittite died!' "...

And David said to the messenger, "Thus shalt thou say to Joab, 'Let this thing not be evil in thy eyes, for the sword devoureth this way and that. Increase thy fight against the city and destroy it!' And thou encourage him."

And the wife of Uriah heard that her husband Uriah had died, and she mourned for her husband. And when the mourning was past, David sent and took her to his house, and she became his wife, and she bore him a son. But the thing that David did was evil in the eyes of the Lord.

(2 Sam. 11:2-21, 25-27)

Nathan's Parable

And the Lord sent Nathan to David, and he came to him and said to him, "There were two men in a city, one rich and one poor. The rich man had flocks and herds, very many. And the poor man had nothing but one little ewe lamb which he had bought and reared. And she grew up with him and together with his children, she ate from his bread, and drank from his cup, and lay in his lap, and she was for him as a daughter. And a passerby came to the rich man, and he was reluctant to take from his own flock and herd to prepare for the guest that had come to him, and he took the lamb of the poor man and prepared it for the man who had come to him."

And David grew very wroth against the man, and he said to Nathan, "As the Lord liveth, the man who hath done this surely deserveth death. And he shall pay fourfold for the lamb, because he did this thing, and because he had no pity."

And Nathan said to David, "Thou art that man! Thus saith the Lord God of Israel, 'I anointed thee king over Israel, and I saved thee from the hand of Saul. And I gave thee the house of thy master, and the wives of thy master into thy bosom, and I gave thee the house of Israel and Judah, and if that were little, I would have added thee more and more. Why didst thou despise the word of the Lord, to do the evil in His eyes? Thou hast smitten Uriah the Hittite with the sword, and taken his wife to be thy wife, and him thou hast slain with the sword of the Children of Ammon. And now the sword shall not depart from thy house for ever, because thou hast despised Me and hast taken the wife of Uriah the Hittite to be thy wife!' Thus saith the Lord, 'Behold, I will raise up evil against thee from thy own house, and I will take thy wives before thy eyes and give them to thy neighbor, and he will lie with thy wives before the eyes of this sun! For thou hast acted in secret, and I will do this thing in front of all Israel and before the sun!' "

And David said to Nathan, "I have sinned against the Lord!"

And Nathan said to David, "The Lord also hath put away thy sin; thou shalt not die. But because thou hast greatly blasphemed the Lord with this thing, the child that will be born unto thee shall surely die!"

And Nathan went to his house.

And the Lord struck the child that the wife of Uriah bore unto David, and he became very sick. And David besought the Lord for the child, and David fasted, and when he turned in for the night he lay on the earth. And the elders of his house came to him to lift him up from the earth, but he would not, nor did he break bread with them.

And it came to pass on the seventh day that the child died. And the servants of David were afraid to tell him that the child had died, for they said, "Behold, while the child was alive we spoke to him and he hearkened not unto our voice, and how can we tell him that the child died? He may do himself some harm." But when David saw that his servants were whispering, he understood that the child had died, and said to his servants, "Has the child died?" And they said, "It died."

And David rose up from the earth, and washed and

anointed himself, and changed his clothes, and entered the house of the Lord and worshiped, and returned to his house and asked for bread, and they put it before him, and he ate. And his servants said to him, "What is this thing which thou hast done? For the living child thou hast fasted and wept, and when the child died thou didst rise and eat bread?"

And he said, "As long as the child was alive I fasted and wept, for I said, 'Who knoweth, perhaps the Lord will have mercy upon me and the child will live.' I shall go to him, but he will not return to me."

And David comforted his wife Bathsheba, and went in unto her and lay with her, and she bore a son and she called his name Solomon, and the Lord loved him.

(2 Sam. 12:1-25)

Amnon and Tamar

And it came to pass thereafter that Abshalom the son of David had a beautiful sister and her name was Tamar, and Amnon the son of David loved her. And it distressed Amnon so much that he fell ill because of Tamar his sister, for she was a virgin, and it seemed impossible in the eyes of Amnon to do anything to her.

And Amnon had a friend and his name was Jonadab son of Shimeah, David's brother, and Jonadab was a very astute man. And he said to him, "Why, O prince, art thou thus wasting away day by day? Wouldst thou not tell me?" And Amnon said to him, "I love Tamar, the sister of my brother Abshalom." And Jonadab said to him, "Lie down on thy bed and feign sickness. And when thy father cometh to see thee tell him, 'Let my sister Tamar come to me and break bread for me, and let her dress the food before my eyes that I see and eat from her hand.'"

And Amnon lay down and feigned sickness, and the king came to see him, and Amnon said to the king, "Let, I pray thee, my sister Tamar come and make two cakes before my eyes that I may eat from her hand."

And David sent for Tamar to the house saying, "Pray, go to the house of thy brother Amnon, and prepare food for him." And Tamar went to the house of Amnon her brother, and he was lying, and she took the dough and kneaded it and made cakes before his eyes, and baked the cakes. And she took the pan and poured them out before him, but he refused to eat. And Amnon said, "Everybody get out from here!" And everybody went out.

And Amnon said to Tamar, "Bring the food to the chamber, and I will eat from thy hand!" And Tamar took the cakes which she had made and brought them to Amnon her brother into the chamber. And she presented them to him that he eat, and he seized her and said to her, "Come, lie with me, my sister!" And she said to him, "No, my brother, do not violate me, for such a thing is not done in Israel, do not this vile deed! And I, where shall I take my shame? And thou wilt be like one of the vile men in Israel! Instead, speak to the king for he will not withhold me from thee!"

But he did not want to hearken to her voice, and overpowered her and violated her and lay with her. And then Amnon hated her with a very great hatred, for greater was the hatred wherewith he hated her than the love wherewith he had loved her. And Amnon said to her, "Up, get out!"

And she said to him, "O no, because this evil is greater than the other one which thou hast done to me, to drive me away!" But he did not want to hearken to her. And he called his young manservant and said, "Take this one away from me and out, and shut the door after her!" And she had on a striped robe, for that is what the virgin daughters of the king wore for a mantle, and his servant brought her out and shut the door behind her.

And Tamar put ashes upon her head, and rent the striped robe she had on, and laid her hand on her head, and went and kept on screaming. And her brother Abshalom said to her, "Hath thy brother Amnon been with thee? But now, my sister, keep quiet: he is thy brother, set not thy heart upon this thing." And Tamar stayed in her brother's house desolate.

And King David heard all these things and he became very wroth. And Abshalom spoke to Amnon neither good nor bad; but he hated Amnon because he had violated Tamar his sister.

And it came to pass two years later that Abshalom held a sheep-shearing in Baal-Hazor which is in Ephraim, and Abshalom invited all the sons of the king. And Abshalom went to the king and said, "Behold, thy servant holdeth a sheep-shearing, let the king and his servants come with thy servant." And the king said to Abshalom, "No, my son, let not all of us go, lest we become too heavy for you." And he urged him, but he did not want to go, and he blessed him. And Abshalom said, "If not, let at least my brother Amnon come with us." And the king said to him, "Why should he go with thee?" And Abshalom urged him, and he sent with him Amnon and the king's sons.

And Abshalom commanded his young men saying, "Watch, and when Amnon's heart is merry with wine I will say to you, 'Smite Amnon,' and kill him. Fear not, for is it not that I have commanded you? Be courageous and be men of valor."

And the young men of Abshalom did to Amnon as Abshalom had commanded, and all the king's sons rose, and mounted each man his mule, and fled.

(2 Sam. 13:1-29)

Abishag the Shunammite

And King David was old, stricken in years, and they covered him with clothes but he could not get warm. And his servants said to him, "Let them seek for my lord the king a young girl, a virgin, and let her stand before the king and be him a stewardess, and let her lie in thy bosom, that the king may get warm."

And they sought a beautiful girl in all the borders of Israel, and found Abishag, the Shunammite, and brought her to the king. And the girl was very beautiful, and she became stewardess to the king, and served him, but the king knew her not.

(1 Kings 1:1-4)

Solomon's Judgment

Then came two women, harlots, to the king and stood before him. And one of the women said, "Please, my lord, I and this woman dwell in one house, and I bore a child with her in the house. And it came to pass on the third day after I gave birth that also this woman bore a child, and we were alone, no stranger was in the house except for us two in the house. And the son of this woman died in the night, for she lay upon him. And she arose during the night and took my son from beside me, and thy handmaid was asleep, and she laid him in her bosom, and she laid her dead son in my bosom. And I awoke in the morning to suckle my son, and behold, he is dead. And I looked closely at him in the morning, and behold, it was not my son to whom I had given birth."

And the other woman said, "Not so, for my son is the one alive, and thy son is the one dead." And this said, "No, for thy son is the dead one and my son the one alive." And they argued before the king.

And the king said, "This one sayeth, 'This is my son, the one alive, and thy son is the dead one,' and this one sayeth, 'No, for thy son is the dead one and my son the one alive.'" And the king said, "Get me a sword!" And they brought the sword before the king. And the king said, "Cut the live child in two, and give half to the one and half to the other!"

And the woman whose son was the one alive said to the king, for her heart was filled with pity for her son, and said,

"Please, my lord, give her the living child, but do not slay him!" And the other said, "Neither I nor thee shalt have him; cut him in two!"

And the king answered and said, "Give her the living child, and slay him not; she is his mother!"

And all Israel heard the judgment which the king had judged, and they feared the face of the king for the wisdom of God was in him to make judgment.

(1 Kings 3:16-28)

Solomon's Wisdom

And God gave wisdom to Solomon, and very much understanding, and greatness of heart even as the sand which is on the seashore. And the wisdom of Solomon excelled the wisdom of all the Children of the East, and all the wisdom of Egypt. And he was wiser than all men, than Ethan the Ezrahite, and Heman, and Kalkol, and Darda, the sons of Mahol; and his fame was in all the nations around. And he spoke three thousand proverbs, and his songs were a thousand and five. And he spoke of the trees, from the cedar which is in Lebanon unto the hyssop which grows in the wall, and he spoke of the beasts and the birds, and of the creeping things and the fish. And they came from all the peoples to hear the wisdom of Solomon, from all the kings of the earth who heard of his wisdom.

(1 Kings 5:9-14)

The Queen of Sheba

And the Queen of Sheba heard the fame of Solomon because of the name of the Lord, and she came to test him with riddles. And she came to Jerusalem with a very heavy army, camels carrying spices and gold very much, and precious stones, and she came to Solomon and said to him everything that was in her heart. And Solomon replied to all her words, there was nothing hidden from the king that he did not tell her. And the Queen of Sheba saw all the wisdom of Solomon, and the house that he had built. And the food of his table, and the seat of his servants, and the position of his attendants, and their clothes, and his cupbearers, and the burnt offerings which he offered up in the House of the Lord, and no spirit was left in her.

And she said to the king, "True was the thing which I heard in my country about thy words and thy wisdom. And I disbelieved the things until I have come, and my eyes have seen, and behold, not even half had been told to me. Thou hast added wisdom and good beyond the fame which I had heard. Happy are thy men, happy thy servants, those who stand before thee always and hear thy wisdom! Blessed be the Lord thy God who delighteth in thee to place thee upon the throne of Israel, for the Lord loveth Israel for ever, and He made thee king to do justice and righteousness."

And she gave the king a hundred and twenty talents of gold, and very many spices and precious stones; never again came so much in spices as that which the Queen of Sheba gave King Solomon. And also the fleet of Hiram which brought gold from Ophir brought from Ophir very many sandalwood trees and precious stones. And the king made the sandalwood supports for the House of the Lord and for the house of the king, and harps and psalteries for the singers; never again came so much sandalwood, nor was it seen, until this day. And King Solomon fulfilled all the wishes the Queen of Sheba had, beside that which he gave her of his royal bounty. And she returned and went to her country, she and her servants.

(1 Kings 10:1-13)

Solomon's Sins

And King Solomon loved many foreign women, also the daughter of Pharaoh, and Moabites, Ammonites, Edomites, Zidonites, Hittites. From the nations of whom the Lord had said to the Children of Israel, "Go not among them and they shall not come among you, lest they bend your heart after their gods"—Solomon cleaved to them in love. And he had wives, princesses, seven hundred, and concubines three hundred, and his women turned away his heart.

And it came to pass at the time of Solomon's old age that his wives bent his heart after other gods, and his heart was not complete with the Lord his God as was the heart of his father David. And Solomon went after Astarte the goddess of the Zidonians, and after Milcom, the abomination of the Ammonites. And Solomon did what was evil in the eyes of the Lord, and was not fully after the Lord as was David his father. Then Solomon built a high place for Kemosh, the abomination of Moab, on the mountain which faces Jerusalem, and for Moloch, the abomination of the Children of Ammon. And so he did for all his foreign wives: they burnt incense and sacrificed for their gods.

And the Lord became wroth with Solomon for he turned away his heart from the Lord the God of Israel who had appeared to him twice, and commanded him this thing: that he go not after other gods. But he kept not that which the Lord commanded. And the Lord said to Solomon, "Because this was done by thee, and thou hast not kept My covenant and My statutes which I commanded thee, I will surely tear away the kingdom from thee and give it to thy servant. But I will not do it in thy days for the sake of thy father David; from the hand of thy son will I tear it away. Howbeit, I will not tear away the entire kingdom: I will give one tribe to thy son for the sake of My servant David, and for the sake of Jerusalem which I have chosen."

(1 Kings 11:1-13)

Elijah in the Desert

And Elijah the Tishbite, of the inhabitants of Gilead, said to Ahab, "As the Lord the God of Israel liveth, before whom I have stood, there will be neither dew nor rain these years, except according to my word." And the word of the

Lord was unto him saying, "Go hence and turn east, and hide by the brook Kerith which is before the Jordan. And it shall be that from the brook shalt thou drink, and I have commanded the ravens to feed thee there."

And he went and did according to the word of the Lord, and went and dwelt by the brook Kerith which is before the Jordan. And the ravens brought him bread and meat in the morning, and bread and meat in the evening, and from the brook he drank. And it came to pass after days that the brook dried out for there was no rain in the country.

(1 Kings 17:1-7)

The Widom of Zarephath

And the word of the Lord was unto him saying, "Arise, go to Zarephath which is by Zidon, and dwell there. Behold I commanded there a woman, a widow, to feed thee." And he arose and went to Zarephath, and he came to the gate of the city, and behold, there was a woman there, a widow, gathering wood. And he called to her and said, "Fetch me, I pray thee, a little water in the vessel, that I drink." And she went to fetch it, and he called to her and said, "Fetch me, I pray thee, some bread in thy hand!"

And she said, "As the Lord thy God liveth, I have no cake, only a handful of flour in a jar and a little oil in a cruse, and behold, I will gather two sticks and then go and prepare it for me and my son, that we eat it and die."

And Elijah said to her, "Fear not, go, do as thou hast said, but first make me thereof a small cake, and bring it out to me, and for thyself and thy son make thereafter. For thus saith the Lord, the God of Israel, 'The jar of flour shall not come to an end, and the cruse of oil shall not be wanting until the day on which the Lord will give rain upon the face of the earth.' "

And she went and did according to the word of Elijah, and she ate, and he and her house, many days. The jar of flour did not come to an end and the cruse of oil was not wanting, according to the word of the Lord which He spoke through Elijah.

(1 Kings 17:8-16)

Elijah Resurrects the Child

And it came to pass after these things that the son of the woman, the mistress of the house, fell sick, and his sickness was very sore until no breath was left in him. And she said to Elijah, "What have I to do with thee, O man of God? Art thou come unto me to remind me of my sin and to kill my son?"

And he said to her, "Give me thy son!" And he took him from her bosom and carried him up into the loft in which he dwelt, and lay him down on his bed. And he called to the Lord and said, "Oh Lord, my God, dost Thou evil even unto the widow with whom I sojourn, to slay her son?" And he stretched himself upon the child two times, and called to the Lord and said, "Oh Lord, my God, return, I pray thee, the soul of this child into him!"

And the Lord hearkened unto the voice of Elijah, and the soul of the child returned into him, and he lived. And Elijah took the child and carried him down from the loft into the house, and gave him to his mother. And Elijah said, "See, thy son liveth!"

And the woman said to Elijah, "Now I know that a man of God art thou, and the word of the Lord in thy mouth is true."

(1 Kings 17:17-24)

Elijah and the Baal Prophets

And it came to pass after many days that the word of the Lord was to Elijah in the third year saying, "Go, show thyself to Ahab, and I will give rain upon the face of the earth."

And Elijah went to show himself to Ahab, and the

famine was intense in Samaria. And Ahab called Obadiah who was over the house, and Obadiah feared the Lord greatly. And it had come about when Jezebel cut off the prophets of the Lord that Obadiah took a hundred prophets and hid them, fifty men in a cave, and fed them bread and water. And Ahab said to Obadiah, "Go into the land, to all sources of water and all the brooks, perhaps we shall find grass and we can save the life of horse and mule and we shall not be cut off from the beasts."

And they divided the country between them to pass through: Ahab went one way alone, and Obadiah went the other way alone. And while Obadiah was on his way, and behold, Elijah encountered him, and he recognized him and fell upon his face and said, "Is it thou, my lord Elijah?"

And he said, "I indeed. Go and tell thy master, 'Behold, Elijah!' "

And he said, "What have I sinned that thou wouldst deliver thy servant into the hand of Ahab to kill me? As the Lord thy God liveth, there is no nation and kingdom to which my lord hath not sent to seek thee, and when they said, 'Not here,' he made that kingdom and nation swear that they found thee not. And now thou sayest, 'Go tell thy master, Behold Elijah'? And it will come to pass that as soon as I leave thee the spirit of the Lord will carry thee off, whereto I shall not know, and I shall come and tell Ahab, and he will not find thee, and will slay me, and thy servant hath feared God since my youth. Has it not been told my lord what I did when Jezebel slew the prophets of the Lord, and I hid of the prophets of the Lord a hundred men, fifty men in a cave, and fed them bread and water? And now thou sayest, 'Go tell thy master, Behold Elijah,' and he will slay me!"

And Elijah said, "As the Lord of Hosts liveth, before whom I have stood, this very day I shall show myself to him!"

And Obadiah went to meet Ahab, and told him, and Ahab went to meet Elijah. And when Ahab saw Elijah he said to him, "Is it thou, thou troubler of Israel?" And he said, "Not I have troubled Israel, but thou and thy father's house, having forsaken the commandments of the Lord, and thou hast gone after the Baals. And now, send and gather to me all Israel on Mount Carmel, and the prophets of the Baal, four hundred and fifty, and the prophets of the Asherah, four hundred, that eat at the table of Jezebel."

And Ahab sent to all the Children of Israel, and gathered the prophets on Mount Carmel. And Elijah approached all the people and said, "How long will ye sit on the fence? If the Lord is God, go ye after Him, and if the Baal, go ye after him!" And the people answered him nothing. And Elijah said to the people, "I alone am left a prophet of the Lord, and the prophets of the Baal are four hundred and fifty men. Let two bullocks be given to us, and let them choose one bullock and cut it in pieces and place it upon the wood, and put no fire to it, and I will do the other bullock and will place it upon the wood, and will put no fire to it. And call ye on the name of your god, and I will call on the name of the Lord, and the god who answereth by fire he is God."

And all the people answered and said, "So be it."

And Elijah said to the prophets of the Baal, "Choose yourselves one bullock, and do it first, for ye are many, and call ye on the name of your god, and put no fire."

And they took the bull which was given them, and did so, and called on the name of the Baal from the morning until noon, saying, "O Baal, answer us!" And there was neither voice nor answer. And they leapt around the altar which they made. And it came to pass at noon that Elijah began to mock them and said, "Cry aloud, for surely he is a god; he may be musing or is busy, or he hath an errand, or perhaps he is asleep and must be awakened." And they cried aloud, and cut themselves as was their custom, with swords and lances, until the blood gushed out upon them.

And noontime passed and they prophesied until the time of the evening offering, but there was neither voice nor answer nor notice. And Elijah said to all the people, "Come near me!" And all the people came near him, and he repaired the altar of the Lord which had been demolished. And Elijah took twelve stones, as the number of the tribes of the sons of Jacob to whom had been the word of the Lord saying, "Israel shall be thy name." And he built of the stones an altar in the name of the Lord, and he made a trench of about two measures of seed in capacity round about the altar. And he arranged the wood and cut up the bullock and put it upon the wood. And he said, "Fill four jars of water and pour it upon the burnt offering and the wood." And he said, "A second time!" And they repeated it, and he said, "A third time!" and they did it a third time. And the water flowed around the altar, and also the trench was filled with water.

And at the time of the evening offering Elijah the prophet came near and said, "O Lord, God of Abraham, Isaac, and Israel, this day it shall become known that Thou art God in Israel and I am Thy servant, and that according to Thy word did I all these things. Answer me, O Lord, answer me, that this people know that Thou art the Lord the God, and that Thou hast turned their heart backward!"

And the fire of the Lord fell and consumed the burnt offering and the wood and the stones and the dust, and licked up the water that was in the trench. And all the people saw it, and they fell on their faces, and said, "The Lord is the God! The Lord is the God!"

And Elijah said to them, "Seize the prophets of the Baal! Let no man of them escape!" And they seized them and took them down to the river Kishon, and slaughtered them there.

And Elijah said to Ahab, "Go up, and eat and drink, for there is the sound of the rustle of rain." And Ahab went up to eat and drink, and Elijah went up to the top of Mount Carmel, and he crouched down to the earth and put his face between his knees. And he said to his page, "Go up, I pray thee, and look towards the sea!" And he went up and looked and said, "There is nothing." And he said, "Go back," seven times. And it came to pass at the seventh that he said, "Behold a small cloud, like the hand of a man, is rising from the sea." And he said, "Go up and say to Ahàb, 'Hitch up and go down lest the rain hold thee up.' "

And it came to pass in the meanwhile that the heaven became black with heavy clouds, wind, and there was a great rain. And Ahab drove and went to Jezreel. And the hand of the Lord was upon Elijah, and he girded his loins and ran before Ahab until thou comest to Jezreel.

(1 Kings 18:1-46)

Elijah on Mount Horeb

And Ahab told Jezebel all that Elijah had done, and that he had slain all the prophets with the sword. And Jezebel sent a messenger to Elijah saying, "So let the gods do unto me, and even more so, if by this time tomorrow I make not thy soul as the soul of one of them!"

And he saw, and arose, and went for his life, and came to Beer-Sheba which is in Judah, and left his page there. And he went into the desert, one day's journey, and came and sat down under a broom tree, and he yearned that his soul die and said, "It is too much; now, O Lord, take my soul, for I am no better than my fathers." And he lay down and slept under a broom tree, and behold, an angel touched him and said to him, "Get up, eat!" And he looked around, and behold, at his headside a baked cake and a cruse of water. And he ate and drank, and lay down.

And the angel of the Lord returned a second time, and touched him and said, "Get up, eat, for the journey before thee is too great!" And he got up and ate and drank, and he walked by the strength of that eating forty days and forty nights, until the mountain of God, Horeb. And he came there to a cave, and spent the night there. And behold, the word of the Lord was to him, and He said to him, "What hast thou here, Elijah?" And he said, "I have been jealous and zealous for the Lord, the God of Hosts, for the Children of Israel have forsaken Thy covenant, and demolished Thy altars, and slain Thy prophets with the sword. And I alone was left, and they sought my soul to take it."

And He said, "Go out and stand upon the mountain before the Lord."

And behold, the Lord passed by, and there was a great and strong wind, which rendeth mountains and breaketh rocks before the Lord. But the Lord was not in the wind.

And after the wind there was an earthquake. But the Lord was not in the earthquake.

And after the earthquake fire. But the Lord was not in the fire.

And after the fire the sound of fine silence.

And it came to pass when Elijah heard it that he wrapped his face in his mantle, and went out, and stood at the entrance of the cave. And behold, a sound came to him and said, "What hast thou here, Elijah?" And he said, "I have been jealous and zealous for the Lord, the God of Hosts, for the Children of Israel have forsaken thy covenant, and demolished Thy altars, and slain Thy prophets with the sword, and I alone was left, and they sought my soul to take it."

And the Lord said to him, "Go, return on thy way to the desert of Damascus, and come and anoint Hazael king over Aram. And Jehu the son of Nimshi anoint king over Israel, and Elisha the son of Shaphat of Abel-Meholah anoint prophet in thy stead."

(1 Kings 19:1-16)

Elijah and Ahaziah

And Ahaziah fell down through the lattice in his upper chamber which was in Samaria, and became sick. And he sent messengers and said to them, "Go, inquire of Baal-Zebub, the god of Ekron, whether I will recover of this sickness."

And the angel of the Lord spoke to Elijah the Tishbite,

"Arise, go up to meet the messengers of the king of Samaria, and speak to them, 'Is there no God in Israel that ye go to inquire of Baal-Zebub, the god of Ekron?' Therefore, thus saith the Lord, 'The bed upon which thou hast lain down, thou shalt not get up from it, for surely thou shalt die.' " And Elijah went away.

And the messengers returned to him and he said to them, "Why have ye returned?" And they said to him, "A man came up to meet us and said to us, 'Go return to the king who hath sent you, and speak to him, "Thus saith the Lord, 'Is there no God in Israel that thou sendest to inquire of Baal-Zebub, the god of Ekron? Therefore, the bed upon which thou hast lain down, thou shalt not get up from it, for surely thou shalt die.' " ' "

And he spoke to them, "What manner of man was he who came up to meet you and told you these things?" And they said to him, "A hairy man, and girt with a leather girdle around his loins." And he said, "It was Elijah the Tishbite."

And he sent to him a captain of fifty with his fifty men, and he went up to him, and behold, he sat on top of the mountain. And he said to him, "Man of God! The king spoke, come down!" And Elijah answered him and spoke to the captain of fifty, "If indeed I am a man of God, let fire come down from heaven and consume thee and thy fifty." And fire came down from heaven and consumed him and his fifty.

And he sent to him again another captain of fifty and his fifty, and he spoke and said to him, "Man of God! Thus saith the king, 'Come down quickly!' " And Elijah answered and spoke to them, "If I am a man of God, let fire come down from heaven and consume thee and thy fifty." And the fire of God came down from heaven and consumed him and his fifty.

And again he sent a third captain of fifty and his fifty. And the captain of fifty came and fell on his knees before Elijah, and besought him and spoke to him, "Man of God!

Let, I pray thee, my life and the life of thy servants, these fifty, be dear in thy eyes! Behold, fire came down from heaven and consumed the first two captains of fifty and their fifties, and now, let my soul be dear in thy eyes!"

And the angel of the Lord spoke to Elijah, "Go down with him, fear him not!" And he arose and went down with him to the king.

And he said to him, "Thus saith the Lord, 'Because thou hast sent messengers to inquire of Baal-Zebub, the god of Ekron — is there no God in Israel to inquire of His word? — therefore the bed upon which thou hast lain down, thou wilt not get up from it, for surely thou shalt die.'"

And he died according to the word of the Lord, which Elijah spoke, and his son Jehoram reigned in his stead.

(2 Kings 1:2-17)

The Translation of Elijah

And it came to pass that the Lord carried up Elijah to heaven in a whirlwind. And Elijah and Elisha went forth from Gilgal, and Elijah said to Elisha, "Sit, I pray thee, here, for the Lord hath sent me to Beth-El." And Elisha said, "As the Lord liveth, and as thy soul liveth, I shall not leave thee." And they went down to Beth-El.

And the sons of the prophets who were in Beth-El came out to Elisha, and said to him, "Knowest thou that this day the Lord will take away thy master from thy head?" And he said, "I also know it. Be silent!"

And Elijah said to him, "Sit, I pray thee, here, for the Lord hath sent me to the Jordan." And he said, "As the Lord liveth, and as thy soul liveth, I shall not leave thee." And the two of them went together.

And fifty men of the sons of the prophets went and stood opposite afar off, and the two of them stood by the Jordan. And Elijah took his mantle, and rolled it up and smote the waters, and they divided hither and thither, and the two of them went across on dry ground.

And as they were crossing Elijah said to Elisha, "Ask, what shall I do for thee ere I am taken away from thee?" And Elisha said, "Let there be, I pray thee, double of thy spirit upon me." And he said, "Thou hast asked a hard thing. If thou see me being taken away from thee, so shall it be unto thee, and if not, it shall not be."

And it came to pass as they went on, walking and talking, and behold, a chariot of fire and horses of fire, and they separated them, and Elijah went up to heaven in the whirlwind.

And Elisha saw it and cried out, "My father, my father! Chariot of Israel and its horsemen!" And he saw him no more.

And he took hold of his garments and rent them in two. And he lifted up the mantle of Elijah which had fallen off him, and returned and stood on the bank of the Jordan. And he took the mantle of Elijah which had fallen from him, and smote the waters and said, "Where is the Lord, the God of Elijah?" And he too smote the waters, and they divided hither and thither, and Elisha went across.

And the sons of the prophets who were in Jericho opposite saw him and said, "The spirit of Elijah resteth upon Elisha." And they came to meet him, and bowed down to earth before him.

(2 Kings 2:1-15)

Elisha Heals the Bitter Waters

And the men of the city [Jericho] said to Elisha, "Behold, the site of the city is good, as my lord seeth, but the waters are bad, and the land miscarrieth." And he said, "Fetch me a new cruse, and put salt into it." And they brought it to him. And he went out to the source of the waters, and cast the salt there and said, "Thus saith the Lord, 'I have healed these waters. No more will there be from here death and miscarriage.'" And the waters were healed, unto this day, according to the word of Elisha which he spoke.

(2 Kings 2:19-22)

Elisha Multiplies the Oil

And a woman, of the wives of the sons of the prophets, cried unto Elisha saying, "Thy servant, my husband, died, and thou knowest that thy servant feared the Lord, and the creditor is come to take my two children to be his slaves."

And Elisha said to her, "What shall I do for thee? Tell me, what hast thou in the house?" And she said, "Thy handmaid hath nothing in the house save a flask of oil."

And he said, "Go, borrow vessels from the outside, from all thy neighbors, empty vessels, not a few. And come, shut the door behind thee and behind thy children, and pour into all those vessels, and set aside those that are full."

And she went from him, and shut the door behind her and behind her children. They brought to her and she poured. And it came to pass when all the vessels were filled that she said to her son, "Give me another vessel," and he said to her, "There are no more vessels." And the oil ceased.

And she came and told the man of God, and he said, "Go and sell the oil, and pay thy creditor, and thou and thy sons live on that which is left."

(2 Kings 4:1-7)

Elisha Resurrects the Dead Child

And it came to pass one day that Elisha passed to Shunem, and there was a great woman, and she prevailed upon him to eat bread with her, and every time he passed by he would turn in there to eat bread. And she said to her husband, "Behold, I pray thee, I know that he is a holy man of God who passeth by us frequently. Let us make him a small chamber atop the wall, and put a bed there for him, and a table and a chair and a lamp, so that when he cometh to us he should turn in there."

And the day was that he came there and turned into the upper chamber, and lay down there. And he said to his page Gehazi, "Call this Shunammite woman." And he called her, and she stood before him. And he said to him, "Tell her, 'Behold thou hast expended all this care upon us, what can I do for thee? Is there anything thou wantest to say to the king, or to the commander of the army?' " And she said, "I dwell among my own people." And he said, "Still, what can I do for her?" And Gehazi said, "But she has no child, and her husband is old." And he said, "Call her." And he called her, and she stood in the door. And he said, "About this season, at the time of life, thou shalt embrace a son." And she said, "Nay, my lord, man of God, do not mislead thy handmaid."

And the woman conceived and bore a son, about that season, at the time of life, as Elisha had spoken to her.

And the child grew, and it came to pass one day that he went out to his father, to the reapers. And he said to his father, "My head, my head!" And he said to the servant, "Carry him to his mother." And he carried him and brought him to his mother, and he sat upon her knees until midday, and died.

And she went up and lay him down upon the bed of the man of God, and shut the door on him and went out. And she called her husband and said, "Send me one of the servants and one of the she-asses, and I shall run to the man of God, and come back." And he said, "Why dost thou go to him? This day is neither new moon nor Sabbath?" And she said, "Peace." And she saddled up the she-ass and said to her servant, "Lead and go! Do not slow down the riding because of me, unless I tell thee." And she went and came to the man of God on Mount Carmel.

And it came to pass when the man of God saw her from afar, that he said to his page Gehazi, "Behold, that Shunammite woman. Now pray run to meet her and say to her, 'Is it peace with thee? Is it peace with thy husband? Is it peace with the child?' " And she said, "Peace." And she came to the man of God to the mountain, and seized his feet, and Gehazi came near to thrust her away, but the man of God said, "Leave her be, for her soul is bitter, and the

Lord hath hidden it from me and hath not told me."

And she said, "Did I ask a son from my lord? Did I not say, 'Do not deceive me'?"

And he said to Gehazi, "Gird thy loins and take my staff in thy hand and go. If thou meetest a man, greet him not, and if a man greet thee, answer him not, and place my staff upon the face of the boy."

And the mother of the boy said, "As the Lord liveth, and as thy soul liveth, I shall not leave thee!" And he arose and went after her. And Gehazi passed before them, and he placed the staff upon the face of the boy, and there was no voice and no sound. And he came back to meet him and told him, saying, "The boy did not wake up."

And Elisha went into the house, and behold, the boy was dead, laid upon his bed. And he entered, and shut the door upon the two of them, and prayed to the Lord. And he went up and lay upon the child, and put his mouth on his mouth, and his eyes on his eyes, and his hands on his hands, and stretched himself upon him, and the flesh of the child became warm. And he returned and walked in the house, once to and once fro, and then went up and stretched himself upon him, and the boy sneezed up to seven times, and the boy opened his eyes. And he called to Gehazi and said, "Call this Shunammite woman!" And he called her and she came. And he said to her, "Take thy son!"

And she came and fell at his feet, and bowed down to the earth, and took her son and went out.

(2 Kings 4:8-37)

Elisha Cures the Poisonous Food

And Elisha returned to Gilgal, and there was famine in the land, and the sons of the prophets sat before him. And he said to his page, "Put the big pot on the fire and cook pottage for the sons of the prophets." And one went out into the field to gather herbs, and found a field vine and plucked from it a lap full of field gourds, and brought them back, and shredded them into the pot of pottage, for they knew them not. And they poured out for the men to eat, and it came to pass as they ate of the pottage that they cried out and said, "Death is in the pot, O man of God!" And they could not eat it.

And he said, "Then get flour!" And he cast it in the pot, and said, "Pour for the people!" And they ate, and there was nothing bad in the pot.

(2 Kings 4:38-41)

Elisha Multiplies the Bread

And a man came from Baal-Shalishah, and brought the man of God firstling bread, twenty barley breads, and fresh fruit in his sack. And he said, "Give it to the people and let them eat!" And his servant said, "What shall I give? This before a hundred men?" And he said, "Give it to the people and let them eat, for thus saith the Lord, 'They shall eat and leave over.' " And he put it before them, and they ate and left over, according to the word of the Lord.

(2 Kings 4:42-44)

Elisha Cures the Leper

And Naaman, the commander of the army of the king of Aram, was a great man before his master, and much esteemed, for through him the Lord had given deliverance to Aram. And the man was a valiant hero, but a leper. And Aram went forth in bands, and they captured in the land of Israel a little girl-child, and she became [a handmaid] unto Naaman's wife.

And she said to her mistress, "I wish that my lord were before the prophet who is in Samaria! Then he would cure him of his leprosy!"

And he went and told his master saying, "Thus and thus hath spoken the girl who is from the land of Israel." And the king of Aram said, "Go, come and I will send a letter to the king of Israel."

And he went and took in his hand ten talents of silver and six thousand pieces of gold, and ten suits of clothes. And he brought the letter to the king of Israel saying, "And now, when this letter cometh to thee, behold, I am sending to thee my servant Naaman, and thou cure him of his leprosy."

And it came to pass when the king of Israel read the letter, that he rent his clothes and said, "Am I God, to put to death or to let live, that this one sendeth to me to cure a man of his leprosy? But know ye, I pray you, and see that he looketh for a pretext against me!"

And it came to pass when Elisha, the man of God, heard that the king of Israel hath rent his clothes that he sent to the king saying, "Why hast thou rent thy clothes? Let him, I pray thee, come to me and know that there is a prophet in Israel."

And Naaman came with his horses and chariots, and stopped in front of the door of Elisha's house. And Elisha sent to him a messenger saying, "Go and wash seven times in the Jordan, and thy flesh shall return to thee and thou shalt become clean."

And Naaman became wroth and went and said, "Behold, I thought to myself, 'He will surely come out and stand and call on the name of the Lord his God, and wave his hand over the place and cure the leper. Are not Abana and Parpar, the rivers of Damascus, better than all the water of Israel? Can I not wash in them and become clean?' " And he turned away and went off in anger.

And his servants approached him and spoke to him and said, "My father! Had the prophet said a great thing to thee, wouldst thou not have done it? How much rather then since he said to thee 'Wash and become clean'?"

And he went down and immersed himself in the Jordan seven times, according to the word of the man of God, and his flesh returned as the flesh of a little boy, and he became clean.

And he returned to the man of God, he and all his camp,

and came and stood before him and said, "Behold, I pray thee, I know that there is no God in all the earth save in Israel! And now, accept, I pray thee, an offering from thy servant."

But he said, "As the Lord liveth before whom I have stood, I will not accept!" And he urged him to accept, but he refused. And Naaman said, "If not, let thy servant be given two mules' load of earth, for thy servant shall no more offer burnt offering and sacrifice to other gods but to the Lord. Only may the Lord forgive this thing to thy servant: when my master goes to the house of Rimmon to worship there, and he leans on my hand, and I worship in the house of Rimmon—when I worship in the house of Rimmon, may the Lord forgive thy servant for this thing."

And he said to him, "Go in peace!"

(2 Kings 5:1-19)

Elisha Causes the Axe to Swim

And the sons of the prophets said to Elisha, "Behold, pray, the place in which we dwell before thee is too strait for us. Let us, pray, go to the Jordan, and let each of us take from there a beam, and let us make ourselves there a place to dwell." And he said, "Go." And one said, "Be willing, pray, to come with thy servant." And he said, "I will go." And he went with them, and they came to the Jordan, and cut the trees. And it came to pass as one was felling the beam, that the iron fell into the water, and he cried and said, "Alas, my lord, for it was borrowed!" And the man of God said, "Where did it fall?" And he showed him the place. And he cut a stick and cast it there, and the iron swam up. And he said, "Take it out for thee!" And he stretched forth his hand and took it.

(2 Kings 6:1-7)

Elisha Captures the Aramaeans

And the king of Aram fought against Israel, and took

counsel with his servants saying, "In such and such a place will I camp." And the man of God sent to the king of Israel saying, "Beware of passing in this place for there is Aram encamped."

And the king of Israel sent to the place of which the man of God had told him and warned him, and guarded himself there, not once and not twice.

And the heart of the king of Aram raged over this thing, and he called his servants and said to them, "Can you tell me who among us is for the king of Israel?" And one of his servants said, "Nay, my lord the king, but Elisha the prophet who is in Israel telleth the king of Israel the words which thou speakest in thy bedchamber." And he said, "Go and see where he is, and I will send and take him." And it was told him saying, "Behold, he is in Dothan." And he sent there horses and chariots and a great host, and they came in the night and surrounded the city.

And the servant of the man of God arose early in the morning, and went out, and behold, a host surroundeth the city, and horse and chariot. And his page said to him, "Alas, my lord, what shall we do?"

And he said, "Fear not, for more are they that are with us than those with them." And Elisha prayed and said, "O Lord, open, pray, his eyes that he may see!" And the Lord opened the eyes of the page, and he saw, and behold, the mountain full of horses and chariots of fire round about Elisha. And they came down to him, and Elisha prayed to the Lord and said, "Smite, pray, this nation with blindness!" And He smote them with blindness according to the word of Elisha.

And Elisha said to them, "This is not the way and this is not the city; come after me and I will take you to the man whom ye seek." And he led them to Samaria.

And it came to pass when they came to Samaria that Elisha said, "O Lord, open the eyes of these, that they may see!" And the Lord opened their eyes and they saw, and behold, they were in the midst of Samaria.

And the king of Israel said to Elisha when he saw them, "Shall I smite, smite them, my father?" And he said, "Smite them not, those whom thou hast captured with thy sword and thy bow, those wouldest thou smite? Set bread and water before them, and let them eat and drink and go to their master."

And he prepared a great meal for them, and they ate and drank, and he sent them off, and they went to their master. And the troops of Aram did no more come to the land of Israel.

(2 Kings 6:8-23)

The Anointing of Jehu

And the prophet Elisha called one of the sons of the prophets and said to him, "Gird up thy loins and take this vial of oil in thy hand and go to Ramoth-Gilead. And when thou comest there thou shalt see Jehu the son of Jehoshaphat the son of Nimshi, and go and make him rise from the midst of his brothers, and take him into an inner chamber. And take the vial of oil and pour it upon his head and say, 'Thus saith the Lord, I have anointed thee king over Israel.' And then open the door and flee, tarry not."

And the youth, the young prophet, went to Ramoth-Gilead. And he came and behold, the captains of the host were sitting, and he said, "I have a word to thee, O captain." And Jehu said, "To which of us?" And he said, "To thee, O captain."

And he rose and went inside, and poured the oil upon his head, and said to him, "Thus saith the Lord, the God of Israel, 'I have anointed thee king over the people of the Lord, over Israel. And thou shalt smite the house of Ahab thy master, and I will avenge the blood of my servants the prophets, and the blood of all the servants of the Lord, from the hand of Jezebel. And all the house of Ahab shall perish, and I will cut off from Ahab every one who urinates against the wall, and him that is shut up and left in Israel. And I will make the house of Ahab like the house of Jeroboam the son of Nebat, and like the house of Baasha the son of Ahijah. And the dogs shall eat Jezebel in the portion of Jezreel, and none will bury her.' " And he opened the door and fled.

And Jehu went out to the servants of his master, and they said to him, "Is it peace? Why did this madman come unto thee?" And he said to them, "Ye know the man and his talk."

And they said, "It is not true. Pray, tell us!" And he said, "Thus and thus he spoke to me, saying, 'Thus saith the Lord, I have anointed thee king over Israel.' "

And they hastened and every man took his garment, and put it under him at the top of the stairs, and they blew the shofar and said, "Jehu reigns!"

(2 Kings 9:1-13)

The Death of Elisha

And Elisha fell sick of the sickness of which he was to die. And Joash king of Israel went down to him, and wept upon his face and said, "My father, my father! The chariot of Israel and its horsemen!"

And Elisha said to him, "Take bow and arrows!" And he took unto him bow and arrows. And he said to the king of Israel, "Place thy hand upon the bow!" And he did place his hand, and Elisha put his own hands upon the hands of the king.

And he said, "Open the window to the east!" And he opened it, and Elisha said, "Shoot!" And he shot. And he said, "An arrow of deliverance to the Lord, and arrow of deliverance from Aram! And thou shalt smite Aram in Aphek until extinction."

And he said, "Take arrows!" And he took. And he said to the king of Israel, "Beat them against the earth!" And he beat them three times and stopped.

And the man of God was wroth with him and said,

"Hadst thou beaten five or six times, thou wouldst have smitten Aram until extinction, but now thou shalt smite Aram only three times."

And Elisha died, and they buried him. And the bands of Moab came into the land at the beginning of the year. And they were about to bury a man, and behold, they saw the band, and they cast the man into the tomb of Elisha, and the man went and touched the bones of Elisha, and came to life and stood up on his feet.

(2 Kings 13:14-21)

Isaiah and Hezekiah

In those days Hezekiah fell sick unto death, and the prophet Isaiah the son of Amoz came to him and said to him, "Thus saith the Lord, 'Endow thy house, for thou shalt die and live not.'"

And he turned his face to the wall, and prayed to the Lord saying, "I beseech Thee, O Lord, remember that I walked before Thee in truth and with a whole heart, and did that which was good in Thy eyes." And Hezekiah wept a great weeping.

And it came to pass ere Isaiah came out of the middle court, that the word of the Lord was to him saying, "Return and tell Hezekiah, the prince of My people, 'Thus saith the Lord, the God of thy father David, I have hearkened unto thy prayer, I have seen thy tears, behold I will heal thee. On the third day thou shalt go up to the House of the Lord. And I will add fifteen years to thy days, and I will deliver thee from the hand of the king of Assyria, and this city, and I will protect this city for My sake and for the sake of My servant David.'"

And Isaiah said, "Fetch a cake of figs." And they fetched, and put it on the boil, and he lived.

And Hezekiah said to Isaiah, "What is the sign that the Lord will heal me, and that on the third day I shall go up to the House of the Lord?"

And Isaiah said, "This is for thee the sign from the Lord: If the Lord will do the thing He had spoken: Shall the shadow go forward ten degrees, or go back ten degrees?" And Hezekiah said, "It is easy for the shadow to lengthen ten degrees. Nay, let the shadow go backwards ten degrees."

And the prophet Isaiah called on the Lord, and He made the shadow go back ten degrees which it had gone down on the dial of Ahaz, backwards ten degrees.

(2 Kings 20:1-11)

Isaiah's Consecration

In the year of king Uzziah's death I saw the Lord sitting on a high and exalted throne, and His train filled the hall. Seraphim stood above Him: each one had six wings, with two he covered his face, with two he covered his feet, and with two he flew. And one called to the other and said, "Holy, holy, holy is the Lord of Hosts, the whole earth is full of His glory!" And the doorposts shook from the voice of the call, and the house filled with smoke. And I said, "Woe to me, for I am undone, for a man of unclean lips am I, and in the midst of a people of unclean lips I dwell, for my eyes have seen the King, the Lord of Hosts!"

And one of the Seraphim flew to me, and in his hand a burning coal which he had taken with tongs from the altar. And he touched it to my lips and said, "Behold, this has touched thy lips, and thy sin is departed and thy iniquity purged."

And I heard the voice of the Lord saying, "Whom shall I send, and who will go for Us?" And I said, "Here am I, send me."

And He said, "Go and tell this people, 'Hear ye indeed, but understand not, and see ye indeed, but perceive not.' Make the heart of this people fat, and its ears heavy, and blind its eyes, lest it see with its eyes, and hear with its ears, and its heart understand, and it return and be healed."

And I said, "How long, O Lord?"

And He said, "Until the cities remain desolate without inhabitants, and houses without man, and the land be utterly waste. And the Lord will remove man, and great will the forsakenness be in the country. But a tenth will yet be in her, and then that too shall again be consumed, as a terebinth and oak which, when felled, leave behind a trunk, a holy seed shall be its trunk."

(Isa. 6:1-13)

The Parable of the Vineyard

Let me sing of my friend, the song of my beloved about his vineyard: My friend had a vineyard upon a fruitful hill. And he dug it through, and cleared it of stones, and planted it with choice vines, and built a watchtower in its midst, and also hewed out a vat in it, and he hoped that it would bring forth grapes, but it brought forth rottenness.

And now, O dwellers of Jerusalem and men of Judah, judge, I pray you, between me and my vineyard! What more could be done to my vineyard than what I have done? Why did I hope for grapes and it brought forth rotten fruit?

But now, pray, I shall inform you of what I shall do to my vineyard: remove its hedge and it will become a grazing place, pull down its fence and it will be a stamping ground. And I will lay it waste; it will neither be pruned nor dug, and the brier and the thorn will overrun it, and I shall command the clouds to rain no rain upon it.

For the vineyard of the Lord of Hosts is the House of Israel, and the man of Judah is the plant of His delight, and He hoped for justice, but behold, violence; for righteousness, but behold, outcry.

(Isa. 5:1-7)

Jeremiah's Consecration

And the word of the Lord was to me saying, "Before I

fashioned thee in the belly I knew thee, and before thou emerged from the womb I sanctified thee, and ordained thee a prophet unto the nations."

And I said, "Ah, O Lord God! Behold I cannot speak, for I am but a boy!"

And the Lord said to me, "Say not 'I am a boy,' because wherever I shall send thee thou shalt go, and whatever I shall command thee thou shalt speak. Fear not their faces, for I am with thee to deliver thee, saith the Lord."

And the Lord stretched forth His hand and touched my mouth, and the Lord said to me, "Behold, I have put My words into thy mouth! See, I have set thee this day over the nations and over the kingdoms, to root out and to pull down and to destroy and overthrow, but [also] to build and to plant."

(Jer. 1:4-10)

The Throne-Chariot

The word of the Lord was to Ezekiel the son of Buzi the priest, in the land of the Chaldaeans, on the River Kebar, and the hand of the Lord was there upon him. And I saw, and behold, a whirlwind came from the north, a great cloud, and fire flashing about, and brightness was around it, and from its midst as the color of electrum from the midst of fire. And from its midst the likeness of four living creatures, and this was their appearance: the likeness of man had they, and each had four faces, and four wings had each of them. And their legs were straight legs, and their feet were like the feet of a calf, sparkling like the color of burnished brass. And they had human hands under their wings on their four sides, and all four had faces and wings. Their wings were joined to one another, they turned not when they went; each one went in the direction of his face. And the likeness of their faces were: the face of a man and the face of a lion on the right side of all four, and the face of an ox on the left side of all four, and all the four had also the face of an eagle. And their wings were divided from above, each had two wings joined to those of the others, and two which covered their bodies. And each of them went straight forward, wherever the spirit went, they went; they turned not as they went. And the likeness of the living creatures was like coals of fire burning like the appearance of torches; it moved to and fro between the living creatures. And the fire had a radiance, and a lightning issued forth from the fire. And the living creatures ran back and forth, like the appearance of lightning flashes. And I saw the living creatures, and behold, a wheel upon the earth was next to each living creature, at its four faces. The appearance of the wheels and their work was like the color of beryl, and all four had one likeness, and their appearance and their work was as it were wheels within wheels. They went, when they moved, toward their four sides, they turned not when they went. And as for their rims, they had a great height and an awesomeness, and their rims were full of eyes all around, to all four of them. And when the living creatures went, the wheels went with them, and when the living creatures rose up from the earth, the wheels too rose up. Wherever the spirit went, there they went, as the spirit went, and the wheels rose up over against them, for the spirit of the living creature was in the wheels. When they went, they went; and when they stopped, they stopped; and when they rose high above the earth the wheels too rose over against them, for the spirit of the living creature was in the wheels.

And over the head of the living creature there was a likeness, a firmament like unto the color of the terrible ice, stretched over their head above. And beneath the firmament their wings were straight, one over against the other, and each had two covering his body. And I heard the sound of their wings as the sound of great waters, as the voice of the Almighty, when they went, the voice of a tumult, as the din of an armed camp. And when they stopped, they let down their wings. And there came a voice from above the firmament which was over their heads. And when they stopped they let down their wings.

And above the firmament which was over their heads there was the appearance of sapphire stone, the likeness of a throne, and upon the likeness of the throne the likeness of the appearance of a man, over it above. And I saw as the color of electrum, as the appearance of fire, enclosing it round about, from the appearance of his loins upward; and from the appearance of his loins downward I saw as the appearance of fire. And radiance was round about him. As the appearance of the bow in the clouds in the day of rain, so was the appearance of radiance round about. This was the appearance of the likeness of the glory of the Lord. And I saw, and fell upon my face, and heard a voice speak. And He said unto me,

"Son of man, stand on thy feet, and I will speak unto thee."

And the spirit entered into me as He spoke to me, and set me upon my feet, and I heard Him who spoke to me. And He said to me,

"Son of man, I send thee to the Children of Israel, to rebellious nations who rebelled against Me, they and their fathers have transgressed against Me unto this very day..."

(Ezekiel 1:3-2:3)

The Vision of the Dry Bones

The hand of the Lord was upon me, and He carried me out in the spirit of the Lord, and set me down in the midst of the valley, and it was full of bones. And He made me pass over them round about, and, behold, they were very many upon the face of the valley, and, behold, they were very dry. And He said to me, "Son of Man! Can these bones live?" And I said, "Lord God, Thou knowest." And He said to me, "Prophesy, Son of Man, about these bones, and say to them, 'O ye dry bones, hear the word of the Lord! Thus saith the Lord God to these bones, Behold, I bring spirit into you and ye shall live! And I will put upon you sinews, and will bring flesh upon you, and will stretch skin over you, and will put spirit into you, and ye shall know that I am the Lord!' " And I prophesied as I was commanded, and there was a sound as I prophesied, and, behold, a commotion, and the bones came together, bone to its bone. And I saw, and behold, there were upon them sinews, and flesh came up, and skin stretched upon them on the top, but spirit was not in them. And He said to me, "Prophesy to the spirit, prophesy, Son of Man, and say to the spirit, 'Thus saith the Lord God, From the four winds come, O spirit, and breathe into these slain ones so that they may live!' " And I prophesied as He commanded me, and the spirit came into them and they lived, and they stood up on their feet, an army, very, very great. And He said to me, "Son of Man! These bones are all the House of Israel. Behold, they say, 'Our bones are dried up, and lost is our hope, we are cut off!' Therefore prophesy and say to them, 'Thus saith the Lord God, Behold, I open your tombs, and I will bring you up from your graves, O My people, and will take you to the Land of Israel. And ye shall know that I am the Lord, I spoke and I did it, saith the Lord.' "

(Ezekiel 37:1-14)

Jonah and the Fish

And the word of the Lord was unto Jonah the son of Amittai, saying, "Arise, go to Nineveh, the great city, and call over it, for their evil is come up before Me."

And Jonah rose up to flee to Tarshish from before the Lord, and he went down to Jaffa, and found a ship Tarshish bound, and paid its fare, and boarded it to go with them to Tarshish from before the Lord.

And the Lord flung a great wind upon the sea, and there was a fierce storm in the sea, and the ship was about to be wrecked. And the mariners were afraid, and each cried to his gods, and they cast the vessels which were in the ship into the sea to lighten it. And Jonah had gone down into the hold of the ship, and lay down and fell asleep. And the captain went to him and said, "How canst thou sleep? Arise, call on thy God, perchance God will consider us and we shall not perish!"

And they said to one another, "Come, let us cast lots that we know because of whom is this evil upon us." And the lot fell upon Jonah. And they said to him, "Pray, tell us why is this evil upon us? What is thy work, and whence comest thou? What is thy country and of what people art thou?"

And he said to them, "I am a Hebrew, and I fear the Lord, the God of heaven, who made the sea and the dry land."

And the men were sore afraid, and said to him, "What is it thou hast done?" Because the men knew that he was fleeing from before the Lord, for he had told them. And they said to him, "What shall we do unto thee that the sea calm down for us?" For the sea raged more and more.

And he said to them, "Take me, and fling me into the sea, and the sea shall calm down for you. For I know that because of me is this great storm upon you."

And the men strove to return to the shore but could not, for the sea raged more and more at them. And they called on the Lord, and said, "We beseech Thee, O Lord, let us not perish because of the soul of this man, and lay not innocent blood upon us, for Thou, O Lord, hast done as it pleased Thee!"

And they took Jonah, and flung him into the sea, and the sea ceased raging. And the men feared the Lord with a great fear, and offered up sacrifices to the Lord and made vows.

And the Lord ordained a great fish to swallow Jonah, and Jonah was in the belly of the fish three days and three nights. And Jonah prayed to the Lord his God from the belly of the fish. . . . And the Lord spoke to the fish and it vomited Jonah out upon the shore. . . .

And the word of the Lord was unto Jonah a second time saying, "Arise, go to Nineveh the great city, and call upon her the call which I shall bid thee." And Jonah arose and went to Nineveh according to the word of the Lord, and Nineveh was a great city unto God, of three days' journey. And Jonah began to enter the city a day's journey, and he called and said, "Forty days more, and Nineveh shall be overthrown!" And the people of Nineveh believed in God, and proclaimed a fast, and put on sackcloth, from their great ones to their little ones. And the word reached the king of Nineveh, and he arose from his throne, and took off his mantle, and covered himself with sackcloth and sat in ashes. And he had it proclaimed in Nineveh in behalf of the king and his nobles saying, "Man and beast and cattle and flocks, none shall taste anything! Let them neither graze nor drink water! But let man and beast cover themselves with sackcloth, and let them call on the Lord mightily, and let every man turn from his evil way, and from the violence which is in their hands. Who knoweth, perhaps God will turn and relent, and turn from his fierce wrath, and we shall not perish."

And God saw their acts, that they turned from their evil way, and God relented of the evil which He had said He would do to them, and did it not.

And it seemed very wrong to Jonah, and he waxed wroth. And he prayed to the Lord and said, "I pray Thee, O Lord, was not this what I said while I was still in my country? This I tried to prevent by fleeing to Tarshish, for I knew, for I knew that Thou art a merciful and compassionate God, long-suffering and of great kindness, who relenteth of evil. And now, O Lord, pray, take my soul from me, for it is better for me to die than to live."

And the Lord said to him, "Dost thou well to be wroth?"

And Jonah went out of the city, and sat down to the east of the city, and made himself there a booth, and sat under it in the shadow, until he would see what will be in the city. And the Lord ordained a castor plant, and made it come up over Jonah to be a shadow over his head, to save him from his plight. And Jonah rejoiced over the castor plant with a great joy. And God ordained a worm, at the rise of dawn next morning, and it smote the castor plant and it withered. And it came to pass when the sun rose that the Lord ordained a soft east wind, and the sun struck the head of Jonah, and he fainted, and he wished to die, and said, "It is better for me to die than to live."

And God said to Jonah, "Dost thou well to be wroth about the castor plant?" And he said, "I do well to be wroth even unto death."

And the Lord said, "Thou hast pitied the castor plant for which thou hast not labored, nor hast thou raised it, which shot up in a night and perished in a night. Should I then not pity Nineveh the great city, in which are more than twelve times ten thousand men who knew not between right and left, and also much cattle?"

(Jon. 1:1-2:2, 11; 3:1-4:11)

The Vision of the Horsemen

On the twenty-fourth day of the eleventh month, which is the month of Shevat, in the twelfth year of Darius, the word of the Lord was unto Zechariah the son of Berechiah the son of Iddo, the prophet, saying, I saw in the night, and behold, a man riding on a red horse, and he stood among the myrtles which were in the depth, and behind him red, speckled, and white horses. And I said, "What are these, my Lord?" And the angel who spoke to me said, "I shall show thee what these are." And the man who stood among the myrtles spoke and said, "These are they whom the Lord hath sent to walk to and fro in the earth." And they answered the angel of the Lord who stood among the myrtles and said, "We walked to and fro in the earth, and behold, the whole earth sitteth and is tranquil." And the angel of the Lord spoke and said, "O Lord of Hosts, how long wilt Thou not have mercy upon Jerusalem and upon the cities of Judah with which Thou hast been angry these seventy years?" And the Lord answered the angel who spoke to me with good words, words of consolation. And the angel who spoke to me said to me, "Call and speak, 'Thus saith the Lord of Hosts, I am jealous for Jerusalem and Zion with a great jealousy, and I am wroth with a great wrath at the nations which are tranquil. For I was displeased [with Jerusalem] but a little, but they helped for [great] evil.' Therefore thus saith the Lord, 'I shall return to Jerusalem in mercy, and My House shall be built in her midst, saith the Lord of Hosts, and a line shall be stretched over Jerusalem.' And cry again and say, 'Thus saith the Lord of Hosts, My cities will yet spread abroad in prosperity, and the Lord shall yet comfort Zion, and shall yet choose Jerusalem!' "

(Zech. 1:7-17)

Satan and the High Priest

And he showed me Joshua the high priest standing before the angel of the Lord, and Satan stood on his right side to accuse him. And the angel of the Lord said to Satan, "The Lord rebuke thee, O Satan, and the Lord who hath chosen Jerusalem rebuke thee! Is this not a brand plucked out of the fire?"

And Joshua was clothed in filthy garments, and he stood before the angel. And he spoke and said to those who stood before him saying, "Remove the filthy garments from him!" And he said to him, "See, I have taken away thy sins from thee, and have clothed thee in festive garments." And I said, "Let them put a mitre upon his head!" And they put the pure mitre upon his head, and clothed him in the garments, and the angel of the Lord stood there.

And the angel of the Lord cautioned Joshua saying, "Thus saith the Lord of Hosts, If thou shalt walk in My ways, and if thou wilt keep My charge, and wilt also judge My house and also guard My courts, I will give thee free access among these who stand here. Hearken, O Joshua the high priest, thou and thy friends who sit before thee, for they are men of portent, for behold, I will bring My servant Zemah ("The Shoot"). For behold, the stone that I have put before Joshua, upon one stone seven eyes; behold, I will engrave an inscription upon it, saith the Lord of Hosts, and I will remove the iniquity of that land in one day. On that day, saith the Lord of Hosts, ye shall invite every man his neighbor, under the vine and under the fig tree."

(Zech. 3:1-10)

The Four Chariots

And I turned and lifted up my eyes and saw, and behold, four chariots coming forth from between the two mountains, and the mountains are mountains of brass. In the first chariot red horses, and in the second chariot black horses. And in the third chariot white horses, and in the fourth chariot grizzled bay horses. And I spoke and said to the angel who was talking to me, "What are these, my Lord?" And the angel answered and said to me, "These are the four winds of heaven, coming out from having waited upon the Lord of the whole earth. The one in which are the black horses goes to the land of the north, and the white ones go out after them, and the grizzled go to the land of Yemen ("The South"), and the bay go forth, and they sought to go, to walk to and fro in the earth." And he said, "Go, walk to and fro in the earth!" And they walked to and fro in the earth.

And he shouted out at me and spoke to me saying, "See, those which go to the land of the north will leave my spirit in the land of the north."

(Zech. 6:1-8)

The Shoot and the Priest

Thus saith the Lord of hosts saying, "Behold the man, Shoot is his name, and he shall shoot up out his place, and he shall

build the Temple of the Lord. And he shall build the
Temple of the Lord, and will bear the glory, and he will sit
upon his throne and rule. And the priest will be upon his
throne and the counsel of peace shall be between them."

(Zech. 6:12-13)

Job's Story

There was a man in the land of Uz, Job by name, and the
man was wholehearted and just, and God-fearing, and
shunned evil. And there were born unto him seven sons
and three daughters. And his possessions were seven
thousand sheep and three thousand camels, and five
hundred teams of oxen, and five hundred she-asses, and
very many servants, and that man was greater than all the
children of the east.

And his sons went and held a feast: each day in the house
of one of them, and they called their three sisters to eat and
drink with them. And it came to pass when the days of the
feasting were over that Job sent and sanctified them, and he
rose early in the morning and offered burnt offerings,
according to their number, for Job said, "Maybe my sons
sinned and cursed God in their heart." Thus did Job all the
days.

And there was a day on which the sons of God came to
wait on the Lord, and also Satan came among them. And
the Lord said to Satan, "Whence comest thou?" And Satan
answered the Lord and said, "From roaming the earth and
walking to and fro in it." And the Lord said to Satan, "Hast
thou given attention to My servant Job, for there is no
wholehearted and just man like unto him in the earth, who
feareth God and shunneth evil?"

And Satan answered the Lord and said, "Is it for naught
that Job feareth God? Is it not that Thou hast protected
him and his house and all he hath round about? Thou hast
blessed the work of his hands and his possessions are spread
out in the land. But shouldst Thou put forth Thy hand and

touch anything he hath, he shall surely curse Thee to Thy face!"

And the Lord said to Satan, "Behold, all he hath is in thy hand, only put not thy hand forth against his own self."

And Satan went forth from the face of the Lord.

And it came to pass one day that his sons and daughters were eating and drinking wine in the house of their brother, the firstborn. And a messenger came to Job and said, "The cattle were plowing and the she-asses grazing near them. And Sheba fell upon them, and took them, and they smote the servants with the edge of the sword, and only I alone escaped to tell thee."

This one was still speaking when another came and said, "The fire of God fell from heaven and burned up the flocks and the servants and consumed them, and only I alone escaped to tell thee."

This one was still speaking when another came and said, "The Chaldaeans deployed three bands and fell upon the camels and took them, and smote the servants with the edge of the sword, and only I alone escaped to tell thee."

While he was still speaking yet another came and said, "Thy sons and daughters were eating and drinking in the house of their brother, the firstborn, and behold, a great wind came from out of the desert, and touched the four corners of the house, and it collapsed upon the young people and they died, and only I alone escaped to tell thee."

And Job arose and rent his coat, and cut his head, and fell down upon the earth and prostrated himself. And he said, "Naked did I come out of the womb of my mother, and naked shall I return there. The Lord hath given, and the Lord hath taken away, may the name of the Lord be blessed!" And despite all, Job did not sin, and ascribed no impropriety to God.

Again there was a day on which the sons of God came to wait upon the Lord, and also Satan came among them to wait on the Lord. And the Lord said to Satan, "Whence comest thou?" And Satan answered the Lord and said,

"From roaming the earth and walking to and fro in it." And the Lord said to Satan, "Hast thou given attention to My servant Job, for there is no wholehearted and just man like unto him in the earth, who feareth God and shunneth evil? And he still holdeth to his virtue, and thou hast incited Me against him, to swallow him up for no cause." And Satan answered the Lord and said, "Skin for skin, and everything a man hath he will give for his life. But shouldst Thou put forth Thy hand and touch his bone and his flesh, he shall surely curse Thee to Thy face!"

And the Lord said to Satan, "Behold, he is in Thy hand, but spare his life."

And Satan went forth from the face of the Lord, and smote Job with sore boils from the sole of his foot to his pate.

And he took a potsherd to scrape himself with, and he sat in the midst of ashes. And his wife said to him, "Doest thou still hold to thy virtue? Curse God and die!" But he said to her, "Thou speakest like one of the base women. Will we accept the good from God, and not accept the evil?" And despite all, Job did not sin with his lips.

And the three friends of Job heard of all the evil that had come upon him, and they came, each from his place, Eliphaz the Yemenite, and Bildad the Shuhite, and Zophar the Naamathite, and they got together to go and bemoan him and comfort him. And they lifted up their eyes from afar, and recognized him not, and they lifted up their voice and wept, and each rent his mantle, and sprinkled ashes upon their heads towards heaven. And they sat with him on the earth seven days and seven nights, and none spoke a word to him for they saw that his pain was very great.[4]

(Job 1:1-2:13)

[4] Job 2:14 to 42:9 contains discussions between Job, his friends, and God, about the power of God, the secrets of nature, and the nature of good and evil, in a highly poetic language and a very difficult style. The conclusion, 42:10-17, tells that God restored to Job everything he had lost.

Nebuchadnezzar's Dream

In the second year of the reign of Nebuchadnezzar he dreamt dreams and his spirit was troubled, and his sleep was broken. And the king commanded to call the magicians, and the soothsayers and the sorcerers and the astrologers, to tell the king his dreams, and they came and stood before the king. And the king said to them, "I dreamt a dream, and my spirit is troubled to know the dream."

And the astrologers spoke to the king in Aramaic, "O king, live forever! Tell thy servants the dream, and we will give the interpretation."

The king answered and said to the astrologers, "The thing is gone from me. If ye let me not know the dream and its interpretation, ye shall be cut in pieces and your houses shall be made into a dung heap. And if ye present the dream and its interpretation, ye shall receive from me gifts and rewards and great honor. Therefore present to me the dream and its interpretation."

They answered a second time and said, "Let the king tell the dream to his servants, and we shall present the interpretation."

The king answered and said, "I know of certainty that ye wish to gain time, because ye see that the thing is gone from me. If ye will not let me know the dream, there is but one law for you: for ye have prepared false and corrupt words to speak before me till the time be changed. Therefore tell me the dream, and I shall know that ye can present me its interpretation."

The astrologers answered before the king and said, "There is not a man upon the earth who could present the king's matter: for no king, lord, or ruler hath asked such a thing of any magician, soothsayer, or astrologer. It is indeed a hard thing that the king asketh, and nobody else can come who could present it before the king, save the gods whose dwelling is not with flesh."

For this reason the king was angry and very wroth, and

said to destroy all the wise men of Babylon. And the decree went forth that the wise men be killed. And they sought Daniel and his friends to be killed.

Then Daniel answered with counsel and wisdom to Arioch the captain of the king's guard who went forth to slay the wise men of Babylon. He answered and said to Arioch, the king's officer, "Why is the decree so adamant from before the king?" Then Arioch informed Daniel of the matter. And Daniel went and asked of the king that he give him time to present the interpretation to the king. . . .

Then Arioch quickly brought Daniel before the king, and he said to him, "I have found a man of the captivity of Judah who will let the king know the interpretation."

The king answered and said to Daniel, whose name was Belteshazzar, "Canst thou indeed let me know the dream which I saw and its interpretation?"

Daniel answered before the king and said, "Neither the wise men, nor the soothsayers, nor the magicians, nor the astrologers can present to the king the secret which the king asked. But there is God in heaven, who revealeth secrets and letteth King Nebuchadnezzar know what will be in the end of the days. Thy dream and the visions of thy head upon thy bed are these: Thou, O king, upon thy bed thoughts came to thee about what will come to pass hereafter, and He who revealeth secrets let thee know what will be. And I, this secret was revealed to me not for any wisdom that hath come to me more than to any living, but in order to let the king know the interpretation, and to make known to thee the thoughts of thy heart.

"Thou, O king, sawest, and behold, a great image. This image was mighty, and its brightness excelled: it stood before thee, and its appearance was awesome. The head of that image was of fine gold, its breast and arms of silver, its belly and thighs of brass, its legs of iron, its feet—part of them of iron and part of them of clay. Thou looked until a stone was cut without hands, and smote the image upon its feet of iron and clay, and broke them in pieces. Then the iron, the clay, the brass, the silver, and the gold were all broken in pieces together, and became like the chaff from the summer threshing floors, and the wind carried them, so that their place was not found. And the stone that smote the image became a great mountain, and filled the whole earth.

"This is the dream. And let me now tell its interpretation before the king. Thou, O king, king of kings, unto whom the God of heaven gave kingship, power, and strength, and glory, and wherever the sons of man dwell He hath given the beasts of the field and the fowl of heaven into thy hand, and made thee rule over all of them — thou art the head of gold. And after thee will arise another kingdom, inferior to thee, and yet another third kingdom of brass, which will rule over the whole earth. And the fourth kingdom will be strong as iron, since iron breaketh in pieces and beateth all, and as iron shattereth so it will break everything in pieces and crush. And that thou sawest feet and toes part potter's clay and part iron [means that] the kingdom will be divided: there will be in it of the firmness of iron inasmuch as thou sawest the iron mixed with miry clay. And the toes of its feet part iron and part clay [means] that part of the kingdom will be strong, and part of it brittle. And that which thou sawest, iron mixed with miry clay — they will mix with the seed of men but will not cleave one to the other, just as iron mixeth not with clay. And in the days of those kings the God of heaven will raise a kingdom which shall never be destroyed, and its dominion shall not be left to others. It shall break in pieces, and put an end to, all those kingdoms, and it shall stand for ever. And that which thou sawest that a stone was cut from the mountain without hands and broke in pieces the iron, the brass, the clay, the silver, and the gold [means that] the great God hath let the king know what shall be hereafter. And the dream is certain, and its interpretation sure."

Then the king Nebuchadnezzar fell upon his face, and bowed down to Daniel, and commanded that presents and

precious things be offered to him. The king answered
Daniel and said, "It is true that your God is the God of gods
and the Lord of kings, and the revealer of secrets that thou
couldst reveal this secret." And the king made Daniel a
lord, and gave him many great gifts, and made him ruler
over the whole province of Babylon and chief governor
over all the sages of Babylon.

(Dan. 2:1-16, 25-48)

The Three Youths in the Fiery Furnace

King Nebuchadnezzar made an image of gold, its height
was sixty cubits, its width six cubits, and he set it up in the
plain of Dura, in the province of Babylon. And King
Nebuchadnezzar sent to gather the satraps, the prefects, the
governors, the judges, the treasurers, the counselors, the
sheriffs, and all the rulers of the provinces, to come to the
dedication of the image which King Nebuchadnezzar had
set up. And a herald called aloud, "To you it is
commanded, O peoples, nations, and tongues! At the time
you hear the sound of the horn, the pipe, the zither, the
trigon, the psaltery, the bagpipe, and all kinds of music, ye
shall fall down and worship the image of gold which King
Nebuchadnezzar hath set up! And he who falleth not down
and worshipeth not shall in the same hour be cast into the
furnace of burning fire." ... At that time some Chaldeans
came forward and brought accusations against the Jews ...
saying, ... "There are some Jewish men whom thou hast
appointed over the work of the province of Babylon,
Shadrach, Meshach, and Abed-Nego, and these men have
not regarded thee, O king, they serve not thy gods nor
worship the image of gold which thou hast set up."

Thereupon Nebuchadnezzar, greatly incensed and
wroth, commanded that Shadrach, Meshach, and Abed-
Nego be brought. So these men were brought before the
king. Nebuchadnezzar spoke and said to them, "Is it true,
O Shadrach, Meshach, and Abed-Nego, that ye serve not

my gods and worship not the image of gold which I set up?" ... Shadrach, Meshach, and Abed-Nego answered and said to the king, "It is unnecessary for us to answer thee in this matter. If our God, whom we worship, is able to deliver us, He will deliver us from the furnace of burning fire and from thy hand, O king. And even if not, be it known to thee, O king, that we will not serve thy gods, and will not worship the image of gold which thou hast set up."

At this Nebuchadnezzar was filled with fury, and the form of his face changed against Shadrach, Meshach, and Abed-Nego. And he spoke and commanded that they stoke the furnace seven times more than usual. And he commanded the mightiest men in his army to bind Shadrach, Meshach, and Abed-Nego, and to cast them into the fiery furnace. Thereupon these men were bound in their footwear, trousers, headgear, and clothes, and were cast into the furnace of burning fire. And because the king's commandment was adamant, and the furnace exceeding hot, the flame of its fire slew the men who led Shadrach, Meshach, and Abed-Nego. And these three men, Shadrach, Meshach, and Abed-Nego, fell down bound into the furnace of burning fire.

Then Nebuchadnezzar, alarmed, rose up in haste, and spoke and said to his counselors, "Did we not cast three men bound into the fire?" And they answered and said to the king, "True, O king!" He answered and said, "Behold, I see four men unbound walk in the fire, without being hurt, and the appearance of the fourth is like unto a son of the gods!"

And Nebuchadnezzar went near the door of the furnace of burning fire, and spoke and said, "Shadrach, Meshach, and Abed-Nego! Servants of God Most High! Come out! Come here!" Thereupon Shadrach, Meshach and Abed-Nego came out from the midst of the fire.

And the satraps, the prefects, the governors, and counselors of the king, who were gathered together, saw these men, that the fire had no power over their bodies, and the hair of their head was not singed, and their footwear had not changed, and the smell of fire had not penetrated them. And Nebuchadnezzar spoke and said, "Blessed be the God of Shadrach, Meshach, and Abed-Nego, who sent His angel and delivered His servants who trusted in Him, and who invalidated the command of the king, and gave their bodies rather than serve or worship any god except their own God. Therefore I decree that every people, nation, and tongue who speak disparagingly of the God of Shadrach, Meshach, and Abed-Nego be cut in pieces and their houses be made a dung heap, because there is no other god able to deliver thusly."

And thereafter the king raised Shadrach, Meshach, and Abed-Nego high in the province of Babylon.

(Dan. 3:1-2, 4-6, 8, 12-14, 16-30)

The Vision of the Four Beasts

In the first year of Belshazzar king of Babylon Daniel saw a dream and visions of his head on his bed. Then he wrote the dream and told the headings of the matter. And Daniel spoke and said, "I saw in my vision of the night, and behold, the four winds of heaven swept down upon the great sea. And four great beasts came out of the sea, one unlike the other. The first was like a lion and had eagle's wings. I beheld until its wings were plucked, and it was taken from off the earth, and it was made to stand on feet like a man, and a man's heart was given to it.

"And behold, the other beast, the second, like a bear, and it raised itself to one side, and three ribs in its mouth between its teeth. And they spoke thus unto it, 'Arise, eat much flesh.'

"After this I saw, and behold, another one, like a leopard, and it had on its back four bird's wings, and the beast had four heads, and dominion was given to it.

"After this I saw in visions of the night, and behold, a

fourth beast, dreadful and terrible, and exceedingly strong, and it had big teeth of iron. It ate, and crunched, and what was left he stamped with its feet, and it was unlike all the beasts that preceded it, and it had ten horns. I was looking at the horns, and behold, another small horn came up among them, and three of the first horns were uprooted before it, and behold, in this horn there were eyes like the eyes of a man, and a mouth which spoke great things.

"I was looking until thrones were set up, and the Ancient of Days sat: His clothes were like white snow, and the hair of His head like pure wool, His throne fiery flames, and its wheels burning fire. A river of fire issued and came forth before Him, thousand thousands ministered unto Him, and myriad myriads stood before Him. The judgment was set and the books were opened.

"And then I saw, because of the voice of great words which the horn hath spoken, and I was looking until the beast was slain and his body destroyed, and it was given to burning fire. And the other beasts, their dominion was ended, but their lives were spared for a time and a year.

"And I saw in visions of the night, and behold, with the clouds of heaven came one like a Son of Man, and he came to the Ancient of Days, and they brought him before Him. And given to him were dominion, and glory, and kingship, and all the peoples, nations, and tongues worshiped him. His dominion is an everlasting dominion, which shall not pass, and his kingship shall not be destroyed.

"And I Daniel, my spirit was grieved in my body, and the visions of my head affrighted me. I approached one of them standing there, and asked him about all this. And he spoke to me and let me know the meaning of the things. Those great beasts, which are four—four kings shall arise from the earth. But the saints of the Most High shall receive the kingdom, and shall possess the kingdom for ever and ever. Then I wanted the certainty about the fourth beast which was unlike all the others, exceedingly terrible, its teeth of iron, and its nails of brass, which devoured, crunched, and what was left stamped with its feet; and about the ten horns which were on its head, and the other horn which came up and before which three horns fell, and which had eyes and a mouth speaking great things, and whose appearance was greater than that of the others.

"I saw that this horn made war with the saints and prevailed against them. Until the Ancient of Days came, and judgment was given the saints of the Most High, and the time came when the saints took possession of the kingdom.

"He spoke thus: The fourth beast is the fourth kingdom which shall be on earth and which shall be unlike all kingdoms, and it shall consume the whole earth and shall stamp it and crush it. And the ten horns—from that kingdom ten kings shall arise, and then another one shall arise after them, and he shall be unlike the first ones, and he shall subdue three kings. And he shall speak words against the Most High, and shall annihilate the saints of the Most High, and shall intend to change times and laws, and they shall be given into his hands until a time, and times, and half a time. But judgment shall sit, and his dominion shall be taken away to be destroyed and annihilated to the end. And the kingdom and the dominion and the greatness of the kingdom under the whole heaven shall be given to the people of the saints of the Most High, whose kingdom is an eternal kingdom, and all dominions shall worship and obey Him.

"Until here is the end of the matter. I Daniel was greatly affrighted by my thoughts, and my color changed; but I kept the matter in my heart."

(Dan. 7:1-28)

Belshazzar's Vision

Belshazzar the king made a great feast to a thousand of his lords, and drank wine with them. And while he tasted the wine, he commanded to bring the golden and silver vessels which his father Nebuchadnezzar had taken from the Temple of Jerusalem, so that the king and his lords, and his wives and concubines might drink from them. . . . And they drank the wine, and praised the gods of gold, silver, brass, iron, wood, and stone.

In that hour the fingers of a man's hand appeared and wrote above the chandelier on the plaster wall of the king's palace, and the king saw the fingertips of the hand which wrote: And the color of the king changed, and his thoughts frightened him so that the joints of his loins were loosed, and his knees hit against one another.

And the king cried aloud to call in the conjurers, the astrologers, and the soothsayers. And the king spoke and said to the wise men of Babylon, "Whosoever readeth this writing and telleth me its interpretation, shall wear purple, and a chain of gold around his neck, and shall rule as the third in the kingdom."

Then came all the wise men of the king, but they could not read the writing nor tell the king its interpretation. Then King Belshazzar was greatly affrighted, and his color changed, and his lords were confused. And prompted by the words of the king and his lords the queen came to the banqueting hall, and the queen spoke and said, "O king, live for ever! Let thy thoughts not frighten thee, and let thy color not change. There is a man in thy kingdom in whom is the spirit of the holy gods, and in the days of thy father light and understanding and wisdom like unto the wisdom of the gods were found in him. And thy father King Nebuchadnezzar make him master of the magicians, conjurers, astrologers, and soothsayers—so did thy father the king, because an outstanding spirit and knowledge, and ability to interpret dreams, and to declare riddles, and to solve problems were found in that Daniel whose name the king changed into Belteshazzar. Now therefore let Daniel be summoned and he will present the interpretation."

When Daniel was brought before the king the king spoke and said to him, "Art thou Daniel who is of the exiles of Judah, whom my father the king brought from Judah? I have heard of thee that the spirit of the gods is in thee, and that light, understanding, and great wisdom are found in thee. And now, the wise men and the conjurers were brought before me to read this writing and to let me know its interpretation, but they could not present the meaning of the words. And I have heard about thee that thou art able to make interpretations and solve problems. If thou canst read the writing and let me know its interpretation, thou shalt wear purple, and a chain of gold around thy neck, and thou shalt rule as the third in the kingdom."

Then Daniel answered and said before the king, "Let thy gifts be thine, and thy rewards give to others, but I will read the writing to the king and let him know the interpretation. Thou, O king, God Most High gave thy father Nebuchadnezzar kingship, and greatness and glory and majesty. And because of the greatness which He gave him all peoples and nations and tongues trembled and feared before him, whom he wanted he killed and whom he wanted he let live, whom he wanted he raised up and whom he wanted he humbled. But when his heart became haughty and his spirit overbearing, he was deposed from his royal throne, and his glory was taken from him. And he was driven from the sons of man, and his heart was made like the beasts, and his dwelling place was with wild asses, they fed him grass like cattle, and his body was wet with the dew of heaven, until he knew that God Most High ruleth the kingdom of man, and that He appointeth over it whomever He wanteth. And thou, his son Belshazzar, hast not humbled thy heart, although thou hast known all this, but hast risen up against the Lord of Heaven, and they have brought the vessels of His House before thee, and thou and thy lords and thy wives and concubines have drunk wine from them, and hast praised gods of silver and gold, brass, iron, wood, and stone, which see not and hear not and know not, and hast not glorified the God in whose hand is thy life-breath and whose are all thy ways. Therefore He sent the fingers of a hand from before Him and they wrote this writing. And this is the writing that is written: Mene, Mene, Tekel, Upharsin. And this is the interpretation of the words: Mene—God hath numbered (*mana*) thy kingdom and ended it. Tekel—thou art weighed (*tekilta*) in the balances and found wanting. Peres—thy kingdom is broken (*perisath*) and given to Media and Persia."

Then Belshazzar said, "Clothe Daniel in purple and put a chain of gold around his neck and proclaim of him that he should be the third ruler in the kingdom." In that same night Belshazzar the Chaldean king was killed.

(Dan. 5:1-2, 4-30)

Daniel in the Lions' Den

All the presidents and the satraps importuned the king and spoke to him thus, "King Darius, live for ever! All the presidents of the kingdom, the prefects and the satraps, the counselors and the captains have consulted together to have a royal decree issued and a prohibition established that whosoever shall turn with a request to any god or man for thirty days save thee, O king, be cast into the lions' den. . . ."

And when Daniel knew that the decree was signed, he went to his house, whose upper chamber had windows opening toward Jerusalem, and three times every day he knelt down and prayed and gave thanks before God, exactly as he had done before. Then these men rushed in and found Daniel praying and beseeching before his God. Whereupon they went and spoke before the king concerning the king's decree, "Hast thou not signed a prohibition that whosoever shall turn with a request to any god or man for thirty days save thee, O king, be cast into the lions' den?"

The king answered and said, "The word is firm, according to the laws of Media and Persia which change not."

Then they answered and said before the king, "This

Bible   119

Daniel, who is of the children of the exile of Judah, hath
disregarded thee, O king, and the decree thou hast signed,
and three times a day he maketh his supplication."

When the king heard these words he was much
displeased with it, but he set his heart to save Daniel, and
he tried until sunset to rescue him. Then those men rushed
in upon the king and said to him, "Know, O king, that it is
the law of Media and Persia that an edict or prohibition of
the king must stand and cannot be changed."

Then the king said, "Fetch Daniel and cast him into the
lions' den." And the king spoke to Daniel and said, "Thy
God whom thou worshipeth steadfastly shall deliver thee!"

And a stone was brought and laid upon the mouth of the
den, and the king sealed it with his seal and the seal of his
lords that the matter of Daniel should not be changed.
Then the king returned to his palace, and passed the night
fasting, nor were concubines brought before him, and his
sleep fled from him. Then the king arose early in the
morning, and hastened to the lions' den. And when he
reached it he called with a sorrowful voice, and said to
Daniel, "Daniel! Servant of the living God! Thy God,
whom thou worshipest steadfastly, could He save thee from
the lions?"

Then Daniel said unto the king, "O king, live for ever!
My God hath sent His angel and hath closed the mouth of
the lions, and they harmed me not because I was found
innocent before Him, and even before thee, O king, I have
committed no transgression."

This was most pleasing to the king, and he commanded
that Daniel be brought up from the den. And Daniel was
brought up from the den, and no injury was found in him
because he trusted his God.

And the king commanded and they brought those men
who had accused Daniel, and they cast them into the lions'
den, them, their children and their wives, and even before
they reached the bottom of the den the lions overpowered
them and crunched their bones to pieces.

Then king Darius wrote to all the peoples, nations, and tongues that dwelt in all the earth, "May your peace be great! I issue a decree that in all the dominion of my kingdom they should tremble and fear before the God of Daniel, for He is the living God, who endureth for ever, and His kingdom shall not be destroyed, and His reign will last unto the end. He redeemeth and saveth, and He worketh signs and wonders in heaven and in earth, who delivered Daniel from the hand of the lions."

And this Daniel prospered in the kingdom of Darius and in the kingdom of Cyrus the Persian.

(Dan. 6:7-8, 11-29)

2

APOCRYPHA

These are books written mostly in Hebrew or Aramaic by Jewish authors from ca. the second century B.C.E. to ca. the first century C.E. Thus most of them were extant at the time when the Talmudic sages undertook the formidable task of establishing the Biblical canon of sacred books, which they did about 90 C.E. Having found these writings spurious and even heretical, or else too mysterious, too esoteric, or too profound to be made accessible except to the initiated few, the sages concluded that the Apocrypha were in any case not divinely inspired, and therefore they excluded them from the canon. Hence the Talmudic name of these books, *S'farim Ḥitzonim*, or "extraneous books."

A collection of these books, in Greek and Latin translations, was incorporated into the canon of the Roman Catholic and Greek Orthodox churches under the name Apocrypha, literally books that are "hidden away." In the Septuagint (MSS A, B) fifteen apocryphal books are included, of which only one, the Book of Wisdom of Ben Sira (see below), is mentioned in the Talmud. The other most important Apocrypha are the four Books of the Maccabees, Tobit, Judith, the Wisdom of Solomon, and Esdras IV. While the authors of most of these books are unknown, it is evident that they continued the literary traditions of the Bible, producing theocentric historical and moralistic writings in the spirit of the Biblical books, although in general of an inferior literary quality.

The Apocrypha fall into several distinct literary types: historical, legendary, prophetic, apocalyptic, and didactic.

A valuable historical book is 1 Maccabees, which recounts the exploits of Judah Maccabee and his family, who fought for and achieved the liberation of the Jews of Palestine from the rule of Antiochus Epiphanes (r. 175–164 B.C.E.). It was written in Hebrew by a Palestinian Jew ca. 100 B.C.E., and covers the period from 175 to 134 B.C.E.

2 Maccabees is an abridgment of a lost five-volume history by Jason of Cyrene, and covers the first fifteen years of the Maccabean struggle (175–160 B.C.E.). It was written between 125 B.C.E. and 70 C.E., and, because of its emphasis on the miraculous, has little historical value.

Among the several legendary apocryphal books are the Additions to Daniel, brief legends which include the story of Susanna and the Elders (given below in full), and the two-part legend of Bel and the Dragon, both written originally in Hebrew or Aramaic in the third or second century B.C.E. To this group belongs the story of Tobit (of which substantial excerpts are given here), which was written probably in the second century B.C.E.

The prophetical Apocrypha include the Book of Baruch, attributed to the scribe of Jeremiah, written probably in Hebrew by several authors who lived in or before the first century B.C.E.

An apocalyptic (or revelatory) apocryphal book is 2 Ezra (also known as 4 Esdras), which describes revelations received by Ezra in Babylonia during the sixth century B.C.E., and which was written (except for chapters 1-2 and 15-16, which are of later provenance) in the first century C.E., probably in Aramaic.

To the didactic genre belong the Wisdom of Ben

Sira (also known as Ecclesiasticus), written in Hebrew by a Palestinian Jew in ca. 180 B.C.E., and the Wisdom of Solomon, which seems to have been composed in Greek by a Jew, probably in Alexandria, between 100 B.C.E. and 50 C.E.

Another type of extraneous books are those known as Pseudepigrapha, literally "false, or spurious, writings." These writings are attributed by their anonymous authors to ancient Biblical heroes, beginning with Adam and Eve, Enoch, the twelve sons of Jacob, etc. They deal, typically, with the mysteries of Creation, the workings of good and evil, and the apocalyptic future, which is their favorite subject. Their number is indeterminate, and still growing due to such unexpected discoveries as the Dead Sea Scrolls, some of which are definitely of apocalyptic character. The first selections presented below (in chronological order of the topics they discuss) from the Book of Jubilees and the Enoch literature, will give the reader a taste of the specific features characterizing this pseudo-Biblical literature. The Book of Jubilees, written in Hebrew, stems from the second century B.C.E. (several manuscripts of major parts of it were discovered at Qumran by the Dead Sea). The Book of Enoch (or 1 Enoch) was written in Hebrew or Aramaic in the second or first century B.C.E. A later version, known as 3 Enoch, was composed in Hebrew in the third century C.E.

Creation

On that day God created for them the seas according to their gathering places, and all the rivers, and the gatherings of the waters in the mountains and in the whole earth, and all the lakes, and all the dew of the earth, and the seed which is sown, and everything that is eaten, and fruit-bearing trees, and the forests, and the Garden of Eden for rest. And all these four great things He did on the third day....

(Jub. 2:7)

Adam and Eve

In the first week of the first jubilee Adam and his wife were in the Garden of Eden for seven years tilling and keeping it, and We instructed him to do everything that is suitable for tillage. And he worked and was naked and knew it not, and was not ashamed, and he protected the garden from the birds and the beasts and the cattle, and gathered its fruit and ate, and put aside the residue for himself and his wife.

(Jub. 3:15-16)

Enoch in Paradise

From thence I went to another place of the earth, and He showed me mountains of fire which burnt day and night. And I went beyond it and saw seven magnificent mountains, all differing from each other, and the stones were magnificent and beautiful, all magnificent, glorious of appearance and of fair exterior.... And the seventh mountain in their midst, and in their height they resembled a royal throne. And they were encircled by fragrant trees. And among them was a tree such as I had never yet smelled, neither was any among them like it, nor were others like it. And its fragrance was better than all fragrance, and its leaves and blossoms and wood would never wither, and its fruit was beautiful, and its fruit resembled the dates of a palm....

Then Michael, one of the holy and glorious angels who was with me, and was their leader, said unto me: "This fragrant tree, no mortal can touch it without permission, until the great judgment, when He shall take vengeance on all and bring everything to its consummation for ever. And then it will be given to the righteous and the meek. From its fruit will be given life to the elect: it shall be transplanted to the north, to the holy place, to be the Temple of the Lord, the Eternal King."

(1 Enoch 24-25)

And I came to the Garden of Righteousness, and saw beyond those trees great trees growing there and their fragrance was good, and they were very beautiful and glorious, and the Tree of Knowledge of which they eat and acquire great knowledge. That tree is in its height like the fir, its leaves are like the leaves of the carob tree, and its fruit is like the clusters of the vine, very beautiful, and the fragrance of the tree wafts afar. And I said: "How beautiful is this tree, and how pleasant is its appearance." Then Raphael, the holy angel who was with me, answered me and said: "This is the Tree of Knowledge, of which your old father and your old mother who were before you have eaten, and they learned knowledge, and their eyes opened, and they knew that they were naked and they were driven out of the Garden."

(1 Enoch 32:3-6)

The Sons of God and the Daughters of Man

And it came to pass when the children of man had multiplied in those days, and beautiful and comely daughters were born unto them, that the angels, the children of heaven, saw them and lusted after them. And said one to the other: "Come, let us choose ourselves wives from among the daughters of man, and beget children."

And Shemhazai, who was their leader, said to them: "I fear you will not agree to do this deed, and I alone shall carry the great sin."

And they all answered him and said: "Let us all swear an oath, and all bind ourselves by imprecations, all of us among ourselves, not to abandon this plan but to do this thing accordingly." Then they all together swore and bound themselves by imprecations. And they were in all two hundred angels who descended in the days of Jared on the summit of Mount Hermon, and they called the mountain Hermon [i.e., "Imprecation"] because there they had sworn and bound themselves by imprecations.

And these are the names of their princes: Shemhazai, the greatest among them, Arkiba, Ramel, Kokhviel, Tamiel, Daniel, Zakiel, Barkiel, Azael, Armaros, Batriel, Ananiel, Zaqiel, Shamshiel, Satarel, Turel, Yomiel, Sahriel. These were their chiefs of tens.

And they, and all the others together with them, took unto themselves wives, and each chose for himself one, and they began to go in unto them, and they cleaved to them, and instructed them in charms and enchantments, and taught them the cutting of roots and plants. And the women became pregnant, and they bore great giants, three thousand cubits in height, who consumed all the fruits of the efforts of men. And when men could no longer provide food for them, the giants turned against them and devoured the men. And they began to sin against the birds and the beasts, and the reptiles, and the fish, and devour one another's flesh, and drink the blood. Then the earth laid accusation against the violent ones.

And Azazel taught men to make swords and knives and shields and breastplates, and made known to them the metals of the earth and the art of working them, and bracelets and ornaments, and the use of antimony, and the beautifying of the eyelids, and all kinds of precious stones, and all coloring tinctures. And there was much evil, and they committed fornication, and they went astray, and corrupted all their ways.

Shemhazai taught them enchantments, and the cutting of roots; Armaros the resolving of enchantments; Barkiel the gazing in the stars; Kokhviel astrology; Zakiel the knowledge of the clouds; Arqiel the signs of the earth; Shamshiel the signs of the sun; and Sahriel the phases of the moon. And as the children of man perished, they cried, and their cry went up to heaven....

(1 Enoch 6-8)

Then the Lord said to Raphael: "Bind Azazel hand and foot, and cast him into the darkness, and make an opening in the desert which is in Dudael, and cast him into it. And place upon him hard and sharp rocks, and cover him with darkness, and let him abide there forever. And cover his face so that he may not see light. And on the day of the great judgment he will be cast into the fire. And heal the earth which the angels have corrupted." And to Gabriel the Lord said: "Go forth against the bastards and the despicable ones, and against the children of fornication." And the Lord said to Michael: "Go, bind Shemhazai and his companions ... for seventy generations under the hills of the earth, until the day of their judgment and of their annihilation.... In those days they shall be taken to the abyss of fire...."

(1 Enoch 10:4-13)

The Tower of Babel

In the thirty-third jubilee, in the first year of the second week, Peleg took to himself a wife whose name was Lomna, the daughter of Shinar. And she bore him a son in the fourth year of that week, and he called his name Reu ("Evil"), for he said: "Behold, the children of man have become evil through the evil purpose of building for themselves a city and a tower in the land of Shinar." For they wandered from the land of Ararat eastward to Shinar, and in his days they built the city and the tower, saying: "Let us ascend thereby to heaven."

And they began to build, and in the fourth week they burnt brick in fire, and the bricks served them for stone, and the mortar with which they cemented them together was asphalt which comes out of the sea and out of fountains of water in the land of Shinar. And they built it: forty years and three years were they building it. . . .

And the Lord descended, and we descended with Him, to see the city and the tower which the children of man had built. And He confounded their language, and they no longer understood one another's speech, and they ceased to build the city and the tower. . . . And the Lord sent a mighty wind against the tower and overthrew it upon the earth. And behold, it is the tower which is between Asshur and Babylon in the land of Shinar.

(Jub. 10:18-26)

Sheol (the Underworld)

Would that you had ears, O earth,
And that you, O dust, had a heart;
Then you might go and announce in Sheol,
And say to those that are dead:
"Better off are you than we the living."

(Apoc. of Bar. I, 11:6-7)

And I Baruch said: "Behold, Lord, You did show me great and wonderful things; and now show me all things for the sake of the Lord."

And the angel said to me: "Come, let us go."

And I went with the angel from that place, to a distance of about 185 days' walk. And he showed me a valley and a dragon, and its length was about two hundred plethra. And he showed me Sheol, and its appearance was darkness and impurity. And I said:

"Who is this dragon, and what is this place around him?"

And the angel said: "The dragon is he who eats the bodies of those who have spent their lives in evil, and he is nourished by them. And this is Sheol, which itself also resembles him, in that it also drinks about a cubit from the sea, but the sea does not diminish at all." . . .

And I Baruch said to the angel: "My Lord, let me ask you one thing. Since you did say to me that the dragon drinks one cubit of the sea, tell me also how big is his belly?"

And the angel said: "His belly is as Sheol, and it is as big as the distance to which a plummet can be thrown by three hundred men...."

(3 Bar. 4:1-6, 5:1-2)

Gehenna

And God will imprison the angels who have shown wickedness in the burning valley which my grandfather Enoch had formerly shown to me in the west among the mountains of gold and silver and iron and purified metal and tin. And I saw that valley in which there was a great convulsion and a convulsion of the waters. And when all this came to pass, a smell of sulphur arose from that metal which was molten in fire and from the convulsion which issued from that place, and it became attached to those waters. And the valley of the angels who had caused mankind to sin burned beneath that land. And through those valleys flowed rivers of fire, in which were punished the angels who had led astray those who dwell upon the earth.

(1 Enoch 67:4-7)

And the judgment was held first over the stars, and they were found guilty, and went to the place of condemnation, and they were cast into a valley full of fire and flames, and full of pillars of fire. And the seventy shepherds were judged and found guilty, and they were cast into the depths of that fire. And I saw at that time, and behold, a valley like unto it was opened in the midst of the earth, and it was full of fire, and they brought those blinded sheep, and they were all judged and found guilty and cast into that valley of fire, and they burned....

(1 Enoch 90:24-27)

The Man from the Sea

And it came to pass after seven days that I dreamed a dream by night. And I saw, and behold, a violent wind arose from the sea and stirred up all its waves. And I saw, and behold, the wind caused a form like that of a man to come up from the heart of the seas. And I saw, and behold, that man flew with the clouds of heaven. And wherever he turned his face to look, everything seen by him trembled; and wherever the voice went out of his mouth, all that heard his voice was burnt, as the wax melts when it feels the fire.

And after this I saw, and behold, there was gathered from the four winds of heaven an innumerable multitude of men to make war against the man who had come up out of the sea. And I saw, and behold, he cut out a great mountain for himself, and flew upon it. . . .

And after this I saw, and behold, all who were gathered against him to do battle with him were seized with great fear; yet even so fight they did. And when he saw the assault of the multitude as it came, he neither lifted up his hand, nor held sword nor any other weapon. But I saw only that he sent out of his mouth, as it were, a fiery stream, and out of his lips a flaming wind, and out of his tongue he shot forth a storm of sparks. And all these were mingled together, the fiery stream, the flaming wind, and the storm, and fell upon the assault of the multitude. . . And it burned them all up, so that suddenly nothing more was to be seen of the innumerable multitude, save only dust of ashes and smell of smoke. And I saw this and was amazed.

And afterwards I saw the man come down from the mountain, and call upon him another multitude which came in peace. . . .

(4 Ezra 13)

Zion the Mourner

I lifted up my eyes, and behold, I saw a woman standing on the right side, mourning and weeping with a great voice, and her soul was greatly aggrieved, and her clothes were rent, and ashes were upon her head. And I left off from my thoughts, which I had been thinking, and turned to her and said: "Why are you weeping? And why are you aggrieved in your soul?" And she said to me: "Let me be, my lord, and let me continue to weep and to mourn, for I am very bitter of soul and very afflicted." And I said to her: "What happened, tell me!" And she said to me: "I was barren, I your handmaid, and bore not unto my husband whom I had for thirty years. And during those thirty years I prayed to the Most High, hourly and daily, day and night. And it came to pass after the end of thirty years that God heard the voice of your handmaid, and saw my misery, and listened to my supplication, and gave me a son. And we rejoiced in him greatly, I and my husband and all the people of my city, and we gave much glory to God Almighty. And I reared my son with great travail. And it came to pass when he grew up that I went to take him a wife and I made a day of feasting. And when my son came to his wedding chamber, he fell down and died. And we overturned all the lamps, and all the people of my city arose to comfort me, and I lay silent until the second day, until nightfall. And when all of them ceased to comfort me, for I lay silent, I arose in the night and fled and came out into this field as you can see. And I have it in my heart never again to return to the city, but here I shall remain, and shall neither eat nor drink but shall mourn without cease, and fast until I die."

And I left the thoughts which I had been thinking before, and answered her angrily and said: "O you most foolish of women! Do you not see our mourning and that which has befallen us? For Zion, the mother of us all, is in great grief, and she is brought down very low, and the mourning is very great! And now all of us do mourn, and you, too, mourn with us, for all of us are aggrieved! And you are aggrieved because of one son? Go, ask the earth, and she will tell you that she must mourn for the many who grew up upon her. And all those who were born upon her at first, and the others who had come to her, behold, almost all of them have gone into perdition, and into destruction go all their multitudes. Who, then, should mourn more: the earth who lost such a great multitude, or you who grieve over a single son? And should you say to me, 'My lament is not like the lament of the earth, for I have lost the fruit of my womb, whom I bore in pain and brought forth in sorrows; while the earth is as the way of the earth, many go from her as against those who come,' then I answer you, just as you bear in pain so also the earth gave her fruit, man, in the beginning, unto Him who made her. And now, overcome your pain, and bear with a stout heart the misfortune that has befallen you. And if you acknowledge the sentence of God, you will receive again even your son, and will be blessed among women! Go therefore to the city, to your husband."

But she said to me: "I shall not do that, and I shall not return to the city, but here I shall die."

And I continued to speak to her and said: "Do not this thing, but recognize with me the pain of Zion and find comfort in the sorrow of Jerusalem!"

"*For see, our Temple is desolate,* 　　*And our altar destroyed*
　Our sanctuary ruined 　　*And our tent despoiled.*
　Our harp has been muted 　　*And our song silenced*
　Our joy is gone 　　*And our light extinguished*
　The Ark of our Covenant is robbed 　　*And our Holies defiled*
　Our Name is profaned 　　*And our honor disgraced*
　Our nobles are dishonored 　　*And our elders despised*
　Our priests are burned 　　*And our Levites captured*
　Our virgins defiled 　　*And our women ravished*
　Our pious men seized 　　*And our children taken*
　Our youths became slaves 　　*And our heroes powerless.*"

And it came to pass as I was speaking to her and behold, suddenly her countenance shone exceedingly, and her appearance became like the lightning. And I was sore afraid to approach her, and I was considering to know what this was. And behold, suddenly she uttered a great and terrible cry, so that the earth shook at her voice. And I saw, and behold, there was no longer a woman but a city builded, and the place of great foundations became visible. And I was affrighted and called out in a loud voice and said: "Where is the angel Uriel who came to me at first? For it is he who brought me to this great wonderment of the heart. And now my end is come to naught and my prayer is futile."

And while I was still speaking these words, behold the angel came who had come to me at first, and he saw me lying on the ground as one dead, and my spirit afflicted. And he took hold of my right hand, and strengthened me, and raised me up on my feet, and said to me: ...

"This is the meaning of the vision: The woman whom you saw is Zion whom now you see as a builded city...."

(4 Ezra 9:38-10:44)

Judith and Holofernes

And in those days Judith the daughter of Merari ... sat in her widowhood in her house for three years and four months. And she had made herself a tent on the roof of her house, and put sackcloth upon her loins, and wore the garments of her widowhood. And she fasted all the days of her widowhood, except for the Sabbath eves and the Sabbaths, and the eves of the New Moon and on the New Moon, and on the feasts and the holidays of the House of Israel. And she was very beautiful and goodly of appearance. And her husband Menasseh had left her gold and silver, and menservants and maidservants, and flocks and fields, and she dwelt with them. And nobody said a bad word about her, for she feared the Lord very greatly.

And she heard ... that Uzziah had sworn that after five days he would deliver the city to the Children of Assyria. And she sent her old handmaid who managed all that she had, and called Uzziah and Kabri and Karmi, the elders of the city. And they came to her, and she said to them:

"Hear me, O you, the heads of those who dwell in Bethulia. Not right is the thing you spoke today before the people . . . saying that you would deliver the city to your enemies, unless the Lord turns against them to help you. And now, who are you that you should try the Lord today and should stand in the place of God among the people. . . . If He does not want to help us within five days, behold, He can save us any day He chooses, or can annihilate us before our enemies. And you, do not frustrate the counsel of the Lord our God, for God is not a man to be threatened, and not a son of man to recant. Therefore let us wait for His salvation, and let us call upon Him to help us, and He will hear our voice if it please Him. . . ."

And Uzziah said to her: "All that you have spoken you have spoken with a good heart, and nobody will gainsay your words. . . . But the people were very thirsty, and they forced us to do as we have spoken to them, and to render an oath which we will not leave unfulfilled. But now, beseech God for us, for you are a God-fearing woman, so that God should send rain to fill our cisterns and we faint no more."

And Judith said to them: "Hear me, and I shall do a thing whose fame will reach many generations of our people! Stand at the gate tonight, and I shall go out with my maid, and within the days after which you said you would deliver the city to our enemies the Lord will send succor to Israel through me. But do not search for what is in my heart to do, for I shall not tell you until I have accomplished the deed."

And Uzziah and the chiefs said to her: "Go in peace, and the Lord be before you to take vengeance on our enemies."

And they left the tent and went to their posts.

And Judith fell upon her face and put ashes upon her head, and uncovered the sackcloth which she was wearing. And it was the time of the evening incense offering in the House of the Lord in Jerusalem, and Judith cried with a loud voice to the Lord and said:

"O Lord, God of my father Simeon, into whose hands You gave a sword to take vengeance on the strangers who loosened the girdle of a virgin to defile her, and uncovered the thigh to her shame, and desecrated the womb to her disgrace ... Behold, the Children of Assyria have brought a great army, prided themselves of horses and riders, gloried in the arm of the footsoldier, trusted in shield and lance, and bow and sling. And they know not that You, O Lord, put an end to war, The Lord is Your name. O break their power with Your strength, and bring low their force with Your wrath, for they plan to desecrate Your Temple, to defile the tent of the dwelling of Your glorious name, and cut down with iron the horn of Your altar: Look at their insolence, send Your ire upon their heads, and give to the hands of the widow the strength which I desire! ..."

And it came to pass when she ceased crying to the God of Israel, and ended all these words, that she arose from the ground, and called her maid, and went down into the house in which she dwelt on the Sabbath and holidays. And she took off the sackcloth which she had on, and removed the garments of her widowhood, and washed her body in water, and anointed it with oil of myrrh, and braided the hair of her head, and covered it with a tiara, and put on the clothes of her joy in which she would wrap herself in the days of her husband Menasseh. And she put sandals on her feet, and adorned herself with chains, armlets, rings, and earrings, and all her jewelry, and made herself very beautiful to all who saw her.

And she gave her maid a skin full of wine and a cruse of oil, and filled her bag with corn and figs and fine bread, and laid the vessels upon her. And they went out to the gate of the city of Bethulia, and found Uzziah and the elders of the city Karmi and Kabri standing upon it. And when they saw her—and her face had altered and her garments were changed—they were exceedingly amazed at her beauty, and they said to her:

"May the God of our fathers give you favor and fulfill

your wish, to the glory of the Children of Israel and the exaltation of Jerusalem!" And they bowed down before her.

And she said to them: "Order the young men to open for me the gate of the city, so that I can go out to do the thing whereof you spoke to me."

And they ordered the young men to open for her, as she said. And so they did, and Judith and her maid went out. And the people looked after her until she descended from the mountain and crossed the valley, and then they could no longer see her.

And they went in the valley, and were met by a patrol of the Children of Assyria. And they took her and asked her saying: "Of what people are you? From where do you come? And where are you going?"

And she said: "I am a daughter of the Hebrews, and I am fleeing from them for they are delivered to you to be consumed. And behold, I am going to Holofernes, your commander, to declare him words of truth, and to show him the way he should go in order to take possession of the whole mountain, without losing a single one of his men."

And when the men heard her words and saw her face, they were greatly amazed at her beauty, and said to her:

"You have indeed saved your life by hastening to come down to our lord. And now go to his tent, and from there they will accompany you until they hand you over to him. And when you stand before him, fear not in your heart, but tell him your words, and it will be well with you."

And they chose a hundred men from among them, and escorted her and her maid, and took them to the tent of Holofernes. And there was a rush in the whole camp, for her coming became known in the tents, and they came and surrounded her, and she was standing outside the tent of Holofernes until they told him about her. And they marveled at her beauty, and marveled at the Children of Israel because of her, and said to one another: "Who can despise this people in whose midst there are such women? But it is better not to leave a single one of them alive, because if some are let go, they can lead astray the whole earth."

And all those who were sitting and eating with Holofernes came out, and all his servants, and they brought the two women into the tent. And Holofernes was lying on his couch, under a canopy which was woven of purple and gold and emeralds and precious stones. And they told him of her, and he came out in front of his tent, and silver torches went before him. And it came to pass when Judith came before him and before his servants, that they all marveled at her beauty. And she fell down upon her face, and prostrated herself before him, and his servants raised her up.

And Holofernes said to her: "Be strong, fear not in your heart, for I would do no harm to anybody who chooses to serve Nebuchadnezzar, the king of the whole earth. And your people who dwell on the mountain, had they not scorned me, I would not have lifted my spear against them; but they did this to themselves. And now tell me, why did you flee from them and come to us? If you came in order to save your life, take courage! You will live this night and thereafter as well. For there is none to harm you, but good will be done to you as is done to the servants of my lord, the king Nebuchadnezzar!"

And Judith said to him: "Accept the words of your handmaid, and allow your servant to speak, and I shall tell no lie to my lord this night. If you will listen to the words of your handmaid, God will do good to you, and my lord will not be prevented from carrying out his plans. For as Nebuchadnezzar, the king of the whole earth, lives, and as his kingship lives who sent you . . . not only men will serve him through you, but also the beasts of the field and the cattle, and the birds of heaven, through your might, will live in the days of Nebuchadnezzar and of all his house. For we have heard of your wisdom and of the plans of your heart, and it has been told to the whole land that you are the bravest in his whole kingdom, great in wisdom, wonderful in strategy of war....

"It is true that our people are not punished and the sword has no power over them as long as they sin not against their God. And now, so that my lord return not empty, know that death will fall upon them, and they will be caught in a sin which will arouse the wrath of their God when they commit evil. For when their food gave out and they lacked water they decided to slaughter the animals and all that which God has commanded them in His Tora not to eat. And they resolved to use for their own needs the firstfruits of the wheat, and the tithes of the wine and the oil which they had consecrated and preserved for the priests who stand in Jerusalem before our God, although an ordinary person is not allowed even to touch it with his hands. And they have already dispatched messengers to Jerusalem, for also the people who dwell there did likewise, to bring them permission from the community of elders. And when they will bring them the answer and they will do it, then they will be delivered up to you to destroy them on that day.

"Therefore I, your handmaid, knowing all this, fled from them, and God sent me to do things for you about which the whole earth will be amazed when they hear them. For your handmaid is a fearer of God, night and day I serve the God of heaven. And now, my lord, let me stay with you, and let your handmaid go out at night into the valley, and I shall pray to God, and He will tell me when they have committed the sin. And I shall come and tell you, and you will march out with your whole army, and no man among them will stand up before you. And I shall lead you into the midst of Judah, until you come up against Jerusalem, and I shall set your seat in her midst, and you will drive them as a flock which has no shepherd, and no dog will open its mouth against you, for all this was said to me in my prophecy and told to me, and I was sent to tell you."

And her words were pleasing in the eyes of Holofernes and in the eyes of all his servants, and they marveled at her wisdom, and said: "There is none like this woman in beauty and in wisdom from one end of the earth to the other!"

And Holofernes said to her: "Well did God do to send you before the people, so that there should be strength in our hands, and destruction for those who scorn my lord. And now, behold, you are beautiful of countenance and goodly in your words, and if you will do as you said your God will be my God and you will dwell in the house of the king Nebuchadnezzar, and your name will go forth in the whole earth."

And he commanded that they take her to the place where there were the silver vessels which he had, and said that they put before her of his food, and of his wine to drink. But Judith said: "I shall not eat of it, lest it become a stumbling. I shall have enough of that which was brought with me."

And Holofernes said to her: "And if that which is with you will be finished, from where shall we bring to give you the like of it, since nobody is with us here from your people?"

And Judith said to him: "By your life, my lord, your handmaid will not finish that which is with her until the Lord fulfills through me what He intended."

And the servants of Holofernes led her into the tent, and she slept until midnight, and arose toward the morning watch. And she sent to Holofernes saying: "Command, O my lord, that they allow your handmaid to go out to pray."

And Holofernes commanded the watchman saying: "Do not stop her."

And she stayed in the camp three days, and she went out every night into the valley of Bethulia, and she bathed there in the well of water. And she came up and prayed to the Lord, the God of Israel, that He let her way succeed for the succor of her people. And she returned cleansed, and sat in the tent until she brought her bread in the evening.

And it came to pass in the fourth day that Holofernes gave a feast to his servants alone, and did not invite any of the officers. And he said to Bagoas, the eunuch who was in charge of everything he had: "Go now, persuade the Hebrew woman who is with you that she come to us to eat and to drink with us. For, behold, it would be a shame for us if we let such a woman go away without being with her, for if we do not take her, she will laugh at us."

And Bagoas came out from before Holofernes, and went to her and said: "Let this beautiful girl not refuse to come to my lord and to find favor before him, and to drink wine with us to rejoice, and to be this night like one of the daughters of Assyria who stand in the house of Nebuchad-nezzar."

And Judith said to him: "And who am I to disobey my lord? All that is good in his eyes I shall quickly do, and this will be a joy for me until the day I die."

And she arose, and adorned herself in her dress and all her jewelry, and her handmaid went and spread out for her before Holofernes on the floor the skins which she had taken from Bagoas for her use every day, so that she might recline on them at the time of the meal.

And Judith came and lay down. And the heart of Holofernes went out to her, and his soul was moved, and he desired her very much to lie with her, for he was awaiting the hour to seduce her from the day he first had seen her.

And Holofernes said: "Drink, and make your heart merry with us."

And Judith said: "Behold, I shall drink, my lord, for more enriched is my life today than in all the days since I was born."

And she took that which her handmaid had prepared, and she ate and drank before him. And Holofernes took great delight in her, and drank wine amply, more than he had ever drunk on any day since he was born.

And it came to pass at night that his servants hurried to take their leave of him, and Bagoas shut the dwelling from without, and bid those who were standing there to go away from his master, and they went to their dwellings, for all were tired from the heavy drinking. And Judith remained alone in the tent, and Holofernes was fallen upon his couch, for he was flushed with wine. And Judith said to her handmaid to stand outside her room and wait for her going out as she did every day, for, she said, "I shall go out to my prayer." And she told Bagoas the same thing.

And all of them went out from before her, and nobody remained in the room, and Judith approached the couch and said in her heart:

"O Lord, God of all power! Look now upon the work of my hands to raise up the glory of Jerusalem! For now is the time to help Your inheritance, and to do my will, and to break the enemies who arose against us!"

And she stepped to the post of the couch which was next to the head of Holofernes, and took down his sword from there. And she went to the couch and gathered the hair of his head in her hand, and said:

"Strengthen me, O God of Israel, this day!"

And she smote his neck with all her strength, twice, and severed his head from his body. And she rolled down his corpse from the couch, and pulled down the canopy from the posts, and then she went out and gave the head of Holofernes to her handmaid. And she hid it in her food bag, and the two of them went out together as usual, and crossed the camp, and went around the valley, and went up the mountain to Bethulia, and came to the gate.

And Judith called from afar to the watchmen: "Open, open the gate, for the Lord our God is with us to perform more mighty deeds in Israel, and a strong arm over our enemies, as He did this day!"

And when the people of the city heard her voice, they hurried to go down to the gate, and called the elders of the city. And they all came running, from the great ones to the little ones, for her coming was like unto a miracle, and they opened the gate and gathered them in, and made a fire to give light, and surrounded them round about. And Judith lifted up her voice and said to them:

"Hallelujah! Praise the Lord who did not remove His

mercy from the House of Israel, and destroyed our enemies by my hands this night!"

And she took the head out of the bag and showed it to them and said:

"See the head of Holofernes, commander of the army of Assyria, and see the canopy under which he lay in his drunkenness, and the Lord smote him by the hand of a woman! And as the Lord lives who preserved me in the way I went, the appearance of my face enticed him to his downfall, and he did no base deed to me to defile me or disgrace me."

And all the people were shaken greatly, and they bowed down and prostrated themselves before the Lord, and said with one mouth: "Blessed be You, our God, who have destroyed this day the enemies of Your people!" ...

And when the servants of Holofernes saw that he was slain, fear fell upon them, and none of them stood up in front of his neighbor, and they fled and ran away as one man, and took to all the paths of the valley and the mountain. . . .

And many wanted to marry Judith, but no man knew her all the days of her life, from the day on which her husband Menasseh died. And she grew old in the house of her husband, and reached one hundred and five years, and she set free her maid, and she died in Bethulia, and they buried her in the tomb of her husband Menasseh.

(Judith 8-16)

Susanna and the Elders

There lived a man in Babylon and his name was Jehoiakim. And he had married a woman by the name of Susanna daughter of Hilkiah, and she was exceedingly beautiful and God-fearing. And her parents were pious people who had taught their daughter the Tora of Moses. And Jehoiakim was very wealthy, and he had an orchard next to his house, and the Jews would gather in his house because he was the most respected among them.

In a certain year two of the elders were appointed judges. Of them did the Lord speak when He said, "From Babylon will wickedness issue forth, from the elders of the judges who only appear as if they were leaders of the people." And those two elders would frequent the house of Jehoiakim, and all the people who had disputes would come to them.

And when the people would leave, Susanna would come to the orchard of her husband. And the two elders would watch her day after day, walking about, and they lusted for her. And their minds became perverted, and they lowered their eyes so as not to look to heaven and not to remember the true judgment. And the two were greatly troubled by her, but they did not tell one another of their frustration, for they were ashamed to speak of their desire to come to her which agitated them. So they tried eagerly, day after day, to watch her.

And they spoke to one another: "Let us go home, for the time of the meal has arrived." And they left the orchard and took leave of one another. But then they turned back, and came to the place, and asked one another: "What is the matter?" And they admitted their desire, and agreed on a time when they might find her alone.

And they observed the time, and Susanna came as she had done every day, she and her two maids alone. And she wished to take a take a bath in the orchard in the heat of the day. And she said to her maids: "Bring me oil and ointments, and lock the gates of the orchard." And they went out by the rear doors to bring her what they were ordered, and they did not see the elders because they were hidden.

And when the maids left, the two elders arose and ran up to Susanna and said: "Look, the gates of the orchard are locked, and no one can see us. And now listen to us, and let us come to you. And if not, we shall testify against you that a youth came to you, and that is why you sent away your maids."

And Susanna groaned and said: "Woe to me, whether I

do this or not. For if I do this, I shall be put to death, and if I do not do it, I shall not escape your hands. And now it is better that I do not do it, and fall into your hands rather than sin before the Lord."

So Susanna cried out with a loud voice, and also the two elders shouted against her. And one of them ran and opened the gates of the orchard. And when the sound of the cries was heard in the house, they came to see what had happened to her. And when the elders had their say, the servants were greatly ashamed for such a thing had never been told about Susanna.

Next day, when the people gathered in the house of Jehoiakim her husband, the two elders came, and they were full of evil thoughts about Susanna, to kill her. And they said before the people: "Fetch Susanna the daughter of Hilkiah, her who is the wife of Jehoiakim." They sent for her, and she came, and her father and mother, and her children, and all her relatives. And Susanna was very delectable and beautiful to look at.

And the evildoers commanded that they uncover her head, for she was veiled, in order that they might sate themselves on her beauty. And the people around her wept, and all those who saw her.

Then the two elders stood up in the midst of the people, and put their hands upon her head. And Susanna wept and looked up to heaven, for her heart trusted God.

And the elders said: "While we were walking alone in the orchard, this woman came with her two maids, and she locked the gates of the orchard, and sent away the maids. Then there came to her a youth who had been hiding there, and lay with her. And we, from the corner of the orchard, saw this shameful deed, and ran up to them. But, although we saw them together, we could not catch the youth for he was stronger than we. But we caught this woman and asked her who was the youth. But she refused to tell us. And we are witnesses to all this."

And the congregation believed them for they were of the

elders of the people and its judges, and they sentenced her to death.

And Susanna cried with a loud voice, saying: "O eternal God, You know that which is hidden, and know everything before it happens! You know that they are lying in accusing me. And behold, I shall die, although I am innocent of what they accuse me!"

And the Lord heard her voice. And as they were leading her out to die, the Lord God gave His Holy Spirit upon a youth by the name of Daniel. And he cried with a loud voice: "I am innocent of the blood of this woman!"

And all the people turned to him and said: "What is this thing you are saying?"

And he stood up in their midst and said: "Are you fools, O Children of Israel? You have not examined, and you know not the truth, and yet you condemn a daughter of Israel! And now, return to the court of law, for these two have testified falsely against her!"

And all the people hastened to return, and the elders said to him: "Come and sit with us, and tell us, for God has given you the wisdom of old age."

Then Daniel said to them: "Separate and move far away the one from the other, and I shall examine them."

When they separated the one from the other, he called the first one and said to him: "O you, who have spent your days in wickedness, now the sins which you have committed from old have caught up with you. You passed false judgments, found the innocent guilty and the guilty innocent, although the Lord has said, slay not the innocent and the righteous. And now, if you have really seen this, tell me, under what kind of tree did you see them together?"

And the elder said: "Under a mastic tree."

And Daniel said: "Now surely you have perjured yourself! Already the angel of God has received word from God to rend you into two!"

And he made him stand alone, and ordered the other to

be brought in, and said to him: "O you seed of Canaan, and not of Judah! Beauty has led you astray, and lust has made your heart corrupt! This is how you have acted towards the daughters of Israel, and they, because they were afraid of you, submitted to you. But one daughter of Judah did not submit to your evil design. And now tell me, under what kind of tree did you catch them together?"

And the elder said: "Under a holm oak."

And Daniel said to him: "How well you, too, have lied! By your head! The angel of God stands here with his sword in his hand to cut you into two, and to destroy both of you!"

And the whole congregation burst into loud cheers, and they blessed God who saves those who put their hope in Him. And they rose up against the two elders, for Daniel proved through their own mouths that they were false witnesses, and they did to them as they had conspired to do to others. And they did according to the Tora of Moses, and put them to death, and thus innocent blood was saved on that day.

And Hilkiah and his wife praised God for their daughter, and so did her husband Jehoiakim and all her relatives, because no shameful thing was found in her.

And Daniel became great in the eyes of the people from that day onwards.

(Additions to Dan.)

Bel and the Dragon

When King Astyages was gathered to his fathers, Cyrus the Persian inherited his kingdom. And Daniel was a confidant of the king and was honored more than all his companions. And the people of Babylon had an idol and its name was Bel [i.e., Baal], and they gave him to eat every day twelve bushels of wheat and forty sheep and six large containers of wine. And the king, too, worshiped it, and came every day to prostrate himself before it. And Daniel prostrated himself before his God. And the king said to him: "Why do you not worship Bel?" And he answered: "Because I do not serve idols, the work of human hands, but only the living God, the creator of heavens and earth, the master of all flesh." The king said to him: "Do you not think that Bel is a living god? Do you not see how much he eats and drinks every day?" And Daniel laughed and said: "Let yourself not be deceived, O king, for it is clay inside and brass on the outside, and has never eaten or drunk anything." And the king became wroth, and he called his priests and said to them: "If you do not tell me who eats all the food presented to Bel, you will surely die. And if you show me that indeed Bel eats it, Daniel will die for having spoken sedition against Bel." And Daniel said to the king: "Let it be as you have said." And Bel had seventy priests, each with wives and children. And the king went with Daniel to the temple of Bel. And the priests of Bel said: "Behold, we shall go outside, and you, O king, place the food and the wine before Bel, and lock the door and seal it with your ring. And let it be that if tomorrow you will not find that everything has been eaten by Bel, we shall die, or else Daniel will die for having told lies about us." And the matter seemed light in their eyes, for they had made a secret door under the table, and through it they would always enter and take out the food with them. And when they went out, the king placed the food before Bel, and Daniel ordered his lads to bring ashes, and they strewed it all over the temple before the eyes of the king alone. And then they went out and locked the door and sealed it with the signet ring of the king, and went away. And during the night the priests came, as was their wont, they, and their wives and children, and ate everything and drank. And early next morning the king arose and Daniel with him. And the king said: "Are the seals whole, O Daniel?" And he said: "They are whole, O king." And when they opened the door, the king looked at the table and called out with a loud voice: "Great are you, O Bel, and there is no untruth in you at all." And Daniel laughed, and held onto the king lest he enter the temple, and said to him: "Look at the floor and see whose footprints are these!" And the king said: "I see the footprints of men, women, and children." And the king became wroth and summoned the priests and their wives and their children, and they showed him the secret doors through which they had come and eaten everything that was on the table. And the king put them to death, and gave everything as a present to Daniel, and had the temple of Bel destroyed.

And there was there a great dragon, and the people of Babylon worshiped him. And the king said to Daniel: "Surely you cannot say that this is not a living god, therefore prostrate yourself to him." And Daniel said: "I prostrate myself to the Lord my God, for he is the living God. And if, O king, you will let me, I shall kill the dragon without a sword or a club." And the king said: "Behold, I am giving him into your hands." And Daniel took pitch and lard and hair and cooked them together and made loaves of them and put them into the mouth of the dragon, and the dragon swallowed them and burst. And Daniel said: "Now look at that which you feared." And when the people of Babylon heard this, they became very wroth and murmured against the king and said: "The king has become Jewish; he destroyed Bel, he killed the dragon, and slaughtered the priests." And they came to the king and said: "Give Daniel into our hands, and if not, behold, we shall slay you and your house." And when the king saw that they were pressing him hard, he delivered Daniel to them under duress. And they cast him into the lions' pit, and he was there six days. And in the pit there were seven lions, and every day they would put before them the bodies of two men and two sheep, but during those six days they gave them nothing, so that they would eat Daniel.

And in the land of Judah there was the prophet Habbakuk, and he cooked pottage, and mixed bread into the pot, and was going out into the field to take it to the reapers. And the angel of God said to Habbakuk: "Take the food which is in your hand to Babylon for Daniel who is in the lions' pit." And Habbakuk said: "O Lord, I have never seen Babylon, and I do not know the pit." And the angel of God took hold of his head and lifted him up by his hair, and carried him in a storm, and put him down in the land of Babylon, over the pit. And Habbakuk called saying: "Take the food which God has sent you." And Daniel said: "Verily you remembered me, O God, and did not forsake those who love You." And Daniel arose and ate, and the angel of God instantly returned Habbakuk to his place.

And on the seventh day the king went to mourn for Daniel, and he came to the pit, and saw, and behold, there was Daniel sitting. And the king cried with a great voice saying: "Great are You, O Lord, the God of Daniel, and there is none else beside You." And he brought him up from the pit and cast into the pit those who had planned evil against him, and in a moment the lions tore them to pieces before his eyes.

(Additions to Dan.)

The Story of Tobias

[The pious Tobit of Nineveh, blinded by a film on his eyes, sends his son Tobias to recover a deposit of ten talents of silver he had left twenty years earlier with Gabael of Rages in Media. Tobias is accompanied by the angel Raphael disguised as a young Hebrew and answering to the name Azariah. They arrive at Ecbatana, where lives Tobit's kinsman Raguel with his wife Edna and his daughter Sarah.]

On that very day it came to pass that Sarah the daughter

of Raguel in Ecbatana of Media was scolded and cursed by one of her father's maidservants. For she had been given to seven men, and Ashmodai, the evil demon, had killed them all before they could be with her as is the way of women. And the maidservant said to her: "You are the one who slays her husbands. Behold, you have already been given to seven men, and are still not called after the name of any one of them. Why do you plague us with your husbands who died? Go with them, and let us never see a son or a daughter from you!"

And Sarah sorrowed in her heart on that day, and she wept, and went up to the upper story of her father's house, and was about to hang herself. But then she spoke in her heart: "People will curse my father and say to him: 'You had one beloved daughter and she too hanged herself because of the calamities.' And thus I would cause the hoary head of my father to go down to Sheol in sorrow. It is better that I do not hang myself but pray to the Lord that I should die and hear no more curses in my life."

And she stretched forth her hands toward the window and prayed, and said: "Blessed be You, merciful God, and blessed be Your name forever, and let all Your works bless You for all eternity. And now I have lifted up my face and my eyes to You. Speak and let me be gathered from the earth and let me hear no more curses. And You know, my Lord, that I am pure of all impurity with men, and have not polluted my name, nor the name of my father in the land of my captivity. I am the only one of my father, and he has no other child who could inherit him, nor has he a brother's son or a relative for whom I should preserve myself to become his wife. And I already have lost seven husbands. Why should I go on living? And if it pleases You not to slay me, O Lord, listen to my disgrace."

At the same time the prayers of both were heard before the glory of God. And He sent Raphael to heal both of them: Tobit, by removing the white film from his eyes so that he should see with his eyes the light of God, and Sarah the daughter of Raguel, to give her to wife to Tobias son of Tobit by ridding her of Ashmodai the evil demon. For Tobias had to inherit her from among all those who sought to take her. And at one and the same time Tobias entered his house from the courtyard, and Sarah the daughter of Raguel descended from the upper story....

And the youth [Tobias] went forth, and the angel with him, and also the dog went forth with him, and they journeyed together until the night came down upon them, and they stopped for the night at the river Tigris. And the youth went down to wash his feet in the river Tigris, and a great fish leaped out of the water and wanted to swallow the foot of the youth, and he cried out. And the angel said to the youth: "Catch the fish, and hold it fast." And the youth held the fish, and pulled it out to the dry land. And the angel said to him: "Cut up the fish and take out its gall and its heart and its liver, and keep them with you. And throw away the intestines. For its gall and its heart and its liver are good for a remedy." And the youth cut up the fish, and collected the gall and the heart and the liver. And he roasted the fish and ate, and salted what was left over of it.

And the two of them journeyed together until they approached Media. And the youth asked the angel and said to him: "Azariah my brother, what remedy is there in the heart of the fish and in its liver and gall?" And he said to him: "If you smoke the heart of the fish and its liver before a man or a woman who has been harmed by a demon or by an evil spirit, all affliction will flee from them never to return. And if the gall is smeared on the eyes of a man which are covered by a white film, the white film will dissolve and the eyes will be healed."

And when they came to Media and approached Ecbatana, Raphael said to the youth: "Tobias my son!" And he said to him: "Here am I." And he said to him: "Tonight we shall lodge in the house of Raguel who is your kinsman. And he has a daughter whose name is Sarah. And he has no male child, nor another daughter, but only Sarah alone.

And you are her closest relative of all the people to inherit her. And you will merit to inherit also all that which her father has. And the girl has a good mind, and she is a woman of valor, and is very beautiful, and her father is of a fine family. And it is your due to marry her. And now listen to me, my brother, and tonight I shall speak for the girl to her father so that we take her for you as a bride. And when we return from Rages we shall have the wedding. And I know that Raguel cannot deny her to you, nor can he betroth her to another man, for in that case he would incur the death penalty according to the law of the Book of Moses, since he will know that you have the right of inheritance from among all men, to take his daughter to wife. And now listen to me my brother, and I shall speak for the girl tonight, and we shall betroth her to you, and when we return from Rages we shall take her and carry her with us to your house."

And Tobias answered and said to Raphael: "Azariah my brother, I have heard that she had been given to seven men and they all died in their wedding chamber during the night in which they went in unto her. And I also have heard them say that a demon has killed them. And now I am afraid, for while no evil befalls her, he who wants to approach her is killed by the demon. And I am the only son of my father, and should I die I would bring down the lives of my father and my mother in sorrow to their grave, and they have no other son to bury them."

And Raphael said to him: "Do you not remember the command of your father which he has commanded you to take a wife from your father's house? And now, listen to me, my brother, and think nothing of the demon but take the girl, and I know that this night she will be given to you to be your wife. And when you enter the wedding chamber, take of the liver of the fish and its heart, and put them on the coals of the incense, and the smell will rise, and the demon will smell it and flee, and will never again appear to her. And when you wish to be with her, first both of you should rise and pray and request of the Lord the God of heavens that His mercy and salvation be upon you, and fear not, for she has been destined for you since the six days of Creation, and you will save her. And she will go with you, and I hope that you will have from her sons."

And when Tobias heard the words of Raphael, and learned that she was a sister from the seed of his father, he loved her very much and his heart was bound to her. And when they came to Ecbatana, he said to him: "My brother Azariah, lead me on a straight path to our brother Raguel."

And he led him to the house of Raguel, and they found him sitting at the gate of the courtyard, and they greeted him first. And he said to them: "Rejoice greatly, O my brothers, may your coming be in peace!" And he led them into the house.

And he said to Edna his wife: "How similar is this youth to my brother Tobit!" And Edna asked them and said: "From where are you, my brothers?" And they told her: We are of the Children of Naftali who were exiled to Nineveh." And she said to them: "Do you know Tobit our brother? And they said to her: "We know him." And she said to them: "Is he in peace?" And they said to her: "He is in peace and alive." And Tobias said: "He is my father."

And Raguel arose and kissed him and wept, and spoke and said to him: "Blessing upon you, my son, good and beautiful son of his father! But woe that he is so severely ill, for he is a righteous man who practices charity, and he was stricken with blindness!" And he fell on the neck of Tobias his brother and cried. And also his wife Edna cried on him, and their daughter Sarah, too, cried. And Raguel slaughtered a ram from the flock and received them with a pleased soul.

And when they had immersed themselves and washed and sat down to eat, Tobias said to Raphael: "My brother Azariah, speak to Raguel that he should give me Sarah my sister to wife." And Raguel heard it and said to the youth: "Eat and drink, and let your heart be merry this night, for there is no other man besides you, my brother, who would be suited to marry my daughter. And likewise, I could not give her to anybody else besides you, for you are my nearest relative. However, I want to tell you the truth, my son. I have given her to seven men from among my brothers, and all of them died during the night in which they came to her. And now, my son, eat and drink, and may the Lord have mercy on you."

And Tobias said: "I shall not eat from now on, and shall not drink, until you fulfill my wish."

And Raguel said to him: "So I shall do. She is given to you according to the law of the Book of Moses. It has been decreed from heaven that she be given to you. Take your sister, from now on you are her brother and she your sister. She is given to you from today for ever. And may the Lord of heaven make you succeed, my son, this night, and show you mercy and give you peace."

And Raguel called Sarah his daughter, and she came to him, and he took her right hand and gave it to him, and said: "Take her according to the Tora and the law written in the Book of Moses, to give her to you to wife. Take her and go in peace to your father, and the God of heaven give you luck in your peace!"

And he called her mother and said that they bring writing utensils, and he wrote out a marriage contract, and thereby he gave her to him as a wife, according to the law of the Tora of Moses. And thereafter they began to eat and to drink.

And Raguel called Edna his wife and said to her: "My sister, prepare a separate room, and take them there." And she went, and made the bed in the room as he had said, and led her there, and she cried over her, and wiped off her tears and said to her: "Be strong, my daughter, may the Lord of heaven give you joy instead of your sorrow. Be strong, my daughter!" And she went out.

And it came to pass when they finished eating and drinking, they wanted to sleep, and accompanied the youth and took him to the room. And Tobias remembered the words of Raphael, and he took the liver of the fish and its heart out of the bag in which they were, and put them on the coals of the incense. And the smell of the fish was heavy, and the demon fled to the edge of Upper Egypt, and Raphael went and chained him there and captured him suddenly. And they went and closed the door of the room, and Tobias arose from the bed and said: "My sister, arise, let us pray and request our Lord that He do to us mercy and salvation."

And she arose, and they began to pray and to ask for salvation, and he said: "Blessed are You, O God of our fathers, and blessed is Your name for all generations of the world. Let the heavens and all Your creatures bless You for all generations. You made Adam and made Eve for him as his wife, a help-meet and a support, and of the two of them was born the seed of the children of men. You said, *It is not good that the man should be alone; I will make him a help-meet for him* (Gen. 2:18). And now, not for lust do I take this sister of mine, but in truth, in order to procreate offspring, to praise Your name forever and ever. Command therefore that I and she find mercy and grow old together." And they said to each other, "Amen, Amen." And they slept in the night.

And Raguel arose and called the servants of his house, and they went and dug a grave, for he said: "If he has died, we will be held up to derision and shame." And when they finished to dig the grave, Raguel went into the house and called his wife, and said: "Send one of the maids, and let her go and see whether he is alive. And if he is dead, we shall bury him and nobody will know." And they sent the maid, and lit the candle, and opened the door, and she found them sleeping side by side. And the maid went out and told them that he was alive and no evil had befallen him. And they blessed the God of heaven and said: "Blessed are You, O God, may You be blessed with all the pure blessing by all generations. And blessed are You that You caused us joy, and that it did not happen as we thought it would, but with Your great mercy You did this to us. And blessed are You that You had mercy on these two who are the only begotten children of their parents. Give them, O Lord, mercy and salvation, and fill their lives with joy and mercy." And he told the servant of his house that they fill the grave with earth before the rise of dawn. . . .

And when the fourteen days of the wedding feast were over . . . Tobias left the house of Raguel in peace and returned to Nineveh. And Raphael said to Tobias: "Take the gall of the fish into your hand." And the dog went with them after Tobias. And Hannah was sitting and watching the road for her son. And she saw that he was approaching and said to his father: "Behold, your son is coming, and with him the man who had accompanied him." And Raphael said to Tobias: "Go to your father. I know that his eyes will open. Anoint his eyes with the gall of the fish, and the remedy will contract and dissolve the film from the eyes of your father, and he will look at you and will see the light."

And Hannah ran to him and fell upon the neck of her son, and said to him: "I have seen you, my son, now I can die!" And she wept.

And Tobit got up, and stumbled as he went out the door of the courtyard. And Tobias went to him and got hold of him and took the gall of the fish and put it upon his eyes, and said: "Courage, my father!" And he applied the remedy and repeated it. And with his hands he wiped off the film from the corners of his eyes. And he fell upon his neck and wept and said to him: "My son, I can see you, light of my eyes!"

And he said: "Blessed be God, and blessed His great name, and blessed be all His holy angels. May His great name be with us, and blessed be the angels for all the generations. For He afflicted me, and, behold, I can see my son Tobias!"

And Tobias went in, full of joy, and blessed God with his

whole mouth. And he told his father that he had succeeded in his journey, that he had brought the money, and that he had taken Sarah the daughter of Raguel to wife, and that she was here, and near the gate of Nineveh.

And Tobit went forth to receive his daughter-in-law before the gate of Nineveh, rejoicing and blessing God. And when the people of Nineveh saw him walking and stepping out with all his strength, and nobody led him, they were amazed. And Tobit declared before them that God had mercy on him. And Tobit approached Sarah the wife of Tobias, and blessed her and said to her: "Come in peace, my daughter, and blessed be God who led you to us, my daughter. Come into your house in peace, in blessing, and in joy."

On that day there was great rejoicing for all the Jews in Nineveh.

(Tobit 3:7-17; 6:1-8:21; 10:7-11:18)

3

TALMUD

The Talmud is second only to the Bible in its importance and influence as a source book of Jewish religion. The term "Talmud" (literally "study") is generic: there are actually two Talmuds, the larger and more authoritative Babylonian Talmud containing the teachings of the Babylonian Jewish sages (the so-called Amoraim) who lived in the third to fifth centuries, and the smaller Jerusalem (or Palestinian) Talmud which presents the teachings of the sages who lived in the Land of Israel in the third and fourth centuries. Both Talmuds are structured in the form of commentaries on the Mishna, the code of traditional law compiled about 200 C.E. by Rabbi Y'huda haNasi in the Galilee, which contains the teachings of the earlier sages (the so-called Tannaim) who lived in the first and second centuries C.E. In distinction from the Mishna, which is always brief and succinct, the voluminous Talmudic commentary appended to it is called the Gemara. The Jerusalem Talmud contains ca. 800,000 words; the Babylonian ca. 2,500,000 words. In the two Talmuds references are made to ca. two hundred Tannaim and no less than two thousand Amoraim. Both Talmuds are written partly in Hebrew and partly in Aramaic; the latter was the colloquial tongue in Palestine and in Babylonia in those days.

The material contained in both Talmuds consists either of records of legal discussions which took place in the Talmudic academies and of the decisions in which these discussions resulted (the so-called Halakha), or of nonlegal material designated by the term Agada or Hagada, which is of a most varied character and which has been discussed in section II of the Introduction.

As the Bible, so the Talmud too is suffused with an all-pervasive moral consciousness. Its fundamental purpose is to teach the law of the Lord and to edify by showing the ways of God in a dozen different literary genres. One of these many Talmudic literary forms is that of the legend, of which the Hebrew designation is Agada in the narrow sense.

Most Talmudic legends are elaborations of Biblical stories. Narratives given in the Bible in a brief form are amplified by many additional details, obscure statements are explained, and new events, thoughts, and dialogues are added. Persons who remain unnamed in the Bible are named and identified, often two different individuals are stated to have been one and the same, and the effects of one act or event on another are explored. Occasionally the Talmudic Agada preserves an older, more complete version of a legend of which merely an abridged or even expurgated version is found in the Bible. Thus, to mention only one example, the Bible tells that the sin of Ham was that he gazed disrespectfully at the nakedness of his drunken father Noah (Gen. 9:20-28); the Talmud, in the name of Rab, refers to what must have been the original full form of the story: Ham unmanned Noah, and this is why he drew upon his head the severe curse of his father (B. Sanh. 70a).

Compared to the Bible and the Midrash literature (see below, Part 4), each of which spanned more than a millennium, the Talmud originated, developed, and was brought to a conclusion within a relatively short period, a mere five hundred years. Nevertheless the Babylonian Talmud was destined to become the central subject of study for traditional Jews from its completion to the Enlightenment some thirteen centuries later, and the basis of all successive Halakhic law codes, from that of Isaac Alfasi (1013–1103) to the *Shulḥan 'Arukh* of Joseph Caro (1488–1575), which is still considered authoritative by Orthodox Jews all over the world.

Compared to the importance of the Talmud as the source of Halakha, its Agadic parts were considered by traditional Jews of much lesser interest, and were largely neglected. Although compilations of the Agadic passages were made—foremost among them is the *'En Ya'aqov* (1515–16) by R. Levi ibn Ḥaviv—the study of the Talmudic and Midrashic Agada came into its own only after the emergence of the modern "science of Judaism" in the nineteenth century.

This part presents a selection of legends from the Talmudic Agada, culled from both the Babylonian and the Palestinian Talmud, and arranged according to subject matter, to wit: Of God; Creation, Eden, Gehenna; Sea Lore; Angels and Demons; Biblical Heroes; Between Israel and Edom (Greece, Edom, Jews and Gentiles, Israel and the Nations); Sages and Saints; and Sin and Repentance. Needless to say, these selections exemplify only a small part of the many subjects which figure in the Talmudic Agada.

One important characteristic of Agadic literature is that one and the same story appears in several variants in different parts of the Talmud, or in both the Palestinian and the Babylonian Talmuds, or in a Talmudic source as well as in one or more Midrash collections. These versions may be centuries apart and may exhibit considerable differences in style, detail, and elaboration. In making the selection from among such parallel passages, the oldest extant version was, in general, preferred, except for cases in which a later variant was obviously of a higher literary quality and hence more attractive.

OF GOD

The Nightwatches

R. Eliezer said: "There are three watches in the night ... and their signs are: in the first watch, the donkey brays; in the second, the dogs bark; in the third, the baby suckles at its mother's breast and the woman chats with her husband."

R. Yitzḥaq bar Sh'muel said in the name of Rav: "There are three watches in the night, and in each the Holy One, blessed be He, sits and roars like a lion and says: 'Woe to the children because of whose sins I destroyed My House and burnt My Temple and exiled them among the nations of the world.'"

In the hour when Israel enters the synagogues and houses of study and says: "May His Great Name be blessed," the Holy One, blessed be He, shakes His head and says: "Happy the king who is thus praised in his house; woe to the father who exiled his children and woe to the children who were exiled from the table of their father!"

(B. Ber. 3a)

R. Yishma'el Blesses God

R. Yishma'el ben Elisha' the High Priest said: "Once I entered the innermost sanctuary to burn incense, and I saw Aktariel Yah, the Lord of Hosts, sitting on a high and exalted throne. He said to me: 'Yishma'el My son, bless Me!' I said to Him: 'May it be the will before You that Your compassion overcome Your wrath, and that Your compassion overrule Your attributes of justice, and that you deal with Your children with the attribute of compassion, and that You let them enter inside the line of justice.' And he inclined his head toward me."

(B. Ber. 7a)

The Earthquake

Once when Rav Q'tina was on his way, an earthquake struck just as he reached the door of the house of a necromancer who used bones. He said: "Does the necromancer know what is this earthquake?" Thereupon the necromancer called out to him: "Q'tina, Q'tina, why should I not know it? When the Holy One, blessed be He, remembers His children who dwell in misery among the nations of the world, He lets two teardrops fall into the Great Sea and their sound is heard from one end of the world to the other, and this is an earthquake." Rav Q'tina said: "This necromancer is a liar and his words are lies. If he were right, there should be two quakes." But not so; for, in fact, two quakes do come. The true reason why Rav Q'tina disagreed with the necromancer was to prevent the world from going astray after him. And Rav Q'tina himself said that God clapped His hands together.[1] R. Nathan said: "He gives a sigh." The rabbis said: "He kicks the firmament." Rav Aḥa bar Yaʿaqov said: "He stamps His foot under the Throne of Glory."

(B. Ber. 59a)

The Work Day of God

Rav Y'huda said in the name of Rav: "The day has twelve hours. During the first three the Holy One, blessed be He, sits and busies Himself with the Tora. The next three hours He sits and adjudges the whole world. When He sees that the world has become liable to destruction, He rises from the Throne of Judgment and sits on the Throne of Mercy. In the third, He sits and nourishes the whole world, from the horns of the *reem* to the eggs of lice. In the fourth, He sits and plays with Leviathan."

However, Rav Aḥa said: "Since the Temple was de-

---

[1] And this caused the earth to quake.

stroyed, there is no more play for the Holy One, blessed be
He." What then does He do in the final three hours? He sits
and teaches children Tora.

What does He do during the night? If you wish, I say, He
does as He does at daytime; and if you wish, I say, He rides
His light Cherub, and soars across eighteen thousand
worlds; and if you wish, I say, He sits and listens to the song
from the mouths of the heavenly animals.

(B. 'Avoda Zara 3b)

CREATION, EDEN, GEHENNA

The Work of Creation

R. Y'huda bar Pazi expounded: "In the beginning the
world was water in water. How do we know this? [For it is
written:] *The spirit of God hovered over the face of the water*
(Gen. 1:2). Then He made it into snow ... then He made it
into earth. And the earth stands on waters ... and the
waters stand on mountains ... and the mountains stand on
wind ... and the wind is suspended from tempest ... and
the tempest was made by the Holy One, blessed by He, into
a kind of amulet and He hung it on His arm...."

(Y. Ḥagiga 77a mid.)

R. L'azar [El'azar] said: "... This is like unto a king who
built a palace in a place of gutters, in a place of refuse, in a
place of offal. If someone comes and says, 'This palace
stands in a place of gutters, in a place of refuse, in a place of
offal,' does he not offend? Thus he who says, 'In the
beginning the world was water in water,' certainly does
offend."

(Y. Ḥagiga 77c bot.)

The Foundations of the World

R. Yose said: "Woe to the creatures who see and do not
know what they see, who stand and do not know on what

they stand! On what does the earth stand? On pillars ... the pillars on the water ... the water on the mountains ... the mountains on the wind ... the wind on the tempest ... and the tempest is suspended from the arm of the Holy One, blessed be He. ..." And the sages said: "The earth stands on twelve pillars. ..." Others say, on seven pillars. R. El'azar ben Shamu'a said: "On one single pillar and its name is *Tzaddiq* [Righteous], as it is written, *The Tzaddiq is the foundation of the world* (Prov. 10:25)."

(B. Ḥagiga 12b)

The Prince of the Sea

R. Y'huda said in the name of Rav: "In the hour when the Holy One, blessed be He, wanted to create the world, He said to the Prince of the Sea:[2] 'Open your mouth and swallow all the waters that are in the world!'[3] He said before Him: 'Master of the World! It is sufficient [for me] to remain with what I have.' Instantly He kicked him and killed him, as it is written, *With His power he quieteth the sea, and by His understanding He smiteth Rahav* (Job 26:12)." R. Yitzḥaq said: "From here we learn that the name of the Prince of the Sea is Rahav, and were it not for the waters which cover him, no creature could stand its smell."

(B. Baba Bathra 74b)

The Male and Female Waters

R. Levi said: "The Upper Waters are male and the Lower Waters female. What does it mean *Let the earth open* (Isa. 45:8)? Like unto this female who opens up for the male. ..." R. Aḥa taught in the name of R. Shim'on ben Gamliel: "Why is the early rain called *r'vi'a*?[4] Because it copulates with the earth."

(Y. Ber. 14a mid.)

[2] The celestial patron of the sea.

[3] So that the dry land should become visible.

[4] Literally, "copulation."

The Creation of Man

R. Yoḥanan bar Ḥanina said: The day consisted of twelve hours. In the first hour, Adam's dust was gathered; in the second, it was made into a clod; in the third, his limbs were shaped; in the fourth, a soul was cast into him; in the fifth, he arose and stood on his feet; in the sixth, he gave names to the animals; in the seventh, Eve joined him; in the eighth, they ascended to bed as two and descended as four [since Eve conceived Cain and Abel]; in the ninth, he was commanded not to eat of the tree; in the tenth, he sinned; in the eleventh, he was judged; and in the twelfth he was expelled from Eden and departed.

(B. Sanh. 38b)

How the Gazelles Are Born

Knowest thou the time when the gazelles of the rock give birth, or canst thou mark the time when the hinds do calve? (Job 39:1). The gazelle is cruel to her offspring. In the hour when she kneels down to give birth, she goes up to the top of the mountain so that her young should fall down from it and die. But I [God] keep an eagle ready to receive the young upon its wings, and the eagle places it before her. And should the eagle come a moment too early or a moment too late, the young gazelle would instantly die....

As for the hind, her womb is tight. In the hour when she kneels down to give birth, I keep a snake ready for her to bite her at the opening of the womb that it become loose for the birth. And should the snake come a moment too early or a moment too late, the young gazelle would instantly die.

(B. Baba Bathra 16b)

The First Nightfall

The rabbis taught: "On the day on which Adam the first man was created, when the sun set upon him he said: 'Woe is to me, because I sinned,[5] darkness rises up over me, and the world will return to Tohu vaBohu, and this is the death which was decreed upon me from heaven.' He sat fasting and crying all night, and Eve cried opposite him. When the pillar of dawn rose, he said: 'This is the wont of the world.' He stood up and sacrificed an ox whose horns preceded its hooves . . . ."[6]

(B. 'Avoda Zara 8a)

The Shortening of the Days

The rabbis taught: "When Adam the first man saw that the days were growing shorter[7] he said [i.e., thought]: 'Woe is me, perhaps because I have sinned the world grows dark over me and returns to Tohu vaBohu, and this is the death which was decreed upon me from heaven.' He went and sat fasting eight days. When he saw the *Tequfa* of Teveth,[8] and saw that the days were growing longer, he said: 'This is the order of the world.' He went and celebrated eight days of festivity . . . ."

(B. 'Avoda Zara 8a)

The Garden of Eden

Seven things were created before the creation of the world: the Tora, Repentance, the Garden of Eden, Gehenna, the Throne of Glory, the Temple, and the Name of the Messiah.

(B. Pes. 54a)

---

[5] According to Talmudic legend Adam and Eve sinned by eating of the forbidden fruit on the very first day of their lives.

[6] I.e., was created by God with fully grown horns. Ordinary oxen have hooves when born, but their horns grow only later.

[7] As the winter solstice approached.

[8] The winter solstice.

About the Garden of Eden Resh Laqish said: "If it is located in the Land of Israel, its gate is Beth Shean; if in Arabia, its gate is Beth Gerem; and if between the two rivers, its gate is Dumasqanin."

(B. 'Er. 19a)

When Alexander of Macedonia passed by a source, he sat down to eat his bread. He had with him salted fishes, and when he washed them they emitted a fragrance. Thereupon he said: "It would seem that this source comes from the Garden of Eden." Some say that he took from the water and washed his face in it, and some say that he went along the course of water until he reached the gate of Paradise. He raised his voice and cried: "Open me the gate!" He was answered: *"This is the gate of the Lord, the righteous shall enter it"* (Ps. 118:20). He said: "I too am king, and am highly regarded. Give me something!" They gave him a skull. When he subsequently weighed it against all his gold and silver, it outweighed everything. He said to the rabbis: "What is this?" They answered him: "The skull is the [housing of the] eyes of flesh and blood which are never satisfied." He said to them: "What proves this?" Thereupon they took a little earth and covered the skull with it, and it was instantly reduced to its proper weight.

(B. Tam. 32b)

It was taught: It took five hundred years to walk around the Tree of Life. R. Yuda b. Ilai said: "This was not the circumference of its crown, but the size of its trunk. And all the divisions of the waters of Genesis branched out from beneath it . . . ." It was taught: The Tree of Life measured one sixtieth of the Garden, and the Garden one sixtieth of Eden.

(Y. Ber. 2c bot.)

R. Sh'muel b. Nahmani said: "This is Eden which has never been exposed to the eyes of any creature. Should you say,

Where then did Adam dwell? He was in the Garden. Should you say, Are not the Garden and Eden one and the same? Not so, for it says: *'And a river went out of Eden to water the Garden'*—The Garden is one thing and Eden is another."

(B. Ber. 34b)

R. Y'hoshu'a b. Levi said: "The whole world is watered by the residue of the Garden of Eden."

(B. Ta'an. 10a)

Our rabbis taught: The sun is red at sunrise because it passes by the roses of the Garden of Eden; and at sunset, because it passes the gate of Gehenna.

(B. Baba Bathra 84a)

Gehenna

It is taught: The House of Shammai said: There are three classes on the Day of Judgment: one of the totally pious, one of the totally wicked, and one of the intermediate. The totally pious are instantly inscribed and sealed for eternal life; the totally wicked are instantly inscribed and sealed for Gehenna; ... the intermediate descend to Gehenna, and scream, and rise up. ... Those of Israel who sin with their body and those of the heathen who sin with their body descend to Gehenna and are punished there for twelve months. After twelve months their bodies are consumed, their soul is burnt, and a wind scatters them under the soles of the feet of the pious. ... But the heretics, and the informers, and the unbelievers who deny the Tora, and those who deny the Resurrection of the Dead, and those who turned aside from the ways of the community, and those who spread terror in the land of the living, and those who sin and cause the public to sin like Jeroboam ben Nevat and his comrades, descend into Gehenna and are punished there for countless generations. ... Gehenna will cease, but they will not cease.

(B. Rosh. Hash. 16b-17a)

R. Yohanan said: "Every drop that the Holy One, blessed be He, let fall upon the generation of the Deluge He first brought to a boil in Gehenna and then poured it over them...." Both Y'huda son of R. Hizqiya and Rabbi said: "The Holy One, blessed be He, punishes the wicked in Gehenna for twelve months. First he causes a cold to enter them, and then He makes them enter the fire, and they say, 'Hoy, hoy!' And then He makes them enter snow, and they say, 'Woe, woe!' "

(Y. Sanh. 29b bot.)

R. Yirm'ya bar El'azar said: "Gehenna has three gates: one in the desert, one in the sea, and one in Jerusalem...."

In the name of the Rabban Yohanan ben Zakkai it was taught: "There are two palm trees in the Valley of Ben Hinnom, and smoke ascends from between them . . . and there is the gate of Gehenna...."

(B. Er. 19a)

The Work of the Chariot [9]

Once Rabban Yohanan ben Zakkai was traveling on the road, riding on an ass, and Rabbi El'azar ben 'Arakh was walking behind him on foot. Rabbi El'azar said to Rabban Yohanan: "Rabbi, teach me a chapter in the Work of the Chariot." Rabban Yohanan answered him: "Did not the sages warn that one is not allowed to teach about the Chariot unless the student is wise and understands it himself?" El'azar thereupon said to him: "Rabbi, allow me, then, to say something before you." He said to him: "Speak." As soon as Rabbi El'azar ben 'Arakh began discussing the Work of the Chariot, Rabban Yohanan ben Zakkai got off the ass, saying: "It is not seemly that I should listen to the glory of my Creator while riding on an ass."

[9] This Talmudic term refers to God's throne of glory, which, following Ezekiel 1, was imagined as a combination of a throne and a chariot.

They went and sat down under a tree, and fire descended from heaven and enveloped them, and ministering angels danced before them like people attending a wedding who rejoice before the bridegroom. One angel spoke up from the midst of the fire and said: "As you say, El'azar ben 'Arakh, so indeed is the Work of the Chariot." Instantly all the trees opened their mouths and sang the song, *Then shall all the trees of the wood sing for joy* (Ps. 96:12).

When Rabbi El'azar ben 'Arakh finished discussing the Work of the Chariot, Rabban Yoḥanan ben Zakkai stood up, kissed him on his forehead and said: "Blessed be the Lord, God of Abraham, Isaac, and Jacob, who gave our Father Abraham a wise son who knows how to expound the glory of our Father in heaven! There are those who expound beautifully but do not fulfill the commandments beautifully, and there are those who fulfill beautifully but do not expound beautifully. El'azar ben 'Arakh, however, expounds beautifully and fulfills beautifully. Happy are you, our Father Abraham, that from your loins issued El'azar ben 'Arakh!"

When Rabbi Yosef haKohen and Rabbi Shim'on ben N'tan'el heard this, they too began discussing the Work of the Chariot. They say that it was a day in the period of Tammuz [midsummer], and the earth trembled, and the rainbow appeared in the clouds, and a heavenly voice was heard saying to them: "Behold, the place is vacant for you, and the banqueting couch is spread for you, you and your disciples are invited to be of the Third Party ... of the seven Parties of the Pious in the Future Time."

(Y. Ḥagiga 77a)

The Four Who Entered Paradise

The rabbis taught: "Four entered the *Pardes,*[10] and they are:

---

[10] *Pardes* is the same word as Paradise, both being derived from the Persian. In Hebrew it generally means "orchard," but here it refers to metaphysical and mystical studies.

Ben ʿAzzai, Ben Zoma, Aḥer,[11] and R. Akiba." R. Akiba said to them: "When you reach the stones of pure marble, say not, 'Water, water,' for it is written, *He that speaketh falsehoods shall not be established before Mine eyes* (Ps. 101:7).[12] Ben ʿAzzai gazed about and died. . . . Ben Zoma gazed about and was stricken. . . .[13] Aḥer cut down shoots.[14] R. Akiba came out in peace.

(B. Ḥagiga 14b)

The Death of Ben Zoma

Once when Rabbi Y'hoshuʿa was walking on the road, he saw Ben Zoma approaching him. Rabbi Y'hoshuʿa greeted him, but Ben Zoma did not respond. Rabbi Y'hoshuʿa asked: "From where and where to, Ben Zoma?" He then answered: "I was contemplating the Work of Creation, and found that there was between the Upper Waters and the Lower Waters not more than a handbreadth. It is written here 'hovering' (Gen. 1:2), and elsewhere it is written, *As an eagle that stirreth up her nest, hovereth over her young* (Deut. 32:11). Just as the hovering mentioned there means touching and yet not touching, so the hovering mentioned here means touching and yet not touching." Rabbi Y'hoshuʿa said to his disciples: "Alas, already Ben Zoma is outside." and within a few days Ben Zoma passed away.

(Y. Ḥagiga 77a-b)

---

[11] Aḥer (lit. "Another") is the name given to R. Elishaʿ ben Abuya after he had become an apostate, and the rabbis refused to refer to him by his own name.

[12] R. Akiba here warns his colleagues against referring to the watery state of the world prior to Creation which was considered offensive to God. Cf. Y. Ḥagiga 77c bot.

[13] Probably meaning that he lost his mind.

[14] I.e., attacked the basic doctrines of Judaism.

SEA LORE

The Tall Tales of Rabba bar Bar Ḥana[15]

Rabba said: "The seafarers told me: The wave which sinks the ship appears to have a white fiery edge on its top. And we beat it with a stick on which is engraved '*I am that I am* (Exod. 3:14), Amen, Amen, Selah,' and it subsides."

Rabba said: "The seafarers told me: Between wave and wave there are three hundred parasangs, and the height of a wave is three hundred parasangs. Once we were on a trip and a wave lifted us up until we could see the resting place of a small star, and it had the area upon which forty measures of mustard seed could be sown. And had it lifted us higher, we would have been roasted by its breath. And one wave called to its companion: 'My comrade, have you left anything in the world which you did not inundate? So let me go and annihilate it!' He said to him: 'Go and see the might of your Master. I cannot cross over the sand even as much as the thickness of a thread. . . .'"

Rabba said: "I myself saw a one-day-old gazelle which was like Mount Tabor. And how big is Mount Tabor? Four parasangs. And the size of its neck was three parasangs, and the resting place of its head was one and a half parasangs. When it eliminated, its excrement dammed up the Jordan."

And Rabba bar Bar Ḥana said: "I myself saw a frog which was like the fort of Hagronya. And how big is the fort of Hagronya? Sixty houses. A snake came and swallowed it. A raven came and swallowed the snake. And it went and sat on a tree. Come and see how strong that tree was." Rav Papa bar Sh'muel said: "Had I not been there I would not have believed it."[16]

And Rabba bar Bar Ḥana said: "At one time we were

---

[15] These stories can be compared to tall tales told by seamen from Marseilles and other ports.

[16] Evidently a sarcastic statement.

traveling on a ship and we saw a dead fish in whose nostril a little worm had lodged. The water washed the fish ashore. From it sixty cities were destroyed, and from it sixty cities ate, and from it sixty cities salted meat, and from one of its eyeballs they filled three hundred barrels with oil. And when we returned after a twelve-month year we saw that they had sawed its bones into beams and rebuilt from them those cities."

And Rabba bar Bar Ḥana said: "At one time we were traveling on a ship and saw a fish upon whose back sand had settled and a meadow grew out of it. We thought it was dry land and went up, and baked and cooked on its back. And when it felt the heat, it turned over, and had the ship not been nearby we would have drowned."

And Rabba bar Bar Ḥana said: "At one time we traveled on a ship, and the ship sailed between one fin and the other fin of a fish three days and three nights. The fish swam in one direction, and we in the opposite." And should you think that the ship did not sail fast, when Rav Dimi came he said: "While a kettle of water was brought to boil it sailed sixty parasangs. When a hunter shot an arrow, the ship overtook it." And Rav Ashi said: "It was but a sea *gildana* [a small fish] which has only two fins."[17]

And Rabba bar Bar Ḥana said: "At one time we were going in a ship and saw a bird which stood in the water up to its ankles and its head was in the firmament. And we said: 'There is no deep water here,' and we wanted to go down to cool ourselves. But a heavenly voice issued forth and said to us: 'Do not get out here, for a carpenter dropped an axe here seven years ago and it still has not hit the bottom. Not because the water is deep but because of the strong currents.'" Rav Ashi said: "That was the *Ziz Sadai*."[18]

And Rabba bar Bar Ḥana said: "At one time we were

---

[17] Another sarcastic comment.

[18] A huge legendary bird, cf. Ps. 50:11.

traveling in the desert and saw geese whose feathers had fallen out because of their fat and under which a stream of fat flowed. We said to them: 'Will we have a share of you in the World to Come?' One of them lifted up its wing, and another its thigh."[19]

And Rabba bar Bar Ḥana said: "At one time we were traveling in the desert and an Arab nomad attached himself to us. He took up some dust, smelled it and said: 'This road leads to a certain place.' We said to him: 'How far are we from water?' He said to us: 'Give me dust.' We gave him, and he said: 'Eight parasangs.' Later we gave him dust a second time. He said that we were three parasangs away. We exchanged the dust from different places, but could not mislead him.

"He said to me: 'Come, I shall show you the dead of the desert.'[20] I went and saw them, and they looked like people who had gotten intoxicated and were lying on their backs. One of them had his knee propped up, and the Arab, riding on his camel and holding his lance upright, passed under his knee and did not touch him. I cut off the corner of the purple-blue Tallith of one of them, and we could not advance. He said to me: 'Perhaps you took something from them? Return it, for it has been made known to us that he who takes anything from them cannot go away from here.' I went and returned it, and we were able to go on.

"The Arab then said to me: 'Come, I shall show you Mount Sinai.' I went and saw that it was surrounded by scorpions which stood about like white asses. I heard a heavenly voice which said: 'Woe to Me that I swore to exile the Children of Israel; and now that I have sworn, who will release Me from My vow?' When I came before the rabbis, they said to me: 'Every Abba[21] is an ass, and every bar Bar Ḥana is a fool. You should have said, 'You are released!' "

"He said to me: 'Come, I shall show you the ravines of

[19] To indicate the portions of the questioners.

[20] The generation which came out of Egypt and died in the desert.

[21] The name Rabba is considered a contraction of R. Abba.

Korah.'²² I saw two crevices and they belched smoke. The
Arab took a ball of wool, dipped it in water, and stuck it
onto the tip of his lance and held it there. And when he
pulled it back, it was singed. He said to me: 'Listen to what
you hear.' And I heard that they were saying, 'Moses and
his Tora are true and we are liars.' He said to me: 'Every
thirty days Gehenna brings them back here, like meat in a
caldron, and they say this: Moses and his Tora are true and
we are liars.'

"He said to me: 'Come, I shall show you where the earth
and heaven kiss each other.' I took my bread basket and put
it into the window of heaven. After I had prayed, I looked
for it, but could not find it. I said to him: 'Are there thieves
here?' He said to me: 'The wheel of heaven has turned
away. Wait here until tomorrow, and you will find it.' "

(B. Baba Bathra 73a-74a)

Other Tall Tales of the Sea

R. Yoḥanan related: "At one time we were going in a ship
and saw a fish which stuck its head out of the sea, and its
eyes were like two moons, and it blew water out of its two
nostrils like the two streams of Sura."

Rav Safra related: "At one time we were going in a ship
and saw a fish which stuck its head out of the sea, and it had
horns, and on them was engraved, 'I am a small creature in
the sea and I measure three hundred parasangs, and I am
going into the mouth of Leviathan.'" Rav Ashi said: "That
was the sea goat which searches for food and has horns."

R. Yoḥanan related: "At one time we were going on a
ship, and we saw a box which was full of precious stones
and pearls, and wound around it was a kind of fish called
karsha. A diver went down to fetch it, and the *karsha*
noticed him and wanted to bite his hip. But he threw a skin
of vinegar at it and it swam off. A heavenly voice issued

²² Which swallowed up Korah and his cohorts; cf. Num. 16:31-32.

forth and said to us: 'What do you want with this box of the wife of R. Ḥanina ben Dosa, who will in the future put the purple-blue into it for the pious in the World to Come?' "

R. Y'huda of India related: "At one time we were going on a ship and saw a precious stone around which a sea dragon had wound itself. A diver went down to fetch it. The sea dragon came and wanted to swallow the ship. A raven came and bit off his head. The water turned to blood. Another sea dragon, its comrade, came, took the precious stone, put it on him, and he came alive. He came, wanted to swallow the ship. Again, a bird came, bit off his head. The diver took the precious stone, threw it into the ship. There were there salted birds with us. We put the precious stone upon them. They took it and flew off with it."

The rabbis taught: "It happened to R. Eliezer and R. Y'hoshu‘a that they were coming in a ship, and R. Eliezer was asleep and R. Y'hoshu‘a was awake. R. Y'hoshu‘a gave a start and R. Eliezer woke up. He said to him: 'What is it, Y'hoshu‘a, why did you give a start?' He said to him: 'I saw a great luminary in the sea.' He said to him: 'Perhaps you saw the eyes of Leviathan, as it is written, *His eyes are like the eyelids of the morning* (Job 41:10).

(B. Baba Bathra 74a-b)

ANGELS AND DEMONS

The Two Angels

It was taught: R. Yose bar Y'huda said: Two ministering angels accompany man on the eve of the Sabbath from the synagogue to his home; one a good angel and one an evil one. And when he arrives home and finds the candle burning, the table laid, and his bed made up, the good angel exclaims, "May it be the will of God that it be even thus on another Sabbath," and the evil angel unwillingly responds, "Amen." But if not, the evil angel exclaims,

"May it be the will of God that it be thus on another Sabbath," and the good angel unwillingly responds, "Amen."

(B. Shabbath 119b)

The Kiss of the Shekhina

The Rabbis taught: There were six over whom the Angel of Death had no power. They were Abraham, Isaac, and Jacob; Moses, Aaron, and Miriam... R. El'azar said: "Miriam, too, like Moses, died through a kiss of the Shekhina."

(B. Baba Bathra 17a)

Ilfa and R. Yoḥanan

Ilfa and R. Yoḥanan were studying the Tora. They were lacking sustenance. They said: "Let us go and engage in business and provide for ourselves, and we shall make the verse *There shall be no needy among you* (Deut. 15:4) come true for us." They went and sat under a ruined wall and ate bread. Two ministering angels came, and R. Yoḥanan heard one of them saying to the other: "Let us throw this wall upon them and kill them, for they have abandoned the life eternal and occupy themselves with the life of the hour." The other angel said to him: "Let us leave them alone, for there is one of them for whom the hour is favorable."[23] R. Yoḥanan heard this but Ilfa did not. R. Yoḥanan said to Ilfa: "Did you hear anything?" He said to him: "No." He said to himself: "Since I heard it and Ilfa did not, this indicates that it is for me that the hour is favorable." And he said to Ilfa: "I am turning back and fulfill on myself the verse, *For the poor shall never cease out of the land* (Deut. 15:11)" R. Yoḥanan returned and Ilfa did not return. When at last Ilfa returned, R. Yoḥanan ruled.[24]

[23] I.e., one of them will become great in the Tora.
[24] I.e., was head of the yeshiva.

They said to Ilfa: "Had you remained here and studied, you would have ruled."

(B. Ta'anith 21a)

The Evil Inclination

And the land shall mourn...(Zech. 12:12). What is the reason for this mourning? R. Dosa and the rabbis differ on it. R. Dosa says: "They will mourn over the Messiah who will be slain," and the rabbis say: "They will mourn over the Evil Inclination which will be killed."...Rabbi Y'huda explained: "In the future time[25] the Holy One, blessed be He, will bring the Evil Inclination and slaughter it in front of the pious and in front of the wicked. To the pious it will appear like a high mountain, and to the wicked it will appear like a thread of hair, and both will cry. The pious will cry and say: 'How were we able to conquer such a high mountain?' And the wicked will cry and say: 'How were we unable to conquer this thread of hair?'"

(B. Suk. 52a)

The Angel of Death

Resh Laqish said: "Satan, the Evil Inclination, and the Angel of Death are one and the same."... In a Baraitha it is taught: He descends and leads astray, ascends and accuses, obtains permission and takes the soul.

(B. Baba Bathra 16a)

The rabbis taught: When there is an epidemic in town, one should not walk in the middle of the street, as the Angel of Death walks then in the middle of the streets: since permission has been granted him he walks about openly. When there is peace in town, one should not walk along the sides of the streets: since the Angel of Death has no permission he hides as he stalks.

[25] I.e., in the Messianic days.

The rabbis taught: When there is an epidemic in town one should not enter the synagogue alone, for the Angel of Death keeps his gear there. This, however, applies only to a synagogue in which no children study and no ten men pray.

The rabbis taught: When dogs howl, the Angel of Death has come to town. When dogs frolic, the prophet Elijah has come to town. This is so, however, only if there is no female among the dogs.

(B. Baba Qama 60b)

They said about the Angel of Death that he is all full of eyes. When the hour comes for a sick person to die, he positions himself above his head with his sword drawn in his hand, and a drop of gall hangs on it. When the sick person sees him, he trembles [with fear] and opens his mouth, whereupon the Angel flings the drop into his mouth. From it he dies, from it he putrefies, from it his face turns green.

(B. 'Av. Zar. 20a)

Rava was sitting in front of R. Naḥman as the latter lay in the throes of death. R. Naḥman said to him: "O Master, tell the Angel of Death that he should not torture me." Rava answered him: "O Master, are you not an important man?"[26] He said: "Who is important, who is honored, who is respected by the Angel of Death?" Rava then asked him: "O Master, appear to me after your death!" He appeared to him. Rava asked him: "O Master, did you suffer pain when your soul departed?" He answered: "It was like the removing of a hair from the milk. But if the Holy One, blessed be He, should say to me, 'You can go back into that world,' I would not do it, so great is the fear of the Angel of Death."

(B. Mo. Qat. 28a)

---

[26] Therefore you yourself could influence the Angel of Death.

Elihoreph and Ahijah were two scribes of Solomon. One day he saw the Angel of Death looking at them and grinding his teeth in anger. Thereupon the king uttered a magic word and therewith transported them into a cave so as to protect them. But the Angel of Death went and took them from there. Then he went and stood before Solomon and grinned at him. Solomon said to him: "Earlier you gnashed your teeth, and now you grin at us?" He answered him: "The Merciful One commanded me to take Elihoreph and Ahijah from the cave, and I thought, Who will put these two into the place from which I am sent to take them? And He put it into your heart to do so, so that I be able to accomplish my task." Thereupon Solomon went and took their bodies from there to take care of their funeral.

(Y. Kil. 9, 32c)

The Angel of Death has no permission to enter the City of Luz. Instead, the old people who dwell there, when they become weary of life, go outside the wall and die.

(B. Sot. 46a)

The Angel of Death was unable to approach R. Hiyya. One day he took the appearance of a beggar, and knocked on his door saying: "Give me some bread!" They gave him, and the Angel of Death said to him: "O Master, you have pity on a beggar, why have you no pity on me?"[27] And he revealed himself to him and showed him a rod of fire. Thereupon R. Hiyya surrendered his soul.

(B. Mo. Qat. 28a)

When the time came for R. Y'hoshu'a b. Levi to die, the Angel of Death was told: "Go and have your will on him!" He went and showed himself to R. Y'hoshu'a who said to him: "Show me my place in the Other World." The Angel said: "All right." R. Y'hoshu'a said: "Give me your knife,

---

[27] I.e., why do you not let me do my job?

for I may be affrighted by it while on the way." He gave it
to him. When they arrived there, the Angel lifted up R.
Y'hoshu'a over the wall of Paradise and showed him his
place. Whereupon R. Y'hoshu'a jumped over to the other
side. But the Angel of Death got hold of the corner of his
robe. R. Y'hoshu'a said: "I swear that I shall not return!"
The Holy One, blessed be He, said: "If he ever had an oath
of his annulled, he must return; but if not, he does not have
to." The Angel of Death said to him: "Give me back my
knife!" But he did not give it back to him. Then a heavenly
voice was heard saying to him: "Return it to him for it is
needed for the creatures!" Elijah announced in front of
him: "Make room for the son of Levi! Make room for the
son of Levi!"

(B. Ket. 77a)

R. Ḥanina bar Papa was an intimate of the Angel of Death.
When the time came for his soul to rest, they said to the
Angel of Death: "Go, have your will on him!" He went to
him and showed himself to him. R. Ḥanina said to him:
"Give me thirty days to go over my studies, for they say,
Hail to him who comes here bringing his studies with
him!" He granted him his request, and when the thirty
days were up he came and showed himself again. R. Ḥanina
said to him: "Show me my place!" He said to him: "All
right." R. Ḥanina said: "Give me your knife, lest I become
frightened on the way." The Angel said to him: "You want
to do to me as your colleague did!" R. Ḥanina said: "Bring a
Tora scroll and see whether there is anything written in it
which I did not fulfill." The Angel said to him: "Have you
embraced those afflicted with *Ra'athan* (a skin disease) and
studied the Tora (as R. Y'hoshu'a ben Levi did)?" And
nevertheless, when he was about to die, a pillar of fire
separated him from the rest of the world, and it is known
that such a separation through a pillar of fire only takes
place when a man dies who is either unique in his
generation or had only one counterpart. Thereupon R.

Alexandri approached R. Ḥanina and said to him: "Acquiesce in your death, for the honor of the sages." But he did not listen to him. "Do it for the honor of your father." But he did not listen to him. "Do it for your own honor." Thereupon he died.

(B. Ket. 77b)

A messenger was sent to fetch the soul of Rabba bar Naḥmani. But the Angel of Death could not approach him because he did not interrupt his studies even for one moment. Then a wind blew up and howled between the branches, and he thought it was a troop of horsemen. He said: "Let me die rather than be delivered into the hands of the pagan authority." As he was dying he exclaimed: "Clean, clean!" A heavenly voice was heard: "Happy are you, O Rabba bar Naḥmani, for your body is pure and your soul departed in purity!" A tablet fell from the firmament in Pumbeditha and upon it was written: "Rabba bar Naḥmani has been summoned to the heavenly academy."

(B. Bab. Metz. 86a)

Rav Joseph wept when he came to this verse: *But some are swept away without judgment* (Prov. 13:23). He said: "Is there anyone who passes away before his time?" Yes, as in the story of Rav Bibi bar Abbaye, who had frequent contact with the Angel of Death. Once the Angel of Death said to his messenger: "Go, fetch me Miriam the women's hairdresser!" He went and brought him Miriam the children's nurse. He said to him: "But I told you Miriam the women's hairdresser!" He answered, "If so, I shall take her back." But he said to him: "Since you have brought her, let her remain. But how were you able to overpower her?" He answered: "She took a shovel in her hand and raked the oven, and then, when she put the shovel on her knee, she burnt herself, whereupon her star (luck) was shaken, and so I brought her." Rav Bibi bar Abbaye said to him: "Have you permission to act thus?" He answered him: "Is it not written, *Some are swept away without judgment?*"

(B. Hag. 4b-5a)

R. Y'hoshu'a ben Levi said: "Three things were told to me by the Angel of Death: Do not take your robe in the morning from the hands of a servant to put it on; do not wash your hands with the help of somebody who has not yet washed his hands; and do not stand before the women when they return from a funeral, for I come and dance before them with my sword in my hand, and I have permission to destroy...."

(B. Ber. 51a)

Lilith

Lilith is a demoness who has a human face and has wings.

(B. Nid. 24b and Rashi, ibid.)

Lilith has long hair.

(B. Er. 100b)

Rabbi Ḥanina said: "It is forbidden to sleep alone in a house, for he who sleeps alone in a house, Lilith gets hold of him."

(B. Shab. 151b)

Rabba bar Bar Ḥana said: "Once I saw Hormin [Ahriman] son of Lilith run on top of the battlements of the wall of Mahoza. And a horseman was riding beneath the wall and could not overtake him. At one time they saddled for him [Hormin] two mules on two bridges of the river Rognag, and he jumped from the one to the other, back and forth, and all the time held in his hands two cups of wine and poured the wine from the one into the other, and not a drop fell to the earth. And that day was [stormy like the one of which it is written] *They [the waves] mounted up to heaven, they went down to the deeps* (Ps. 107:26). And when the house of government [of the demons] heard about this, they put him to death [because it is not done among the demons to show themselves to humans, and he uncovered their secrets]."

(B. Bab. Bath. 73a-b, and Rashi, ibid.)

Rabbi Yirm'ya ben El'azar said: "All those years in which Adam the first man was in isolation from Eve he begat spirits and demons and Lilin...." Rabbi Meir said: "Adam the first man was very pious. When he saw that through him the punishment of death was ordained, he sat in fasting for 130 years, and separated himself from the woman for 130 years, and put fig belts on his flesh for 130 years. But we are talking [about spirits, demons, and Lilin] whom he begot through spontaneous emission of seed."

(B. Er. 18b)

Solomon, Ashmodai, and the Shamir

Solomon said: *I got me... male demons and female demons* [28] (Eccles. 2:8).... What for did he need them?

For it is written, *The Temple when it was in building was built of whole stones, and there was neither hammer nor axe nor any tool of iron heard in the House while it was in building* (1 Kings 6:7).[29] Solomon said to the rabbis: "How can this be accomplished?" They said to him: "There is the Shamir,[30]

---

[28] This is the Talmudic interpretation of *shidda w'shiddot* in Eccles. 2:8 whose original meaning is unclear.

[29] The rabbis explain that iron, of which swords, instruments of killing, are made, could not be used in building the Temple, the holy house of God.

[30] Rashi explains: "A creature from the six days of Creation which no hard object can resist." It seems to have been imagined as a worm, the size of a barleycorn. Cf. B. Sota 48b.

which Moses took to cut the stones of the Ephod."[31] He said to them: "Where can it be found?" They said to him: "Bring a male demon and female demons, pressure them, perhaps they know and will reveal it to you." He brought a male demon and female demons, and pressured them. They said: "We do not know it. Perhaps Ashmodai, the king of the demons, knows." He said to them: "Where can he be found?" They said to him: "He can be found on a certain mountain. He has dug himself a cistern and filled it with water and covered it with a rock and sealed it with his seal, and every day he goes up to the firmament and studies in the academy of the firmament, and then comes down to the earth and studies in the academy of the earth. And he examines his seal, and uncovers the pit, and drinks, and recovers it and seals it, and goes away."

Solomon dispatched Benayahu ben Yehoyada. He gave him a chain on which was engraved the Name, and a ring on which was engraved the Name, and balls of wool, and skins of wine. He went, dug a pit under it, and let the water run out, then plugged it up with the balls of wool, and dug a pit over it and poured into it the wine and plugged it up. Then he went and climbed up a tree.

When Ashmodai came, he examined the seal, uncovered it, found wine in it, and said: "It is written, *Wine is a mocker, strong drink is riotous, and whosoever reeleth thereby is not wise* (Prov. 20:1), and it is written, *Harlotry, wine and new wine take away the heart* (Hos. 4:11). I shall not drink." When he became thirsty, he could not resist; he drank, became drunk, and lay down to sleep.

Then Benayahu approached, put the chain around him, and locked it. When he awoke and struggled, Benayahu said to him: "The Name of your Master is upon you! The Name of your Master is upon you!" Then he seized him and led him away. . . .

---

[31] The twelve precious stones on the breastplate of Aaron, cf. B. Sota 48b.

When they came to Solomon's court, they did not bring him to Solomon for three days.... When he was finally brought before the king, he took a reed, measured four cubits, and threw it before him. He said to him: "When you die, you will have nothing in this world but four cubits of the grave. But now you have subjugated the whole world, and were not satisfied until you have subjugated me too." He said to him: "I want nothing of you. I want to build the Temple and need the Shamir." He said to him: "It is not entrusted to me. It is in entrusted to the Prince of the Sea,[32] and he gives it to nobody except the wild cock on whom he relies because of its oath that he will return the Shamir to him."

"And what does the wild cock do with it?" "It takes it to mountains which have no vegetation, and places it upon the ridge of the mountain, and the mountain splits open, and it takes seeds from trees and casts them there and they grow." This is why we translate the name of the wild cock "mountain splitter."

They searched for the nest of the wild cock which had the young in it and covered the nest with a clear glass. When it came it tried to enter the nest but could not. It went, brought the Shamir, and placed it on it. They then gave a loud shout, and the wild cock dropped the Shamir. Thereupon it went and strangled itself because of its oath.

Solomon kept Ashmodai with him until he built the Temple. One day he was alone with him and said to him: " ... In what way are you demons superior to us humans?" He said to him: "Remove my chains and give me your ring, and I shall show you my superiority." He removed his chains and gave him his ring. He swallowed it, set one of his wings into the firmament and the other into the earth, and hurled Solomon to a distance of hour hundred parasangs. Solomon made the round of doors begging, and wherever he came he said, *I, Koheleth, was king over Israel in Jerusalem*

---

[32] The Prince of the Sea is the mythical heavenly ruler of the sea.

(Eccles. 1:12). When he came to the Sanhedrin, the rabbis said: "Since a fool does not constantly repeat the same thing, what can this mean?" They said to Benayahu: "Does the king ask you to come to him?" He said to them: "No." They sent to the queens: "Does the king come to you?" They sent them the reply: "Yes, he does come." They sent word to them: "Observe his feet."[33] They replied that he was coming in stockings, and that he demanded to have sex with them at the time of their menstrual impurity, and demanded it also from his mother Bathsheba.

They went to Solomon, and gave him a ring and a chain upon which the Name was engraved. When he entered, Ashmodai saw him and flew away.

(B. Gittin 68a-b)

The Curious Acts of Ashmodai

[While Benayahu led Ashmodai in his chains] they came to a palm tree. Ashmodai rubbed against it and uprooted it. They came to a house, and he made it collapse. They came to the hut of a widow; she came out and begged him not to destroy it. Thereupon he twisted his shoulder away from it and a bone broke in his body. He said: "This is what is written, *A soft tongue breaketh the bone* (Prov. 25:15)." He saw a blind man err about on the road, and he set him right on his way. He saw a drunk err about on the road, and he set him right on his way. He saw people rejoicing at a wedding, and he wept. He heard a man say to the cobbler, "Make me shoes for seven years," and he laughed. He saw a magician make magic, and he laughed.

Upon arriving at Solomon's court, they did not bring him to Solomon for three days. The first day he said to them: "Why did the king not ask for me?" They said to him: "He was prevented by drinking." He took a brick and placed it

---

[33] According to Talmudic belief the demons had birds' feet which they could not change. Cf. B. Ber. 6a.

on top of another. They went and told Solomon. He said to them: "This is what he meant: 'Go, give him more.'" Next day he said to them: "And why did the king not ask for me today?" They said to him: "He was prevented by eating." He took the brick off the other and placed it on the ground. They went and told Solomon. He said to them: "This is what he meant: 'Go, take the food away from him.'" Finally, on the third day he was brought before the king.

Benayahu asked him: "Why, when you saw the blind man lost on the road, did you set him on his way?" He said to him: "It was proclaimed about him in heaven that he was a completely righteous man, and he who performed a service for him would merit the World to Come."

"And why, when you saw that drunk lost on the road, did you set him on his way?" He said to him: "It was proclaimed about him in heaven that he was a totally wicked man, and I performed a service for him so that he should consume his world."[34]

"And why did you cry when you saw that rejoicing?" He said to him: "The groom was destined to die within thirty days, and the bride was destined to wait thirteen years for her minor brother-in-law."[35]

"And why did you laugh when you heard that man say to the cobbler that he should make him shoes for seven years?" He said to him: "He had not even seven days left to live, and wanted shoes for seven years."

"And why did you laugh when you saw that magician make magic?" He said to him: "He was sitting on top of a royal treasure; he should have conjured up what was beneath him."

---

[34] I.e., he should have nothing left by way of rewards in the Other World.

[35] Until he would reach adulthood and could perform the *Halitza* ritual for her, thereby setting her free to marry again.

BIBLICAL HEROES

Human and Divine Beauty

R. Banaa[36] marked the burial caves.[37] When he came to the cave of Abraham, he encountered Eliezer the servant of Abraham standing before the door. He said to him: "What is Abraham doing?" He said to him: "He lies between the arms of Sarah, and she contemplates his head." He said to him: "Go and tell him that Banaa is at the door." Abraham said to him: "Let him enter, for it is well known that there is no evil inclination in this world."[38] He entered, looked, and exited.

When he came to the cave of Adam the first man, a heavenly voice issued forth and said: "You saw the likeness of My image [i.e., Abraham], but My image itself [Adam] you cannot see." "But I must mark the cave!" "The measure of the outside equals the measure of the inside...."

R. Banaa said: "I looked at Adam's two heels, and they seemed like two wheels of the sun." Before Sarah all others are like apes before Adam. Adam before the Shekhina is like an ape before Adam.

(B. Baba Bathra 58a)

Eve and the Serpent

When the serpent mounted Eve, he injected filth into her. Israel who stood at Mount Sinai, their filth ceased; the

---

[36] One of the great men of his age to whom permission was given to enter the tomb of the patriarchs.

[37] The tombs were caves in mountainsides. R. Banaa measured them inside and then marked the corresponding area over them outside so as to demarcate the area which, if a person entered it, would render him ritually unclean.

[38] I.e., there is no sexuality in the World to Come, and hence no need to be reticent because of Sarah's presence.

other nations who did not stand at Mount Sinai, their filth
has not ceased....

(B. Shab. 146a)

The Generation of the Deluge

The Rabbis taught: The generation of the Deluge became
overbearing because of the benefits with which the Holy
One, blessed be He, showered them.... They said: "We do
not need Him at all, except perhaps for the drops of rain.
But we have rivers and wells which satisfy our demands."
The Holy One, blessed be He, said: "Since they anger Me
with the benefits I showered upon them, I shall punish
them with the same...." R. Yose said: "The generation of
the Deluge became overbearing because of the eyeball
which is like water, therefore He punished them with
water...." R. Yohanan said: "They caused domestic
animals to copulate with wild beasts, and beasts with
animals, and all of them with man, and man with all of
them."

(B. Sanhedrin 108a)

How the Phoenix Became Immortal

Rav Ḥana bar Bizna said: "Eliezer said to Shem the Elder:[39]
"How did you manage in the ark?" He said to him: "We
had great trouble in the ark. The creatures which were used
to eating by day, we fed by day; those which were used to
eating by night, we fed by night. As for the *zaqita*,[40] father
did not know what it ate. One day he was sitting and
cutting open a pomegranate. A worm fell out of it. The
zaqita ate it. Thenceforth he mashed up reeds for it and

---

[39] The eldest son of Noah. The Talmud, typically, overlooks the time
element: Abraham, whose servant was Eliezer, lived ten generations after Noah!

[40] Probably the chameleon.

when they became wormy it ate them. The lion was stricken by fever and hence ate nothing. As for the phoenix, father found him in a corner of the ark. He said to him: "Don't you want to eat?" He said to him: "I saw you were too busy, so I did not want to trouble you." He said to him: "May it be the will of God that you should never die!"

(B. Sanhedrin 108b)

The Vindication

R. Levi said: "On the day on which Abraham weaned his son Isaac he gave a great banquet. All the nations of the world were whispering and saying: "Did you see that old man and that old woman who brought a foundling from the marketplace and now say, He is our son? And not only that, but they are giving a great banquet to make us believe their words." What did our father Abraham do? He went and invited all the notables of the generation, and our mother Sarah invited their wives, and each one of them brought along her child but did not bring along her wetnurse. And a miracle occurred to our mother Sarah, and her breasts opened up like two springs, and she suckled all of them. But still they were whispering and saying: "If ninety-year-old Sarah gave birth, could hundred-year-old Abraham beget?" Instantly the features of Isaac's face changed and he became similar to Abraham. They all proclaimed and said: *Abraham begot Isaac* (Gen. 25:19).

(B. Baba Metzia 87a)

Abraham the Astrologer

R. Eliezer of Moda'im said: "Astrology was in the heart of our father Abraham, so that all the kings of the East and of the West frequented his doorstep." R. Shim'on ben Yoḥai said: "A precious stone hung from the neck of our father Abraham. All the sick who looked at it were instantly healed. And when Abraham passed away from the world, the Holy One, blessed be He, hanged it upon the wheel of the sun."

Abbaye said: "This is why people say, when the day breaks, sickness breaks."[41]

(B. Baba Bathra 16b)

Eliezer in Sodom

There were four judges in Sodom: Liar, Prevaricator, Falsifier, and Misjudger. If somebody struck his fellow man's wife and she miscarried, they said to the woman's husband: "Give her to him until he makes her pregnant." If somebody cut off the ear of his fellow's ass, they said to the owner of the ass: "Give it to him until the ear grows back." If somebody wounded his fellow, they said to the one who sustained the wound: "Give him a payment for having bled you." He who crossed a river on a ferry[42] paid four *Zuzim.* He who waded through the water had to pay eight *Zuzim.*

Once a launderer happened to come there. They said to him: "Pay four *Zuzim.*" He said to them: "I came through the water." They said to him: "Pay eight *Zuzim,* since you crossed in the water." He did not pay. He [the ferryman] wounded him. He went before the judge. He said to him: "Pay him for having bled you, and [pay him] eight *Zuzim* for having come through the water."

Eliezer the servant of Abraham happened to come there. They wounded him. He went before the judge. The judge said to him: "Pay him for having bled you." Eliezer took a stone and wounded the judge. The judge said to him: "What is this?" He answered: "Give to this man the payment that you now owe me, and my own money will remain as it is."

They had a bed on which they laid the visitors. If he was

---

41 I.e., the patient becomes better.
42 Here the storyteller evidently has Babylonian conditions in mind. In Sodom there were neither rivers nor ferries.

too long for the bed, they cut off his feet. If he was too short, they stretched him.[43] Eliezer the servant of Abraham happened to come there. They said to him: "Come, lie down on the bed." He said to them: "On the day on which my mother died I made a vow that I shall not lie in a bed."

When a poor man came there, each one of them would give him a denar on which the donor's name was written. But they gave him no bread. When he died, they came and each one took back his denar. They made a stipulation among themselves: Whosoever invites a stranger to a wedding feast, his cloak will be taken away. There was a wedding feast. Eliezer happened to come there, and they gave him no bread. When they sat down to eat, Eliezer went and sat down at the end at the table. They said to him: "Who invited you?" He said to the one who sat next to him: "You invited me." The one who sat next to that man grabbed his cloak and ran out. And so Eliezer did to all of them, until all went away, and he ate the meal by himself.

There was a girl who would take out bread to the poor in her water jar. The matter became known. They smeared her body with honey and put her on top of a wall. The hornets came and killed her.

(B. Sanhedrin 109b)

Sisterly Love

Rav said: "Leah argued[44] with herself and said: 'Twelve tribes are destined to issue from Jacob. Six have been born by me and four by the two concubines, which makes ten. If this one with whom I am pregnant will be a male, my sister Rachel will not have even as many sons as one of the concubines.' Instantly it changed into a daughter, as it is written, *And she called her name Dinah* (Gen. 30:21)."

(B. Ber. 60a)

---

[43] This legendary motif duplicates that of Procrustes' bed.
[44] Hebrew *danah*, from which Rav derives the name Dinah.

The Coffin of Joseph

The rabbis taught: Come and see how dear were *mitzvot* [good deeds] to our Master Moses. While all Israel was busy with the spoils of Egypt, he devoted himself to *mitzvot*.... And whence did our Master Moses know where Joseph was buried? They said: Serah the daughter of Asher alone remained from that generation. Moses went to her and said to her: "Do you know where Joseph is buried?" She said to him: "The Egyptians made him a metal coffin and sank it into the Nile so that its waters become blessed." Moses went and stood on the bank of the Nile. He said to him: "Joseph, Joseph, the time has arrived of which the Holy One, blessed be He, swore that 'I shall redeem you!' And the oath has come which you made Israel swear.[45] If you show yourself, good and well; if not, behold, we are freed of your oath." Instantly the coffin of Joseph swam up.... Moses took it and took it with him, and all those years that Israel wandered in the desert, these two boxes, one of the dead [Joseph] and one of the Shekhina [i.e., the Ark of the Covenant], went side by side. But is it the wont of the dead to go with the Shekhina? They said: "This one fulfilled that which is written in this one."

(B. Sota 13a-b)

The End of Og

The rabbis taught: "He who sees the rock which Og, king of the Bashan, wanted to hurl at Israel must give thanks and praise before God." Concerning that rock we have a tradition: Og said: "How large is the camp of Israel? Three parasangs. I shall go and uproot a mountain of three parasangs, and hurl it upon them and kill them. He went and uprooted a mountain of three parasangs and put it on

---

[45] Joseph made Israel swear that they would take his bones to the Land of Promise, cf. Exod. 13:19.

his head. Thereupon the Holy One, blessed be He, sent ants into it, and they made a hole in it and it fell down around his neck. He wanted to lift it up again, but his teeth grew out to this side and that side, so that he could not remove the mountain.

How tall was Moses? Ten cubits. He took an axe with a handle of ten cubits, jumped up ten cubits, and struck Og at his ankle and killed him.

(B. Ber. 54a-b)

Moses in Heaven

R. Y'hoshu'a ben Levi said: "In the hour when Moses ascended on high, the ministering angels said before the Holy One, blessed be He: "Master of the World! What is this man born of woman doing among us?" He said to them: "He came to receive the Tora." They said before Him: "This precious treasure was hidden with You for 974 generations before the world was created, and now You want to give it to flesh and blood?" ... The Holy One, blessed be He, said to Moses: "Give them a reply." He said before Him: "Master of the World! I am afraid lest they burn me with the breath of their mouths!" He said to him: "Take hold of My Throne of Glory and answer them!" ... R. Naḥum said: This teaches us that the Almighty spread over him the radiance of his Shekhina and His cloud. Then Moses said before Him: "Master of the World! The Tora which You are about to give me, what is written in her?[46] *I am the Lord thy God who brought you out of the Land of Egypt* (Exod. 20:2)." He said to the angels: "Did you go down to Egypt? Were you enslaved by Pharaoh? What need do you have for the Tora? Again, what is written in her? *Thou shalt have no other gods* (Exod. 20:3). Do you dwell among the peoples? What else is written in her? *Remember the Sabbath day to keep it holy* (Exod. 20:8). Are you

---

[46] The Tora is personified as a female.

doing any work that you should need a rest? What else is written in her? *Thou shalt not take* (Exod. 20:7). Is there a giving and taking among you? What else is written in her? *Honor thy father and mother* (Exod. 20:12). Do you have father and mother? What else is written in her? *Thou shalt not murder. Thou shalt not commit adultery. Thou shalt not steal* (Exod. 20:13). Is there envy among you? Is there an evil inclination among you?"

Instantly they confessed to the Holy One, blessed be He, that Moses was right . . . and every one of them became a friend to Moses and revealed something to him. . . . Even the Angel of Death revealed something to him . . . for had he not told him, Moses would not have known how to stop the plague.[47]

(B. Shab. 88b-89a)

Moses and Satan

And R. Y'hoshu'a ben Levi said: "In the hour when Moses ascended to the heights he said to Israel: 'After forty days, at the beginning of the sixth hour, I shall return.' At the end of the forty days Satan came and confused the world. He said to them: 'Your Master Moses, where is he?' They said to him: 'He ascended to the heights.' He said to them: 'The six hours have come and gone.' But they paid no attention to him. He said: 'He died.' But still they paid no attention to him. Then he showed them the image of his bier, whereupon they said to Aaron, '*This Moses, the man who brought us up from Egypt, we do not know what is become of him* (Exod. 32:1).' "

And R. Y'hoshu'a ben Levi said: "In the hour when Moses descended from before the Holy One, blessed be He, Satan came and said before Him: 'Master of the World! The Tora, where is she?' He said to him: 'I gave her to the earth.' Satan went to the earth and said to her: 'The Tora, where is

[47] Cf. Num. 17:12-13.

she?' She said to him: '*God understandeth her way, and He knoweth her place* (Job 28:23).' Thereupon he went to the Sea, but the Sea said to him: 'She is not with me.' He went to the Deep, but the Deep said to him: 'She is not in me, as it is written, *The Deep saith, She is not in me, and the Sea saith, She is not with me* (Job 28:14). *Perdition and Death say, We have heard a rumor thereof with our ears* (Job 28:22).' Satan returned and said before the Holy One, blessed be He: 'Master of the World! I searched in the whole earth and found her not.' He said to him: 'Go to the Son of Amram!' He went to Moses and said to him: 'The Tora which the Holy One, blessed be He, gave you, where is she?' He said to him: 'Who am I that the Holy One, blessed be He, should give me the Tora?' The Holy One, blessed be He, said to Moses: 'Moses! Are you a liar?' He said before Him: 'Master of the World! You have a hidden treasure in which You delight every day. Can I claim this benefit for myself?' The Holy One, blessed be He, said to Moses: 'Since you have belittled yourself, she will be called by your name, as it is written: *Remember the Tora of Moses My servant* (Mal. 3:22).' "

(B. Shabb. 89a)

On the Wings of the Shekhina

Mount Nebo[48] is in the territory of Reuben.... And where was Moses buried? In the territory of Gad.... And how far is it from the territory of Reuben to that of Gad? Four miles. Who took him those four miles? This teaches us that Moses was lying on the wings of the Shekhina....

(B. Sota 13b)

Moses in Akiba's Academy

Rav Y'huda said in the name of Rav: "In the hour when Moses ascended the heights he found the Holy One, blessed

---

[48] The mountain on which Moses died.

be He, sitting and tying crownlets for letters.[49] He said
before Him: 'Master of the World! Who prevents you from
leaving the letters as they are?' He said to him: 'There is a
man who will live after many generations, and Akiba ben
Joseph is his name, and he will build on every thorn[50] heaps
and heaps of Halakhot.' He said before Him: 'Master of the
World! Show him to me!' He said to him: 'Turn around!'
He went and sat at the back of eight rows of R. Akiba's
disciples, and he did not comprehend what they were
saying. His strength failed him.[51] When R. Akiba reached a
certain point, his disciples said to him: 'Rabbi, from where
do you know this?' He said to them: 'It is a Halakha of
Moses from Mount Sinai.' Moses was satisfied. He returned
and came before the Holy One, blessed be He. He said
before Him: 'Master of the World! You have such a man,
and You give the Tora through me?' He said to him: 'Be
silent! This is how it emerged in the thought before Me.'
He said before Him: 'Master of the World! You showed me
his teaching, show me his reward!' He said to him: 'Turn
around!' He turned around and saw how they tore his flesh
with iron combs.[52] He said before Him: 'Master of the
World! Is this the Tora and is this its reward?' He said to
him: 'Be silent, this is how it emerged in the thought before
Me!' "

(B. Menahot 29b)

How David Escaped Yishbi

*And Yishbi-benov who was of the sons of the giants, the weight of
whose spear was three hundred shekels of brass weight, he being
girded with the new armor, and he wanted to slay David* (2 Sam.
21:16). . . .

[49] In the handwritten Tora scrolls, certain letters bear decorations
which look like three-pointed crownlets.
[50] I.e., a pointed protuberance of these crownlets.
[51] I.e., he was confused and upset.
[52] I substituted this statement from B. Ber. 61b for the words in our
text here.

One day David went out to fill up breaches. Satan came and appeared to him in the form of a deer. He shot an arrow at him but did not hit him. He chased after him until he came to the land of the Philistines. When Yishbi-benov saw him, he said: "This is the one who killed my brother Goliath." He tied him up, he pressed him down, put him under the beam of a press. But a miracle happened to him: The earth under him became soft. . . .

That day was the Sabbath eve. Avishai ben Tzeruya[53] was washing his head in four pitchers of water. He saw spots of blood in the water. Some say that a dove came and fluttered before him. He said: "The community of Israel is likened to a dove. . . . Hence this indicates that David is in distress." He went to his house but did not find him there. He said: "We have learned that one does not ride on the king's horse, one does not sit on his throne, and one does not use his scepter. But what about a time of danger?" He went, asked in the House of Study. They said to him: "In time of danger it is permitted." He mounted David's mule, and rode off. The earth jumped for him.[54] While riding he saw Yishbi's mother 'Orpa who was busy spinning. When she saw him she grabbed the spindle and threw it at him. She wanted to kill him. She said to him: "Young man, bring me the spindle!" He threw it at her head and killed her.

When Yishbi-benov saw him he said: "Now there are two against me and they will kill me." He grabbed David, tossed him up into the air, and held up his spear under him, saying: "He will fall on it and be killed." But Avishai uttered the Name of God, and made David remain suspended between heaven and earth. And why did not David himself utter the Name? The prisoner cannot free himself from prison. Avishai asked David: "How did you get here?" He said to him: "Thus said the Holy One,

---

[53] One of the officers of David; cf. 2 Sam. 21:17.
[54] I.e., he reached the place where David was with miraculous speed.

blessed be He, to me, and thus did I answer Him."[55] He said to him: "Change your prayer, let your grandson sell wax, but you do not worry."[56] He said to him: "If so, help me!" Avishai uttered the Name and brought him down.

Yishbi ran after them. When they reached Qubi[57] they said: "Here we stop." When they came to Be-Tre they said: "Two young lions kill the old lion." They said to Yishbi: "Go, you will find your mother 'Orpa in her grave." When they mentioned the name of his mother, he lost his strength, and they killed him.

(B. Sanh. 95a)

The Shafts and the Songs of Ascents

R. Yoḥanan said: "In the hour in which David dug the shafts,[58] the Abyss rose and threatened to inundate the world. David said fifteen Songs of Ascents[59] and made it subside." If so, why should they be called "Songs of Ascents"? They should rather be called "Songs of Descents." However, this is what was taught: In the hour in which David dug the shafts, the Abyss rose and threatened to inundate the world. David said: "Is there anybody here who knows whether it is permitted to write the Name of God on a potsherd and cast it into the Abyss so that it will subside?" No one said a word. David said: "If anyone knows the answer and remains silent, let him suffocate!" Thereupon Ahitophel[60] drew a conclusion from a minor to a major issue: "If, in order to make peace between man and

---

[55] God had asked David how he wished to be punished for his sins, and he chose to fall into the hands of his enemy.

[56] A proverb meaning, "Do not worry about future generations."

[57] A place in Israelite territory.

[58] According to Talmudic belief, under the altar in the Temple there were perpendicular shafts which reached down into *Tehom*, the Abyss.

[59] Psalms 120-134.

[60] Ahitophel was David's counselor, cf. 2 Sam. 15:12.

wife, the Tora said, 'Let My Name which is written in holiness be blotted out by water,'[61] it certainly should be permitted for the purpose of bringing peace to the whole world." And he said: "It is permitted." David wrote the Name on a potsherd and threw it into the Abyss, whereupon the waters of the Abyss sank down sixteen thousand cubits.

When David saw that it had sunk down that much, he said: "The higher it is the better it waters the world." And he said the fifteen Songs of Ascents, and brought it up fifteen thousand cubits, and made it remain at a depth of one thousand cubits.

(B. Sukka 53a-b)

The Shafts of the Temple—Another Version

In the hour when David came to dig the foundations of the Temple, he dug down fifteen hundred cubits and did not find *Tehom* [the Abyss]. Finally he found a potsherd and wanted to lift it up. It said to him: "You cannot lift me up." He said to it: "Why?" It said: "For I am here to press down the Abyss." He said to it: "And since when have you been here?" It said to him: "Ever since the hour when the Merciful One let His voice be heard at Mount Sinai, saying, *I am the Lord thy God* (Exod. 20:2). At that time the earth trembled and sank, and I was put here to press down the Abyss." Nevertheless David did not listen to it. As soon as he lifted it up, the Abyss rose and threatened to inundate the world.

(Y. Sanh. 29a bot.)

David's Harp

R. Osha'ya said in the name of R. Aḥa: "David said: 'Never did I sleep through midnight.'" R. Zera said: "Until

---

[61] The reference is to the ordeallike ritual described in Num. 5:11-31: A married woman suspected of adultery was given water to drink in which curses written on a scroll had been blotted out. The text of these curses contained the name of God.

midnight David would sleep on and off like a horse; thereafter he would gird himself with strength like a lion." Rav Ashi said: "Until midnight he pored over the words of the Tora, thereafter he sang songs and praises. . . ." And how did David know when the hour of midnight arrived? . . . Rav Aḥa bar Bizna said in the name of R. Shim'on the Just: "A harp was hanging above the bed of David, and when midnight arrived, a north wind came and played on its strings. Thereupon he got up and studied the Tora until the pillar of the dawn rose."

(B. Ber. 3b)

The Death of David

David said before the Holy One, blessed be He: "Master of the World! Let me know my end!" He said to him: "It is a decree from before Me that no flesh and blood is told the time of his end." Then David asked: "And what is the measure of my days?" God answered: "It is a decree from before Me that no man is told the measure of his days." "Let me know on what day shall I expire!" He said to him: "You will die on a Sabbath." "Let me die on the first day of the week!" He said to him: "On that day the time of the rule of your son Solomon will have to begin, and one rule must not impinge on the other—not even as much as a hair's breadth." "Let me die on the eve of the Sabbath!" He said to him: *A day in Thy courts is better than a thousand* (Ps. 84:11)—better for Me is one day during which you sit and study the Tora than a thousand burnt sacrifices which your son Solomon will offer up before Me on the altar."

From then on David sat and studied every Sabbath throughout the day. On the day on which he was to die, the Angel of Death came to him but could not touch him for his mouth never ceased studying. The Angel said: "What shall I do to him?" He had a garden behind his house, and the Angel of Death went and shook the trees. David rose to see what the noise was and as he went down the stairs, a step broke under his feet. He fell silent, and his soul departed.

(B. Shab. 30a-b)

The Gates of the Sanctuary

David said before the Holy One, blessed be He: "Master of the World! Forgive my sin with Bathsheba." He said to him: "It is forgiven." He said to Him: "Give me a sign in my life!" He said to him: "In your lifetime I shall not let it be known, but in the lifetime of your son Solomon I shall."

When Solomon built the Temple he wanted to place the Ark into the Holy of Holies, but its doors would not open. Solomon recited twenty-four songs of praise, but was not answered. He said, *Lift up your heads, O gates, and raise yourselves, O everlasting doors, and let the king of glory enter* (Ps. 24:7). Thereupon the gates ran after him and threatened to swallow him up. They said: *Who is the king of glory?* He said to them: *The Lord, strong and mighty* (Ps. 24:8), and he repeated the verse but was not answered. But when he said, *O Lord God, turn not away the face of Thine anointed, remember the good deeds of David Thy servant* (2 Chron. 6:24), instantly he was answered and the doors opened. In that hour the faces of all those who hated David turned black like the underside of a pot, and the whole people and all Israel knew that the Holy One, blessed be He, had forgiven David that sin.

(B. Shab. 30a)

The Cherubim

Rav Q'tina said: "When the Israelites would go up on pilgrimage to the Temple, they would draw away the curtain for them and show them the Cherubim which were intertwined in one another, and say to them: 'See, your love before the God is like the love of male and female.'"

(B. Yoma 54a)

Resh Laqish said: "When strangers entered the Temple and saw the Cherubim intertwined in one another, they brought them out into the marketplace and said: 'That these Israelites, whose blessing is a blessing and whose curse is a curse, should occupy themselves with such things!' And they mocked them, as it is written, *All those who used to honor her mocked her because they saw her shameful nakedness* (Lam. 1:8)."

(B. Yoma 54a-b)

The Foundation Stone

When the Ark was taken away, there was under it a rock since the days of the first prophets and its name was *Shetiyya* [Foundation].[62] It was three fingers high above the ground, and on it the High Priest would place the censer on Yom Kippur....

(M. Yoma 5:2)

It does not say, "when it was hidden," but "when it was taken away." This is in conformity with him who said, "The Ark was exiled to Babylonia...." But R. Y'huda ben Laqish said: "The Ark was hidden in the very place where it used to stand...." R. Naḥman said: "It is taught that the Sages said: 'The Ark was hidden in the chamber of the store-house for wood.'" R. Naḥman bar Yitzḥaq said: "We, too, learned that it happened to a priest who was busy in the woodshed and noticed that one floor tile differed from the others. He went to tell his friend, but before he could finish what he wanted to say his soul departed. Then they knew for sure that the Ark was hidden there." What was he doing there? R. Ḥelbo said: "He was busy with his axe." In the house of R. Yishma'el it was taught: "Once two

---

62 The Shetiyya stone, which formed the floor of the Holy of Holies in the Jerusalem Temple, can still be seen today in the center of the Dome of the Rock.

blemished priests were sorting out the wormy wood, and the axe of one of them slipped from his hand, and fire issued forth and consumed him."

(B. Yoma 54a)

It was called *Shetiyya* [Foundation]. We learned that from it was the world founded. . . . R. Yitzḥaq Nappaḥa [the smith] said: "The Holy One, blessed be He, cast a stone into the sea and from it the world was founded."

(B. Yoma 54b)

The Wonders of the Temple

R. Hoshaʻya said: "In the hour when Solomon built the Temple he planted in it all kinds of golden delicacies and they produced fruits in their proper time. And when the wind blew at them the trees let their fruits fall, and from them there was livelihood for the priesthood. But when strangers entered the Temple they dried up. . . . In the future the Holy One, blessed be He, will restore them to us."

(B. Yoma 39b)

R. Aḥa bar Yitzḥaq said: "In the hour when Solomon built the Temple he fashioned all kinds of golden trees in it. And in the hour when the trees outside bore fruit, those which were inside bore fruit. . . . " When did they wilt? R. Yitzḥaq Ḥinena bar Yitzḥaq said: "In the hour when Manasseh set up an idol in the Temple[63] they wilted."

(Y. Yoma 41d mid.)

Rabba bar Bar Ḥana said: "From Jerusalem to Jericho there are ten parasangs, and the noise of the hinges of the Temple doors could be heard over eight Sabbath areas. The goats in Jericho sneezed from the scent of the incense, the women in

[63] Cf. 2 Kings 21:7.

Jericho did not have to perfume themselves because of the scent of the incense, and brides in Jerusalem did not have to adorn themselves because of the scent of the incense."

(B. Yoma 39b)

Appointment with Death

There were two Ethiopians who served Solomon, *Elihoreph and Ahijah, the sons of Shisha, scribes* (1 Kings 4:3) of Solomon. One day Solomon saw that the Angel of Death was brooding. He said to him: "Why are you brooding?" He said to him: "Because I was asked to fetch these two Ethiopians who sit here." Thereupon Solomon delivered them to the demons and sent them off to the district of Luz.[64] As soon as they approached the district of Luz, they died. On the morrow Solomon saw that the Angel of Death was merry. He said to him: "Why are you merry?" He said: "Because you sent them to the place where I was required to take their lives." Instantly Solomon said: "The feet of man vouch for him: they take him to the place where he is required to be."

(B. Sukka 53a)

Elisha of the Wings

Once the government issued a decree against Israel: Whoever puts on the Tefillin [phylacteries] will have his brain pierced through. But Elisha put them on and went out into the street. An inquisitor saw him, but Elisha fled before him. The inquisitor ran after him, and as he was about to overtake him, Elisha took the Tefillin off his head and held them in his hand. He said to him: "What is that in your hand?" He answered: "The wings of a dove." He

---

[64] In order to save their lives. According to Talmudic view, the Angel of Death had no power in the city of Luz; cf. B. Sota 46b. See also the parallel story above, in the section "The Angel of Death."

opened his hands and the wings of a dove were found in them. Therefore he was called Elisha of the Wings.

(B. Shabbat 49a)

The Keys of the Temple

In the hour in which Nebuchadnezzar came here, when he reached the neighborhood of Antiochia, the Great Sanhedrin went out to meet him, and said to him: "The time has arrived for this House [the Temple] to be destroyed." He said to them: "Give me him whom I made king over you,[65] and I shall go my way." They returned and said to Jehoiachin king of Judah: "Nebuchadnezzar wants you." When he heard this, he took the keys of the Temple, went up to the roof of the Holy Hall, and said before Him: "Master of the World! In the past we were considered trustworthy by You, and Your keys were delivered to us. Now that we are not considered trustworthy, behold, Your keys are delivered to You." There are two traditions. One says, he threw them upwards and they have not yet fallen down, and the other says he saw a kind of a hand take them from his hand. When the noblemen of Judah saw this, they went up to the tops of their roofs and threw themselves down and died. . . .

(Y. Sheqalim 50a mid.)

The rabbis taught: When the First Temple was destroyed, the young priests assembled in groups with the keys of the Temple in their hands, and went up to the roof of the Temple, and spoke before the Lord: "Master of the World! Since we have not merited to be Your faithful treasurers, let the keys be delivered to You!" And they threw them up

[65] In 2 Kings 24:17-25:1 ff. this incident is told about Zedekiah, king of Judah.

into the air, and the shape of a hand came out and took the
keys from them. And then they jumped down from the roof
into the fire. . . .

(B. Ta'anit 29a)

BETWEEN ISRAEL AND EDOM

Alexander and Shim'on

We have learned: The 25th of Teveth is the Day of Mount
Gerizim, on which there is no fasting. For on that day the
Samaritans petitioned Alexander of Macedonia that he
should destroy the house of our God, and permission was
given to them. The rabbis came and informed Shim'on the
Just, the High Priest. What did he do? He put on the
priestly garments and wrapped himself in priestly garments, and gathered some of the nobility of Israel with
lighted torches in their hands, and all night long they
marched, some on one side of the High Priest and some on
the other side, until the pillar of dawn rose. When the pillar
of dawn rose, Alexander said to the Samaritans: "Who are
these people?" They said to him: "Jews, who have rebelled
against you." When he reached Antipatris, the sun had
risen and he met the Jews. When he saw Shim'on the Just,
he got off his chariot and prostrated himself before him.
The Samaritans said to him: "A great king like you bow
down to this Jew?" He said to them: "The image of this
man appears before me and leads me in my victories." He
said to them: "Why did you come?" They said: "Can it be
that you should be misled by strangers to destroy the House
in which we pray for you and for your kingdom that it be
not destroyed?" He said to them: "Who are those
strangers?" They said to him: "These Samaritans who stand
before you!" He said to them: "Behold, they are delivered
into your hands!" Instantly they pierced their heels, tied
them to the tails of their horses, and dragged them over

thorns and thistles until they reached Mount Gerizim. When they reached Mount Gerizim they plowed it and sowed it with horse-beans, as the Samaritans wanted to do to the House of our God. And they made that day a holiday.

(B. Yoma 69a)

The Origin of Hanukka

What is Hanukka? Our rabbis taught: On the 25th of Kislev begin the eight days of Hanukka during which one must neither mourn nor fast. When the Greeks entered the Temple they defiled all the oils in the Temple and when the rule of the House of Hashmonai prevailed and they defeated them, they searched but found only one cruse of oil which was left with the seal of the High Priest unbroken. And the oil in it sufficed only to burn one day. A miracle occurred, and they could burn from it for eight days. A year later they established those eight days and made them into holydays, with the recitation of the Hallel and songs of thanks.

(B. Shab. 21b)

King Monobaz the Righteous

It is told of King Monobaz[66] that in years of drought he gave away to charity his treasures and the treasures of his fathers. His brothers and the house of his father got together against him and said to him: "Your fathers gathered treasures and added to those of their fathers, and you are squandering them." He said to them: "My fathers gathered treasures for this world, but I gathered treasures for the world above. . . . My fathers gathered treasures in a place in which violence rules, but I gathered treasures in a place in which violence does not rule. My fathers gathered treasures

[66] King Monobaz of Adiabene (first cent. C.E.) converted to Judaism.

which yield no fruit, but I gathered treasures which yield fruit.[67] My fathers gathered treasures of money, but I gathered treasures of souls. My fathers gathered treasures for others,[68] but I gathered treasures for myself. My fathers gathered for this world, and I gathered for the World to Come."

(B. Baba Bathra 11a)

Yoḥanan and Vespasian

Abba Siqra, the head of the zealots of Jerusalem, was the son of Rabban Yoḥanan ben Zakkai's sister. Yoḥanan sent for him saying: "Come to me in secret." When he came, Yoḥanan said to him: "How long will you act thus and kill the world with hunger?"[69] He said to him: "What shall I do? If I say anything to them they will kill me." He said to him: "Find a way for me to escape from the city; perchance there will be some succor." He said to him: "Pretend to be ill, and let all the world come to ask about you. And take something putrid and place it next to you, and they will say that you died, and let only your disciples come in to you, and let nobody else come in, lest they notice that you are light of weight, for they know that a living person is lighter than a dead one."

So he did.[70] R. Eliezer walked on one side of him, and R. Y'hoshu'a on the other side. When they came to the gate, the guards wanted to stick their lances into R. Yoḥanan. But Abba Siqra said to them: "The Romans will say, they

---

[67] In the World to Come.

[68] I.e., for their heirs.

[69] When the Romans besieged Jerusalem, there was a famine in the city.

[70] The story here jumps ahead of itself. It must be understood that after the faked death of Rabban Yoḥanan, his disciples took him to be buried outside the city, thus to smuggle him out. The zealots allowed no living person to leave the city.

pierced their master!" They wanted to push him. He said to them: "They will say, they pushed their master!" Then they opened the gate for him and he was taken out.

When he reached Vespasian, he said: "Peace be unto you, O king! Peace be unto you, O king!" He said to him: "You have incurred two death sentences. One, because I am not king and you called me king; and the other, because if I am king, why did you not come to me before this?" He said to him: "As for your saying that you are not king, you are about to become king, for were you not king, Jerusalem would not be delivered into your hands. . . . And as for your saying that if you are king why did I not come to you before this, the zealots who are among us did not let me come."

In the meantime a messenger came from Rome and said to Vespasian: "Rise, for Caesar died and the notables of Rome decided to seat you on top."[71]

Vespasian had put on one shoe, and wanted to put on the other, but it did not go on. He wanted, then, to take off the first shoe, but it did not come off. He said: "What is this?" Rabban Yoḥanan said to him: "Be not concerned. Good news has come to you, and it is written, *Good news maketh the bones fat* (Prov. 15:30)." "But what is its remedy?" "Let a person, whom you hate, come and pass in front of you, for it is written, *A broken spirit drieth the bones* (Prov. 17:22.)" He did so, and the second shoe could be put on.

Vespasian said to him: "I am going away, and shall send here another man.[72] However, ask something of me and I shall give it to you." He said to him: "Give me Yavne and its sages, the dynasty of Rabban Gamliel, and a physician to heal R. Tzadoq."

(B. Gittin 56a-b)

---

[71] I.e., they elected you Caesar.

[72] His son Titus, who was to capture Jerusalem and destroy the Temple.

The Punishment of Titus

Vespasian went away and sent Titus. This is that Titus who reviled and blasphemed toward Above. What did he do? He got hold of a whore and entered the Holy of Holies, and spread out a Tora scroll and on it committed a transgression. And he took a sword and ripped off the veil,[73] and a miracle occurred and blood oozed out, and he thought that he had killed God. . . . Abba Ḥanan said: *"Who is mighty like unto Thee, O Lord?"* (Ps. 89:9) — who is like unto You, mighty and hard? For You heard how that man reviled and blasphemed, and You kept silent."

What did Titus do? He took the Veil and made a kind of sack out of it, and brought all the Vessels which were in the Temple and put them into it, and loaded them on a ship to go and pride himself in his city. A storm on the sea arose against him to drown him. He said: "It seems to me that the God of this people has no strength except in water. Pharaoh came, He drowned him in water;[74] Sisera came, He drowned him in water;[75] and now again He rises against me to drown me in water. If He is mighty, let Him go up to the dry land and make war against me there!" A heavenly voice issued and said to him: "Wicked son of a wicked father, son of the son of the wicked Esau, I have a small creature in My world, and it is called a gnat. Go up to the dry land and make war against it."

A gnat came and entered Titus' nose, and gnawed at his brain for seven years. One day he passed the door of a smith. The gnat heard the pounding of his hammer, and fell silent. Titus said: "So there is a remedy." Every day they brought a smith and he pounded before him. To a Gentile smith he gave four Zuzim, but to a Jewish smith he said: "It

---

[73] The curtain that separated the Holy of Holies from the Holy House.

[74] Cf. Exod. 14:27 ff.

[75] Cf. Judg. 5:21.

should be enough for you to see your enemy in this state."
He did so for thirty days; thereafter the gnat got used to it.

We learned that R. Pinḥas ben 'Aruba said: "I was among
the notables of Rome, and when he died, they opened his
brain and found in it a creature like a swallow, weighing
two selas. . . . Abbaye said: "We have been told that its beak
was of copper and its claws of iron."

When Titus died he said to them: "Burn me and scatter
the ashes upon the seven seas, so that the God of the Jews
should not find me and make me stand in judgment before
Him."

Onkelos bar Kalonikos was the son of the sister of Titus.
He wanted to become a proselyte. He went and had the
spirit of Titus brought up through necromancy. He said to
him: "Who is respected in that world?" He said to him:
"Israel." "Should one join them?" He said to him: "Their
religious rules are many and you will not be able to keep
them. Instead go and persecute them in your world, and
you will become a chief, as it is written, *Her adversaries are
become the head* (Lam. 1:5). All those who oppress Israel
become heads." Onkelos said to him: "What is your
punishment?" He said to him: "That which I decreed upon
myself. Every day they gather my ashes, and judge me, and
burn me, and scatter the ashes upon the seven seas."

(B. Gittin 56b-57a)

The Fall of Betar

R. Yoḥanan said: "The voice of Hadrian Caesar killed
eighty thousand myriads in Betar."[76] R. Yoḥanan said:
"Eighty thousand pairs of trumpeteers surrounded Betar,
and each of them was in charge of several troops. And there
in the fortress was Bar Koziba and he had two hundred

---

[76] The fortress in the Judean hills where Bar Kokhba (originally
called Bar Koziba), leader of the Jewish revolt against the Romans
(132-35), made his last stand.

thousand men, each of whom had cut off a finger. The sages
sent a message to him: "How long will you make Israel
blemished?" He replied: "How else is it possible to test
them?" They said to him: "Whosoever cannot uproot a
cedar from Lebanon while riding on his horse should not be
admitted to your troops." And Bar Koziba had two
hundred thousand of the first group, and two hundred
thousand of the second. And when he went out to battle he
said: "Master of the World! Help not and hinder not! *Hast
not Thou, O God, cast us off? Come not out, O God with our
hosts!* (Ps. 60:12)."

For three and a half years Hadrian surrounded Betar, and
R. El'azar of Moda'im sat on sackcloth and ashes and prayed
every day and said: "Master of the World! Sit not in
judgment today! Sit not in judgment today!" Hadrian
wanted to go away [to give up the siege]. A Kuthite
[Samaritan] said to him: "Do not go for I can see what has
to be done in order to deliver you the city." The Samaritan
entered through the sewers, and found R. El'azar standing
and praying. He did as if he were whispering something
into R. El'azar's ear. The people of the city saw it and took
the Samaritan to Ben Koziba. They said to him: "We saw
this old man speaking to your uncle."[77] Bar Koziba said to
him: "What did you tell him, and what did he tell you?"
He said to him: "If I tell you, Hadrian will kill me, and if I
do not tell you, you will kill me. It is better for me that
Hadrian should kill me and not you. R. El'azar said to me, 'I
shall deliver the city.' " Bar Kokhba went to R. El'azar of
Moda'im, and said to him: "What did this Samaritan tell
you?" He said to him: "Nothing." "What did you tell
him?" He said to him: "Nothing." Bar Kokhba thereupon
gave his uncle a kick and killed him. Instantly a heavenly
voice issued forth and said: *"Woe to My worthless shepherd
who deserts the flock! May the sword smite his arm and his right
eye! Let his arm be wholly withered, his right eye utterly*

[77] R. El'azar was Bar Kokhba's uncle.

blinded!(Zech. 11:17). You killed R. El'azar of Moda'im, the arm of all Israel and their right eye. Therefore your arm will wither and your right eye be blinded!" Instantly Betar was captured and Bar Koziba was killed.

They went and brought his head to Hadrian. He said to them: "Who killed him?" A Samaritan said: "I killed him." He said to him: "Show me his body!" He showed him his body. They found a snake wound around it. Hadrian said: "Had not God killed him, who could have killed him? . . ." And they continued to kill the people of Betar until the horse sank in blood to its nose, and the blood rolled rocks the weight of forty measures, and the blood flowed into the sea. . . . And should you say that Betar was near the sea, not so, for it is forty miles from the sea.

They said: They found three hundred brains of babes on one stone, and they found three baskets of Tefillin capsules of nine measures, and some say nine of three measures, each.

It was taught: Rabban Shim'on ben Gamliel said: "Five hundred schools were in Betar, and the smallest of them had no less than five hundred children. And they would say: 'If the enemy should come upon us we shall go forth against them with these pencils and shall stab their eyes.' And when the sins caused Betar to fall, they wound each one of the children in his scroll and burned him. And I alone remained of all of them. . . ."

The wicked Hadrian had a big vineyard, eighteen by eighteen miles, like from Tiberias to Sepphoris, and he surrounded it with a fence made of the bodies of those killed in Betar, all standing up with their hands straight. And he did not let them be buried, until another king arose and had them laid to rest.

(Y. Ta'aniyot 68d–69a)

Shim'on bar Yoḥai

Once R. Y'huda and R. Yose and R. Shim'on ben Yoḥai

were sitting, and Y'huda ben Gerim [son of proselytes] came and sat down with them. R. Y'huda began and said: "How pleasant are the works of this nation [the Romans]. They established marketplaces, built bridges, created bathhouses." R. Yose kept silent. R. Shim'on ben Yoḥai said: "Everything they did they did only for their own needs. They established marketplaces in order to seat whores in them; bathhouses in order to pamper themselves there; bridges in order to levy tolls on them." R. Y'huda ben Gerim went and repeated their words to others, and they became known to the Romans. They said: "Y'huda, who praised us, should be praised; Yose, who kept silent, shall be exiled to Sepphoris; and Shim'on who defamed us, shall be killed."

Thereupon R. Shim'on and his son hid in the House of Study. His wife brought them every day bread and a jug of water, and they ate. When the persecution became more severe, he said to his son: "Women are weak.[78] It can come about that they will torture her and she will reveal to them where we are." So they went and hid in a cave. A miracle occurred: A carob tree was created for them, and a source of water. They took off their clothes and sat up to their necks in the sand, and studied all day. At the time of the prayers they put on their clothes and prayed, and then took them off again so that they should not be worn out. After they had stayed twelve years in the cave, Elijah came and stood at the entrance of the cave and said: "Who will inform Bar Yoḥai that Caesar has died and his edicts have been cancelled?" Thereupon they came out and saw people plowing and sowing. R. Shim'on said: "They abandon the life eternal and devote themselves to the life of the hour." And wherever they directed their glance everything was consumed by fire. A heavenly voice issued forth and said to them: "Did you come out in order to destroy My world?

[78] This is the only meaning, fitting into the context of the story, of the popular Talmudic saying quoted here which literally means "The mind of woman is light."

Go back to your cave!" They returned and stayed there for
another twelve months. Then they said: "The punishment
of the wicked in Gehenna is twelve months." A heavenly
voice issued forth and said: "Leave your cave!" They went
out, and wherever R. El'azar struck, R. Shim'on healed. He
said to him: "My son, the world has had enough of me and
you!"

On the eve of the Sabbath, at dusk, they saw an old man
carrying two bunches of myrtles and running. They said to
him: "What are these for?" He said to them: "For the honor
of the Sabbath." "But would not one be enough for you?"
"One is for *Remember the Sabbath day* (Exod. 20:8), and one
for *Observe the Sabbath day* (Deut. 5:12)." R. Shim'on said to
his son: "See, how dear are the commandments to Israel!"
Whereupon their minds were relieved.

(B. Shab. 33b)

Body and Soul

Antoninus said to Rabbi Y'huda the Prince: "The body and
the soul can free themselves from punishment. How? The
body can say: 'The soul is guilty for from the day that it
departed from me I have been lying in the grave like a
dumb stone.' And the soul can say: 'The body is guilty, for
from the day that I departed from it I have been flying
about in the air like a bird and sin not.' "

Rabbi said to him: "I shall tell you a parable. To what can
this be likened? To a king of flesh and blood who had a
beautiful orchard, and there were in it fine fruits. And he
put into it two watchmen, one lame and one blind. The
lame said to the blind: 'I see fine fruit in the orchard; come
take me on your back and we shall get them and eat them.'
The lame rode on the back of the blind, and they took and
ate. Days later the owner of the orchard came and said to
them: 'The fine fruits, where are they?' The lame said to
him: 'Do I have feet to walk on?' The blind said to him: 'Do
I have eyes to see?' What did the king do? He made the

lame man ride on the back of the blind and punished them together. Thus the Holy One, blessed be He, brings the soul, casts it into the body, and punishes them together."

(B. Sanh. 91a–b)

The Lion of the Supernal House

Caesar said to R. Y'hoshu'a ben Ḥananya: "Your God is likened to a lion, as it is written, *The lion hath roared, who will not fear?* (Amos 3:8) What is His greatness? A hunter can kill a lion." He said to him: "He is not likened to such a lion. He is likened to a lion of Be 'Ilai.[79] He said to him: "I want you to show it to me." He said to him: "You cannot see it." He said to him: "Indeed, I want to see it." R. Y'hoshu'a asked God for mercy, and the lion was brought from its place. When it was at a distance of four hundred parasangs, it roared a single time, and all the bridges and walls of Rome collapsed. When it was at a distance of three hundred parasangs, it roared a second time, and the molars and front teeth of the people fell out, and Caesar himself fell from his throne to the floor. He said to him: "I beg of you, ask for mercy so that it should return to its place." He asked for mercy, and the lion returned to its place.

(B. Hullin 59b)

The Earthen Vessel

The daughter of Caesar said to R. Y'hoshu'a ben Ḥananya: "Why is glorious wisdom contained in an ugly vessel like you?" He said to her: "Does your father keep his wine in earthen vessels?" She said to him: "In what else should he keep it?" He said to her: "You people of importance should keep it in gold and silver!" She went and told her father. He put the wine into golden and silver vessels, and it soured.

---

[79] According to Rashi, the name of a forest. Literally, "Supernal House."

They went and told him. He said to his daughter: "Who told you this?" She said to him: "R. Y'hoshuʻa ben Ḥananya." He called him and said to him: "Why did you tell that to my daughter?" He said to him: "What she told me, I told her."

Caesar said: "But there are also beautiful people who are scholars?" "If they were ugly, they would be even greater scholars."

(B. Taʻanith 7a-b)

Joseph the Sabbath-Lover

In the neighborhood of Joseph the Sabbath-Lover there lived a Gentile who owned much property. The Chaldeans[80] said to him: "Joseph the Sabbath-Lover will consume all your property." Thereupon the Gentile went and sold all his property and bought a jewel which he affixed to his cap. Once, when he crossed a river on a ferry, a gust of wind blew off his cap and carried it into the water, where a fish swallowed it.

On the eve of the Sabbath, the fish was caught and brought to the market. They said: "Who will buy such a fish?" They were told: "Go, take it to Joseph the Sabbath-Lover, for he usually buys fish for the Sabbath." They took it to him and he bought it. When he cut it open, he found in it the jewel, and later sold it for thirteen heaps of golden denars.

Once an old man encountered him and said to him: "He who lends to the Sabbath, the Sabbath pays him back."

(B. Shab. 119a)

The Tora—Our Life Element

The rabbis taught: Once the Greek government[81] issued a

[80] Soothsayers.

[81] Since R. Akiba lived in the second century C.E., the statement "Greek government" must be emended to read "Roman government."

decree prohibiting Israel from studying the Tora. Papos ben Y'huda came and found R. Akiba gathering groups of students in public and teaching the Tora. He said to him: "Akiba, are you not afraid of the government?" He said to him: "I shall tell you a parable. What is this like? It is like the fox who was walking along the banks of the river and saw the fish gathering in one place, then in another. He said to them: 'What are you fleeing from?' They said to him: 'From the nets which people bring to catch us.' He said to them: 'You should come up to the land, and I and you will dwell together as my forebears dwelt with yours.' They said to him: 'Are you the one of whom they say that he is the smartest of the animals? You are not smart but foolish. If we are afraid in the place of our life, how much more should we be afraid in the place of our death!' So it is with us as well. If now, that we sit and study the Tora about which it is written *For she is thy life and the length of thy days* (Deut. 30:20), we are in danger, should we go and cease studying her, how much more would we be in danger!"

(B. Ber. 61b)

SAGES AND SAINTS

The Gates of Nikanor

The rabbis taught: What miracles happened to Nikanor's gates which he had made for the Temple? They said: When Nikanor went to bring the gates from Alexandria of Egypt, on his way back a storm arose in the sea and threatened to sink his ship. They took one of the gates and cast it into the sea, but the sea did not cease from its wrath. They wanted to cast overboard the other gate, whereupon Nikanor rose up and hugged it and said: "Cast me overboard together with it!" Instantly the sea rested from its wrath. And Nikanor was aggrieved because of the first gate. When he reached the port of Acre, the gate appeared and rose up from beneath the ship. And some say that a creature in the sea swallowed it and then spit it out onto dry land. Therefore all the gates that were in the Temple were subsequently exchanged for golden gates except for the gates of Nikanor, because miracles happened to them.

(B. Yoma 38a)

The Death of Shim'on the Just

The rabbis taught: In the year in which the High Priest Shim'on the Just died, he told them that he would die in that year. They said to him: "How do you know?" He said to them: "Every Yom Kippur [Day of Atonement] an old man, dressed in white and wrapped in white, would join me, enter with me into the Holy of Holies, and come out with me. But today an old man dressed in black and wrapped in black joined me. He entered with me but he did not come out with me." After the Feast Shim'on the Just fell ill for seven days and died.

(B. Yoma 39b)

The Whole Tora in a Sentence

It happened that a Gentile came to Shammai and said to him: "Make me a proselyte provided you can teach me the entire Tora while I stand on one foot." Shammai gave him a push with the builder's ell which he had in his hand. Thereupon the Gentile went to Hillel. He accepted him as a proselyte and said to him: "Whatever is hated by you, do it not to your fellow man.[82] This is the whole Tora; the rest is commentary. Go and study!"

(B. Shab. 31a)

---

[82] This, of course, is but the negative formulation of the famous golden rule which reads in the Bible (Lev. 19:18), *Love thy neighbor as thyself.*

The Patience of Hillel

The Rabbis taught: "One should always be mild-tempered like Hillel and not irritable like Shammai." It once happened that two men made a bet. They said: "He who can go and make Hillel angry will get four hundred *Zuzim*." One of them said: "I shall go and make him angry." That day was a Friday and Hillel was washing his head. The man went and came to the door of Hillel's house and said: "Is Hillel here? Is Hillel here?" Hillel wrapped himself up and went out to him and said: "My son, what is your wish?" He said to him: "I have a question to ask." He said: "Ask, my son, ask." "Why are the heads of the Babylonians round?" He said to him: "My son, you have asked an important question. Because they have no clever midwives." The man went away, waited a little while, then returned and said: "Is Hillel here? Is Hillel here?" Hillel again wrapped himself up, and went out to him. He said to him: "My son, what is your wish?" He said to him: "I have a question to ask." He said to him: "Ask, my son, ask." "Why are the eyes of the Palmyrese dripping?" He said to him: "My son, you have asked an important question. Because they live amidst sands." He went away, waited a little while, then returned and said: "Is Hillel here? Is Hillel here?" Hillel again wrapped himself up, went out to him and said: "My son, what is your wish?" He said: "I have a question to ask." He said, "Ask my son, ask." "Why are the feet of the Africans wide?" He said to him: "My son, you have asked an important question. Because they live among swamps." He said to him: "I have many more questions to ask, but I am afraid you will get angry." Hillel wrapped himself up, sat down before him and said: "Ask all the questions you wish to ask." He said to him: "Are you Hillel whom they call the Prince of Israel?" He said to him: "Yes." He said to him: "If you are he, let there not be many like you in Israel!" He said to him: "My son, why?" He said to him: "Because through you I lost four hundred *Zuzim*!" He said to him: "Be careful, you may lose through Hillel four hundred *Zuzim* and again four hundred *Zuzim*, but Hillel will not get angry."

(B. Shab. 30b-31a)

The Disciples of Hillel

The rabbis taught: Hillel the Elder had eighty disciples. The greatest of them was Jonathan ben Uziel, the least of them was Rabban Yoḥanan ben Zakkai. It was said of Rabban Yoḥanan ben Zakkai that he did not leave aside the study of the Bible, Mishna, Gemara, laws and legends, fine points of the Tora and of the Scribes, conclusions from a minor to a major issue, analogies, the Tequfot,[83] the numerical values of words, the discussions of angels and of demons, the lore of palm trees, laundrymen's fables and fox fables, great matters and small matters—great matters such as the work of the Divine Chariot; small matters such as the disputes between Abbaye and Rava—in order to fulfill what is written: [Wisdom saith:] *That I may cause those that love me to inherit substance, and that I may fill their treasuries* (Prov. 8:21). And if the least of them was this versatile, how much greater must have been the greatest of them. They said about Jonathan ben Uziel that when he sat and studied the Tora the birds that flew over him were instantly consumed by fire.

(B. Sukka 28a)

Ḥoni the Rainmaker

Our Rabbis taught: It once happened that most of the

---

[83] *Tequfot* is the Talmudic term for the four turning points in the annual course of the sun: the vernal equinox, the summer solstice, the autumnal equinox, and the winter solstice.

month of Adar had passed but no rains had fallen.[84] They sent for Ḥoni haM'aggel [Ḥoni the Circle Maker]: "Pray so that the rains shall fall!" He prayed, but no rains fell. Thereupon he drew a circle and stood inside it ... and said before Him: "Master of the World! Your children have turned their faces to me for I am like a son of the house before You. I swear by Your Great Name that I shall not move from here until You have mercy on Your children!" Rain began to fall drop by drop. His disciples said to him: "Rabbi, we look to you so that we die not. It seems to us that this rain falls only to release you from your vow." He said to God: "This is not what I asked for, but rains for cisterns, ditches and caves." They then fell with great vehemence until every drop was enough to fill the mouth of a barrel, and the sages estimated that no drop was less than a *log* [about a cup]. His disciples said to him: "Rabbi, we look to you so that we die not. It seems to us that these rains fall only in order to destroy the world." He said before Him: "This is not what I asked for, but rains of goodwill, blessing, and beneficence." Then they fell properly, until all the people had to go up to the Temple Mount because of the rains. They said to him: "Rabbi, just as you prayed that rains should fall, so pray now that they should cease." He said to them: "I have received a tradition that one does not pray for the cessation of too much of a good thing. Nevertheless, bring me a bull of thanksgiving." They brought him a bull of thanksgiving, he placed his two hands on it, and said before Him: "Master of the World! Your people Israel whom You brought out of Egypt, can stand neither too much of a good thing nor too much misfortune. You were angry with them, they could not endure it; You gave them too much of a good thing, they could not stand it. May it be the will from before You that the rains cease and that there be relief for the world." Instantly the wind blew and the clouds were dispersed and

---

[84] The normal rainy season in Israel is from November to April. If no rains fell until Adar (February–March) it was a drought.

the sun shone, and the people went out into the field and brought for themselves mushrooms and truffles.

Shim'on ben Shetah[85] sent word to him: "Were you not Ḥoni, I would excommunicate you.[86] But what can I do to you who lord it over God and He nevertheless fulfills your will, as a son lords it over his father and he nevertheless fulfills his will. The son says: 'Father, take me, bathe me in warm water, rinse me with cold water, give me nuts, almonds, peaches and pomegranates,' and he gives them to him." . . .

What message did the members of the Hall of Hewn Stones[87] send to Ḥoni the Circle Maker? *Thou decreest a thing and it is fulfilled unto thee, and light shineth upon thy ways* (Job 22:28). *Thou decreest a thing* here below, and the Holy One, blessed be He, fulfills your decree from Above. *And light shineth upon thy ways*—you make light shine with your prayer upon a generation which was in darkness. . . .

One day Ḥoni was walking on a road and saw a man who was planting a carob tree. He said to him: "After how many years does this tree yield fruit?" He said to him: "After seventy years." He said to him: "Are you sure you have seventy years to live?" He said to him: "I found carob trees in the world which were planted for me by my fathers; I too plant them for my children." Ḥoni sat down and ate his bread. Sleep came upon him and he slept. A rock surrounded him and covered him from the eyes of people, and he slept seventy years. When he awoke he saw a man gathering carobs from that tree. He said to him: "Are you the one who planted this tree?" He said to him: "I am the son of his son." He said to him: "If so, I slept seventy years!" . . . He went to his house and said to them: "Is the son of Ḥoni the Circle Maker still alive? They said to him:

---

[85] Shim'on ben Shetah (first century B.C.E.) was the *Nasi*, or the *Av Bet Din*, the head of the Sanhedrin, High Court, in Jerusalem.

[86] For having shown disrespect toward God.

[87] A designation of the Sanhedrin.

"His son is no more, but the son of his son lives." He said to them: "I am Ḥoni the Circle Maker." They did not believe him. He went to the House of Study. There he heard the rabbis say: "This teaching is as clear to us as in the years of Ḥoni the Circle Maker. For he, when he came to the House of Study, answered all the questions which the rabbis had." He said to them: "I am he." They did not believe him, and did not pay him the respect that was due to him. He grieved over this, prayed for mercy, and died. Rava said: "This is why people say, 'Either companionship or death.'"

(M. Ta'anit 3:8; B. Ta'anit 23a)

Ḥoni the Circle Maker—Another Version[88]

It happened that they said to Ḥoni the Circle Maker: "Pray that rains should fall." He said to them: "Go out and bring in the Passover ovens lest they melt away in the rain which will come." Then Ḥoni prayed, but no rains fell. R. Yose ben R. Bun said: "Because he did not come in modesty." R. Yudan Geraya [or Ben Gerim] said: "This Ḥoni was the son of the son of Ḥoni the Circle Maker. About the time of the destruction of the Temple he went out to a mountain to the workers. While he was there, rain fell. He entered a cave. There he fell asleep and was sunk in his sleep for seventy years, until the Temple was destroyed and rebuilt a second time. At the end of seventy years he awoke, went out of the cave, and saw a changed world. In the place where there used to be vineyards, there were olive trees, where there used to be olive trees there were wheat fields. He asked the people of the place, and said to them: "What voice [i.e., news] is there in the world?" They said to him: "And don't you know what voice there is in the world?" He said to them: "No." They said to him: "Who are you?" He said to

---

88 While the previous legend places Ḥoni in the first century B.C.E., this puts him in the sixth century B.C.E. when the First Temple was destroyed (in 586 B.C.E.), and the Second Temple built seventy years later.

them: "Ḥoni the Circle Maker." They said to him: "We have heard that when Ḥoni entered the Temple court it became lighted up." He went there, and the court became lighted up. And he applied to himself the verse: *When the Lord brought back those who returned to Zion we were like dreamers* (Ps. 126:1).

(Y. Taʿaniyot 66d bot.)

Ḥoni's Grandsons

Abba Ḥilqiya was the son of the son of Ḥoni the Circle Maker. When the world would be in need of rain, the rabbis would send to him, he would pray for mercy, and rain would come. Once the world was in need of rain. The rabbis sent two rabbis to him so that he should pray for mercy that rain should come. They went to his house but did not find him there. They went to the field and found him digging. They gave him "Peace," but he did not return it to them. Toward evening, when he was carrying the wood he had collected, he carried the wood and the hoe on one shoulder and the cloak on the other.[89] All the way he did not wear his shoes, but when he came to water, he put them on. When he passed thorns and thistles, he lifted up his garments. When he reached town, his wife, all dressed up, came to meet him. When he reached his home, his wife entered first, then he went in, and then the rabbis went in. He sat down to eat bread, and did not say to the rabbis, "Come, eat!" When he gave portions to his children, he gave one piece of bread to the elder and two to the younger.

He said to his wife: "I know that the rabbis came on account of the rain. Let us go up to the roof and ask for mercy. Perhaps it will please the Holy One, blessed be He, and rain will come without credit being given to us." They went up to the roof, he stood in one corner and she in

---

[89] This was an unusual procedure, for normally a worker would put his folded-up cloak on his shoulder to serve as a cushion for the wood, and place the hoe on top of it.

another. Clouds came first from the corner of his wife. When it began to rain, he went down and said to them: "Why did you come?" They said to him: "The rabbis sent us that you ask for mercy concerning the rain." He said to them: "Blessed be God who brought it about that you do not need Abba Ḥilqiya." They said to him: "We know that the rain came because of you. But would you explain to us several things which made us wonder. What is the reason that when we greeted you, you did not return the greeting?" He said to them: "I am a day laborer, and did not want to interrupt my work." "And why did you carry the wood on one shoulder and the cloak on the other?" He said to them: "It is a Tallith that I had borrowed only to wear, but not to use it as a padding under the wood. "Why did you not wear your shoes all the way, but put them on when you reached water?" He said to them: "All the way I could see where I stepped, but in the water I could not see." "Why did you raise your garment when you came across thorns and thistles?" He said to them: "The body heals, but the garment does not heal." "Why, when you reached town, did your wife come to meet you all dressed up?" He said to them: "So that I should not let my eyes stray to another woman." "Why did she enter the house first, and then you entered after her, and only then did we enter?" He said to them: "Because I had not ascertained your morality." "Why, when you sat down to eat bread, did you not say to us, 'Come, eat'?" "Because the bread was insufficient, and I did not want you to thank me for nothing." "Why did you give one piece of bread to the older child, and two to the younger?" He said to them: "The older one stays at home and eats during the day, and the younger sits in the House of Study all day and eats only in the evening." "And why did the cloud come first from the corner where your wife stood, and only thereafter from your corner?" "Because the woman remains in the house and gives bread to the poor, which they can enjoy instantly, while I give them money which they cannot enjoy at once.

Or, possibly, because there are outlaws in our neighborhood, and I asked God that they die, while she asked that they repent."

(B. Ta'anit 23a-b)

Hiding Ḥanan was the son of the daughter of Ḥoni the Circle Maker. When the world was in need of rain the rabbis sent to him the schoolchildren, and they got hold of the end of his cloak and said to him: "Father, father, give us rain!" He said before the Holy One, blessed be He: "Master of the World! Do it for the sake of these who know not the difference between the Father who gives rain and a father who cannot give rain!" And why did they call him Hiding Ḥanan? Because when they would ask him to pray for rain he would hide out of modesty.

(B. Ta'anit 23b)

Rain and Humility

Once the rabbis were forced to decree a fast, but the rain did not fall. R. Y'hoshu'a ordered a fast in the south, and rain fell. And the people of Sepphoris said: "R. Y'hoshu'a ben Levi brought rain for the people of the south, and R. Ḥanina withheld the water from the Sepphoreans." They needed a fast [in Sepphoris] a second time. R. Ḥanina sent and brought R. Y'hoshu'a ben Levi. He said to him: "Would the master come out with us to fast?" They both went out to fast, but no rain fell. He went up and said before them: "Not R. Y'hoshu'a ben Levi brings rain to the southerners, and not R. Ḥanina withholds rain from the Sepphoreans, but the hearts of the southerners are soft, they hear the word of the Tora and humble themselves, and the hearts of the Sepphoreans are hard, they hear the word of the Tora but do not humble themselves." When he returned,[90] he lifted up his eyes and saw that the air was

---

[90] To the place before the synagogue where the people who fasted were gathered.

clear. He said: "After all this fasting, still so clear!"
Instantly rain fell. And he vowed not to do this again,
saying: "Who am I to tell the Creator [God] not to collect
His debt?"[91]

(Y. Ta'aniyot 66c bot.)

Why Rains Fall and Why They Are Withheld

R. Berekhya and R. Ḥelbo Papa in the name of R. L'azar
[El'azar]: "Occasionally rain falls because of the merit of
one man, because of the merit of one blade of grass, because
of the merit of one field."

R. Simon said: "Because of the merit of three things the
rains fall: the merit of the earth, the merit of charity, the
merit of sufferings.... Because of the sins of four things the
rains are withheld: the sin of idolatry, of fornication, of
bloodshed, and the public promise which is not kept...."

(Y. Ta'aniyot 66c mid.)

The Ugly Vessel

Once it happpened that R. El'azar ben R. Shim'on of
Migdal G'dor was coming from the house of his master,
and he was sitting on an ass and riding along the riverbank.
And he was full of joy and pride because he had learned
much Tora. He met a man who was very ugly, and who
greeted him: "Peace be upon you, rabbi!" He did not return
the greeting, but said to him: "You good-for-nothing! How
ugly you are! Are all the people of your city as ugly as you
are?" He said to him: "I do not know, but go and tell the
craftsman who made me, 'How ugly is this vessel which
you made!'"

When R. El'azar became aware that he had sinned, he got
off the ass, prostrated himself before the man, and said to
him: "I humble myself before you; forgive me!" He said to

[91] I.e., not to punish the people for their sins.

him: "I shall not forgive you until you go to the craftsman who made me, and tell him, 'How ugly is this vessel you made!' " R. El'azar walked after him until they reached his city. The people of the city came out to meet him and said to him: "Peace be upon you, rabbi, rabbi, my teacher, my teacher!" The man said to them: "Whom are you calling rabbi, rabbi?" They said to him: "Him who walks behind you." He said to them: "If that one is a rabbi, let there not be many like him in Israel." They said to him: "Why?" He said to them: "This and this is what he did to me." They said to him: "Still, forgive him, for he is a man great in Tora." He said to them: "For your sake I forgive him; only let him not act like this in the future." Instantly R. El'azar ben R. Shim'on entered the House of Study and taught: "A man should always be pliable like a reed and not hard like a cedar. This is why the reed has been destined to provide pens for the writing of Tora scroll, the Tefillin, and the Mezuzot."

(B. Ta'anit 20a-b)

The Sages as Acrobats

They said about Rabban Shim'on ben Gamliel that when he rejoiced at the Joy of the House of Water Drawing,[92] he took eight lighted torches and threw one into the air and caught another, and not one of them touched the other. And when he prostrated himself, he stuck his two thumbs into the ground and bent down and kissed the floor and then straightened up, and nobody else was able to do this. And this is the *qidda* [bow]. Levi tried to show this *qidda* before Rabbi Y'huda the Prince but became lame. . . . Levi juggled before Rabbi with eight knives; Sh'muel before King Sapor with eight cups of wine; Abbaye before Rava with eight eggs, and some say with four eggs.

(B. Sukka 53a)

[92] The great joyous feast celebrated on the last day of the Feast of Tabernacles.

The Two Ways

When Rabban Yoḥanan ben Zakkai fell ill, his disciples came to visit him. When he saw them he began to cry. His disciples said to him: "Light of Israel! Pillar of the right side! Mighty hammer! Why are you crying?" He said to them: "When there are before me two ways, one leading to the Garden of Eden and the other leading to Gehenna, and I do not know along which I shall be led, shall I not cry?"

(B. Ber. 28b)

How Akiba Was Saved

Rav Huna said: "Rav said in the name of R. Meir, and we have learned the same in the name of R. Akiba: 'One should always practice the custom of saying, Everything God does, He does for good.'" It once happened to R. Akiba that he was walking on the road and came to a town. He tried to find lodgings there but they gave him none. He said: "Everything God does He does for good." Then he went out into the field to stay there overnight. He had with him a cock and a donkey and a candle. A wind came and blew out the candle. A cat came and ate the cock. A lion came and ate the donkey. He said: "Everything God does He does for good." In the same night a troop came and captured the town. He said: "Did I not tell you that everything the Holy One, blessed be He, does is for good?" (Rashi: Had the candle remained lighted, the troop would have seen me, and had the donkey brayed or the cock crowed, the troop would have come and captured me.)

(B. Ber. 60b-61a and Rashi, ibid.)

How R. Akiba Became a Sage

The daughter of Kalba Savu'a[93] became engaged to R.

---

[93] One of the richest men in Jerusalem; cf. B. Git. 56a.

Akiba.[94] Kalba Savu'a heard it. He made a vow that his daughter would enjoy nothing of his property. She went and married him. In the winter they slept in straw. She would pick the straw from his hair. He said to her: "If I would have riches I would give you a Jerusalem of gold.[95]

Elijah came, appeared to them in the shape of a man, called through the door and said to them: "Give me some straw, for my wife has just given birth and I have nothing on which to lay her down." Akiba said to his wife: "See, there is a man who has not even straw." She said to him: "Go, attend the House of Study." He went and spent twelve years before R. Eliezer and R. Yishma'el. At the end of twelve years he returned to his house. From behind his house he heard a wicked man say to his wife: "Your father was right in doing this to you. For one thing, Akiba is inferior to you, and for another, he left you in a living widowhood all these years." She said to him: "Were he to listen to me, he would stay there another twelve years." Upon hearing this, Akiba said: "Since she gave me permission, I shall turn back." He turned back, went, and stayed another twelve years.

Thereafter he returned with twenty-four thousand disciples. The whole town went out to meet him, and his wife, too, arose to go to meet him. That wicked man said to her: "And you, where to?" She said to him: "*The righteous man knoweth the soul of his beast* (Prov. 12:10)."[96] She went to show herself to him, but the rabbis who surrounded Akiba pushed her back. He said to them: "Let her be. Mine and yours is hers."[97]

---

[94] R. Akiba was at the time an uneducated and poverty-stricken youth.

[95] Evidently, a piece of jewelry in which a picture of Jerusalem was engraved. Cf. B. Shab. 59a.

[96] I.e., I know that it is Akiba who is approaching.

[97] That is, it is due to her that I studied, and that you studied with me.

Kalba Savu'a heard it, he came and asked about his vow, and it was annulled.

(B. Ned. 50a)

Charity Delivereth from Death

From R. Akiba we learn that Israel has no *Mazal*[98] For R. Akiba had a daughter, and the Chaldeans[99] said to him that on the day on which she would enter her bridal canopy, a snake would bite her and she would die. He was much worried about this thing. On that day his daughter took off her brooch and stuck it into the fence, and it so happened that its point penetrated the eye of a snake. Next morning when she pulled it out, the snake was dragging after it. Her father said to her: "What had you done?"[100] She said to him: "In the evening a poor man came, knocked on the door, but everybody was busy with the banquet so that nobody heard it. I went and took my portion which you had given me and gave it to him." He said to her: "You performed a *mitzva*." R. Akiba went out and expounded: "*Charity delivereth from death* (Prov. 10:2) — and not only from an unnatural death but from death in general."

(B. Shab. 156b)

The Death of R. Akiba

They said that within a few days[101] R. Akiba was arrested and imprisoned in the jail house. Then they also arrested Papos ben Y'huda and imprisoned him next to him. He said to him: "Papos, what brought you here?" He said to him: "Happy are you, R. Akiba, that you were arrested

---

98 *Mazal* is a nation's or person's star or constellation to which his fate is subject.

99 Astrologers, soothsayers.

100 R. Akiba concluded that this must have been a reward for a *mitzva*, a good deed, his daughter had performed.

101 A few days after R. Akiba disobeyed the Roman prohibition against studying the Tora.

because of matters of the Tora, but woe to Papos who was arrested because of matters of no worth!"

When they took R. Akiba out to be executed, it was the time of the *Sh'ma'* prayer. They tore his flesh with iron combs, but he accepted the yoke of the kingdom of heaven. His disciples said to him: "Our Master, thus far?" He said to them: "All my life I worried about the verse, *And thou shalt love the Lord thy God with all thy heart and with all thy soul* (Deut. 6:5), which means even if He takes your soul. I thought: When will I have the opportunity to fulfill this? And now that I do have the opportunity, should I not fulfill it?" And he prolonged [the word] *One*[102] until his soul departed with *One*. A heavenly voice issued forth and said: "Happy are you, R. Akiba, that your soul departed with *One*." The ministering angels said before the Holy One, blessed be He: "Is this the Tora and is this her reward?" He said to them: "*Their portion is in life* (Ps. 17:14)." Again a heavenly voice issued forth and said: "Happy are you, R. Akiba, for you are destined for life in the World to Come!"

(B. Ber. 61b)

Poverty of Scholars, Servitude of Officials

It happened that Rabban Gamliel and R. Y'hoshu'a were sailing on a ship. Rabban Gamliel had bread with him. R. Y'hoshu'a had bread and flour. The bread of Rabban Gamliel ran out and he relied on the flour of R. Y'hoshu'a. He said to him: "Did you know that we would have such a delay that you brought flour?" He said to him: "Once in seventy years a star rises and leads the seamen astray. I said, 'Perhaps it will rise and lead us astray.' " Rabban Gamliel said to him: "So much is in your hand, and you board a ship?"[103] He said to him: "Instead of being surprised at me,

---

[102] The last word of the *Sh'ma'* prayer, which is the Jewish confession of faith.

[103] I.e., you have so much knowledge and yet you must seek your livelihood overseas?

you should be surprised at two disciples whom you have on land, R. El'azar Ḥasma and R. Yoḥanan ben Gudgeda, who know how to calculate how many drops there are in the sea and have no bread to eat and no garment to wear." Rabban Gamliel decided to seat them at the head.[104] When he went ashore he sent for them, and they did not come.[105] He sent for them a second time, and they came. He said to them: "Do you think I am giving you lordship? I am giving you servitude, as it is said, *And they spoke to him saying, If thou wilt be a servant unto this people this day* (1 Kings 12:7)."

(B. Horayot 10a-b)

The Power of R. Ḥiyya

Elijah used to frequent the academy of Rabbi.[106] One day, it was the New Moon, he was late, and did not come at his usual time. Rabbi said to him: "Why was the Master late?" He said to him: "Because I had to awaken Abraham, wash his hands, let him pray, and lay him down; and likewise with Isaac, and likewise with Jacob." "Could you not awaken them together?" "I thought they would pray with such power that they could bring the Messiah before his time."

He said to him: "And are there like them in this world?" He said to him: "There is R. Ḥiyya and his sons." Rabbi decreed a fast. He let R. Ḥiyya and his sons lead the prayers. He said: "He causes wind to blow," and it blew. He said: "He causes rain to fall," and rain came. When he came to say, "He resurrects the dead," the world shook.

They said in heaven: "Who disclosed the secret in the world?" They said: "Elijah." They brought Elijah, and gave him sixty lashes of fire. Thereupon he came and appeared

---

[104] I.e., to give them high positions.

[105] Because of modesty.

[106] R. Y'huda the Prince, compiler of the Mishna, who lived in the second half of the second century C.E.

to them like a bear of fire, went among them and interrupted their prayers.

(B. Baba Metzia 85b)

Prodigies

Abbaye and Rava[107] were sitting before [their teacher] Rabba. Rabba said to them: "Whom does one bless?" They said to him: "The Compassionate One." "And where does the Compassionate One dwell?" Rava pointed to the ceiling; Abbaye went outside and pointed to heaven. Rabba said to them: "Both of you will become rabbis." This is what people say: "The young pumpkin is known by its shaft."

(B. Ber. 48a)

The Pious Men

Abbaye said: "There are in the world no less than thirty-six pious men who receive the face of the Shekhina in every generation...." Not so, for Rava said: "There is a row of pious men eighteen thousand parasangs long before the Holy One, blessed be He." No problem: the one refers to those who look at the shining appearance of God, and the other to those who look at an appearance which is not shining...."

(B. Sanh. 97b)

The Pious and the Dragon

Abayye heard that R. Aḥa bar Ya'aqov was coming to study under him. There was a demon in the House of Study of Abbaye, because of which, even if two students entered it, and even in the daytime, they came to harm. He said to

---

[107] The context of the story shows that Abbaye and Rava were small children when the event related in the story took place.

them: "Let nobody give R. Aḥa lodgings; perhaps a miracle will happen." He went and stayed overnight in that House of Study. The demon appeared to him like a dragon with seven heads. Each time he knelt down while praying, one of its heads fell off. Next day he said to them: "Had no miracle happened, you would have exposed me to danger."

(B. Qid. 29b)

A Golem

Rava said: "If the Just wished to create a world, they could do so. . . ." Rava created a man; he sent him to Rabbi Zera, who spoke to him; when he did not reply, Rabbi Zera told him: "You are a creation of magic; return to your dust." Rav Ḥanina and Rav Oshaya sat every Sabbath eve and studied the *Sefer Y'tzira* (*Book of Creation*), and created for themselves a three-year-old calf, which they then ate.

(B. Sanh. 65b)

The Clever and the Foolish Servants

The rabbis taught: *The spirit returneth unto God who gave it* (Eccles. 12:7). This means: Give her to Him as He gave her to you. Just as He gave her in purity, so you too give her back to Him in purity. A parable: Once a king of flesh and blood distributed royal garments among his servants. The clever among them folded them up and placed them in a box; the foolish among them went and performed work in them. Days later the king asked for his clothes back. The clever servants returned them to him cleaned and pressed; the foolish returned them to him dirty. The king was delighted with the clever servants and was angry with the foolish. He said concerning the clever ones: "Let their clothes be put in the treasure house and they themselves should go to their houses in peace." And concerning the foolish ones he said: "Let their clothes be given to the launderer and they themselves should be detained in the jail house." Thus the Holy One, blessed be He, says concerning the bodies of the righteous: *Let him enter in peace, let them rest on their couches*; and concerning their souls He says: *Let the soul of my lord be bound in the bundle of life* (1 Sam. 25:29). About the bodies of the wicked He says: *There is no peace, saith the Lord, concerning the wicked* (Isa. 48:22); and about their souls He says: *Let the souls of thy enemies be slung out as from the hollow of a sling* (1 Sam. 25:29).

(B. Shab. 152b)

R. Eliezer and R. Yoḥanan

R. Eliezer became sick and R. Yoḥanan went to visit him. He found him in a dark room, whereupon he uncovered his arm and light filled the room. He saw that R. Eliezer was weeping and said to him: "Why are you weeping? If because you have not studied enough Tora—we have learned that it matters not whether one studies much or little, as long as one directs one's heart to heaven. And if because of lack of food—not every man merits two tables.[108] If because you have no children—look: this is a bone of the tenth son I have lost." R. Eliezer said to him: "It is over this beauty of yours which will decay in the dust that I cry." R. Yoḥanan said to him: "Over that you are certainly right to cry." And both of them cried together. Meanwhile he asked him: "Are the sufferings dear to you?" He answered: "Neither they nor their reward." R. Yoḥanan said to him: "Give me your hand!" He gave it to him and he helped him to stand up.

(B. Ber. 5b)

The Gates of Jerusalem

R. Yoḥanan sat and expounded: "In the future the Holy One, blessed be He, will bring precious stones and pearls, of

---

[108] I.e., one in This World and one in the Other World.

thirty by thirty cubits, and will cut openings into them of ten by twenty, and set them up in the gates of Jerusalem."

A disciple mocked him: "At present we cannot find such stones even the size of a dove's egg; how then could there be such?"

After a while that disciple's ship sailed on the sea. He saw the ministering angels who sat and sawed precious stones and pearls which were thirty by thirty cubits and cut into them openings of ten by twenty high. He said to them: "For whom are these?" They said to him that in the future the Holy One, blessed be He, will set them into the gates of Jerusalem.

He went before R. Yoḥanan and said to him: "Expound, Rabbi, it behoves you to expound. As you had said, so I saw."

He said to him: "You good-for-nothing! Had you not seen it you would not have believed? You make a mockery of the words of the sages!" He directed his eye at him, and he became a heap of bones.

(B. Baba Bathra 75a)

Poverty and Riches

R. El'azar ben P'dat lived in great distress. Once he underwent bloodletting and had nothing to eat afterwards. He took a clove of garlic and put it in his mouth. His head became weak and he fainted. The rabbis came to visit him, and saw that he was weeping and laughing in his sleep, and that a ray of fire issued from his forehead. When he woke up, they said to him: "Why did you weep and laugh?" He said to them: "The Holy One, blessed be He, was sitting with me, and I said to him: 'How long do I have to suffer in this world?' And He said to me: 'El'azar My son, if you wish I shall reshape the world from its beginning; perchance you will be born again in an hour of prosperity.' I said before Him: 'All this, and still only perchance?' Then I said to Him: 'Which are more, my past days or those remaining to

me?' He said to me: 'Your past days.' I said to Him: 'If so, I
do not wish it.' He said to me: 'As a reward for having said,
"I do not wish it," We shall give you in the World to Come
twelve rivers flowing with pure balsam oil, like the
Euphrates and the Tigris, in which you will have your pleasure.' I said before Him: 'This, and nothing more?' He said
to me: 'And what shall I give to your companions?'[109] I said
to him: 'But I want only that which no other man has.'[110]
He flicked his finger against my forehead and said to me:
'Take care, El'azar My son, or I shall shoot My arrows at
you.' "[111]

(B. Ta'anit 25a)

Two Stories of Nahum of Gam Zu

I

Why was Nahum called "the man of Gam Zu"? Because
whatever happened to him he said: "This too (*gam zu*) is for
the good." Once Israel wished to send a gift to the house of
Caesar. They said: "Who should go? Let Nahum the man
of Gam Zu go, for he is experienced in miracles." They sent
with him a box full of precious stones. He went and stayed
overnight in a place of lodging. At night his hosts rose up
and took his box, emptied it, and refilled it with dust.
When he reached his destination the servants of Caesar
opened the box and saw that it was filled with dust. The
king wanted to kill all of the Jews. He said: "The Jews mock
me!" But Nahum said: "This too is for the good." And then
Elijah came, appearing to them as one of Caesar's court, and
said to them: "Perhaps this dust is of the dust of their father

[109] I.e., if I give you more, what will remain for your companions?
[110] I.e., I want only those benefits in the World to Come which
would not be given to anybody else.
[111] I.e., God mildly rebuked El'azar for his immodesty in asking too
much of the World to Come.

Abraham. For when he threw the dust it turned into swords, and the straw turned into arrows." At that time there was a country which Caesar could not conquer. They tried some of the dust and conquered it. They took Nahum to their house of treasure and filled his box with precious stones and pearls and sent him off with great honor.

When he came to the same lodging to stay overnight, they said to him: "What did you take to them that they gave you such honors?" He said to them: "What I had taken from here I brought there."

They demolished their lodging and took the dust of it to the house of the king. They said to him: "That dust which was brought here is from our own." They tried it out and found it not to be miraculous, and killed those hosts.

(B. Ta'anit 21a)

II

They said about Nahum the man of Gam Zu that he was blind in both his eyes, both his hands had been severed, both his feet had been cut off, and his whole body was covered with boils. He was lying in a house that was near collapse, and the legs of his bed were kept in bowls of water so that the ants should not crawl up on them. Once his disciples wanted to take his bed out of the house, and after that to take out his belongings. But he said to them: "My sons, first take out the belongings and then take out my bed. For you can be sure that as long as I am in the house, the house will not collapse." They took out the belongings, then took out his bed, and the house collapsed.

His disciples said to him: "Our master, since you are a perfect saint, why did all this come upon you?" He said to them: "My sons, I myself brought it upon myself. For once I was walking on the road towards the house of my father-in-law, and I had with me three donkeys: one laden with food, one with drinks, and one with an assortment of delicacies. A poor man came, stood in my way, and said: 'Rabbi, give me something to eat!' I said to him, 'Wait until I unload the donkey.' Before I could unload the donkey his soul departed. I went and fell upon his face and said: 'My eyes which had no mercy on your eyes, let them become blind! My hands which had no mercy on your hands, let them be severed! My feet which had no mercy on your feet, let them be cut off!' And still I did not feel satisfied, until I said: 'Let my whole body be covered with boils!' "

They said to him: "Woe to us that we saw you thus!" He said to them: "Woe to me if you had not seen me thus!"

(B. Ta'anit 21a)

The Reward of Charity

They told about Benjamin the righteous, who was in charge of the charity box, that one day, in the years of drought, a woman came to him and said to him: "Rabbi, provide for me!" He said to her: "By God, there is nothing left in the charity box!" She said to him: "Rabbi, if you do not provide for me, a woman and her seven children will die!" He rose and provided for her from his own.

Days later he fell ill and was close to death. The ministering angels said before the Holy One, blessed be He: "Master of the World! You have said, 'If somebody keeps alive one soul from Israel, it is as if he had kept alive a whole world.' And Benjamin the righteous, who kept alive a woman and her seven children, should die in his early years?" Instantly they tore up his sentence of death, and it was taught that they added twenty-two years to his years.

(B. Baba Bathra 11a)

The Law Is Not in Heaven

R. Eliezer ben Hyrcanos used all the arguments in the world to support his opinion, but the other sages would not accept them. He said to them: "If the Halakha is as I say, let this carob tree prove it!" It became uprooted and moved to a distance of one hundred cubits, and some say, four hundred cubits. They said to him: "One does not bring proof from a carob tree." He repeated and said to them: "If the Halakha is as I say, let the water canal prove it!" The water in the canal flowed backwards. They said to him: "One does not bring proof from a water canal." He repeated and said to them: "If the Halakha is as I say, let the walls of the House of Study prove it." The walls of the House of Study inclined as if to collapse. R. Y'hoshu'a rebuked them and said to them: "When scholars argue about the Halakha, what concern is that of yours?" The walls did not fall out of respect for R. Y'hoshu'a, and did not straighten up out of respect for R. Eliezer, and to this day they stand inclined. He repeated and said to them: "If the Halakha is as I say, let them prove it from heaven." A heavenly voice issued forth and said: "What do you want with R. Eliezer? The Halakha is always as he says." R. Y'hoshu'a got on his feet and said: "*It* [the Halakha] *is not in heaven* (Deut. 30:12)." What does *It is not in heaven* mean? R. Yirm'ya said: "Because the Tora was given to us from Mount Sinai. We pay no attention to a heavenly voice, for You [God] wrote on Mount Sinai, *Turn after the majority* (Exod. 23:2).[112]

R. Nathan encountered Elijah. He said to him: "What did the Holy One, blessed be He, do in that hour?" He said to him: "He smiled and said: 'My children have defeated Me, My children have defeated Me!'"

(B. Baba Metzia 59b)

R. Ḥanina's Wife

R. Y'huda said in the name of Rav: "Every day a heavenly voice issues forth and says: 'The whole world is nourished for the sake of My son Ḥanina, and My son Ḥanina is content with a measure of carobs from one Sabbath eve to

---

[112] In the original Biblical text these words have the opposite meaning. They are a warning against following the majority in an evil cause.

the next.' " His wife would light the oven every Sabbath eve
and throw into it something that would make smoke,
because of shame.[113] She had an evil woman neighbor who
said: "We know that she has nothing, so what is all this
for?" And she went and knocked on the door of Ḥanina.
Ḥanina's wife was ashamed and withdrew into the
chamber. A miracle happened to her, and the neighbor saw
the oven full of bread and the kneading trough full of
dough. She said to her: "Fetch a shovel, for your bread is
getting charred." She said to her: "That's why I went in." . . .

R. Ḥanina's wife said to him: "How long shall we go on
suffering like this?" He said to her: "What shall we do?"
"Ask for mercy that something be given to you." He asked
for mercy. Thereupon the shape of a hand appeared and
gave him the leg of a golden table. She saw in a dream: in
the Future the righteous will eat at golden tables with three
legs, but R. Ḥanina will eat at a golden table with only two
legs. She said to him: "Is it satisfactory for you that the
whole world should eat at a whole table and we at a
defective table?" He said to her: "What shall we do?" "Ask
for mercy that it should be taken back from you." He asked
for mercy, and it was taken back.

                                    (B. Ta'anit 24b-25a)

The Guests of the King

R. Eliezer said: "Repent one day before your death." His
disciples asked him: "Can a man know on which day he
will die?" He said to them: "Exactly. Let him repent today
in case he die tomorrow. Thus he will be in a state of
repentance all his days." Likewise, Solomon said in his
wisdom: *At all times let thy garments be white, and let thy head
lack no oil* (Eccles. 9:8). Rabban Yoḥanan ben Zakkai said:
"It can be likened to a king who invited his servants to a

---

[113] Lest her neighbors know that she had nothing to cook.

banquet and did not fix a time for them. The clever among them put on their festive clothes and sat at the gate of the royal palace, for they said: "Does the house of the king lack anything?"[114] The foolish among them went to their work, for they said: "Can there be a banquet without preparations?" Suddenly the king asked for his servants. The clever among them entered before him all adorned, and the foolish entered all soiled. The king rejoiced over the clever and was angry at the foolish. He said: "These, who adorned themselves for the banquet, let them sit and eat and drink; these, who did not adorn themselves, let them stand and watch."

(B. Shab. 153a)

The Ruined House of Charity

'Ula and Rav Ḥisda were walking in the street. When they reached the door of the ruined house of Rav Ḥana bar Ḥanilai, Rav Ḥisda collapsed and wailed. 'Ula said to him: "Why are you wailing?" He answered: "How can I not wail, when a house in which there were sixty bakers in the day and sixty bakers at night who would bake for everybody in need; and whose owner would never remove his hand from the purse for the thought that 'perhaps an impoverished person from a good family may come by and would be ashamed to wait until I open the purse for him'; and which had four doors open towards the four winds of the world and he who entered them hungry left well satisfied; and from which they poured out wheat and barley in years of drought, and he who was ashamed to take of it by daytime could come and take by night— and now this house is a heap of ruins and I should not wail?"

'Ula said to him: "R. Yoḥanan said this: 'From the day on which the Temple was destroyed an edict was passed con-

---

[114] Since the royal palace is well supplied, the king can decide any moment to have a banquet.

cerning the houses of the righteous that they be destroyed.' But R. Yoḥanan also said: 'In the future the Holy One, blessed be He, will restore them to their inhabitants. Just as Mount Zion will be raised and inhabited, so the houses of the righteous will be restored by the Holy One, blessed be He, and will be inhabited.' " When 'Ula saw that this did not reassure Rav Ḥisda, he said: "It is sufficient for the servant to be like his master."

(B. Ber. 58b)

SIN AND REPENTANCE

How Aḥer Became a Sinner

Aḥer cut down the shoots. . . . What happened? He saw that Metatron[115] came and was given permission to sit down and write the merits of Israel. He said: "It is taught that On High there is no sitting, no rivalry, no back of the neck,[116] and no tiring. Can it be, God forbid, that there are two powers?"[117] They brought Metatron and gave him sixty fiery lashes, for they said to him: "When you saw Aḥer, why did you not get up?" Then permission was given to him to erase the merits of Aḥer. A heavenly voice issued forth and said: "*Return, ye backsliding children* (Jer. 3:22), all except Aḥer." He said: "Since I have been excluded from That World, let me go and enjoy this world." He went and became a sinner. He went and found a whore and asked for her services. She said to him: "Are you not Elishaʻ ben Abuya?" He tore up a radish from the bed on the Sabbath, and gave it to her. She said: "It is another [Aḥer]."

(B. Ḥagiga 15a)

---

[115] The highest-ranking ministering angel.

[116] For the angels have faces on all sides.

[117] I.e., two divinities.

Aḥer and R. Meir

The rabbis taught: "It happened that Aḥer was riding on a horse on the Sabbath and R. Meir was walking behind him in order to learn Tora from his mouth. He said to him: "Meir, turn back, for I have figured from the steps of the horse that here is the Sabbath boundary.[118] He said to him: "You, too, turn back!" He said to him: "Have I not already told you that I heard from behind the *Pargod* [heavenly curtain]: '*Return, ye backsliding children* (Jer. 3:22), all except Aḥer?' " R. Meir got hold of him and led him to the House of Study. Aḥer said to a child: "Tell me your verse!"[119] He said to him: "*There is no peace, saith the Lord, for the wicked* (Isa. 48:22)." He took him to another House of Study. He said to a child: "Tell me your verse!" He said to him: "*For though thou wash thee with nitre, and take thee much soap, yet thine iniquity is marked before Me* (Jer. 2:22)." He took him to yet another House of Study. He said to a child: "Tell me your verse!" He said to him: "*And thou that art spoiled, what doest thou, that thou clothest thyself with scarlet, that thou deckest thee with ornaments of gold, that thou enlargest thine eye with paint? In vain dost thou make thyself fair* (Jer. 4:30)." And he took him to yet another House of Study, until he took him to thirteen Houses of Study, and all of them read him verses of this kind. . . .

How could R. Meir learn Tora from the mouth of Aḥer? . . . When Rav Dimi came he said: "In the West[120] they said, 'R. Meir ate the fig and threw away the peel.' "

(B. Ḥagiga 15b)

The Punishment of Aḥer

When Aḥer died, they said [in heaven]: "We shall not

---

[118] Beyond which it is forbidden to walk on the Sabbath.

[119] Which the child was studying at that moment. This was considered a kind of oracle.

[120] I.e., Palestine.

punish him, but he will not enter the World to Come. We shall not punish him because he studied the Tora, and he will not enter the World to Come because he sinned." R. Meir said: "It is better that he should be punished and then enter the World to Come. When I die I shall make smoke rise from his grave."[121] When R. Meir passed away, smoke rose from the grave of Aḥer. R. Yoḥanan said: "It was, indeed, a mighty deed to make his master burn! He was one among us and we have no power to save him. If I take him by the hand,[122] who will take him from me?" And he said: "When I die I shall extinguish the smoke from his grave." When R. Yoḥanan passed away, the smoke from Aḥer's grave ceased.

(B. Ḥagiga 15b)

The Fivefold Sinner

R. Abbahu was told in a dream: Let Pentaqaqa [fivefold sinner] pray, and rain will come. Rain fell. R. Abbahu sent for him and had him come to him. He said to him: "What is your work?" He said to him: "Every day I commit five sins: I hire out prostitutes, decorate the theater, carry their clothes to the bath, dance before them, and beat the drum before them." He said to him: "And what good deed did you do?" He said to him: "At one time I was decorating the theater. A woman came and remained standing behind a column weeping. And I said to her: 'What is it?' And she said to me: 'My husband has fallen into captivity, and I want to see what I can do to ransom him.'[123] And I sold my bed and my blanket and gave her their price, and said to her. 'Go, ransom your husband and sin not!'" R. Abbahu said to him: "Worthy are you to pray and to be answered."

(Y. Ta'aniyot 64b bot.)

---

[121] As a sign that Aḥer's soul has begun its punishment in Gehenna.

[122] To lead him to the World to Come.

[123] I.e., she wanted to prostitute herself so as to ransom her husband with her earnings.

The Two Bribes

Imma Shalom, the wife of R. Eliezer, was the sister of Rabban Gamliel. In their neighborhood there was an [apostate] judge who had made it known that he was not taking bribes. They wanted to put him to ridicule. She brought him a golden lamp, went before him, and said to him: "I want to have a share in the estate of my father the Prince." He said to her: "Divide it among yourselves." She said to him: "But it is written in the Tora: Where there is a son, a daughter does not inherit." He said to her: "From the day that you were exiled from your country the Tora of Moses has been revoked, and another Tora given in its place, and in it it is written, the son and the daughter should inherit equally."[124] Next day Rabban Gamliel went and brought him a Libyan donkey. Thereupon the judge said to him: "I looked at the end of the book, and there it is written, I am not come to detract from the Tora of Moses, but I am come to fulfill the Tora of Moses,[125] and in it it is written, Where there is a son, a daughter does not inherit." She said to him: "Let your light shine like a lamp!" Rabban Gamliel said to her: "The donkey came and kicked over the lamp."

(B. Shab. 116a-b)

The Spirit of Idolatry

After their return from the Babylonian exile the Jews *cried with a loud voice unto the Lord their God* (Neh. 9:4). What did they say? Rav said, and according to some, R. Yoḥanan: They said: "Woe, woe! He [the Spirit of Idolatry] destroyed the Temple, and burned the Sanctuary, and killed all the righteous, and exiled Israel from its land, and still he dances among us! Why did you give him to us? Was it not in order

---

[124] No such rule is found in the New Testament, to which the judge seems to refer.

[125] This is a rough rendering of Matthew 5:17.

to receive a reward when we overcame him? We want neither him nor his reward!" Thereupon a tablet fell from the firmament and on it was written, "Truth." Rav Ḥanina said: "From this we understand that the seal of the Holy One, blessed be He, is 'Truth.' " They sat in fasting for three days and three nights, and the spirit was delivered to them. He issued forth from the house of the Holy of Holies appearing like a young lion of fire. The prophet said to them: "This is the Inclination of Idolatry. . . ." When they caught him, a hair was torn out of his mane, and he lifted up his voice and his cry was heard for four hundred parasangs. They said: "What shall we do? Perchance, God forbid, they will take pity on him from heaven?" The prophet said to them: "Cast him into a leaden caldron and cover its mouth with a leaden lid, for lead absorbs sounds. . . ."

They said: "Since this is a time of goodwill, let us ask for divine help against the Inclination of [sexual] Sin. They asked for pity, and it, too, was delivered into their hands. The prophet, however, said to them: "Look, if you kill this one, the world will come to an end." They locked him up for three days, and when they were looking for a fresh egg, they could find none in all the Land of Israel.[126] They said: "What shall we do? If we kill him, the world will come to an end. If we ask for one half[127] they give no halves in heaven." So they blinded his eyes and let him go. And the the result of this was that he no longer arouses the desire of a man towards a kinswoman.

(B. Yoma 69b)

The Impious Daughters

The daughters of Rav Naḥman used to stir the pot with

---

[126] For in the absence of the sexual instinct the hens stopped laying eggs.

[127] I.e., that only the licit sexual urge should survive.

their bare hands.[128] R. 'Ilish raised a problem: "It is written, *One man among a thousand I have found; but a woman among all those I have not found* (Eccles. 7:28). And what about the daughters of Rav Naḥman?" It so happened that they were captured, and R. 'Ilish too was captured with them. One day a man, who knew the language of birds, sat down next to him. A raven came and called out to him. R. 'Ilish said to him: "What did it say?" He said to him: "It said, ' 'Ilish run, 'Ilish run!' " He said: "The raven is a liar, and I do not rely on it." Thereupon a dove came, and cooed. He said to him: "What did it say?" He said to him:" ' 'Ilish run, 'Ilish run!' " He said: "The Community of Israel is likened to a dove;[129] hence this means that a miracle is going to happen to me." Then he said: "I shall go and see whether the daughters of R. Naḥman still maintain their piety, and will take them back with me." He heard them say: "Our captors are men and the Nehardeans [their husbands at home] are men. Let us tell our captors that they should remove us from here, lest people come and hear about us and ransom us."[130] He rose and ran away, he and that man. A miracle happened to him. He got across on a ferry, but that man was found and killed. When the daughters of R. Naḥman returned, he said: "They stirred the pot with magic."[131]

(B. Gittin 45a)

Shim'on ben Shetaḥ and the Witches

There were two Hasids [pious men] in Ashkelon. They ate like one man, and drank like one man, and studied the Tora like one man. One of them died, and no charity was

---

[128] People thought that their exceeding piety saved their hands from being scalded.

[129] Cf. Ps. 68:14.

[130] That is, they were satisfied with their position as concubines of their captors.

[131] That is why their hands were not scalded, and not because of their piety.

done to him.[132] The son of Ma'ayan the custom collector[133] died, and the whole country stopped working to do charity to him. The other pious man saw this; it pained him. He said: "Woe, that Israel has nothing!"[134]

The Hasid who died appeared in his dream and said to him: "Do not despise the children of your Master,[135] I committed a sin and departed with it, and the son of the custom collector performed a good deed and departed with it."

What sin did that pious man commit? God forbid, he committed no sin in all his days. But once he put on the Tefillin of the head before the Tefillin of the hand.[136] And what good deed did the son of Ma'ayan the custom collector perform? God forbid, he never performed a good deed in all his days. But once he prepared a banquet for the council of senators, and they did not come to eat it. He said, "Let the poor eat it so that it should not be wasted." And some say, he passed through the marketplace, and dropped a loaf of bread, and a poor man saw it and took it, and he said nothing to him so as not to shame his face.

Days later [in a dream] that Hasid saw his friend strolling in gardens, in orchards, among springs of water. And he saw the son of Ma'ayan the custom collector with his tongue lolling toward a river, trying to reach the water but unable to do so. And he saw Miriam daughter of 'Ale-B'tzalim [Onion Leaves]. R. L'azar bar Yose said: "He saw her strung up by the nipples of her breasts." R. Yose ben Hanina said: "He saw her with the pivot of the door of Gehenna stuck into her ear." The Hasid said to them: "Why is this?" He [someone in his dream] said to him: "Because she fasted and publicized it." And some say,

132 I.e., they did not bury him properly.
133 Considered a robber in Talmudic law.
134 I.e., woe, that nothing is done for a pious son of Israel.
135 I.e., the Jews.
136 Reversed the proper order.

because she used to fast one day and mark down two.[137] He said to them: "How long will she stay thus?" He said to him: "Until Shim'on ben Shetaḥ[138] comes, when we shall lift it up from her ear and stick it into his ear." He said to them: "And why?" He said to him: "Because he said, 'If I become *Nasi* [head of the community], I shall kill the warlocks.' He has become *Nasi* and has not killed the warlocks. And behold, there are eighty women witches dwelling in a cave of Ashkelon, causing ruination in the world. However, go and tell him."

The Hasid said to them: "I am afraid. For he is the *Nasi* and will not believe me." He said to him: "Yes, he will believe you, for he is modest. And if he does not, this is your sign before him: Put your hand to your eye and take it out and then put it back, and it will go back as it was."

He went and told him the matter. He wanted to perform the sign before him, but they did not let him. R. Shim'on said to him: "I know that you are a pious man. You can do more than that. And, moreover, I did not pronounce that oath with my mouth, I only thought it in my heart."

Instantly R. Shim'on ben Shetaḥ arose, on a rainy day, and took with him eighty young men and gave into their hands eighty clean cloaks, and they put them into eighty new pots, and put them over their heads. He said to them: "When I whistle once, put on your cloaks, and when I whistle a second time, come up all of you together. And when you arrive, each of you should take hold of one of the witches and lift her up from the ground, for it is known of these witches that if they are lifted up from the ground they can do nothing."

He went and stood at the door of the cave. He said to them: "Ho! Ho! Open for me, for I am one of your own!" They said to him: "How did you get here on such a

---

137 Thus deceiving herself in her account with God.

138 Religious head of the Jewish community of Palestine in the first century B.C.E.

day?"[139] He said to them: "I was walking between the raindrops."[140] They said to him: "What did you come here to do?" He said: "To learn and to teach. Let each of us do what he is good at." Thereupon one of them said what she said and conjured up bread. And another said what she said and conjured up meat. A third one said what she said and conjured up cooked food. A fourth one said what she said and conjured up wine. They said to him: "You, what can you do?" He said to them: "I can whistle twice and bring you eighty young men, who will rejoice with you, and gladden you." They said to him: "Yes, we want that."

He whistled once, and they put on their cloaks. He whistled a second time and they all came up together. He said: "Let each of you choose his pair." And they picked up the witches, and went and crucified them. This is what we learned: It happened that Shim'on ben Shetaḥ hanged eighty women in Ashkelon.

(Y. Ḥagiga 77d-78a)

The Book of Life

R. Kruspedai said in the name of R. Yoḥanan: Three books are opened in heaven on New Year: one for the thoroughly wicked, and one for the thoroughly righteous, and one for the intermediate. The thoroughly righteous are forthwith inscribed and sealed for life; the thoroughly wicked are forthwith inscribed and sealed for death; the intermediate are suspended and left in abeyance till the Day of Atonement; if they acquire merits, they are inscribed for life; if not, they are inscribed for death.

(B. Rosh Hash. 16b)

---

[139] Without becoming soaked by the rain.
[140] Which only a witch or warlock can do.

4
MIDRASH

The Hebrew term Midrash (plural: Midrashim) has
several meanings. It can mean a study, an exposition, a
homily or homiletical interpretation, and a book
containing legends and homiletical commentaries on
Scripture. The Midrash literature comprises several
dozen volumes, each containing collections of such
homilies and legends, and, in addition, a large number
of Midrash fragments.

The production of Midrash literature began in the
Tannaitic period (first two centuries C.E.), and the
first Midrashim were those written by the pupils of R.
Yishma'el and R. Akiba, both of whom lived in the
second century C.E. However, even these early
Midrashim were compiled and redacted only in the
fourth century. These Midrashim are called Halakhic,
because they deal primarily with Halakha, that is, the
traditional law, as it can be derived from the Biblical
books Exodus, Leviticus, Numbers, and Deuteronomy.
Since Genesis contains no legislation, there are no
Halakhic Midrashim based upon it. However, even
these Halakhic Midrashim contain varying amounts of
Agadic—that is, legendary—material.

The Agadic Midrashim, in contrast to the Halakhic,
comprise primarily Agadic material—legends,
homilies, and sayings. Some of the material contained
in them is attributed to Tannaim, other parts to
Amoraim. Both the Halakhic Midrashim and the early
classical Agadic ones, which were compiled from 400

to 640, are the products of Palestinian sages. Their language is partly Hebrew and partly Palestinian Aramaic.

These early Agadic Midrashim fall into two types: exegetical and homiletical. A typical exegetical Midrash contains a systematic exposition of each chapter, verse, and often even word of a Biblical book. To this type belong such Midrashim as Genesis Rabba, Lamentations Rabba, etc. A homiletical Midrash comprises comments on only the first verse or verses of the weekly portions of the Pentateuch, or is based on the Biblical portion and prophetic readings (the Haftara) of special Sabbaths and festivals, with each chapter containing a collection of sayings and homilies on one topic. In its classical form, each section of such a Midrash opens with a proem (or proems), an introductory paragraph opening (in Genesis Rabba) usually with a quotation from the Hagiographa which then is explained and connected to the verse which is being discussed.

Thus section 11 of Genesis Rabba begins as follows: "*And God blessed the seventh day* (Gen. 2:3). It is written, *The blessing of the Lord, it maketh rich, and grief shall not continue with it* (Prov. 10:22). *The blessing of the Lord maketh rich*—this is the Sabbath, as it is said, *And God blessed the seventh day; and grief shall not continue with it*—this is mourning, as you say, *The king grieveth for his son* (2 Sam. 19:3)." Having thus established in the proem a homiletical exegesis of Gen. 2:3—namely that, read together with Prov. 10:22, it means that the Sabbath interrupts the mourning ritual—the section then continues with numerous explanations of Gen. 2:3.

Following the Arab conquest (ca. 640), a rich production of Midrashic and Agadic works began, which, however, as far as structure and form are concerned, show a certain decline when compared to the works of the classical period. In the Midrashim of this middle period, which lasted from ca. 640 to ca. 1000, the proem becomes an artifical imitation, the influence of the apocryphal and apocalyptic literature (see Part 2) is strong, and works which are not compilations (as are the classical Midrashim) but the products of one single author appear. Also, pseudepigraphism becomes widespread: authors falsely attribute sayings and statements contained in their books to ancient sages in order to secure a favorable reception for their works. The language is no longer rabbinic Hebrew and Palestinian Aramaic, but becomes a pure and polished, but artificial, Hebrew.

In the late period (ca. 1000–ca. 1200), the Hebrew is completely medieval, the content and form is even more pseudepigraphic, and anthologylike books appear. This is followed by a period of Yalqutim, or anthologies (1200–1500), of which the largest and most important are the Yalqut Shim'oni, assembled in Germany in the early thirteenth century by a certain Shim'on haDarshan, and the Midrash haGadol, from the same century, compiled by a native of Aden, David ben 'Amram 'Adani.

Thus the Midrash literature spans some twelve centuries, and is derived from all parts of the Jewish Diaspora. It supplied reading fare for the semilearned Jews for whom the study of the Talmud proved too onerous. It had a major share in keeping alive among them a knowledge of Hebrew, providing a familiarity with the Agadic work of the ancient rabbis, and strengthening their moral and religious convictions.

From a purely literary point of view the Midrash is at its best when it elaborates in flowing narrative form a brief story from the Bible, or when it illustrates a point with a parable. Other Midrashim of high literary quality are those telling about the doings of post-Biblical heroes, sages, leaders, or common men. Most of the material presented in this part belongs to these three types.

Several excerpts from Midrash sources which have a definite folktale flavor were included in part 6. Folktales.

CHRONOLOGY OF THE MIDRASHIM QUOTED

A Midrash may have been redacted (i.e., put in final shape) several centuries after the material contained in it was first assembled. In such a case I have assigned it to the date of its redaction. While the dates of the major Midrashim are firmly established, those of the minor ones and of the fragments frequently remain unknown.

2nd century	Avot diR. Nathan
	Shiur Qoma
3rd century	Sefer haRazim
4th century	Genesis Rabba
	Canticles Rabba
	Sifre on Numbers and Deuteronomy
	Sefer Hekhalot
	Massekhet Hekhalot
	Ma'ase diR. Y'hoshu'a ben Levi
5th century	Leviticus Rabba
	Lamentations Rabba
	Esther Rabba
	Pesiqta diR. Kahana
	3 Enoch
7th-9th centuries	Midrash Yona
	Divre haYamim Shel Moshe Rabbenu
	P'tirat Moshe

8th century	Seder Eliyahu Rabba
	Deuteronomy Rabba
	Ecclesiastes Rabba
	Massekhet Kalla
	Pirqe R. Eliezer
8th-9th centuries	Alfa Beta diR. Akiba
9th century	Pesiqta Rabbati
9th-10th centuries	Tanḥuma
	Tanḥuma edited by S. Buber
	Agadta diV'ne Moshe
10th century	Agadat B'reshit
	Shir haShirim Zuta
	Kisse v'Ippodromin shel Sh'lomo
10th-11th centuries	Ḥay Gaon (939–1038)
	Midrash l'Ḥanukka
10th-12th centuries	Midrash T'hillim
11th century	Midrash 'Aseret haDibrot
	Midrash waYosha'
	Midrash Abkir
	Midrash Konen
	Alfa Beta diBen Sira
	Agadat Mashiab
	Sefer haYashar
11th-12th centuries	Exodus Rabba
	Ma'ayan Ḥokhma
	T'fillat R. Shim'on ben Yoḥai
12th century	Numbers Rabba
	Midrash Temura
	Midrash Abba Gorion

13th century	D'mut Kisse Shel Sh'lomo
	Yalqut Shim'oni
	Midrash haGadol
14th century	Midrash Gadol uG'dola
	Aboab, Isaac, M'norat
	haMaor
	Yalqut haMakhiri
Of unknown date	Midrash Ele Ezkra
	Midrash Gan'Eden
	v'Gehinnom
	Midrash Goliath haP'lishti
	Ma'ase Avraham Avinu
	Massekhet Gehinnom
	Massekhet Ḥibbut haQever
	Seder Maḥanot
	Seder Y'tzirat haV'lad

CREATION, EDEN, GEHENNA

The Six Days of Creation

First Day. He took a lump of snow from beneath the Throne of Glory and cast it upon the face of the waters in the middle of the world, and it became the earth.... And He took the *Shetiyya* [Foundation] Stone and laid it in the place of the Temple and upon it the world became founded.... And He called to the earth and she stood in her place, to move neither here nor there, like a ship in the sea.... And when His light shone on the Land of Israel, it shone first in the Temple and from there it lighted up the whole world.... How did He light it up? He put on His Tallith and wrapped Himself in His light and lighted up the world.... And the waters covered the earth all that day, and the earth was melting away, until He clothed Himself in majesty, and His Glory radiated out ... and He girded

Himself in girders of strength, and stopped it with his strength....

Second Day. He said to the waters: "Divide yourselves into two halves, and let one half of you go up and one half down." And they rebelled, and all of them went up. The Holy One, blessed be He, said to them: "I said, Let one half of you go up, and you, all of you went up!" The waters said: "We shall not go down!" They were insolent before the Creator, therefore they are called *insolent waters*[1] (Isa. 43:16). What did the Holy One, blessed be He, do? He stretched forth His little finger and tore them into two parts, and half of them fell down against their will.... And the Holy One, blessed be He, wanted to burn them, until they stood and beseeched Him. He said to them: "Be it known to you that I shall seek to make my children pass in shoes in your midst. If I want to make you into a sea, you will be a sea; if dry land, you will be dry land."... After He divided the waters He created Erels, angels, Wheels, Seraphim, and Hashmals,[2] and blew into the fire and heated up the seven circles of Gehenna.

Third Day. He created all the trees and arbors in the Garden of Eden, and in This World He created all the food trees and the trees bearing no fruit. When the cedars of Lebanon and the trees of Bashan and all the tall trees saw that they were created first in the earth, instantly they became haughty and overbearing. The Holy One, blessed be He, said: "I hate pride and haughtiness. There is none proud in the world except Me." Instantly he created iron. And when the trees saw that he created the mountain of iron, they wept. This is why they are called "weeping trees."... The Holy One, blessed be He, said to them: "Why are you weeping?" They said to Him: "Because You created the mountain of iron so that they should uproot us

---

[1] This is the Midrashic interpretation of the expression actually meaning "mighty waters."

[2] Erels and Hashmals are kinds of angels.

from our stems. And we thought that there is nothing on earth as high as we are. And now there is created a destroyer to ruin us." The Holy One, blessed be He, said to them: "From you yourselves will come the handle for the axe which will cut you down. And I shall make it so that you should rule over it, and it should rule over you." And He made peace between them.

Fourth Day. He took fire and sealed it and stamped it and called its name sun, for it serves[3] the world. On the same day He took light and sealed it and stamped it and called its name moon . . . and it serves at night to light up the world when it is dark like a house of prison. And both were equal. . . . Both were great, until the moon complained against the sun and said before the Holy One, blessed be He: "Master of the World? . . . You created the sun and the moon. It is fitting that one of them should be greater than the other." The Holy One, blessed be He, said: "It is revealed and known before Me that it is in your mind that I should make you greater and should diminish the sun. Since you complained against him, you go and diminish yourself to one sixtieth of the light of the sun." Instantly the moon said before Him: "Master of the World! Because of one word that I said, I should be punished so severely?" He said to her: "In the future I shall restore you to equal the light of the sun. . . ."

Fifth Day. The Holy One, blessed be He, took light and water and created of them Leviathan and his wife, and all the fish of the sea, and He hung the whole world on the fins of Leviathan. He mixed the swamp of water and from it were created Ziz[4] of the field, and all the fowl of heaven, and he hung the feet of Ziz of the field on the fins of Leviathan, and its head is opposite the Throne of Glory. And He created a Wheel[5] on the earth and its head is

---

[3] In Hebrew a pun: sun — *shemesh*; serve — *m'shamesh.*

[4] A fabulous gigantic bird.

[5] This is the literal meaning of the Hebrew *ofan,* but it means a wheel-like angel.

opposite the Holy Beasts,[6] and he is the interpreter between Israel and their Father in heaven.... And his name is Sandalfon, and he ties crowns for the Master of Glory from the [words of the prayer] "Holy" and "Blessed is He" and "Amen, may His Great Name be blessed," which the Children of Israel recite in the synagogue. And he adjures the crown with the Ineffable Name, and goes and ascends to the head of the Lord....

Sixth Day. He took water and dust and light, and created Behemoth in the Thousand Mountains, and the Ox which pastures a thousand mountains every day. And they gambol every day in the Garden of Eden before the Creator. And He created animals and beasts and creeping things, and then gathered all the Ministering Angels groups by groups and said to them: *Let us make man* (Gen. 1:26). They said before Him: *What is man that Thou shouldst be mindful of him?* (Ps. 8:5). And this was the whole party of Michael. Instantly He burned them with His great fire and left of them only Michael alone. And He called the whole party of Gabriel, and they spoke as the former spoke to Him, and He burned them with His great fire and left of them only Gabriel alone. And He called the party of Laviel. They said before Him: "Master of the World! Who can tell You what You should do? Do as You wish in Your world, for this befits You." The Holy One, blessed be He, said: "You have properly looked out for yourself, for you have healed that which your comrades had destroyed." Instantly He changed his name and called his name Raphael [God heals], and placed into his hands all kinds of remedies in the world. He said to Michael: "Go, bring Me dust from the place of the Temple." He did so. The Holy One, blessed be He, heaped it in His hand and made it into Adam the first man. And the Holy One, blessed be He, appointed Michael and Gabriel over Israel. He appointed Raphael over all kinds of remedies and placed into his hand models of all

[6] Who carry God's Throne of Glory.

things which are in the world, such as the models of the
Upper Waters, and models of the Lower Waters. And even
if all those who walk on earth would assemble, they would
not be able to make anything like one model. And there is
no single grass or tree below which does not have its Prince
above, who covers it with a web, brings it in its due time,
and makes it grow.

(Konen, BhM 2:24-27)

Three Drops of Creation

What did God do? He opened the Tora, and took from her
a name which had not been delivered to any creature. And
He made three drops from it fall into the sea, and all of it
became filled with water and the Holy Spirit. And the
Shekhina of Holiness was hovering and blowing over it.
Then He opened the Tora again and took from her a second
name and took out of it three drops of light: one for the
light of This World, one for the light of the World to
Come, and one for the light of the Tora. He opened the
Tora a third time, and took out from there three drops of
fire and from that fire the whole world became heated,
except for the fire of the sons of man. When the Holy One,
blessed be He, saw fire on His right, light on His left, and
water beneath Him, He took them and mixed them
together two by two. He took fire and water and mixed
them together and made of them heaven, which is fire and
water.[7] And made of them a tent of darkness and the
Clouds of Glory. He took fire and light[8] and made of them
the Holy Beasts.

(Konen, BhM 2:24)

The Secrets of Creation

R. Shim'on ben Zoma sat lost in thoughts, and R. Y'hoshu'a

[7] In Hebrew *shamayim,* heaven, sounds similar to *esh-mayim,* fire-
water.

[8] The text has "fire and water," which is evidently a mistake.

passed by him and greeted him once, and twice, and he did not answer. The third time he answered him as if in confusion. He said to him: "Ben Zoma, whence the feet?"[9] He said to him: "I was contemplating." He said to him: "I call heaven and earth as my witnesses that I shall not move from here until you let me know whence the feet?" He said to him: "I was considering the work of Creation, and found that there were only two or three fingers between the Upper Waters and the Lower Waters. It does not say here, *And the spirit (wind)*[10] *of God blew over the face of the water*, but *hovered* (Gen. 1:2). Like unto this bird which flaps its wings, and its wings touch and yet do not touch." R. Y'hoshu'a returned and said to his disciples: "Ben Zoma is gone!" And within a few days Ben Zoma was in the World to Come.

(Gen. Rab. 2:4)

The heavens, from what place were they created? From the light of the garment of the Holy One, blessed be He, into which He is clothed. He took of it and spread it out like a cloth, and the heavens continued to stretch farther and farther until He said to them: "Enough!" ... The earth, from what place was it created? From the snow which is beneath the Throne of Glory. He took and cast it upon the waters, and the water froze and became the dust of the earth.

The hooks of the heavens are fastened to the waters of the ocean, for the waters of the ocean are between the edges of the earth and the edges of heavens, and the edges of heavens are spread over the waters of the ocean. The middle of heavens rises upwards, their globe is like a stretched-out tent whose edges are low and whose middle is high, and the children of Adam sit under it. So are the heavens: their edges are low and their middle high.

(Pirqe R. Eliezer, ch. 3)

---

9 I.e., where were you in your thoughts?

10 The Biblical word *ruah* means both "spirit" and "wind."

Introduction to the Book of Secrets [11]

This is a book of the books of secrets which was given to Noah son of Lamekh son of Methuselah, son of Enoch son of Jered son of Mahalel, son of Kenen son of Enosh son of Seth son of Adam, from the mouth of the angel Raziel, in the year of his going into the ark, prior to his entrance. And he wrote it with a sapphire stone, well explained, and from it Noah learned the work of miracles and the secrets of knowledge, and the values of understanding, and thoughts of modesty, and ideas of advice, to explore the degrees of the heights, and to roam about in all that is in the seven heavenly dwellings, and to scrutinize all the constellations and to study the way of the sun, and to explain the hidden things of the moon, and to know the paths of *the Bear, the Orion and the Pleiades* (Job 9:9), and to tell what are the names of the guards of each firmament and their kingdoms, and with what they can succeed in every thing, and what are the names of their servants. To know from it the work of death and the work of life, to understand the evil and the good, to search times and moments, to know the time of birth and the time of dying, the time of wounding and the time of healing, to interpret dreams and visions, to incite to battle and to settle wars, to rule over spirits and plagues, to send them so that they go as servants, to look into the four winds of the earth, to be wise about the sound of thunders, to relate what is the work of lightnings, to tell what will be in every month, to understand the affairs of every year, whether for satiety or for hunger, for crops or for drought, for peace or for war. To be like one of the terrible ones and to know the songs of the Above.

And from the wisdom of the secrets of this book Noah learned and understood how to make an ark of gopher

---

[11] The *Book of Secrets* (*Sefer haRazim*) is a Jewish-Hellenistic book of magic written in Hebrew in the third century C.E., and discovered and edited by Mordecai Margalioth, Jerusalem-Tel Aviv, 1967 (in Hebrew).

wood and to find refuge from the flood of the waters of the Deluge, to take with him two and two and seven and seven animals, and to put in of every food and every victual. And he placed this book into a golden box and brought it first into the ark to know from it the times of day and to search from it the times of night, and in what season he should stand up and cry for succor. And when they came out of the ark he used it all the days of his life, and at the time of his death he gave it to Abraham, and Abraham gave it to Isaac, and Isaac to Jacob, and Jacob to Levi, and Levi to Kehath, and Kehath to Amram, and Amram to Moses, and Moses to Joshua, and Joshua to the elders, and the elders to the prophets, and the prophets to the sages, and thus every generation, until King Solomon arose, and the Book of Secrets was revealed to him. And he became very knowledgeable in books of understanding, and ruled over all he wished, all the spirits and the plagues which roam about in the world, and he tied and released,[12] and sent and fetched, and built and succeeded with the wisdom of this book. For many books were delivered into his hand, and this one was found to be clearer and more honored and more solid than all the others. Happy the eye which looks at it, happy the ear which understands its wisdom, for in it are the seven firmaments and all that is in them. From their camps we shall learn to understand everything and to succeed in every act, to think and to do from the wisdom of this book.

(Sefer haRazim, pp. 65-66)

The World Proclaims Its Creator

An unbeliever came to R. Akiba and said to him: "Who created this world?" He said to him: "The Holy One, blessed be He." He said to him: "Show me a proof." He said to him: "Come back tomorrow." Next day he came. R.

---

[12] Or: prohibited and permitted.

Akiba said to him: "What is this you are wearing?" He said to him: "A garment." He said to him: "Who made it?" He said to him: "The weaver." He said to him: "I don't believe you. Show me a proof!" He said to him: "What can I show you? Don't you know that the weaver made it?" He said to him: "And you, don't you know that the Holy One, blessed be He, created His world?" The unbeliever went away. R. Akiba's disciples said to him: "What is the proof?" He said to them: "My sons, just as the house proclaims the builder, and the garment proclaims the weaver, and the door the carpenter, so the world proclaims the Holy One, blessed be He, that He created it. May His name be praised and exalted for ever and for all eternity."

(Temura, BhM 1:113-14)

The Size of the Throne

The high and exalted Throne, its length is eight hundred thousand myriads of parasangs, and its width is five hundred thousand myriads of parasangs, and its height is three hundred thousand myriads of parasangs. And these figures are in parasangs of the Holy One, blessed be He, blessed be His name and praised His memory, and each parasang of His is two thousand cubits, and His cubit is four spans, and His span is from one end of the world to the other. . . .

(Mass. Hekhalot, BhM 2:41)

The Arm of God

The length of the world is five hundred years and its width is five hundred years, and it is round, and the Great Sea, which is called Ocean, surrounds it. And the Great Sea stands on the fins of Leviathan, and Leviathan dwells in the midst of the Lower Waters, and appears in them as but a small fish in the sea. And the Lower Waters stand on the shore of the waters of Ocean and appear in them as but a small well which is on the shore of the sea. This is how the Lower Waters are compared to the waters of Ocean. And the waters of Ocean stand on the shore of the Waters of Genesis, and the waters of Ocean appear compared to them as a small well which is on the shore of the sea. And the Waters of Genesis stand on the shore of the Weeping Waters, and appear compared to them as a small well on the shore of the sea. And the Weeping Waters hang and stand on the Lowermost Earth. And the Lowermost Earth is stretched out upon the waters ... and the waters on pillars of *Ḥashmal*,[13] and the pillars of *Ḥashmal* on the Mountain of Hailstones, and the Mountain of Hailstones on the Storehouses of Snow, and the Storehouses of Snow on the Storehouses of Water and Fire, and the Storehouses of Water on the Sea, and the Sea on the Abyss [*Tehom*], and the Prince of the Abyss is like unto three ox-heads, and he stands between the Upper Abyss and the Lower Abyss, and says to the Upper Abyss, "Let your waters diminish," and to the Lower Abyss, "Let your waters spring up." ... And the Abyss stands on *Tohu,* and *Tohu* is like unto a green line which surrounds the whole world like a thread, and it mediates between the edges of heaven and the edges of the earth, and from there darkness comes forth. And *Tohu* stands on *Bohu* which is smooth stones which are sunk into the Abyss, and from them issue waters. ... And *Bohu* stands on the sea, and the sea stands on the Sweet Waters, and the Sweet Waters on the mountains, and the mountains on the wind, and the wind on the wings of storm ... and the storm is tied to *'Aravot* [heavens] and *'Aravot* are suspended from the arm of the Holy One, blessed be He.

(Konen, BhM 2:32-33, abridged)

The Tora Written on the Arm of God

We know that prior to the creation of the world there

---

[13] A mythical, glittering, fiery substance associated with the Throne of God, cf. Ezek. 1:27, where it is usually translated "electrum."

existed no skins of parchment upon which to write the Tora, for there were as yet no animals. How, then, was she written? On the arm of the Holy One, blessed be He, with black fire upon white fire. And the Holy One, blessed be He, took her and placed her before Him and was gazing at her.

('Aseret haDibrot, BhM 1:62)

The Feet of the Shekhina

The Lower Earth is suspended from the hooks of *'Aravot.* And the plain of *'Aravot* is in the Lower Earth and in it are the feet of the Beasts and the Wheels and the Seraphim. And over the horns of the Beasts is the Firmament, and over that Firmament is the Throne of Glory. And the feet of the Shekhina rest upon their heads.

(Konen, BhM 2:33)

Marble and Water

He who is unworthy to see the King in his beauty, the angels say to him, "Enter!" He enters. Instantly they press him and cast him into the fiery stream. And at the gate of the sixth Hall it seems as if thousands of myriads of waves of water were buffeting him, although not even a single drop of water is there, only the air of the glitter of pure marble stones with which the Hall is paved, and the glitter of whose appearance is more terrible than that of water. And the servants (i.e., the angels) stand facing him, and if he says, "These waters, what is their nature?" they instantly run after him to stone him, and say, "O you empty of deeds! Can you not see with your eyes? Are you, perchance, of the seed of those who kissed the Golden Calf, and are not worthy of seeing the King in his beauty?" Then a heavenly voice issues forth from the seventh Hall, and the herald comes forth before him and blows and winds the horn to let them know: "Well did you say, he is surely from the seed of those who kissed the Calf, and he is not worthy of seeing the King in his beauty!" And he moves not from there until they wound his head with iron sickles. This should be a sign for generations lest a man err at the sixth gate, and, upon seeing the glitter of the air of the stones, ask and say, "It is water!" and lest he thereby bring himself into danger. For even if he is not worthy of seeing, if he does not ask them about the air of the glitter of pure marble stones with which the Hall is paved, they do not destroy him but judge him to be meritorious.

(*Hekhalot* text, Ms. Munich 22d. 162b)

The World Stands on the Spirit

It happened that the royal authority asked R. Akiba: "On what does the world stand?" He said to him: "On the spirit." He said to him: "Show me!" He said to him: "Bring me camels loaded with salt." They brought him camels loaded with salt. He led them in all corners of the house. He said to them: "What do you see?" They said to him: "Camels loaded with salt." He said to them: "Bring me a rope." They brought him a rope, and he tied it around their necks. He gave the rope to two men. He said to them: "This one should pull from this side, and the other one from the other side." Until he strangled them. After he strangled them, he said to them: "Make them stand up!" They said to him: "O, you sage of the Jews! After you strangled them you say, Make them stand up?!" He said to them: "And what did you take away from them?" From here you learn that the world stands on nothing but the spirit which is superior and highly praiseworthy. And she was from the beginning, for it is said, *And the spirit of God hovered over the face of the waters* (Gen. 1:2). And there are two things about which we do not find that they were created, the spirit and the water, and they were from the beginning. . . .

(Temura, BhM 1:109)

Peace in High Places

Bar Kappara expounded: "Even the Supernal Ones need peace, as it is said, *Dominion and fear are with Him, He maketh peace in His high places* (Job 25:2). How? The firmament is of water, as it is said, *Who layest the beams of Thy upper chambers in the waters* (Ps. 104:3), and the stars are of fire, as it is said, *Praise ye Him, all the stars of light* (Ps. 148:3), and they are in peace the one with the other. These do not cause the firmament to boil, and the firmament does not extinguish them. Therefore it is said, *He maketh peace in His high places.*

And these angels, their bodies are created from the water, and they are frozen and they stand like glass as it is said, *His body is like the beryl* (Dan. 10:6), and their heads are of fire, as it is said, *And his face as the appearance of lightning* (ibid.), and it is written, *And his eyes like torches of fire* (ibid.). The one does not cause the other to boil, and the other does not extinguish the one. This is what is written, *He maketh peace in His high places.*

(Gadol uG'dola, BhM 3:128-29)

The Tree of Life

The Tree of Life stands in the middle of the Garden and its height is five hundred years' journey. And the souls of the just go up the Tree of Life to heaven, and from heaven to the celestial Garden of Eden, like a man who goes up and down a ladder. It is planted on a source of living water. And the size of the Garden is a thousand years' journey.

(Konen, OM, p. 255)

R. Y'hoshu'a ben Levi in the Garden of Eden

R. Y'hoshu'a ben Levi was a complete saint, and when his time came to depart from the world, the Holy One, blessed be He, said to the Angel of Death: "Do to him all his needs, whatever he asks of you." He went to him and said: "Your time has come to depart from the world, but whatever you ask of me I shall do for you." When R. Y'hoshu'a ben Levi heard this he said to him: "I ask of you that you show me the place of the Garden of Eden." He said to him: "Come with me and I shall show it to you." He said to him: "Give me your sword, lest you frighten me with it." Instantly he gave him the sword, and the two of them went until they reached the walls of the Garden of Eden. And when they reached the walls of the Garden of Eden, outside the wall the Angel of Death took R. Y'hoshu'a ben Levi and lifted him up and put him down on top of the walls of the Garden of Eden. He said to him: "Look at your place in the Garden of Eden." R. Y'hoshu'a ben Levi jumped down from the wall and fell into the Garden of Eden. But the Angel of Death held onto his robe. He said to him "Come out of there." R. Y'hoshu'a ben Levi swore by the Name of God, "I shall not come out of here." And the Angel of Death had no permission to enter there. The Ministering Angels said before the Holy One, blessed be He: "Master of the World! See what Ben Levi did! With force he took his share in the Garden of Eden." The Holy One, blessed be He, said to them: "Go and investigate whether before this he ever swore and transgressed his oath. In that case, he will have to transgress it now as well." They went out and investigated and said: "In his whole life he never transgressed his oath." The Holy One, blessed be He, said to them: "If so, he should not go out from there." When the Angel of Death saw that he could not make him come out, he said to him: "Give me the sword!" But R. Y'hoshu'a did not want to give it to him until a heavenly voice issued and said: "Give him the knife, for it is needed for the creatures." R. Y'hoshu'a said to him: "Swear to me that you will not show it to the creatures in the hour when you take the soul of a man." For before that, in whatever place he found a man he used to slaughter him in front of everybody like an animal, even in the bosom of his mother. And in that hour he swore to him, and R. Y'hoshu'a gave him the sword.

And Elijah began to proclaim before R. Y'hoshu'a and said: "Make room for Bar Livai!" He went and found R. Shim'on ben Yoḥai, who was seated on thirteen couches of the pious. He said to him: "Are you Bar Livai?" He said to him: "Yes." He said to him: "Did you ever see the rainbow in your lifetime?" He said to him: "Yes." He said to him: "If so, you are not Bar Livai." And it was not the case, for the rainbow was never seen in his lifetime, and why did he say that it was seen? In order not to praise himself. And why did Shim'on ben Yoḥai ask him about the rainbow? Because it is a sign of the covenant between the Holy One, blessed be He, and the earth, and whenever the rainbow appears the Holy One, blessed be He, has pity on His world.[14] And whenever there is one pious man in the world, the world does not need the rainbow, because for the sake of one pious man the world stands. . . . This is why he asked him about the rainbow.

(Ma'ase diR. Y'hoshu'a ben Levi, BhM 2:48-49)

The Creatures of Tevel

In Tevel[15] there are 365 kinds of creatures. Some of them are men with heads like those of oxen and their bodies are like those of oxen, and they talk like humans. And some of them have two heads and four ears and four eyes and two noses and two mouths and four hands and four legs but one body, and when they sit they look like two men and when they walk they look like one man. And when they eat and drink they quarrel with one another saying: "You ate more than I, and you drank more than I." And should you say they are wicked, God forbid, they are totally pious.

(Konen, BhM 2:36)

[14] According to Gen. 9:11-17 God placed the rainbow in the sky as a sign of the covenant to remind Him that He promised Noah never to bring another Deluge on the earth.

[15] One of the nether worlds.

Gehenna and Its Princes

The north of the world is Gehenna.... At its back are the storehouses of the fire of Gehenna and the storehouses of snow and hailstones and steam and frost and darkness and storm wind, and it is a thousand times thousand seven hundred and five years.[16] And there are also in it, a walk of five years, the dwellings of demons and harmful demons and destructive spirits. And there is Gehenna, and its size is 2,100 years, and there the wicked are punished in the seven circles of Gehenna, and there is the party of Samael, and the north wind does not cover it.... And there is a distance of five years between the dwellings of the demons and the settled parts of the northern wind. And were it not so, they would destroy the whole world.

The Prince of Gehenna, Kipod is his name, and his second comrade is Negadsagiel, and the third prince is Samael, and they are appointed over three great gates. One gate is in the desert, and there went down Korah and his company to Sheol (the underworld), and Negadsagiel is appointed over it. The second gate is in the Sea of Tarshish, and Kipod is appointed over it. The third gate is in the Valley of Ben Hinnom opposite Zion and Jerusalem.

(Konen, BhM 2:30)

The Compartments of Gehenna

There are seven compartments in Gehenna, and these are their names: *Sheol* [Hades], whose size is three hundred years' journey and in it are punished Korah and his community for twelve months, like meat in a caldron; *Abaddon* [Perdition], whose size is three hundred years, and in it perish the souls of the wicked; *B'er Shaḥat* [Well of Ruination], whose size is three hundred years, and in it are punished the robbers and the thieves and they who deprive

---

[16] I.e., it would take 1,705,000 years to go from one end to the other.

the hired workers of their wages; *Bor Sh'on* [Tumultuous Pit] in which there are two wells which are filled one from the other and empty one into the other, and they are never filled; *Tit haY'ven* [Miry Clay], whose size is three hundred years, and in it are punished those who committed incest, and they sink into it and never come up; Death's Shadow or *Duma* [Silence], whose size is three hundred years, and in it those who envy the sages are punished with all kinds of punishments; *Lowest Earth,* whose size is three hundred years, and in it sink down into darkness those Jews who contradict the sages. . . .

And there are seven houses: In the first house are opened many pits, and lions of fire stand there, and when people fall into them they instantly devour them, and after the fire has consumed them they regain their former shape and fall down again. In the second house there are ten thousand myriads of the nations of the world, and Absalom is appointed over them to punish them. And a heavenly voice says: "Let him be for the sake of his father's [David's] merits." And a cruel angel stands and beats the nations with a rod of fire, and his name is Qoshiel [Severity of God]. And Absalom was absolved from the punishment for the sake of his fathers who said at Mount Sinai, *All that the Lord hath spoken we will do and obey* (Exod. 24:7). And the wicked are punished there twice a day.

And in the third house are punished another ten thousand myriads of the aforementioned nations of the world, and they are punished with rods of fire like the first ones. And the name of the angel appointed over them is Shoftiel [My Judge Is God]. And Korah and his community are there, and Korah is appointed over them. And Korah was absolved of the punishment for the merits of Levi son of Jacob, and his community is absolved of the punishment because their fathers said at Mount Sinai, *We will do and obey.* In the fourth house are punished another ten thousand myriads of the aforementioned nations of the world, with rods of fire, like the first ones, and Jeroboam son of Nevat is appointed over them, and the angel who beats them is called Mattaniel [My Gift Is God]. And Jeroboam was saved from the punishment for the sake of Ephraim son of Joseph who was a completely pious man, and because his fathers said at Mount Sinai, *We will do and obey.*

In the fifth house are punished another ten thousand myriads of the nations of the world every day, like the first ones, and Ahab is with them, and the name of the angel who beats them is Oniel [My Power Is God]. And Ahab escaped these punishments because his fathers said at Mount Sinai, *We will do and obey.* In the sixth house are punished every day ten thousand myriads of the aforementioned nations of the world, like the first ones, and Micha [the judge who set up a graven image] is with them, and the angel who beats them is called Hadriel [My Splendor Is God]. And Micha escaped all these punishments because his fathers said at Mount Sinai, *We will do and obey.* In the seventh house are punished every day ten thousand myriads of the aforementioned nations of the world, like the first ones, and with them is Elisha' Aḥer, he is Elisha' ben Abuya [the Talmudic sage who became an unbeliever]. And the name of the angel who is appointed over them is Rogziel [My Wrath Is God], and Elisha' Aḥer is punished with them.

(Konen, OM, 1:256-57)

The Fires of Gehenna

R. Yoḥanan began: "... There are five kinds of fire in Gehenna: A fire which eats and drinks, one which drinks but eats not, one which eats but drinks not, one which neither drinks nor eats, and then there is a fire which eats fire. There are in it embers as big as mountains, and embers like hills, and embers like the Dead Sea. And there are in it embers like big rocks, and there are in it rivers of pitch and of sulphur which flow and boil with broom shrubs.

The punishment of the wicked: Angels of destruction

throw him down on his face before the fire of Gehenna.
And Gehenna opens wide her mouth and swallows him. . . .
This happens to him who has not a single good deed in his
hand which could tilt the scales to the side of merits. But he
who has in his hand Tora and good deeds, and many
sufferings have come to him, he is saved from the
punishment of Gehenna.

(Mass. Gehinnom, BhM 1:147)

The Angels of Destruction

R. Yishma'el said: "Metatron, the Prince of the Face, said to
me: 'Come and I shall show you the souls of the wicked,
where they go down, and the souls of the average people
where they stand.' And he said: 'The souls of the wicked are
taken down to Sheol by two angels of destruction, and they
are *Za'afiel* [My Wrath Is God] and *Samkhiel* [My Support Is
God]. Samkhiel is appointed over the souls of the average
people to support them and to cleanse them with the great
mercy of God; Za'afiel over the souls of the wicked to
make them go down from before the Holy One, blessed be
He, from the judgment of the Shekhina, with rods of
burning coal.' And I approached him, and he took me by
the hand and showed me everything with the fingers of his
hand. . . ."

(Seder Maḥanot, BhM 5:186)

The Quarters of Gehenna

In the southern quarter . . . is the entrance to Gehenna, and
the wicked enter there and turn and see the eastern quarter,
and view the honor of the pious, and they are ashamed and
regretful, and say: "Woe to us that we sinned and that we
did not occupy ourselves with the Tora and with the
commandments!" And angels of destruction drive them
with thorns until they reach the depth of Gehenna which is
in the northern quarter.

And between the entrance of Gehenna and the settled part of the south there is a distance of 104 years' journey. And as soon as the soul flies out of her body, the angels of destruction seize her and, before you could blink an eye, they hurl her to the angels of wrath, and the angels of wrath hurl her into Gehenna, as it is written, *And the souls of thy enemies, them shall he sling out as from the hollow of a sling* (Sam. 25:29), and they torture her in Gehenna.

(Konen, OM 1:256-57)

Sins and Judgment

When a man dies and lies on his bier, the ministering angels walk in front of him and the people walk after him. If the people say of him: "Happy was this man, he was good and pleasant in his life," the ministering angels tell him, "Write!" and he writes and they sign it. Moreover, two ministering angels accompany the man in the hour of his death, and they know if he was a thief, or if he muzzled an animal while threshing, or if he oppressed, and, more than that: the very beams of his house and its stones testify about him. And he who repented is taken to the Garden of Eden, and if he died without repentance he is taken to Gehenna.

(Gan 'Eden w'Gehinnom, BhM 5:50)

The Courts of Gehenna

There are five law courts set up in Gehenna, and Isaiah saw all of them. He entered the first court and found there two men who were carrying water jars on their shoulders and were filling them and pouring the water into a pit but the pit never filled up. Isaiah, peace be upon him, said before the Holy One, blessed be He: "Reveal the secret, reveal the secret of this!" The Holy Spirit answered him: "These are men who coveted what their fellow men had, and because of it they are punished in this manner." He entered the second court and found there two men who were strung up by their tongues. And he said to the Holy One, blessed be He: "Reveal the secret, reveal the secret of this!" He answered him: "These are men who slandered, and because of it they are thus punished." He entered the third court and found there men who were strung up by their genitals. He said: "Reveal the secret of this!" He said to him: "These are men who left their wives and fornicated with daughters of Israel, and because of it they are thus punished." He entered the fourth court and found there two women strung up by their breasts. He said: "Reveal the secret of this!" He said: "These are women who uncovered their heads and opened up their garments and sat in the marketplace and suckled their children in the marketplace in order to make the hearts of men incline towards them and to cause them to sin, and because of it they are thus punished." He entered the fifth court and found there the pashas and the deputies and the cashiers, and the wicked Pharaoh sitting above them and guarding the entrance of Gehenna and saying to them: "You should not have learned from me when you were in Egypt!" And he still sits and guards every entrance of Gehenna.

(Gan 'Eden w'Gehinnom, BhM 5:50-51)

BIBLICAL HEROES

Adam the Androgyne

Thou hast formed me from the back and the front (Ps. 139:5).[17] R. Yirm'ya ben El'azar said: "In the hour in which the Holy One, blessed be He, created Adam the first man, He created him as an androgyne. This is meant by what is written, *Male and female created He them, and called their name Adam* (Gen. 5:2)." R. Sh'muel bar Naḥman said: "In the hour in which the Holy One, blessed be He, created Adam the first man,

---

[17] This is the Midrashic interpretation of the verse.

He created him with two visages, and then sawed him into two and made him two backs, a back here and a back there."

(Gen. Rab. 8:1)

Adam the Giant

R. Tanhuma in the name of R. B'naya and R. Berekhya in the name of R. El'azar said: "He created him in the form of a Golem [a lifeless clod], and it was lying and extending from one end of the world to the other. This is meant by what is written, *Thine eyes did see my Golem* (Ps. 139:16)."

R. Y'hoshu'a ben R. N'hemya and R. Y'huda ben R. Simon in the name of R. El'azar said: "He created him filling the whole world."

(Gen. Rab. 8:1)

Creation by Theft

A Roman matron asked R. Yose: "Why did God create woman by theft?" He said to her: "A parable: if somebody deposited with you an ounce of silver in secret, and you return to him a pound of gold openly, is this a theft?" She said to him: "But why in secret?" He said to her: "At first He created her for him, and he saw her full of secretions and blood, and he rejected her. Thereupon He created her a second time while he was asleep." She said to him: "I can add to your words: I was spoken for to marry the brother of my mother, but because I grew up with him in one house I seemed ugly in his eyes, and he went and married another woman and she is not more beautiful than I."

(Gen. Rab. 17:7)

Adam's Wedding

The Holy One, blessed be He, loved Adam the first man with love abounding in that He created him from a pure place. And from which place did He take him? From the place of the Temple, and brought him into His mansion, as it is said, *And the Lord took the man and put him into the Garden of Eden to work it and to guard it* (Gen. 2:15). And should you say, "What work was there in the Garden of Eden? Perchance to prune the vines, to plow and harrow the soil, or to harvest and to bind sheaves? Was it not that all the trees grew by themselves? And should you say, there was work in the Garden of Eden, namely to water the garden; is it not that a river flowed and issued forth from Eden, as it is said, *A river went out of Eden to water the garden* (Gen. 2:10)? No, [the work Adam did was] to occupy himself with the words of the Tora and to guard the way of the Tree of Life, and the Tree of Life is none other than the Tora, as it is said, *A tree of life is she for them that lay hold upon her* (Prov. 3:18). And Adam was strolling about in the Garden of Eden as one of the Ministering Angels. The Holy One, blessed be He, said: "I am one in My World, and he is one in his world; I—there is no procreation before Me, and he—there is no procreation before him. Hereafter the creatures will say, 'Since there is no procreation before him, it is he who created us.' *It is not good that the man should be alone; I will make him a helpmeet for him* (Gen. 2:18)." ...

When the earth heard this language, she trembled and shook, and said before her Creator: "Master of all the worlds! There is no strength in me to nourish the flock of man!" The Holy One, blessed be He, said to her: "I and you together will nourish the flock of man." And they divided among them: the night for the Holy One, blessed be He, and the day for the earth. What did the Holy One, blessed be He, do? He created the sleep of life, so that a man lies down and sleeps, and this is for him nourishment, and healing, and life, and rest.... And the Holy One, blessed be He, supports the earth and waters her, and she gives her fruit and nourishment to all the creatures. But the nourishment of men, *in toil shalt thou eat it all the days of thy life* (Gen. 3:17).

However, the Holy One, blessed be He, had pity on him, and in order not to cause him pain *He caused a deep sleep to fall upon the man, and he slept* (Gen. 2:21). And He took a bone of his bones and flesh from his heart and made it into a helpmeet, and made her stand up in front of him. He awoke from his sleep and saw her standing before him, and instantly he embraced and kissed her and said: "Blessed are you to the Lord! Your bone is of my bone, and you are worthy of being called Woman."

The Holy One, blessed be He, prepared ten canopies for Adam the first man in the Garden of Eden, and all of them of precious stones and pearls and of gold. But is it not that for every bridegroom they make only one canopy, and even for a king they make only three canopies? However, the Holy One, blessed be He, made ten canopies for Adam the first man in order to honor him, as it is said, *Thou wast in Eden the garden of God; every precious stone was thy covering, the carnelian, the topaz, and the emerald, the beryl, the onyx, and the jasper, the sapphire, the carbuncle, and the smaragd, and gold* (Ezek. 28:13)—these are the ten canopies. And the angels were beating drums and dancing like females. And the Ministering Angels were like groomsmen who guard the canopy. And as the prayer-leader [Ḥazzan] stands and blesses the bride in her canopy, so God stood and blessed Adam and his helpmeet.

(Pirqe R. Eliezer, ch. 12)

The Origin of Fire

When the sun sank at the outgoing of the Sabbath, and darkness came nearer and nearer, Adam was terrified, as it is written, *Surely the darkness shall bruise me* (Ps. 139:11). He said: "The serpent, about whom it is said, *He shall bruise thy head and thou shalt bruise his heel* (Gen. 3:15), is coming to attach himself to me!" What did the Holy One, blessed be He, do? He made him find two flints which he struck against each other, and light came forth, and he uttered a blessing over it. This agrees with Sh'muel, for he said: "Why do we recite a blessing over the candle at the termination of the Sabbath? Because fire was then created for the first time."

(Gen. Rab. 11:2)

The Fragrant Garments of Adam

Adam the first man, who was the firstborn of the world, was the first to wear priestly garments, as it is said, *And the Lord God made for Adam and for his wife garments of skin and clothed them* (Gen. 3:21). Adam handed over the garments to Seth, and Seth to Methuselah, and Methuselah to Noah, and Noah to Sem who was the firstborn of Noah, and Sem gave them to Abraham, and Abraham to Isaac, and Isaac to Esau who was the firstborn. And when Isaac saw that Esau's wives worshiped idols, he took the garments from Esau and placed them into the safekeeping of Rebekah. When Jacob stood up and took the firstborn's right from Esau, Rebekah said, "Since Jacob has taken the right of the firstborn, it is lawful that he should wear these garments." He entered to his father, who smelled the fragrance which he had smelled when he was tied upon the altar.

(Agadat B'reshit, ed. Buber, p. 86)

The Fall of Man

Samael was the greatest prince in heaven. The celestial animals and the Seraphim had six wings each, but Samael had twelve. He took his cohorts and went down, and saw all the creatures whom the Holy One, blessed be He, had created, and found among them none as astute and malicious as the serpent. And the serpent's appearance was like that of a camel. And Samael mounted him and rode him. And the Tora cried and shrieked and said: "Samael, the world has just been created, is this the time to rebel against God?"

The serpent went and said to the woman: "Is it true that you are commanded not to eat the fruit of this tree? She said to him: "Yes." The serpent said: "This is but a commandment of jealousy, for in the hour in which you eat of it you will be like unto God. Just as He creates worlds and then destroys them, so you too will be able to create worlds and to destroy worlds. Just as He slays and gives life, so you too will be able to slay and to give life." Then the serpent went and touched the tree. The tree cried out and said: "You evil one, do not touch me!" The serpent went and said to the woman: "Behold, I touched the tree and did not die. You too can touch it and will not die." The woman went and touched the tree, and in that moment she saw the Angel of Death coming towards her. She said: "Now I shall die, and the Holy One, blessed be He, will make another woman and give her to Adam. I would rather make him eat with me, if we die, we shall both die, and if we live, we shall both live."

And she took of the fruit of the tree and ate, and gave of the fruit also to her husband that he too eat with her. When Adam ate of the fruit of the tree he saw that he was naked, and his eyes opened and his teeth were set on edge. And he said to her: "What is this you gave me to eat which opened my eyes and set my teeth on edge? I know that just as my teeth were set on edge so will the teeth of all generations be set on edge."

(Pirqe R. Eliezer. ch. 13)

The Birth of Cain

When Eve gave birth to Cain she saw that his appearance was not of This World but of the Supernal World. She looked at him and said: *I have gotten a man from the Lord* (Gen. 3:1).

(Pirqe R. Eliezer, ch. 21)

Cain and Abel

And Cain spoke unto Abel his brother. What did he say to him?
"Let us divide the world. And since I am the firstborn, I
shall take a double share." Abel said to him: "Cannot be."
Cain said: "In that case I shall take one thing in addition to
my share: the place where your offering was accepted."
Abel said to him: "You will not take it." And over this
matter they fell to quarreling. Some say that Cain said to
Abel: "Let us divide the world." Abel said: "All right."
Abel took the flock and Cain the land to work. And they
agreed between them that one will not have anything from
the share of the other. When Abel took his flock, he began
to graze the flock, and Cain pursued him from mountain to
valley and from valley to mountain, until they got hold of
each other, and Abel defeated Cain who fell down under
him. And when Cain saw this, he began to cry: "Abel, my
brother, do no evil to me!" And Abel had compassion on
him and let off him, whereupon Cain arose and killed him.

As soon as he killed him he said: "I shall flee from my
father and my mother for there is nobody from whom they
will demand him but me, for there is none other in the
world save me and him."

Instantly the Holy One, blessed be He, revealed Himself
to Cain and said to him: "From your parents you can flee,
from Me you cannot flee. . . ." And He said to him: *Where is
Abel thy brother?* (Gen. 4:9) And God said to him: "Woe to
Abel that he had pity on you and did not kill you when you
fell down under him, and you stood up and killed him!"

And how did Cain kill Abel? He inflicted on him wound
after wound, blow after blow, with a rock, on his hand and
on his feet, for he did not know from where his soul would
depart, until he reached his neck. And when the Holy One,
blessed be He, said to him, *Where is Abel thy brother?* he said:
"I know not; *am I my brother's keeper?* (ibid.) You are the
keeper of all the creatures and You demand him from my
hand?" To what can this be likened? To a thief who stole

vessels at night and was not caught. In the morning the
gatekeeper caught him, and said to him: "Why did you
steal the vessels?" He said: "I am a thief, and I have not
abandoned my vocation. But you, your vocation is in the
gate, to watch; why did you abandon your vocation? And
now you are telling me this?" Likewise Cain said: "I killed
him, because You created in me the Evil Inclination. You
are the keeper of all, and You let me kill him. You are the
one who killed him. For had You accepted my offering like
his, I would not have become jealous of him!"

Instantly the Holy One, blessed be He, answered him:
*What has thou done? The voice of thy brother's blood crieth unto
Me* (Gen. 4:10) — unto Me — against Me. This can be likened
to two who engaged in a fight, and one of them killed the
other, and there was an officer present and he did not
separate them. Against whom will everybody speak? Is it
not against the officer? Therefore it is written *crieth unto
Me,* read *crieth against Me.*

Cain said to Him: "Lord of the World! I did not know,
for I had never seen a slain man all my life. How could I
have known that if I strike him with a stone he will die?"

Instantly He answered him: *Cursed art thou from the
ground* (Gen. 4:11). Cain said to Him: "Lord of the World!
Are there, perchance, informers before You who denounce
a person to You? My father and my mother are on earth
and yet they do not know that I killed Abel, and You in
heaven, how do You know?" He said to him: "You fool! I
bear the whole world...." Cain said to Him: "You bear the
whole world, but my sin you cannot bear? *My punishment is
greater than I can bear*" (Gen. 4:13).

He said to him: "Since you made repentance, go forth
and be exiled from this place." As he went forth, in every
place where he went the earth trembled under him, and the
animals and the cattle trembled and said: "What is this?"
And they said to one another: "Cain killed Abel his
brother, and the Holy One, blessed be He, decreed upon
him, *A fugitive and a wanderer shalt thou be.*" They said: "Let

us go to him and devour him." And they gathered and came to him. In that hour his eyes overflowed with tears, and he said, *Whither shall I go from Thy spirit? Or whither shall I flee from Thy presence? If I ascend up into heaven, Thou are there, if I make my bed in the nether world, Thou are there. If I take the wings of the morning, and dwell in the uttermost parts of the sea, even there would Thy hand lead me, and Thy right hand would hold me.* (Ps. 139:7-10).

(Tanḥ. B'reshit 9)

R. Yoḥanan said: "Abel was stronger than Cain, for what the Scripture says, *and Cain rose up,* teaches us that he had fallen under Abel. But Cain said to him: Only we two are in the world; what will you tell Father? Abel was filled with compassion for him, and thereupon Cain instantly rose up against him and killed him. Hence people say, Do not good to the wicked and the wicked will not reach you."

R. Shim'on ben Yoḥai said: "Abel's argument against God was a very hard thing to say, and his mouth could not utter it. It can be likened to two gladiators who were standing and fighting before the king. Had the king wanted it, he could have separated them. But the king did not wish to separate them, and one of them overcame the other and killed him. [And as the defeated gladiator was dying] he cried out and said: Who will demand my life from the King? Thus *The voice of thy brother's blood crieth unto Me from the ground.*"

(Gen. Rab. 22:8, 9)

The Tower of Babel

They said: "Once in 1,656 years a Deluge comes upon the earth,[18] the heaven collapses, and the upper waters fall

---

[18] The rabbis figured that the Deluge took place 1,656 years after the creation of the world, and attributed this knowledge to the people of the Tower.

upon us. Therefore, come, let us make ourselves towers, so that if the heaven should fall, they should hold it up."

(Tanḥ. Buber, 1:27a)

The generation of the dispersion said: "Once in 1,656 years the firmament collapses. Therefore let us build pillars: one in the north, one in the south, one in the west, and this one to support it in the east."

The generation of the dispersion said of God: "It is not right that He should select for Himself the supernal realms and give us only the lower ones. Let us make us a tower. We will set an idol on its top, and put a sword in its hand so that it will seem to wage war against God."

The generation of the Deluge was immersed in violence and no remnant was left of it. But because the generation of the dispersion loved one another . . . a remnant was left of it. Rabbi said: "Great is peace, for even if Israel engages in idolatry, while there is peace among them, God, as it were, says: 'I cannot prevail against them since there is peace in their midst.' "

(Gen. Rab. 38:1, 6)

R. Huna said: "Their work was accomplished with great ease: a man laid one brick, and behold—two were laid. He put mortar for one, and behold—he had four done.

"The one third of the tower which remained standing is so huge that if you climb up to its top, the palm trees below will appear to you like locusts."

(Gen. Rab. 38:1, 6, 7)

The people of the tower were "men of falsehood" (Ps. 26:4). They went and said to Abraham: "Come and dwell with us. For you are a hero, and we see that God sits on high and has left us down below." Whereupon the Holy Spirit cried: "You cannot sit quietly even for one hour!" Abraham said: "What do you want of the Holy One, blessed be He, who dwells on high? Did He perchance tell you, 'Go, toil and maintain Me?' He creates and maintains, He makes and carries, what do you want of Him?" But they said: "Let us build a city and a tower, and let us set our idol on its top, and let us wage war against Him." Abraham said to them: "Why all this?" They said to him: "So that He should not do to us as He did to our ancestors."

(Tanḥ. Buber 1:50a-b)

The Childhood of Abraham

Said the narrator: At that time[19] the mother of Abraham our father, peace be upon him, went and took a man, by the name of Terah, and she conceived from him. And it came to pass after about three months that her belly had grown big and her face green, and Terah her husband said to her: "What is the matter, my wife, your face has turned green and your belly is big?" She said to him: "Every year this illness, which is called *qoltzani*, [20] comes upon me." Terah said to her: "Show me your belly, for it seems to me that you are pregnant, and if so, it is not proper that we transgress the commandment of our god Nimrod."[21] He put his hand upon her belly. The Holy One, blessed be He, made her a miracle, and the child went up under the chest. And Terah examined her with his hand but found nothing. He said to her: "You were right in what you said." And the thing could not be seen and did not become known until the months of the child were complete. And because of her great fear she went out of the city and went the way of the desert, near a river, and there she found a big cave and entered it. And the next day the pangs of childbirth got hold of her, and she bore a son. And she saw that the whole

---

[19] I.e., after Nimrod decreed that all the male children born be killed.

[20] Arabic term, meaning vomiting.

[21] Nimrod had ordered that all pregnant women must go to a special house, where the male newborns were killed.

cave shone like the sun from the light of the child's face, and she rejoiced greatly. And he was Abraham our father, peace be upon him. And she opened her mouth and said: "I bore you at this time when Nimrod rules, and he killed because of you seventy thousand male children, and I fear for you very much, for should he learn about you he would kill you, and therefore it is better that you die in this cave and my eyes should not see you slaughtered upon my breast." And she took the garment which was upon her and dressed him, and left him in the cave, and said: "May your god be with you, may he not leave you nor abandon you." And she went her way.

Said the narrator: Abraham our father, peace be upon him, while he was still in the cave, had no wetnurse to suckle him. He cried and God heard his weeping and sent the angel Gabriel to keep him alive and to give him milk. And the angel caused milk to come out of his right finger and he sucked from it until Abraham was ten days old and began to walk on the earth and went out of the cave and went to the bank of the river. And when the sun set and stars came out he said: "These are God." Then, when the pillar of dawn rose, he could not see the stars and said: "I shall not serve these, for they are not God." Then he saw the sun and said: *"This is my God and I shall praise Him* (Exod. 15:2)." And when the sun set he said: "This is not God." He saw the moon and said: "This is my God, and I shall serve him." When it darkened he said: "This is not God. They have a Mover." He was still talking, and, behold, the angel Gabriel came and said to him: "Peace be upon you, Abraham." He said to him: "Upon you be peace! Who are you?" He said to him: "I am the angel Gabriel, the messenger of the Holy One, blessed be He." In that hour he went to a source which he found there and washed his face and his hands and his feet, and prayed to God, blessed be He, with kneeling and prostration.

Said the narrator: The mother of Abraham our father, peace be upon him, remembered him and wept a great weeping and went forth from the city to seek her son in the cave where she had left him, and she found him not, and she multiplied the weeping over him more and said: "Woe to me that I bore you to be a prey to the beasts of the field, to the bears and to the lions and to the wolves." And she went to the banks of the river and found there her son but she knew him not for he had grown very much in stature. She said to him: "Peace be upon you." And he replied to her: "And upon you be peace. What are you walking in these deserts?" She said to him: "I came out from the city to seek my son." He said to her: "And your son, who brought him here?" She said to him: "I was pregnant from Terah my husband and at the time of birth I feared for my son who was in my belly, that our king Nimrod ben Canaan should not kill him as he killed seventy thousand children by number, and I came to a cave near this river, and the pangs of birth came upon me, and I bore a son and left him in the cave and went to my house, and now I came to seek him and found him not." Abraham said to her: "These things you said, that you left the child, how many days old is he?" She said to him: "About twenty days." He said to her: "Is there a woman in the world who will leave her small son in the desert alone, and will come to look for him twenty days later?" She said to him: "Perhaps the god had mercy on him." He said to her: "I am your son for whose sake you came to this river." She said to him: "My son, you grew this much, and you are walking on your feet, and speaking with your mouth, and all this in twenty days?" He said to her: "Yes, so that it become known to you, my mother, that there is in the world a great and fearsome God, who lives and exists, sees and is not seen, and He is in heaven, and *the whole earth is full of His glory* (Isa. 6:3)." She said to him: "My son, is then another god besides Nimrod?" He said to her: "Yes, my mother, the God of heaven, and the God of the earth, and the God of Nimrod ben Canaan. Therefore, go to Nimrod and announce to him this thing."

(Ma'ase Avraham Avinu, BhM 1:26-28)

Abraham the Astrologer

Abraham was an astrologer and he saw in the stars that he would not beget, neither he nor Sarah. And all the other astrologers saw it likewise. Therefore he spoke to the Holy One, blessed be He: "It is not possible that I should beget, and even though everybody said so, I did not believe it until I myself saw it in the stars."

The Holy One, blessed be He, said to him: "Do no longer observe those things, leave behind you that skill.... And what did all of them say to you? That Abram will not beget and Sarai will not bear.... When will you two have offspring? When *thy name shall no more be called Abram, but thy name shall be Abraham* (Gen. 17:5), and your wife Sarai, *thou shalt not call her name Sarai, but Sarah shall be her name* (Gen. 17:15). That is, Abram does not beget, but Abraham begets; Sarai does not bear, but Sarah bears."

(Agadat B'reshit, ed. Buber, p. 73)

Isaac's Paternity

And these are the generations of Isaac Abraham's son: Abraham begot Isaac (Gen. 25:19). Do I not know that Abraham begot Isaac? R. Ḥanania Rabba said: "A parable. It is like a dove whom the hawks and the ravens pursued. She fled from them and entered and sat in her nest, and the people said: "These eggs are from the hawk," and others said: "They are from the raven." One of them said to them: "As long as they are eggs it is not known whether they are from the raven, or they are from the hawk. But let them be until they hatch and become chicks, then you will know from whom they are!"

Thus Sarah wandered much: to Pharaoh, to Abimelech. People began to say: "She did not conceive except from Pharaoh," and others said: "She did not conceive except from Abimelech." The Holy One, blessed be He, said to them: "*Let the mouth of them that speak lies be stopped* (Ps. 63:12). Wait until she bears, and you will see to whom he

resembles." Instantly the Holy One, blessed be He,
commanded the angel who is in charge of the shape of the
foetus, and said to him: "Shape him not to be like his
mother, but to be like his father, so that everybody should
know that he is from nobody else but his father." Instantly
he emerged resembling his father. This is why it is said,
Abraham begot Isaac.

(Agadat B'reshit, ed. Buber, p. 75)

The Captain and His Ship

As soon as Sarah died, suddenly old age jumped upon
Abraham. A parable: There was a valiant sea captain who
had a ship. He conquered the seas and the winds. When
pirates came upon him, he stood up and slew all of them.
After a time he sailed into the entrance of a harbor, and a
hard wind came upon him, and his ship broke. He began to
beseech people for mercy: "I beseech you, save me!" They
said to him: "Yesterday you were a conqueror of the seas, a
killer of pirates, and now you beg of others that they save
you?" He said to them: "As long as I had my ship I was
valiant and needed no help, but now that my ship broke,
my strength broke."

Thus Abraham was valiant. Pirates came upon him, but
he stood up and slew all of them. . . . They said to him:
"Yesterday you were a ruler of the whole world . . . and now
you say, *I am a stranger and a sojourner* (Gen. 23:4)? He said
to them: "And what shall I do, since my wife died. . . . "
Instantly, *and Abraham became old* (Gen. 24:1).

(Agadat B'reshit, ed. Buber, pp. 66-67)

The Akeda

I

As Isaac was walking with his father, what did Satan do? He
came and stood on the right side of Isaac, and said to him:

"O you miserable boy, son of a miserable woman! How many fasts did your mother observe, and how many prayers did she offer until finally you came to her. And now this old man became demented because of his old age and he is going to slaughter you!"

Instantly Isaac turned to his father and said: "Father, do you see what this man says to me?" He said to him: "He came to cause you worry. The Holy One, blessed be He, *will provide for Himself a lamb* (Gen. 22:8)." Instantly *they came to the place which God had told him of, and Abraham built the altar there* (Gen. 22:9). And why did Isaac not build it with him? Because Abraham said, lest a stone or a bundle fall upon him and make a blemish in him and render him unfit for a sacrifice. He built the altar, arranged the wood and tied Isaac on top of it. Abraham took the knife to slay him. Isaac said to him: "Father, tie my hands and feet, for the soul is unruly, lest when I see the knife coming toward me I tremble and become unfit for a sacrifice." His father tied him down. As he was about to put the knife to his throat, the angels came and cried and sobbed before the Holy One, blessed be He. What did they cry? "Where is the reward for all those wayfarers who were coming from every place and lodging with Abraham, who ate for nothing, and [through whom Abraham] made You a blessing in the world? Are You violating the covenant in which You said to Abraham *I will establish My covenant with Isaac* (Gen. 17:21)? And, behold, the knife is on his throat! How long will You wait?" Instantly the Holy One, blessed be He, said to Michael: "What are you standing? Do not let him do it." Michael began to call him, and said, "Abraham, Abraham!" twice. For Abraham rushed to slay Isaac and Michael shouted at him like a man who shouts when seized with pain: "What are you doing?" Abraham turned his face to him, and Michael said to him: "What are you doing? *Lay not thy hand upon the lad* (Gen. 22:12)."

(Pes. Rab. pp. 170b-171a)

II

A parable. There was a king who said to his friend: "I desire to see a peacock on my table." His friend instantly went and brought the peacock and put it on the table. He ran to fetch the knife to slaughter it. The king shouted and said: "What are you doing? Did I say to you that I desire to see a peacock on my table slaughtered? No, alive! And since you brought the knife, behold, here is a pheasant before you, slaughter it instead of the peacock."

Thus the Holy One, blessed be He, said to Abraham: "I desire to see Isaac, your only one, on Mount Moriah, and offer him there as an offering." When Abraham offered him there *and laid him on the altar, upon the wood and stretched forth his hand and took the knife to slay his son* (Gen. 22:9-10), the Holy One, blessed be He, shouted, *and the angel of the Lord called unto him from heaven . . . and said, Lay not thy hand upon the lad . . .* (Gen. 22:11-12), and since you have brought the knife to slaughter him, behold, here is before you an animal, slaughter it instead of your son."

(Agadat B'reshit, ed. Buber, p. 62)

III

Take, please, thy son (Gen. 22:2). "Please" is the language of request. This can be likened to a flesh-and-blood king who had to face many wars. And he had a hero who was victorious in all the battles. At a later time the king had to engage in a very fierce battle. He said to that hero: "I beg of you, help me in this battle lest the commanders of my soldiers say that those earlier wars had no importance." Likewise the Holy One, blessed be He, said to Abraham: "I tried you in nine tests and you passed them. Now, pass this test lest they say, those earlier ones had no importance." He said: *Take, please, thy son.* He said to Him: "Which son?" He said to him: *Thine only son.* He said to Him: "This is an only son to his mother, and that one is an only son to his mother."

He said to him: *Whom thou lovest.* He said to Him: "I love
both of them." He said to him: *Whom thou lovest most.* He
said to him: "Are there boundaries in the bowels?[22] He said
to him: *Even Isaac, and get thee into the land of Moriah.* Why
Get thee . . . ? Because this last test was like the first test. In
the first test He said to Abraham, *Get thee out of thy country
and from thy kindred* (Gen. 12:1), and in the last test He said,
Get thee into the land of Moriah. Thereupon, *Abraham rose
early in the morning, and saddled his ass* (Gen. 22:3). Did that
righteous man not have many servants that he himself
saddled his ass? He did it to show his eagerness.

*On the third day Abraham lifted up his eyes, and saw the place
afar off* (Gen. 22:4). Why on the third day and not on the
first day or on the second day? So that the nations of the
world should not say, "God confused him, and he went and
slaughtered his son." *And he saw the place afar off.* Abraham
said: "What shall I do? If I reveal the matter to Sarah,
women's mind is light in small matters, and how much
more so in such a great thing as this! And if I do not reveal it
to her and take him away from her, when she sees that he is
gone she will kill herself." What did he do? He said to
Sarah: "Prepare food and drink for us, and let us eat and be
merry." She said to him: "Wherein does this day differ from
others, and what is the meaning of this joy?" He said to her:
"Old people like us, a son was born to us in our old age, this
is enough of a reason to eat and drink and be merry." She
went and prepared the food. In the midst of eating he said
to her: "You know that when I was three years old I knew
my Creator, and this boy is big and has not been educated.
There is a place at some distance from us where they
educate boys, I shall take him there to be educated." She
said to him: "Go in peace." Thereupon, *And Abraham rose
early in the morning.* Why in the morning? He said: "Perhaps
Sarah will go back on her word and will not let me go. I
shall rise early before she rises."

---

22 I.e., I love them both equally.

And he took two of his young men with him (Gen. 22:3). He said: "While I sacrifice him let them guard our belongings."

Satan approached them on the way and appeared to him in the shape of an old man. He said to him: "Where are you going?" He said to him: "To pray." He said to him: "If a person goes to pray, why does he have fire and a knife in his hand and wood on his shoulder?" He said to him: "Perhaps we shall tarry a day or two, and shall slaughter and bake and eat." He said to him: "Old man, was I not present when the Holy One, blessed be He, said to you, 'Take your son'? An old man like you should go and destroy his son who was given to him when he was a hundred? Have you not heard the saying, 'He destroyed that which was in his hand, and went begging from others'? And even if you say you will have another son, will you listen to the Tempter and destroy a soul which will make you guilty before the Judgment?" He said to him: "It was not the Tempter but the Holy One, blessed be He. I shall not listen to you!"

Thereupon Satan left him and appeared like a youth, and stood on the right side of Isaac and said to him: "Where are you going?" He said to him: "To study Tora." He said to him: "In your life or in your death?" He said to him: "Is there a man who studied after his death?" He said to him: "O you miserable one, son of a miserable woman! How many days did your mother fast until you were born, and this old man has become crazy and he goes to slaughter you!" He said to him: "Even so, I shall not transgress the wish of my Creator, and the command of my father."

He turned and said to his father: "Father, see what this one says to me!" He said to him: "Pay no attention to him, for he came only to wear us down."

When Satan saw that they did not accept his arguments, he went and turned himself into a big river before them. Unhesitatingly Abraham waded into the water, and it reached up to his knees. He said to his young men: "Follow me!" They followed him. When they reached the middle of the river the water reached to his neck. In that hour

Abraham lifted up his eyes to heaven and said before Him: "Master of the World! You chose me, you set me apart, and revealed Yourself to me, and said to me, 'I am one and only and you are one and only. Through you My name will become known in My world. And sacrifice your son Isaac as a burnt offering before Me.' And I did not hold back, and behold I strive to fulfill Your command. And now the water reaches the soul. If I or my son Isaac drown, who will fulfill Your word? Who will declare the oneness of Your name?"

The Holy One, blessed be He, said to him: "By your life, the oneness of My name will be declared by you in the world!" Instantly the Holy One, blessed be He, rebuked the source and the river dried up and they stood on dry land.

What did Satan do? He said to Abraham: "I heard from behind the Curtain that a lamb is destined to be the burnt offering and not Isaac." He said to him: "This is the punishment of the liar: even if he tells the truth they don't believe him."

Instantly, Abraham *saw the place afar off.* How did it appear from afar? It teaches us that at first the place was a valley, and when the Holy One, blessed be He, decided to let His Shekhina dwell on it and to make it a sanctuary, He said: "It is not the way of a king to dwell in a valley, but on an elevated, exalted, and beautiful place which is visible to all." Instantly the Holy One, blessed be He, motioned to the surroundings of the valley that the mountains shall gather to one place to establish a place for the Shekhina. Therefore it is called Mount Moriah ["Mount of Fear"] because it became a mountain out of the fear of the Holy One, blessed be He.

And he saw the place afar off. He said to Isaac: "Do you see what I see?" He said to him: "I see a beautiful, splendid mountain, and a cloud is tied over it." Abraham then asked his young men: "Do you see anything?" They said to him: "We see nothing but deserts." He said to them: *Abide ye here with the ass* (Gen. 22:5).... In that hour great fear and dread fell upon Isaac, for he saw nothing in his father's hand for the sacrifice, and he felt what was about to happen. This is why he said, *Where is the lamb for a burnt offering?* Abraham said to him: "Since you said so, the Holy One, blessed be He, has chosen you." Isaac said to him: "If he has chosen me, behold, my soul is given to Him. But I am terrified about my blood." Nevertheless, *They went both of them together* (Gen. 22:8) in certainty; one to slaughter and one to be slaughtered. And Isaac was thirty-seven years old in the hour of his Binding.

And they came to the place which God had told him of . . . and he bound Isaac his son (Gen. 22:9). When he came to slaughter him, Isaac said to him: "Father, bind my hands and feet, for the soul is unruly, and when I see the knife I may tremble, and the sacrifice will become unfit. I beg of you, do not make a blemish in me." Instantly, *And Abraham stretched forth his hand and took the knife to slay his son* (Gen. 22:10). He said to him: "Father, do not inform my mother when she stands over the pit, or when she stands on the roof, lest she throw herself down and die."

Instantly the two of them built the altar, and Abraham bound Isaac on the altar, and he took the knife to slaughter him, until one quarter of his blood came out of him. And Satan came and pushed Abraham's hand and he dropped the knife. And when he stretched forth his hand to take it, a heavenly voice issued and said to him from heaven: *Lay not thy hand upon the lad* (Gen. 22:12). And failing this, Isaac would have been slaughtered.

In that hour Satan went to Sarah and appeared to her in the shape of Isaac. When she saw him, she said to him: "My son, what did your father do to you?" He said to her: "My father took me, and led me up mountains and down valleys, and took me up to the head of a mountain, and built an altar, and arranged the wood, and bound me on top of it, and took the knife to slaughter me, and had not the Holy One, blessed be He, said to him, *Lay not thy hand upon the lad*, I would have been slaughtered." Before he finished what he had to say, Sarah's soul departed.

In that hour Abraham said before the Holy One, blessed be He: "Master of the Worlds! A man tests his fellow man because he does not know what is in his heart, but You, who knows what the hearts and the kidneys advise, You had to test me thus?" He said to him: "For now I know that you are a fearer of God." And the Holy One, blessed be He, instantly opened the heavens and the darkness, and said: *By Myself I swear* (Gen. 22:16). Abraham said to Him: "You have sworn, and I have sworn that I shall not descend from this altar until I tell You what I must tell You." He said to him: "Speak." He said to Him: "Did You not say, *Count the stars, if thou be able to count them . . . thus shall thy seed be* (Gen. 15:5)?" He said to him: "Yes." He said to Him: "From whom?" He said to him: "From Isaac." He said to Him: "Just as it was in my heart to answer You and to say to You, 'Yesterday You told me, *For in Isaac shall seed be called to thee* (Gen. 21:12), and now You are telling me to sacrifice him as a burnt offering,' but I subdued my inclination and did not argue with You, thus when the children of Isaac will sin and enter into straits, You should remember for them the Binding of Isaac, and let it count before You as if his ashes were heaped upon the altar, and forgive them, and redeem them from their straits." The Holy One, blessed be He, said to him: "You spoke your mind, and I shall speak Mine: In the future the children of Isaac will sin before Me, and I shall judge them on New Year. But if they beg me that I shall seek merit for them and remember the Binding of Isaac, let them blow the shofar of this before Me." Abraham said to Him: "What is the shofar?" He said to him: "Turn around!" Instantly, *And Abraham lifted up his eyes, and looked, and behold behind him a ram caught in the thicket by his horns* (Gen. 22:13). It was one of the ten things created on Friday at dark. The Holy One, blessed be He, said: "Let them blow before Me the horn of a ram, and I shall save them and redeem them from their sins. And I shall break the yoke of the Exile from off them and shall lead them to Zion."

(Tanh. waYera, 22-23)

Jacob at Bethel

Rabbi Levi said: "In that night the Holy One, blessed be He, showed Jacob all the signs. He showed him a ladder standing from the earth to the heaven, as it is said, *And he dreamed, and behold a ladder set up on the earth, and the top of it reached to heaven* (Gen. 28:12). And the ministering angels were ascending and descending thereon, and they beheld the face of Jacob, and they said: 'This is a face like the face of the Holy Beast on the Throne of Glory.' The Holy One, blessed be He, showed him the four kingdoms, their rule and their destruction: He showed him the celestial prince of the kingdom of Babylon ascending and descending seventy rungs; and He showed him the prince of the kingdom of Media ascending and descending fifty-two rungs; and He showed him the prince of the kingdom of Greece ascending and descending 180 rungs; and He showed him the prince of the kingdom of Edom ascending, but he was not descending, but was saying, *I will ascend above the heights of the clouds; I will be like the Most High* (Isa. 14:14). Jacob replied to him: *Yet thou shalt be brought down to Sheol, to the uttermost parts of the pit* (Isa. 14:15).

"Jacob rose up early in the morning in great fear, and said: *How dreadful is this place! This is none other but the house of God* (Gen. 28:17).

"And Jacob returned to gather the stones, and he found them all turned into one stone, and he set it up for a pillar in the midst of the place, and oil descended for him from heaven, and he poured it thereon. What did the Holy One, blessed be He, do? He placed His right foot on it, and sank the stone to the bottom of the abyss, and He made it the keystone of the earth, like a man who sets a keystone in an arch; therefore it is called the Foundation Stone, for there is the navel of the earth, and therefrom was all the earth stretched out, and upon it the Sanctuary of God stands."

(Pirqe R. Eliezer, ch. 35)

When the Prince Returns from Barbary

Those angels who served Jacob in the Land of Israel, when he was about to leave it and go abroad, he saw that they flew away from him, and other angels descended and served him abroad. When he came to return to his father, the Holy One, blessed be He, said to the first angels who had served him in the Land of Israel: "You are not going to receive My son?"

A parable. This is like unto the son of kings who left Rome and its senate and went to the people of Barbary. And his father gave him many legions to serve him. After a time, when he was about to return from Barbary, the king said to his senate: "Shall we not go out to receive my son, who is returning?" And the son was afraid to come. When he lifted up his eyes and saw his father and all his senate who had come out to meet him, he began to rejoice. Thus Jacob, when he came back to his father, the Holy One, blessed be He, said to the first angels: "Let us go down and receive Jacob." Jacob heard that Esau was approaching, and began to be afraid. The Holy One, blessed be He, said to him: "Lift up your eyes and see who comes to receive you." Instantly, *And Jacob said when he saw them, This is God's camp* (Gen. 32:3).

(Agadat B'reshit, ed. Buber, pp. 109-10)

Jacob and Leah

And the Lord saw that Leah was hated (Gen. 29:31). By whom was she hated? By her husband. Why? Because she argued with him. When? *Jacob served seven years for Rachel and they seemed unto him but a few days, for the love he had to her* (Gen. 29:20). *And Jacob said unto Laban: Give me my wife. . . . And it came to pass in the evening that he took Leah his daughter and brought her to him, and he went in unto her* (Gen. 29:20-23). All night he made love to her thinking she was Rachel. When the morning rose, *behold it was Leah* (Gen. 29:25). He said to her: "O, you daughter of the deceiver, why did you deceive me?" She said to him: "And you, did you not deceive your father? When he said to you, *'Art thou my son Esau?'* (Gen. 27:24) and you said, *'I am Esau thy firstborn'?* (Gen. 27:19). And you say 'Why did you deceive me?' Did not your father say to Esau, *'Thy brother came with guile and hath taken away thy blessing'?* (Gen. 27:35)." And because of these words with which she reproached him, he began to hate her. The Holy One, blessed be He, said: "There is no remedy for her except in having sons; behold, I am giving her sons, and her husband will incline to her." Therefore, *And the Lord saw that Leah was hated, and He opened her womb* (Gen. 29:31)

(Agadat B'reshit, ed. Buber, p. 99)

Esau and Ishmael Conspire

Wicked Esau wanted to kill Jacob because of the blessings which his father Isaac bestowed upon Jacob. What did the wicked Esau do? He went to Ishmael and said to him: "Let us counsel together, you and I, and we shall rule the whole world." He said to him: "How?" Esau said to him: "You know that your father loved you in his soul, but after Isaac was born, your father came and expelled you, and made you leave his house without anything, for his wife had told him, *Cast out this bondswoman and her son* (Gen. 21:10), and she did not let you inherit anything of that which your father had, even one penny. . . . And it was not enough that Isaac did that to you, but he cast out me too. And now you know that it is unlawful for a son to kill his father, but a brother can kill his brother for his inheritance, for thus we find that Cain killed his brother Abel. . . . And now the law permits you to kill your brother who deprived you of all your fortune and of all that you had. And I likewise shall kill my brother, and then we shall inherit the whole world, and we two shall be the rulers over everything that our father Abraham had."

Ishmael said to him: "I cannot believe you, because you are fickle." Esau said to him: "If I take your daughter to wife, will you believe me?" He said to him: "Yes." Whereupon Esau *took unto the wives that he had Mahalath the daughter of Ishmael ... to be his wife* (Gen. 28:9).

In that hour Ishmael thought to himself: "If I kill my brother Isaac, the Holy One, blessed be He, will find me guilty and will bring a curse on me and my seed as He did to Cain whom He cut off from this world. It is better for me to leave that which would be mine so that I do not inherit the curse of God."

But wicked Esau did not think thus, but with the great cunning which he had he said in his heart: "When Ishmael kills father, I shall then come against him with the law and shall say to him: 'Why did you kill father?' And he will instantly be found guilty and I shall kill him, and then I shall kill my brother Jacob, and I shall be king over the whole world."

The Holy One, blessed be He, said to him: "Evil one, you think in your mind that I do not know what you are thinking in your heart. Whereas I stand in every place and know all the thoughts of the heart. . . . By your life, I was there and I shall make public to all those who walk in the earth what you wanted to do, as it is said, *I have made Esau bare, I have uncovered his secrets* (Jer. 49:10)."

(Agadat B'reshit, ed. Buber, p. 92, in the notes.)

Jacob Institutes the Sh'ma'

From whence did Israel merit the Sh'ma' prayer? El'azar ben Aḥmi said, "From our father Jacob. In the hour when our father Jacob was near death, he cogitated in his heart and said, 'My grandfather Abraham begot two sons, Isaac and Ishmael. And my father Isaac worshiped the Holy One, blessed be He, but Ishmael worshiped stars and idols. And thus my father Isaac begot two sons, me and Esau. I worship

God, but Esau worships idols. I begot twelve sons, perchance they will not worship the Holy One, blessed be He? Perchance there will be among them idol worshipers?' What did he do? He called all his sons and gathered them before his bed, and when they came to him he said to them, 'Hear what I am telling you!' They said to him, 'What is your wish?' He said to them. 'Hear your father Israel, hear the Holy One, blessed be He, whom your father worships, and worship Him.' They said to him, 'The Lord our God, the Lord is one.' And to this day they observe it every day, and say, 'Hear, O Israel, the Lord our God, the Lord is one!' Hear, O Israel, you who are in the Cave of Machpela, the Lord our God, the Lord is one!"

Hence they merited the Sh'ma' prayer from our father Jacob.

(Deut. Rab., ed. Liebermann, p. 67)

Pharaoh's Plan

Pharaoh said to the Israelite midwives: "If the child is a male, kill him, and if a female do not kill her, but if she lives, let her live, and if she dies, she dies." They said to him: "How shall we know [before the child emerges] whether it is male or female?" R. Ḥanina said: "Pharaoh divulged them a great sign: if its face is downward, know that it is male for he looks towards his mother, the earth, from which he was created. And if its face is upward, it is female, for she looks towards her creation, the rib." ...

The Holy One, blessed be He, said to him: "You evil one! He who gave you this advice was a fool. You should have killed the females. If there are no females from where would the males take women? One woman cannot marry two men, but one man can marry ten women or even a hundred."

(Exod. Rab. 1:14)

Miriam's Advice

Amram was the head of the Sanhedrin at that time. When Pharaoh issued the decree and said, *Every son that is born [to the Israelites] ye shall cast into the river* (Exod. 1:22), Amram said: "Israel procreates in vain." Instantly he sent away Jochebed and removed himself from intercourse. And when he divorced his wife she was three months pregnant. All Israel rose and divorced their wives. His daughter Miriam said to him: "Your decree is harder than that of Pharaoh. For Pharaoh issued a decree only against the male children, but you—against both males and females. Pharaoh is wicked and there is a doubt whether his decree will be carried out, but you are pious and your decree will certainly be carried out." He rose and returned his wife. All Israel rose and returned their wives.

(Exod. Rab. 1:13)

Moses Is Tested

Pharaoh used to kiss and to embrace the child Moses and he took Pharaoh's crown and put it on his own head, as he was to do to him when he grew up. And the magicians of Pharaoh sat there and said: "We are afraid of this child who took your crown and put it on his own head. Perhaps this is the one of whom we said that he will take the kingship from you." Some of them said that he should be killed; others that he should be burnt. But Jethro who sat among them said: "This child has no understanding. Test him by bringing before him gold and glowing coals on a plate. If he stretches forth his hand for the gold, he has understanding, and kill him. And if he stretches his hand for the coals, he has no understanding and he should not be killed." Instantly they brought it before him, and he stretched his hand to take the gold. But the angel Gabriel came and pushed his hand so that he grabbed the coal and put his hand with the coal into his mouth and burnt his tongue.

And from this he became heavy of mouth and heavy of
tongue.

(Exod. Rab. 1:26)

Moses Kills the Egyptian

*When Moses was grown up he went out unto his brethren and
looked on their burdens. And he saw an Egyptian smiting a
Hebrew* (Exod. 2:11). Who was that Egyptian? He was the
father of that man who blasphemed, as it is written, *The son
of an Israelitish woman whose father was an Egyptian . . . blasphemed the Name and cursed* (Lev. 24:10-11). That
Egyptian was smiting a Hebrew, who was the husband of
Sh'lomith the daughter of Dibri (ibid.). How did this
happen? The Egyptian was a taskmaster in charge of 120
men, and he was taking them out to their work at cockcrow.
And since his wont was to take them out, he would come
and go in their houses. He saw Sh'lomith the daughter of
Dibri that she was beautiful of countenance, free of all
blemish. He put his eyes on her. He arose at cockcrow and
took her husband out of his house. And that Egyptian
returned and had intercourse with his wife, and she
thought that it was her husband. Her husband returned,
found the Egyptian leaving his house, asked her and said:
"Did he touch you?" She said to him: "Yes, and I thought
that he was you." When the taskmaster saw that he had
found out about the thing, he returned to the work of rigor,
and was smiting him. Moses saw through the Holy Spirit
what he had done to his wife and how he was smiting him.
He said: "Is it not enough that you violated his wife, now
you are smiting him?" *And he looked this way and that way*
(Exod. 2:12). What is *this way and that way?* He saw that he
had violated his wife and that he had returned and was
smiting her husband. *And he saw that there was no man*
(ibid.). What does the Scripture mean, *that there was no
man?* It teaches that Moses caused a court of justice of
Ministering Angels to convene. He said to them: "Shall I

slay this one?" They said to him: "Slay!" *And he smote the Egyptian* (ibid.). With what did he smite him? Some say he took a mud shovel and bashed in his head. And some say, he uttered over him the Name and killed him. . . .

(HaGadol, Exod., p. 29)

Moses and the Lions

Moses and Aaron came to Egypt, and they came to the house of Pharaoh. And in the gate to the house of Pharaoh there were two young lions because of whom no man was able to approach the gate of the king, because of their fear, for they tore to pieces everyone whom they saw, until the keeper of the lions came and removed them. And when they heard that Moses and Aaron came, the keepers of the lions let them loose and left them at the door of the gate, following the advice of Balaam the sorcerer and the magicians of Egypt. And when Moses and Aaron came to a door of the gate, Moses stretched out his rod over the lions, and they rejoiced at his coming, and went after him and gamboled before him as dogs do gambol with their masters when they come from the field. And when Pharaoh and his servants saw this, they were sore afraid of them and said to them: "What is this thing, and what do you want?" And they said: "The God of the Hebrew called us saying, 'Let My people go so that they serve Me.' "

(Divre haYamim shel Moshe, BhM 2:8)

Pharaoh's Magicians

We have learned that in the hour when Jochebed the mother of Moses became pregnant, wicked Pharaoh saw in his dream a ewe crouching and giving birth to a lamb. Then he saw a pair of scales suspended between the earth and the firmament, and they brought the lamb and put it on one of the two pans of the scales. Then they brought all the silver and gold of Egypt and placed into the other pan, and the lamb outweighed it all. Then they brought all the weapons of Egypt and then added them to the silver and the gold, but the lamb still outweighed it. In the morning Pharaoh sent for his magicians and soothsayers and told them his dream. They said to him: "The ewe you saw crouching is this People of Israel which dwells in Egypt. The lamb which it bore—a male child is going to issue from that people and he will destroy Egypt and will conquer countries for that people." He said to them: "Is he born yet?" They said to him: "Not yet, but last night his mother conceived him." He said to them: "How can he be killed?" They said to him: "His death can be through water." For the magicians see and yet see not, and it seemed to them that he would die through water, and they thought that he would drown in water, and they did not know that he was to be punished because of the Waters of Meribah.[23] Pharaoh said to his magicians: "And now, what measures can we take against this thing?" They said to him: "Appoint officials over all the pregnant women who are in the Land of Egypt, and let them search thoroughly and investigate every pregnant woman and let them write down her name in notebooks, and after nine months let them investigate them, and issue a decree that they should throw the newborn babes into the Nile, for when he enters the water he will have no deliverance, because there is his place of death." . . .

And they counted nine months. But they did not know that all prophets are born as seven-months children, and Moses was the father of prophets.

(HaGadol, Exod. pp. 22–24)

The Two Magicians

There were two magicians among the Egyptians, Yoḥni and Mamre by name (who were none other than Iannes and Iambres, the two sons of Balaam). They said to Pharaoh: "If

[23] Cf. Num. 20:1-13.

all this is done by the hand of God himself, we are helpless; but if by the hands of angels, we can shake them." Instantly they performed their magic and caused the angels to tumble into the sea. The angels cried: "Help us, O God, for the waters have reached the soul!" God sent Michael to succor the drowning angels. He grabbed the two magicians by their hair, and dashed their heads against the waves.

(Abkir in Yalqut Shim'oni, Exod. 235)

The Reluctant Pharaoh

The rabbis said: . . . The Egyptians said to Pharaoh: "Come, let us turn against this nation[the Children of Israel]." He said to them: "You fools, until now we eat of what is theirs, how can we turn against them? Were it not for Joseph we would not be alive." When he did not listen to them, they removed him from his throne for three months, until he said to them: "Whatever you want, I am with you." Whereupon they put him back on the throne.

(Exod. Rab. 1:8)

God Assumes the Shape of a Mare

Pharaoh and his men rode on stallions, and God appeared to them in the shape of a mare which ran into the sea, and all the stallions of the Egyptians ran after her and drowned together with their riders.

Some say that when Pharaoh saw that he could not control his stallion, he exchanged it for a red charger, but in that instant God appeared to him riding on a red mare; when Pharaoh thereupon took a white stallion, God too changed over to a white mare; and finally both rode on black horses, and Pharaoh was plunged into the deep.

The rabbis said that the Children of Israel all appeared to the Egyptians as if they were mares, and the Egyptians felt like lustful stallions and they ran after them until they drowned in the sea. Rabbi Simon said: "God forbid! The

Children of Israel did not appear like mares, but the waves of the sea assumed the shape of mares, and the Egyptians were like lustful stallions, and they ran after them until they drowned in the sea." And the Egyptian said to his horse: "Yesterday I pulled you to the Nile and you did not want to come after me, and now you drown me in the sea!" And the horse answered its rider: "See what is in the sea! A miracle is in the sea!"

(Shir HaShirim Zuta, Buber 15;
Cant. Rab. on Cant. 1:9; etc.)

Moses Divides the Sea

Moses said before the Holy One, blessed be He: "Master of the World! And I, what shall I do?" He said to him: "Take the staff which I gave you and go to the sea as My emissary and speak to it: 'I am the emissary of the Creator of the beginning. Uncover your paths to My sons so that they go through you.' " Instantly Moses went to the sea and spoke to it the words of the Holy One, blessed be He. And the sea answered Moses: "I shall not do as you say, for you are born of a woman, and not only that, but I am three days older than you, for I was created on the third day and you were not created until the sixth day." Instantly Moses reported the words of the sea to the Holy One, blessed be He. And the Holy One, blessed be He, said to Moses: "If a slave refuses to obey his master, what do they do to him?" Moses said: "They beat him with a rod." The Holy One, blessed be He, said to him: "So you too, *lift up thy rod and stretch out thy hand over the sea and divide it* (Exod. 14:16). Instantly, *And Moses stretched out his hand over the sea* (Exod. 14:21) and divided it. And Israel was afraid to go into the sea, until Nahshon ben Aminadav jumped and went down first into the sea, and after him went all Israel, *on ground and the waters were a wall unto them on their right hand, and on their left.* Thus the *Lord saved Israel that day out of the hand of the Egyptian* (Exod. 14: 19-30).

(WaYosha', BhM 1:38-39)

Twelve Paths in the Sea

When the waters of the sea saw how greatly the Holy One, blessed be He, loved Israel, they humbled themselves in order to give honor to Israel. The sea itself humbled itself and made itself into twelve cuts as against the twelve tribes of Israel, and lifted up its waves to a height of six hundred miles and froze itself in that position and transformed its salt waters into sweet water, and it became for them like walls with windows in them through which the tribes of Israel could see one another. And they praised the Holy One, blessed be He with songs and paeans, and walked in the sea like a man who walks in his house, until they came out to the dry land.

(WaYosha', BhM 1:51)

The Divine Judgment

In the hour in which the Holy One, blessed be He, wanted to drown the Egyptians, up rose their celestial prince 'Uzza and said before Him: "Master of the World! You are called righteous and just, and there is before You neither injustice nor forgetfulness nor partiality. Why do You want to drown my children in the sea? Did they, perchance, drown any of Your children? And if it is because of the hard enslavement with which my children enslaved them, they already have taken their compensation for it: they took their vessels of silver and vessels of gold." In that hour the Holy One, blessed be He, gathered the whole supernal family and said to them: "Adjudicate between Me and 'Uzza, the prince of Egypt. True, at the beginning I brought famine upon them and raised for them Joseph my beloved, who saved them with his wisdom, and all of them became slaves to him, and thereafter My children went there as foreigners because of the famine and they enslaved them with all the hard labor in the world, and they cried because of the amount of labor, and their cry for help ascended before Me, and I sent My faithful emissary Moses and Aron to Pharaoh and they went before Pharaoh and said to him, 'Thus speaks the Lord, Let My people go so that they serve Me.' And the kings of the east and of the west sat there before that wicked one, and he began to pride himself and said, 'Who is the Lord that I should listen to his voice? How is it that he did not come before me as all the kings of the world? And why did he not bring me a present as did all the kings? I do not know this god of whom you speak.' What did he do? He went back to search in his books and found nothing written about the mission. He answered and said to his servants, 'Have we heard that he is the son of sages, the son of ancient kings?' And he said to My emissary, 'What are the works of this god?' They answered him and said, 'He is the God of gods and the Lord of lords, He created the heaven and the earth.' He answered and said to My emissaries, 'There is no god in the whole world who could do these deeds, but I alone, for I created myself and the river Nile.' And because of this thing, because he denied Me, I sent him ten plagues until he let My children go against his will. And with all this he has not refrained from his wickedness, but he again pursues them to make them return to his enslavement. Since all this was done to him and he still did not recognize Me, We want to drown him in the sea, him and all his hosts." Instantly the whole supernal family answered and said: "You have a great cause to drown them in the sea." When 'Uzza saw this, he began to speak: "Master of the Worlds! I know that they are guilty, but may it be the will before You that You behave toward them with the quality of mercy. Have mercy on the work of Your hands!" And the Holy One, blessed be He, wanted to have mercy on them until Gabriel, the celestial prince of Israel, came and took a form of a brick which the children of Israel had made in Egypt, and showed it before the Holy One, blessed be He, and said before Him: "Master of the Worlds! You wish to have mercy on this accursed people which enslaved Your children with such hard labor?" And the Holy One, blessed be He, returned from the quality of mercy and sat on the chair of judgment, and drowned them in the sea.

(WaYosha', BhM 1:39-40)

Fruits Plucked from the Sea

The sea was not rent asunder for them until they entered it down to their noses; but thereafter it became dry land for them. R. N'horai expounded: "A daughter of Israel went across in the sea with her son in her arms, and he wept, and she stretched forth her hand and took an apple or a pomegranate from the sea and gave it to him."

(Exod. Rab. 21:10)

Moses Breaks the Tables

How did Moses break the Tables of the Law? At the time when he ascended and took them and descended, he was filled with great joy. When Israel sinned, he said: "If I give them [the Ten Commandments] I shall impose on them hard commandments and cause them to become guilty and liable to a death sentence from heaven, for it is written thus, *Thou shalt have no other gods before Me* (Exod. 20:3)." So he turned back. But the elders saw him and ran after him. Moses held on to one end of the Tables and they pulled the other end, and the strength of Moses was greater than the strength of seventy elders. . . . Moses looked at the Tables and saw that the writing on them was flying away, and the hands of Moses grew heavy, and the Tables dropped from his hands and broke.

(Yalqut Shim'oni, §393)

The Death Wish of Moses

Moses said: "Lord God, You began to show me Your power in the burning bush. Now, in my old age I beseech You, have pity on Your people, Your flock, and forgive them and atone for them. And as for me, Your servant, I beseech You, be not like a king of flesh and blood who, as long as his servant is young and strong, loves him, but when the servant grows old, hates him. But You, *do not cast me away at the time of old age* (Ps. 71:9)."

(P'tirat Moshe, BhM 1:118)

The Stone Breasts

The Holy One, blessed be He, made for them portents and miracles in the Valleys of Arnon like unto the miracles He made for them at the Dead Sea. And what were the miracles in the Valleys of Arnon? A man could stand on this mountain and speak with his friend on the other mountain although the distance between them was seven miles, and the path descended into the valley and ascended [on the other side]. And the way of Israel passed through the valley. All the nations gathered there, people on end, and some of them sat [waiting for Israel] in the valley, and the valley above was full of caves. And opposite the caves there was a mountain with rocks in the shape of breasts (*shad*) as it is said, *And the slope (eshed) of the valleys* (Num. 21:15). The people entered into the caves saying, "When Israel enters the valley, those of us who are in the valley will stand up before them, and the others of us will be above them in the caves, and we shall slay all of them."

When Israel reached that place, the Holy One, blessed be He, did not make it necessary for them to go down into the valleys but beckoned to the mountains, and the breasts of the mountain entered into the caves [on the opposite side], and they all died. And the mountains leaned their heads against each other and became a paved road, and it could not be recognized which mountain leaned over to the other.

That valley is the boundary between the territory of the Land of Israel and the territory of the Land of Moab, as it is said, *For Arnon is the border of Moab, between Moab and the Amorites* (Num. 21:13). The mountain which was in the

Land of Moab, in which there were the caves, did not shake, but the mountain from the Land of Israel shook, the mountain in which there were those rocks like breasts, and it leaned against the mountain opposite it. And why did it shake? Because it was of the Land of Israel. It was like unto a slave woman who saw the son of her master approaching, she jumped up and ran towards him to receive him. The rocks entered the caves and smashed all those warriors.

(Num. Rab. 19:25)

Moses Serves Joshua

Moses said: "For thirty-six years Joshua served me in the desert...." And when the decree arrived that Moses must die, and the Holy One, blessed be He, said to him, "*Behold, thy days approach that thou must die, call Joshua* (Deut. 31:14), and command Joshua." Moses the righteous thought: "Perhaps it is because of the hour of Joshua my disciple that I die, for he will lead Israel and stand at their head, and it is because of this that it was decreed upon me that I shall not enter the Land and shall not eat of its fruits. It is better that Joshua be the leader and I live and enter the Land of Israel."

What did he do? From the first of Shevat until the sixth of Adar he went morning and evening and served Joshua like a disciple his master, and those thirty-six days counted for Moshe a day a year.

How did Moses serve Joshua? Every day, at midnight, Moses rose and went to the door of Joshua, and took the keys and opened the door and entered and took the robe and shook it out and placed it at the head of Joshua, and took his shoes and prepared them and put them at the side of the bed, and took his Tallith and his cover and his cloak, and the golden helmet and the crown of pearls, and inspected them and cleaned them and arranged them before him on a golden board. Then he brought a jug of water and a golden bowl, and put them before the board, and Joshua had still not awakened from his sleep. And then

Moses ordered the boy to sweep Joshua's house of tent just as the tent of Moses [used to be done], and sent for and brought in the golden throne, and spread a sheet of byssus and all kinds of precious and beautiful vessels, as is the custom of kings.

And then he issued a proclamation: "Moses stands in the tent of Joshua, and all those who want to pay obeisance to Joshua, let them come and do so, for the word has come from the Holy One, blessed be He, that Joshua be the leader of Israel."

In that hour, each and every one in Israel who heard the proclamation was afraid and trembled and said: "I feel a pain in my head," so as not to go. And they cried and said: "Woe to you, Israel, that your king is a boy!"

When Moses saw that Joshua had awakened from his sleep, he entered and took his robe and covered his body. And Joshua put it on with a trembling soul, and fell upon the feet of Moses, and said to him: "Do not slay me, my Master, in the middle of my days, because of the rulership that has come to me from the Holy One, blessed be He!"

Moses said to him: "My son, be not afraid, you have no sin in this. As you served me, so I shall serve you." And against his will he stood and served him, and against his will he put on him the rays of radiance. When he was properly wrapped, they came and told them: "All Israel is late in coming!" Instantly Moses took Joshua and brought him out from his tent. When the two of them reached the door of the tent, Moses made him walk in front of him, against his will. When Israel saw Joshua walking in front, they all trembled and stood on their feet. And the two of them went to the place of the great ones, to the golden throne, and Moses made him sit on it against his will. When Israel saw this, they all wept, and also Joshua wept and said: "Greatness and honor, I don't want it!"

A heavenly voice issued and said to Moses: "You have only five hours of life left!"

Moses instantly cried out and said to Joshua: "Sit like a

king before the people!" And both expounded before all
Israel as one. A heavenly voice issued and said: "You have
only four hours left!"

Moses said before the Holy One, blessed be He: "Master
of the World! If it is because of my disciple that You reject
me, I behave like a disciple before him, he is like the High
Priest and I am like an ordinary priest, he is like a king, and
I am like a slave." The Holy One, blessed be He, said: "I
have sworn by My great name, which cannot be contained
by the heavens and the heavens of heavens, that you will not
cross this Jordan."

(P'tirat Moshe, BhM 1:123-24)

The Death of Moses

When Moses saw that the decree about him had been
sealed, he decided to fast. He drew a small circle, stood in it
and said: "I shall not move from here until You annul that
decree!" And he put on sackcloth, covered himself with
ashes, and stood in prayer and supplication before the Holy
One, blessed be He, until the heaven and the earth and the
orders of creation shook and said: "Has perchance the
pleasure of the Holy One, blessed be He, arrived to renew
His world?" But a divine voice was heard saying: "The
pleasure of the Holy One, blessed be He, has not yet arrived
to renew His world."

What did the Holy One, blessed be He, do in that hour?
He proclaimed in all the gates of the firmaments, in every
court of law, that they should not accept the prayer of
Moses and should not take it up before Him, because the
decree about him had been sealed. That angel who is
appointed over proclamations is called Akhraziel [The
Crier of God]. In that hour the Holy One, blessed be He,
called out in a hurry and said to the ministering angels: "Go
down in a hurry and lock up the gates of all the
firmaments!" For the voice of the prayer became powerful
towards the Above, and they wanted to go up to the

firmament because of the voice of Moses' prayer. His prayer was like a sword, which cuts and gashes and cannot be stopped. For his prayer was like the Ineffable Name which he had learned from Zagzagel, the great scribe of the Sons of the Height.

When the Ofanim [Wheels] of the Chariot and the Seraphim of flame saw that the Holy One, blessed be He, said, "Do not accept the prayer of Moses!" and that He did not honor his request and did not give him life and did not let him enter the Land of Israel, they said: *Blessed be the Glory of the Lord from His place* (Ezek. 3:12), for He gives no special consideration to anybody, either to a little man or to a great man."

In that hour Moses said before the Holy One, blessed be He: "Master of the World! Revealed and known to You are all my efforts and the troubles I had with Israel to make them believe in Your Name. How much I suffered because of them until I established the Tora and the commandments among them. I thought: just as I saw their anguish, so I shall see their reward. And now that the reward of Israel has come, You tell me, *Thou shalt not go over this Jordan* (Deut. 3:27)? . . . Is this the reward of forty years' toil which I toiled so that they should become a holy and faithful people?"

The evil angel Samael, who is the head of all Satans, counted the hours until the death of Moses, saying: "When will the end come? The moment in which Moses will die? So that I can go down and take his soul from him? . . ." This is how the evil Samael waited for the soul of Moses, and said: "When will Michael weep and I fill my mouth with laughter?" Finally Michael said to him: "What, you evil one! I weep and you laugh?"

Thus one hour passed for Moses, and in that hour he said before the Holy One, blessed be He: "Master of the World! If You do not let me enter the Land of Israel, allow me to stay in This World so that I should live and not die!" But the Holy One, blessed be He, said to him: "If I do not cause you to die in This World, how will I resurrect you in the World to Come?"... Moses said to Him: "Master of the World! If You do not let me enter the Land of Israel, allow me to be like one of the beasts of the field which eat grass, drink water, and live, and see the world! Let my soul be like one of them!" But He said to him: "You ask too much!" Then Moses said before Him: "Master of the World! If not, let me stay in This World like this bird which flies on the four winds of the world and gathers its food every day, and at eventide returns to its nest! Let me be like one of them!" But He said to him: "You ask too much!"

When Moses saw that no creature could save him from the way of death... he took a scroll and wrote on it the Ineffable Name. But before he could complete the Song [i.e., Deut. 32] the moment in which he was to die arrived. In that hour the Holy One, blessed be He, said to Gabriel: "Gabriel, go and fetch the soul of Moses!" But Gabriel said before Him: "Master of the World! He who outweighs six hundred thousand men, how can I see him die? And he who has in him these words, how can I do him harm?" Then He said to Michael: "Go and fetch the soul of Moses!" But he said before Him: "Master of the World! I was his teacher and he was my pupil; I cannot see him die!" Then God said to the evil Samael: "Go and fetch the soul of Moses!"

Instantly Samael clothed himself in wrath and girded on his sword and wrapped himself in cruelty, and went to encounter Moses. When he saw him sitting and writing the Ineffable Name, and the radiance of his appearance was like the sun, and he resembled an angel of the Lord of Hosts, Samael was sore afraid of Moses. He thought: "It is clear why the angels could not take the soul of Moses!..." And he fell to trembling and shook like a woman in childbirth, and could not open his mouth to address Moses, until Moses turned to him and said: "What are you doing here?" Then Samael said to him: "I have come to take your soul." Moses asked: "Who sent you?" He answered: "He who created all creatures." Moses said: "You will not take my soul!" But Samael said: "The souls of all the mortals are delivered into my hand!" Moses said: "I have more strength than all other mortals!" Samael asked: "And what is your strength?" He said: "I am the son of Amram who emerged from his mother's womb circumcised, so that there was no need to circumcise me. On the very day on which I was born I was able to open my mouth and to walk, and I spoke to my father and my mother, and I did not even suck milk. And when I was three months old I prophesied and said that I would receive the Tora from the midst of flaming fire. And when I walked out I entered the palace of a king and took the crown from his head. And when I was eighty years old I performed miracles and signs in Egypt, and led out six hundred thousand in full view of all Egypt. And I clove the sea into twelve parts. And I turned the water of Mara [Bitterness] into sweet water. And I ascended and trod a path in heaven. And I took part in the battle of angels and received the Tora of fire, and dwelt under the Throne of Fire, and sheltered under the Pillar of Fire, and spoke with Him face to face. And I vanquished the Supernal Family and revealed their secrets to the children of man, and received the Tora from the right hand of the Holy One, blessed be He, and taught it to Israel. And I waged war against Sihon and Og, two idolatrous heroes who were so tall that the waters of the Deluge could not reach even to their ankles. And I bade the sun and the moon stand still on the top of the world, and hit them with the staff which is in my hand and killed them. Who is there among the mortals who could do all this? Begone, you evil one! You have nothing to say here! Go, run from me! I shall not give my soul to you!"

Instantly Samael returned and gave account before the Power [God]. The Holy One, blessed be He, said to him: "Return, and fetch the soul of Moses!" Thereupon Samael drew his sword from its sheath and faced Moses. Moses fell into a rage, took the staff which was in his hand, on which was engraved the Ineffable Name, and struck Samael with all his might. Samael fled from before him, and Moses ran after him with the Ineffable Name, and took the ray of majesty from between his eyes and blinded him. Thus far Moses succeeded. After a moment a divine voice was heard saying: "The time of your death has arrived!" Moses said before the Holy One, blessed be He: "Master of the World! Remember the day when You revealed Yourself to me on Sinai. Remember the time when I stood on the mount forty days and forty nights! I beseech You, do not deliver me into the hands of the Angel of Death!" A divine voice was heard: "Fear not, I Myself shall attend to you and to your burial!"

In that hour Moses stood and sanctified himself like the Seraphim, and the Holy One, blessed be He, descended from the highest heaven of heavens to take the soul of Moses. Three ministering angels were with him: Michael, Gabriel, and Zagzagel. Michael arranged the couch of Moses, Gabriel spread a purple garment for his head, and Zagzagel for his feet. The Holy One, blessed be He, then said to Moses: "Moses, close your eyes!" He closed his eyes. He said to him: "Place your hands upon your chest!" He placed his hands upon his chest. He said to him: "Straighten your legs!" He straightened his legs.

In that hour the Holy One, blessed be He, called the soul from his body. He said to her: "My daughter! I allotted to you a hundred and twenty years in the body of Moses. Now your time has come to leave it. Come out, do not tarry!" But she said before Him: "Master of the World! I know that You are the God of all the spirits; and all the souls, those of the living and those of the dead, are delivered into Your hand. You created me and You formed me, and You placed me into the body of Moses for a hundred and twenty years. Is there a body in the world purer than the body of Moses? Therefore I love him and do not want to leave him."

The Holy One, blessed be He, said to her: "Soul, go out, do not tarry, and I shall take you up into the highest heaven of heavens, and shall seat you under My Throne of Glory, next to Cherubim and Seraphim and heavenly hosts."

She said before Him: "Master of the World! Two angels, 'Uzza and 'Azael, descended from the place of Your Shekhina, and they became desirous of the daughters of man and corrupted their ways on earth, until You suspended them between the earth and the firmament. But the son of Amram, from the day that You revealed Yourself to him in the bush, has never touched his wife. I beseech You: Allow me to stay in the body of Moses!"

In that hour the Holy One, blessed be He, kissed him and took the soul of Moses with a kiss on his mouth. And the Holy One, blessed be He, wept, and the heavens wept, and the earth wept.

(Deut. Rab. 11:10)

Aaron the Peace Maker

We have learned in the *Avot of R. Nathan*[24]: "Hillel the Elder said: Be of the disciples of Aaron who loved peace, and pursued peace, etc." This teaches us that Aaron used to inquire even after the peace of the traitors of Israel, and the wicked of Israel. And when one of them planned to commit a transgression he said to himself: "Woe to me, tomorrow Aaron will come and inquire after my peace; what shall I answer him?" And he was ashamed and did not do wrong.

And likewise if a man provoked his fellow man, Aaron would go to him and say to him: "My son, why did you provoke your friend? He has just now come to me and cried and wailed and said to me, 'Woe to me that I have provoked my friend who is greater than I.' And, see, he is waiting in the marketplace. Go, in your kindness, and ask his forgiveness." And so Aaron spoke to his fellow man as well. When they went out to the marketplace and met, they embraced and kissed each other. And this is how Aaron

[24] An early Midrash containing ethical teachings.

acted all the days until he made peace between all men.

And likewise if a man provoked his wife and sent her away from his house, Aaron would make peace between them. If the man wronged the woman, Aaron said to her: "Behold, I shall vouch for him that he will no longer beat you and will not curse you from now on." And thus also he spoke to the man: "Behold, I shall vouch for her that she will not wrong you from now on." And this is how Aaron acted all the days until he made peace between man and wife. And the woman would conceive and give birth and say: "This son would not have been given me except for the merit of Aaron." And they would name him Aaron. And the sages of blessed memory said: "More than three thousand in Israel were named Aaron. And when he died, more than twenty-four thousand sons and sons of sons mourned him. . . ."

(Gadol uG'dola, BhM 3:128)

Rahab and the Spies

There is nobody as beloved before the Holy One, blessed be He, as an emissary who is sent out to fulfill a commandment and gives his soul for its success, and there was no man who was sent to fulfill a commandment and gave his soul to succeed in his mission like unto those two whom Joshua bin Nun dispatched, as it is said, *And Joshua bin Nun sent out of Shittim two spies secretly* (Josh. 2:1) Who were they? Our masters taught, "They were Pinhas and Kaleb, and they went and gave their souls and succeeded in their mission." What is "secretly (*heresh*)?" Read "pot (*heres*)." For they made themselves appear as potters and cried, "Behold, pots, let him who wishes come and buy!" so that nobody should suspect them, and that the people should not call them spies. *And they went and came to the house of a harlot* (ibid.) She arose and received them. The king of Jericho found out about them and heard that they had come to search out the land. When they came to search for them, what did Rahab do? She took them to hide them. Pinhas said to her: "I am a priest (*kohen*), and priests are like angels. And an angel, if he so wishes, he is visible, and if he so wishes, he is invisible." And whence do we know that she hid only Kaleb? For it is said, *And the woman took the two men and hid him* (Josh. 2:4).

(Tanḥ. Buber, Num. pp. 31b-32a)

Ruth and Boaz

Many times did He save them (Ps. 106:43). This refers to people. When distress overtakes a man, he instantly repents and the Holy One, blessed be He, saves him. Thus the first time and the second, if he repents, good, and if not, He brings upon him distress. Why? Because it is hard for the Holy One, blessed be He, to stretch forth His hand against a man. What then does He do to him? When he sins, at first He stretches forth His hand against his property. From whom do we learn this? From Naomi and her sons, and Elimelech who was the head of the generation. When famine came, what did he do? He left the Land of Israel and went to the Land of Moab. And the Holy One, blessed be He, was wroth with him, for he was a prince of the generation. The Holy One, blessed be He, said to him: "If My children were to do likewise, they would leave the Land of Israel a wilderness." What is written there? *And Elimelech the husband of Naomi died* (Ruth 1:3). His sons should have learned from the fate of their father and returned to the Land of Israel. Instead what did they do? *They took themselves wives of the women of Moab* (Ruth 1:4). They did not immerse them, they did not convert them. *And they dwelt there about ten years* (ibid.) All those ten years the Holy One, blessed be He, warned them. When He saw that they did not repent, He began to stretch forth His hand against their camels and their flocks. They still did not repent. When He saw that they did not repent, thereupon *Mahlon and Chilion died both of them* (Ruth 1:5).

This shows that it is hard before the Holy One, blessed be He, to stretch His hand forth against a man. What then does He do to them? He causes them to become impoverished until they must sell all they have. When a man sins the first time, what does the Holy One, blessed be He, do to him? He brings poverty upon him, so that he must sell his field. If he repents, fine; and if not, He causes him to sell his house. If he repents, fine, and if not, He makes him sell his daughter. If he repents, fine, and if not, He is forced to sell himself into slavery.

R. Shim'on ben Yoḥai said: "Elimelech and Mahlon and Chilion were leaders of their generation. And why were they punished? Because they left the Land of Israel and settled abroad. . . ."

In that hour when Ruth went to Boaz, her mother-in-law said to her: *Behold, he winnoweth barley tonight in the threshing floor* (Ruth 3:2). Boaz was a prince. Could it be that he himself winnowed in the threshing floor? Because his generation was wanton in fornication and robbery, therefore he went out to watch over his threshing floor. Naomi said to Ruth: *Wash thyself, therefore, and anoint thee . . .* and thereafter *get thee down to the threshing floor.* But Ruth did not do as her mother-in-law had said to her. What did Ruth do? She went down to the threshing floor and only thereafter *did she accomplish to all that her mother-in-law bade her* (Ruth 3:6). Why? Because she said, "This generation is wanton in fornication; if they see me adorned they will say 'Perhaps she is a harlot.' "

And when Boaz had eaten and drunk and his heart was merry (Ruth 3:7). What is *his heart was merry*? It means that he occupied himself with the Tora. . . . *And she came softly* (ibid.); this means secretly. *And it came to pass at midnight that the man was startled and turned himself* (Ruth 3:8). What does *turned himself* mean? That he touched her head and thought it was a spirit. *And he said: "Who art thou?" And she said: "I am Ruth thy handmaid"* (Ruth 3:9). And he said to her: "What did you come here to do?" She said to him: "I came to fulfill the Tora. . . . Arise and fulfill the Tora!" He said to her: "Since you came to fulfill the Tora, *Tarry this night, and in the morning, if he will redeem thee, well* (Ruth 3:13). For Boaz had an older brother whose name was Tov [Well]. [In the morning] *Boaz went up to the gate and sat him down there* (Ruth 4:1), and said to him: "Sit down and let us look into the Tora." Boaz said to Tov: *Naomi that is come back and out of the field of Moab selleth the parcel of land which was our brother Elimelech's and I thought to disclose it unto thee, saying: "Buy it!"* (Ruth 4:3-4), for you are older than I in the matter of the redemption. *If thou wilt redeem it, redeem it* (ibid.). And he [Tov] said to Boaz, *Redeem it.* In that hour Boaz redeemed that which Naomi sold.

(Tanḥ. Buber, Num. 54a-b)

The Parable of the Two Wives

When Job was smitten, Eliphaz, the firstborn son of Esau, was his friend. And Eliphaz was a righteous man . . . and he said to Job: "You said, 'Why am I not like Abraham?' Have you been tried like Abraham? Abraham was tried and did not kick,[25] but you do kick . . . ." A parable. This is like unto a man who had two wives, one with a marriage contract of ten thousand [denars], and the other with a marriage contract of four thousand. The one with the four thousand said to him: "Why do you not give me the same honor you give to my co-wife?" He said to her: "Your marriage contract is for four thousand, and your co-wife's for ten." Thus Job said: "Why do you not give me the same honor you gave to Abraham?" He said to him: "Have you been tried like Abraham?" Job said to them: "And I, did I not bring in four crowns, *Whole hearted and upright and God-fearing and a shunner of evil?* (Job 1:1)." They said to him: "Abraham was tried with ten tests and hence had ten crowns. He was called Steadfast, he observed the five books

---

[25] I.e., show insubordination toward God.

of the Tora even before they were given, was called hawk, was called rock, was called prince, was called lord, was called God, was called prophet, was called God-fearing— behold these are ten tests." Eliphaz said to Job: "Do you perchance have these qualities?"

(Agadat B'reshit, Buber, pp. 111-12)

Saul and the Witch of En-dor

R. Levi in the name of R. Ḥama bar Ḥanina: "It would have been better had Saul asked the Urim w'Tummim of above, and not a ghost and a familiar spirit of below." What was Saul like in that hour? Resh Laqish said: "Like a king who entered a city and decreed and said, 'All the cocks which are here must be slaughtered tonight!' When he wanted to leave, he said, 'Is there a cock here to crow?' They said to him, 'Is it not you who decreed and said, 'All the cocks which are here must be slaughtered'? So Saul removed those who divined by a ghost and a familiar spirit from the land, and then he said, '*Seek me a woman that divineth by a ghost* (1 Sam. 28:7).' Nevertheless, *His servants said to him, 'Behold, there is a woman that divineth by a ghost at En-dor'* (ibid.). *And Saul disguised himself and put on other raiment* (1 Sam. 28:8)— clothes of a common man—*and went, he and two men with him* (ibid.)—they were Abner and Amasa.... *And they came to the woman by night* (ibid.). Was it nighttime? No, but it teaches us that the hour was dark for them as the night. And he said, '*Divine for me I pray thee, by a ghost, and bring up for me whomsoever I shall name unto thee* (ibid.).' *And the woman said to him, 'Behold, thou knowest what Saul hath done, how he hath cut off those that divine by a ghost or a familiar spirit out of the land; wherefore then layest thou a snare for my life to cause me to die? And Saul swore to her by the Lord, saying: 'As the Lord liveth, there shall no punishment happen to thee for this thing* (1 Sam. 28:9-10).' "

What was Saul like in that hour? Resh Laqish said: "Like a woman who was with her lover and swore by the life of her husband. So Saul was consulting a ghost and a familiar spirit and saying, '*As the Lord liveth, there shall no punishment happen to thee for this thing.'* The woman did what she did and said what she said and brought up Samuel. When she saw him she became affrighted, as it is said, *And when the woman saw Samuel, she cried with a loud voice; and the woman spoke to Saul, saying: 'Why hast thou deceived me? For thou art Saul'* (1 Sam. 28:12)."

From whence did she know that he was Saul? Because a spirit comes up one way for a commoner and another way for a king. For a commoner it comes up with its face downward, while for a king his face is upward. *And the king said unto her: "Be not afraid; for what seest thou?" And the woman said unto Saul: "I see gods coming up from the earth"* (1 Sam. 28:13). When Saul heard "gods," he became affrighted. Some say: "Righteous men came up with him in that hour."

And he said unto her: "What is his form?" (1 Sam. 28:14). Did he, then, not recognize him? Three things were said about him who brings up a dead man in necromancy: He who brings him up sees him but does not hear his voice; he who needs him hears his voice but does not see him; and he who does not need him does neither hear nor see. Thus the woman who brought up Samuel saw him but did not hear him; Saul who needed him heard his voice but did not see him; Abner and Amasa who did not need him did neither see nor hear him. . . .

And Samuel said to Saul: "Why hast thou disquieted me, to bring me up? (1 Sam. 28:15)." He said to him: "Did you have to incite the wrath of your Creator precisely through me? You made me into an idol! Do you not know that just as those who serve idols are punished thus also those who are served as idols are punished?" Some say that Samuel thought that the Day of Judgment had arrived, and he brought up Moses with him, for the word "god" refers to Moses as it is said, *See, I have sat thee a god to Pharaoh* (Exod. 7:1).

And Samuel said . . . "Because thou didst not hearken to the voice of the Lord . . . the Lord will deliver Israel also with thee into the hands of the Philistines (1 Sam. 28:18-19)." Saul said to him: "And if I run away?" Samuel said: "If you run away you will be saved. And if you accept the punishment, *Tomorrow thou and thy sons shall be with me* (ibid.)." R. Yoḥanan said: " 'With me' means in my precinct."

When Saul heard the words of Samuel he was affrighted. Abner and Amasa said to him: "What did Samuel tell you?" He said to them: "He said to me, 'Tomorrow you go down to battle and you will be victorious. And more than that, your sons will become great princes.' " He took his three sons and went into battle.

Resh Laqish said: "In that hour the Holy One, blessed be He, called the ministering angels and said to them: 'Come and see a creature I created in the world! It is customary in the world that a man who goes to a banqueting hall does not take his sons along because that would be unseemly; but this one goes out to war and knows that he will be killed and yet takes his sons with him and rejoices that the punishment will strike him!' "

(Lev. Rab. 26:7)

Abishai Saves David

It is written, *Let not the mighty man glory in his might* (Jer. 9:22). This was said about King David. They said: When David fought he would throw and kill eight hundred men in one throw, and would draw his sword against three hundred men at once. When David saw this he prided himself and said: "There is none like me in the world and after me there will be none like me." The Holy One, blessed be He, said to him: "Do not pride yourself of your bravery. You count it, but soon you will see that it does not come from your bravery." What did the Holy One, blessed be He, do to him? He caused a deer to run before him. And Abishai was sitting with him. David and Abishai went after it until they went too long after the deer, and they lost their way. And a shoelace of Abishai fell. In the meantime, while he tied it, David went on until he saw a beautiful tower. He went and entered it and saw an old woman—she was the mother of Goliath the Philistine, and she was sitting and spinning with a spindle. And she recognized him that he was the one who had killed her son, Goliath the Philistine, but he did not recognize her. She went and tore her thread. She said: "My son, hand me my spindle." He said to her: "By your life, my lady." When he bent down to lift up that spindle, she instantly hid him in her palm,[26] and put him under the legs of the bed on which she was sitting, in order to break all his limbs. Instantly the Holy One, blessed be He, before whom there is no forgetting and no favoritism, caused a hole to open up under him so that he fell into it. And when the brother of Goliath the Philistine came, his mother instantly went out to meet him and said to him: "Do you know, my son, whom I caught?" He said to her: "No." She said: "Behold, I caught David who killed your brother." He said to her: "My mother, what did you do with that wicked one? Give him to me and I shall kill him." She said: "Go and you will see him under the legs of the bed, for I broke all his bones." He went and saw him, and saw him sitting in the hole. When he saw it, he said to his mother: "He is alive." He went and took his spear and went outside and stuck that spear into the ground with its point towards the sky in order to receive him on his spear. He went and took David and threw him upwards and his spear was under him. But the Holy One, blessed be He, caused him to stop in the air. In the meantime Abishai came and saw what was happening. He went to the brother of Goliath the Philistine and said to him: "Give me your spear and I shall kill him." He said to him: "Take it." When he took it, Abishai went and killed that wicked one. And then instantly David fell down. And they returned to their place.

---

[26] She was a giantess.

Then they said: "Whose is the bravery? It is not his but it belongs to the Holy One, blessed be He." This is what is written: *And Abishai succored David and smote the Philistine* (2 Sam. 21:17).

(Goliat haPlishti, BhM 4:140-41)

Solomon's Throne

R. Hosha'ya said: "Solomon's throne was made like the quadriga of Him who spoke and the world was, the Holy One, blessed be He. *There were six steps to the throne,* as against the six firmaments." But are there not seven firmaments? R. Abin said: "Where the King [God] dwells is an honored place [and therefore could not be represented on earth]."

(Num. Rab. 12:17; Esth. Rab. *ad* 1:2, par. 12)

R. Yoḥanan said: "The Holy One, blessed be He, seated Solomon on his throne and made him king over those above and those below, and made him a throne below which reproduced the appearance of the Throne of Glory which is above. Just as in the throne above there are four living creatures: man, lion, ox, and eagle, so in the throne of Solomon there were shapes of man, lion, ox, and eagle."

R. Ḥiyya said: "Solomon made his throne in the likeness of the Throne of Glory, with the help of the Holy Spirit. Behind the throne there was a likeness of the Wheel and of Cherubim, and before the throne he placed likenesses of heavenly animals and heavenly wheels. And sixty warriors were stationed there, and on its front were engraved the sixty letters of the priestly blessing."

R. El'azar said: "Solomon's throne was studded with precious stones and pearls, to make it glitter like the very heavens in purity, and also cattle, beasts, and birds were attached to the throne, an impure one opposite a pure one, the lion opposite the ox."

R. Eliezer said: "The likeness with the lion face stood in

strength, and its two front legs were raised up towards the horns of the ox, and the horns of the ox reached forward towards it like two rods."

R. Yoḥanan said: "King Solomon placed them at the throne, one to the right and one to the left: the lamb on the right, and the lion on the left, the gazelle on the right and the bear on the left, the deer on the right and the elephant on the left, the *reem* [unicorn] on the right and the griffin on the left. And at the end of all of them he placed a man, and opposite him a demon. And on top he placed the *ziz* [a gigantic bird] and opposite it an eagle, and he put a dove and opposite it a hawk. And inside there was a tablet engraved with a serpent on a pole."

R. Yoḥanan said: "In what manner did Solomon ascend the throne and sit on it? The ox took him upon its horns and passed him on to the lion, and warned it saying: 'Be careful with King Solomon so that nothing bad should happen to him.' And the lion passed him on to the ram, and the ram to the panther, and the panther to the lamb, and the lamb to the wolf, and the wolf to the gazelle, and the gazelle to the bear, and the bear to the deer, and the deer to the elephant, and the elephant to the *reem* , and the *reem* to the griffin, and the griffin to the man, and they all said to him in a great voice: 'Behold, we have been peaceable with you, O King of Peace, be you a witness between us!' And the man passed him on to the demon, and the demon flew with him and took him between heaven and earth, and then took him to his place and seated him upon the throne, which was of pure gold studded with precious stones and pearls. And the demon ascended to the firmament and brought the sapphire stone and placed it under his feet. . . . "

In that hour a dove of fine gold brought the book of Deuteronomy to the king, placed it on his knees, and called on him to obey what is written in it. And the book was with him and he read in it all the days of his life.

R. Yoḥanan said: "All the animals raised their voices which made the whole world tremble. . . . The hawk cried, and from its voice all the sleepers of Jerusalem awoke. The serpent hissed with his mouth and all the sick of Jerusalem became cured by its voice."

R. El'azar said: "What was the manner in which Solomon sat on the throne? He took the Tora, looked into it, and began to judge Israel. In that hour the lion called out: *Thou shalt not respect persons in judgment* (Deut. 16:19). The ox repeated and said: *Neither shalt thou favor a poor man in his cause* (Exod. 23:3). The ram answered: *For the judgment is God's* (Deut. 1:17). The panther called out in wrath: *Justice, justice shalt thou follow* (Deut. 16:20)."

His disciples asked R. Yoḥanan: "Why were there palms and clothes of byssus?" He answered them: "The trees stood high above the throne and they were sunk into the domes, and byssus and purple ropes were hanging over Solomon's head. And clothes of byssus were attached to the trees, and all kinds of colors played through them, and when the wind entered them they covered the whole throne and everything around it for a hundred cubits, and they looked like the appearance of lightning and like the appearance of torches of fire, and like the appearance of the rainbow. And to the mouths [of the animals] were attached golden bells, and the wind entered them and they chimed."

R. Ḥiyya taught: "There were seventy thousand golden chairs around the throne, on which sat the sages and their disciples and the priests and the Levites and the princes of Israel. And in the throne room itself there were seventy chairs on which sat the seventy elders. And opposite [the king's throne] there were two chairs: one for the seer Gad and the other for the prophet Nathan. And on his right there was a chair for Bathsheba, his mother, so that she should hear his wisdom...."

Two lions were standing one to his right and one to his left. When the king came to ascend the throne, the left lion stretched forth his hand and took the crown and placed it on the king's head. And the right lion took the golden scepter and put it into the king's hand. Then a silver dragon ran forward through a contrivance and bowed down before the king, and the eagles spread their wings. When he came to issuing his verdict, the lions opened their mouths opposite him and shone like torches of fire, and opened their mouths and gnashed their teeth, and carried the king into the hall of the gate. And the king was afraid to issue his verdict lest he did not decide rightly, and he looked at Gad the seer and Nathan the prophet, and they decided through prophecy, and the king agreed with them in his wisdom. And they would announce it to the seventy elders, and the elders to the princes of Israel, and the princes to the emissaries of the law court, and they would lead forth the man whether to life or to death. . . .

When the king pronounced the judgment, the lions would lick the soles of his feet, and the Holy Spirit would chirp and say: "King Solomon be blessed," and all those who stood there replied: "Let the kingdom of the House of David be established solidly!"

(Kisse w'Ippodromin, BhM 5:34-37)

What Happened to the Throne After Solomon's Death?

Our sages said that in the hour when King Ahasuerus ascended his royal throne, he wanted to sit on the throne which Solomon had made in his great wisdom and with the understanding of the Holy One, blessed be He. Israel said before the Holy One, blessed be He: "Master of the World! That evil one should sit in the place in which King Solomon sat and judged Israel? Do it for Your Name, and let not Your Throne of Glory be sullied!"

And the sages said: "How did the golden throne reach Media?" The sages said: "After the death of Solomon, Shishak king of Egypt went up to the land of Israel and seized the throne of Solomon as a settlement for his daughter (who was Solomon's wife), and took it down to

Egypt.... Subsequently Sanherib went up and seized the throne in Egypt and took it back to the land of Israel because he wanted to fight the Jews. At that juncture Sanherib fell into the hands of Israel, and Israel captured his fortune, and the throne returned to its place. And King Hezekiah sat on it and partook of the honor and became elevated in his kingship and succeeded....

And in the days of King Joshiah, Pharaoh king of Egypt went up and fought Joshiah and took the throne from Jerusalem and brought it to Egypt. And he wanted to sit on it but did not know its custom nor how one sits on it, and the lion hit him on his hip and he became crippled, and this is why he is called Pharaoh Nekho which is rendered in Targum "Pharaoh the lame."

And when Nebuchadnezzar went up against Egypt, he found the throne there and took it and carried it to Babylon. And he, too, tried to ascend it and sit on it and thus judge Zedekiah king of Judah in Babylon.... But Nebuchadnezzar did not know the custom of the throne, went up to sit on it, and the lion which is on the left side hit him so that he fell down from the blow and suffered from it until the day of his death.

And when Darius the Mede became king and destroyed Babylon, he too took the throne and carried it to Elam which is in Media. But nevertheless no man ever sat on it. And when Ahasuerus became king, he sent and fetched him sages to make a throne like it, but they could not, so he had another throne made for himself and sat on it. And when King Ahasuerus saw that throne, he desired to sit on it, more than did Nebuchadnezzar and Darius and Pharaoh, but could not. And he brought craftsmen from Tyre and Alexandria to make another throne like it, but they could not. However, they made him another beautiful throne. And the craftsmen worked on it for three years. And in the third year of his reign he sat on that throne which the craftsmen from Tyre and Alexandria made for him.

(D'mut Kisse Shel Sh'lomo, BhM 2:83-85)

When Solomon died, Shishak king of Egypt came up and took the throne from them, saying: "I take it as a settlement for my daughter." When Shishak made war against Zerah the Ethiopian, the latter took it from him. When Asa king of Judah made war against Zerah (2 Chron. 14:8-14) the throne fell into his hands and he took it from him.

It is taught: Asa and all the kings of Judah sat on it, and when Nebuchadnezzar went up and destroyed Jerusalem, he took it into exile to Babylon. And from Babylon it got to Media, and from Media to Greece, and from Greece to Edom [Rome]. R. El'azar son of R. Yose said: "I saw its broken parts in Rome." Nebuchadnezzar sat on it, Cyrus sat on it, but when Ahasuerus came to sit on it they did not let him for they said to him: "He who is not a cosmocrator [world ruler] in the world cannot sit on it." So he went and had another, similar, throne made for himself.

(Esth. Rab. *ad* 1:2, par. 12)

Solomon's Hippodrome

R. Yohanan asked R. Zera: "How many chariot races did King Solomon hold every year?" He answered him: "Twelve, as against the twelve officers [of his realm, cf. 1 Kings 4:7], and each of them held it in his month. . . . " The thirteenth officer (1 Kings 4:19) did not organize chariot races but foot races, and those young runners had their knees cut so that they could run so fast that no horse or other animal could overtake them. And from which tribe were they? R. Yose said: "From Naftali, as it is written, *Naftali is a hind let loose* (Gen. 49:21)." R. Yohanan said: "From the tribe of Gad, as it is written, *And the Gadites there separated themselves unto David . . . and they were as swift as the roes upon the mountains* (1 Chron. 12:9)." And how many were they? Ten thousand youths. They were the young men of the king who were fed from the table of the king. They had their races in the month of Teveth. And what did they carry? Golden shields.

How large was the hippodrome? Three parasangs long and one parasang wide. In its middle there were built two structures, made of net work, and all kinds of beasts and birds were set into them, and the horses and the runners raced around them eight times every day. On top of each tower there were two golden lions. These lions emitted all kinds of fragrances, which originated from the Garden of Eden, in order to show Israel a sample of the World to Come which they would see in the future with their own eyes. From the mouths of two of the lions issued forth spiced wines, and from the other two issued spices. . . .

R. Yoḥanan said: "There were four factions in the hippodrome of the king, and in each there were four thousand men, and in each faction there were structures and over them capitals fortified with iron, brass, and gold, and on each capital there were seven platforms, one on top of the other, and four tiers one on top of the other, and each tier sat a hundred men. And to each faction [led] two gates of olive wood, and in them were set all kinds of golden vessels and precious stones and pearls, and Cherubim and palm trees set in gold, and their light shone far beyond Jerusalem. And before each faction there were flutes and pipes which were played high on top and were playing the flute according to its rhythm."

R. Yose said: "They were divided into four groups: the king and his servants and the sages and the students and the priests and the Levites were dressed in sky-blue; all Israel [who lived in Jerusalem] was dressed in white; those who had come from the towns and the villages and the other places were dressed in red; and the nations of the world who had come from great distances to bring offerings to the king were dressed in green." His disciples said to him: "Why were there these four kinds of clothes?" He said to them: "As against the four turns of the sun (*t'qufot*): from the autumnal equinox until the winter solstice the days are like the blue of the sky; from the winter solstice to the vernal equinox the snow falls and they were dressed in white; from

the vernal equinox to the summer solstice the sea is good
for sailing and they dressed in green; and from the summer
solstice to the autumnal equinox the fruits are beautiful and
red, and then they wore red clothes."

(Kisse w'Ippodromin, BhM 5:37-39)

The Death of Absalom

Absalom was a hero of great strength, and his sword was
girded on his loins. Why then, when he was caught in the
tree by his hair, did he not draw his sword and cut off his
hair and get down? Because he saw Gehenna which opened
up beneath him, and he said: "It is better for me to hang by
the hair of my head than to go down into the fire."
Therefore he remained hanging. R. Yose said: "Gehenna
has seven gates, and Absalom entered five of them. David
heard, and began to lament and to mourn, and called
Absalom 'My son, my son!' five times, and thereby brought
him back from the five gates."

(Pirqe R. Eliezer, ch. 53)

The Righteous of Nineveh

How did the people of Nineveh repent of their evil ways?
Each one of them did law and justice. . . . Even if a man sold
a ruinous house to his fellow man, and he came to rebuild it
and found in it a treasure of silver and gold, what did he
do? He called the man who had sold him the ruinous house
and said: "The treasure I found in this ruin belongs to you."
The seller replied and said to the buyer: "When I sold you
the ruinous house, I sold you everything in it, therefore
these treasures belong to you." When neither the seller nor
the buyer wanted to take it, they both went to the judge.
The buyer said to the judge: "Your Honor, when I bought
this ruin from this man, I bought nothing but the ruin, and
when I searched in it I found in it precious stones and
pearls, and now let him take them from me, and let him not

leave them with me, for the Holy One, blessed be He, destroys the world because of robbery." The seller said to the judge: "I, when I sold him this ruin, sold it to him with everything that was in it. Just as you are fleeing from robbery, so I, too, am fleeing from robbery, for he who robs from his fellow man even as much as a penny's worth, is as if he had taken his soul from him." What did the judge do? He searched the deed of that ruin, and went back four generations, and found the heir of that man who had hidden the treasure in it, and returned it to its rightful owner.

(Yona, BhM 1:101)

In the Fiery Furnace

The Holy Spirit said to Israel: I adjure you that if the kingdom issues decrees oppressing you, do not rebel against it because of anything that it decrees, but obey the word of the king. But if it decrees that you must desist from studying the Tora and from the commandments and from the Sabbath, do not obey them. *I [counsel you] keep the king's command* (Eccles. 8:2) in everything that the kingdom needs, but in regard of the oath of God *be not hasty to go out of his presence, stand not in an evil thing* (Eccles. 8:2-3). Why? Because they prevent you to fulfill the commandments only in order that you deny the Holy One, blessed be He. Therefore, be *in regard of the oath of God.*

And this is what Hananiah, Mishael, and Azariah did in the hour when Nebuchadnezzar set up the image. They said to him: "What do you think? That you will throw us into the fiery furnace and the Holy One, blessed be He, will not save us? Whether He saves us or saves us not, we shall not worship the image."

They said to him: "Whatever you decree upon us, dues and taxes and head taxes, we shall obey you. But to deny the Holy One, blessed be He, in that we shall not obey you." When Nebuchadnezzar heard this, he began to rage. And when they lighted the furnace they cast them bound into it. When they descended into the furnace they lifted up their eyes to the Holy One, blessed be He, and said: "Master of the Worlds! You know that we did not put our trust in our deeds but only in Your Name."

Instantly the angels wanted to descend to release them. The Holy One, blessed be He, said to them: "Is it for your name that they descended into the furnace? They descended for the sake of My name, and I shall go down and release them." Instantly the Holy One, blessed be He, released them and caused the furnace to float and brought it up and made it level with the ground, for it had been a pit. When the angel saw this he said to them: "Come out of there, for the Holy One, blessed be He, has released you and made miracles for you and made the furnace level with the ground, come out." They said to him: "We shall not come out except by [the word of] Nebuchadnezzar, lest they say, 'They fled from the furnace.' *We keep the king's command.* By his word we entered here and by his word we shall go out."

When Nebuchadnezzar came, he saw them and was amazed. He began to shout to them, as it is said, *He spoke and said, Shadrach, Meshach, and Abed-nego,*[27] *ye servants of God Most High, come forth and come hither* (Dan. 3:26). Instantly they said to the angel: "Now we shall go out."

(Tanḥ. Buber 1:38-41)

Vashti's Downfall

R. Abbahu said: "When Israel eats and drinks they engage in words of Tora and songs before the Holy One. But when the nations of the world eat and drink they engage in indecent talk." These said, "The Median women are the most beautiful," and the others said, "The Persian women are the most beautiful." Ahasuerus said to them: "The vessel

---

[27] These are the Babylonian names of Hananiah, Mishael, and Azariah.

I am using is not from Media and not from Persia, but from Chaldea, and there is none like it in the whole world!" He said to them: "Do you wish to see her?" They said to him: "We do, provided that she be naked."

Thereupon Ahasuerus commanded *that they bring Vashti the queen before the king with the royal crown* (Esth. 1:11), that nothing should be on her except the crown, and that she be naked.

But the queen Vashti refused (Esth. 1:12). She sent him words which touch the heart. She said to him: "Why do you demand this? If they find me ugly, you will be disgraced, and if they find me beautiful, they will plan to kill you and will violate me."

When the king insisted she sent him this message: "O, you fool, your heart went out because of your wine. Know that I am the daughter of Belshazzar, the son of Nebuchadnezzar who was praised among kings, and rulers were like nothing before him, and you could not have been even a chief of equerries in the house of my father, not even a questor to run before his chariot. Not even the convicts of my father were judged naked."

And the king was very wroth and his anger burned in him (ibid.). R. Yoḥanan said: "All those seven years from the time when Vashti was executed until the time when Haman was crucified, his anger burned in him."

When Ahasuerus sobered up from his wine he asked for Vashti. They said to him: "You had her killed." He said to them: "Why?" They said to him: "Because you said she should come before you naked and she did not come." He said to them: "I did wrong. Who gave me the advice to kill her?" They said to him: "The seven princes of Persia and Media." He had them killed instantly.

(Abba Gurion, BhM 1:3-5)

R. Levi said: "A picture of Vashti was hanging over the bed of Ahasuerus. When women entered, he would look at them and at the picture of Vashti, and there was none like

Vashti. But when Esther entered, she was more beautiful than the picture of Vashti. Thereupon he took down the picture of Vashti and hanged up a picture of Esther."

(Abba Gurion, BhM 1:6)

The Parable of the Sow

After these things did the king Ahasuerus promote Haman (Esth. 3:1). To what can this be likened? To a man who had a she-ass, and a mare, and a sow. He gave the sow food without measure, but to the she-ass and the mare he gave food in measure. The she-ass said to the mare: "We who do work for our owner, he gives us in measure, and to the sow [who does no work he gives] without measure." The mare said to the she-ass: "The hour will come and you will see." When Calendas [a feast day] came, they took the sow and killed her. Thus it is said, *After these things did the king Ahasuerus promote Haman*, and thereafter, *They hanged Haman* (Esth. 7:10).

(Abba Gurion, BhM 1:6-7)

Haman's Holocaust Prevented

Haman went to the House of Study and found there Mordecai sitting at the head of the children. They were covered with dust and sackcloth on their hips, and they were mourning and weeping. He counted them: Twenty-two thousand. And he put iron rings on their necks and chains on their feet, and placed guards over them, and said: "I shall first slaughter these, and then I shall hang Mordecai." And their mothers brought them bread and water and said to them: "Our sons, eat and drink before you die." But they placed their hands on their books and swore: "By the life of Mordecai our master, we shall neither eat nor drink, but will die fasting." And each one of them rolled up his book and returned it to his master, saying: "We had thought that the merit of this Tora will give us long life, as it is said, *For that is thy life and the length of thy days* (Deut. 30:20). But now that we have not merited it, take your book from our hands." Instantly they all uttered bitter cries, and their mothers lowed like cows outside, and their sons like calves inside, until their cry, and the cry of the Fathers of the World, ascended to heaven. At the hour of two at night their weeping was heard before the Holy One. He said to the Ministering Angels: "I hear the voice of kids and of sheep!" In that hour Moses arose before the Holy One, blessed be He, crying and said: "Master of the World! It is revealed and known before You that it is not the voice of kids and sheep but the voice of the small ones of Your people Israel who have been fasting for three days and three nights and are bound in chains, and tomorrow they will stand to be slaughtered like kids and sheep, and the heart of the enemy rejoices over them." In that hour the pity of the Holy One was aroused, and He broke the seals and tore up the decree, and cut down the horn of the evil one, and frustrated the plan of the wicked Haman, and turned his thought against him, and lifted up the horn of Israel and caused salvation to grow for them. R. Ḥelbo said: "The world exists only because of the breath of the mouth of the children of the House of Study, and thus also the plan of the wicked Haman was frustrated only because of them."

(Abba Gurion, BhM 1:14-15)

Haman and Mordecai

R. Levi said: When Mordecai saw Haman approaching him leading the horse, he said: "It seems that this evil one comes to kill me." And his pupils were sitting before him and studying. He said to them: "Get up and flee, lest you be burned by my embers!" They said to him: "Whether for death or for life, we are with you and shall not leave you!" What did he do? He wrapped himself in his Tallith and stood in prayer before the Holy One, blessed be He, and his pupils sat and studied. He said to them: "What are you studying?" They said to him: "The Commandment of the *Omer* [sheaf] which Israel used to offer up in the Temple on this day." He said to them: "This *Omer*, what was it of, of gold or of silver?" They said to him: "Of barley." He said to them: "And how much was its value? Ten *qentars*?"[28] They said to him: "Its value is ten *manehs*."[29] He said to them: "Get up, for your ten *manehs* have defeated the ten thousand *qentars* of silver which Haman offered the king for permission to slay the Jews (Esth. 3:9)." When Esther heard of Haman's plot she sent out heralds to the whole city and said: "Let no man open his store in the market! Let all the people go out, for the chief of the Jews is about to be crucified!"

When Mordecai finished his prayer, Haman said to him: "Put on this royal purple, and put this crown on your head, and mount this horse." He said to him: "You fool in the world! Do you not know that I am wearing sackcloth and ashes? Can a man put on the purple of the king without having washed? Do you want to spurn the royalty?" Haman went to the bathmaster but did not find him. What did he do? He girded himself until his midriff, and entered the bathhouse, mixed it, wiped it, and went in and washed him. When he finished, Mordecai put on the purple. Then Haman said to him: "Put this royal crown on your head." Mordecai said to him: "Can a man put the royal crown on his head without having his hair cut? Why do you want to spurn the royalty?" Haman went to fetch the barber, but could not find him. What did he do? He took the barber's tools and sat and cut Mordecai's hair. While he was sitting and cutting his hair he began to moan. Mordecai said to him: "What is the matter?" Haman said to him: "Woe to me! What has come upon me! I who functioned as *comes panton* [chief of all], who functioned as *comes calator* [chief of

[28] Centenarium, or 100,000 sesterces.

[29] A *maneh* or *mina*—a weight in gold or silver equal to one hundred shekels.

appointments], who functioned as the *magister* of the palace, have now become a bathmaster and a barber!" Mordecai said to Haman: "Don't I know that your father in the village of Krinus is the bathmaster and the barber? And these are the barber's utensils." When Haman finished cutting his hair, he said to Mordecai: "Get up and mount this horse!" Mordecai said to him: "I have no strength, for I am an old man." Haman said to him: "And I, am I not old?" Mordecai said to him: "Was it not you who brought all this upon yourself?" Haman said to him: "Get up, I shall bend my back for you, so you can step on me and mount this horse, so as to fulfill on you that which is said in your book, *Thine enemies shall dwindle away before thee, and thou shalt tread upon their high places* (Deut. 33:29)."

When Mordecai mounted the horse he began to praise the Holy One, blessed be He, and said: "*I will extol Thee, O Lord, for Thou hast raised me up.* (Ps. 30:2)."

(Lev. Rab. 28:6)

THE EXILE: WOES AND TRIUMPHS

Mother Zion

Jeremiah said: When I went up to Jerusalem, I lifted up my eyes and saw a woman sitting on top of the mountain. She was dressed in black, her hair was disheveled, and she was crying and begging: who will comfort her? And I, too, was crying and begging, who will comfort me? I approached her and spoke to her. I said to her: "If you are a woman, speak to me, and if you are a spirit, get away from me!" She answered and said: "Do you not recognize me? I am she who had seven sons. Their father went to lands across the sea, and while I was going up and crying over him, behold, a messenger came and said to me, 'The house collapsed over your seven sons and killed them.' Now I do not know over whom I should cry and over whom I should dishevel my hair." I answered and said: "You are not better than my Mother Zion, for she has become a pasture for the beasts of the field." She answered and said: "I am your Mother Zion, I am the mother of seven, as it is written, *She that hath borne seven languisheth* (Jer. 15:9)."

(Pes. Rab. 131b)

Jerusalem the Mourner

A parable: There was a flesh-and-blood king who was attacked by enemies and they put his house to the torch. And he sat and was silent, for he thought: "What shall I do? Shall I get up and run out of my house? I shall not, lest they say, he fled because he had no power." He sat in his place, and the fire almost reached him. His friends entered and said to him: "Our Lord the king, why do you sit when there is a conflagration in your house?"

Thus the Holy One, blessed be He; in the hour when the enemy entered and put the Temple to the torch, He sat and cried: "What shall I do?" Asaf entered to Him and said to Him: "Master of the World! Fire consumes Your house, and you sit? Arise, go out of Your house!"

In that hour all the prophets returned and gathered and went to Jerusalem to comfort her. The Holy One, blessed be He, said to them: "Who is it whom you should comfort first, Me or Jerusalem? If a son dies, whom do people comfort? Is it not the father? If a house burns down, whom do people comfort? Is it not its owner? How much more so do I need to be comforted first! Nevertheless, go and comfort her, comfort Jerusalem!"

All of them gather and go to her. As soon as she sees them she says to them: "Go away, I do not need the consolation of my children!" Instantly they go before the Holy One, blessed be He, and say before Him: "She does not want to accept our consolation." He says to them: "It behooves no one else to go to her, but Me. I Myself shall go and comfort her, because I exceeded in meting out punishment."

Instantly the Holy One, blessed be He, goes to her and says to her: "Wherefore are you so embittered?" She says before Him: "Master of the World! I am not embittered because You exiled me among the nations of the world, and cursed me with bad curses, and my face became black like the bottom of a pot. Despite all that I sanctified Your great name." He said to her: "I was wroth with you because you transgressed My Tora." She said before Him: "Master of the World! Since the day that You exiled me among the nations of the world, it is meet that I should not observe Your commandments." He said to her: "Already the time of your Redemption has arrived!" Instantly she says before Him: "I shall not be comforted until You show me the downfall of those wicked who tortured me and blasphemed Your name!" Instantly, He says to her: "I shall feed them their own flesh, as it is said, *I will feed them that oppress thee with their own flesh, and they shall be drunken with their own blood as with sweet wine, and all flesh shall know that I the Lord am thy Savior, and thy Redeemer, the Mighty One of Jacob* (Isa. 49:26)."

(Yalqut Shim'oni. Ekha 1031)

Israel Reproaches God

Israel stood up to pour out their complaint before their Father in Heaven saying: "You let much anguish fall upon us. Which shall we hold on to and which shall we leave? You cast upon us great trouble and a heavy burden. You said to us, 'Build Me a House, but even while you are building it, occupy yourselves with the Tora.'" This is the complaint of His children.

And the answer of their Father in Heaven is this: "In the exile there was great idleness among you, and I was yearning and waiting to hear the voice of the words of the Tora from your mouths. You did not act properly, and I did not act properly. You did not act properly in that you argued against Me, so that I became angry with you and arose and brought utter destruction upon My city and My

352 GATES TO THE OLD CITY

House and My children. And I did not act properly in that I
arose against you and sealed your fate with a cruel decree
against you. But certainly an attribute which stands for ever
and all eternity [i.e., divine mercy] will overcome an
attribute [i.e., divine wrath] which has a limited duration
and lasts only a year, or two, or ten, or thirty, or at the
utmost a hundred years, and then passes. But you were right
in reproaching Me, and I have already accepted your
reproach."

(*Sefer Hekhalot* attributed to the Tanna
R. Yishma'el the High Priest, p. 10a)

The Partridge and the Hawk

As long as the kings of the nations are in peace, Israel is not
in peace. A parable. This is like a partridge which used to
sing in the house of its master. He would sit and eat, and the
partridge would sing. After a time its master brought a
hawk. When the partridge saw it, it fled and hid under the
bed, and did no longer open its mouth. The king came to
partake of a meal. He said to his friend: "Why does the
partridge not sing?" He said to him: "Because you brought
in a hawk upon it, and it sees the hawk and is afraid and
does not sing. But, remove the hawk and it will sing again."

Thus Israel in this world. They dwell outside the Land of
Israel, and the kings of the nations dwell in their land. And
the Holy One, blessed be He, says to Israel: "Why do you
not sing My praise?" Moses[30] said to him: "Master of the
World! As long as the kings of the nations are in Your land,
Israel is not visible in the world. But, remove them, and
Israel will become visible." And even the Holy One, blessed
be He, as it were, is not visible in the world, until He uproot
the kingdom of Edom.[31]

(Agadat B'reshit, ed. Buber, p. 116)

[30] That is, the spirit of Moses in the World to Come.
[31] I.e., Rome.

WARRIORS AND MARTYRS

The High Priest's Daughter

Our masters taught: In the days of the kingdom of the wicked Greeks they decreed upon Israel that whosoever has a bolt in his house must engrave into it that Israel has no share and no inheritance in the God of Israel. Instantly Israel went and uprooted the bolts which were in their houses. And they also decreed that whosoever has an ox must write on its horns that Israel has no share in the God of Israel. Israel went and sold their oxen. And they also decreed that they must couple with their wives while they menstruate. Israel went and separated themselves from their wives. And they also decreed that whosoever takes a wife, she must first have intercourse with the general,[32] and then she could return to her husband. And this thing was in force for three years and eight months, until the daughter of Yoḥanan the high priest got married. As they were about to take her to that general, she uncovered her head and rent her garments and stood naked before the people. Instantly Judah Maccabi and his brothers became filled with wrath at her and said: "Take her out to be burnt, and let this thing not be revealed to the government, because of the mortal danger, for she had the audacity to show herself naked before this whole people." But she said to him: "How shall I become disgraced before my brethen and friends and shall not become disgraced in the eyes of that uncircumcised and impure man to whom you want to deliver me and to take me to lie with him!"

When Judah and his friends heard this they took counsel together to kill the general. Instantly they dressed the girl in royal robes and made her a canopy of myrtles, from the house of the Hasmonaeans to the house of the general. And all the harpists and violinists and singers came and made music and danced until they reached the house of the

[32] The Greek governor of Palestine.

general. When the general heard this, he said to his lords and servants: "Look at them! They are of the great ones of Israel, of the seed of Aaron the priest, how they rejoice to do my will. They deserve great honor." And he commanded that his lords and servants should be led out, and Judah and his friends entered with his sister to the general, and they cut off his head and despoiled everything he had and killed his lords and servants, and defeated the Greeks completely, except for the essence of the kingdom. And Israel who were in the city were in fear and trembling because of those youths of Israel. A heavenly voice issued and said: "Victorious are the youths who went to make war in Antioch!" And those young men returned and closed the gates, and repented and occupied themselves with the Tora and works of charity.

(L'Hanukha BhM 1:133-34)

The Miraculous Battle

Their sword shall enter into their own heart, and their bows shall be broken (Ps. 37:15). R. Shim'on ben Yohai said: This refers to the Greeks who made war with the House of Hashmonai and his sons. In the hour in which they entered the Temple, a Greek went and took a Tora scroll, and brought Hannah the daughter of Yohanan the High Priest, like whose beauty there was not in the world, and she was married to El'azar ben Hashmonai. And that Greek wanted to violate her before her husband and her father. Yohanan the High Priest said: "I and my three sons and you, Hashmonai, and your seven sons make twelve, as against the twelve tribes. I am sure that the Holy One, blessed be He, will perform a miracle through us." Instantly El'azar lifted up the sword and killed that Greek, and said: "*My help cometh from the Lord, who made heaven and earth* (Ps. 121:2)."

R. Yitzhaq said: "There were sixty times ten thousand times a thousand troops, and in each of them there were a thousand men, who came with the wicked Galiscas to fight the House of Hashmonai. And that wicked one said: "What is there for us to fear? They are twelve against a great army. Should you say their God will bring out stars from their courses and make war against us, and the stars will despoil us, as He did to Sisera—we shall smear ourselves with pigs' blood and with horses' semen, so that they cannot touch us. And should you say, He will bring a deluge—He swore by his great name that He will not bring a deluge upon the world. Should you say He will send snakes and scorpions and bears as He did with the Kuthites—we are riding on elephants which those animals cannot touch."

And Israel stood in prayer and said: "Master of the World! It is revealed and known before You that we did rise to give battle to them only for the sake of Your great name, that it not be humiliated among the nations, and if You do not make a miracle through us they will say, 'He has no counsel,' whereas it is written about you, *Great in counsel and mighty in work* (Jer. 32:19)."

Instantly the compassion of the Holy One, blessed be He, was aroused and He said: "Be quiet, My sons, stand up and see the vengeance of the Lord which He will wreak in the nations." And He brought all the celestial princes of seventy nations, and said to them: "Each one of you will slay your own in the army of that wicked one, and if one of them escapes from you, your soul will be taken for his soul." They instantly descended upon the earth, and when a Greek put an arrow in his bow to shoot at Israel, the angel made it turn back and it struck him in the heart. And the House of Hashmonai looked at one another and said: "*The Lord will fight for you and you keep silent!* (Exod. 14:14)."

(L'Ḥanukka, BhM 1:135-36)

The Sons of Miriam bat Tanhum

Hadrian Caesar came and captured a widowed woman, Miriam bat Tanhum by name, and her seven sons. He said to her: "Who are you?" She said: "I am a widow." "And who are these children who stand next to you, from where do you have them?" She said to him: "They are my sons." He took them and imprisoned each of them separately.

He brought the first, the oldest of them, and said to him: "Bow down to this deity as your brothers have done." He said to him: "God forbid that my brothers should have bowed down to idols. Even so I shall not bow down to the work of human hands." Instantly they took a sword and cut off his head.

He brought the second one and said to him: "Bow down to this deity as your brothers have done." He said to him: "God forbid that my brothers should have bowed down. Even so I will not bow down to the work of human hands." Instantly they took a sword and cut off his head.

[Each of the sons was thus executed.]

He brought the seventh, the youngest of them all. He said to him: "Come and bow down to this." He said to him: "God forbid. I shall not bow down to the work of human hands. For this is how we swore to the Holy One, blessed be He, that we shall not serve any other god. And the Holy One, blessed be He, swore to us that He will not exchange us for another people." He said to him: "You do not have to bow down to this god. Look, I shall throw to you this ring, and you lift it up from before the image, so that all the people who stand about should say, 'He listened to the words of Caesar and bowed down to it.'" He said to him: "Woe to you, Caesar, because of your own words. If you, who are flesh and blood, are ashamed in front of flesh and blood like yourself, should I not be ashamed before the King of kings of kings?" He said to him: "Does, then, the world have a God?" He said to him: "Did you see a lawless world?"[33] He said to him: "And does your God have a head?" He said to him: "It has already been said, *His head is as the most fine gold* (Song 5:11)." He said to him: "And does your God have ears?" He said to him: "Already it has been said, *And the Lord hearkened and heard* (Mal. 3:16)." He said

[33] I.e., did you imagine that there is no law governing the world?

to him: "And does your God have eyes?" He said to him: "Surely it has already been said, *The eyes of the Lord run to and fro* (Zech. 4:10.)" He said to him: "And does your God have a nose?" He said to him: "Surely it has already been said, *And the Lord smelled the sweet savor* (Gen. 8:12)." He said to him: "And has your God a mouth?" He said to him: "Surely it has already been said, *And all the hosts of them by the breath of His mouth* (Ps. 33:6)." He said to him: "And does your God have a palate?" He said to him: "Surely it has already been said, *His palate is most sweet, yea, he is altogether lovely* (Song 5:16)." He said to him: "And has your God hands?" He said to him: "Surely it has already been said, *Yea, My hand hath laid the foundation of the earth, and My right hand hath spread out the heavens* (Isa. 48:13)." He said to him: "And does your God have feet?" He said to him: "Surely it has already been said, *And His feet shall stand in that day upon the Mount of Olives* (Zech. 14:4)." He said to him: "And does your God have strength?" He said to him: "Surely it has already been said, *Behold, the Lord's hand is not shortened that it cannot save* (Isa. 59:1)." He said to him: "Since your God has strength, and his eyes see, and his ears listen, why did he not reveal himself and save you from my hands?" He said to him: "O you fool in the world! You are not worthy of miracles to be performed through you. And we, we have deserved death. If you do not kill us, God has many killers. God has many panthers, many snakes, many scorpions, many lions, which can attack us." Instantly Caesar commanded that he be killed.

In that hour their mother said to him: "By the life of your head, Caesar! By the life of your head, Caesar! Give me my son so I can kiss him!" They gave him to her. She stroked him, embraced him, and kissed him. And she took her breast and put it into his mouth[34] And honey and milk

[34] They used to suckle their children up to three years of age, as is still done among the Arabs, cf. R. Patai, *Sex and Family in the Bible and the Middle East*, pp. 192 ff.; *Society, Culture and Change in the Middle East*, p. 97.

dripped and fell on the earth. And again she said: "By the life of your head, Caesar! By the life of your head, Caesar! Put the sword on my neck and the neck of my son together!" Caesar said to her: "God forbid! I shall do no such thing." Instantly they took a sword and cut off his head.

The sages figured out the age of that child. It was found that he was two years and six months and seven and a half hours old.

In that hour the nations of the world tore their hair and beard and wept a great weeping, and said: "What did the Father of these do that they are thus slain because of him?" In that hour[35] their mother said to them: "My sons, go and tell your father Abraham, Let your mind not be elated. You say, 'I built an altar and sacrificed my son upon it,' but I built seven altars and sacrificed my seven sons on them." And their mother spoke again: "My sons, happy are you that you did the will of your Father who is in heaven, and that you were not in the world except to sanctify His great name through you." Instantly she prostrated herself and ascended the roof and threw herself down and died. A heavenly voice issued forth and said to her: "Of you speaks the verse, *Joyful is the mother of children* (Ps. 113:9)."

(Seder Eliyahu Rabba, ed.
Friedmann, pp. 151-53)

The Ten Martyrs

After the destruction of the Temple the impudence of the generation became overbearing and they said: "What did we lose by the destruction of the Temple? There are among us scholars who lead and instruct the world in His Tora and in His commandments." Instantly the Holy One, blessed be He, put it into the heart of Caesar of Rome to study the Tora of Moses from the mouth of sages and elders. And he

[35] The mother here addresses her sons after their execution.

started with the Book of Genesis and he studied until he reached *And these are the ordinances* (Exod. 21). When he reached the verse, *He that stealeth a man and selleth him, or if he be found in his hand, he shall surely be put to death* (Exod. 21:16), he instantly commanded that they fill his palace with locks, and he sent to fetch ten sages of Israel. And they came before him, and he seated them on golden chairs. He said to them: "I have to ask of you a matter of profound law. Do not tell me anything but the law and the truth and the ordinance." They said to him: "Speak." He said to them: "He who has stolen a man from among his brothers of the Children of Israel and made use of him and sold him, what is his punishment?" They said to him: "The Tora said, *He shall surely be put to death.*" He answered and said to them: "If so, you are guilty and must die." They said to him: "Why?" He said to them: "Because of the selling of Joseph whom his brothers sold. Were they alive, I would sentence them to death, but since they are not alive, you will carry the sin of your fathers." They said to him: "Give us three days' time. If we shall find a defense, good; and if not, do to us as you wish." Caesar gave his consent, and they went and beseeched R. Yishma'el the High Priest that he should utter the Great Name and ascend to the firmament and find out there whether this indeed was a decree from God, blessed be He.

And R. Yishma'el purified himself by immersion and by sanctifications, wrapped himself in Tallith and Tefillin, and uttered to the Ineffable Name in full. Instantly the spirit carried him and took him up until the sixth firmament. There the angel Gabriel met him and said to him: "Are you Yishma'el with whom your Creator praises Himself every day saying that He has a servant on earth who is like the image of His countenance?" He said to him: "I am he." He said to him: "Why did you come up here?" He said to him: "Because the Evil Kingdom has issued a decree against us, to cause ten sages of Israel to perish, and I have come up to know whether this decree is from the Holy One, blessed be

He." Gabriel said to him: "If the decree has not been sealed, can you annul it?" He said to him: "Yes." He said to him: "What with?" He said to him: "With the Name of the Blessed One." Instantly Gabriel replied and said: "Happy are you, children of Abraham, Isaac, and Jacob, that the Holy One, blessed be He, revealed to you that which He did not reveal to the Ministering Angels."

Gabriel said to him: "Yishma'el, my son, by your life, I heard from behind the Curtain[36] that ten sages of Israel have been delivered to be slain by the Evil Kingdom." R. Yishma'el said to him: "Why?" He said to him: "Because of the selling of Joseph, whom his brothers sold. For the Divine Quality of Justice brings accusations every day before the Throne of Glory and says: 'Did You write in Your Tora even one single letter in vain? Is it not that You have not yet punished the Tribes[37] who sold Joseph, neither them nor their seed?' Therefore the decree has been issued to deliver ten sages of Israel to be slain by the Evil Kingdom." R. Yishma'el said to him: "Until now the Holy One, blessed be He, has not found anybody to punish for Joseph's sale except us?" Gabriel said to him: "By your life, my son Yishma'el, from the day on which the Tribes sold Joseph the Holy One, blessed be He, has not found in one generation ten men as righteous and pious as the Tribes. Therefore the Holy One, blessed be He, punishes you. But the truth is yours."

When the evil Samael saw that the Holy One, blessed be He, wished to put the seal on the decree to deliver ten righteous men into the hands of the Evil Kingdom, he rejoiced greatly and prided himself as if saying, "I defeated Michael the Prince." Instantly the wrath of the Holy One, blessed be He, was kindled against evil Samael, and He said to him: "O Samael, do you want to release ten sages of Israel

---

[36] The Curtain (*Pargod*) separates God from all the other heavenly beings.

[37] That is, the sons of Jacob from whom the tribes of Israel were destined to descend.

from being slain, or to take upon yourself leprosy in the World to Come? You must make a choice!" The evil Samael said to Him: "I shall not release the ten righteous men from being slain. I rather accept Your decree as You have said." Instantly the wrath of the Holy One, blessed be He, was kindled against Samael, and even before he finished his words the Holy One, blessed be He, called Metatron, the Great Scribe, the Prince, and said to him: "Write and seal: six months of leprosy, eruption, scurf, spots, jaundice and bad boils upon the evil Edom,[38] and brimstone and fire upon man and beast, and upon the silver and the gold, and upon everything they possess, until one will say to the other, 'Here you have Rome and everything that is in her, for a penny,' and his friend will answer, 'I do not want them for I have no enjoyment from them.'"

When R. Yishma'el heard this, his mind quieted down. And he walked in heaven, here and there, and saw an altar near the Throne of Glory. He said to Gabriel: "What is this?" He said: "It is an altar." He said to him: "And what do you sacrifice on it every day? Are there bulls and lambs in heaven?" He said to him: "We sacrifice on it souls of righteous men every day." He said to him: "Who sacrifices them?" He said to him: "Michael, the Great Prince."

Thereupon R. Yishma'el descended from heaven and reached the earth and told his colleagues that already the decree had been issued and written and sealed. And they mourned on the right that such a cruel decree had been issued against them, and rejoiced on the left that the Holy One, blessed be He, found them equal to the Tribes in the weight of righteousness and piety. And they sat in pairs, R. Yishma'el and R. Shim'on ben Gamliel, R. Akiba and R. Hanina ben Teradyon, R. El'azar ben Shamu'a and R. Y'shevav the Scribe, R. Hanina ben Hakhinai and R. Yuda ben Bava, R. Hutzpit the Interpreter and R. Yuda ben Dama.

[38] Edom is the Talmudic-Midrashic name of Rome, whose heavenly patron was Samael.

Entered Caesar, and the great ones of Rome after him. He said to them: "Who should be slain first?" R. Shim'on ben Gamliel answered: "I am the prince, son of the prince, from the seed of David king of Israel, peace be upon him, I shall be slain first." R. Yishma'el the High Priest answered and said: "I am the High Priest, son of the High Priest, from the seed of Aaron the Priest. I shall be slain first, and let me not see the death of my colleagues." Caesar said: "This one says, I shall be slain first, and this one says, I shall be slain first. Therefore, draw lots between them." And the lot fell on R. Shim'on ben Gamliel, and Caesar commanded his head be cut off first, and they cut it off. And R. Yishma'el the High Priest took it in his lap and cried over it with a bitter soul and said: "Is this the Tora and is this its reward? The tongue which explained the Tora in seventy languages, how it now licks the dust!" And he mourned and cried over R. Shim'on ben Gamliel. Caesar said to him: "What is this, what is this? You are old and you are crying over your friend, whereas you should be crying over yourself." R. Yishma'el said to him: "I am crying over myself, for my friend was greater than I in Tora and in wisdom, and I am crying because he preceded me to the Supernal Yeshiva."

While he was still speaking and mourning and crying the daughter of Caesar looked down the window and saw the beauty of R. Yishma'el the High Priest, and her compassion was stirred over him, and she sent word to her father that he should grant her one request. And Caesar sent back to her: "My daughter, whatever you wish I shall do, except R. Yishma'el and his colleagues." She sent to him: "I beg of you to let him live." He sent to her: "I have already sworn." She sent to him: "If so, I beg of you to order that they peel off the skin of his face so that I can look at it in place of a picture." Instantly he ordered that they peel off the skin of his face. And when they reached the place of the Tefillin,[39]

---

[39] One of the two Tefillin (phylacteries) is worn on top of the forehead at the hairline, the other on top of the left arm.

he uttered a great and bitter cry, and heaven and earth shook. He cried a second time, and the Throne of Glory trembled. The ministering Angels said before the Holy One, blessed be He: "Such a righteous man, to whom You have shown all the hidden treasures of the supernals and secrets of the infernals, should be slain and die an unnatural death at the hands of this evil one? Is this the Tora and is this its reward?" He said to them: "Let it be, so that his merits stand for the generations after him!"

The Holy One, blessed be He, said: "What shall I do to My children? It is a decree, and none can annul it!" A heavenly voice issued and said: "If I hear another sound, I shall turn the whole world into Tohu vaBohu [primordial chaos]." When R. Yishma'el heard this, he fell silent.

Caesar said to him: "Until now you did not weep and did not cry, and now you cry?" He said to him: "I cry not for my soul but for the commandment of the Tefillin which departs from me." Caesar said to him: "Still you trust in your god?" He said to him: "Yes. *Though He slay me, yet I will trust in Him* (Job 13:15)." Instantly the soul of R. Yishma'el departed.

After him they took out R. Akiba ben Yosef, who used to explain the crowns of the letters and reveal meanings in the Tora as they were handed to Moses on Mount Sinai. And as they were taking him out to be slain, a letter came to Caesar that the king of Araby attacked his land. He had to go, and he ordered that R. Akiba be imprisoned in the jail house until he would return from the war. And when he did return from the war he ordered that they bring him out. And they combed his flesh with iron combs, and at each stroke R. Akiba said: "The Lord is righteous, *The Rock, His work is perfect, for all His ways are justice, a God of faithfulness and without iniquity, just and right is He* (Deut. 32:4)." A heavenly voice issued and said: "Happy are you, R. Akiba, that you were just and right, and your soul departed with *just and right.*"

And when he died, Elijah the prophet of blessed memory

came and took him on his shoulder and carried him five parasangs. And R. Y'hoshu'a haGarsi met Elijah and said to him: "Are you not a Kohen?"[40] He said to him: "The body of a righteous man does not cause defilement." And Y'hoshu'a haGarsi went with him until they came to a cave, a very beautiful one, and when they entered it they found there a beautiful bed and a burning candle. Elijah of blessed memory took Akiba by his shoulders and R. Y'hoshu'a by his legs, and laid him down upon that bed. And the Ministering Angels cried over him thirty days and thirty nights, and then they buried him in that cave. And the following day Elijah of blessed memory took him and led him to the Supernal Yeshiva to expound the crowns of the letters, and all the souls of the righteous and the pious gathered to listen to his teachings.

And after him they took out R. Ḥanina ben Teradyon. They said of R. Ḥanina ben Teradyon that he was pleasing in the sight of God and man, and that never did his lips utter a curse of a fellow man. And when Caesar in Rome ordered that the study of the Tora be prohibited, what did R. Ḥanina ben Teradyon do? He stood up and gathered groups in public, and sat in the market places of Rome, and studied and occupied himself with the Tora and expounded it. And Caesar ordered that he be wrapped into a Tora scroll and be burned. The executioner took him, and wrapped him into a Tora scroll, and lit the fire, and took sponges of wool and soaked them in water and put them over his heart so that his soul should not depart quickly.

And R. Ḥanina's daughter stood there and said: "Woe to me, Father, that I see you thus!" And he answered her and said to her: "How good it is for me, my daughter, that you see me thus!" And his disciples stood about him and said: "Our master, what do you see?" He said to them: "I see the scrolls being consumed by fire and the letters flying away."

---

[40] A Kohen must not touch a dead body, which would cause him ritual defilement.

And he began to cry. His disciples said to him: "Why are you crying?" He said to them: "If I alone would be burned, it would not be difficult for me, but I am being burned and the Tora scroll with me!"

The executioner said to him: "Rabbi, if I take away the sponges of wool from over your heart so that your soul depart quickly, will you bring me to the life of the World to Come?" He said to him: "Yes." He said to him: "Swear to me!" He swore to him. As soon as he swore, the executioner increased the fire and took away the sponges, and his soul departed. And the executioner, too, threw himself into the fire and was consumed. A heavenly voice issued and said: "R. Ḥanina ben Teradyon and the executioner are invited to the life of the World to Come."

And after him they took out R. Yuda ben Bava who all his life never tasted more sleep than the sleep of a horse,[41] from his eighteenth to his eightieth year. And the day on which they took him to be slain was the eve of the Sabbath, and they took him out to be slain after the ninth hour.[42] And he began to beseech them: "By your life, wait a little longer until I fulfill a commandment which the Holy One, blessed be He, commanded me." They said to him: "Still you trust in your god?" He said to them: "Yes." "And is there any power left in your god that you trust him?" He said to them: "*Great is the Lord and highly to be praised, and His greatness is unsearchable* (Ps. 145.3)." They said to him: "If he has power, why did he not save you and your colleagues from the hands of the kingdom?" He said to them: "We owe death to the great and terrible King, and He delivered us into the hands of this king, in order to demand our blood from him." They went and told the king what he had said. The king sent for him and said to him: "Is it true what they told me about you, or not?" He said to him: "It is true." Caesar said to him: "How insolent you Jews are! Even when

41 A horse sleeps standing, on and off, for short periods of time.
42 The ninth hour after sunrise, i.e., in the afternoon.

you stand at the door of death you are still insolent!" R. Yuda said to him: "Woe to you, Caesar, evil son of an evil father. God saw the destruction of His House and the slaying of His pious and righteous, and did not become zealous to take vengeance at once."

His disciples said to him: "Our master, you should have flattered him." He said to them: "Have you not learned that he who flatters the wicked, his end is that he falls into their hands?"

He said to him: "By your life, Caesar, wait until I fulfill one commandment, and its name is Sabbath, and it is the World to Come." He said to him: "This request of yours I shall grant you." Instantly he began the *Kiddush* [sanctification] of the day, *And the heaven and the earth were finished*, etc. (Gen. 2:1),[43] and he said it melodiously, in a loud voice, and all those who stood around him were amazed. And when he reached *In it He rested from all His work which God in creating had made* (Gen. 2:3), they did not let him finish and Caesar ordered that he be slain, and they slew him and his soul departed. A heavenly voice issued and said: "Happy are you R. Yuda that you were like an angel and your soul departed with *God*." And Caesar ordered and they cut him into pieces and threw them to the dogs, and he was neither mourned[44] nor buried.

And after him they took out R. Yuda ben Dama. That day was the eve of Shavuout [Pentecost]. R. Yuda said to Caesar: "By your life, wait awhile until I fulfill the commandment of the feast of *'Atzeret*, and sanctify it in order to praise the Holy One, blessed be He, who gave us the Tora.[45] Caesar said to him: "You still trust in the Tora and in God who gave it?" He said to him: "Yes." Caesar said

---

[43] The beginning of the blessing recited Friday evening.

[44] The mourning ritual could not be performed because his corpse was not available.

[45] 'Atzeret, another name for Shavuot, is the holiday commemorating the Revelation of the Tora on Mount Sinai.

to him: "What is the reward of your Tora?" He said to him: "David, peace be upon him, said about it, *Oh how abundant is Thy goodness which Thou has laid up for them that fear Thee* (Ps. 31:20)." Caesar said to him: "There are no fools in the world like you Jews, who think that there is another world." He said to him: "There are no fools in the world like you who do not believe in the living God, and woe to you, woe to your shame and woe to your disgrace, when you will see us with God in the light of life, and you will dwell in the nethermost Sheol [underworld] in the lowest compartment." Instantly the wrath of Caesar was kindled and he ordered that they tie him by the hair of his head to the tail of a horse, and he ordered that he should be dragged along all the streets of Rome, and then he ordered him to be cut into pieces.

And Elijah of blessed memory came and took the limbs and buried them in a cave near the river which flows before Rome, and for thirty days all the Romans heard the sound of mourning and crying in that cave, and they went and told it to Caesar. He said to them: "Even if the world is turned into Tohu vaBohu, I shall not rest until I fulfill my will on those ten old men as I have sworn." And there was there one of the sages of Rome and he said to Caesar: "My lord Caesar, know that you acted foolishly in this, and you made a very great error in stretching out your hand against the people of the Lord without mercy. Know that at the end you will have bitterness, for it is written in the Tora of the Jews, *God merciful and gracious, long suffering* (Exod. 34:6), and, moreover, it is written in their Tora, *and He repayeth to them that hate Him to their face, to destroy them* (Deut. 7:10)." When Caesar heard this, his wrath was kindled against that elder and he ordered him to be strangled. When the elder heard this, he hurried and circumcised himself instantly. After he was strangled, they could not find him, and they did not know where he was. And Caesar became greatly affrighted, but his anger did not subside, and his hand was nevertheless stretched forth.

And after him they took out R. Ḥutzpit the Interpreter. It was said about R. Ḥutzpit the Interpreter that he was one hundred and thirty years old when they took him out to be slain, and he was beautiful of countenance and beautiful of appearance and was like an angel of the Lord of Hosts. They went and told the king about his beauty and his praise, and said to him: "By your life, my lord, have mercy on this old man." Caesar said to R. Ḥutzpit: "How old are you?" He said to him: "One hundred and thirty but for one day. And my request to you is that you wait until my day is completed." Caesar said to him: "What is it to you whether you die today or tomorrow?" He said to him: "So that I fulfill two more commandments." He said to him: What commandments do you want to fulfill now?" He said to him: "To read the evening and morning *Sh'ma'* prayer, to proclaim the rule of the great and terrible one and only Name over me." Caesar said to him: "You insolent and arrogant people! How long will you trust in your god who has no power to save you from my hands? For, behold, my fathers destroyed his temple, and cast out the bodies of his servants in the environs of Jerusalem and there was none to bury them, and now your god is old and has no power to save any more. For if he had power, he would take his vengeance and the vengeance of his people and the vengeance of his Temple as he did with Pharaoh and Sisera and all the kings of Canaan."

When R. Ḥutzpit heard this, he wept a great weeping, and took hold of his garments and rent them because of this blasphemy of the Name, blessed be He, and His profanation, and said to Caesar: "Woe to you, Caesar, what will you do on the Last Day, when the Holy One, blessed be He, punishes Rome and your gods!" The king said: "How long shall I argue with this one?" And he ordered that he be slain, and they stoned him and hanged him. Then Caesar's lords and sages came and beseeched his face to let him be buried for they had pity on his hoary head. And the king said that they could bury him. And his disciples came and buried him, and mourned him with a very great and heavy mourning.

And after him they took out R. Ḥanina ben Ḥakhinai. And that day was the eve of Sabbath. And he used to sit all his days in fasting from the age of twelve until ninety-five. His disciples said to him: "Rabbi, do you wish to taste something before you are slain?" He said to them: "Until now I have fasted and have neither eaten nor drunk, and now I do not know what way I shall go,[46] and you are telling me to eat and to drink?" He began the sanctification of the day, *And the heaven and earth were finished*, until *and He hallowed it* (Gen. 2:1-3), and they did not let him finish it but slew him. And a heavenly voice issued forth and said, "Happy are you, R. Ḥanina ben Ḥakhinai, for you were hallowed, and your soul departed in holiness with the word *hallowed*."

And after him they took out R. Y'shevav the Scribe. It was said about R. Y'shevav the Scribe that he was ninety years old on the day on which they took him out to be slain. When they took him out, his disciples came and said to him: "Our master, what will happen to the Tora?" He said to them: "My sons, the Tora will be forgotten by Israel, because the evil nation raised its face in insolence and took counsel to cause our feet to perish from under us, and I wish I could be an atonement for the generation. But I can see that there will be no street in Rome in which there will be no people cut down by the sword, for the evil nation will spill innocent blood of Israel." They said to him: "Our master, and what will happen to us?" He said to them: "Support one another, and love peace and justice. Perchance there is hope."

Caesar said to him: "Old man, how old are you?" He said to him: "Today I am ninety years old. And I had not yet come forth from the womb of my mother when a decree was passed by the Holy One, blessed be He, to deliver me

[46] I.e., whether I shall go to the Garden of Eden or to Gehenna.

and my colleagues into your hand, in order to demand our blood from your hand." He said to him: "Is there a second world?" He said to him: "Yes. And you, woe and woe to your shame when the blood of His pious men will be avenged on you." Caesar said: "Hurry to slay him, this one too, and let me see the strength and the power of his god, and what he will do to me in the second world." He ordered, and they burned him.

And after him they took out R. El'azar ben Shamu'a. On that day, it was said about R. El'azar ben Shamu'a, he was one hundred and five years old, and from his childhood until the end of his days nobody ever heard him utter an unseemly word, and he never quarreled with his colleagues, either in word or in deed, and he was modest and humble of spirit, and he sat fasting eighty years. And the day on which he was to be killed was Yom Kippur, and his disciples came before him and said to him: "Our master, what do you see?" He said to them: "I see R. Yuda ben Bava being carried on his bier, and the bier of R. Akiba ben Yosef next to him, and they are arguing about an issue of Halakha." They said to him: "And who decides between them?" He said to them: "R. Yishma'el the High Priest." They said to him: "Who is victorious?" He said to them: "R. Akiba, because he labored on the Tora with all his strength." He said to them: "My sons, I can also see that the soul of each righteous man cleanses itself in the waters of the Shiloah in order to enter today in purity the supernal Yeshiva, to listen to the expositions of R. Akiba ben Yosef which he expounds to them about issues of the day, and each angel brings chairs of gold to each righteous man to sit on in purity."

Caesar ordered that he be slain. And a heavenly voice issued and said: "Happy are you R. El'azar ben Shamu'a that you were pure and your soul departed in 'purity'."

                                        (Ele Ezk'ra, BhM 2:64-72)

MEN OF VIRTUE: SAGES AND SAINTS

For the Sake of Peace

Great is peace for whose sake the Name of the Holy One, blessed be He, which is written in holiness, is blotted out in water in order to improve peace between man and wife.[47]

R. Meir was sitting and expounding on Friday night, and a woman was there who listened to his voice, and it was sweet for her, and she stayed there until he finished. Then she went home and found that the candle had gone out. Her husband said to her: "Where were you?" She said to him: "I was sitting and listening to the voice of a preacher." Her husband swore: "You will not enter here until you spit into his face!" And he threw her out of his house. And she spent three months outside, until R. Meir heard about it. He went to her and found her among the women. He said: "Perchance there is one among you who knows an incantation for the eye, for my eye has been bothering me." Her women neighbors said to her: "Behold God has fulfilled your wish to make him stumble. Spit into his face and it [48] will leave." R. Meir said to her: "Tell your husband, 'You said once, and I spat seven times.' " R. Meir's disciples said to him: "To such an extent you humbled the Tora?"[49] He said to them: "Sufficient to the servant is to be like his master. Should it not be sufficient for Meir to be equal to his Creator? For, behold, His Great Name written in holiness is blotted out in water in order to make peace between man and wife."

(Gadol uG'dola, BhM 3:127)

---

[47] The reference is to the *Sota* ritual (Num. 5:23 ff) in which a woman suspected of adultery is subjected to an ordeal-like rite. The name of God is written on a parchment, then blotted out in water. The woman drinks this water; if she is guilty she dies; if innocent, she is blessed with children.

[48] The spirit which was believed to cause eye trouble.

[49] I.e., yourself, who are a vessel of the Tora.

The Son's Sacrifice

Once the king issued a decree that every man who sits idly should be punished by having his hands and feet cut off. Day after day the son of a man ground flour in his mill, while the man sat on the bed. One day the servants of the king came there. The son said: "Father, turn the mill, and I shall sit on the bed." The servants of the king found him sitting on the bed, and brought him before the king, and cut off his hands and his feet. And this brought him to the life of the World to Come, for he saved his father.

('Aseret haDibrot, BhM 1:76)

The Futility of Idolatry

It happened to a Jew who was lame, that he heard that there was an idol in a certain place, and that all the sick people in the world went there and were healed. He went there to be healed. He entered the house of idolatry with the other sick. At midnight a man came with a small vial of oil in his hand and anointed all the sick, and they were healed. When he reached the Jew he said to him: "Are you not a Jew?" He said to him: "Yes, I am." "And why did you come here?" "To be healed." The man said: "Don't you know that I myself am a demon, and I am doing these things so as to lead people astray after idolatry, in order to make them perish from the world? But you, by your life, tomorrow your time would have arrived to be healed, and because you have come here you will never be healed."

Therefore, one is duty-bound to distance himself from idolatry, and even if they come to take his life he should not worship idols.

('Aseret haDibrot, BhM 1:71)

All Depends on the Woman

It happened to a pious man who was married to a pious woman that they had no children from each other. They said: "We are useless for the Holy One, blessed be He." They arose and divorced each other. The man went and married a wicked woman, and she turned him into a wicked man; and the woman went and married a wicked man and turned him into a righteous man. Hence: all depends on the woman.

(Gen.Rab. 17:7)

How R. Akiba Became a Scholar

What were the beginnings of R. Akiba? They said that he was forty years old and had learned nothing. Once he was standing at the mouth of a well. He said: "Who hewed this stone?" They told him: "The water, which constantly falls upon it day after day." They said to him: "Akiba, have you not read, *"The waters wear the stones* (Job 14:19)?" Instantly R. Akiba considered: "If something soft can carve something hard, the words of the Tora which are hard like iron, how much more will they carve my heart which is flesh and blood." He went and began to study Tora. He went together with his son and sat before a teacher of small children. He said to him: "Rabbi, teach me Tora." R. Akiba held one end of the writing board, and his son held the other end. The teacher wrote the Alef Bet, and he learned it. Alef Tav,[50] and he learned it. The book of Leviticus, and he learned it. He went and sat before R. Eliezer and before R. Y'hoshu'a. He said to them: "My masters, open for me the meaning of the Mishna." When they told him one Halakha, he went and sat alone and said: "This Alef, why was it written? This Bet, why was it written? This word, why was it written?" He returned and asked them, and stopped them with his words.

R. Shim'on ben El'azar said: "I shall tell you a parable. To what can the matter be likened? To a stone-cutter who was cutting in the mountains. Once he took his axe in his hand

---

[50] *Tav* is the last letter of the Hebrew alphabet.

and went and sat down on the mountain and chipped away
small pieces of stone from it. People came and said to him:
"What are you doing?" He said to them: "I want to uproot
the mountain and to cast it into the Jordan." They said to
him: "You cannot uproot the whole mountain." But he
went on chipping until he reached a big rock. He dug under
it, uprooted it, and cast it into the Jordan, saying to it, "Not
this is your place, but that is your place." This is what R.
Akiba did to R. Eliezer and R. Y'hoshu'a. . . .

(Avot diR. Nathan A, p. 28-29)

Damages

It happened that a man disobeyed the words of R. Akiba,
and uncovered the head of a woman in the marketplace. She
went to R. Akiba, and he sentenced him to paying her four
hundred *Zuzim* [silver coins]. He said to him: "Rabbi, give
me time." He gave him time. When he came out, his friend
said to him: "I shall give you an advice so that you will not
have to pay her even as much as a penny." He said to him.
"Tell me." He said to him: "Go, buy oil for an *Isar* [a small
coin], and break the cruse at the door of that woman." What
did that woman do? She came out from her house,
uncovered her head in public, and daubed the oil with her
hand on her hair. And the man brought witnesses and came
before R. Akiba and said to him: "To this contemptible
woman shall I pay four hundred *Zuzim* ? For the sake of one
Isar's worth of oil she did not save her honor but came out of
her house, uncovered her head in the public, and daubed
the oil with her hand on her hair." R. Akiba said to him:
"Your argument is worthless, for he who wounds himself,
even though it is forbidden, is not guilty, but if others
wound him they are guilty. Thus she who damaged herself
is not guilty, but you who damaged her must go and give
her the four hundred *Zuzim*."

(Avot diR. Nathan A. p. 15)

The Role of Medicine

Once R. Yishma'el and R. Akiba were walking in the streets of Jerusalem, and a third man was with them. They met a sick man who said to them: "My masters, tell me with what can I be healed?" They said to him: "Do thus and thus, until you become healed." He said to them: "And who smote me?" They said to him: "The Holy One, blessed be He." He said to them: "If so, you have injected yourselves into a matter which is not yours. He smote me and you heal me. Are you not transgressing His will?" They said to him: "What is your work?" He said to them: "I am a cultivator of the soil. And here is the scythe in my hand." They said to him: "Who created the vineyard?" He said to them: "The Holy One, blessed be He." They said to him: "If so, you inject yourself into a matter which is not yours. He created it, and you cut its fruits from it." He said to them: "Don't you see the scythe in my hand? If I don't go out and till it, and cover it, and manure it, and weed it, it will yield nothing." They said to him: "O you fool in the world! Because of your work you have not heard that it is written, *As for man, his days are as grass* (Ps. 103:15). Just as the plant, if it is not weeded and manured and plowed, it does not grow; or if it grows but does not drink water and is not manured, it does not live but dies, so the human body: the manure is the medicine and all kinds of remedies, and the tiller of the soil is the physician." He said to them: "I beg of you, punish me not!"

(Temura, BhM 1:107)

Ashmodai and R. Shim'on in Rome

R. Shim'on ben Yoḥai was sent from Jerusalem to Rome to Caesar. While he was on the ship, Ashmodai, the prince of the demons, appeared to him in a dream and said to him: "Tell me what you want me to do for you!" R. Shim'on said to him: "And who are you?" He answered: "I am

Ashmodai. The Holy One, blessed be He, sent me to perform a miracle for you." R. Shim'on said: "Master of the World! To Hagar, the slave woman of Sarah, You sent an angel, and to me You send the prince of the demons?" Ashmodai said to him: "In any event, the miracle will take place, whether I or an angel fulfill your wish." And Ashmodai further said to him: "For the time being I leave you, and I shall enter into the daughter of Caesar and shall weaken her, and shall call your name, 'R. Shim'on! R. Shim'on!' until you come. And they will ask of you that you persuade me to leave that house, and I shall say, 'I shall not leave it until they do what R. Shim'on wants.' "

And Ashmodai went away, and came to the house of Caesar and did everything as he had told R. Shim'on. And Caesar's daughter was there, and he entered into her, and as soon as he did she began to break all the vessels which were in the palace of her father, and she cried, "R. Shim'on! R. Shim'on ben Yoḥai!"

A few days later the ship arrived with R. Shim'on on board, and they went and announced it to Caesar. Caesar sent for him and said to him: "What is your wish?" He said: "The Jews of Jerusalem sent you a present." Caesar said: "I will not accept anything from you, and I want nothing of you except that you expel this demon from my daughter, for I have nobody to rule after me but her, for I have no other children." R. Shim'on went and said to him: "Ashmodai, get out of this girl!" He answered: "I shall not get out until they fulfill all your wishes." And so he repeated several times: "I shall not leave until they fulfill all your wishes."[51]

The king went and sent for all his elders, princes, and servants, and said to them: "What do you suggest should be done with my daughter who is possessed by this demon, since we have prohibited the Jews from circumcising their

---

[51] The text omits R. Shim'on's wishes, but what they were becomes evident from the sequel.

sons, and from observing the Sabbath, and their wives from keeping the rules of menstruation, and it is the rule of our kingdom that once an edict is issued it can never again be rescinded, and if a king retracts it he is removed from his kingship, according to the laws of Media and Persia."

Up stood one of his councilors and said to him: "My lord king, I shall tell you a thing through which your daughter can be healed and all your decrees can be annulled, for this decree imposed on the Jews is harmful for us and for you."

The king said to him: "Speak."

He said: "If somebody has an enemy, what does he want for him: that he be poor or rich?"

The king said to him: "Poor."

The councilor said to him: "The main custom of the Jews is to work all week and earn money, and on Friday they spend all of it in honor of the Sabbath. And since you have prohibited them from observing the Sabbath, the Sabbath expenses are being retained by them, and they save much money, and they will rebel against you. But if you restore the Sabbath to them, they will spend much money on it and will become poor."

The king said to them: "Restore the Sabbath to them."

The councilor then continued: "If a man has enemies, what will he wish them to be: many or few?"

The king said: "Few."

The councilor said: "My lord king, the Jews perform the circumcision on their sons when they are eight days old. While one survives, a hundred die."

The king said: "Restore them also circumcision."

The councilor then said: "My lord king, this is how it is with the rules of menstruation: if you allow the women of Israel to observe these rules they will not have numerous offspring, for they will observe seven days of blood and seven days of purification."[52]

---

[52] During those fourteen days every month intercourse is forbidden.

The king said: "Let them observe the rules of menstruation as they did before."

Then the king said to R. Shim'on: "I have granted your requests. Now go and tell the demon that he should go out of my daughter."

R. Shim'on commanded Ashmodai, and he went out of the daughter of the king.

And the king returned to R. Shim'on the present he had brought him, and he gave him many more presents, and wrote him a letter to the governor whom he had in Jerusalem. And R. Shim'on returned to Jerusalem joyful and with a happy heart, and the evil decrees were annulled.

(T'fillat R. Shim'on ben Yoḥai, BhM 4:117-18)

OF BIRTH AND DEATH

The Formation of the Embryo

How is the formation of the embryo? R. Yoḥanan said: What is the meaning of the verse, *Who doeth great things and unsearchable, marvelous things without number* (Job 5:9)? These are the great things and the marvelous things which the Holy One, blessed be He, does in the formation of the embryo. For in the hour when a man comes to serve his bed with his wife, the Holy One, blessed be He, calls the angel in charge of pregnancy and says to him: "Know that So-and-so emits seed tonight for the formation of an embryo, and you go and guard that drop and take it in a cup and winnow it in the threshing floor to make it into 365 parts."[53] And so he does, and takes the drop and brings it before the Holy One, blessed be He, and says before Him: "Master of the World! I did all that which You have commanded me. And this drop, what will happen to it?

[53] According to Talmudic tradition the human body comprises 365 parts.

Decree upon it according to Your will." Instantly the Holy One, blessed be He, decrees upon it whether it will be mighty or weak, tall or short, male or female, foolish or wise, rich or poor. But whether pious or wicked He does not decree upon it, for we have learned, "Everything is in the hands of heaven, except the fear of heaven."

Instantly the Holy One, blessed be He, beckons the angel in charge of the souls and says to him: "Bring Me that particular soul!" For this is how it is done when they are created from the day the world was created until the world comes to an end. Immediately the soul comes before the Holy One, blessed be He, and prostrates itself before Him. In that hour the Holy One, blessed be He, says to it: "Enter into this drop!" But the soul opens its mouth and says to Him: "Master of the World! I am satisfied with the world I have been in from the day in which I was created. If it please You, do not make me enter this evil-smelling drop, for I am holy and pure." The Holy One, blessed be He, says to it: "The world which I make you enter is better than the world in which you have been, and when I created you I did not do so except for this drop." Then the Holy One, blessed be He, places it against its will into that drop, and the angel comes and puts the soul into the bowels of its mother. And He posts there two angels who guard him that he should not fall out, and they put a burning candle upon his head. And he looks and can see from the beginning of the world to its end.

And in the morning the angel takes him and leads him to the Garden of Eden and shows him the righteous who sit in glory and says to him: "Do you know whose was that soul?"[54] He says to him: "No." He says to him: "That man whom you see in that glory and in that exaltation was created like you in the bowels of his mother, and likewise that one, and that one. And they observed the laws and ordinances of the Holy One, blessed be He. If you will do

---

[54] The soul of one of the righteous.

like them, after your death you will be rewarded, as they were, with this exaltation and this glory, as you see them. And if not, your end will be to go to the place which I am now going to show you."

And in the evening the angel takes him to Gehenna and shows him the wicked whom angels of destruction punish and beat and smite with rods of fire, and they scream: "Woe and alas!" But the angels have no pity on them. And the angel says to him: "My son, do you know who are these who are being burnt?" And he says to him: "No." And he says to him: "Know, that they were formed from evil-smelling drops in the bowels of their mother, and they emerged into the world, but they did not heed the warnings nor observe the laws of the Holy One, blessed be He. Therefore they came to this shame. And now, my son, know that your end is to leave this place and to die. Therefore be not wicked but be righteous, and you will live forever."

And the angel guides him from the morning to the evening. And he shows him every place which the sole of his foot will tread, and the place in which he will be buried. And then he shows him the world of those who are good and of those who are evil. By eventide he returns him into the bowels of his mother. And the Holy One, blessed be He, makes for him doors and a bolt, and says to him: *Thus far shalt thou come and no further* (Job 38:11).

And the embryo lies in the bowels of his mother nine months. The first three months he dwells in the lower compartment, the three middle months in the middle compartment, and the last three months in the upper compartment. And he eats of everything his mother eats, and drinks of what his mother drinks, and does not eliminate excrement, for would he do so his mother would die.

And when his time comes to emerge into the world, he argues: "Did I not already say before Him who spoke and caused the world to be that I am satisfied with the world in which I have been dwelling?" And He says to him: "The world which I make you enter is good. Moreover, against your will are you formed in the bowels of your mother, and against your will are you born and do you emerge into the world!" Instantly he cries. And why does he cry? Because of that world in which he was and which he leaves behind. And when he emerges, He hits him under his nose and puts out the candle which is over his head, and brings him out against his will, and he forgets everything he saw.

(Seder Y'tzirat haV'lad, BhM 1:153-54)

The Birth of R. Yishma'el

They said about R. Yishma'el the High Priest that he was one of the seven beauties which were in the world, and his face was like unto an angel of the Lord of Hosts. When most of the days of his father R. Yose had passed, his wife said to him: "My lord, my husband, what is this I see many men succeeding in their seed, and we have not succeeded in children, for we have no heir, neither son nor daughter." R. Yose said: "This is the thing that causes this to them: Because their wives guard themselves when they come out of the house of submersion.[55] If they meet something untoward, they return and immerse themselves a second time, and therefore they succeed in their seed." She said to him: "If this thing prevents, I take it upon myself to be careful in those things." And when she went to submerge, and came out of the house of submersion, she met a dog. She returned and submerged a second time. She met a camel,[56] and returned and submerged, and thus she did eighty times. The Holy One, blessed be He, said to Gabriel: "This pious woman has suffered enough. Go and show

---

[55] The ritual bath, the *miqve,* in which an observant Jewish woman must submerge seven days after the cessation of the menses each month.

[56] Both the dog and the camel are unclean animals and hence were considered as falling into the category of "untoward things."

yourself to her in the shape of her husband." Instantly
Gabriel went and sat at the door of the house of
submersion, and he appeared to her in the shape of her
husband R. Yose, and he got hold of her and led her home.
And that night she conceived R. Yishma'el. And he became
beautiful of countenance and beautiful of appearance like
the image of Gabriel. And this is why Gabriel accompanied
him when he ascended to the Firmament.

(Ele Ezk'ra, BhM 2:64-65)

The Wish to Die

It happened to a woman who had become very old and she
came before R. Yose ben Halafta. She said to him: "Rabbi, I
have become too old, and from now on my life is a hideous
life, for I can taste neither food nor drink, and I wish to pass
from this world." He said to her: "What *mitzva* do you
regularly perform every day?" She said to him: "Even if I
have something I like, I always leave it and go to the
synagogue every day, early in the morning." He said to her:
"Refrain from going to the synagogue for three consecutive
days." She went and did so, and on the third day she fell ill
and died.

(Yalqut Shim'oni, § 771)

The Angel of Death

How does a man die? Angels come to him: one is of the
ministering angels, one of the angels of death, and one is a
scribe, and one who is in charge of him and says to him:
"Get up, your end has come!" He says to them: "My end
has not yet come!" Instantly he opens his eyes and sees an
angel whose size is from one end of the world to the other.
From the soles of his feet to the top of his head he is full of

eyes. His garment is fire, his clothes are fire, all of him is fire, and a knife is in his hand and a drop of a gall hangs on it. From it he dies, from it he becomes putrid, from it his face turns green. And he dies not until he sees the Holy One, blessed be He, for it says, *For man shall not see Me and live* (Exod. 33:20). In their life they cannot see Him, but they see Him in their death. Instantly he testifies about himself, telling everything he did in This World. He testifies and the Holy One, blessed be He, signs. If he was pious, he delivers his soul to its owner (i.e., God). If he was totally wicked, he stiffens his neck and strengthens his Evil Inclination.

They asked R. Eliezer: "How is the rule of the beating of the grave?" He said to them: "When a man leaves the world, the Angel of Death comes and sits on his grave and beats it with his hand and says to him: 'Get up, tell me your name!' He says to him: 'It is revealed and known before Him who said and the world was that I do not know what is my name.' Instantly he causes spirit and soul to enter his body, and makes him stand in judgment and finds him guilty." R. Y'hoshu'a ben Levi said: "A kind of chain is in the hand of the Angel of Death, half of it is fire and half of it iron. He beats him with it once—his limbs fall apart; a second time—his bones fall apart. And the ministering angels come and gather them, and make them stand up. And he beats him a third time, and asks an account of him, and punishes him according to his deserts, one day, a second day, this is how they punish him. The third day they punish him with beatings. He beats his two eyes because he did not see and speak. And his ears, because he did not hear and speak. And his lips, because he uttered words of obscenity with his lips. And his tongue, because he bore false witness. And his feet, because he made them hasten to transgression."

(Mass. Hibbut haQever, BhM 1:150-51)

All his life Moses had wished to bless Israel, but the Angel of Death did not allow him to bestow the blessing. What did Moses finally do? He seized the Angel of Death, cast him down under his feet, and blessed Israel in his very presence.

(Pes. diR. Kahana, ed. Mandelbaum, 2:444)

R. Meir said: "The Angel of Death came to Moses and said to him: 'The Holy One, blessed be He, has sent me to you, since you have to depart today.' Moses said: 'Begone, for I want to praise the Holy One, blessed be He. . . .' The Angel of Death said: 'Moses, what are you boasting? He has many who praise Him. The heaven and the earth praise Him every hour, as it is written, *The heavens declare the glory of God* (Ps. 19:2).' Moses said to him: 'But I shall bid them be silent and shall praise Him, as it is written, *Give ear, ye heavens, and I will speak* (Deut. 32:1).'

"The Angel of Death came to him a second time. What did Moses do? He uttered the Ineffable Name, whereupon the Angel of Death fled. . . . When he came back a third time, Moses said: 'Since it is from God, I must acquiesce in the judgment.' "

(Deut. Rab. 11:5)

It happened in the days of R. Shim'on b. Ḥalafta that he went to a circumcision feast. The father of the child gave a banquet and gave them seven-year-old wine to drink. He said to them: "From this wine I shall lay aside for the wedding of my son!" They feasted until midnight. R. Shim'on b. Ḥalafta, who trusted in his strength against demons, left at midnight to go back to his town. On the way he met the Angel of Death, and saw something strange about him. He said to him: "Who are you?" He answered: "The messenger of God." R. Shim'on said to him: "And why your peculiar expression?" He answered: "Because of the way people talk. They say, 'We shall do this and this,' and none of them knows when he is called to die. That man with whom you feasted and who said to you, 'From this wine I shall lay aside for the wedding of my son,' his turn will come in thirty days."

R. Shim'on said to him: "Show me my turn!" But he answered him: "I have no power over you, and over those like you, because sometimes the Holy One, blessed be He, wants their good deeds and lengthens their lives."

(Deut. Rab. 9:1)

When a man's end comes and he must take leave of this world, the Angel of Death comes to take his soul. The soul is like a tube full of blood which has little tubes branching off from it into the whole body. The Angel of Death takes hold of the top of the tube and pulls it; from the body of a just man he pulls it gently, as if he were removing a thread from the milk; but from the body of an evil man he pulls it out like water gushing forth out of the opening of a channel.

(Tehillim, ed. Buber, 51b)

When a man's time comes, the angel who assisted at his birth comes and says to him: "Do you recognize me?" The man answers, "Yes," and goes on to say: "Why did you come for me today of all days?" The angel answers him: "In order to take you away from the world, for your time has come to depart." Instantly the man begins to cry and lets his voice be heard from one end of the world to the other. But no creature recognizes and hears his voice, except for the cock. And the man says to the angel: "You did remove me from two worlds and placed me into this world; why, then, do you want to take me away again?" The angel answers him: "Did I not tell you that you were created against your will, were born against your will, have lived against your will, and will give account before the Holy One, blessed be He, against your will?"

(Tanh. Peq. 3, ed. Warsaw, n.d.,133b)

ANGELS, DEMONS, AND GHOSTS

Demonic Offspring

R. Simon said: "All the hundred and thirty years that Eve was separated from Adam, male spirits became hot from her and she bore from them, and female spirits became hot from Adam and bore from him."

(Gen. Rab. 20:11; 24:6)

The Translation of Enoch

R. Yishma'el said: Metatron, the Prince of the Face, told me: When the Holy One, blessed be He, wanted to take me up to heaven, at first He sent the Prince Anpiel to me, and he took me from their midst in their sight and made me ride on a great Cherub and in a chariot of fire and with horses of fire and Attendants of honor, and took me up with the Shekhina into the heaven on high. When I arrived there, the Holy Beasts and the Seraphim and the Cherubim and the Wheels of the chariot and the Attendants of consuming fire smelled my smell from a distance of 5,360 myriads of parasangs, and said: "What is this smell of a woman-born here? And what is the reason that a white drop[57] should come up to heaven on high?" The Holy One, blessed be He, answered and said: "My servants, My hosts, My Cherubs, and My Wheels, let your heart not feel bad about this thing, for all My children have denied Me and the great kingdom, and have worshiped idols, and I removed My Shekhina from their midst. And this one whom I took is My reward for all My labors under all the heavens."

And it is also written there: R. Yishma'el said: Metatron, the Prince of the Face, told me: When the Holy One, blessed be He, took me to serve under the Throne of Glory

---

[57] I.e., a human being who developed out of a drop of semen.

and the Wheel of the chariot and all the courses of the Shekhina, my flesh became flame of fire, and my sinews flaring fire, and my bones embers of broom-brush, and my eyelids radiance like the firmament, and my eyeballs torches of fire, and the hair of my head flashes of flame, and all my limbs wings of burning fire, and the body of my stature scorching fire, from my right side searing flames of fire, and from my left burning torches, and round about me soared winds of storm.

(Tziyoni, Hekhalot-fragment, BhM 2:XIV)

Metatron

R. Yishma'el said: In that hour I questioned the angel Metatron, Prince of the Face. I said to him: "What is your name?" He answered: "I have seventy names, corresponding to the seventy languages of the world, and all of them are [based] on the name of the King of kings of kings. But my King calls me 'Youth.'"

R. Yishma'el said: I said to Metatron: "Why are you called by the name of your Creator with seventy names? You are greater than all the [celestial] princes, higher than all the angels, more beloved than all the servants, more honored than all the hosts, and more exalted than all the powers in sovereignty, greatness, and glory. Why, then, do they call you 'Youth' in the heavenly heights?" He answered and said to me: "Because I am Enoch the son of Jared. For when the generation of the Deluge sinned and turned to evil deeds and said to God, *Depart from us! For we desire not the knowledge of Thy ways* (Job 21:14), the Holy One, blessed be He, took me from their midst to be a witness against them in the heavenly heights to all those who walk on earth so that they should not say, 'The Merciful One is cruel! What was the sin of all those people, their wives, their sons and their daughters, their horses, their mules, their cattle, and all the birds of the world whom the Holy One caused to perish from the world together with them in the waters of the Deluge?' And lest they say, 'If the generation of the Deluge sinned, the beasts and the birds, what was their sin to be destroyed together with them?' Therefore the Holy One, blessed be He, brought me up to the heavenly heights before their very eyes and in their lifetime, to be a witness against them in the Future to Come. And the Holy One, blessed be He, appointed me to be a prince and a ruler among the ministering angels."

R. Yishma'el said: Metatron, the Prince of the Face, said to me: "From the day that the Holy One, blessed be He, banished Adam the first man from the Garden of Eden, the Shekhina rested upon a Cherub beneath the Tree of Life, and the ministering angels would gather and come down from heaven in companies and in bands and cohorts from the firmament, and in camps and troops from heaven, to do His will in the whole world. And Adam the first man and his generation [?] sat at the gate of the Garden of Eden to gaze at the image of the brilliance of the Shekhina, for her radiance went forth from one end of the world to the other, 365,000 times more brightly than the wheel of the sun. Anyone who beheld the brilliance of that Shekhina would not be touched by flies or gnats and would not become sick or feel pain, nor could evil overpower or harm him; and, moreover, even angels had no power over him. When the Holy One, blessed be He, went in and out of the Garden of Eden, and from Eden to the Garden, and from the Garden to the firmament, and from the firmament to the Garden of Eden, all gazed at the brilliance of the image of His Shekhina and were unharmed—until the coming of the generation of Enosh who was the chief of all the idolaters in the world.

"What did the men of his generation do? They went from one end of the world to the other, and each of them brought silver, gold, precious stones, and pearls in mountains and hills, and fashioned them into idols in the four winds of the world. And in each wind they set them up as idols, about a thousand parasangs in size. And they brought down the sun and the moon, the stars and the constellations, and placed them before the idols, to their right and to their left, to serve them in the way they served the Holy One, blessed be He, as it is written, *All the hosts of heaven standing by Him on His right hand and on His left* (1 Kings 22:19). And how did they have the strength to bring them down? Because 'Uzza, 'Azza, and 'Aza'el taught them sorceries, so that they could bring them down and serve them, for otherwise they would not have been able to bring them down.

"In that hour the ministering angels banded together to lodge a complaint before the Holy One, blessed be He, and they said before Him: 'Master of the World! Why do You concern Yourself with the sons of man, as it is written, *What is man that Thou shouldst remember him?* (Ps. 8:5) It does not say, What is Adam, but What is Enosh, because Enosh was the head of idolatry. Why did You leave the supernal heavens of heavens, the abode of the Glory of Your Name, and the high and exalted Throne which is in the heights of 'Aravot, and come and dwell with men who worship idols, and who equated You with idols? What is Your concern with those who dwell on earth, who serve idols?' Instantly the Holy One, blessed be He, removed His Shekhina from the earth, from their midst. In that hour the ministering angels came, and the cohorts of the hosts, and the armies of 'Aravot, a thousand companies, and myriads of hosts, and they took trumpets and seized shofars, and surrounded the Shekhina with songs and tunes, and she ascended to the heavenly heights, as it is said, *God is gone up amidst shouting, the Lord amidst the sound of the shofar* (Ps. 47:6).

"In that hour three of the ministering angels, 'Uzza, 'Azza, and 'Aza'el, came and accused me in the heavenly heights, and they said before the Holy One, blessed be He: 'Did not the First Ones properly speak before You when they said, Do not create man?' But the Holy One, blessed be He, replied: *'I have made and will bear, yea, I will carry and*

will deliver (Isa. 46:4).' When they saw me they said before
Him: 'Master of the World! What is the nature of this one
who ascends the height of heights? Is he not of the
children's children of those who perished in the waters of
the Deluge? What has he to do in the firmament?' Again
the Holy One, blessed be He, replied and said to them:
'What is your nature that you dare to interrupt Me? I have
chosen this one in preference to you all, to be a prince and a
ruler over you in the heavenly heights.' Instantly they all
arose and went to meet me, prostrated themselves before
me, and said: 'Happy are you, and happy your parents,
because your Creator has favored you!' And since I am
young in their company, and a mere youth among them in
days and months and years, therefore they call me Youth."

R. Yishma'el said: The angel Metatron, Prince of the
Face, said to me: "When the Holy One, blessed be He,
took me from the generation of the Deluge, He brought
me up on the wings of the spirit of the Shekhina to the
highest firmament, and made me enter the great palaces
which are in the height of the 'Aravot of the firmament,
where are the Throne of Glory of the Shekhina and the
Chariot, the troops of wrath, the hosts of fury, the fiery
Shin'anim,[58] the blazing Cherubim, the glowing Ophanim
["Wheels"], the servants of flame, the lightning
Hashmalim, and the flashing Seraphim. He stationed me
there to serve the Throne of Glory day by day."

R. Yishma'el said: The angel Metatron, Prince of the
Face, said to me: "When the Holy One, blessed be He,
wanted to bring me up to the heights, at first He sent me
the Prince Anpiel Yah, and he took me from their midst,
before their very eyes, and he made me mount in great
glory a fiery chariot with fiery horses and glorious servants,

---

[58] A type of angel, based on Ps. 68:18. Also the other terms denote
various angels.

and he brought me up with the Shekhina to the heavenly heights. As soon as I reached the heavenly heights, the Holy Beasts, the Ophanim, the Seraphim, the Cherubim, the Wheels of the Chariot, and the servants of consuming fire smelled my odor from a distance of 365,000 myriads of parasangs, and they said: 'What is this smell of a woman-born, and why does this white drop[59] ascend on high to serve among those who hew flames?' The Holy One, blessed be He, replied and said to them: 'My servants, My hosts, My Cherubim, My Ophanim, and My Seraphim, let this not displease you, for all mankind has denied Me and My great kingdom, and has gone and worshiped idols. And I have removed My Shekhina from their midst and brought her up to the heights. And this one, whom I have taken from their midst, is the elect of the world and outweighs them all in faith, righteousness, and perfect conduct. This one whom I have taken is My reward from My world under the whole heaven. . . .'

" . . . In that hour the Holy One, blessed be He, gave me wisdom upon wisdom, understanding upon understanding, subtlety upon sublety, knowledge upon knowledge, mercy upon mercy, Tora upon Tora, love upon love, grace upon grace, charm upon charm, humility upon humility, might upon might, strength upon strength, power upon power, splendor upon splendor, beauty upon beauty, countenance upon countenance; and I was honored and adorned with these all good and praiseworthy qualities more than the children of the heights.

"In addition to all these qualities, the Holy One, blessed be He, laid His hand on me and blessed me with one thousand and three hundred and five times thousand blessings. I was raised up and made high as the length and breadth of the world. And He caused me to grow seventy-two wings, thirty-six on one side and thirty-six on the other, and each wing was like the whole world. And He set

[59] See footnote 57.

into me 365,000 eyes, and each eye was like the Great Luminary. And He left no sort of splendor, brilliance, countenance, and beauty of the luminaries of the world that He did not set into me."

R. Yishma'el said: Metatron, Prince of the Face, said to me: "After all this, the Holy One, blessed be He, made for me a throne like the Throne of Glory, and he spread over me a canopy of splendor, brilliance, countenance, beauty, loveliness, and grace, like unto the canopy of the Throne of Glory in which are set all kinds of luminaries that are in the world. And He placed it at the door of the Seventh Hall and seated me upon it. And the herald went forth into every firmament saying: "I have made Metatron My servant, a prince and a ruler over all the children of the heights, except for the eight great, honored, and terrible princes who are called by the name of the Lord their king. All the angels and all the princes who have anything to say before Me must go before him and speak to him. And whatever he says to you in My name you must obey and do, because the Prince of Wisdom and the Prince of Understanding serve him to teach him the wisdom of the supernals and of the infernals, and the wisdom of This World and of the World to Come. Moreover, I have put him in charge of all the treasuries of the Halls of 'Aravot, and all the storehouses which I have in the heavenly heights."

R. Yishma'el said: The angel Metatron, Prince of the Face, said to me: "The Holy One, blessed be He, from that time on revealed to me all the mysteries of the Tora, all the secrets of the perfect wisdom, and all the thoughts of the hearts of the creatures; and all the mysteries of the world, and all the orders of creation are revealed before me as they are revealed before the Creator. And I expected to behold deep secrets and wonderful mysteries. For before a man thinks in secret, I see it, and before a man acts, I see it. And there is nothing in the heights or deep in the world which is concealed from me."

R. Yishma'el said: Metatron, Prince of the Face, said to

me: "Because of the love the Holy One, blessed be He, had for me more than for all the children of the heights, He made me a garment of glory in which there were all kinds of luminaries, and He clothed me in it. He fashioned for me a glorious cloak in which there were brightness, brilliance, splendor, and luster of every kind, and He wrapped me in it. And He made me a royal crown in which were set forty-nine stones of countenance like the wheel of the sun, and its brilliance went out to the four winds of the 'Aravot of the firmament, and to the seven firmaments, and the four winds of the world. And He placed it upon my head, and He called me 'The Lesser Lord' in the presence of His whole family in the heights, as it is said, *My name is in him* (Exod. 23:21)."

R. Yishma'el said: The angel Metatron, Prince of the Face, who dwells in the heights, said to me: "Because of the abundant love and great compassion with which the Holy One, blessed be He, loved and cherished me more than all the children of the heights, He wrote with His finger [as] with a pen of flame, upon the crown which was on my head, the letters by which heaven and earth were created, the letters by which seas and rivers were created, the letters by which mountains and hills were created, the letters by which stars and constellations, lightning and winds, thunder and voices, snow and hail, storm and tempest were created, the letters by which all the necessities of the world and all the orders of creation were created. Time after time each letter made images of lightnings flare up, time after time images of torches, time after time images of flames, time after time images of the rising of the suns, the moon and the stars."

R. Yishma'el said: The angel Metatron, Prince of the Face, said to me: "When the Holy One, blessed be He, placed this crown upon my head, all the princes of kingdoms who are in the heights of 'Aravot of the firmament, and all the legions of every firmament trembled before me. Even the prince of the Erelim and the princes of the Tafsarim[60] who are greater than all the ministering angels who serve before the Throne of Glory trembled and recoiled when they saw me. And even Samael, the Prince of the Accusers, who is greater than all the princes of kingdoms who are in the heights, was afraid of me and trembled. Even the angel of fire, the angel of hail, the angel of wind, the angel of lightning, the angel of storm, the angel of tempest, the angel of thunder, the angel of snow, the angel of rain, the angel of day, the angel of night, the angel of the sun, the angel of the moon, the angel of the stars, the angel of the constellations, who lead the world by their hands, trembled and recoiled in alarm when they saw me."

R. Yishma'el said: The angel Metatron, Prince of the Face, who dwells in the highest heaven, said to me: "When the Holy One, blessed be He, took me into service, to serve the Throne of Glory, the Ophanim of the Chariot, and all the needs of the Shekhina, instantly my flesh turned into flame, my sinews into blazing fire, my bones into embers of broom-fire, my eyelids into lightning flashes, the wheels of my eyes into fiery torches, the hairs of my head into flames and flares, all my limbs into wings of burning fire, and the body of my stature into blazing fire. On my right—those who hew flames of fire, on my left—burning torches, round about me flew wind, tempest and storm, and the roar of earthquake upon earthquake was before and behind me."

R. Yishma'el said: The angel Metatron, Prince of the Face, the glory of the height of all, said to me: "At first I sat upon a great throne at the door of the Seventh Hall, and judged all the children of the heights, the supernal family, by permission from the Holy One, blessed be He. And I distributed greatness, royalty, rank, sovereignty, glory, praise, diadem, crown, and honor to all princes of kingdoms, while I sat in the supreme Yeshiva. The princes of kingdoms stood around me, to my right and my left, by

---

[60] The name of yet another type of angel.

permission from the Holy One, blessed be He. But when Aher[61] came to gaze at the vision of the Chariot and set eyes upon me, he was affrighted and trembled before me, and his soul was terrified into departing from him because of his fear, dread and terror of me when he saw me seated upon a throne like a king, with ministering angels standing about me as servants, and all the princes of kingdoms crowned with crowns surrounding me. In that hour he opened his mouth and said: 'There are indeed two powers in heaven!' Instantly a divine voice issued from heaven, from the presence of the Shekhina, and said, *'Return, ye backsliding children* (Jer. 3:22) — except Aher.' In that hour Anpiel Yah, the honored, glorified, beloved, wonderful, terrible, and awesome prince, came at the behest of the Holy One, blessed be He, and flogged me with sixty fiery lashes, and made me stand on my feet."[62]

(Excerpts from 3 Enoch 3-16)

The Sons of God and the Daughters of Man

The children of the sons of God and the daughters of man were called by seven names: *Emim* [Fearsome], because their fear fell upon all those who saw them; *Rephaim* [Weakeners], because the hearts of all those who saw them became weak like wax; *Gibborim* [Heroes], because the marrow in their hipbone measured eighteen cubits; *Zamzummim* [Strategists], because they were great in planning wars; *'Anaqim* [Giants, but here interpreted as Embracers], because many necklaces embraced their long

---

[61] Aher ("Other") was the name given by the Talmudic sages to their colleague Elisha ben Abuya (second century C.E.) after his apostasy. Our text explains that Aher's apostasy was due to his error in mistaking Metatron for a second deity.

[62] Although Metatron committed no sin, he was punished in accordance with the Talmudic tenet which holds that both the idolaters and the idols worshiped by them undergo punishment.

necks, or because they embraced and stopped the wheel of the sun and said, "Give us rain!"; *'Avvim* [Devastators], because they laid the world waste and were in turn wasted from the world, or because they were experts in the knowledge of dusts like snakes which in the Galilee are called *'Ivvim; Nefilim* [Fallen Ones], because they caused the world to fall, and fell from the world, and because with their fornication they filled the world with bastard children.

(Gen. Rab. 26:7)

The sons of God had intercourse with the virgins, the unmarried women, the married women, and even with the males and the animals.

(Tanh. Buber, pp. 23-24)

Why did the animals perish in the Deluge? Because they too corrupted their acts, and one species copulated with another: the horse with the donkey, the lion with the ox, the snake with the turtle.... Because the animals, the beasts, and the birds also sinned, they too were destroyed together with man.

(Tanh. Buber, p. 45)

Naama, the sister of Tubal-Cain, was the most beautiful woman on earth. It was she whose sight caused the ministering angels to sin.

(Tanh. Buber, p. 131)

Rabbi said: "The angels who fell down from the abode of their holiness, from heaven, saw the daughters of Cain walk about with the flesh of their shame uncovered, and their eyes painted black like harlots, and they went astray after them and took wives from among them...." R. Y'hoshu'a ben Qorḥa said: "The angels are searing fire, and when they copulated, the fire penetrated flesh and blood. Did the fire not burn them? No, because when the angels fell down from heaven, from the abode of their holiness, their strength and stature became like those of the sons of Adam, and their bodies turned into clumps of clay...." R. Tzadoq said: "From them were born the giants who strutted about tall-statured, and engaged in all kinds of plunder, violence, and bloodshed...." R. Levi said: "They begot children, and were fruitful and multiplied, bearing something like large worms, six in every litter, and as soon as they were born they stood up on their feet and spoke in the Holy Tongue, and began to dance and prance.... Noah warned them: 'Repent of your evil ways and deeds lest God bring the waters of the Deluge upon you and destroy all the seed of the sons of Adam.' But they said: 'We shall practice self-restraint so as not to beget offspring.' What did they do? When they went in unto their wives, they spilled their seed upon the earth so as not to beget children.... Furthermore they said: 'If He brings the waters of the Deluge upon us from above, we are so tall of stature that the water can never reach up to our necks; and if He brings up the waters of the deep against us, we shall seal the sources of the deep with the soles of our feet....'" But the Holy One, blessed be He, heated up the water of the deep so that it scalded their flesh and burned off their skin...."

(Pirqe R. Eliezer, ch. 22)

There was a pious virgin, and when the sons of God came down to the earth they said to her: "Listen to us!" But she said: "I shall not listen to you unless you do this: give me your wings...." They gave her their wings, and she thereupon flew up to heaven, thus escaping from sin. And she took hold of the throne of God. And the Holy One, blessed be He, spread His cloud over her, and accepted her, and set her among the stars, namely into the constellation Virgo. And the angels remained on earth, and could not ascend until they found the ladder which our father Jacob saw in his dream.

(Fragment, BhM 5:156)

The sons of God were none other than the sons of Cain who were of exceeding beauty and tall of stature.... Even the married women would leave their husband and choose them because of their beauty. And how do we know that the sons of Cain were called the sons of God? From what Eve said [when she bore Cain]: *I have gotten a man from God* (Gen. 4:1).

The sons of God were 'Uzza and 'Azael, who dwelt in the firmament, and descended to earth intent on a test.... God said to them: "If you were to dwell on earth like these sons of Adam, and were to see the beautiful women among them, the Evil Inclination would instantly enter you and make you sin." But they said to Him: "We are going down, and we shall not sin." They went down and saw the daughters of man.... As soon as they saw they wanted to return to the firmament, and said: "Master of the World! We have enough of this test." But He said to them: "You have already become defiled and cannot be purified again...."

R. Eliezer ben R. Yosef said: "They were suspended on iron chain and fastened to the Mountains of Darkness."

(Agadat B'reshit, ed. Buber, Intr., pp. xxxviiif.)

His disciples asked R. Yosef: "What about 'Azael?" He said to them: "When the generation of the Deluge arose and served idols, the Holy One, blessed be He, grieved. Thereupon the two angels, Shemhazai and 'Azael, arose and said to Him: 'Master of the Universe! Did we not tell You, when You created Your world, *What is man that Thou shouldst be mindful of him?* (Ps. 8:5)' He said to them: 'It is revealed and known to me that, should you dwell on earth, the Evil Inclination would overpower you, and you would become worse than the sons of Adam.' They said to Him: 'Give us permission and we shall dwell among the people, and You will see how we shall sanctify Your name.' He said to them: 'Go down and dwell among them.'

"Immediately upon their descent they engaged in

corruption with the daughters of man who were beautiful, and were unable to control their inclination. Shemḥazai saw a girl, Istahar by name, desired her, and said to her: 'Give in to me!' She said to him: 'I shall not, unless you teach me the Ineffable Name by pronouncing which you fly up to the firmament.' He taught her that Name, she uttered it, and flew up to the firmament, thus escaping defilement. The Holy One, blessed be He, said: 'Since she removed herself from sin, go and set her among these seven stars so that she be remembered by them forever.' And she was set in the Pleiades.

"When Shemḥazai and 'Azael saw this, they went and took wives and begat sons, Hivva and Hiyya. And 'Azael made all kinds of many-hued dresses and jewelry for the women which entice men to sinful thoughts. Thereupon [the chief angel] Metatron sent a messenger to Shemḥazai saying: 'The Holy One, blessed be He, will surely destroy His world and will bring a Deluge upon it.' Shemḥazai began to cry and to grieve for the world and for his sons: What will his sons do, what will they eat, once the world is destroyed? For each of them ate every day a thousand camels and a thousand horses and a thousand oxen.

"One night Hivva and Hiyya both had dreams. One of them saw a huge slab of stone spread over the earth like a table, engraved with many lines of inscription. And an angel came down from the firmament and in his hand was something like a knife with which he scraped off and erased all those lines, leaving but four words. The other saw in his dream a great orchard planted with all kinds of fine trees, and angels came with axes in their hands and cut down all the trees, leaving only one with three branches. When they awoke they rose, frightened, and went to their father. He said to them: 'The Holy One, blessed be He, will bring a Deluge, and none will remain save Noah and his sons.' When they heard this they cried and wept. He said to them: 'Do not grieve, for your names will not be forgotten by mankind. For each time logs will be hewn or stones hoisted or ships hauled, your names will be mentioned: Hivva and Hiyya [i.e., Heave-Ho! and Hey-Ho!].' This gave them reassurance.

"Shemḥazai himself repented, and suspended himself from heaven, head down and feet up. To this day he hangs thusly in penitence between heaven and earth. 'Azazel, however, did not repent but has continued in his misdeeds, enticing the sons of Adam to sinful acts with the many-hued clothes of women. This is why Israel used to sacrifice a ram on the Day of Atonement, to atone for the Children of Israel, and a ram to 'Azazel to bear the sins of Israel, and he is the 'Azazel of the Tora."

(Abkir, BhM 4:127-28;
Yalqut Shim'oni, Gen. § 44)

Like the Grass of the Field

When the time would come for the Israelite women in Egypt to give birth, they would go and bear in the field under the apple tree.... And the Holy One, blessed be He, would send an angel from the heavens above and he would clean the newborn babes and preen them like a wild animal which preens its young. And he would give them two round stones, one of oil and one of honey. And as soon as the Egyptians noticed them they wanted to kill them, but a miracle happened to the children and they were swallowed up by the earth. And the Egyptians would bring oxen and plow over them. And after they went away they sprouted up and emerged like the grass of the field. And when they grew up they came in droves to their houses. And when the Holy One, blessed be He, revealed Himself at the sea, they recognized Him first.

(Exod. Rab. 1:12)

And it came to pass when the Children of Israel heard that which Pharaoh had ordered—to throw the newborn male children into the Nile—that some of them separated themselves from their wives, while others cleaved to them to bear sons, and then the mothers left their children in the field. And the Lord, who had sworn to their fathers to make their seed as the dust of the earth, sent them His angels, to wash them and to anoint them and to swaddle them, and to give them two smooth pebbles from the earth, from one to suck milk and from the other to eat honey. And he made their hair grow long, until their knees, to cover them and to adorn them and pamper them, in His compassion for them. And it came to pass when God, blessed be He, pitied them and wished to multiply them on the face of the earth, that He commanded Tevel,[63] His earth, to receive them and to guard them until they would grow up. And thereafter the earth opened and spewed them out, and they sprouted up like the grass of the earth. And each one of them returned to his father and each to his family and cleaved to them. And they made booths in the ground in the earth and hid them there. And the Egyptians were plowing on their backs, but could not harm them. . . .

(Divre haYamim Shel Moshe, BhM 2:1-2)

Moses and the Serpent[64]

Moses said: Satan came in the shape of a serpent and attacked me and swallowed me from my head until the circumcision, and he could never touch the sign of the covenant. Zipporah considered and said: "I know that this is for no other reason but the sin that we committed by not circumcising our son Eliezer." Instantly Zipporah *took a flint and cut off the foreskin of her son* and took of the blood and cast it upon my feet. In that hour a heavenly voice issued and said to the serpent! "Spit him out!" And so he did, as it

---

[63] One of the names of the earth or of the world.

[64] This legend elaborates the brief and enigmatic story in Exod. 4:24-25 according to which it was God who wanted to kill Moses when he and his family spent the night in the desert.

is said in Scripture, *So he let him alone.* Then she said: *A bridegroom of blood in regard of circumcision* (Exod. 4:26). Thus my wife saved me from two deaths....

(WaYosha‘, BhM 1:43-44; cf. B. Ned. 32a)

Moses Faces the Angels

In the hour when Moses ascended to the height, a cloud came and crouched before him. And our master Moses did not know whether to ride on it or to hold onto it. Instantly the cloud opened its mouth, and Moses entered into it, and he walked in the firmament like a man who walks on earth.... He was encountered by the gatekeeper angel Qemuel who is appointed over twelve thousand angels of destruction who stand over the gates of the firmament. He shouted at Moses and said to him: "How dare you, Ben Amram, to come to this place of fiery angels?" Moses said to him: "I am come not on my own, but by permission of the Holy One, blessed be He, to receive the Tora and to bring it down to Israel..." But since Qemuel did not let him pass, Moses dealt him a blow and caused him to perish from the world.

And Moses continued his way in the firmament until he was encountered by the angel Hadarniel. It is said about the angel Hadarniel that he is taller than his comrades by sixty myriad parasangs, and every word that issues from his mouth twelve thousand lightnings of fire issue from his mouth with it. And when he saw Moses he shouted at him and said to him: "How dare you, Ben Amram, come to this place of supernal saints?" When Moses heard his voice, he became affrighted of him, and tears streamed from his eyes, and he was about to fall down from the cloud. Instantly the compassion of the Holy One, blessed be He, was aroused over Moses and He said to Hadarniel: "Ever since the day I created you angels you are full of discord. In the beginning, when I wanted to create Adam the first man, you took the role of accusers before Me and said to Me, *What is man that*

Thou shouldst remember him (Psalm. 8:5). And My wrath was aroused against you and I burnt of you many legions with My little finger. And now you oppose My faithful servant whom I brought up here to receive the Tora and take it down to My chosen children. For were it not for the Tora which Israel will receive, you have no dwelling in the firmament."

When Hadarniel heard this, he instantly made himself zealous before the Holy One, blessed be He, and said before Him: "Master of the World! It is revealed and known before You that I did not know that He came with Your permission. Now I shall be his messenger and shall go before him as a disciple before his master." Instantly Hadarniel bent himself and went before Moses until he reached the fire of Sandalfon. Hadarniel said to Moses: "Come, turn back, for I cannot endure the fire or Sandalfon lest he burn me!"

When Moses saw Sandalfon, he instantly got affrighted, and he was about to fall down from the cloud, and tears flowed from his eyes, and he asked mercy before the Holy One, blessed be He, and He answered him. And because of His great love for Israel, the Holy One, blessed be He, Himself came down from His Throne of Glory and stood before Moses until he passed on from the fire of Sandalfon. It is said of Sandalfon that he is taller than his comrades by five hundred years' journey. And Sandalfon stands behind the Chariot (*Merkava*) and ties crowns for his Creator. And the Ministering Angels do not know the place of the Holy One, blessed be He. But Sandalfon adjures the crown with which they crown the place of the Holy One, blessed be He, in holiness, and the crown of itself rises up and settles upon the head of its Master. Instantly all the Supernal Hosts tremble with fear, and the Holy Beasts fall silent, and the holy Seraphim roar like lions and say, *Holy, holy, holy is the Lord of Hosts, the whole earth is full of His glory* (Isa. 6:3).

Come and see the praise of the Holy One, blessed be He: for in the hour when the crown reaches His head, the Lord holds His head to receive the crown from His servants, and all the Beasts, and Seraphim, and the Wheels of the Chariot, and Supernal Hosts, and Hashmalim and Cherubim join together and pride themselves and give praise to the majesty of the Lord, and declare His kingship, and all say with one voice, The Lord was king, the Lord is king, the Lord will be king for ever and ever.

And when Moses passed on from Sandalfon, he encountered Rigyon, the river of fire, whose coals burn the Ministering Angels, and all of them immerse themselves in it and become renewed every morning. And this Rigyon issues from before the Holy One, blessed be He, from beneath the Throne of Glory, and it is made of the sweat of the four Beasts which are under the Throne of Glory and of the sweat of fire and of the dread of the Holy One, blessed be He. And of that sweat of fire is made that river. And the Holy One, blessed be He, sits on the Seat of Judgment and judges even the Ministering Angels. And when the Ministering Angels come to be judged they renew themselves by submerging in that river of fire.

Instantly the Holy One, blessed be He, made Moses pass on from there, and he encountered Galetzur who is called Raziel. And why is his name Galetzur? Because he reveals (*m'galle*) the reasons of the Rock (*Tzur*, i.e., God). And he is called Raziel, because he hears behind the Curtain the secrets of God, (*raze El*), that which has been decreed to come to pass, and he announces it in the world. It is said of Galetzur that he stands before the Throne and his wings are spread out to receive the breath of the mouth of the Beasts, and were it not so, all the Ministering Angels would be burnt by the breath of the mouth of the Beasts. And Galetzur has yet another task: he takes a kind of an iron pan which is of fire, and receives in it the fiery coals of the River Rigyon, and places it opposite the kings, and rulers, and princes of the world so that their splendor should succeed and their fear fall upon the world.

When Moses saw him he trembled, and instantly the

Holy One, blessed be He, took him and caused him to pass on from there. And then he encountered a legion of angels of dread who surround the throne of Glory, and who are stronger and mightier than all the angels, and they wanted to burn him with the breath of their mouth. Instantly the Holy One, blessed be He, spread the splendor of His glory over Moses and said to him: "Give them an answer!"

[Follows, in great detail, the standard argument: the angels do not need the Tora because its laws do not apply to them, and therefore they should not object to it being given to Israel.]

Instantly all the Ministering Angels returned and accepted the words of the Holy One, blessed be He. And the Holy One, blessed be He, taught Moses the whole Tora in forty days. And when Moses was about to descend and saw the dread of the angels and the legions of the angels of dread, the angels of fiery sweat, the angels of fright, the angels of trembling, he was instantly seized with trembling and forgot it in one moment. Instantly the Holy One, blessed be He, called Y'fefiya ["The Beautiful One"], the heavenly prince of the Tora, and he gave Moses the Tora all arranged and ordered, and all the Ministering Angels became his loving friends, and each of them gave him some healing substance and secrets of Names which are derived from each weekly portion of the Tora and all their uses. . . . And even the Angel of Death gave him something. . . . And this is the honorable use which the angels gave him through Y'fefiya, the prince of the Tora, and through Metatron, the Angel of the Face, and Moses gave it to Eleazar, and Eleazar to his son Phinehas who is none other than Elijah, the great and dear priest of blessed memory, Amen.

(Ma'ayan Ḥokhma, BhM 1:58-61)

Samael and Job

R. Ḥama ben R. Ḥanina said: In the hour when Israel came out of Egypt, up rose the angel Samael to accuse them. R.

Ḥama ben R. Ḥanina explained in the name of his father: A parable. This is like unto a shepherd who was leading his flock across a river. A wolf came to attack the flock. The shepherd, who was experienced, what did he do? He took a big ram and delivered it to the wolf, saying, Let the wolf fight with this one until we cross the river, and than I shall bring him over. Thus in the hour when Israel came out of Egypt, up rose the angel Samael to accuse them. He said before the Holy One, blessed be He: "Master of the World! Until now this people worshiped stars, and You would part the sea for them?" What did the Holy One, blessed be He, do? He delivered him Job who was one of the counselors of Pharaoh, and said to him: "Behold, he is in your hand!" For the Holy One, blessed be He, said: "While he occupies himself with Job, Israel will descend into the sea and ascend, and then I shall save Job." This is to what Job referred, "*He hath set me up for His mark* (Job 16:12) and delivered me into the hand of Satan so that Israel should not emerge guilty in judgment."

(Exod. Rab. 21:7)

The Size of the Shekhina

The body of the Shekhina is 236 times a myriad of parasangs—118 myriads from her hips upward, and 118 from her hips downward. And these parasangs are not like our parasangs, but like her parasangs which equal a thousand times thousand cubits. And a cubit of her is four handbreadths and a span; and a handbreadth of her reaches from one end of the world to the other.

(Alfa Beta diR. Akiba, BhM 3:29; taken from *Shi'ur Qoma*, attributed to R. Yishma'el)

Seraphim and Satan

How many Seraphim are there? Four, corresponding to the

four winds of the world. And how many wings do they have? Six, corresponding to the six days of Creation. And how many faces do they have? Sixteen faces, four towards each wind. And the size of the Seraphim and their height— each of them corresponds to the seven firmaments. The size of their wings—each wing is like the fullness of the firmament. The size of their faces—each face is like the face of the East, each emits light like the radiance of the Throne of Glory, which even the Holy Beasts and the Wheels of Splendor and the Cherubim of Majesty cannot look at, for he who looks at it, his eyes grow dim from the great radiance which is upon it. And why is their name called Seraphim? Because they burn (*sorfim*) the ledgers of Satan. Every day Satan sits with Samael, the celestial prince of Rome, and with Dumiel, the celestial prince of Persia, and enters the sins of Israel into ledgers. And they give them to the Seraphim so that they present them to the Holy One, blessed be He, to destroy Israel from the world. But the Seraphim know the holy secrets: that the Holy One, blessed be He, does not want this nation of His to fall. What do the Seraphim do? Every day they take the ledgers from the hands of Satan and burn them in the flaming fire which is opposite the high and exalted Throne, so that they should not come before the Holy One, blessed be He, in the hour when He sits in judgment and judges the whole world in truth.

(Sefer Hekhalot, attributed to the Tanna
R. Yishma'el the High Priest, pp. 8a-b)

Lilith

When the Holy One, blessed be He, created Adam the first man single, He said: *It is not good for the man to be alone* (Gen. 2:18), and He created for him a woman from the earth like him, and called her Lilith. Instantly they began to quarrel. She said: "I shall not lie beneath," and he said, "I shall not lie beneath but above, for your place is beneath and mine above." She said to him: "Both of us are equal for both of us are of earth." And they did not listen to each other. When Lilith saw this, she uttered the Ineffable Name and flew off into the air of the world.

Thereupon Adam rose in prayer before his Creator and said: "Master of the World! The woman whom You gave me fled from me." Instantly the Holy One, blessed be He, sent three angels [Senoi, Sansenoi, and Semangelof] after her to bring her back. And the Holy One, blessed be He, said to Adam: "If she wants to return, good and well, and if not, she will have to take it upon herself that every day one of hundred of her children should die."

The angels left Adam and went after her. They overtook her in the sea, in the strong waters in which the Egyptians were to drown in the future. They told her the word of God, but she did not want to return. They then said to her: "We shall drown you in the sea." She said to them: "Let me be, for I was not created except for weakening the newborn children: the males until their eighth day, and the females from their birth until twenty days."

When they heard her words, they pressed her to take her, whereupon she swore to them in the name of the Living and Enduring God that "Each time when I see you or your names or your likeness on an amulet, I shall not harm that child." And she took it upon herself that a hundred of her children should die every day. Therefore every day one hundred of the demons die, and this is why we write the names of the three angels on amulets for little boys, for Lilith sees them and remembers her oath, and the child recovers."

(Alfa Beta diBen Sira, OM, p. 47)

A Ghost Story

It happened to a pious man that he once gave a denar to a poor man in a year of drought. His wife reproached him, whereupon he went and stayed overnight in the cemetery.

He heard two spirits talking to each other. One of them said: "My friend, come let us roam about in the world and see what misfortunes are about to befall the world." The other spirit answered: "My friend, I cannot leave because I am buried in a mat of reeds. But you go, and then tell me whatever you hear." She[65] went and returned, and the other said to her: "My friend, did you hear from behind the Curtain in heaven what misfortunes will befall the world?" She said to her: "I heard that all those who will sow at the first rainfall, hail will ruin their crops." The pious man went and sowed at the second rainfall. The crops of everybody else were ruined by hail, but his crops were not ruined.

Next year he again spent the night in the cemetery and heard two spirits talk to each other. One said to the other: "Come, let us roam in the world and see what misfortunes will befall the world." She said to her: "My friend, did I not tell you that I cannot get out because I am buried in a reed mat? However, you go, and then tell me what you heard." She went and came back, and the first one said to her: "Did you hear anything from behind the Curtain?" She said: "I heard that those who will sow at the second rain will be hit by blight." He went and sowed at the first rain. Blight came to the world and the crops of everybody were blighted, but his were not blighted. His wife said to him: "Why is it that the misfortune that comes to the world hits the crops of everybody, but your crops are not hit and not blighted?" He told her the whole story. Days later a quarrel broke out between the wife of that pious man and the mother of that girl who was buried in a reed mat. She said to her: "Come and I shall show you your daughter who is buried in a reed mat!"

Next year he went and spent the night in the cemetery and heard those two spirits talk to each other. One said to the other: "My friend, come let us roam in the world and

---

[65] The word for "spirit" — *ruaḥ* — is feminine in Hebrew.

hear what they say behind the Curtain." The other one said to her: "My friend, let me be. Things we say to each other have become known among the living."

(Avot diR. Nathan A, p. 16-17; B. Ber. 18b)

THE MESSIAH

The Birth of the Messiah

R. Aybo in the name of R. Yudan said: It happened to a man who was plowing when his ox lowed. An Arab passed by and said to him: "Untie your ox and untie your plow." He said to him: "Why?" The Arab answered: "Because the Temple of the Jews has been destroyed." The Jew said to him: "How do you know?" "From the lowing of your ox." While he was occupied with it, the ox lowed a second time. The Arab said: "Tie your ox, tie your plow, for the Redeemer of the Jews has just been born." The Jew said to him: "And what is his name?" He answered: "Menahem is his name." "And what is his father's name?" He said: "Hezekiah." The Jew said to him: "And where do they dwell?" He said to him: "In Birat 'Arava which is in Bethlehem of Judea."

That man thereupon sold his ox, sold his plow, and bought felt clothes for children. He went from town to town and from city to city until he came to that place. All the villagers came to buy from him, but that woman, the mother of that babe, bought nothing. He said to her: "Why are you not buying children's clothes?" She said to him: "My child was born under a bad sign." He said to her: "Why?" She said: "Because on the day of his birth the Temple was destroyed." He said to her: "As sure as God lives, through him it was destroyed and through him it will be rebuilt." [She said to him: "I have no money." He said to her: "I do not mind,] come and buy of these clothes for your child, and after a time I shall come to your house and get from you their price." She bought and went. Some days later that man said: "Let me go and see that child, and find out how he is." He came to her and asked her: "That child, how is he?" She said to him: "Did I not tell you that he was born under a bad sign? For since that time winds and storms came and took him and went their way." He said to her: "And I, did I not tell you that through him the Temple was destroyed and through him it will be rebuilt?"

(Lam. Rab. 1:51, p. 36, ad Lam. 1:16, ed. Buber 45a-b.
The addition in brackets is from Y. Ber. 5a.)

Praise of the Messiah

The garment in which the Holy One, blessed be He, clothes the Messiah will go and shine from one end of the world to the other, and Israel will use its light and say to the Messiah: "Happy is the hour in which the Messiah was created, happy the womb from which he issued, happy the generation whose eyes saw, happy the eye which merited to see him, for the opening of his mouth is blessing and peace, and his speech is pleasure for the spirit, and splendor and pomp are in his garments, and safety and security in his words, and his tongue is forgiveness and pardon, and his prayer a sweet savor, and his supplication holiness, and purity is in his study."

(Pes. diR. Kahana, ed. Mandelbaum, p. 470)

The Hiding Messiah

The first redeemer, Moses, revealed himself and then was hidden. R. Berekhya in the name of R. Levi said: "As the first redeemer, so the last redeemer, the Messiah. The first redeemer, that is Moses, revealed himself to them and then was hidden from them." How long was he hidden from them? R. Tanḥuma said: "Three months." Thus also the last redeemer will be revealed to them and then will be hidden from them. How long will he be hidden from them? R. Tanḥuma in the name of R. Ḥama ben R. Hosha'ya said: "Forty-five days. Thereafter he will again be revealed to them." And where will he lead them? Some say to the Judean Desert, and some say to the desert of Sihon and Og. All those who believe in him and go after him will eat roots of wormwood and leaves of saltworth. And all those who do not go after him will go and submit to the nations of the world, and at the end the nations of the world will kill them. R. Yitzḥaq bar Marion said: "At the end of the forty-five days the Holy One, blessed be He, will bring manna down for them."

(Num. Rab. 11:2)

The Messianic Days

It was taught in the name of the rabbis: In the septenary in which the Son of David comes, in the first year there will be insufficient food; in the second, arrows of famine are sent out; in the third, great famine; in the fourth, neither famine nor abundance; in the fifth, great abundance, and a star will grow from the east, it is the star of the Messiah, and it will abide in the east for fifteen days, and if it tarries longer it will be to the good of Israel; in the sixth, voices and rumors; in the seventh, wars. And the end of the seventh will expect the Messiah, and the Children of the West will become overbearing and will come and will maintain a reign with insolence, and they will come to Egypt and capture all the captivity.

The False and the True Messiah

... another king will come from the *Maghreb* [West], and he will be worse and more hostile than the others. His marks will be: he will be a hundred cubits [tall] and eleven spans wide and will have much hair on his face. He will conquer the entire West. And there will be evil and warlike men who will gather around him from the whole world, and will say that he is the Messiah. And this rumor will spread throughout the world and the whole world will be subjugated by him, and he will kill those who do not submit to him. The Israelites will endure much suffering and misery, and they will flee. In the whole world there will be oppression. They, however, will go into the mountains and will reach their utter ends. And the army of Gog and Magog will go with that king. They will be recognized by having four eyes, two in the front and two in the back. All people will have to endure much suffering and trouble, but the Israelites even more.... Then a man will appear in a remote place and every Israelite will leave his dwelling, and all of them will gather. That man will be of the Children of Ephraim. They will go to that wicked one who says, I am the Messiah, your king, your treasure. The Israelites will tell him: "We ask of you three signs to convince us." He will say: "What signs do you ask for? Let me see!" They will answer: "We demand the following signs: That you take the staff which our Teacher Moses turned into a snake before Pharaoh, and do the same. And that the Staff of Aaron, which was dry wood, should promptly bring forth fresh leaves and fruits. And as yet another sign we ask that you produce that vessel full of manna, which Aaron has preserved. Perform these signs and we shall know that you are telling the truth." But that wicked one will not be able to perform even one of them.

Then Michael and Gabriel will come to the camp of the Israelites, and will slay him who claims to be the Messiah. And the Messiah son of Joseph will also be killed, and the banner of the Messiah son of David will appear. He will kill the whole army of Gog and Magog.

(The Story of Dan. pp. 415, 417-21)

And in those days an insolent king will arise over a poor and destitute people.

Rab Huna in the name of Rabbi Levi said: Israel will be gathered in Upper Galilee, and Messiah ben Joseph will oversee them, and they will ascend from there, and all

Israel with him, to Jerusalem. And he will go up and rebuild the Holy House and offer up sacrifices, and fire will descend from heaven. And he will smite all the nations of the world, and march against the Land of Moab and slay half of it and the rest he will capture in captivity, and they will pay him tribute. And in the end he will make peace with Moab. And they will sit for forty years in safety, eat and drink [as it is written:] *Aliens shall be your plowmen and your vinedressers* (Isa. 61:5).

And after all this Gog and Magog will hear it and come up against them. And they will enter and kill Messiah son of Joseph in the streets of Jerusalem. And Israel will see it and say: "The Messiah is lost to us, and no other Messiah will come!" And four families will mourn over him, except the family of the House of David, and the Holy One, blessed be He, will go out and fight with them. And the Mount of Olives will split asunder from his arrows, and the Holy One, blessed be He, will descend upon it, and Israel will flee and escape. And this will be the plague, and Israel will thereafter be exiled to marshy deserts to graze in the salty shrubs and roots of broom bushes forty-five days. And Clouds of Glory will surround them, and there Israel will hide. And all those who have evil thoughts in their hearts about the Holy One, blessed be He, the clouds will eject them and the nations of the world will slay them. And many from Israel will go out to the nations of the world, and they will have no share with Israel in the World to Come. But those who will suffer from eating salt plants for forty-five days will be addressed by a Divine Voice saying: "Go down to Babylonia for there you will be saved." And the Divine Voice rings out again: "Go to Edom, and perform there My vengeance!" And Israel will come to Rome, and the Divine Voice issues a third time saying: "Do to her as Joshua did to Jericho!" And they will march around the city and blow the shofars, and at the seventh time they blow a *t'ru'a: Hear, O Israel, the Lord our God, the Lord is one!* And the wall of the city will crumble, and they enter it and find its young men lying dead in its streets.

Thereafter they will gather all its booty, and Israel will seek their God and David their king. And instantly King Messiah will reveal himself to them and say to them: "I am he, King Messiah, for whom you were waiting." And he will say to them: "Take the silver and the gold!" And they will take it and go up. And a fourth Divine Voice issues and says: *A voice crieth in the wilderness* (Isa. 40:3). And a fifth Divine Voice proclaims: *Comfort ye, comfort ye, My people* (Isa. 40:1). And Elijah announces to Israel: *Thy God reigneth!* (Isa. 52:7). . . . And an eighth Divine Voice proclaims and says: *Bid Jerusalem to take heart* (Isa. 40:2). And a ninth Divine Voice says: *Open ye the gates that the righteous nation that keepeth faithfulness may enter it* (Isa. 26:2). And a tenth Divine Voice says: *Lift up, O Gates, your heads* (Ps. 23:7), and let the dead live. And then the exiles will gather. And then it will be fulfilled that *There shall step forth a star out of Jacob* (Num. 24:17). And thus be it the will before our Father in Heaven that this verse be fulfilled, *And He will set up an ensign for the nations, and will assemble the dispersed of Israel* (Isa. 11:12) in our days and in the days of all Israel.

(Agadat Mashiaḥ, BhM 3:141-43)

Resurrection

And why will then be such a great earthquake? So that the bones which were trampled into the earth and built into buildings and burnt into bricks and buried under ruins should come up, so that bone go to its bone. And the Holy One, blessed be He, will stretch sinews upon them and cover them with flesh and will envelop them with skin, but there will be no spirit in them. And then the Holy One, blessed be He, will cause the dew of life to descend from heaven in which there is the light of the life of the soul. And he who had a blemish will at first rise with his blemish, and if he was old he will come back with his old age and the weakness of his flesh, so that they should not say: "These are other creatures." And then the Holy One, blessed be He, will heal them. And for whom is this Resurrection of the dead? For all those who were pious in Israel at first, and also for those who sinned and repented. But those whose sins were more numerous than their merits and did not repent will not rise in the Days of the Messiah. And Israel will marvel and say: "From whence did all these come suddenly?" And the nations of the world will also marvel.

And the nations which will remain will become proselytes. And when they come before King Messiah he will command them to make swords and wars cease. And then Sodom and Gomorrah will be settled, their towns and all the surroundings, so that the Land of Israel should not be left blemished by a desolation in its midst. And he will also make all evil animals cease from the land. And those people whom King Messiah will find alive will live a long life and then will die. And no man will die as a youth or a young man. And he will uproot death from the world. And those who will die in the days of the Messiah will live in the life of the World to Come because of the merits of the totally saintly. And in those times, when the Temple will be revealed and Jerusalem will descend from heaven and station itself like a pillar of fire from the earth to the firmament, all those who will want to come to Jerusalem will see that pillar of fire from their countries and will walk in its light until they reach Jerusalem. For that light will be greater than the light of the sun and the moon, and it will make their light dim. And they will dwell in their kingdom until the end of the world, or, as some say, until seven thousand years will be completed from the days of creation.

(Hai Gaon, *Responsum*, in Eliezer Ashkenazi, ed., *Ta'am Z'qenim*, pp. 60a-b)

Elijah and the Messiah

Open to me, my sister, my love (Song 5:2). This refers to the days of Gog and Magog when Israel will have to hide in caves and crevices, and God knocks. R. Shim'on ben Zoma said: God said to Israel, *Open to Me, My sister.* And they are looking, and God will make miracles for them, and they will see the Messiah standing on top of the Desert of Moab, and with him four hundred men. And God will give them Redemption. And the crevices will open for them from there, from the Desert of Moab until Mount Horeb, and Israel will go and take the Desert of Horeb, for behold God's name is written upon it, and they will come and take Ammon and Moab. And behold, the Kings of the North will hear that Ammon and Moab were killed, and they all will gather and come and establish the kingship in Damascus. And also the Kings of the West and the South will gather, and come and take counsel with Midian. And Israel will be in pain: shall they leave their brethren, the sages of Midian—this cannot be; or shall they leave their brethren the sages of Jerusalem—this cannot be. And God will open a door for Elijah and he will go out to Midian and leave the sages who are in Jerusalem. And what does Elijah do? That whole desert which stretches from Jerusalem to Midian, is full of crags and evil beasts, but God makes miracles for him and he [Elijah] comes and stands before the Messiah in Midian, and the Messiah takes leave from that place. And Elijah stands there. In that hour he takes out the Book of Yashar of which this Tora of ours is not more than a single line. The earth opens under them, and consumes them with fire and becomes for them a great grave. And the Messiah comes from Midian and takes all its booty, and goes to Damascus and takes all its booty. Until the kingdom of Edom [i.e., Rome] falls. And a door opens from there to Rome. Then God says to them: "Return to Jerusalem, for behold, you are like this sleeper who is asleep. And behold, the Kings of the East have gathered in Tarmod [Palmyra]. And Israel comes from Rome and offers up sacrifices in Jerusalem for seven days, and God lets wind blow and says to Israel: "Return to Palmyra to face the

Kings of the East!" And the kings of the nations say:
"Permission has been given to rebuild the Temple!" And
they come to burn it, and God goes forth and fights them.
And the Messiah comes to Tyre and Sidon and Palmyra and
to Rabba of Ammon. . . .

(Yalqut haMakhiri, *ad* Isa. 11:4, p. 89)

5
KABBALA

The bulk of the selections contained in this part comes from the Zohar (written by Moses de Leon in Spain in the late thirteenth century), which is as it should be, since the Zohar outweighs in importance and influence all the other Kabbalistic writings together. The appearance of the Zohar was the culmination of a mystical trend which had spread among the Jews of Germany, southern France, and Spain from about 1150. That is, chronologically, Jewish mysticism stood between the Muslim mysticism which originated in the eighth century in Persia and reached its golden age from the eleventh to the thirteenth centuries, and the Christian mysticism which, although it had important forerunners such as Meister Eckhardt and Jan van Ruysbroeck, flourished in the sixteenth century with Jakob Böhme, St. Teresa, and St. John of the Cross.

Mystical traditions, to be sure, existed within Judaism for more than a millennium prior to the great breakthrough in the twelfth century. They go back to esoteric and theosophical currents which are well documented in the writings of the great Hellenistic Jewish philosopher Philo of Alexandria (first century C.E.), in apocalyptic apocryphal books, in the Talmud (especially in the so-called Merkaba—"chariot"—mysticism), as well as in the Hekhalot ("Heavenly Halls") literature, the *Sefer Yetzira* ("Book of Creation"), written probably in Palestine between the third and the sixth centuries, and the ancient Jewish books of magic composed in Talmudic times in Babylonia. However, for several centuries thereafter these traditions remained all but forgotten. Thus, for instance, the mystical aspect of the encyclopedic work *Kifayat al-'Abidin* ("Guide for the Servants of God"), written in Arabic by Abraham, the son of Maimonides (1186–1237), draws only on Muslim Sufi sources and betrays no familiarity with Jewish mystical traditions.

The more remarkable is the emergence in the twelfth century of the movement of the *Haside Ashk'naz*, the devout, or pious, of Germany (and France), and the contemporaneous growth of the Kabbala in Provence, where the *Sefer haBahir* appeared in 1180. From Provence the Kabbala rapidly spread to northern Spain, where, in the early thirteenth century, an important center came into being in Gerona. By the second half of the thirteenth century many Kabbalists were active in various parts of Spain, the foremost of them being Moses de Leon (c. 1240–1305), author of the Zohar, or Book of Splendor, considered the "Bible" of the Kabbala. A contemporary of de Leon was Abraham Abulafia (1240–after 1292), who wrote no less than twenty-six prophetic books, of which, however, only one, the *Sefer haOt* ("Book of the Sign"), survived.

The literary development of the Kabbala continued in Spain in the fourteenth and fifteenth centuries, but the movement itself did not spread beyond the narrow circle of the scholarly elite. With the expulsion from Spain in 1492, Messianism became an essential part of Kabbalistic teachings, which in the sixteenth century rapidly developed into a veritable mass movement and gave rise to a flood of Kabbalistic writings produced by its scholarly devotees in Italy, North Africa, Germany, Greece, Turkey, and Palestine, with the Safed center surpassing all others in importance and influence. Within a generation after the Spanish expulsion the little town of Safed in the Galilee became the undisputed center of the Kabbala, and before the end of the century the books written by the Safed Kabbalists were avidly read, and their teachings absorbed, everywhere in the Jewish world. The undisputed master was Yitzhaq Luria (1534–1572), whose teachings were made available in the writings of his foremost disciple, Hayyim Vital (1542–1620). Next to him Moses Cordovero (1522–1570), Joseph Caro (1488–1575, the author of the *Shulhan 'Arukh*), Jacob Berab (c. 1474–1546), Joseph Taitazak (1487–1545?), David ibn Abi Zimra (1479–1573), Solomon Alqabetz (1505–1584, the author of the *Lekha Dodi*), and many others lived, taught, and wrote in Safed in the sixteenth century. Thereafter, Jewish mysticism continued to produce a gradually dimishing literary crop until the nineteenth century, when much of its traditions was taken over, and transformed, by Hasidism (see Part 7).

As far as the legends found in Kabbalistic sources are concerned, they are, as one would expect, suffused with a mystical tone of spirituality. Although Biblical figures still appear in them, they are secondary in importance to the Talmudic sages, who are represented as teachers of secret esoteric lore (foremost among them being R. Shim'on ben Yohai, the pseudepigraphic author of the Zohar, and his son R. El'azar), and about whom many hagiographic stories are told. Another type of Kabbalistic story is mythological: it tells of angels (e.g., Metatron, Gabriel, the Angel of Death) and divine personages (God the King, his mate the Shekhina-Matronit, the personified Community of Israel, Zion, etc.). Kabbalistic stories pay much attention to mythical cosmogony—the seven worlds, the Garden of Eden, Gehenna, the Bird's Nest—as well as to the evil spirits (Samael, Lilith) who lurk everywhere and are out to bring ruination to man.

In the Kabbalistic view, which is expressed eloquently in many a mystical story, the human soul is a battleground between the Good and the Evil ("the Other Side"), between the Sparks and the Husks, and it is man's cosmic task to help the Good to victory over Evil.

The selections in this part date from the thirteenth to the eighteenth century. Their original language is Aramaic (the Zohar) or Hebrew. The style is often obscure, because the Kabbalists had a predilection for using an inordinate amount of technical terms and phrases which mean something quite different from what they appear to say. The epithets themselves by which the major figures of the Kabbalistic mythology are designated are so many and varied that they can easily lead to confusion. Thus God is called, in addition to the old Talmudic name "the Holy One, blessed be He," also the Ancient One, the Ancient of Days, the Long of Face (which Scholem interprets as the Patient One), the Small of Face (Scholem: the Impatient One), the One Name, the King, Zoharariel ("the Splendor of the Lion of God"), Adiryaron ("the Mighty One Sings"), Aktariel ("My Crown Is God"), Tetrasia ("Fourfold God," referring to the Tetragrammaton), Heaven, etc. The feminine emanation of God is termed the Daughter, Malkuth ("Kingship"), Shekhina ("Dwelling"), Matronit ("Matron" or "Lady"), Pearl, Precious Stone, Discarded Cornerstone, Female, Moon, Hart, Earth, Night, Garden, Well, Sea, the Supernal Woman, the Light-Woman, the Community of Israel, etc.[1] The evil powers are called the Other Side, the Left, the Left Side, the North Side, etc. Lilith, the female embodiment of evil, is called Northerner, Husk, Serpent, the Tortuous Serpent, Woman of Harlotry, End of all Flesh, End of

[1] Cf. R. Patai, *The Hebrew Goddess,* p. 143.

Days, the Alien Crown, the Alien Woman, the Slave Woman, the Impure Female, or, most cautiously, That Certain Woman (*P'lonit*), etc.

Because of the peculiarities of the Kabbalistic texts, when rendering them into English I often had to interpolate explanatory words or phrases into the body of the translation, while in other cases footnotes had to be appended to the texts so as to make clear the meaning of obscure references.

CHRONOLOGY OF THE SOURCES QUOTED

13th century	The *Zohar* by Moses de Leon
	Seder Gan Eden
	Qabbalot R. Ya'aqov w'R. Yitzhaq (ed. G. Scholem)
	Bahya ben Asher, *Biur 'al haTora*
	Moses ben Solomon of Burgos
14th century	School of RaShBA (R. Sh'lomo ben Avraham)
	Zohar Hadash
	Sefer Tashaq by R. Yosef (ed. J. Zwelling)
15th-16th centuries	Meir Arama, *Sefer Meir T'hillot*
16th century	Moses Cordovero, *Pardes Rimmonim*
	Yitzhaq Luria's teachings as presented by Hayyim Vital
	Shivhe haARI

16th-17th centuries	Abraham Azulai
17th century	Nathan Spira, *Tuv haAretz* Naphtali Bacharach, *'Emeq haMelekh* Yalqut R'uveni
18th century	Ḥayyim Yosef David Azulai

OF BODY AND SOUL

The Creation of Man

R. Hizqiya began: When the Holy One, blessed be He, created the world, he fashioned man in His image, and formed him in His form so that he should persevere in the Tora and walk in His ways. Therefore man was created from the dust of the lower Temple and was fashioned, and the four sides of the world were joined together in that place which is called the Holy House. And those four sides of the world joined together with the four sides which are the elements of the Lower World: Fire, Wind, Water, and Dust. And once those four sides were joined together with the four elements of the world, the Holy One, blessed be He, fashioned from them one body in the supernal image. And that body is composed of two worlds: the Lower World, and the Supernal World.

(Zohar 2:23b)

The New Tora

There was a Tora before the Holy One, blessed be He, before she was given to those below, and the numbers of her letters were before Him, and she was not composed of words as she is now, and the reason was that she should be capable of any arrangement according to what would take place in the world. But in consequence of the sin of Adam

the first man He arranged the letters which were before
him into words which tell about death, and Levirate
marriage, and the like. And had Adam not sinned, and
there would have been no death, He would have arranged
the letters into words telling of other matters. This is why
there are in the Tora neither vowels nor divisions of verses,
nor cantillation signs, as an allusion to the Tora which was
in the beginning a heap of letters, unarranged. And the
ultimate intention of the Holy One, blessed be He, is that
when King Messiah comes, and He *will swallow up death
forever* (Isa. 25:8), there will be no death, no impurity, and
the like, and the Holy One, blessed be He, will take apart
words of the Tora and attach a letter from one word to a
letter from another word, to combine words whose
meaning will be different, and this is the new Tora which
will issue from Me. For verily, the Tora is eternal, and the
Tora Scroll will be then as she is now, and the Holy One,
blessed be He, will teach us how to read it properly
according to the order of the letters which will combine to
make a word and will teach us the division and joining of
the words.

(Azulai, D'vash l'Fi, 50a quoting a Ms. of R.
Eliyahu Kohen of Smyrna [d. 1729])

Partners in Creation

The Holy One, blessed be He, said: "I and My Shekhina are
partners in [the creation of] the soul, and his father and
mother are partners in the body. For his father emits the
seed [for the fashioning] of the white of the eyes and of the
bones and the sinews and the brain, and the woman [gives]
the black of the eyes and the hair, and the flesh and the
skin." And likewise, the heaven and the earth and all their
hosts participate in his creation. The angels—from them is
the Good Inclination and the Evil Inclination,[2] so that man

2 The Evil Inclination originates from the fallen angel Samael.

be fashioned from both. The sun and the moon—to give him light by day and by night. Beasts, animals and birds and fishes, to nourish himself from them. All the trees and seeds of the earth, to nourish himself from them. What did the Holy One, blessed be He, do? He uprooted his father and his mother from the Garden of Eden, and took them with Him to be with Him in the joy of their children. And there is no joy like the joy of Redemption, as it is written, *Let the heavens be glad and let the earth rejoice, and let them say among the nations, The Lord reigneth* (1 Chron. 16:31).

                              (Ra'aya Mehemna, Zohar 3:119b-120a)

The Fate of the Soul

Come, see: We have learned that even in this world, when men sleep in their beds, and their souls leave the bodies and roam about in the world, not every soul rises and roams to see the glory of the face of the Ancient of Days. But to the extent that a man had always been attracted to God, and according to his works, so his soul rises up. But if he became unclean when he sleeps, and the soul leaves his body and all the unclean spirits take hold of her and she cleaves to them in those lower grades where they roam the world, and they let her know things which are about to happen in the world. And at times they tell her false things and mock her, and this has already been stated elsewhere. And if the man is worthy, when he sleeps and his soul rises up, she roams about and cuts through those unclean spirits and all proclaim and say: "Make room, make room! This one is not of our side!" And she goes up among the holy ones [angels] and they tell her a word of truth. And when she descends, all those bands of evil spirits want to approach her in order to learn that word, and they tell her other things, and that word which she received from those holy ones is among those others like a grain among the chaff. And that one word of truth is all that a man can obtain while he is still alive and his soul is in this world. In a similar manner, when the souls leave the body in this world, they try to rise up, and there exist many gatekeepers and bands of harmful spirits. If the souls are of their side [i.e., evil], they all seize them and deliver them to the hands of the angel Duma to be taken to Gehenna. Then they ascend and seize them and take hold of them and proclaim about them: "These are they who transgressed the commands of their Master." And they roam about with the souls in the whole world. And thereafter they return them to Gehenna, and thus they do for twelve months. After twelve months they are assigned to their proper places. But those souls who are worthy ascend on high, as has been explained, and attain their proper places. Come, see: Happy are the righteous; for them many boons are hidden in That World.

(Zohar 1:130a-b)

The Letter of Identity

When the soul leaves this world and enters the cave of Adam,[3] and the Fathers are there, they give him a letter of identity, and then the soul enters the Garden of Eden. When she approaches it, she encounters there the Cherubim, and that *Flame of revolving sword* (Gen. 3:24). If she had merits, they inspect the letter of identity, and open a door for her, and she enters. And if not, they push her out. And she sits there all the time that she sits there, and clothes herself there in the image of this world. And on New Moons and Sabbaths, when she wants to ascend to the Garden of Eden, the righteous who are in the Garden of Eden give her a letter of identity. And she ascends by means of that pillar,[4] and encounters the guardians of the walls of Jerusalem. If she had merits, they open the gate for her and she enters; and if not, they take from her that letter of identity and push her out.

(Sitre Tora, Zohar 1:81b)

---

[3] I.e., the Cave of Machpela.
[4] Which is in the middle of the earthly Garden of Eden, as explained in Zohar Gen. 2, p. 14 of the Sullam edition.

The Way of the Spirit

R. El'azar and R. Abba were going from Tiberias to Sepphoris. While they were walking they met a Jew. He joined them. R. El'azar said: "Let each of us say a word of Tora!" He began and said: "*Prophesy, Son of man, prophesy to the spirit and say to the spirit,* etc. (Ezek. 37:9). From this verse we know the place from whence the spirit issues. Verily, man cannot rule the spirit, but the Holy One, blessed be He, rules over everything, and at His word Ezekiel prophesied. Moreover, that spirit was in a body in this world, and this is why he prophesied about her: *From the four winds come, O spirit* (ibid.)—from that place which was delimited by its pillars in the four sides of the world."

Up jumped that Jew before him. R. El'azar said to him: "What have you seen?" He said: "I saw something." He said to him: "What is it?" He said to him: "If the spirit of man clothes itself in the Garden of Eden in a bodily form of This World, it should have been written, 'Thus saith the Lord, From the Garden of Eden come, O spirit.' Why 'From the four winds'?" He said to him: "The spirit does not descend to This World until it rises from the Garden of the Earth to the Throne which stands on four pillars. After it rises up there, it imbibes from that throne of the King, and comes down to This World. The body is taken from the four sides of the world, and the spirit is likewise taken from the four sides of the Throne which rests upon them."

That man said to him: "I jumped before you because I saw something of this kind. For one day I was walking in the desert and I saw a tree, delightful to behold, and there was a cave beneath it. I approached and saw that the cave emitted fragrances of all kinds, of all the fragrances of the world. I took courage and entered that cave, and went down a number of steps to a place in which there were many trees and fragrances and savors which I could not endure. And there I saw a man with a scepter in his hand. And he stood in a door. When he saw me, he was surprised and rose and said: 'What are you doing here, and who are you?' I was much afraid. I said to him: 'My master, I am one of the Company. This and this is what I saw in the desert, and I entered the cave and came down here.' He said to me: 'Since you are of the Company, take this bundle of writings and give it to the Company, to those who know the mysteries of the souls of the righteous.' He struck me with that scepter and I fell asleep. In my sleep I saw many troops and camps coming on the road to that place. And that man struck them with that scepter and said: 'Go the way of the trees!' While they went they flew in the air and rose up, and I did not know where they went. And I heard voices of troops, and did not know who they were. I awoke, and saw nothing, and was afraid in that place. Then I saw that man, and he said to me: 'Did you see anything?' I said to him: 'I saw this and this in my sleep.' He said: 'That is the way in which the spirits of the righteous go to the Garden of Eden, to enter it. And what you heard were the voices of those who stand in the Garden in the likeness of This World and they rejoice at the spirits of the righteous who come there. Just as the body is built in This World from a mixture of four elements and is formed in This World, so the spirit is formed in the Garden from a mixture of the four winds which stand in the Garden, and the spirit is clothed there and is formed in the shape of the likeness of the body which is formed in This World, and were it not for those four winds which are the airs of the Garden, the spirit would not be formed in a shape at all and would not be clothed in them. Those four winds are bound up with one another as one, and the spirit is formed and is clothed in them, as the body is formed of a mixture of the four elements of the world. Therefore, *From the four winds come, O spirit*—from those four winds of the Garden of Eden in which the spirit is clothed and formed. And now, take this bundle of writing and go your way and give it to the Companions.'"

Rabbi El'azar and those Companions came and kissed him on his head. R. El'azar said: "Blessed be the Merciful

One who sent you here, for certainly this is the explanation of the word, and the Holy One, blessed be He, put that verse in my mouth!"

He gave them that bundle of writings. When R. El'azar took it and opened it, walls of fire burst forth and surrounded him. He saw in the writings what he saw, and it flew away from his hands. R. El'azar wept and said: "Who can stand in the treasury of the King! .... Blessed be this way and this hour in which we met you!"

(Zohar 2:13a-b)

Planetary Influences

[At the birth of] every man, in whom there are four elements, four angels descend with him on his right, and four on his left. The four on his right are Michael, Gabriel, Raphael, and Nuriel, and the four on his left are Sin, Destroyer, Anger, and Wrath. From the side of the body Metatron descends upon him from the right side, and Samael from the left. And there is no man in whom the four elements would not be present, but the order of the four angels depends on the order in which the elements are assembled in him. If his sign[5] ("*mazal*") is the Lion, the first is Michael, after him Gabriel, after him Nuriel, and after him Raphael. If his sign is the Ox, then the first is Gabriel, after him Michael, after him Nuriel, and after him Raphael. If his sign is the Eagle, the first is Nuriel, after him Michael, after him Gabriel, and after him Raphael. And if his sign is Man, the first is Raphael, after him Michael, after him Gabriel, and after him Nuriel. And they all are of the right side. And those of the right side, which is the side of Michael, all their four faces (lion, bull, eagle, and man) are compassion, acts of charity, and his face is white. And if that man occupies himself with the Tora, he performs acts of

---

[5] The Hebrew word *mazal*, here translated as "sign," also means the constellations in the zodiac which are mentioned in the sequel.

charity, is pious, and wise. But if he does not occupy himself with the Tora, he is the opposite, for he then is from the side of the Evil Inclination, and he is a robber, a wicked man, and there is no piety in him, for the ignorant are not pious.

On the side of Gabriel (which is the left side), there are also four faces which are punishing, that is, have the quality of stern judgment over the wicked. And they taunt the wicked, for, as we have established, it is permitted to taunt the wicked in this world.

He whose sign is the Eagle is not very compassionate, and is not strong in stern judgment, but is mediocre in the Good Inclination, in his good qualities, as well as in the Evil Inclination, in the bad qualities. And he has a white-and-red face.

And he whose sign is Man is from the good side and included in him are good qualities, and he is pious, wise, mighty in the Tora, fears sin, and is filled with all the good qualities. And the color of his face is black. And if he is from the side of the Evil Inclination, he is full of all the bad qualities.

(Zohar 2:42a)

Of Good and Evil

Before a man comes into this world and emerges from the womb of his mother, *A man wrestles with him* (Gen. 32:25). This is Gabriel who wrestles with that dust of the ground about which it is said *The Lord God formed man of the dust of the ground* (Gen. 2:7), and teaches him seventy languages. And God created for man a Good Inclination, which teaches him seventy languages, and an Evil Inclination, which wrestles with him. For it is said, *Because he touched the hollow of his thigh, even the sinew of the thigh vein* (Gen. 32:33), and made him forget the seventy languages which the Good Inclination had taught him.

And prior to all this, four angels descend with him, about

whom it is said, *He will give His angels charge over thee* (Ps. 91:11). If he has ancestral merits, one, Michael, descends with him, because of the merits of Abraham; the second, Gabriel, because of the merits of Isaac; and the third who descends with him is Nuriel because of the merits of Jacob. And the fourth is Raphael, because of the merits of Adam the first man. The Good Inclination is above him. But if he has no merits, these four descend with him: Sin, Destroyer, Anger, and Wrath; and the Evil Inclination is above them to judge him in the World to Come. Therefore, it was explained, if he is evil, the Evil Inclination judges him; if righteous, the Good Inclination judges him; if mediocre, both together judge him. Therefore, if he is mediocre, Gabriel, who is the Good Inclination, and Samael, who is the Evil Inclination, judge him together.

(Zohar 2:41b-42a)

THE MYSTERIES OF EDEN

The Bird's Nest

Rabbi Shim'on said: "Come and see: In the lower Garden of Eden there is a place, hidden, secret, and unknown. It is embroidered in several colors, and in it are concealed a thousand palaces of longings. And nobody can enter them save the Messiah who dwells all the time in the Garden of Eden. And the whole Garden encompasses a multitude of bands of just men, and the Messiah stands over them and over many hosts and camps of the souls of the just who are there. And on New Moons, feasts, and Sabbaths the Messiah enters that place to find pleasure in those palaces. In the midst of those palaces there is another secret and hidden place which is totally unknown, and it is called Eden, and nobody can find it. And the Messiah is hidden there until the time when a place called the Bird's Nest is revealed to him. This is the place proclaimed by that Bird [i.e., the

Shekhina] which is stirred up in the Garden of Eden every day.

In that place are woven likenesses of all the other nations which band together against Israel to harm it. The Messiah enters that place, lifts up his eyes, and sees the Patriarchs visiting the ruins of the House of God. And when he sees Rachel with tears upon her face, and the Holy One, blessed be He, comforting her, but she refusing to be comforted, the Messiah too lifts up his voice and cries. And the whole Garden of Eden quakes, and all the Just who are there cry and lament with him. And the firmament which is above the Garden and the one thousand and five hundred myriads of supernal hosts are seized by a trembling which reaches the Supernal Throne. Then the Holy One, blessed be He, beckons to that Bird, which thereupon enters its nest, and settles down next to the Messiah, and utters cries and calls. Then, from inside the Holy Throne, that Bird's Nest and the Messiah are called three times, and they all ascend on high. And the Holy One, blessed be He, proclaims to them that He will destroy the guilty kingdom [Rome] through the hands of the Messiah, and avenge Israel. And all those good things which He prepared for Israel He will give to His people. And then the Bird's Nest and the Messiah return to their place.

(Zohar 2:8a)

We have learned: The Garden of Eden has three walls, and between them many spirits and souls walk about and enjoy the scents which are delightful for the Just, although they are not allowed to enter. And there are certain days in the year, namely the days of Nisan and the days of Tishri, when those spirits roam about and appear on top of the walls of the Garden in the likeness of birds which chirp every morning. And that chirping is a praise of the Holy One, blessed be He, and a prayer for the life of the humans of this world. For in those days Israel busies itself with fulfilling the commandments of the Master of the World. All this is in the lower Garden of Eden. And the Holy One, blessed be He, shows them a secret place, well hidden, which no eye has seen except God, and that palace is called Bird's Nest.

(Zohar 3:196b)

The rabbis taught: The Holy One, blessed be He, made the Garden of Eden below on earth, and it is opposite the Throne of Glory and the curtain of the fearful ice. R. Shim'on said: "Eden, which is above it, nourishes the Garden below. Three times every day that Eden on high lets drops fall upon the Garden, with all kinds of good fragrances and supernal splendors and enjoyments and longings, and from that fragrance and longing and enjoyment which descend upon the Garden is nourished the whole world."

(Zohar Ḥadash, Gen. p. 13c)

The Garden of Eden was created prior to the creation of the world, together with all its equipment, and all its plants, and the firmament which is over it and the ground which is under it. And 361 years and three hours and two minutes later were created the heaven and the earth. When the Holy One, blessed be He, created the Garden of Eden, He took snow from beneath the Throne of Glory, and from it was fashioned the soil of the Garden. And its ground touches and yet does not touch this earth, for it is above all the lands. The firmament which is above the Garden has the glitter of all the colors, like unto the sapphire stone. And the name of the Holy One, blessed be He, is engraved in the middle of the firmament. And in its four corners there are four rings, and in each ring there are four wheels. And in the middle of the firmament there is a column which is set into the soil of the Garden, and [its top] is fastened to the Throne of Glory, and it is covered by a Cloud of Glory. And the angel Gabriel, clothed in linen, mounts it once a day, gets hold of the rings of the firmament, whereupon the column turns and the firmament rotates, and the letters of the Ineffable Name protrude and sparkle and move up and down.

Then a voice calls: "Prepare yourselves, O camps of the holy Just! Happy are you that you have been worthy of this!" And there is the sound of a melody as the firmament travels in response to the man clothed in linen. Then he departs, and the firmament stands still, but the column continues to make music and to go up and down as long as the light of splendor continues to shine from above the column. And the Just stand facing the light and enjoy it until midnight.

At midnight, the Holy One, blessed be He, comes to join the company of the Just, and a voice is heard around the firmament, and the column makes music, and the ground of the Garden rises, and the Just go up from their bridal canopies to receive their Creator, and the whole Garden becomes filled with His Glory. In that hour the male and the female souls couple, as they did prior to being created. And from the joy of their desire to see the delightfulness of God they all produce fruit, and their fruit which is drawn out from them gives rise to the souls of the proselytes. Happy is he who is found worthy in This World to be present in that hour at the rejoicing of the Tora!

The light of the splendor of the Holy One, blessed be He, remains in the Garden of Eden after He ascends, and all the Just sing as He ascends in the morning. The ground of the Garden is then covered by the dew with which the Holy One, blessed be He, will resuscitate the dead; and the Just come forth and taste of it, as do the ministering angels on high.

When the Messiah comes out and takes hold of the four rings and raises his voice, the whole firmament over the Garden trembles. And seven angels are detailed to him, and they say to him: "Elect of God! Be silent, for the time has come for the Evil Kingdom to be uprooted from its place!" And the voice is heard from the houses of prayer and houses of study where they say with all their strength: "Amen! May

His Great Name be blessed for ever and ever!" Then the
Holy One, blessed be He, shakes all the firmaments, and
lets two tear drops fall into the Great Sea; and the Just go
back, and the Messiah goes back into that palace which is
called Bird's Nest.

(Seder Gan'Eden, BhM 3:132-33)

The simple meaning of the verse *And out of the ground made
the Lord God grow every tree* proves that there is a Garden of
Eden on earth, and there is the Tree of Life and the Tree of
Knowledge. The Tree of Life gives long life to those who eat
of it, and the Tree of Knowledge gives them will and
choice, whether in matters of the intellect or in matters of
the body.

Both trees were in the middle of the Garden, and
although they were two, and two trees cannot both be
exactly in the middle, they were one below and two above,
for they had a common trunk and they were divided into
two above, and thus both were exactly in the middle.

And you know that all these things were in the Garden of
Eden on earth, but all were shaped and modeled after
intellectual things which are in the supernal Garden of
Eden.

According to the Kabbalistic interpretation, the Tree of
Life and the Tree of Knowledge above are [the Sephirot of]
Tiferet [Beauty] and *'Atara* [Crown], and Adam sinned in act
and thought with the Tree of Knowledge and its [supernal]
counterpart. When Adam sinned, he did not deny the One
Name [i.e., God], because, although he saw the Tree of Life
in front of him, he thought that the Tree of Knowledge was
the essence of all things, and was attracted to it, because
good and evil comprise all the opposites, and according to
them are performed all the acts in both the supernal spheres
and the lower ones.

Adam was placed in the Garden to have pleasure and
delight at will. His sustenance came from the trees of the
Garden, his drink from the rivers of Eden, and his clothes

from the Clouds of Glory. His dwelling there was a great enjoyment, exceedingly great in the pleasure of the soul, and a little in the pleasure of the body, in repose, delight, and enjoyment, the like of which do not exist elsewhere, for they all are of the intellect. His soul and body were one in comprehending his Creator. And this is why God withheld from him the Tree of Knowledge which causes inclination towards the desires, but the Tree of Life which gives eternal life was at first not withheld from him. But after he sinned and ate of the Tree of Knowledge, that act caused him to be attracted to desires and to be occupied with the needs of the body more than with the needs of the soul, as we all are to this day. And he caused that which he desired to be removed from him, and thus he brought it upon himself that his days be shortened and that death have power over him.

(Baḥya ben Asher, Biur 'al haTora 1:67-69)

The Reward of Midnight Study

At midnight, when the cocks awaken, the North Side is stirred up by the winds. Up rises the scepter which is on the South Side, and strikes that wind, whereupon it subsides and becomes fragrant.[6]

Then the Holy One, blessed be He, rises, as is His wont, to play with the righteous in the Garden of Eden in that hour. Happy is the share of the man who rises to play with the Tora, for the Holy One, blessed be He, and all the righteous in the Garden of Eden, all of them listen to his voice. And more than that: The Holy One, blessed be He, draws over him a thread of grace to be protection for him in this world so that those above and those below protect him.

R. Ḥizqiya said: "Whosoever studies the Tora in that hour surely has a permanent share in the World to Come." R. Yose said: "What does it mean 'permanent'?" He said to

---

[6] I.e., the good South Side overcomes the evil North Side.

him: "This is how I have learned: Every midnight, when the Holy One, blessed be He, awakens in the Garden of Eden, all the plants of the Garden are watered more abundantly from that stream which is called the Primeval Stream, the Stream of Delights, whose waters have never ceased to flow. He who stands and studies the Tora, that stream, as it were, is poured over his head and waters him together with those plants which are in the Garden of Eden. And more than that: Since all the righteous who are in the Garden of Eden listen to him, he has an equal share in the waters of that stream. Thus he is found to have a permanent share in the World to Come."

(Zohar 1:92a-b)

God Plays with the Righteous

R. Yitzḥaq said: "It is written, *A river went forth from Eden to water the Garden* (Gen. 2:10). This is the support on which the world stands, and it waters the Garden, and the Garden is watered from it, and from it it bears fruits. And all the fruits blossom in the world and they are the maintenance of the world, the maintenance of the Tora. And what are they? The souls of the righteous, which are the fruit of the work of the Holy One, blessed be He. Therefore, every night the souls of the righteous go forth, and when the night divides[7] the Holy One, blessed be He, comes to the Garden of Eden to play with (or: delight in) them." With whom? R. Yose said: "With all of them, whether their dwelling place is in that world, or their dwelling is in this world, with all of them the Holy One, blessed be He, plays at midnight."

Come, see: The Supernal World needs to be aroused by the Lower World. And when the souls of the righteous issue forth from this world and go up on high, they all clothe themselves in supernal light, in the image of glory, and with them the Holy One, blessed be He, plays and He desires

---

[7] I.e., at midnight.

them, for they are the fruit of His work. And this is why Israel, who have holy souls, are called sons to the Holy One, blessed be He, as it is written, *Ye are sons to the Lord your God* (Deut. 14:1)—sons, truly the fruit of His work.

R. Yesa said: "Even with those who are in this world? How?" He said to him: "At midnight all those who are righteous in truth, all of them arise to read in the Tora and to sound the praises of the Tora. And this is what has been taught: The Holy One, blessed be He, and all those righteous who are in the Garden of Eden, all of them listen to their voices, and a thread of grace is drawn over them by day, as it is written, *By day the Lord commandeth His grace, and by night His song is with me* (Ps. 42:9). Hence praises which rise up at night before Him are the perfect praises."

(Zohar 1:82b)

DEATH AND PUNISHMENT

When the Soul Departs

When the Left awoke at the time of Creation, a strife arose, and in that strife the fire of wrath became strong, and from that strife emerged Gehenna, and Gehenna arose in the Left and adheres to it. The wisdom of Moses pondered this and observed the work of Creation. In the work of Creation there was a strife of the Left against the Right, and in that strife in which the Left arose Gehenna emerged, and the Pillar of the Middle, which is the Third Day, adhered to it, rose up between them, and separated the strife and brought harmony between the two sides. And Gehenna descended down below, and the Left became included in the Right, and there was peace everywhere.

(Zohar 1:17a)

When a man departs from this world, if he was virtuous his soul leaves and is crowned in its place. And if not, many destructive gatekeepers are prepared to drag him down into Gehenna and to deliver him into the hands of Duma, to be surrendered to the overseer of Gehenna. And with him are twelve thousand myriads of attendants, and they all are appointed over the souls of the guilty.

Come and see: There are seven compartments in Gehenna and seven entrances, and the souls of the guilty come there, and many pure gatekeepers watch over the gates, and at every gate there is one overseer over them. And the souls of the guilty are delivered to those attendants by Duma. And when they are delivered into their hands, they close the gates of the flaming fire. For there are gates behind gates, and all gates open and then close: Those on the outside open, and those on the inside close. And on every Sabbath they all open, and the guilty come up to those outer gates, and there they meet other souls which tarry at the outer gates. When the Sabbath goes out, a herald stands at every entrance and says: *The wicked shall return to Sheol* (Ps. 9:18).

(Zohar 1:237b)

The Angel of Death

All the dead of the world die through an angel of destruction, except for those who die in the Holy Land. And all of them die through an angel of destruction who is the Angel of Death; but those who die in the Holy Land do not die through him but through an angel of mercy who rules in the Land. And Moses and Aaron and Miriam died outside the Holy Land but still died through the Holy One, blessed be He.

(Zohar 2:151b)

The red color is Gabriel. He is the one who destroyed Sodom, he is of the left side. He is appointed over all the judgments of the world from the left side, to be executed by the Angel of Death, who is the master of slaying the house of the king. And all of them carry out their tasks. The angel Gabriel has the task of taking the holy soul, and the Angel of Death has the task of taking the soul with the Evil Inclination. However, the holy soul does not leave the body until it sees the Shekhina.

(Sitre Tora, Zohar 1:99a)

R. Y'huda said: "*Have the gates of death been revealed to thee? Or hast thou seen the gates of the shadow of death?* (Job 38:17). This verse was addressed by the Holy One, blessed be He, to Job when He saw that Job was distressed over the justice of the Holy One, blessed be He. The Holy One, blessed be He, said to him: 'Am I the one who slays the children of men? Many gates are open on the left side, and Death rules over them, and all of them are hidden from the children of men who do not know those gates.' Death and the Shadow of Death are together, and they are one couple. Death, as it has been said, is the Angel of Death, and it has been explained. The Shadow of Death is he who rides him [Samael]; and he is his shadow and his strength, and they couple and become one, in one union."

(Zohar 1:160b)

Death and Judgment

It has been taught: On that stern and frightful day when a man's time comes to depart from the world, the four quarters of the world stand in stern judgment, and judgments are stirred up from the four quarters of the world. And the four elements [which are in the body of man] begin to strive, and quarrel breaks out among them, and each of them wants to depart to its own quarter. And a herald goes out and proclaims in that world, and he is heard in 270 worlds. If the man is worthy, all the worlds rejoice over his coming, and if not, woe to that man and woe to his share!

It has been taught: At that time, when the herald

proclaims, a flame comes forth from the north side and goes and burns in the River of Fire, then divides toward the four quarters of the world, and consumes the souls of the guilty. That flame goes up and down in the world, and then that flame alights on the wings of a black cock, which flaps its wings, and crows at the door between the gates.

It has been taught: In the hour when the soul of a man departs, all his relatives and friends from the Other World go with his soul and show it the place of delight and the place of punishment. If he was worthy, he sees his place, and enters, and sits down, and enjoys the supernal delights of that world; and if he was not worthy, the soul remains in this world until the body is interred in the earth. When it is interred, many executors of the law [i.e., angels of destruction] take hold of him until he reaches Duma [the Nether World], and they deposit him in his dwelling place in Gehenna.

(Zohar 1:218b)

Come and see: For seven days the soul goes from the house to the grave and from the grave to the house, and mourns over the body. And three times every day the soul and the body are chastised together, and nobody in the world knows it or pays attention to it to arouse the heart. Thereafter the body is banished and the soul goes and is cleansed in Gehenna, and comes out and flies about in the world and visits its grave until it clothes itself into whatever it clothes itself. After twelve months all is at rest: the body has sunk into the dust, and the soul has been gathered and lighted up in the spirit in the garment in which it is clothed.

(Zohar 1:226b)

R. Y'huda said: "Why are the sinners punished with the fire of Gehenna? Because Gehenna is fire which burns day and night, just like the sinners who are heated up with the fire of the Evil Inclination to transgress the commandments of the Tora. Each time they get heated up with the Evil

Inclination the fire of Gehenna burns higher. One time the Evil Inclination was not found in the world because it was subdued with an iron signet ring and thrown into the hole of the Great Tehom [abyss]. And throughout that time the fire of Gehenna remained extinguished and did not burn at all. When the Evil Inclination returned to its place and the sinners of the world rose to warm themselves by it, the fire of Gehenna rose again and burned, for Gehenna does not burn except for the heat of the strength of the Evil Inclination of the sinners. And with that heat the fire of Gehenna burns day and night and subsides not."

(Zohar 2:150b)

The Souls of the Sinners

The sinners of the world who have not returned to their Master with a full repentance — naked did they come into this world and naked will they return there. And their souls go with longing towards other souls who have no clothes at all, and they are punished in Gehenna which is in the earth by that fire from above. And there are of them those who scream and go forth, and they are the sinners of the world who in their heart did think of repentance but died before they could repent. They are punished there in Gehenna, and then they scream and go forth. And the Holy One, blessed be He, has prepared for these sinners a place in the compartments of Sheol, and there they scream repentance, and that repentance comes before the Holy One, blessed be He, and breaks all the bolts of the gates of the compartments of Gehenna, and reaches that place of those sinners and kicks them, and that will to repentance is thus awakened in them as before, while they were still alive. And those souls scream wishing to escape the compartments of Sheol. And there is no good will which would be lost before the Holy King.

(Zohar 2:150a-b)

Sabbath in Gehenna

Every Sabbath eve, when the day becomes sanctified, heralds go out to all those compartments of Gehenna announcing: "Cease punishing the sinners, for the Holy King approaches and the Day is about to be sanctified, and He protects all!" Instantly the punishment ceases, and the guilty have a respite. But the fire of Gehenna does not let off from those who never observed the Sabbath. Since they had not observed the Sabbath there, therefore they have no respite forever. And an angel whose name is Santriel ["My Guardsman is God"] goes and fetches that body of the sinner and brings it to Gehenna before the eyes of the guilty, and they see how it has bred worms. The soul of such a sinner has no respite in the fire of Gehenna. And all those guilty who are there surround that body and proclaim over it: "This person is guilty, for he regarded not the honor of his Master, he denied the Holy One, blessed be He, and denied the whole Tora. Woe to him! It had been better for him not to be created and not to be subjected to this punishment and this disgrace!"

R. Y'huda said: "After the Sabbath goes out that angel comes and takes back that body to its grave, and both the body and the soul are punished, each in its own way."

And all this takes place while the body is still well preserved. But once the body is decayed, it no longer suffers all these punishments. While the body is intact in all its parts in the grave, both the body and soul are punished, each with a suitable punishment. But when the body disintegrates, the punishment of the soul ceases. He who can leave Gehenna leaves, and he who can find rest has rest. And he who must become ashes and dust under the feet of the pious turns to ashes and dust — to each one is done what is suitable for him.

(Zohar 2:251a)

Those who corrupted their ways on earth and did not consider the honor of their Master in this world, all of them

are punished there for uncounted generations and do not
come out of there on Sabbaths and New Moons, and festive
times and holidays. In that place the fire subsides and they
are not punished, but they do not come out of there like the
other guilty ones who have a respite. But all those who
desecrated the Sabbath and the festive times and considered
not at all the honor of their Master nor respected it but
desecrated it in public—just as they did not observe the
Sabbaths and festive times in this world, likewise those
times will not be observed for them in that world, and they
have no respite.

(Zohar 2:150b)

MYSTERIOUS WORLDS

The Path of the Sun

We have learned: R. Shim'on said: "Come and see: The sun
was not made by the Holy One, blessed be He, except to
serve the sons of man. Come, see: The sun goes in 390 places
of habitation on earth, and it goes up and down, and it has
definite grades and degrees."

R. Yose said to him: "How does it go up?" Rabbi said:
"We have learned from the masters of the Yeshiva that the
world is a wheel like a ball, and that the sun rises from the
east and goes in a circle until it comes down, and then it
becomes evening. And in that hour the sun goes and sets in
circles of definite grades, and sets and circles the whole
earth and the inhabited parts. And when it sets and
disappears from us, it becomes dark for us and it shines on
those who dwell under us according to the inhabited parts
and the roundness of the earth. And then it goes and sets,
and divides between the water which is under the ocean sea
and the water which goes up, and it divides in the middle
of the waters, in order to prevent the stream of water which
issues from Gehenna from crossing and harming the sons of

man. And this is why it is not called *Shimsha* [Sun], but *Shammasha* [Servant], because it is a servant of all men."

R. El'azar said to him: "If the sun would not swim in the ocean sea it would burn the whole world to ashes. It goes down under the inhabited earth and it touches that grade which is called *Karbisa* in the Greek language. And from that grade it begins to ascend, and the sound of its wheels is heard in all the firmaments in its journey as it goes with its song which it sings. And no man has ever existed who heard it except Moses, who was a confidant of the King, and Joshua, who was his attendant. For when Joshua needed the sun and heard the sound and the roar of the sun's song, he could not endure it. What is written? *Sun upon Gibeon dom [stand still]* (Josh. 10:12). What does *dom* mean? It means, 'Stop singing a song, stop the sound of your singing and roaring!' For he heard the sound of its journey."

R. Ba said: "The sun makes 640 journeys, as the numerical value of the letters of the word *shemesh* [sun], between the day and the night, and it circles the whole world round about, in order to soften and warm the earth and to make grasses and crops abundant and fruits and trees grow."

(Zohar Ḥadash 15a)

The Seven Worlds and Their Inhabitants

There are seven worlds, one above the other, just as there are seven firmaments one above the other. And they are: *Eretz, Adama, Arqa, Gay, N'shiyya, Tziyya, Tevel.*

Tevel [World] is above all of them. When Adam was expelled from the Garden of Eden, he was hurled from there to that one which is called *Eretz* [Earth]. And that is a dark place in which there is no light at all, and it serves no purpose. When Adam entered it he was frightened with a great fright, and the flame of the revolving sword was burning on all sides in *Eretz*. When the Sabbath came, and Adam thought of repentance, the Holy One, blessed be He, brought him out to the place called *Adama* [Soil]. Here there is light which shines, and the images of the stars and the constellations. And there is light there. And there are there the forms of tall men who issued from Adam in the 130 years in which he copulated with female spirits, and they are always sad, for there is no joy in them. And they roam about and go up to this world, and they are transformed here into the evil side,[8] and they return there, and say a prayer, and sit down in their places there, and they sow seeds and thresh and eat. And there is no wheat there, nor any of the seven kinds of field crops. In this place were born Cain and Abel.

When Cain sinned, the Holy One, blessed be He, exiled him to that place which is called *Eretz* from that place which is called *Adama*. And he said: *Whosoever findeth me will slay me* (Gen. 4:14) — this is that flame of the revolving sword. And he was afraid, and thought of repentance, and the Holy One, blessed be He, removed him to *Arqa* [Aramaic for "earth"]. And he was there and he begot children in *Arqa*. And in *Arqa* there is light from the light of the sun. And they sow seeds and plant trees, but there is no wheat there, nor any of those seven kinds of field crops. All those who are there are of the descendants of Cain, and they have two heads. Some of them are tall men and others are small, and there is no complete mind in them as in the other men here. At times they are pious and turn to the good side, and at times they turn to the evil side. And they beget and die like all other men. Adam was in *Adama* until he begot Seth, and from there he went up four levels and went to the place called *Tevel*. And this *Tevel* is higher than all the levels. When he came here he came to the place of the Temple which is called by the names of those places in which he dwelt. . . . Adam jumped over three places: *Gay, N'shiyya, Tziyya. Gay* [Valley] is a large place, and in it is the width and length of Gehenna. In *Gay* and *N'shiyya* and

---

[8] I.e., become evil spirits.

Tziyya are dispersed those who built the Tower [of Babel] and there they begot, because they angered the King of the World. Therefore it [*Gay*] is near the burning fire, and the people there are rich in every richness and dusts of gold and precious stones. He who enters there and becomes defiled [or: affected] by the desire for that riches, they give it to him. And at times he goes to the place which is called *N'shiyya* [Forgetfulness] because everything becomes forgotten there. And he goes to this *Gay* and knows not the place from which he came. This *Gay* is in the middle between Above and Below, and it is called *Gey Ben Hinnom* [i.e., Gehenna]. And a strap stretches from there up to *Tevel*, and here too it is called *Gey Ben Hinnom*, and there is the heat of Gehenna. The people who are there, they all know magic and precious wisdoms. And there they sow and plant trees, but there is no wheat there, nor any of the seven kinds. In *N'shiyya* there are people, all of whom are dwarfed and puny, and they have no noses but only two holes in which the wind goes in and out. And everything they do is instantly forgotten, and this is why it is called *N'shiyya*. And they sow and plant trees, but there is no wheat there, nor any of the seven kinds.

Tziyya [Parched Land] is a place like its name. There is dryness in it everywhere. And there are there people beautiful to look at. And since it is *Tziyya*, if a place with a source of flowing water becomes known to them they go there. And at times they come up from the place in which the waters come up to this *Tevel*. And they are more faithful than other people. And among them are five dwellings and great riches, and they sow a little because of the dryness which is there, and they plant trees and they do not succeed. And their desire is toward the people who live here. And of all of them there is none who eats bread as those who live here in *Tevel*.

Above all of them is *Tevel*. Something like all those worlds is in this *Tevel*, and all those names are here as well, because this is the seventh. There are here, like there, places of boundaries and places of walking, and each of them is called like that place below. And all those dwellings of people differ from one another, as it is written, *How manifold are Thy works, O Lord! In wisdom hast Thou made them all* (Ps. 104:24).

(Sitre Tora, Hashmatot, Zohar 1:253b-254a)

Another Version

The names of the order of the world are: *Eretz* [Earth], *Adama* [Soil], *Ḥarsa* [Clay], *Yabasha* [Dry Land], *Arqa* [Aramaic for "earth"], *Tevel* [World], *Ḥeled* [World]. And there are no human habitations in them, but there are demons. And there are 365 kinds of creatures in *Tevel.* Some of them with a head like a lion and a body like a man's ; some of them with a head like a man's and a body like a lion; and some of them with a head like a snake and a body like a man's; and some of them the other way round. And some of them have two heads and four hands and one body and one stomach and two legs. When they sit they are like one man. But when they eat and drink they are like two persons. And when they eat they [the two heads] quarrel among themselves, and say to each other: "You ate more than I, and you drank more than I!"

(Yalqut R'uveni, 1:6-7, quoting Azulai)

Cain in the Nether World

When Cain was cast out from the face of the earth, he descended into Arqa [one of the seven nether earths], and there begot offspring. And he became confounded there, for he knew nothing. And that earth consists of two parts: one of darkness and one of light. And there are there two chief rulers, one having dominion over the darkness, and one over the light, and they are accusing each other. But when Cain arrived, they made peace and joined together. . . . And their names are Afrira and Qastimon, and

their appearance is like that of holy angels with six wings.
One has the likeness of an ox, and the other that of an eagle.
And when they unite they appear in the likeness of a man.
When they are in darkness they turn into the likeness of a
two-headed serpent, crawl like a snake, then fly over the
abyss and swim in the great sea. And when they reach the
place in which are chained 'Uzza and 'Azael, the latter
become restless and excited, and leap unto the mountains of
darkness, and think that the Holy One, blessed be He, is
about to pass judgment on them. And those two chiefs
swim in the great sea, and then fly off into the night to
Naamah, the mother of demons, after whom went astray
the ancient saints. They want to approach her, but she leaps
away six thousand parasangs, and assumes many shapes in
the eyes of the sons of man so that they go astray after her.
Then the two chiefs fly and soar about in the world, and
return to their abode, and, with the spirit of evil instincts,
they arouse desires in the sons of Cain to beget children.

(Zohar 1:9b)

THE MATRONIT

The Black Matronit

In the hour when the Matronit adorns herself and wishes to
approach her Husband, and she adorns herself, and says to
her hosts: "*I am black* (Song 1:5) — from the side of the
Below, *and comely* (ibid.) — from the completion of the side
of the Above."

(Zohar Ḥadash, Shir, 138)

The Matronit Laments

At midnight the Matronit enters that point in Zion, the
place of the Holy of Holies. She sees that it has been
destroyed, and the place of the house of her dwelling and

her couch have been defiled. She cries and laments. She goes up and down, from the Above to the Below, and from the Below to the Above. She looks at the place of the Cherubim. She cries with a bitter voice and lifts up her voice and says: "My couch, my couch! O house of my dwelling! About this place it is written, *On my bed at night I sought Him whom my soul loveth, I sought Him but I found Him not* (Song 3:1). My bed, couch of the Matronit!" She keens and cries and says: "My couch! Place of my Temple! Place of fine pearls on the Curtain! Cover of the Holy Ark, which was studded with two thousand myriads of precious stones, row after row, line after line facing each other! Rows of pomegranates were arranged upon you on four sides. The world existed for your sake. In you the Master of the World, my Husband, would come to me, and lie between my arms, and everything I would ask of Him He would do. At this time He would come to me, put in me His dwelling, and play betwixt my breasts. My couch, my couch! Don't you remember how we would come to you in joy and with a happy heart, and those young maidens would come to meet me, beating their wings in joy to receive me? The dust in you would rise from its place! And see how the Ark of the Tora which was here has been forgotten! From here did nourishment go out to the whole world, and light and blessings to all. I am looking for my Husband, but He is not here. I am looking in every place! At this time my Husband would come to me, and around him many pious youths, and all those maidens[9] were ready to receive Him, and we would hear from afar the sound of a pair of bells tinkling on His feet so that I should hear His approach even before He came to me. All my maidens praised and hailed before the Holy One, blessed be He.

"Thereafter each went to the place of his seat, and we remained alone. We embraced with kisses of love. My

---

[9] This is one of the extremely few indications in the Kabbalistic literature of the existence of male and female angels.

Husband, my Husband! Where did you go? Now is the time when I would see You. I am looking in every place, but You are not here. Where shall I look for You, where shall I not search for You? This is Your place, this is the time for You to come to me. Behold I am here! Have You forgotten me? Don't You remember our days of love when we were lying in tight embrace and Your image impressed itself upon me, and my image impressed itself upon You, like this seal which leaves its impress upon a sheet of writing? Here I left my image upon You so that You play with my image while I am in the midst of my hosts."[10]

She bursts forth weeping and cries: "My Husband, my Husband! The light of my eyes has become dark! Don't you remember how You stretched forth Your arm under my head, and I enjoyed Your strength, and Your right arm embraced me in love and with kisses, and You vowed to me that You would never forsake my love, and said to me, *If I forget thee, O Jerusalem, let My right hand be forgotten* (Ps. 137:5)."

And the Holy One, blessed be He, calls her and goes down to her and talks to her. And about this it is written, *Thus saith the Lord: Refrain thy voice from weeping, and thy eyes from tears . . . for there is hope for thy future* (Jer. 31:16, 17).

(Zohar Ḥadash, p. 183)

The Motherly Matronit

When a man passes from this world to his world, he tarries in the Garden of Eden of below until his wife comes, and then they go up to the yeshiva of the firmament, and are crowned with the crown of the Holy One, blessed be He, surrounding the body of the Holy King. And the Matronit sits in the middle, and the pious and the righteous round

---

[10] According to Kabbalistic mythology, the hosts of heaven are entrusted to the Matronit; cf. Patai, *The Hebrew Goddess,* pp. 199-202.

about, and they suck from that central point which is the Shekhina, and she gives them from that point food, manna, of the dew and the overflow of heaven from above.

> (Sefer Tashaq, Ms. folio 40a; ed. by
> Jeremy Zwelling. By permission.)

THE LEGEND OF LILITH

The Birth of Lilith

Lilith is called Northerner, because *Out of the north the evil breaks forth* (Jer. 1:14). Both Samael, king of the demons, and Lilith were born in a spiritual birth androgynously. And Samael and Grandmother Lilith — she is the Northerner — for both of them the Tree of the Knowledge of Good and Evil is an epithet. And the sin of Adam caused it that both of them came and confused the whole world, the Upper one and the Nether one.

> (Moses ben Solomon of Burgos, ed. Scholem)

Samael resembles the form of Adam, and Lilith the form of Eve. Both were born in an androgynous form, corresponding to the form of Adam and Eve: below and above, two twin forms. And Samael and Grandmother Eve [i.e., Lilith], who is the Northerner, are emanations from beneath the Throne of Glory. And the sin [of Adam] caused this evil.

> (R. Ya'aqov and R. Yitzḥaq)

In the beginning the Holy One, blessed be He, created Eve, and she was not flesh but the scum of the earth and its impure sediments, and she was a harmful spirit [i.e., Lilith]. And the Holy One, blessed be He, took her away from Adam and gave him another in her stead.

> (Yalqut Reubeni, B'reshit 34b)

Lilith and Adam

When the letters of the name of Adam descended below, together in their completeness, the male and the female were found together, and the female was attached to his side, until God cast a deep slumber upon him, and he fell asleep. And he lay in the place of the Temple below. And the Holy One, blessed be He, sawed her off him, and adorned her as they adorn a bride, and brought her to him. . . . In an ancient book I found that this [refers to] the primeval Lilith who was with him and conceived from him, but was not a helpmeet for him. . . .

(Zohar 1:34b)

After the primeval light was hidden, a husk was created for the brain, and that husk spread out and brought forth another husk which was Lilith. And when she emerged, she went up and went down towards the little faces [i.e., children], and wanted to attach herself to them and be shaped after them, and did not want to depart from them. But the Holy One, blessed be He, removed her from there and placed her down below.

When He created Adam, in order to perfect this world, as soon as Lilith saw Eve affixed to the side of Adam, and saw in them the beauty of the Above, and saw their perfect image, she flew off from there and wanted, as before, to attach herself to the little faces. But the guardians of the gates of Above did not let her. The Holy One, blessed be He, rebuked her, and cast her into the depths of the sea, and she remained dwelling there until Adam and his wife sinned. Then the Holy One, blessed be He, brought her up from the depths of the sea and gave her power over all those children, the little faces of the sons of man, who are liable to punishment because of the sins of their fathers. And she went and roamed the world.

She approached the gates of Paradise on earth, and saw the Cherubim guarding the gates of Paradise, and sat down facing the Flaming Sword, for she originated from that flame. When that flame revolved, she fled. And she roams in the world, and finds children liable to punishment, and caresses them, and kills them. And all this is because of the diminishing of the moon which reduced its light. . . .

When Cain was born, she could not attach herself to him. But later she approached him and bore spirits and winged demons. For 130 years Adam had intercourse with female spirits, until Naamah came. Because of her beauty the sons of God went astray after her, 'Uzza and 'Azael, and she bore from them, and from her spread evil spirits and demons in the world.

(Zohar 1:19b)

Come and see: There is a female, a spirit of all spirits, and her name is Lilith, and she was at first with Adam. And in the hour when Adam was created and his body became completed, a thousand spirits from the left [evil] side clung to that body until the Holy One, blessed be He, shouted at them and drove them away. And Adam was lying, a body without a spirit, and his appearance was green, and all those spirits surrounded him.

In that hour a cloud descended and pushed away all those spirits.

And when Adam stood up, his female was attached to his side. And that holy spirit which was in him spread out to this side and that side, and grew here and there, and thus became complete. Thereafter the Holy One, blessed be He, sawed Adam into two, and made the female. And He brought her to Adam in her perfection like a bride to the canopy.

When Lilith saw this, she fled. And she is in the cities of the sea, and she is still trying to harm the sons of the world.

(Zohar 3:19a)

And the Serpent, the Woman of Harlotry, incited and seduced Eve through the husks of Light which in itself is holiness. And the Serpent seduced Holy Eve, and enough said for him who understands. And all this ruination came about because Adam the first man coupled with Eve while she was in her menstrual impurity — this is the filth and the impure seed of the Serpent who mounted Eve before Adam mounted her. Behold, here it is before you: because of the sins of Adam the first man all the things mentioned came into being. For Evil Lilith, when she saw the greatness of his corruption, became strong in her husks, and came to Adam against his will, and became hot from him, and bore from him many demons and spirits and Lilin.

(Bacharach, 'Emeq haMelekh 23c-d)

Lilith and Naamah

For 130 years Adam kept separate from his wife and did not beget. After Cain killed Abel, Adam did not want to copulate with his wife. Rabbi Yose said: "From the hour in which death was decreed upon him and upon the whole world, he said: 'Why should I beget children for terror?' and instantly separated from his wife."

And two female spirits [Lilith and Naamah] would come and copulate with him and bear children. And those whom they bore are the evil spirits of the world who are called Plagues of Mankind. And they lead the sons of man astray, and dwell in the doorway of the house, and in the cisterns and in the latrines. . . . But if the holy name Shaddai with supernal crowns is found in the doorway of a man's house, they all flee and go away from there.

And we have learned that in the hour in which man descended to earth in the supernal image, in the image of the Holy One, and the higher and lower beings saw him, they all approached him and proclaimed him king over this world. After the Serpent mounted Eve and injected filth into her, she gave birth to Cain. From thence descended all the wicked generations in the world. And the abode of demons and spirits is from there and from his side.

Therefore, all the spirits and demons have one half from man below, and the other half from the angels of the supernal realm.

Thereafter Adam begot on those spirits daughters who are like the beauty of those above and those below. And all went astray after them. And there was one male who came into the world from the spirit of Cain's side, and they called him Tubal-Cain. And a female came forth with him, and the creatures went astray after her, and her name was Naamah. From her issued other spirits and demons. And they hover in the air and tell things to those others found below. And this Tubal-Cain brought weapons of killing into the world. And this Naamah became aroused and adhered to her [evil] side. And to this day she exists, and her abode is among the waves of the great sea. And she comes forth, and makes sport with the sons of man, and becomes hot from them in the dream, in that desire which a man has, and she clings to him, and she takes the desire and from it she conceives and brings forth other kinds [of spirits] into the world. And those children whom she bears from the sons of man come to the women, and they conceive from them and bear spirits. And all of them go to Lilith the Ancient, and she rears them.

(Zohar 3:76b)

At times it happens that Naamah goes forth into the world to become hot from the sons of man, and a man finds himself in a connection of lust with her, and he awakens from his sleep and takes hold of his wife and lies with her. And this desire comes from that lust which he had in his dream. Then the child that he begets comes from the side of Naamah, for the man was driven by his lust for her. And when Lilith comes and sees that child, she knows what happened, and she ties herself to him and brings him up like all those other sons of Naamah. And she is with him many times, but does not kill him. This is the man who becomes blemished on every New Moon, for she never gives him up. For month after month, when the moon becomes renewed in the world, Lilith comes forth and visits all those whom she brings up, and makes sport with them, and therefore that person is blemished at that time.

(Zohar 3:77a)

Lilith and Blindragon

The Dragon Above is the Blind Prince who has the likeness of an intermediary groomsman between Samael and Lilith, and his name is *Tanin'iver*, Blindragon. And he is like a blind dragon . . . and it is he who brings about the adhesion and coupling between Samael and Lilith. Had he been created whole, in the completeness of his emanation, he would have destroyed the world in one minute.

(Moses Cordovero, *Pardes Rimmonim*, 186d)

And he [Blind Dragon] is castrated so that he cannot beget, lest [his offspring] annihilate the world.

(Bacharach, 'Emeq haMelekh, 121b)

Blind Dragon rides Lilith the Sinful — may she be extirpated quickly in our days, Amen! — And this Blind Dragon brings about the union between Samael and Lilith. And just as *the Dragon that is in the sea* (Isa. 27:1) has no eyes, likewise Blind Dragon that is above, in the likeness of a spiritual form, is without eyes, that is to say, without colors.

(Bacharach, 'Emeq haMelekh, 84b)

The Blind Dragon is between Samael and the Evil Lilith. And he brings about a union between them only in the hour of pestilence, the Merciful One save us! And he is castrated so that the eggs of the viper should not come forth into the world. For were it not so, they would annihilate the world.

And that kind which is called Lilin are full of hair from their heads down to their feet, but on their heads they have no hair, and all their body and face is full of hair. And this Lilith has fourteen evil times and evil names and evil factions. And all are ordained to kill the children — may we be saved! — and especially through the witches who are called *Kinder Benimmerins* in the language of Ashkenaz [Germany].

(Bacharach, 'Emeq haMelekh 140b)

Lilith and Her Competitors

Then came two women harlots to King Solomon. They were Lilith and Igrat. Lilith who strangles children because she cannot make of them a veil for herself to serve as a hiding place for her. And the second is Igrat. One night King David slept in the camp in the desert, and Igrat coupled with him in his dream. And he had emission, and she conceived and bore Adad [king of Edom]. When they asked him, "What is your name?" he said, "*Sh'mi Ad, Ad sh'mi* [My name is Ad, Ad is my name]," and they called him Ashm'dai. He is Ashmodai, king of the demons, who deprived Solomon of his kingship and sat on his throne, and therefore *he was of the seed of the king of Edom* (1 Kings 11:14), for he came from the side of the kingdom of evil. These two women strangled the son of the Shunamite woman....

All [the four queens of the demons, Lilith, Igrat, Mahalath and Naamah] and all their cohorts give birth to children, except Lilith alone, who does not bear, but is just a fornication in the world....

(School of the RaShBA)

And know that the kabbalists have written that the woman from the land of Egypt whom his mother took for Ishmael was the daughter of Kasdiel the Egyptian sorcerer. And when Ishmael divorced her, according to the instructions of his father [Abraham], as it is mentioned in the Pesiqta, she was pregnant. And she bore a daughter, and she was Mahalath daughter of Ishmael. And the mother and the

daughter participated in that desert in many sorceries. And
a spirit ruled over it, Igratiel by name. And that spirit was
attracted to Mahalath, who was very beautiful, until she
conceived from him and bore a daughter, and called her
name Igrat, after the name of the spirit. And thereafter
Mahalath became the wife of Esau, and she left the desert.
Not so her daughter Igrat, for she and Naamah and Lilith
and Nega' rule over the four *tequfot* [the two solstices and
the two equinoxes]. And they said that Lilith fornicates
with all men, and Naamah only with the Gentiles, and
Nega' only with Israel, and Igrat is sent out to do harm on
the nights preceding the Sabbaths and Wednesdays. And
behold, Lilith is *the scant measure that is abominable* (Mic.
6:10), which Igrat and Naamah carry to the Land of Shinar,
as Zechariah (5:11) said.[11] And about this it is said to the
fearers of God, *neither shall any plague (Nega') come nigh thy
tent* (Ps. 91:10).

(Meir Arama, Sefer Meir T'hillot, p. 91b)

Know that there are seventy heavenly patrons, one
appointed over each nation, and they all are under the rule
of Samael and Rahab. Rahab was given as his share all the
borders of Egypt, which measures 400 by 400 parasangs.
Samael was given four kingdoms, and in each of them he
has a concubine. The names of his concubines are: Lilith,
whom he took as his consort, and she is the first one; the
second is Naamah; the third, Even Maskit; and the fourth,
Igrat daughter of Mahalath. And the four kingdoms are:
first, the kingdom of Damascus, in which is found the
house of Rimmon; the second, the kingdom of Tyre, which
is opposite the land of Israel; the third, the kingdom of
Malta, which formerly was called Rhodos (?); and the
fourth, the kingdom called Granata [Granada], and some

---

[11] The author identifies the "two women" mentioned by Zechariah
with Igrat and Naamah, just as he identifies "Wickedness" with
Lilith.

say that it is the kingdom of Ishmael. And in each of these four kingdoms dwells one of the four aforementioned concubines.

(Nathan Nata Spira, *Tuv haAretz*, p. 19)

Lilith the Seducer

And she [Lilith] goes and roams the world at night, and makes sport with men and causes them to emit seed. And wherever men are found sleeping alone in a house, they [these spirits] descend upon them and get hold of them and adhere to them and take desire from them and bear from them. And they also afflict them with disease, and the men do not know it. And all this is because of the diminishing of the moon.

(Zohar 1:19b)

The male is called Samael, and his female is always comprised in him. Just as it is in the Side of Holiness, so it is in the Other [Evil] Side: male and female are contained in one another. The female of Samael is the Serpent, called Woman of Harlotry, End of All Flesh, End of the Days. The two evil spirits cling together as one. The male spirit is scattered, and the female spirit is spread out in many ways and paths, and she clings to that male spirit. She adorns herself with many jewels like a despicable harlot, and she stands at the crossroads and on the pathways to seduce the sons of man. The fool who comes near, she grabs him and kisses him, and pours for him wine of dregs, of the gall of vipers. As soon as he drinks it, he goes astray after her. When she sees that he has gone astray after her from the way of truth, she divests herself of all those ornaments which she has put on for that fool. Her ornaments for the seduction of the sons of man are: her hair is long and red like the rose, her cheeks are white and red, in her ears hang six ornaments, Egyptian cords dangle from her nape, all the jewels of the land of the east, her mouth is set like a narrow door comely in its decor, her tongue is sharp like a sword, her words are smooth like oil, her lips are beautiful, red like the rose, sweetened with all the sweetness of the world. She is dressed in scarlet and adorned with forty ornaments less one. That fool goes astray after her, and drinks from her cup of wine, and commits fornications with her, and goes astray after her. What does she [thereupon] do? She leaves him asleep on the couch, departs for the Above, denounces him, and takes permission, and descends. That fool awakens, and thinks to make sport with her as before, but she removes her ornaments from her, and turns into a menacing giant. She stands before him clothed in garments of flaming fire, inspiring terror and making his body and soul tremble. She is full of frightening eyes, a drawn sword is in her hand, and a bitter drop hangs from that sword. And she kills that fool and casts him into Gehenna.

Jacob went to her and came to her place, and saw all the ornaments of her house, but escaped from her. This enraged her male, Samael; he descended to attack Jacob, but could not prevail over him.

(Zohar, Sitre Tora, 1:148a-b)

And that spirit which is called Asirta becomes stirred up ... and goes to the female who is beneath all females. And she is Lilith the mother of demons. And a man may become stirred up by that evil spirit called Asirta, which attaches himself to that man and ties himself to him permanently. And on every New Moon that spirit of evil appearance becomes stirred up by Lilith, and at times that man suffers harm from the spirit, and falls to the ground and cannot get up, or even dies.

(Zohar 2:267b)

And behold, the harsh husk, that is Lilith, is always in the sheet of the bed of a man and a woman who copulate, in order to take the sparks of the drops of seed which go waste, because it cannot be without this, and she creates from them demons, spirits and Lilin. And there is an incantation to drive away Lilith from the bed and to bring forth holy souls, which is mentioned in the holy Zohar.

(Bacharach, 'Emeq haMelekh, 19c)

The remedy against Lilith is this: In that hour in which a man copulates with his wife, he should concentrate in his head on the holiness of his Master and say this:

> *O you who are wrapped in velvet,*
> *You have appeared!*
> *Release, release!*
> *Neither come nor go!*
> *Neither you nor yours!*
> *Go back, go back!*
> *The sea is raging,*
> *Its waves call you.*
> *I hold on to the Holy One,*
> *Wrap myself in the King's holiness.*

Then let him cover his head and his wife for one hour, and do thus each time for three days of the receiving. For a grafting which is not received within three days will not be received at all. But in the book which Ashmodai gave to King Solomon it says for thirty days, and it says that after he finished the act he should sprinkle clear water around the couch.

(Zohar 3:19a)

Lilith is a harlot who fornicates with men. She has no mating with her husband, for He [God] castrated the male and cooled the female. And she becomes hot from the fornication of men, through spontaneous emission. And enough of this.

Samael is called the Slant Serpent, and Lilith is called the Tortuous Serpent (Isa. 27:1). She seduces men to go in tortuous ways.

The Alien Woman is Lilith, and she is the sweetness of

sin and the evil tongue. And from the lips of the Alien Woman honey flows. And although the Impure Female has no hands and feet for copulation, for the feet of the serpent were cut off, nevertheless the Female in her adornments looks as if she had hands and feet. And it is the mystery of her adornments that she can seduce men.... And she leaves the husband of her youth [Samael] and descends and fornicates with men who sleep below in the impurity of spontaneous emission, and from them are born demons and spirits and Lilin, and they are called the Sons of Man.

(Bacharach, 'Emeq haMelekh, 84b, 84c, 102d-103a)

The Two Liliths

Grandmother Lilith the Great—Samael the great demon and great king over all demons has intercourse with her. And Ashmodai king of the demons has intercourse with Little Lilith.

The demon whose name is Qaftzefoni, on rare occasions, when permission is granted him, has intercourse with, and attaches himself to, and loves, a creature whose name is Lilidtha [Lilith], and she resembles Hagar the Egyptian.

A great jealousy sprang up between Samael the greatest prince of all and Ashmodai king of the demons over Lilith who is called Lilith the Maiden, and who has the form of a beautiful woman from the head to the navel, and from the navel down [she is] flaming fire. Like mother like daughter ... And there is no good intention in her but only to arouse wars and all kinds of destruction. And they are occupied with war, the war between Lilith the Daughter, and Grandmother Lilith.

(R. Ya'aqov and R. Yitzḥaq)

The ancient ones explained that there are two Liliths, one little and one great. The great one is the spouse of Samael, and she is a woman of harlotry, and the little one is the spouse of Ashmodai. And about this Lilith, the bride of Samael, the Geonim explained that she controls 480 legions as is the numerical value of her name. And on the Day of Atonement they go forth into the deserts, they march, and she screeches, for she is the princess of screeching. And Mahalath daughter of Ishmael, she too is a concubine of Samael, and the two [Lilith and Mahalath] go forth with 478 legions. She goes and sings in the Holy Tongue songs and paeans. And when the two meet on the Day of Atonement they quarrel there in the desert. They strive, the one with the other, until their voices rise up to heaven, and the earth shakes with their clamor. And all this is brought about by the Holy One, blessed be He, so that they should not accuse Israel while they [Israel] pray. And others wrote that that husk [i.e., demoness] is called Meshullahel [Messenger of God], and the reason is that she sends out evil angels, may the Merciful One destroy them! And we found it written that the wicked Samael and the evil Lilith have the likeness of a couple which, with the intermediacy of a groomsman, receives an emanation of evil and insolence, flowing from the one to the other. And about this mystery it is written, *And on that day the Lord with His sore and great and strong sword will punish Leviathan the Slant Serpent, and Leviathan the Tortuous Serpent, and He will slay the Dragon that is in the sea* (Isa. 27:1). Leviathan is the connection and coupling between the two who have the likeness of serpents. Therefore it is doubled: the Slant Serpent corresponding to Samael, and the Tortuous Serpent corresponding to Lilith.

(Moses Cordovero, *Pardes Rimmonim*, 186d)

Lilith the Queen

Lilith, the Queen of Zemargad, launched an attack and seized [the sons of Job] and killed the young men....

(Targum, Job 1:15)

Lilith the Destroyer

When the Holy One, blessed be He, will bring about the destruction of the wicked Rome, and turn it into a ruin for all eternity, He will send Lilith there, and let her dwell in that ruin, for she is the ruination of the world. And to this refers the verse, *And there shall repose Lilith and find her a place of rest* (Isa.34:14).

(Zohar 3:19a)

Lilith the Child Killer

And she [Lilith] goes out into the world and seeks her children. And she sees the sons of man and clings to them, in order to kill them, and to become absorbed into the souls of the children of the sons of man, and she goes off with that child. But three holy spirits arrive there and fly before her and take that child from her and place him before the Holy One, blessed be He, and there he studies before Him. Therefore the Tora warns, *Be sacred* (Lev. 19:2). If a man is holy, he is not harmed by her, for the Holy One, blessed be He, orders those three holy angels whom we have mentioned, and they guard that child, and she cannot harm him. But if a man is not holy, and draws a spirit from the impure side, then she comes and makes sport with that child, and when she kills him she penetrates that soul [which departs from the child] and never leaves it.

(Zohar 3:76b-77a)

This Lilith—the Merciful One save us!—has dominion over children who issue from a man who has intercourse at candlelight, or with his wife naked, or at times when he is forbidden to have intercourse. All those children who issue from these mentioned, Lilith can kill them any time she wants to, because they are delivered into her hand. And this is the secret of the children laughing in their sleep when they are small: it is from Lilith who plays with them. And I heard that when a small child laughs during the Sabbath night or the night of the New Moon, it is because Lilith is playing with him, and it is well that his father or mother or anyone who sees him laugh should tap his nose with his finger and say: "Go from here, you accursed one, for you have no resting place here!" Let him say this three times, and each time he recites this incantation let him tap the child's nose. And this is very good, for it is in the power of Lilith to kill them when she wants to. And since she has permission to kill these infants, these souls are called Oppressed Souls.

(Bacharach, 'Emeq haMelekh, 84b)

And the Kabbalists said that the prince who serves before her is called Sariel [My Prince is God], and they have received the tradition that this prince is the greatest king of the demons who rule in the air.

In the middle of the night of Yom Kippur [Day of Atonement], forced by the acts of the sages and elders, Sariel comes against his will, together with 131 warriors, flying in the air, and their faces are aflame with sparks of fire. And the scribe whose name is Pifiron brings, written and sealed by the hand of Sariel, all the secrets of the firmament, and reveals them to the elders.

And from the emanation of Lilith's prince come spirits and demons and Lilin, and evil spirits who have the likeness of humans.

And just as all that time that Adam was separated from Eve he begot spirits and demons and Lilin and all kinds of harmful spirits, likewise Above, so to speak, a spirit of spiritual seduction emerged from Lilith and brought accusations against the attribute of the Foundation of the World.[12] And from that time on alien and evil cohorts were born, destroyers of the world of Above and of Below. And the Holy Seed had no power to materialize, except in two or three persons such as Seth, Enoch, Metushelah, Noah, Sem, and Eber, but most of the world were idolaters.

(Yalqut R'uveni 147a)

---

[12] One of the divine attributes.

Lilith—God's Consort

One day the companions were walking with Rabbi Shim'on bar Yoḥai. Rabbi Shim'on said: "We see that all these nations have risen, and Israel is lower than all of them. Why is this? Because the King [God] sent away the Matronit from Him, and took the slave woman [Lilith] in her place. Who is this slave woman? The Alien Crown, whose firstborn the Holy One, blessed be He, killed in Egypt. At first she sat behind the handmill, and now this slave woman inherited the place of her mistress." And Rabbi Shim'on wept and said: "The King without the Matronit is not called king. The King who adhered to the slave woman, to the handmaid of the Matronit, where is His honor? He lost the Matronit and attached Himself to the place which is called slave woman. This slave woman was destined to rule over the Holy Land of below, as the Matronit formerly ruled over it. But the Holy One, blessed be He, will ultimately bring back the Matronit to her place as before. And then, what will be the rejoicing? Say, the rejoicing of the King and the rejoicing of the Matronit. The rejoicing of the King, because He will return to her and separate from the slave woman, and the rejoicing of the Matronit, because she will return to couple with the King.

(Zohar 3:69a)

Lilith's End

And know that Lilith too will be killed. For the groomsman [Blind Dragon] who was between her and her husband [Samael] will swallow a lethal potion at a future time, from the hands of the Prince of Power. For then, when he rises up, Gabriel and Michael will join forces to subdue and bring low the government of evil which will be in heaven and earth.

(Bacharach, 'Emeq haMelekh, 84d)

Lilith's Children

The Lilin multiply like humans, eat and drink and die. And
they are from the six earths which lie beneath us. And Lilith
came against the will of Adam and became hot from him.
And they [the inhabitants of *Adama*, the second from below
of the seven earths] are always sad, full of sorrow and sighs,
and there is no joy at all among them. And those cohorts
can fly up from there to this world on which we stand, and
they become harmful demons. And then they return there
and offer prayers to God, the Creator of the world....
                    (Bacharach, 'Emeq haMelekh, 179d-180a)

And they say that of the offspring of Ashmodai and Lilith
his wife was fashioned a great prince in heaven who rules
over eighty thousand destroyers and despoilers, and he is
called Sword of Ashmodai the King. And his face flames
like the fire of flame.
                              (R. Ya'aqov and R. Yitzḥaq)

MYSTERIES IN HISTORY

The Book of Raziel

When Adam was in the Garden of Eden, the Holy One,
blessed be He, sent down to him a book by the hand of
Raziel the holy angel, who is in charge of the supernal holy
mysteries. And in it were inscribed supernal inscriptions
and sacred wisdom. And seventy-two kinds of wisdom were
explained from it,[13] [branching out] into 670 inscriptions of
supernal mysteries. In the middle of the book there was an
inscription of wisdom to reveal the 1,500 keys which were
not delivered to the supernal holy ones [the angels], and all
of them were hidden in the book, until it reached Adam.

---

[13] I.e., the mysteries of the seventy-two-letter name of God.

When it reached Adam, the supernal angels·gathered in order to learn and to hear, and they said, *Be thou exalted, O God, above the heavens, Thy glory be above the earth* (Ps. 57:6).

In that hour a sign was given to the holy angel Hadarniel, and he said to him: "Adam, Adam! Hide the glory of your Master, for no permission has been given to the Supernals to know the glory of your Master except to you." And that book was hidden and secreted with Adam until he went out from the Garden of Eden. And at the beginning he studied it and every day used that treasure of his Master, and supernal mysteries became revealed to him, which were not known to the supernal servants. When he sinned and transgressed the command of his Master, that book flew away from him, and Adam beat his head and cried, and entered the waters of Gihon up to his neck, and the water made his body full of mold and mildew, and his splendor changed.

In that hour the Holy One, blessed be He, signaled to Raphael, and he returned to him that book, and Adam pored over it. And he left it to his son Seth, and thus to all his descendants, until it reached Abraham, and from it Abraham learned how to gaze at the glory of his Master. And thus also to Enoch was given a book, with which he gazed at the supernal glory.

(Zohar 1:55b)

Adam Confronts the Dying

God decreed death upon Adam but He took pity on him, and buried him, in the hour in which he died, near the Garden. What did Adam do? He made a cave and hid himself in it, he and his wife. Whence did Adam know [that that cave was near the Garden]? He saw a faint light issue from that place, which came from the Garden of Eden, and felt a great desire to be buried there. And that was a place near the gate of the Garden of Eden.

Come, see: When a man departs from the world he sees

Adam the first man, who asks him why did he leave the world and how did he die. And the man answers him: "Woe, it is because of you I had to leave the world." And Adam responds: "My son, I transgressed one commandment and was punished for it. See how many duties and prohibitions of your Master have you transgressed!"

(Zohar 1:57b)

Who Was Cain's Father?

R. Ḥiyya said: "The sons of God were the sons of Cain. For when Samael mounted Eve, he injected filth into her, and she conceived and bare Cain. And his aspect was unlike that of the other humans, and all those who came from his side were called sons of God."

(Zohar 1:37a)

The Demonic Brood of Adam and Eve

R. Yitzḥaq said: From the hour in which Cain killed Abel, Adam separated himself from his wife, [and] two female spirits came and copulated with him, and he begot spirits and demons which roam in the world. And this should not be difficult for you [to understand], for when a man dreams, female spirits come and play with him and get hot from him and thereafter bear [those demons] which are called the Plagues of Mankind. And they turn into a likeness of men, but they have no hair on their head. . . . And in a similar manner male spirits come to the women of this world who become pregnant from them and give birth to spirits, and all of them are called Plagues of Mankind. After 130 years Adam clothed himself in zeal and had union with his wife and begot a son and called his name Seth.

(Zohar 1:54b-55a)

The Magicians' Downfall

R. El'azar said: "In the days of Enosh men were knowledgeable in the art of magic and sorcery, and in the knowledge of restraining the hosts of heaven. And from the day when Adam came out from the Garden of Eden and brought out with him the knowledge of tree leaves, there was nobody who would have used it, for Adam, his wife, and those who issued from him, all refrained from it until Enosh came. When Enosh came, he saw them and saw their skills which can change the supernals. And they[14] utilized them and performed with them magic and sorcery, and they studied them, until that knowledge spread to the generation of the Deluge, and all of them practiced it for evil. And they fortified themselves with those skills to oppose Noah, and said that the punishment of the world could not descend upon them, for they would use that skill to repel all the masters of punishment.[15] And from Enosh they all were permitted to utilize those skills." R. Yitzḥaq said: "All the righteous who were among them thereafter, in that generation, such as Jered, Methuselah, and Enoch, endeavored to oppose them, but they could not prevail, until the sinful spread out, rebelled against their Master, and said, *What is the Almighty that we should serve Him?* (Job 21:15). Can it be that they said such a foolish thing? Since they knew all those magic arts and all those who were appointed over the world and in command of them, they relied on this—until the Holy One, blessed be He, returned the world to morsels. In the beginning the world was water in water, and He returned it to that primordial state. But it was not completely destroyed, for He in His mercy looked upon it.

"In the days of Enosh even the small children of that

---

[14] I.e., Enosh and his generation.

[15] I.e., the divine forces, such as the angels of destruction, who mete out punishment.

generation all were knowledgeable in the supernal art and all were looking at it."

R. Yesa said: "If so, they were foolish that they did not know that the Holy One, blessed be He, had decided to bring the Deluge upon them and that they would perish in it." R. Yitzḥaq said: "They surely knew it, but they clung to the foolishness in their hearts for they knew that this angel was in charge of fire and that angel was in charge of water, and they thought that they knew how to prevent them so that they should not be able to carry out the punishment upon them. But they did not know that the Holy One, blessed be He, rules the earth, and that from Him issues the punishment of the world. They saw that the world was entrusted to the hands of those celestial officers, and that all the affairs of the world depended on them, and because of this they were not looking to the Holy One, blessed be He, and were not paying attention to His works until the earth was destroyed, although the Holy Spirit proclaimed every day and said: *Let the sinners be consumed out of the earth and let the wicked be no more* (Ps. 104:35). And the Holy One, blessed be He, postponed their punishment while those righteous men, Jered, Methuselah, and Enoch, were alive. But when they departed from the world, the Holy One, blessed be He, let the punishment descend upon them and they perished.

(Zohar 1:56a-b)

The Fallen Angels

Among the demons are those who have the form of he-goats, and of them are those that serve as mounts for 'Uzza and 'Azael. These two alone have a really human form, and when they fell down from heaven they were influenced by the power of the air which is over us, and assumed bodily form like that of men. And the supernal power that had been in them grew weak, and they were engulfed by the power from below. But the offspring which issued from

them was tall of stature, with a superior figure and greater
strength than all children of men.

(R. Ya'aqov and R. Yitzḥaq)

When the Shekhina said to the Holy One, blessed be He,
"Let us make man," 'Uzza and 'Azael said: "What is man
that you should know him? Why do You wish to create
man when You know that he will sin before You with his
woman who is darkness, for light is male and darkness
female, and darkness is the left [i.e., evil] side of creation?"
Thereupon the Shekhina said to them: "The very thing of
which you accuse man will cause your downfall...." They
desired the daughters of man, went astray after them, and
the Shekhina cast them down from their holiness.

The companions said: "Is it not that 'Uzza and 'Azael
were not lying in what they said, for it was certainly
through woman that Adam was destined to sin?" He said to
them: "This is what the Shekhina said: 'You, more than the
rest of the heavenly host, have taken occasion to accuse
man. Only if you were better in your acts than man would it
behoove you to accuse him. But he will sin with one woman
only, while you will sin with many, for your concupiscence
is stronger than that of man.... And more than that: when
man sins, he will repent, return to his Master, and repair his
guilt [while you will persist in your sin].'"

R. Shim'on said: "Had God not created the Good
Inclination and the Evil Inclination, which are light and
darkness, the human creature would have had neither merit
nor guilt. But since he has been created with both, it is
written, *See, I have set before thee today life and death* (Deut.
30:19)."

(Zohar 1:23a)

As soon as *the sons of God saw the daughters of man* they
desired them, and the Holy One, blessed be He, cast them
down. They were 'Uzza and 'Azael, from whom were
derived the souls of the "mixed multitude." They are the

Nefilim [Fallen Ones], for they fell into fornication with women who were beautiful. And because of that the Holy One, blessed be He, cast them down from the World to Come, so that they have no share in it, and gave them their deserts in This World.

(Zohar 1:25a-b)

When the Holy One, blessed be He, saw that the fallen angels had led the world astray, He bound them in chains of iron to the mountains of darkness. He cast 'Uzza in the depth of the mountains, and covered his face with darkness, because he struggled and rebelled against [Him who dwells] On High.... However, 'Azael, who did not struggle, He placed on the side of the mountain and lighted up the darkness for him.

Men who know the places [of these fallen angels] come to them, and are instructed by them in enchantment and sorcery and magic. Those mountains of darkness are called "Mountains of Yore" because darkness preceded light.... And Laban and Balaam learned sorcery from them.... And 'Uzza and 'Azael would tell the men [who come to them] of the supernal things which they knew of old on high, and would speak to them of the holy world in which they used to dwell....

(Zohar 3:208a)

When a man goes to them, as soon as he reaches the peak of the mountain 'Azael, who is called "open of eye," sees him. 'Azael then tells 'Uzza, and they call out, whereupon great fiery beasts gather and surround them. And they send a small *unima*—an animal like a cat with the head of a serpent and with two tails and with small hands and feet—to meet the man. When he sees it, he covers his face [in terror. But] he brings with him some ashes from the burning of a white cock, and throws them in its face, whereupon the *unima* [is tamed and] comes with him. Thus he can reach the top of the chain which is stuck in the ground and extends to the abyss. And there in the abyss there is a bolt which is fastened into the lowest abyss, and the end of the chain is attached to it. When the man reaches the top end of the chain he kicks it three times, whereupon 'Uzza and 'Azael call him. And he falls on his knees and closes his eyes until he reaches them. Then he sits down before them, and all those animals surround him from all sides. He opens his eyes and sees them and trembles, and falls on his face and prostrates himself before them. Thereafter they teach him sorcery and magic, and he stays with them fifty days. When the time comes for him to go his way, the *unima* and all those beasts go before him, until he emerges from the mountains and from that dense darkness.

(Zohar 3:212a-b)

The Tower of Babel

R. Abba said: "They had folly in their hearts, but they also came with an evil scheme to move away from the supernal authority to another authority, and to exchange His glory for a strange glory. And in all this there is a supernal mystery of wisdom. . . ."

The builders of the tower were the descendants of the primeval Adam who rebelled against his Master and brought death into the world.

(Zohar 1:75a)

"City and tower" refer to supernal wisdom. For they knew that the Holy Name cannot be attacked on earth except with a "city and tower." . . . And they acted with wisdom to establish on earth the rule of the Other Side [i.e., Satan] whom the Lord of all the earth had driven away from his place, and to make a dwelling place for the Other Side on earth. . . .

The builders of the tower spoke in the Holy Tongue to all the holy hosts, and thus succeeded. When the Holiness descended, all those hosts became confounded, the higher ones went down, and the lower ones departed.

(Sitre Tora, Zohar 1:74b, 75a)

Why was their language confounded? While all of them spoke the Holy Tongue, that tongue was of great help to them; in both act and word of mouth it helped them to attain what their hearts intended, and thus it facilitated the building of that place as they wanted. This is why their language was confounded, so that they should be unable to attain their wish by speaking the Holy Tongue. When their language was changed, they could no longer succeed in their work, for the supernal hosts can speak and understand only the Holy Tongue. Thus when their language was confounded their power was weakened and their strength broken. Come and see: a word uttered by those below in the Holy Tongue is heard and listened to by the hosts of heaven, but no other language is known and understood by them.

(Zohar 1:75b)

Since they were of one mind and spoke the Holy Tongue, it said of them *nothing will be withholden from them which they propose to do* and the supernal jurisdiction had no power over them. If so, how much more must this apply to us or to fellow students who occupy themselves with the Tora, and are of one heart and one mind. R. Yose said: "From this we learn that those who are quarrelsome cannot survive: for as long as those people were of one mind and one heart, even though they rebelled against the Holy One, blessed be He, the supernal jurisdiction had no power over them, but as soon as they were divided, *the Lord scattered them abroad.*"

(Zohar 1:76b)

In Gay, N'shiyya, and Tziyya [the fourth, fifth, and sixth of the seven nether earths] are scattered those who built the tower, and there they begot offspring, because they angered the supernal Holy King.

(Zohar Ḥadash, Gen., p. 9b)

R. Ḥiyya began and said: "Come and see: It is written, *As they journeyed east* (*miqedem*). What does *miqedem* mean? Away from the Ancient One [*Qadmon*, i.e., God] of the world.... And they found there [a remnant] of the mysteries of the wisdom of the ancients which was left there by the generation of the Deluge, and it was that which they used to accomplish their work of rebellion against the Holy One, blessed be He."

(Zohar 1:76b)

The Cave of Machpelah

R. Y'huda said: "Abraham knew a sign in that cave, and his heart and his wish were there. Because a long time prior to that he entered the cave and saw Adam and Eve hidden there. And how did he know who they were? Because he saw Adam's visage and gazed at it, and a gate of the Garden of Eden opened for him there, and before it stood that image of Adam. And come, see: whoever looks at the image of Adam can never be saved from death. For in the hour when a man departs from the world he sees Adam and in that hour he dies. But Abraham looked at him and saw his image and remained alive. And he saw a light which shone in the cave, and a lamp burning. Therefore Abraham desired that his dwelling be in that place, and his heart and his wish were always in the cave."

R. El'azar said: "In the hour in which Abraham entered the cave, how did he enter? Because he was running after that calf about which it is written, *And Abraham ran unto the herd and fetched a calf* (Gen. 18:7). And that calf fled until that cave and entered it and then Abraham saw what he saw. Moreover, while he was praying day after day, he went until that field which emitted supernal scents, and he saw light issuing from the cave, and he prayed there. And there the Holy One, blessed be He, spoke to him, and therefore he asked for it, for his desire was always directed towards that place.

Come, see: Had Ephron seen in the cave what Abraham saw in it, he would never have sold it to him. But he certainly saw nothing in it, for it was a thing which was not revealed except to its master.[16]

And come, see: When Abraham entered the cave for the first time, he saw there a light. And the dust raised itself up before him and two graves were revealed to him. While this happened Adam emerged in his image, and saw Abraham and smiled, and thereby Abraham knew that he was destined to be buried there. Abraham said to him: "I beg of you, is there a grave prepared for me here?" He said to him: "The Holy One, blessed be He, had hidden me here, and from that time to the present I had been hidden like a blade of grass until you have come. Now, from now on, there is preservation for me and for the world for your sake."

(Zohar 1:127a-128a)

At the Red Sea

R. Shim'on said: In that hour when Israel were standing at the sea and singing the Song, the Holy One, blessed be He, appeared to them with all His chariots and hosts so that they should know their King who performed for them all those miracles and mighty works. And each one of them knew and saw that which all the prophets of the world could not know and see. For should you say that they did not know and did not attain supernal wisdom, from this very Song you can see that all of them saw in wisdom and knew words and sang them. For were it not so, how could all of them have sung all the words in unison, without varying the one from the other, so that what this one sang that one too sang, without putting one word ahead of the other? All of them sang in one measure, and the Holy Spirit was in the mouth of each of them, and the words were said as if they had issued from one single mouth. Thus surely all of them

---

[16] I.e., to the person to whom it pertains.

saw in supernal wisdom and knew supernal words, and the Holy Spirit was in the mouth of each one of them. And even those who were in their mothers' wombs sang the song as one, and all of them saw what not even the prophet Ezekiel saw. And all of them beheld it as if they saw it eye to eye.

And when they finished the Song, all were intoxicated in their souls and desired to see and behold, and refused to depart from there because of the strength of their desire. In that hour Moses said to the Holy One, blessed be He: "Your children have an overwhelming desire to see You, and refuse to depart from the sea." What did the Holy One, blessed be He, do? He hid His Glory, outside, in the desert, and there revealed it, although not completely. Moses said to Israel: "How many times have I told you to depart, and you refused! Finally, I showed you the Glory of the Holy One, blessed be He, in the desert." Instantly they were seized with desire [and went towards it]. And they did not depart until Moses seized them and showed them the splendor of the glory of the Holy One, blessed be He, in the desert. Then, because of their overwhelming desire and wish to see it, Moses was able to take them, as it is written, *And Moses led Israel onward from the Red Sea and they went out into the wilderness of Shur* (Exod. 15:22). What does the Desert of Shur mean? The desert in which they wanted to see (*shur*) the splendor of the glory of the Holy King.

(Zohar 2:60a)

The Threat of a New Deluge

Come, see: In that hour when Moses broke the Tablets, as it is written, *And he broke them beneath the mount* (Exod. 32:19), the ocean overflowed from its place and went to flood the world. Moses saw that the ocean was coming towards him and was about to flood the world. Instantly *He took the calf which they had made, and burnt it with fire, and ground it to powder, and strewed it upon the water* (Exod. 32:20). Moses rose, faced the waters of the ocean, and said: "Waters, waters, what do you want?" They said: "Is it not that the world exists only because of the Tora of the Tablets, the Tora which Israel has denied. And since they worshiped the golden calf, we want to flood the world." Instantly he said to them: "Lo, everything they did in their sin with the calf is herewith delivered unto you. Is it not enough that thousands of them have fallen?" Instantly, *And he strewed it upon the water*. But the waters did not subside until he took some of the water and made Israel drink it. Thereupon the ocean subsided and returned to its place.

(Zohar 2:113b)

Solomon and The Eagle

A great eagle would come to Solomon every day, and the king would ride on its wings, and it would take him four hundred parasangs in one single hour. Where would it take him? To Tarmod in the desert, in the mountains. There is a place in the mountains of darkness called Tarmod in the desert—and it is not the place of the Tarmodeans [i.e. Palmyra], but Tarmod which is in the desert in the mountains, and there gather all the spirits and devils. And that eagle flies there in one hour, and when it reaches that place it hovers high above it. And Solomon, who has written an amulet, throws it down, and is thus saved from those spirits. And the eagle looks at the darkness of the mountains, at the place where 'Uzza and 'Azael are bound in iron chains fastened into the abyss. Nobody in the world can go there, not even the fowl of the sky, except Balaam. And when the eagle sees the great darkness, it swoops down, and, sheltering King Solomon under its left wing, covers him, and alights upon those chains, and goes and approaches them. And Solomon takes out a signet ring upon which is engraved the Holy Name, and puts it into the mouth of the eagle. Thereupon 'Uzza and 'Azael tell him everything he asks them. It is thence that Solomon knew the supernal wisdom.

(Zohar 3:233a-b)

Jonah in the Whale

R. Y'huda began and said: "*The Lord had prepared a great fish to swallow up Jonah* (Jonah 3:1). That fish was prepared for Jonah to protect him from the rest of the fishes of the sea and to be hidden inside it. When he entered it, Jonah saw from its bowels the whole length and breadth of the sea, like unto a great palace. And the two eyes of that fish were shining like the sun. And a precious stone was in its bowels which gave light for him, and he saw everything that was in the sea and in the abyss. When the fish showed him all that was in the sea and in the abyss, it died, for it could not suffer three days.[17] Then it became an affliction to Jonah."

R. El'azar said: "When Jonah saw all that ease, he rejoiced, whereupon the Holy One, blessed be He, said: 'Is it for this that I brought you here?' What did he do? He killed the fish. When it died, all the other fish of the sea surrounded it. Some bit it from this side, others bit it from that side. When Jonah saw himself in bad straits, instantly he prayed to God. When he prayed his prayer, the Holy One, blessed be He, accepted it, and resuscitated the fish, and it vomited out Jonah to the dry land before the eyes of all. And all saw the works of the Holy One, blessed be He."

(Zohar 2:47b-48a)

SAGES AND SAINTS

To Save a Soul

A poor man lived in the neighborhood of R. Yesa, and nobody paid any attention to him. And he was bashful and did not importune people. One day he fell ill. R. Yesa went to visit him. He heard a voice which said: "Wheel, wheel! Lo, a soul is flying to me, and its day has not yet come! Woe

---

[17] The fish was unable to suffer the presence of Jonah in his bowels for more than three days.

to the people of the place that none is found among them who would make his soul return into him!" R. Yesa got up, and sprinkled an infusion of herbs[18] and spiced wine into his mouth, whereupon sweat broke out on his face and his soul returned into him.

Subsequently R. Yesa [again] came and asked him [how he was]. He said to him: "By your life, Rabbi, the soul had gone out of me, and they brought her before the Throne of the King, and she wanted to be left there. But the Holy One, blessed be He, wanted you to acquire merits, and they proclaimed about you, 'R. Yesa is destined to bring up his soul and to be bound together in one holy place which is destined for the companions when they awaken on earth.' And they prepared three thrones which await you and your friends."

From that day on the people of the place paid attention to him.

Another poor man once came to R. Yitzḥaq who had in his possession only half a silver coin. He said to R. Yitzḥaq: "Save my soul, and the souls of my sons and daughters." He said to him: "How can I save you when I have only half a coin?" He said to him: "With it I shall complete the other half which I have." He took it out and gave it to him. [Later] they showed him in a dream that he was walking on the shores of the Great Sea, and they wanted to cast him into it. And he saw R. Shim'on stretching forth his hands towards him, and that poor man came and pulled him out and placed him into the hands of R. Shim'on, and thus he was saved.   (Zohar 2:61a-b)

The Messenger of God

One day R. Ḥiyya was sitting at the door of the gate of Usha. He saw R. El'azar, and saw that a bird was flying

---

[18] In the original, *Maya digargarin*, that is, "water of garden-rocket," or eruca, a stimulating plant.

towards him. He said to R. El'azar: "This means that even while you are on the road, everyone wishes to follow you." R. El'azar turned his head and saw it. He said: "Surely it has a message for me. For the Holy One, blessed be He, causes everything to deliver His messages and He has many messengers. And say not that only those in whom there is a living spirit, but even those things in which there is no spirit."

(Zohar 2:28a)

R. El'azar Wrapped in Flames

R. Ḥiyya went to see R. El'azar. R. Ḥaggai met him and said to him: "This road, which is set before the Master, where does it lead?" He said to him: "To see R. El'azar." He said to him: "I too shall go with you." He said to him: "If you can understand the meaning of what you will hear, come; and if not, go your way." He said to him: "Let not the Master be concerned with that, for I have heard many mysteries of the Tora and understood them." Thereupon R. Ḥaggai started [to discourse and presented several mystical explanations of Biblical verses]. . . .

R. Ḥiyya went and kissed him and said to him: "You, my son, are more worthy than I to see R. El'azar." . . . When they arrived, they entered and sat down before R. El'azar. He kept silent and they kept silent. R. El'azar retired into his room. He heard a voice which said: "Go and tell them what they want [to know] for they are worthy." He returned to them, and said to them: "If you have heard any word [of Tora], tell me." They said to him: "We are waiting to be illuminated by the purity of the supernal light and to absorb teaching."

R. El'azar began: "*The Lord is in His holy Temple, let all the earth keep silence before Him* (Hab. 2:20). When the Holy One, blessed be He, wanted to create the world, He looked into the thought of the secret of· the Tora, and traced outlines. But the world could not come into being until He created repentance, for repentance is the innermost Supernal Hall, and the deepest mystery, and there were traced and sketched the letters in their engravings. When this was created, He looked at that Hall and sketched before Him the outlines of the whole world. ... When He wanted to create heaven, what did He do? He looked at the primordial light and wrapped Himself into it and created heaven, as it is written, *Thou coverest Thyself with light as with a garment* (Ps. 104:2). And then follows *Thou stretchest out the heavens like a curtain* (ibid.). He looked to make the lower world, and made another Hall and entered it, and from it He looked out and sketched before Him all the worlds below and created them. To this refers the verse, *The Lord is in His holy Temple, let all the earth keep silence before Him. Silence* before Him—he sketched *Silence* before Him, all the points of the whole world, which number sixty-five, as the numerical value of *HaS* ["Silence"], which is sixty and five. And he sketched all of them before Him and thus created the world. Therefore the glory of the Holy One, blessed be He, is revealed only to those who know His ways and walk in them, in truth, as it is proper."

While he was talking to them, a flame came and enveloped him, and they sat outside. They heard a voice say: "O, saintly one, *the King hath brought me into His chambers* (Song 1:4) —into all those places whose keys are delivered into the hands of the exalted face, the holy youth [i.e., Metatron], and all of them are prepared for you and for those who deserve it because of you. And by your life, O holy one, all the hosts of heaven *are glad and rejoice in thee* (ibid.)."

When R. Ḥiyya and R. Ḥaggai saw this, they trembled and great fear fell upon them. They said: "We are not worthy of this. Let us leave and go our way." Still they stayed there all that day and could not see him. And then they said: "It is not the will of the Holy One, blessed be He, that we should stay here." They left and went away.

(Sitre Tora, Zohar 1:89a-90a)

R. El'azar, Elijah, and the Messiah

R. El'azar bar R. Shim'on encountered Elijah who appeared to him in the shape of an old man, and a young boy (i.e., the Messiah) was with him. And there was there a ford across a river of great waters for crossing to the other side. R. El'azar said to him: "Old man, old man! I shall take this child upon my shoulder, and you on my other side, and shall take you across the ford of the water." He said: "Even though you are the master of the generation you cannot take us across!" He said to him: "Old man, old man! If I seize you and him with my two hands I can throw you across to the other side, in half a word." He said to him: "Do you study the Tora?" He said to him: "Yes." He said to him: "And is the Tora not called *Tushiyya* [Salvation] because she weakens (*matteshet*) the strength of a man?"[19] He said to him: "And is she not called health and marrow, as it is said, *It shall be health to thy navel and marrow to thy bones* (Prov. 3:8)? I, too, imbibed much from the Tora like one who imbibes health and My strength became great." He took them across. He said to him: "Old man, old man! Who is this child with you?" He said to him: "I am teaching him Tora." He said to him: "Old man, old man! My power is great in This World and in the World to Come, and for the sake of this child I shall not let the angel of Gehenna touch you, and I shall raise you up into the World to Come with the strength of the power I have there." He said to him: "Rabbi, Rabbi! Your power is great in the World to Come like that of one of the servants of the Holy One, blessed be He, who minister before Him." R. El'azar looked at him but saw him not. He said: "This shows that he was Elijah!" And he rejoiced over the things he did to him.

(Midrash haNe'elam to Lekh L'kha, Zohar Ḥadash 50a)

---

[19] The Hebrew word *tushiyya* (salvation) is here considered as if it were related to the verb *mattish* (fem. *matteshet*), weakens, in conformity with the Talmudic saying, "The Tora weakens the strength of man."

Israel, The Heart of the World

R. Abba said: I remember a word I heard from the Holy Light [R. Shim'on ben Yoḥai] which he, in turn, heard in the name of R. Eliezer.

One day a learned Gentile came to him and said: "Old man, old man, I want to ask you three questions. One is that you say that another Temple will be built for you, whereas only two were destined to be built, the First Temple and the Second Temple. You will not find in the Tora [mention of] a Third Temple and a Fourth Temple. That which had to be built has already been built, and there is no more in it, for Scripture speaks only of two Temples of Israel. And it is written, *Greater will be the glory of this last Temple than that of a first* (Hag. 2:9). Furthermore, you say that you are closer to the Supernal King than all the other peoples. Now, he who is close to the king is always in a state of joy, and is without pain, without fear, and without oppression. But you are always in pain and oppression and sorrow more than all the children of the world. And we, no pain, no oppression and no sorrow ever comes near us. [Therefore] we are close to the Supernal King and you are far from Him, and this is why you have pain, and oppression, mourning, and sorrow, which we do not have. And further, you eat no dead and impure animals so that you be healthy and that your body be in health. We eat whatever we want, and we are powerful in strength and all our limbs are in good shape. But you who do not eat [everything] are weak, all of you suffer from bad diseases, and are frail, more than all other peoples. You are a people hated by your God in every respect. Old man, old man! Do not try to answer me for I shall not listen to you and shall not accept it from you."

R. Eliezer lifted up his eyes and looked at him, and he became a heap of bones. After his wrath subsided, he turned his head back and cried and said: "*O Lord, our God, how mighty is Thy name in all the earth* (Ps. 8:2). How great is the power of the Holy Name in all the earth and how beloved are the words of the Tora, for there exists not even a small thing that would not be found in the Tora, and there is not even a smallest word in the Tora which did not issue from the mouth of the Holy One, blessed be He. These same things which that wretch just asked, one day I myself had asked them of Elijah, and he told me that they were discussed in the heavenly academy before the Holy One, blessed be He. And this is it: When Israel came out of Egypt, the Holy One, blessed be He, wanted to make them on earth like the holy angels Above, and wanted to build them the Holy House and make it descend from the heavens of the firmaments, and to implant Israel as a holy shoot like unto the image of Above. This is what is written, *Thou shalt bring them and plant them in the mountain of Thine inheritance* (Exod. 15:17). In what place? *In the place which Thou hast made, O Lord, for Thee to dwell in* (ibid.). In the place which you have made, O Lord, and in no other. *The place which Thou has made, O Lord, for Thee to dwell in*—this is the Temple. *The Sanctuary, O Lord, which Thy hands have established* (ibid.)—this is the Second Temple. And both were the masterwork of the Holy One, blessed be He. And when they caused wrath before Him in the desert, they died, and the Holy One, blessed be He, brought their children into the Land. [And there they learned the acts of the inhabitants], and the Temple was built by the hand of man. And because of this it did not endure. And Solomon knew that because it was the work of man it would not endure. . . . And in the days of Ezra the sins brought it about that, when they built the Second Temple, there was no permanence in it. All this time the primordial building of the Holy One, blessed be He, was not in the world. . . . And that is the building which we are awaiting, and not a building of man which has no permanence at all. The Holy One, blessed be He, will cause both the First Temple and the Second Temple together to descend to us from Above: the First Temple in concealment, and the Second Temple openly. That Temple which will be openly visible is called the Second Temple, so that the whole world should see the masterwork of the Holy One, blessed be He. And there will be perfect joy and gladness in all its existence. The First Temple, which will be in concealment, will be removed upward on top of the one which will be visible, and the whole world will see clouds of glory surrounding it on top of the visible Temple. And inside those clouds will be the First Temple, hidden in them and reaching until the heights of the glory of heaven. And it is that building that we are awaiting. And until now it has not existed in the world. For even the future city of Jerusalem will not be the work of man, as it is written, *For I, saith the Lord, will be unto her a wall of fire round about* (Zech. 2:9). If this is said about the city, how much more so will it hold good for the Temple which is His dwelling place. This work should have been completed in the beginning, when Israel came out of Egypt, but it was postponed to the End of the Days, until the Last Redemption.

"As for the second question, we are certainly closer to the Supernal King than all the other peoples. It is certainly thus, for the Holy One, blessed be He, made Israel to be the heart of the whole world. Thus Israel is among the other peoples like the heart among the limbs of the body. Just as the limbs cannot exist even for one moment without the heart, so all the peoples cannot exist in the world without Israel. And likewise, Jerusalem in the midst of other countries is like the heart in the midst of the limbs, and this is why she is in the middle of the whole world[20] like the heart in the midst of the limbs. And Israel conducts itself in the midst of the other peoples like the heart in the midst of the limbs. The heart is tender and weak, but it is the [basis for the] existence of all the limbs. Pain and distress and

---

[20] According to an old Jewish legend, often alluded to in the Talmud and the Midrash, Jerusalem, and more precisely, the *Even Shetiyya* (Foundation Stone) in the center of the Temple, is the navel of the earth. Cf. R. Patai, *Man and Temple in Ancient Jewish Myth and Ritual,* 2nd ed., pp. 85, 132, 155.

sorrow are known only to the heart, in which there is existence and in which there is intelligence. As for the other limbs, the king does not come near them for there is no real existence in them and they know nothing. All the other limbs are not close to the king, who is the wisdom and the intelligence which dwell in the brain, only the heart is. All the other limbs are remote from it and know nothing of it. Likewise Israel is close to the Holy King, and the other peoples are far from Him.

"As for the last question, that Israel eat no dead and impure meat, nor the filth and defilement of creeping things as do the other peoples, this is the answer. The heart which is tender and weak and is the king and the existence of all the other limbs, takes as its nourishment only the choicest and purest of all blood, and its food is clean and choice, and it is the most tender and the weakest of all, and it leaves all the refuse to the rest of the limbs. And all the other limbs pay no attention to this, but take all the refuse and the bad. And they therefore are strong, as it can be seen by us. And because of this, there are boils and swellings and sores and leprosy, but the heart has none of these, but is clean and select of all of them, and there is no blemish in it. Likewise the Holy One, blessed be He, takes Israel for Himself, for it is pure and select, and there is no blemish in it, as it is written, *Thou art all fair, my love, and there is no blemish in thee* (Song 4:7)."

R. Yose came, kissed R. Abba's hand, and said: "If I had come to the world only to hear this, it would have been sufficient for me."

(Zohar 3:220b-221b)

How R. Yitzḥaq Escaped Death

One day R. Yitzḥaq sat at the door of R. Y'huda and was sad. R. Y'huda went out, found him at the door where he sat in sadness, and said to him: "Wherein is this day different from the rest of the days?" He said to him: "I came to you to ask you three things. One: when you speak words of Tora and remember some of the words that I have said, mention them in my name. Two: that you train my son Yosef in the Tora. And three: that you go every seven days to my grave, and pray for me." He said to him: "Whence this?" He said to him: "My soul leaves me every night and does not enlighten me with a dream as she used to before; and, moreover, when I pray and come to the words 'He who hears the prayer,' I watch my shadow on the wall and cannot see it, and I think that, since the shadow went away and cannot be seen, a herald had gone out and proclaimed, *Surely a man walketh as a semblance* (Ps. 39:7). As long as the semblance [i.e., shadow] of a man has not gone away he walks and his soul stays in him; once his semblance has gone away and cannot be seen, he must pass away from this world." And he added: "And from this: it is written, *Because our days on earth are a shadow* (Job 8:9)." R. Y'huda said to him: "I shall do all these things which you ask, but I request of you that in That World make sure that my place is next to you, as we have been in This World." R. Yitzḥaq cried and said: "I beseech you that you don't leave me all these days!"

They went to R. Shim'on. They found him studying the Tora. R. Shim'on lifted up his eyes and saw R. Yitzḥaq and saw the Angel of Death run before him and dance before him. R. Shim'on rose, took R. Yitzḥaq by hand, and said: "I decree: he who is used to come in should come in, and he who is not used to come in should not come in!" R. Yitzḥaq and R. Y'huda entered, and thus he tied the Angel of Death outside. R. Shim'on observed R. Yitzḥaq and saw that his time had not yet come, for he had time until the eighth hour of the day.[21] He seated him before R. Shim'on, and he studied with him the Tora. R. Shim'on said to his son R. El'azar: "Sit at the door, and whomever you see don't talk to him, and if he wants to enter here utter an oath that he

---

[21] I.e., until about 2:00 p.m. The hours were numbered from sunrise.

must not enter." R. Shim'on then said to R. Yitzḥaq: "Did
you or did you not see the image of your father today?" For
we have learned that in the hour in which a man departs
from the world his father and his relatives are found there
with him and he sees them and recognizes them. And all
those who will dwell near him in That World in the same
grade they all gather and surround him and go with his soul
until the place where he will dwell. He said: "Until now I
have not seen him." Thereupon R. Shim'on arose and said:
"Master of the World! R. Yitzḥaq is well known to me, and
he is one of those seven eyes[22] here. Behold, I hold him, give
him to me!" A voice issued and said: "The footstool of his
Master is near the wings of R. Shim'on.[23] He is yours, and
you will bring him with you when you enter to occupy
your throne." R. Shim'on said: "Surely."

Meanwhile R. El'azar saw that the Angel of Death had
gone away and he said: "No decree of death can be found in
the place of R. Shim'on ben Yoḥai." R. Shim'on said to his
son R. El'azar: "Come here and take hold of R. Yitzḥaq, for
I see that he is afraid." R. El'azar entered and took hold of
him, and R. Shim'on turned his face to studying the Tora.
R. Yitzḥaq fell asleep, and saw his father. He said to him:
"My son, happy is your portion in This World and in the
World to Come. For you dwell among the foliage of the
Tree of Life in the Garden of Eden. R. Shim'on ben Yoḥai is
a tree great and mighty in both worlds; he holds you among
his branches. Happy is your portion, my son!" He said to
him: "Father, and what am I there?" He said to him: "Three
days ago they hurriedly prepared your place of repose, and
made for you open windows to give you light from four
sides of the world. And I saw your place and rejoiced for I
thought: happy is your portion, my son! Except that your

---

[22] I.e., seven saintly men.
[23] I.e., R. Yitzḥaq (the "footstool" of R. Shim'on) will remain near
the wings of R. Shim'on, will live as long as R. Shim'on lives.

son has not yet acquired sufficient Tora.[24] And lo, now twelve righteous men from among the Companions are prepared to come to you; but before we could leave, a voice arose in all the worlds: 'O you Companions who are standing here, adorn yourselves, for the sake of R. Shim'on: he made a request and it has been granted to him.' And not only that, but seventy places have adorned themselves for his sake, and in every place there are windows opening onto seventy worlds, and each world opens onto seventy corridors and each corridor opens onto seventy supernal crowns. And from there open paths unto the Inscrutable Ancient One. And all this in order to see that supernal bliss which lights up and delights everything, as it is said, *To behold the graciousness of the Lord, and to visit early His temple* (Ps. 27:4). What is to *visit early His temple?* This refers to what is written, *He is trusted in all My house* (Num. 12:7)."

He said to him: "Father, how much time have they given me in This World?" He said to him: "I have no permission to tell, nor is it known to any man, but at the great feast of R. Shim'on[25] you will prepare his table. . . ."

Thereafter R. Yitzḥaq woke up and smiled, and his face shone. R. Shim'on saw it and looked at his face. He said to him: "You have heard a new word." He said to him: "Surely." He told him. He prostrated himself before R. Shim'on.

We have learned: From that day on R. Yitzḥaq took his son by his hand, and taught him Tora, and did not let go of him. When he went before R. Shim'on he seated his son outside and sat before R. Shim'on, and he read before him, *O Lord, I am oppressed, be Thou my surety!* (Isa. 38:14).

(Zohar 1:217b-218b)

---

[24] This reflects R. Yitzḥaq's concern about having the training of his son Yosef in the Tora continued by R. Y'huda, cf. above.

[25] I.e., when R. Shim'on dies.

The Death of R. Eliezer the Great

When R. Eliezer the Great fell ill, that day was the eve of Sabbath, and he seated his son Horkenos on his right side, and revealed to him deep things and mysteries. And he did not accept the words in his mind fully for the thought that his father's mind was confused. When he saw that his father's mind was clear, he received from him 189 supernal secrets. When he reached the subject of the stones of marble which are mixed in the Upper Waters, R. Eliezer cried and stopped talking. He said: "Stand over there, my son!" He said to him: "Father, why?" He said to him: "I saw that I shall soon pass from the world." And he said to him: "Go, tell your mother that my Tefillin [phylacteries] will soon move away to a high place, and after I pass away from the world I shall come here to see them [i.e., members of his family]. She should not weep, for they are my supernal relatives, and not from below, and the mind of man cannot understand this."

While they were sitting, the sages of the generation came to visit him. He cursed them because they had not come to attend to him, for we have learned, "Greater is attendance than study." When R. Akiba[26] came, he said to him: "Akiba, Akiba! Why did you not come to attend to me? He said to him: "Rabbi, I had no time." He became wroth and said: "I wonder about you, whether you will die a natural death." And he cursed him that his death should be the hardest of all.[27]

R. Akiba cried and said to him: "Rabbi, teach me Tora." R. Eliezer opened his mouth with the Work of the Chariot.[28] A fire came and enveloped both of them. The sages said: "This shows that we are not worthy to hear this."

---

[26] R. Akiba was the foremost disciple of R. Eliezer the Great.

[27] About the martyr's death of R. Akiba and his nine colleagues, see "The Ten Martyrs," p. 358.

[28] The mysteries of God's Throne of Glory.

They went outside, and sat there. There was what there was, and the fire went away, and he taught three hundred Halakhot of the intensively bright spot like snow.[29] And he taught him 215 meanings of the verses of the Song of Songs. And tears flowed from the eyes of R. Akiba, and the fire returned as before. When they reached the verse, *Stay me with dainties, refresh me with apples for I am love-sick* (Song 2:5), R. Akiba could not bear it and he lifted up his voice in weeping and sobbed aloud. And he spoke not for fear of the Shekhina who was there.

R. Eliezer taught him all the depths and the supernal secrets which are in the Song of Songs. And he gave him a warning not to use any of its verses,[30] lest the Holy One, blessed be He, destroy the world because of it, for He does not want it to be used by the creatures because of the great holiness that is in it.

Thereafter R. Akiba went out and cried, and tears flowed from his eyes, and he said: "Woe, my Master, woe, my Master, that the world will remain orphaned from you!"

All the other sages entered to him and questioned him, and he answered them. The hour pressed R. Eliezer.[31] He raised his two arms and placed them upon his heart, and said: "Woe, world! Supernal world! You are about to take back and to hide all light and illumination from the world below! Woe to you, my two arms, the two Toras,[32] which will be forgotten today from the world. ... I have learned Tora and understood wisdom and served sages, and if all the children of man were scribes they could not write it! And my disciples have not taken from my wisdom more than the kohl[33] on the eye, and took from my masters only like a

---

[29] A subject in the Mishna tractate Nega'im 1:1, dealing with leprosy, but here evidently having a mystical significance.

[30] For the purpose of performing miracles.

[31] I.e., his time was running out.

[32] I.e., the Written Tora and the Oral Tora.

[33] The powder used for painting the eyelid.

man who drinks from the sea." And he said this only in order to give honor to his masters. And they asked him about the sandal of the *Ḥalitza* ceremony,[34] until his soul went out and he said: "Pure."

And R. Akiba was not there. When the Sabbath departed, R. Akiba came and found that he had died. He rent his garments and scratched all his flesh until blood flowed and soaked his beard. He lamented and cried. He went outside and said: "Heaven, heaven! Tell the sun and the moon that the light which was greater than your light has darkened!"

(Midrash haNe'elam, Zohar, 1:98a-99a)

Why Do Jews Rock When Studying?

R. Yose said: R. Abba and I arose and walked, and the force of the sun was great and oppressed us on the way. We saw trees in the desert and water under them. We sat down under the shadow of a tree of the desert. I asked him: "Why is it that all the peoples of the world do not sway to and fro except Israel alone? For when they study the Tora they sway themselves back and forth without having to learn it, and they cannot stand still." He said to me: "You have reminded me of an important thing, and the people do not know it and pay no attention to it." He sat for a while and cried. He said: "Woe to the children of men who walk about like the cattle of the field without understanding. In this thing alone one can recognize the holy souls of Israel among the souls of the peoples who serve idols. The souls of Israel are cut out from the holy lamp which burns, as it is written, *The candle of the Lord is the soul of man* (Prov. 20:27). And this candle, when it is lighted from the supernal Tora, its light does not rest even for a moment. This is the mystery of the verse, *O God, take Thou no rest* (Ps. 83:2), as it is written, *Ye*

---

[34] Cf. Deut. 25:5-10, but probably its mystical connotations were the subject of discussion.

who mention the Lord, take ye no rest (Isa. 62:6) — you have no rest. The light of the candle, once it unites with the wick, that light never rests but sways back and forth, and does not rest forever. Likewise Israel whose souls are from that light of the candle, as soon as they say a word of Tora, this light is kindled, and they cannot rest but sway to and fro and to all sides like the flame of the candle.... The souls of the idolatrous peoples burn like straw without light, and therefore they hold still and do not sway, for they have no Tora and they do not burn with it and no light issues from them. They stand like trees in the fire which burns without light, and therefore they stand still without any light." R. Yose said: "This is a fine explanation of the matter. Happy is my share that I merited to hear this."

(Zohar 3:218b-219a)

R. Shim'on Annuls God's Decree

I

One day R. Shim'on went out and saw that the world was dark and somber and that its light was blocked. R. El'azar said to him: "Come and let us see what the Holy One, blessed be He, wants." They went and encountered an angel who looked like a huge mountain, and who emitted thirty flames of fire from his mouth. R. Shim'on said to him: "What do you want to do?" He said to him: "I want to destroy the world, because there are not thirty pious men found in the generation...." R. Shim'on said to him: "I beg of you go before the Holy One, blessed be He, and tell Him, 'Bar Yoḥai is found in the world.'" Up went that angel before the Holy One, blessed be He, and said to Him: "Master of the World! It is known to You what Bar Yoḥai has told me." The Holy One, blessed be He, said to him: "Go, destroy the world, and pay no attention to Bar Yoḥai." The angel returned and R. Shim'on saw him and said to

him: "If you do not go away, I shall decree upon you that
you should not ascend to heaven and that you be in the
place of 'Uzza and 'Azael.[35] And when you enter before the
Holy One, blessed be He, tell Him, 'And if there are not
thirty pious men, there are twenty, and if not twenty, there
are ten, and if not ten, there are two, and they are I and my
son, and if there are not two, there is one, and I am he, as it
is written *The righteous is the foundation of the world*[36] (Prov.
10:25)." In that hour a voice issued from heaven and said,
"Happy is your share, R. Shim'on, for the Holy One, blessed
be He, has decreed Above and you annul it Below...."

(Zohar Ḥadash, p. 51b-52a)

II

At one time there was pestilence in Lod. R. Shim'on ben
Yoḥai came to the place. They said to him: "What shall we
do?" He arose and went through the place and saw people
lying about dead. He said: "All this in a place in which I am
present? I decree that the pestilence should cease!" They
heard a heavenly voice saying: "Get out of here, for R.
Shim'on ben Yoḥai is here! For the Holy One, blessed be
He, issues a decree and he annuls it." R. Ḥanina was there;
he went and said to R. Meir: "Rabbi, who can stand up
against the greatness of R. Shim'on? He is like Moses."

(Zohar Ḥadash p. 170a)

A Moment Without Tora

R. Yose went for a walk, and R. Aḥa bar Ya'aqov went
with him. While they walked, R. Yose kept silent and was

---

[35] The fallen angels, who are suspended between heaven and earth.

[36] This is the Midrashic interpretation of the Biblical verse, which
usually is translated, *The righteous is an everlasting foundation*. R.
Shim'on's argument echoes Abraham's bargaining with God over
the fate of Sodom, cf. Gen. 18:23ff.

occupied with worldly thoughts, while R. Aḥa kept thinking about the Tora. As they were walking, R. Yose noticed that a serpent was pursuing him. He said to R. Aḥa: "Do you see that serpent which pursues me?" R. Aḥa said to him: "I don't see it." W. Yose ran, and the serpent after him. R. Yose fell, and blood gushed from his nose. He heard that they [i.e., a voice] were saying: *Only you have I known of all the families of the earth, therefore I will visit upon you all your iniquities* (Amos 3:2). R. Yose said: "If this happened because of one moment, he who abandons the Tora, how much more will he be punished."

(Zohar 2:17b)

The Snake's Mission

The companions were walking and the sun was strong. They saw a field with beautiful grass and water issuing to all sides, and the trees of the field were many. They sat down there. R. El'azar said: "How pleasant is this place to rest in it."

While they were sitting, a big snake came in the strong sunlight and passed in front of them. R. El'azar said to him: "Snake, snake! Veer from your way, for that sinner has repented what he had done and will not again do that thing."

The companions were amazed. R. Abba said: "What is this about?" R. El'azar said to them: "Be silent!" And he said: "Snake, snake! After they had whispered to you from heaven, that man repented and made up his mind that he would never return to that sin. Veer off your way!" The snake stopped in its place and turned neither here nor there. R. El'azar again spoke to it: "Snake, snake! I know what you want. Return from your way, for a wicked idolater came to do wrong to a Jew and now he sleeps in your cave. Go and kill him!"

Instantly that snake turned back and danced and jumped before them. R. El'azar said: "Companions, had we not been here, how many wrongs would this snake have done. For a Jewish man committed a sin, and before he turned in repentance they whispered to this snake to kill him. And that man repented in the meantime, and returned from his sin, and said that he would never again commit that sin. And therefore he was saved from the punishment."

The companions said to R. El'azar: "How did you know?" He said to them: "My father gave me a sign from which I knew it." They said to him: Granted that concerning the snake you were informed. But how did you know about that man who repented and returned from his sin?" He said to them: "When that snake passed us, its scales protruded, and its tail stood up, and it went in a hurry. Another spirit came to him and called before him, 'Return from your way, for that man returned from his sin and repented.' And that evil snake would not obey until they gave him a ransom in place of that man who had been sentenced to death but returned from his sin and repented. For such is the way of the snakes above[37] and below: once permission has been given him, he does not turn back until he completes that evil punishment which he has been permitted to carry out, or unless they give him another sinner in his place as a ransom. For he does not go forth in vain."

They said to him: "Granted all this. But how did you know about that Gentile of whom you said that he was given to the snake in ransom?"

He said to them: "When I spoke to the snake, that spirit which came to him whispered to him that he should turn back for that man had repented, and jumped to its ear and told it."

The companions were amazed. R. El'azar said: "Companions, let us go and see whether that snake has done what it had to do."

They arose and went to a rock in that field, and found

---

[37] The "snake above" is Samael the devil.

that idolater dead and that snake was wound around his heel and did not move away from him. Then it moved away from his head and went to his throat and wound itself around it. And from there it again went down to his heel and remained there. They found there a purse full of denars which he had taken from a Jew on the way. R. El'azar took the purse and said: "Blessed be the Merciful One who carries out His mission through all!"

They returned to the place in which they had been. . . .

While they were sitting there, that Jew whom the idolater had robbed passed by the road, tired and exhausted from the power of the sun. He entered that field and sat down under a tree, and complained to the Holy One, blessed be He, and justified the punishment he had suffered and said: "Master of the World! It is revealed and known before You that I worry not about myself and my body and my money, for surely whatever happened happened justly. But I have an old father and mother and I have nothing with which I could support them, and about this I worry. And also, in that purse there was a bundle of denars which belonged to a poor man who was preparing the wedding of his daughter. What will that poor man do now? Master of the World! Because of this my heart aches!" He sat, cried, and said: "*The ordinances of the Lord are true, they are righteous altogether* (Ps. 19:10). . . ."

R. El'azar and the companions heard this and they approached him and saw that he was sitting under that tree, and took hold of him and brought him into their midst. R. El'azar said: "Fear not, O you truly righteous man! For were you not righteous, the Holy One, blessed be He, would not have caused such a great miracle to happen to you as the one which did happen. And, firstly, take your purse of denars, and see what the Holy One, blessed be He, has done for you."

He went with them and saw the idolater dead, and that the snake had punished him and was wound around his neck as it was at first. That Jew prostrated himself in the dust, and thanked and praised the Master of the World, and arose and kissed the hands of R. El'azar and the companions. He said to them: "Now I know that the Holy One, blessed be He, made this miracle happen because of you. But, O Masters, I cried over my old father and mother and over a poor man who gave me this bundle." He opened the purse and showed them the bundle, and he also showed them the wound that idolater caused him. R. El'azar prayed over the wound and it healed. They then approached that idolater and saw that the snake was still as before. R. El'azar said to it: "Snake, snake! All you did you did well. And you showed your strength and your power and meted out great punishment, and we saw it three times, and you showed us all you did. From now on go and hide in your cave, and I decree upon you that you cause no harm to any creature in the world!" The snake unwound itself, bent its head, and went away.

R. El'azar said to that Jew: "Take the spoils of your enemy. I have here this purse of his full of golden denars. And leave him his clothes and take nothing of his. And go to a man in a certain place, and you will find that his wife has died. Go to him and give him this purse of denars, for that man has a son and Shim'on is his name, and he was taking merchandise across the sea, and in the ship the son of this idolater stole this purse from him and gave it to this wicked man. And tell that Jew that he should give this purse to his son who will soon return to him. And let him give thanks to the Holy One, blessed be He, who returned the loss to its owner."

And he did thus. He took the purse and prostrated himself before R. El'azar, and kissed his hands. The companions were amazed. R. Abba said: "All this way there were miracles in everything we saw you doing, and now this is a miracle of miracles. What is the explanation?"

He said to him: "This thing I knew not through a sign and not through wisdom, but my spirit looked and I saw as if I had seen it with my eyes."

All the companions wondered, and they all went, and that Jew with them, until they came to the father-in-law of R. El'azar. When they came there, they found his father-in-law sitting on his couch and studying the Tora. R. El'azar greeted him, and the companions greeted him, and he rejoiced with them.

(Zohar Ḥadash, pp. 107a-108a)

Sleep Seals the Mouth

R. Berekhya said: "I was sitting in the gate of Rome and saw a man approaching. I went out to meet him and brought him to my house. I tested him in Bible, Mishna, Tosefta, and Agada, and found none of it in him. I scolded him, but he made no reply. He dropped behind the door and fell asleep. I said: 'He and the dog—let them eat together....'

"When he awoke from his sleep, he arose and went to the table. He let his head hang and said nothing. I looked at him and saw that his eyes were smiling. He said to me: 'You have certainly removed yourself from the ways of your Master who prepared a table even before Adam came and before He tested and searched him. If you continue to follow this way your children will not survive.' But instantly he took it back and said: 'They will live and they will survive.' I asked him: 'Why did you take back your word?' He said to me: 'It is forbidden for a man to curse himself, and how much more so to curse others....'

"I then again asked him questions of Bible, Mishna, Tosefta, and Agada, and he was well versed in all of them. I said: 'Why when I tested you at first, did you not answer?' He said: 'I was overcome by sleepiness. For I had not slept two days, and then the sleep came upon my eyes, and I did not answer you.'"

(Midrash haNe'elam, Zohar Ḥadash, p. 60c)

OF SAFED KABBALISTS

The Locusts Averted

An awesome event, which took place in the days of the great rabbi, our master and teacher Yitzḥaq Luria Ashkenazi of blessed memory, and which testifies to the power of charity and shows how hard is the outcry of the poor before the Holy One, blessed be He. For the Lord is near those of a broken heart, to hear their cry....

Once the ARI[38] was sitting in the field near Safed with his ten select disciples, and expounding and revealing to them secrets of the Tora. In the middle of his teaching he suddenly said: "Companions, I hear the voice of a herald who is standing and proclaiming in the firmament of heaven of above, in the supernal Court of Law, and his voice is going to all the firmaments, and he says in this language: 'By the decree of the guardians and by the word of the holy angels, it has been decided that countless locusts will come into the area of Safed, and will eat all grass and all the fruit of the earth, and will leave no livelihood for the inhabitants, because of a poor man, a scholar, and his name is R. Ya'aqov Altaretz, who sits and complains to the Holy One, blessed be He. And the Holy One, blessed be He, cannot restrain Himself from punishing all his bad neighbors who dwell in Safed and who pay no attention to him! Thus far the language of the herald.'"

And the ARI of blessed memory said: "My sons, for God's sake, hurry and let us collect among ourselves some good present, and send it to him. Perhaps the Lord will reconsider the evil He said He would do to His people." Instantly they collected among themselves about three thalers, and the rabbi sent them by the hand of one of the disciples, and his name was our master and teacher R.

---

[38] This is the usual abbreviation of the name of Ashkenazi Rabbi Yitzḥaq (1534-1572).

Yitzḥaq Kohen of blessed memory. And R. Yitzḥaq Kohen
hurried to go, and went to the house of the poor man, and
found him still sitting and crying. He said to him: "Why
are you crying?" He said to him: "Because of my bad luck,
for the earthenware barrels, which I used to fill with water
for the whole week, broke, and now that they broke, with
what shall I buy others? So I sat down and wept before the
Holy One, blessed be He: why must I be in these great
straits? Am I more evil than the whole world?"

And when R. Yitzḥaq Kohen heard these words of the
poor man, he was amazed: How true were the words of the
rabbi! And he gave him the money and said to him: "My
lord, the sage, for God's sake beware from here on, don't
complain of the acts of the Holy One, blessed be He, for this
and this is what happened."

And the poor sage admitted that he was sitting and
weeping and, as it were, complaining about His acts. And
he undertook not to do such a thing again. And he prayed
before God that He should forgive him, and reconsider the
evil which He had decreed. And R. Yitzḥaq Kohen
returned to the Yeshiva of the rabbi and his companions,
and related to them what had transpired. And all the
companions were amazed at the greatness of the perception
of their master.

And the ARI of blessed memory said to them: "The
decree has already been annulled, thank God." And they
returned to their studies. And after they had sat about two
hours, they lifted up their eyes and saw, and behold, locusts
came, a very great and heavy army. And all the disciples
were frightened. But the rabbi said to them: "Fear not, for
the decree has already been annulled, and we have appeased
that poor man. And from now on nothing bad will happen,
thank God."

And so it was. All the locusts were blown out by the wind
to the sea and drowned there, and not a single one of them
reached the land.

And from that day on the people of Safed put their eyes

on that poor man to take care of all his needs. And that man was truly pious and versed in the whole Tora.

(Shivḥe haARI, pp. 2b-3a)

The Soul of Benaya

Once it happened that he (the ARI) entrusted our master R. Ḥayyim with going to the village of 'Akhb'ra,[39] where are the tombs of Abbaye and Rava[40] and there prostrating himself on the graves, so that they should give him a Tora scroll. And so he did, and prostrated himself on their graves and concentrated on what his master had entrusted to him. And they spoke to him and gave him a Tora scroll. And as soon as he returned from them and came to his master, the ARI of blessed memory got up before him and said to him: "Blessed be he who comes!" And he seated him on his right hand, and rejoiced with him greatly. And our master R. Ḥayyim, may God preserve him, was very inquisitive, and when he saw that the ARI gave him all that honor which was not his wont on other occasions, he said to him: "My lord and teacher, wherein is this day different from others that your exalted honor gives me all this honor without any reason?" The ARI of blessed memory said to him: "By your life, it was not before you that I got up, and it was not to you that I said 'Blessed be he who comes,' but to Benaya ben Jehoiada[41] whom I saw entering with you."

And it was wondrous in the eyes of R. Ḥayyim. And neither of them knew for what reason did the soul of Benaya attach itself to R. Ḥayyim on that occasion. But three months later, by which time they both had forgotten the matter, they went together to the village of 'Akhb'ra to

---

[39] Village, three miles south of Safed.

[40] Two Babylonian *Amoraim* (Talmudic sages) of the early fourth century C.E. There is no historic basis for the legend that they were buried in 'Akhb'ra.

[41] A captain of David; cf. 2 Sam. 8:18, etc.

study, and halfway there the ARI stopped and said: "I see that here is Benaya ben Jehoiada buried." And there was there no monument or any sign of a grave. And R. Ḥayyim spoke up and said: "By your life, on that occasion when I went to prostrate myself on the tombs of Abbaye and Rava, before I got there I sat down precisely here and repeated the *Yiḥud*[42] which you gave me so that my mouth and heart should be used to it without an error." The ARI said: "So now it has become known that by the power of the *Yiḥud* which you recited here on his grave, you aroused and brought down his soul into his body, and it also cleaved to you to help you down here in wisdom. And this is the mystery of 'He who sanctifies himself down here, becomes sanctified from Above.'"

(Shivḥe haARI, pp. 12a-b)

The Death of R. Yitzḥaq Luria

Once our master R. Ḥayyim Vital, may god preserve him, asked the ARI of blessed memory about the meaning of a Tosefta passage in the Zohar discussing the two gazelles.[43] The ARI of blessed memory said to him: "By your life, R. Ḥayyim, let me be, for I will not explain it to you, and it will be good for you as well as for me and for the whole world. For there is a great mystery there, and they [in heaven] do not want me to reveal it. But R. Ḥayyim said to him: "You must reveal it to me!" The ARI repeated and said to him: "See, if I reveal it to you, you will in the end regret it with a great regret, and I warn you. But I am forced and ordered not to withhold from you anything you want to ask me, therefore I warn you to leave me alone and do not force me to explain to you this Tosefta." But R. Ḥayyim repeated and said: "Nevertheless, I want you to explain it to

---

[42] A Kabbalistic prayer for the purpose of bringing about the union of God and the Shekhina.

[43] An esoteric passage in Zohar 3:55b.

me." Then the ARI explained the Tosefta to him and revealed to him secrets. And after he revealed them he said that already the decree has been passed that the ARI would die that year, "as a punishment for having revealed to you this secret. And you yourself have brought this misfortune upon yourself, for had you not pressed me so much I would not have revealed it to you, and they would not have punished me from heaven. And I did give you hints several times but you did not want to pay attention to my words. Therefore I am not sorry for myself or for my family, but for you: how can I leave you without the completion of your restoration?" And as for this secret, we have not yet deserved to know it, and it is hidden in the hands of our master and teacher R. Ḥayyim, and he does not reveal it until the word issues from the King of kings of kings, the Holy One, blessed be He.

(Shivḥe haARI, pp. 15a-b)

The Spirit Teaches R. Yosef Caro

I found that the Holy Spirit from above was revealed also to our master R. Yosef Gikatilla, and a *Maggid*[44] came to him every day and revealed secrets of the Tora to him. . . . And it was likewise with R. Yosef Caro,[45] peace be upon him: each time he would recite the Mishna by heart, the *Maggid* would reveal himself to him. And people would hear his voice through the door and through the holes saying: "Peace be upon you, R. Yosef Caro! I am the Mishna. You are studying me, and I came out to teach you understanding. How greatly the Holy One, blessed be He, in the Supernal Yeshiva prides Himself in you, and says 'My son Yosef, such and such are his acts, such and such are his

---

[44] An angelic spirit which regularly addresses an exceptionally saintly Kabbalistic rabbi. Literally "Sayer."

[45] The famous author of the *Shulḥan 'Arukh,* lived 1488-1575; from 1536 on in Safed.

ways, such is his devotion to his studies! Happy is she who bore him, and happy they who sit in his company!' And I, the Mishna, saw your place which is prepared for you in the Garden of Eden. How many benefits are awaiting you in the Garden of Eden! How many enjoyments and delicacies will be yours in the future! Be strong and firm in the fear of God! And now I am come to reveal to you such and such a secret in the Tora." And all the things which the *Maggid* revealed to him he wrote down in a book which he called *The Book of the Maggid.*[46] And nevertheless, he was of little importance compared to the wisdom of the ARI of blessed memory, and he himself sat before the wisdom of the ARI and learned from him secrets of the Tora. . . .

(Shivḥe haARI, p. 17a)

The Penitent

R. Abraham haLevi, peace be upon him, expounded and cautioned about repentance and acts which awaken man to repentance. And he used to lie down naked upon a bed of nettles and say that he who wants to escape the punishment of burning should do likewise. And he ordered that they cast stones upon him and said, "Thus can the sons of man escape from the punishment of stoning." And all the other [mortifications] like these. And confession helps more, for the four deaths of the law court are mentioned in it. And through him there was a great awakening [to penitence] until they found, before the great Italian synagogue, a man who sat in sackcloth three days and three nights, in great weeping. R. Abraham haLevi also used to get up every midnight and knock on the doors of the houses in the holy community of Safed, and call them: "Rise to recite the midnight *Tiqqun,*[47] to study in this hour of grace. And no

---

[46] There is, in fact, a book by Yosef Caro entitled *Maggid Mesharim* ("Sayer of Truth") which has been printed several times.

[47] Kabbalistic prayer for the unification of God and the Shekhina.

midnight passed without the voice of Tora study which could be heard afar.

One day that saintly man fell ill and reached the gates of death. And his master, the ARI of blessed memory, went to visit him, and said to him: "Do you want to go to Jerusalem to pray at the Western Wall so that you should be healed of your sickness?" Instantly R. Abraham vowed to go to Jerusalem the holy city, and right away he was healed of his sickness. Then he sold all the furnishings of his house for the expenses of his trip, for he was very poor, and went to Jerusalem. And when he reached the Western Wall, he made a cut in his garment, as is the law for those who see the Temple in ruins, and instantly the Shekhina revealed herself to him, and he saw her, as it were, as the Prophet Jeremiah had seen her,[48] going from the Holy of Holies, her head disheveled, as it is told in the Midrash Ekha. And R. Abraham recited a dirge about this.... And when R. Abraham saw her in her great anguish, he lifted up his voice in weeping, and cried a great and bitter cry, and, impelled by the power of his great pain, he ran his head into a house which was there, and hit his head against the wall of the house, and fainted because of the great pain, and collapsed. And then he saw that the Shekhina took his head[49] between her knees and wiped away the tears of his eyes, and said to him: "Abraham, my son, be comforted, for *There is hope for thy future... and thy children shall return to their border* (Jer. 31:17)."

Thereafter he regained consciousness as before, and returned to Safed. And his master instantly asked him: "Did you see this and this?" And he said to him, "Yes." And he said to him: "You saw all that as a reward of the repentance which was awakened by you, and because of it they added from heaven twenty-two years to your life, for

---

[48] Reference to a legend. Cf. R. Patai, *Adam waAdama* 2:100-3.

[49] Reading: "his" for "Her" which makes no good sense.

the sake of the Shekhina who is the Oral Law which is built of twenty-two letters of the alef-bet, and for the sake of the soul of the Prophet Jeremiah, peace be upon him who was with you. Now be strong and firm in the fear of the Lord to continue the arousal to repentance among the people of the city. . . ."

(Shivḥe haARI, pp. 23b-24a)

6
FOLKTALES

The great riches and variety of the Jewish folktale make it impossible to present in this part examples of each and every type of it. Even after limiting the selections to *legendary* folktales (thereby excluding the romantic tale, the realistic tale, and several other categories of folktale), the presentation must be illustrative rather than comprehensive. Likewise, the present background notes do not intend to serve as an analytical introduction to the Jewish folktale, not even to its legendary category, but merely to comment upon those few varieties of the Jewish legendary folktale which are presented below in a number of typical specimens.

To begin with, Jewish folktales comprise etiological tales which explain the origins of phenomena encountered in nature (e.g., the sun and the moon, the stars, the sky, the sea, the dry land, the animals, etc.), in human life (e.g., the need to work, the pain of childbirth, the inevitability of death, etc.), or in the relations between one nation and the other (e.g., Israel and the Gentiles). Many of these tales have a distinctly mythical character which I have discussed elsewhere.[1] Most of the selections presented in the Biblical part of this anthology (Part 1) belong to this category, many of whose motifs are well known from folktale collections from all over the world. In the present part these tales

[1] Cf. R. Patai, "What Is Hebrew Mythology?"

of origins are represented by the story of Noah and Satan, which explains the origin of what in modern terminology would be called the phenomenology of drunkenness, and by the story of the Tower of Babel, which explains, on the one hand, the origin of mankind's many languages, and, on the other, the origin of the great towerlike ruins of Babylon.

A second type of Jewish legendary folktale comprises the major themes of the vindication of God's justice, the ultimate inevitability of reward and punishment, the imperative of piety, and the folly of sin. Many Talmudic and Midrashic stories belong to this category (see Parts 3 and 4). In the present part, the stories "Charity Saves from Death," "Always Say 'God Willing' " (from the Gaonic period), "The Gold and the Honey," "A Solomonic Judgment" (tenth century), "The Reward of Study," "The Man Who Never Swore," and "Touch Not a Married Woman" (eleventh century) belong to this type. Quite an elaborate example of the same type is Isaac Arama's fifteenth century story, "The Three Sons," which is an entirely transparent parable illustrating the divine reward and punishment meted out to the pious and the sinful respectively. Here belongs also the sixteenth century folktale "The Two Friends," which tells of the reward of fidelity and which closely parallels Schiller's well-known poem *Die Bürgschaft*, and the nineteenth-century story "The Reward of Charity," by Y'huda Birdogo, which, incidentally, contains the widespread motif of the lost ring found in a fish's belly.

The third category comprises folktales which describe conflicts between demons (or angels) and humans. Their Biblical prototype is the story of Jacob and the Angel; the Talmud and Midrash have several of them, as have the sixth-seventh-century magic bowls from Babylonia. The most elaborate is "The Story of the Jerusalemite," which stems from the tenth to twelfth century and which concludes with the demon daughter of Ashmodai killing her unfaithful human husband.[2] Often the superhuman antagonist of man is the Angel of Death (see "The Angel of Death," sixteenth century); occasionally it is his own sins which appear to him in the shape of horrible demons and dogs (see "Sins and Repentance," seventeenth century).

A fourth group is that of animal tales which are either parables whose purpose is to characterize human behavior and to teach a moral lesson ("The Ape and the Leopard," and "The Grasshopper and the Ant," both by Berekhya haNaqdan, thirteenth century), or else stories about fantastic animals or animal-like plants (e.g., the legend about the Adne Sade, an animal which is tied by its navel string to the earth, which first appears in the Jerusalem Talmud, fourth century; or the Yadu'a, a similar creature which is discussed in seventeenth century folktales). These latter tales, in which free rein is given to folk fantasy, have numerous parallels in the folklore of other peoples. Animal tales which attribute Jewish piety to animals ("The Pious Cow," eleventh century) constitute a separate, typically Jewish folktale category: their purpose is to uphold the pious animals as examples to be followed. The story "The Fox and the Angel of Death" (seventh to tenth century) is placed in this group, although it belongs equally with the preceding group.

Occasionally the point of a folktale is satirical: it holds up to ridicule, or pillories, human vices, follies, stupidities, or abuses. The stories "The Herb of Life" and "Cast Thy Bread Upon the Waters," which date

[2] A scholarly annotated edition of this important folktale, containing one Arabic and two Hebrew texts, was published by Jehuda L. Zlotnik, with a preface and additional notes by R. Patai (Jerusalem: Palestine Institute of Folklore and Ethnology, 1946).

from the Gaonic period, belong to this category, as do the eleventh century tale "No Pity in Woman," evidently written by a sworn misogynist, and the much later (nineteenth century?) stories "The Miser Who Swallowed His Pearls" and "The Girl Swallowed Up by the Stone."

In sharp contrast to the satirical folktale is the heroic or epic one, as exemplified by many stories contained in the late-eleventh-century book *Sefer haYashar*, or "Book of the Straight." The favorite theme of this remarkable book is the great courage in battle exhibited by such Biblical heroes as Abraham, Zepho, Moses, and Joshua and by such non-Biblical mythical warriors as Angias king of Africa, his brother Lucus, his son Nivelus, and many others.

Another type of Jewish folktale can be termed wisdom stories. They tell about the great sagacity or shrewdness of kings, sages, and simple men. Their common feature is that they use their God-given ability for the benefit of the downtrodden, the poor, and those who suffer injustice. The stories "A Solomonic Judgment" (tenth century) and "The Wooden Sword" (nineteenth century?) belong to this category. "The Jewish Virgil Legend," included in this group, is of Gentile origin, and although it tells of a most wise man, it is in fact entirely non-Jewish in character.

A very important figure in the Jewish folktale is the miracle-working rabbi who became dominant in Hasidic folklore (see Part 7). This type of folktale, too, has its prototype in the Biblical miracle stories, and in the Talmudic-Midrashic accounts of the miraculous deeds of sages and pious men. Thus the Golem legends (17th century, see below) have their archetype in brief Talmudic references to sages who made animals or men. To this type belong the stories "R. Ephraim al-Naqawa Arrives in Tlemcen" (after the fifteenth century), "The Death of Abraham Azulai" (nineteenth century), and "The Miracle of the Sailing Ship" (nineteenth century). Often these miracle-working men are "hidden saints" whose piety remains unknown and unrecognized until a crucial point is reached in the story ("The Jar of Tears," "The Butcher's Mitzva," "The Drunkard Saint" all from the nineteenth century).

The last category in this part contains a few examples of legendary folktales about Biblical heroes (Abraham, Joshua, King Solomon), or about non-Jewish heroes of legend (King Midas, Alexander), the latter borrowed from Gentile folklore. As stated in the Introduction (p. xxxix), the story about Joshua is of special interest because it represents a Jewish version of the Oedipus myth, and a typically Jewish one at that.

CHRONOLOGY OF THE SOURCES QUOTED

9th-10th centuries	Midrash Tanḥuma
10th century	M'shalim Shel Sh'lomo haMelekh
10th-11th centuries	Alfa Beta diBen Sira Midrash 'Aseret haDibrot
10th-12th centuries	*Ma'ase Yerushalmi* (Story of the Jerusalemite), ed. J.L. Zlotnik *Sefer haMa'asiyyot*, ed. Moses Gaster
11th century	*Sefer haYashar*, ed. Lazarus Goldschmidt Nissim ben Jacob ibn Shahin, *Ḥibbur mehaY'shu'a*

13th century	Berekhya haNaqdan, *Mishle Shu'alim*
15th century	Isaac Arama, *'Aqedat Yitzḥaq*
16th century	Ma'asiyyot, in OM and BhM
	Delacrut, Matityahu, *Tzel 'Olam*
	Ephraim al-Naqawa
17th century	Shim'on of Tarnow, *Notzer T'ena*
	Shabbatai Bass (Bassista or M'shorer), *Sifte Ḥakhamim*
	Rabbi Loew of Prague and the Golem
19th century	Story about R. Abraham Azulai and about "The Miracle of the Sailing Ship" by Ya'aqov ben Mikhael
	Farhi, Yitzḥaq, *Z'khut haRabbim*
	Y'huda Birdogo's stories
Of unknown dates	Sephardi folktales and folktales from Afghanistan, Georgia (Gruzinia), Iraq, Libya, Morocco, Syria, and Tunisia and from Czechoslovakia and Lithuania

TALES OF ORIGINS
Noah and Satan

When Noah was about to plant a vineyard, Satan came, stood next to him, and said: "What are you planting?" Noah said to him: "A vineyard." He asked him: "What is its nature?" "Its fruits are sweet, whether fresh or dry, and of it one can make wine which gladdens the heart, as it is written, *And wine maketh glad the heart of man* (Ps. 104:15)." Satan said to him: "Come, let both of us be partners in this vineyard." He said to him: "So be it."

What did Satan do? He brought a lamb and slew it under the vine. Then he brought a lion and slew it. Then he brought a pig and slew it. And then he brought an ape and slew it under the vine. And he let their blood run over the vineyard, and he watered it with their blood. Thus he gave a hint to Noah that before a man drinks wine he is innocent as this sheep which knows nothing, and as an ewe which stands dumb before her shearers. If he drinks a proper amount, he becomes as strong as a lion, and says, "There is none like me in the world." If he drinks too much, he becomes like a pig: he soils himself with urine and excrement. If he becomes completely drunk, he becomes like an ape, he stands and jumps about and gambols, and utters all kinds of obscenities in front of everybody, and does not know what he is doing.

And all this happend to Noah the Righteous. And if it was thus with Noah the Righteous, whom the Holy One, blessed be He, explicitly praised, how much more so does it apply to the rest of the sons of man!

(Tanh. Noah, 13)

The Tower of Babel

And the whole earth was one language and one speech (Gen. 11:1). And all the princes of Nimrod and all his great men took counsel at that time: Put and Egypt, and Kush and Canaan, according to their families. And they said to one another: "Come, let us build ourselves a city, and in it a tower, fortified and strong, with its head in heaven, and let us make ourselves a name so that we become the rulers of the whole world and so that the evil of our enemies cease from us, and we rule over them by force and not be dispersed upon the face of the earth because of their wars."

And they went and came before the king and told him these things. And the king thanked them for it, and did as they had said. And all the families gathered, about six hundred thousand men, and they went to search for a very broad country in which to build the city and the tower. And they searched in the whole earth and found but one plain in the east, in the land of Shinar, at a distance of two years' journey. And they all traveled there and settled there.

And they began to make bricks and to burn them in fire, to build the city and the tower which they had planned. And the building of the tower became for them a sin and a transgression. And they began to build it. And as they were building it, they rebelled against the Lord, the God of heaven, and thought in their hearts that they would wage war against Him and would ascend to heaven.

And all those people and all their families divided into three groups. One said, "Let us go up to heaven and wage war against Him." The second said, "Let us go up to heaven and set up there our gods and worship them there." And the third said, "Let us go up to heaven and smite Him with bows and spears."

But God knew all their deeds and all their evil thoughts, and He saw the city and the tower which they were building.

And it came to pass as they were building that they built themselves a great city and a tower in its midst, very, very high and strong. And because of its great height the mortar and the brick did not reach the builders who were on top of it before a full year was spent in climbing up. And thereafter they reached the builders, and gave them the mortar and the bricks, and thus they did every day. And while these climbed up, others went down all day long. And it came to pass that when a brick would fall from their hand and break, they all would weep over it; but when a man would fall down and die, nobody would even look after him.

And the Lord knew their thoughts.

And while they were building they shot arrows toward heaven, and all the arrows fell back down upon them full of blood. And when they saw this they said to one another: "Behold, we slew all those who are in heaven." But this was from the Lord, to mislead them and to wipe them off the face of the earth.

And they built the tower and the city, and worked on this day after day until many days and years had passed.

And God said to the seventy angels who stand first before Him, who are nearest to Him: *Come, let us go down and confound there their language, so that they understand not one another's speech* (Gen. 11:7). And this is what He did to them. And from that day on one forgot the language of the other, and they did not understand how to speak in one language. And it came to pass that when a man said to his fellow man, "Give me a stone to build," he gave him mortar; and when he said, "Give me mortar," he gave him a stone. And when the builder took the mortar from the hand of his fellow, or the stone for which he had not asked, he threw it at his companion and killed him. And they did this for many days, and many of them died as a consequence.

And the Lord smote the three groups which were there, and chastised them according to their deeds and thoughts. Those who said, "Let us go up to heaven and worship there our gods," turned into apes and elephants. And those who said, "Let us smite heaven with arrows," them the Lord slew, one through the hands of the other. And the third group, those who said, "Let us go up to heaven and wage war against Him," the Lord scattered all over the earth. And those who were left, when they knew and understood the evil that had befallen them, abandoned the building and they, too, dispersed upon the face of the whole earth. And they ceased to build the city and the tower. Therefore that place is called Babel, for there the Lord confounded (*balal*) the language of the whole earth. And it is to the east of the Land of Shinar.

And that tower which the sons of man had built—the earth opened up her mouth and swallowed one third of it; and fire came down from heaven and burnt one third; and the third part of it remains to this day. And some of it hangs in the wind of heaven, and the size of its shadow is three days' journey.

(Sefer haYashar, pp. 28-31)

REWARDS AND PUNISHMENTS
Charity Saves from Death

Once Joseph and Uziel were walking along the road, and they saw two poor men coming down from the mountain, carrying wood on their heads. Joseph said to Uziel:

"I see over there a boy, carrying wood on his head, and in the wood there is a scorpion, and the scorpion has no permission to sting him."

He called to the boy and asked him: "Have you done an act of charity while on this road?"

The boy answered him: "A boy went with me to the synagogue, and he was an orphan, and he had nothing to eat, and I gave him of my bread, and he ate together with me."

They said to him: "Happy are you that you were saved from death."

This is what Ben Sira said: "Withhold not your hand from a good deed."

(Alfa Beta diBen Sira, OM 1:39)

Always Say, "God Willing"

I

One should never say anything without adding, "God willing."

Once there was a man who said: "Tomorrow I shall sit

with my bride under my wedding canopy, and shall cleave to her."

They said to him: "Say, 'God willing.'"

He said to them: "Whether God willing or God not willing, I shall sit tomorrow with my bride under my wedding canopy."

And this is what he did: He entered with his bride the wedding canopy, and sat with her all day. At night, both of them went to bed, and before he could approach his bride both died. Next morning they found them dead, one next to the other.

They said: "How true is what Ben Sira said, 'The bride entered her wedding canopy and did not know what would befall her.'" Hence they said: "He who wants to do anything should say, 'God willing,' and if he does not say so, he will never succeed."

(Alfa Beta diBen Sira, OM 1:39)

II

There was a man who was very rich, and he had much land, but had no oxen to plow the land. What did that man do? He took a money-purse in which there were a hundred denars, and went to a city to buy oxen or cows to plow his land. And while he was walking on the road, Elijah of blessed memory met him and said to him:

"Where are you going?"

He said: "To the village to buy oxen or cows."

Elijah said: "Say, 'God willing.'"

He said: "Whether God willing or not, behold, my money in my hand, and I shall do what I have to do."

Elijah said to him: "And not with success."

And he continued his way to do what he wanted to do, and the purse fell out of his pocket, and when he reached the village of the oxen to conclude the purchase, he put his hand into his pocket to pay the money, and found nothing. He instantly returned home, with a bitter soul, and took other money, and went to another village, so that Elijah should not meet him. But as he was walking Elijah of blessed memory met him, and appeared to him as an old man, and said to him: "Where are you going?"

He said to him: "To buy oxen."

He said to him: "Say, 'God willing.'"

He said to him: "Whether God willing or not, behold, my money is in my hand, and I am not afraid of anything."

The man went his way, and while he was walking Elijah cast sleep over him and he lay down by the road and slept. And Elijah took the purse from his hand. And when he awoke he found nothing, and he returned home, distraught, and took a third pouch of money and set out again. Elijah of blessed memory met him and said to him: "Where are you going?"

He said to him: "To buy oxen, God willing."

He said to him: "Go in peace and with success!"

Instantly Elijah returned to him all his money, and put it into his pocket, and the man knew nothing of the money. And he went to buy oxen. And he found there two red heifers in which there was no blemish, and he said to their owners: "How much are these heifers?"

"They said: "One hundred denars."

He said: "I do not have a hundred denars with me."

And he put his hand into his pocket and found there three hundred denars, and he right away purchased the oxen to plow his fields. And thereafter he sold the red heifers to the king for a thousand denars of gold.

Therefore, every man who wants to do anything must say, "God willing," for he does not know what will become of him in this world from evening to morning, for this is what Ben Sira said: "From morning to evening the world can be destroyed."   (Alfa Beta diBen Sira, OM 1:39-40)

The Gold and the Honey

This is a story about a man who lived in the days of Saul

king of Israel. That man had a very beautiful and comely wife. And she was very rich, and that man was very old, and his time arrived to leave for the house of his world. And since the woman was comely, the prince of the country put his eyes on her, and wanted to take her with a high hand. And she did not want in any circumstance, and fear entered her heart without end. And she took all the fortune that she had and put it in jars. And in the mouth of the jars she put honey, and she gave them in safekeeping to a man who was an acquaintance and friend of her husband, in front of witnesses, and she fled from the country.

After a time that prince died and the woman returned to her house. The man in whose hand was the deposit made a betrothal banquet for his son, and he needed honey. He went and found those jars with the honey and took from the honey that little which he found in the mouth of the jars. The end of the matter was that he found that all the jars were full of gold. Instantly he took the fortune and filled the jars with honey.

When the woman returned to her house she went to the man and said to him: "Give me the deposit which I had left in your hand." He said to her: "Go and bring the witnesses in front of whom you gave me the honey, and take your thing." And she went, and brought the witnesses, and he brought out all the vessels and returned them to her in front of the aforementioned witnesses.

When she went to her house, she found that all the vessels were full of honey. She began to cry and to weep. She went to the judge of the state and complained against him. The judge said to her: "Do you have witnesses?" She said to him: "No." He said to her: "My daughter, what can I do for you? Go ask the king, and let him judge you."

She went to Saul, and he sent her to the Sanhedrin. They said to her: "Do you have witnesses that you deposited the money with that man?" She said to them: "I have no witnesses, for I did it with cunning because of the fear of the prince." They said to her: "My daughter, we have no permission to decide except by the mouth of witnesses, for we cannot judge matters which are in the heart."

She went out from before them greatly distraught. On her way back to her house she met David king of Israel, and he was a small boy, a shepherd of the flock, and he was playing with other boys. Instantly she cried and said: "My sons, I complained and they did not give justice to me against the man who deceived me. Listen to my words and give me justice in your mercy!"

He said to her: "Go to the king that he should give me permission, and I shall bring out your judgment to the light." She returned to the king and said: "My lord, I found a boy who, according to his words, knows how to bring out my judgment to the light." He said to her: "Go and bring him before me." And she called him to the king. Saul said to him: "Is it true that you can bring out this judgment to the light?" He said: "If I have permission from you, my trust is in my Creator." He said to her: "Go with him."

He said: "Bring out the vessels which you deposited with that man." She brought out the vessels. He said to her: "Can you recognize that these are the very vessels which you deposited with him?" She said to him: "Yes, my lord." He asked also the man, and he admitted that they were those vessels. He said to her: "Go and bring me other, empty, vessels." She went, and poured the honey into those vessels, and he took the first vessels and broke them in the sight of the people. He searched and found among the shards of the vessels in one place, two gold pieces which were stuck to the sides of the jars.

Instantly David said to the man who had had the deposit: "Go and return the deposit to the woman."

Instantly, when Saul and all Israel heard this, they were amazed about it very much. And they knew that the Holy Spirit was in him.

(M'shalim Shel Sh'lomo haMelekh, BhM 4:150-55)

The Man Who Never Swore

Once there was a man who all his life never wanted to swear, and he was very rich, and in the hour of his departure from the world he called his son and said to him:

"My son, I warn you that you should never swear, neither in truth nor falsely, for all the riches I had I earned only by refraining from swearing. I did not swear even a true oath, and the Holy One, blessed be He, made me succeed every day, and in every merchandise, and in everything I did."

His son answered him: "Father, I shall keep all your commands, I shall never swear."

And when his father departed from the world and left life to all Israel, swindlers came upon the orphan and demanded much money of him. They said to him: "Give us the money your father owed us!" He said to them: "It is not true." They went to the judge and he instructed him to swear. The orphan thought in his heart and said: "What shall I do? If I swear, I desecrate the name of heaven and disobey the command of my father. I shall rather pay them and not swear." He gave them all the money his father had left him, and only a few golden denars remained in his hands. The swindlers came and said to him: "Pay us what you owe us, or swear that you have nothing left." He said: "I shall never swear." They arrested him and put him in jail. And his wife was a pious woman and beautiful, and she was ashamed to ask anything of people, and she took in clothes to wash and thus kept alive her husband in the prison, and her children, and herself.

One day she went to the river with her sons to do some washing, and a ship came there, and when the owner of the ship saw her he desired her very much in his heart, and said to her: "Wash my clothes and I shall give you a gold denar." She said: "So I shall do." She took the denar and gave it to redeem her husband from the jail house, and she washed the clothes. And when she went to return them, the owner of the ship kidnapped her and sailed away. And her sons were standing at a distance and they cried and wept, and went to their father and told him and said: "Our mother has been captured!" He lifted up his eyes towards heaven and said: "Praised be the name of the King of kings of kings, the Holy One, blessed be He, who brought me this far, that I am left without food and without livelihood." And he lifted his eyes towards Heaven and said before him: "Master of the World! Have pity on me and on my little children who are orphans!"

And they went together until they came to a river which was near the sea, and there was there no ford to ford the river. What did that pious man do? He took off his clothes and prepared himself to swim across the river. When he reached the river the river swept him away. But the Holy One, blessed be He, caused him to find a big plank, and he sat on it, until he came to a city. And there the people gave him their flock to take to pasture. And his sons who remained on the bank of the river cried and wept, until a ship came and led them off into captivity.

One day that pious man was sitting on the bank of a river which was full of snakes and scorpions, and remembered how rich he had been and how he remained alone, and he lifted up his voice in weeping and said: "Master of the World! I am left without a wife and without children, and without money, and there is nobody to take pity on me. It is revealed and known before you that my death is better than my life." And he wanted to throw himself into the river. But when he saw the dead who were killed by the snakes and the scorpions, he became frightened, and he saw an image calling to him: "So-and-so, be not afraid, for many years now much money has been set aside for you, and now your time has come, and the Holy One, blessed be He, will raise you up to greatness because you have guarded your lips from swearing, and have not desecrated the name of heaven, and have not neglected the command of your father. Take from there all the money!"

He took the money that was there, and hired many

laborers and built himself great palaces and great towns, and he became king. And at the end the Holy One, blessed be He, made a miracle for him, and returned to him his wife and his children, and made them kings and rulers.

And that man gave charity and praised and thanked the Holy One, blessed be He, for having paid him fully his reward. What caused all this? The guarding of his mouth from swearing. For he did not want to swear even a true oath, for thus said the Holy One, blessed be He: "The angels who sanctify My name in holiness are afraid and humble before Me, and you, man, when you become filled with My good presents, how can your heart rise up to mention My name in vain?"

('Aseret haDibrot, BhM 1:72-74)

Look Not at Strange Women

Matya ben Ḥeresh used to sit and study the Tora, and his face was like the sun and his appearance like the Ministering Angels, full of the fear of heaven. And he never lifted up his eyes to the wife of a fellow man. Once as he was sitting and studying and occupying himself with the Tora in the house of study, Satan passed by and became jealous of him. He said: "Is it possible for a man like this not to sin?" What did Satan do? He went up to the firmament and stood before the Holy One, blessed be He, and said: "Master of the World! Give me permission to try him!" He said to him: "Go!" He went and found him sitting and studying the Tora. What did he do? He assumed the shape of a woman the like of whom there has not been since the days of Naamah the sister of Tubal-Cain after whom went astray the sons of God.

She [i.e., Satan in the guise of a woman] came and stood before him. When he saw her, he turned to the left. Thereupon she sat on his left side, and he turned his face to the right. When he saw her moving from side to side, he said: "I am afraid that the Evil Inclination will overpower me and make me sin." What did that righteous man do? He said to the student who sat before him: "Go and bring fire and nails!" And he put the nails into the fire until they became red like fire and put them on his eyes. When Satan saw this, he trembled and became frightened, and fell on his face, and shook, and went up to the Height and returned before the Holy One, blessed be He, and said before Him: "Master of the World! This and this happened." The Holy One, blessed be He, said to him: "Did I not tell you that you cannot overcome him?" In that hour the Holy One, blessed be He, called Raphael. He said to him: "Go and heal the eyes of R. Matya ben Ḥeresh." Raphael went and stood before him. He said to him: "The Holy One, blessed be He, sent me to you to heal your eyes." He said to him: "Let me be, what was, was." He returned to the Holy One, blessed be He, and said before him: "Master of the World! He said to me this and this." He said to him: "Go, tell him that the Evil Inclination will never rule him." Instantly he went and healed him. Hence the sages said: "He who does not turn his eyes to another woman, the Evil Inclination has no power over him. Therefore one should be careful not to turn one's eyes to another woman, except his own wife, for he who touches another woman is brought by her to poverty, and moreover, she kills him, and woe to him in this world and woe to him in the Other World."

('Aseret haDibrot, BhM 1:79-80)

Touch Not a Married Woman

Rabbi Meir used to make the pilgrimage to Jerusalem on every pilgrim festival and to lodge with R. Y'huda the Cook. And the wife of R. Y'huda was a beautiful and modest woman, and she would honor R. Meir each time he stayed with them. After a time the wife of R. Y'huda died and he married another woman and commanded her and said to her: "A scholar will come here, and his name is R. Meir. Be careful about honoring him, bring him into the house and put food and drink before him, and serve him until he finishes his meal, and then make a beautiful bed for him and nice clothes to lie on them." She said to him: "I shall do according to your command."

When the pilgrim festival arrived, R. Meir went up to Jerusalem and went to lodge in the house of R. Y'huda. He said to her: "Let me see the wife of R. Y'huda." She said to him: "My lord, this is what my husband commanded me: 'When a scholar by the name of R. Meir comes here, be careful about his honor, and put food and drink before him.' And I shall be more careful about your honor than was his first wife." He said to her: "I have no permission to enter at the invitation of his wife, but only at the invitation of the master of the house himself." R. Meir went outside and found R. Y'huda. He said to him: "My first wife died." Instantly R. Meir went to the house of R. Y'huda. His wife stood and prepared food and drink, and brought it before him, and he ate, and she stood and served him.

And R. Meir was a beautiful youth, and she lifted up her eyes to him, and made him drunk, and he knew not between his right hand and his left hand, and she made the bed for him, and R. Meir lay down upon it and fell asleep and slept. Up stood the woman before him and took off his clothes and lay with him until the light of the morning, *and he knew not when she lay down, nor when she arose* (Gen. 19:33), and slept with her all night.

In the morning R. Meir got up and went to the House of Study to pray. When he returned to the house, she put food and drink before him. He ate and drank, and she served him and spoke and laughed before him. And R. Meir said: "How impudent is this woman!" And he looked at the floor and did not want to look at her. She said to him: "Why don't you look at me? All night you were lying with me, and you were not ashamed, and now you are ashamed

of me?" He said to her: "It is not true!" She said to him:
"You don't believe me? You have such and such a sign on
your body." Instantly R. Meir recognized that he had lain
with her, and there was bitterness in his soul, and he cried
and wept, and said: "Woe to me that I lost the Tora which I
had studied! Now what remedy do I have?" He said to
himself: "What shall I do? I shall go to the head of the
yeshiva and spread my talk before him. Whatever he will
impose upon me, I shall accept."

He returned to his house and cried and wept all the way,
and his clothes were rent and ashes on his head. Instantly all
his relatives came out and said to him: "What do you have
in your heart to do?" He said to them: "I shall go the head
of the yeshiva in Babylonia, and whatever sentence he will
pass upon me I shall accept." They said to him: "You did it
unintentionally and not intentionally, and the Holy One,
blessed be He, will forgive you. Do not let your voice be
heard so as not to ruin the reputation of your children." He
said to them: "If I listen to you, the Holy One, blessed be
He, will never forgive my sins, for it is written, *He that
covereth his transgressions shall not prosper* (Prov. 28:13)."

Instantly he went to the head of the yeshiva in Babylonia,
and sat before him. The head of the yeshiva said to him:
"What is your wish?" He said to him: "Father of Israel, this
and this happened to me, and therefore I came before you,
for whatever you will tell me, even if it be death or to feed
me to wild animals, I shall accept." He said to him: "Wait
for a while until we study your case." Next day the head of
the yeshiva said to him: "We studied your case, and we
found that you should be fed to wild animals and to a lion."
R. Meir said to him: "I accept the punishment of heaven."
The head of the yeshiva commanded that they do as he had
said. He called two mighty men from Israel, and said to
them: "Take this one to the forest, to the place where lions
are found, and tie his hands and feet, and leave him there,
and you stand on a tall tree and see what happens to him. If
they eat him, bring me the bones, and I shall make a great

mourning over him for he accepted the punishment of heaven."

Instantly they led him to the forest to the place where the lions pass, and tied his hands and feet, and stood there on the tree to see what would happen to him. At midnight a roaring lion came to him, sniffed him, and went his way. Next day they came before the head of the yeshiva. They said to him: "The lion did nothing to him, but sniffed him and went his way." He said to them: "Do the same to him a second night." They did as he said. At midnight a roaring lion came, turned him over on his face, and went his way. Next day they told the head of the yeshiva what had happened. He said to them: "Do the same to him a third night. If nobody touches him, bring him back to me, for he deserves no punishment from heaven." They went and did so. At midnight a roaring lion came and growled at him, and bit him with its teeth and tore out a rib from its vertebra and ate of it only as much as an olive. Next day they told the head of the yeshiva about it. He said to them: "Bring him to me, since the lion ate of him only as much as an olive." They went and brought him to the head of the yeshiva, and he commanded the doctors that they heal him.

When R. Meir returned to his house, a heavenly voice issued and said: "R. Meir is destined for life in the World to Come!"

Therefore one should be careful not to touch a married woman, nor a betrothed woman, for she causes him to go down to Gehenna and to the nethermost Sheol, and to burn forever....

('Aseret haDibrot, BhM 1:81-83)

The Reward of Study

Once there was a pious man who was seventy years old and had no son. And he had much money, and every day he would go to the synagogue and when the boys would come out from the house of their teacher he would hug and kiss them and say to them: "Tell me your verses!"[3] And each one of them would tell him his verse, and he would cry and say: "Happy are you that you merited sons who occupy themselves with the Tora!" And he would say: "Woe to me that all my fortune will be inherited by others."

What did that pious man do? He stood and distributed all his property among the scholars, saying: "Perhaps I shall have a share in the World to Come together with them."

Instantly the compassion of the Holy One, blessed be He, was aroused and he gave him a son at the age of seventy. When the son was five years old, he made him ride on his shoulder and took him to the House of Study. He said to the teacher: "Which book will my son begin to study?" He said to him: "The Book Leviticus." He said to him: "Let him start with the book of Genesis, which is a praise to the Holy One, blessed be He!" And instantly he opened the Book of Genesis.

One day the son said to his father: "How long will you have me ride on your shoulder? Let me go, I know the way, and can go by myself." He said to him: "Go." As he went, he met a messenger of the king. When the messenger saw that he was very beautiful, he took him and led him into his house.

When the time of the meal came, his father saw that he had not come home, and he went to his teacher and said to him: "My son whom I sent to you, where is he?" He said to him: "I do not know, for today he did not come to school." When his father heard this he cried and wept, and went to the crossroads and asked in all the roads: "Did you see my son? Such and such was his sign." They said to him: "We have not seen him." When he heard this, he and his mother cried and wept, and rolled themselves in ashes, until their weeping rose up to the Heights. In that hour the Holy One,

[3] I.e., the Biblical verses which they learned just before leaving school. This was a favorite method of prognostication in Talmudic and later times.

blessed be He, took pity on them, and He brought a sickness upon the king. And the king said to his servants: "Bring me a book of remedies." And they did so, and the Holy One, blessed be He, turned it into the Book of Genesis. His servant opened it and could not read it. They said to him: "It seems to us that this is a book of the Jews." They looked for Jews but found none. The messenger said to the king: "When I went to a village of Jews, I stole from there a boy. Perhaps he can read it." The king said to him: "Go and bring him to me!" He went and brought him before him. The king said to the boy: "My son, if you can read this book, happy will you be and happy will we be." When the boy saw the book he cried and wept, and fell to the ground full length. The king said: "It seems to me that you are afraid of me." He said to him: "I am not afraid of you. I am the only child of my mother, and the Holy One, blessed be He, gave me to my father when he was seventy years old, and he taught me this book. I can read it well." He opened it from *In the beginning* and read until *And finished were* (Gen. 1:1-2:3). The king said to him: "Can you explain it?" He said to him: "Yes." Instantly the Holy One, blessed be He, gave him knowledge and wisdom and understanding, and he explained everything to him. When the king heard the power of the Holy One, blessed be He, he instantly stood up from his throne and seated the boy in his place until he explained everything to him. The king said to him: "Healing has come to me through you. Ask of me whatever you want and I shall give it to you." The boy said to him: "I ask of you nothing but that you return me to my father and my mother." Instantly the king commanded that they take him to his treasury, and gave him silver and gold and pearls, and returned him to his father and his mother. When his father and mother saw him they gave praise and thanks to the Holy One, blessed be He, and in that hour they rejoiced very greatly. Hence the sages said: "If he who studied only the Book of Genesis got such a reward, he who teaches his son Tora and Mishna, how much greater will be his reward.! And if he who honored his father only one hour received such an honor from the Holy One, blessed be He, he who honors his father and mother day and night, how much greater a reward will the Holy One, blessed be He, give him in This World and in the World to Come!"

('Aseret haDibrot, BhM 1:77-78)

The Weasel and the Well[4]

It happened to a girl who was going to visit her father's house—and she was adorned with silver and gold—that she lost her way and found herself in a deserted place. When midday came, she thirsted, and there was nobody with her. She saw a well with a rope hanging from it. She took the rope, and let herself down into the well, and drank. Then she tried to climb up, but could not. She began to weep and to cry. A man passed by the well and heard the voice. He looked down into the well but could see nothing. He said to her:

"Who are you? Are you of the humans or of the demons?"

She said to him: "I am of the humans."

He said to her: "Perhaps you are one of the demons and want to mislead me?"

She said to him: "No."

He said to her: "Swear to me that you are of the humans."

She swore to him.

He said to her: "What happened to you?"

She told him the whole story.

He said to her: "I shall pull you up if you will become mine."

She said to him: "Yes."

He pulled her up. Once he had pulled her up he wanted

---

[4] This story is the basis of Abraham Goldfaden's popular romantic operetta *Shulamis.*

right away to take her. But she said to him: "From what people are you?"

He said to her: "I am from Israel, and I am from such-and-such a place, and I am a Kohen."

She said to him: "And I, too, am from a certain family which is well known and respected."

And she continued: "A holy people such as yours, which the Holy One, blessed be He, has chosen, and He sanctified you from all Israel, and you want to act like an animal, without a marriage contract and without the sacrament of wedding? Come with me to my father and mother, and I shall become betrothed to you."

And they gave a troth to each other.

She said: "Who shall be the witness between you and me?"

And a weasel passed by near them. He said to her: "Heaven, and the weasel, and the well shall be witnesses that we do not lie to each other."

Both of them went their ways.

And that maiden kept her troth, and she refused all those who came to ask for her hand. And when they persisted, she began to behave as if she were possessed, and tore her clothes and also the clothes of anyone who touched her, until the suitors ceased asking for her hand. And she kept her troth to that man. But he, as soon as he saw her no more, his inclination overpowered him, and he forgot her, and went to his city, and busied himself with his work, and married another woman, and she conceived and gave birth to a son. And when the child was three months old, the weasel killed him. And his wife conceived again, and gave birth to another boy, and he fell into the well. His wife said to him:

"If your sons had died as is the way of all men, I would recite the justification prayer.[5] But since they died a

---

[5] The prayer *Tzidduq hadin* (literally, "justification of the judgment") is recited at the burial to justify the divine judgment which brought about the death.

peculiar death, it must have some special reason. Tell me, what did you do?"

He revealed to her everything that had happened.

She said: "Go to your share which the Holy One, blessed be He, has allotted to you."

He went, and asked about her in her city. They told him that she was possessed, and what she did to everyone who asked for her hand. He went to her father, and told him the story, and said to him: "I accept every blemish found in her." And he called for witnesses.

Then he went to her. She began to act as was her wont. He told her about the weasel and the well.

She said: "I was faithful to my troth." And instantly she returned to normal.

And they were fruitful and multiplied and had many children and much property. And of them it is said, *Mine eyes are upon the faithful of the land that they may dwell with Me* (Ps. 101:6).

(Gaster, *Sefer haMaʻasiyyot*, Hebrew pt., 59-60)

R. Akiba and the Sinner

It happened to R. Akiba that he was walking in the cemetery and met a charcoal burner who carried a load of wood on his shoulders. And he was running under his load like a horse. R. Akiba commanded him to stop. He said to him: "My son, what have you with this hard work? If you are a slave and your master put this yoke on you, I shall ransom you and bring you out to freedom. And if you are poor, I shall make you rich." He said to him: "Let me be, my lord, for I cannot stop." He said to him: "Are you of the children of man or are you of the demons?" He said to him: "I have died, and every day they make me hew wood and place me in the fire." He said to him: "What was your work when you were alive?" He said to him: "I was a tax collector and gave favored treatment to the rich and killed the poor. And not only that, but I lay with a betrothed girl on the Day of Atonement." He said to him: "My son, have you heard from those appointed over you whether you can be helped?" He said to him: "Do not detain me, lest the masters of punishment become angry with me. I have no hope and I have heard of no ransom, but I have heard them say to me, 'If you had a son who would stand in prayer before the congregation and would say, Bless God the Blessed One, we would release you from the punishment.' I have no son, but I left my wife pregnant, and I don't know whether she has given birth to a male or a female. And if she bore a son, who would teach him Tora?" R. Akiba said to him: "What is your name?" He said to him: "Akiba." "And the name of your wife?" "Sosmida." "And the name of your city?" "Aldoqa." In that hour R. Akiba grieved over him, and went from city to city until he reached his city, and asked: "Where is he and his house?" They said to him: "May his bones be ground in Gehenna!" He asked about his wife. They said: "May her name and memory be erased from the world." He asked about his son. They said: "But he is uncircumcised! He has not fulfilled even the commandment of circumcision." Instantly R. Akiba took hold of the son and made him sit before him and taught him Tora. And he did not study until R. Akiba sat fasting over him for forty days. A heavenly voice issued and said: "Are you fasting over this?" He said: "Yes." Then he read with him the Alef Bet, and took him to his house, and taught him the after-meal grace, and the reading of the *Sh'ma*, and the prayers. And he made him stand, and he prayed and said, "Bless God, the Blessed One, for ever and ever!"

In that hour they released his father from the punishment. And he came in a dream and said to R. Akiba: "May your mind rest in the Garden of Eden, for you saved me from the chastisement of Gehenna."

(Isaac Aboab, *Menorat haMaor*, par. 9)

The Waves Save the Saintly

It happened to a pious man who was used to giving charity
that once he went and boarded a ship. The wind came and
sank his ship in the sea. R. Akiba saw him go under, and
went before the law court to testify that he had died and his
wife could remarry. But even before the time came for him
to stand up, that man came and stood before him. He said
to him: "Are you the one who went down in the sea?" He
said to him: "Yes." "And who brought you up from the
sea?" He said to him: "The charity I gave, it brought me up
from the sea." He said to him: "How do you know?" He
said to him: "When I went down into the depths of the
abyss I heard the sound of great noise from the waves of the
sea, saying to one another, 'Run, and let us bring up this
man who practiced charity all his life.'"

(Avot diR. Nathan A, p. 17)

The Rabbi and the Harlot

Our rabbis taught: It happened to a man, Nathan by name,
who was very observant of the commandment of the
Tzitzith.[6] He heard that in the cities of the sea there was a
harlot who took four hundred gold pieces as her hire. He
sent her four hundred gold pieces, and made an assignation
with her. When the time came, he went and sat down at the
door of her house. Her handmaid entered and told her:
"That man, who sent you four hundred gold pieces, is
come, and he sits at the door."

She said to her: "Let him enter."

He entered. She made him seven beds, six of silver and
the seventh of gold. She went and sat down on the top bed,

6 The *Tzitzith* are the four fringes which, following Num. 15:37-40,
are appended to the four corners of the garment known as *Tallith
Qatan* (or "small Tallith"), which is always worn by observant Jews
under their clothes.

naked. He too went and sat down next to her, naked. His four fringes came and hit him in the face. He slid down from the bed and sat on the floor.

She said to him: "By the gods of Rome, I shall not let go of you until you tell me what blemishes you have found in me."

He said to her: "By God, I have never seen a woman as beautiful as you. But our God commanded us one commandment, and *Tzitzith* is its name, and in it it is written, *I am the Lord your God*, twice, telling us that 'I am He who shall punish you in the future, and I am He who shall pay you a good reward.' And the fringes seemed to me to be four witnesses."

She said to him: "By God, I shall not let you go until you tell me your name, and the name of your city, and the name of your master, and the name of the House of Study in which you have learned Tora."

He wrote down the names and gave them to her.

She arose, and gave away all her property: one third to the government, one third to the poor, and one third she took in her hand, except those beds, and she went to the Land of Israel.

She came to Tiberias, to the House of Study of R. Ḥiyya, and said to him: "Rabbi, command concerning me that they make me a Jewess."

He said to her: "My daughter, have you perhaps set your eyes on one of the students?"

She took out the note and gave it to him.

He said to her: "Go, take possession of that which you have bought."

Those beds which she had made for him in sin, now she made for him lawfully. If this was the reward of his merits in This World, how much more must he have received in the world to Come!

(Gaster, *Sefer haMa'asiyyot*, Hebrew pt., 25-26)

The Three Sons

Once there was a great, wise, and just king who let it be
known in his whole realm that crowns of honor and
lordship in the royal house will be given only as a reward of
work and successful acts. And in the course of time three
sons were born of the royal seed, sons without blemish,
good to look at and delightful to contemplate, and the king
loved them and wanted to benefit them, and said to them:

"My sons, my heart wishes to do you good and to elevate
your position, for you have found favor in my eyes more
than anyone else of your age. But all the people in the gates
and all the servants of the king know, and you yourselves
know it very well, that the royal word has gone forth and
the law has been established that honors and greatness will
be given only as a reward of good and outstanding deeds.
Therefore, my sons, hear me, and set out over the great sea,
and roam about wherever you wish, in countries and
kingdoms which you will like. Be strong and let not your
hearts be weak, for in every place where your foot will
tread you will find enough for your needs. But listen to my
voice and rise early and go on your way, and perhaps you
will be transformed into other persons and will be
successful, and will do as you will be able to, and dwell [in
those countries] until I send for you, and you will bring to
me accounts of your deeds and then I shall reward you."

When the sons heard this they were saddened, but the
word of the king was a command for them, and they could
not gainsay it. And they prostrated themselves and went
out from before the king, and they crossed the sea and went
beyond the rivers of Cush, and came to one of the remote
islands. And from afar they saw a big orchard, and they
desired it, and went there, and found the gate open before
them, but three men were sitting at the gate. One was very
old, with a staff in his hand because of the great number of
his days. The second was a man of pains, lame of spirit, and
smitten with boils, and the third one was an old man, very

awesome in the splendor and radiance of his face.

The first man said to them: "Come, my sons, into the orchard, but know that your exit from it is inevitable."

The second man said: "Eat, my sons, as much as you desire, but you shall not put anything in your vessels [cf. Deut. 23:25]."

And the third one said: "When you eat of the fruit of the orchard, beware, my sons, of the beautiful, and choose instead the good."

And the three youths entered the orchard, and looked around, and saw in it many beautiful plants, many beautiful trees, and many delightful flowers, and many fragrant fruits of the finest kinds, and many birds which twittered and sang. And many pools and troughs full of sweet and good water, and many rivers and streams. And there was there gold, and crystal, and onyx, and many precious minerals. And they ate and enjoyed the fruits, and, behold, they were sweet, and drank of the water and it was pleasant. Also the shade and the air of the garden was for them a delight. And they tarried there together, and abided about a fortnight.

And it came to pass thereafter that the days became renewed and matters changed, and the three youths separated. And, behold, one of them was drawn after the pleasures of the orchard and its beautiful and desirable fruits, and he did not turn from them and from their pleasures either to the right or to the left. And, behold, the second one turned away from these pleasures which are the bane of the sense of touch and of the other senses, and put his heart to gathering and accumulating much gold and many precious stones which were found there. And he took them and put them in his bag. And the fortune that he could put in it was not enough in his eyes, and he made a bag out of his coat, and he tied it around his waist, and still continued to search for more methods and means from the trees of the garden to take the treasures out with him. And in doing this he mortified himself, and wasted away his flesh because of the heaviness of the burden and the abstinence from food and drink, for his enormous desire to accumulate more and more riches did not allow him any rest and deprived him of all good.

But the third son was displeased with these two things, and he prepared his heart to understand and grasp the workings of that precious orchard, and to know its pathways, and divisions, and all the details of its kinds of fruits and plants which were there, so as to penetrate their characteristics, dispositions, and nature, to learn and study their changes, wonders, and special powers, to delve into the depths of the differences among them, their forms, and their relationships. He listened to and studied the natures of the many and varied animals which were there, and he stood amazed and awed by what his eyes saw when he contemplated the miracles of their existence. He was full of wonderment at the canals, pools, rivers, and streams which were in the orchard, and he also marveled at the mighty order which was there, in that the canals rose to water the beds of the garden each at its proper times and moments. And [he saw that] the water filled the troughs from which the animals drank, each according to its proper place without any lack. And he turned this way and that way, but could see no gardener, nor any man who would do these things in their proper order, and he concluded in his mind that these miraculous things must certainly be done by a wise craftsman with the greatest depth of wisdom. He must be the owner of the orchard and its master, and nothing found in the orchard or around it can escape his will. And the third son was seized with a great desire to know who the master was whose wisdom has reached such heights. And every day he would walk about in the garden, along its walls, hoping to find a place where he could go to complete his search and find the owner of the orchard, or to encounter him by chance, or to meet somebody who could tell him where the owner was and in what place he could be found. And meanwhile he ate enough of the good fruits of the orchard to satisfy his soul, and drank of its sweet waters, and he also saw that there was nothing wrong in taking a few of the precious stones which were there and putting them into his bosom in order to obtain profit from their powers of remedy, and to strengthen himself with them.

And it came to pass after the days grew long, and each of the three brothers was busy with his preoccupation, each according to his inclination, and each according to his work, that behold a servant of the Cushite king came there and in his hand an epistle signed by the hand of the king saying: "When this missile reaches you, hurry and come quickly, and hasten to me right away!"

And when they heard it, they hurried to the gate through which they had entered, and, behold, the first son who put his heart to eating to satiety of the fruits of the garden and of its delights, those fruits entered into him and made him pampered and soft of nature, and when he went out the gate and the air around him changed, the taste and nature of those foods changed, and his belly became swollen, and his soul blown up from the surfeit of pleasures and softness, and he fell down full length on the earth, and died.

And after him came the second son, weighed down with the silver and gold and all the precious stones, a burden which would have been too much even for a team of mules, and he carried the enormous weight, and his whole figure was so distorted that one could not know whether it was a man or a beast of burden. And when he reached the gate, the gatekeepers came out, and frightened him, and took away from him everything he carried, and then let him pass. And when he came through the gate, the watchmen who go about the garden found him, and got hold of him, and beat him, and took away from him all that had been left in the fold of his garment and in his hands, and nothing was left with that fool, and he was left poor and full of pains, and he went gloomily and peculiarly, smitten by God and tortured.

But the third son was glad to hear the call and said:

"Verily, I have become rich, I found, I saw! This is the day I was hoping for! Now I shall go out and walk wherever I want to, perhaps it will so happen that the desire of my soul will be given to me, that which I asked for, and the goal of my search!" And he remembered what the second man had told him when he arrived there, namely, that he was not permitted to take out anything from there, except that which entered into his bowels. And he quickly took a few of the precious stones which he had put into his bosom, and swallowed them, and it could not be known that they entered into him. And he went and left the garden in great joy and happily, and also the gatekeepers and the watchmen received him with kindness, and let him go with great love.

And when these two men went out of the orchard, before they went far they lifted up their eyes and saw the road on which they had come, and they continued on their way to return to the country from which they had set out. And they went in order to present themselves to the king. And behold, one of them, because of his poverty and his overworked condition, looked miserable, no strength was left in him even to walk, he fell down and crawled on all fours like an ape. And he came to the gate at which the servants of the king sat, and they looked at him, two or three officers, and none of them recognized him, and they wondered whether it was an animal or a man, and they said to one another: "Who would let such a despicable person, forsaken by man, come among us? Let the boys arise and drive him away from here!" And his voice appeared to them like that of a ghost from under the earth, and his words like a whisper from the dust when he said: "I am a son of the royal house. I am at the head of those who sit over the kingdom, and my lord sent me to roam in distant lands, and now he has sent for me in a written epistle, and that is why I came back." And when they heard this, they cursed him, and drove him away saying: "Who are you, you despicable and despoiled one, you full of shame and disgrace, to enter the house of the king? Stop this, get away from here to the dungheap or to the slaughterhouse, or to those in captivity who sit behind the handmill!" And he was driven away, full of anger and despair, and went to the place where the prisoners of the king are kept, and lay down among them in misery, and he did not get to see the face of the king.

And thereafter the third son arrived, running like a gazelle and strong like a lion, beautiful of visage and delightful to see, and the appearance of his countenance answered all questions and showed that he was a man of strength, rich in deeds. And the people were amazed at him and said: "Who is this who approaches us like the image of a guest and a wayfarer? And splendor and glory are before him, like the appearance of princes." And they rejoiced at him and embraced and kissed him and hurried and took him, and brought him before the king, and led him reverently. And when he came before the king, he prostrated himself and greeted him, and he found favor in the eyes of the king, and the king asked him what he had done. And he told the king all that had befallen him, and said: "My lord, the land to which you had sent us is very, very good and broad, and has everything."

And it came to pass as he told the greatest praises of the orchard, its ways and paths, its features and all his own acts, that out of his mouth came the memory of the troughs, the waters, the pools, and the upper and lower terraces. And he took out of his mouth the precious stones and the pearls. And he said: "Has such a thing ever been heard or can it be? Behold, my lord king, this is its fruit." And he related how he, with all the desire of his soul, was searching for the owner of the orchard, whose wisdom he had recognized, in order to know what was his nature, and to shelter in his shadow, for he knew that his palate is sweetness and all of him is delightful.

And the king rejoiced at his words, and also the precious stones which he took out of his mouth found favor in his eyes. And he commanded that they be placed in his treasury, and said to him: "Well did you see, and good was that which was in your heart. And now come and I shall show you the man whom you seek." And he got up from his throne and took him by the hand, and led him into an inner room, and answered him all the questions he asked. There was no thing hidden which he did not tell him. And, behold, the son reached the limit of the pleasure for which he yearned. The king made him great and placed his seat with the seats of all the princes, and there he sat forever.

(Isaac Arama, *'Aqedat Yitzḥaq,* 5:112b-114a)

The Sinner and His Wife

There was a man who was very rich, and he had a very beautiful wife, and he loved her exceedingly. And in his courtyard there were four high walls, strongly fortified, and a door opened into his courtyard from those walls, and he knew that anyone passing through that door would not return to his house in peace, because demons were dancing there. And some say that there was the entrance to Gehenna.

And the man was very evil and godless, and his wife was evil, and they had no children. And she was always desirous of going to that door to see what was behind it, but her husband would not let her, and would always watch over her, because he knew that her mind was directed towards it. But once the king needed that man and sent for him, and the man commanded him who was over his house that he should always be with her and follow her wherever she went. The man went to the king as he had sent for him and tarried there.

In the meantime the woman came and said to him who was over her house: "Listen to me, and do my will, and let me go to the door, and I shall give you everything you want. For know you that if you do to me what I am asking of you I shall greatly reward you." He said to her: "Do not this and do not harm and destroy yourself for nothing. For my master commanded me, saying to watch you like the apple of my eye, for your love is very wonderful for him and you please him. So do not this great evil, and do not bring his white head down to Sheol in evil." She said: "By your life, I shall only approach the door to a distance of a bowshot." But he did not want to give her permission. She, however, made great efforts to go, until she went to the courtyard against his will and without his consent, and there was nobody with them in the house. The man cried out in a loud voice, and clapped his hands, and the man was very much aggrieved, and he ran after her. But she went until she came before the door, and when she came there, somebody from the inside stretched forth his hand and pulled her in to him, and the door closed after her.

The man said: "And I, where shall I come from this great misery which has befallen my master?" Off went the man and hid himself in a room, and remained there until his master returned to his house. And when he came and did not see his wife and his servant, he fell on his face upon the earth and his soul fluttered and he fainted. And all his neighbors came to comfort him, but he refused to be comforted, and said: "That I shall go down to my wife to Sheol in mourning." And he wept over her a great weeping. He went and searched in his whole house, and found not, until he came to his bedroom and heard there somebody moaning and sighing. And he said: "Who are you? Are you my servant whom I heard moaning?" He said to him: "I am your servant who is guilty before you!" And he came to him and fell down before him, and cried and entreated him. The man said to him: "Where is my wife?" He stood up and told him the whole story. He said to him: "I swear, I shall not sit and I shall not be quiet and I shall not rest until I know where she is and in what place she is, and what she is doing there, and whether I can be with her there."

What did he do? He gave everything he had to his relatives and went into captivity [?] until he entered a great forest, and he walked in it six days, and met a man, very big in his stature and black and very ugly. He greeted him and the other returned the greeting. And the man trembled and was very much afraid of him for he had never seen the like of him. The big man said to him: "I know what you wish: you wish to see your wife. If you want to come with me, I shall show you her place and you can talk to her." He said to him: "For all the treasures of the king, if he were to give them to me, I would not go with you." The big man said to him: "Is there in your house any man in whom you trust?" He said to him: "Yes." He said to him: "Bring him to me in eight days from today, and you will find me here." He took leave of him and went and came to his house, and all his friends gathered around him and asked him whether he had found his wife or had heard anything about her. He said to them: "Yes. Is there among you any man who wants to do what I shall command him? If I have done a favor in the world to any one of you, now has come the time and has arrived the hour that he can return to me all that I have done to him all my days."

One of his young men came and said: "My lord, you brought me up and elevated me from my childhood until now, decree upon me all your will and I shall fulfill all your commands, and I shall be careful and observe everything you will command me." He said to him: "You I have wanted, for I have found you faithful and very pleasing, and I trust you. Come with me and do all I shall command you."

And the two went together and came to the forest, to the place where he had been before, and he found the big man there. And the youth was frightened by him and feared him very much. His master said to him: "My son, you must go with this man, and he will take you to the place of my wife, and you will talk to her. And if you can bring her with you I shall give you heavy money and you will inherit everything I have." He said to him: "I shall do as you said."

He went with him and he took him into Gehenna, and

he saw there many people whom he had known suffering their punishment in Gehenna. And his master returned to his house. The youth said to the big man: "Show me the wife of my master." He took him to a room, and it seemed to him that the whole room, the walls and the roof, were covered with fine gold, and the floor was of precious stones, red and fiery. And he saw the wife of his master sit on a golden cathedra, dressed in golden clothes, and her surroundings were gold. It seemed to him that before her was a golden table set, and all kinds of red food. And she had many servants, some of them were cutting her food before her, others were pouring for her white wine into a golden glass.

When he saw her he fell on his face on the ground and said to her: "Blessed be He who gave a portion of His honor to flesh-and-blood creatures, for I have never seen any queen honored this much as I see that they honor you. And yet my master grieves for you, and eats not, all the days he fasts, and he sent me after you that you should come to him if you can."

She said to him: "My lord, hear me. All that you see around me is burning fire: this room, and the table and all the clothes I have on, and the cathedra upon which I sit. And everything I eat is fire: it consumes my body and my flesh until perdition, and the wine is molten lead which I drink every hour. And if the whole world were mine I would give it willingly to go out for one hour to cool myself, for I burn, my soul and my body. And tell this to my husband: that all the sinners of Israel in their body are thus in Gehenna. And tell him that he should repent of the evil deeds, for great is the power of repentance."

He said to her: "And for what sin do you suffer this cruel punishment?"

She said to him: "For many evils and sins which I committed, for I committed adultery with another man, and desecrated the Sabbath, and while unclean because of menstruation I slept with my husband, and I did not pity the poor and the orphans, and I did this and that."

He said to her: "Is it possible for any man to redeem you from this punishment?"

She said to him: "No, because I never had children. But if I had a son from my husband who could say in public, 'Bless the Lord, the blessed,' and the congregation would answer, 'Blessed is the Lord the blessed for ever and ever,' and would recite the entire Kaddish [prayer for the dead], I would be redeemed at the end of my year."

He said to her: "I shall go and relate all this."

And she gave him a ring which was still on her finger, which her husband had given her, and said to him: "Tell him that this should be for a sign that you are telling the truth in all that you say to him."

And he took leave of her, and went his way with the man who brought him there, and he led him until the place from where he took him, and there he took leave of him and went to his house.

When his master saw him he rejoiced greatly, and he related to him everything he had seen, and gave him the sign, and he believed his words. What did that man do? He went to the synagogue and asked mercy before the Holy One, blessed be He, with great weeping and with heartbreak, and he repented completely, and did not move from there until his soul flew away. A heavenly voice came and said: "This man is allotted [a share in] the life of the World To Come, to fulfill what is written, *To cause those that love Me to inherit substance, and that I may fill their treasuries* (Prov. 8:21)."

(Ma'asiyyot, no. 11, OM 2:350-51)

The Two Friends

This is the story of two friends who loved each other with a wonderful love, and the soul of the one was tied to the soul of the other. And because of the many wars they were forced to separate from one another and dwelt in two kingdoms. And it happened one day that one of them came to the city of his friend, and it was reported to that king, and he thought that he was a spy for he had come from the city of his enemy, and he ordered him to be killed. And when the man saw that his evil end had been ordained by the king, he fell before his feet and cried and beseeched him that he should do him one favor. The king said to him: "And what is it?" He said to him: "My lord the king, I was a great merchant, and I have given most of my merchandise to people on trust and did not write notes about it, and my wife and my sons do not know of it, and if I die and do not inform them and do not write notes about the customers, my sons will remain miserably poor, and now let me go to do this and I shall return." The king said to him: "And who will believe that you will return?" He said to him: "My lord the king, behold, this friend of mine who dwells in your city, he will vouch for me." The king said to his friend: "Will you vouch for him that if he does not return within the time that I shall set for him, you will die?" He said to him: "Yes, my lord the king, I shall vouch for him, soul for soul." The king said: "By my life, I shall see whether this great thing will be." Instantly he gave him time to go and to return, one month. And on the last day of the month, the king was waiting all day to see whether the man would come, and the sun was about to set and still the man had not come, and the king ordered that they bring his friend from the house of prison to cut off his head. Instantly they took him out to the square of the city and put the sword on his neck, and, behold, a sound of great noise in the city saying, "Behold the man is coming!" And the man came and saw his friend ready to be killed, and he lifted him up from the earth and took the sword to put it on his own neck, and his friend did likewise, and both of them were holding onto the sword. This one said: "I shall die!" And this one said: "I shall die in your place!" And when the king saw that they acted more wonderfully at the end than in the beginning, he was very much amazed, he and his princes. And the king commanded and they removed the sword from both of them, and he forgave them and gave them great riches and said to them: "I beg of you, since there is such strength of love between you, make me the third of you." And they became friends to the king from that day on, and therefore did our masters say: "Acquire a friend for yourself."

(Ma'asiyyot, BhM 4:143-44)

The Reward of Charity

It once happened in Jerusalem the holy city, may she be rebuilt and reestablished, that there was famine in the city, and all the poor of the city almost died of hunger. And the whole community took counsel and they agreed among them that they would go to a certain lord who was the aide to the king, perhaps he will have pity on them with charity, as the good hand of the Lord is upon him. For the king had three aides: a Jew, a Gentile, and an uncircumcised.[7] And the Jew was liked by the king more than the others, and the Gentile and the uncircumcised (may their name and memory be wiped out) were very envious of that aforementioned Jew....

So the Jews went to the aforementioned Jew to request that he come forth and take pity on them, because of his charitableness. And, God be praised, they found favor in his eyes. And he went and entered into his ledger all the poor of the city who were in need, and also the bashful ones who did not want to accept charity.... And instantly he distributed and gave to the poor enough to supply their needs, and then he said to them:

"Did you distribute all my monies to all the poor of the city, and also to the bashful?"

And they answered him that they had fulfilled the *mitzva* of giving to all the poor of the city, except for one man, a

---

[7] I.e., a Muslim and a Christian.

bashful one, and totally destitute, "whom we have entreated many times, that he accept, but he did not want to accept charity."

And [the lord] pressed that bashful poor man that he should consent to accept charity from his hand, but the man refused. He beseeched him again, perchance he would accept it as a loan, but still he did not want to.

And it came to pass that when the aforementioned aide to the king saw that he did not want to accept from him anything, either as charity or as a loan, he said to him:

"If so, do this: learn a trade to support your soul."

And this seemed good in his eyes, and then he sent to him a craftsman to teach him the trade of fishermen, to catch fish. And for this the lord bought for him a net and all the other things needed for that work, and they made a partnership between them.

Days later they brought a precious stone to the king, and he consulted to make it a *mesirba al-galiun,* that is, a stone at the head of the *pipa.*[8] And he could not find a craftsman expert to carve the stone and to set it into the pipe as his soul desired, and because of this his annoyance grew.

In the meantime the Jewish aide to the king entered before him and found him with his face angry, and he said to him:

"My lord the king, why is your face bad today?"

And he answered him that he had an annoyance in his heart because he could not find a craftsman to set this stone into the head of the pipe, so that when he sits at the head, and each one drinks[9] his pipe, his pipe should be the finest. Then the aide said to him: "Give me the stone, for I have a daughter whose craft it is to carve precious stones and pearls. And give us fifteen days."

And the king rejoiced greatly over this, and he increased

---

[8] I.e., the carved mouthpiece of the narghile, the water pipe.

[9] An Arabism. In Arabic one "drinks" the narghile, because its smoke is drawn through water.

the power of the aforementioned aide, and gave him that stone.

And the Gentile and the uncircumcised, when they saw that the king added greatness to the greatness of the Jew, hated him. And the two conspired to hatch a plot in order to cause him to perish. And they made it known in the house of the king that the aforementioned Jew had become bankrupt, and because of that he took the pearl[10] from the king, in order to sell it or the like. And the words were heard by the king, and he did not believe them, until he heard such things from the mouth of the great ones of the kingdom.

And when the uncircumcised and the Gentile saw that the king believed this rumor, they instantly entered before the king and spoke to him to beat him with words of cunning. But because of the greatness of his love before the king he did not want to punish him. And they entreated the king that they should go to the Jew to bring the pearl in his hand. And they went to fetch him, and they said to him that he bring the stone. And he took the pearl, prepared properly, in order to give it to the king. And it came to pass while they were on their way, in a small ship, that they began to persuade him that he should show them the pearl. But because he recognized in them that they hated him he did not listen to them. And when they saw that their acts were unsuccessful, they said to him:

"It has become known that you had gone bankrupt, and that you stretched forth your hand for it to sell it, and you cannot deny us except if you show it to us."

And his hand held it. And the youth[11] did not tarry to do the thing, and he took it out from his bosom to show it to them. And instantly they pushed his hand, and that pearl fell into the sea. And he became sad in his heart, he went and cried, for he knew that the king would not believe him,

---

[10] That is, the precious stone.
[11] Here the aide is called "youth."

and so he went with them crying in his anguish. And when they came before the king, the king said:

"Where is the precious stone I gave into your hand in order to prepare it?"

And the aforementioned Jew returned word to him:

"What shall I say to my lord, what shall I speak, how shall I justify myself? God found my sin, and now I am in your hand to kill or to let live."

In that hour it appeared to the king that what they slandered him with falsely and with cunning was true: that he had become bankrupt. Nevertheless, because of the king's great love for him he did not want to punish him in any way, and he only pushed him away with a reproach and said to him:

"Go from my face and do not return to see my face, for on the day on which you see my face without this stone, you will die."

And instantly he went away with pain in his soul, and returned to his courtyard, with an anguished face, and he commanded the people of his house:

"If anybody comes to ask for me, say to him that here I sit, and let him come up and come before me."

Let us return to the fisherman, whose work was to catch fish, and he supported himself from this work, with the net which the lord had given him, and he had a share in the catch according to the conditions. And one day when the fisherman went to catch fish as was his wont, a fish came up before him, and behold it was very good. There was none, nor was there created one, like it. And when the fisherman saw that fish, that it was most important, he said:

"I shall surely take this in my own hands to my partner the aide, for this fish is proper and suitable for him, because it is right and proper, and we shall prepare it with our hands and eat of it."

And this is how it was: He went to the courtyard of the aide, and when he came there, the people of the house did not want to open the house for him. And he beseeched them, and they went to ask permission from the lord, the aide to the king, and he returned word to them, "Let him enter, let him enter." And then he entered and sat down before the aide of the king. And it came to pass that when he saw the big fish, that it was very good, he was most delighted, and he himself wanted to deal [with it], and strengthened himself, and he found in its bowels the precious stone which the aforementioned Gentile and uncircumcised had thrown for him into the sea. And then his heart rejoiced and his honor was glad with joy and happiness.

And immediately he went with alertness and with strength girded, until he came before the king and said to him:

"Behold, what is yours is before you!"

And the king rejoiced greatly and said to him:

"My dearly beloved, in any case tell me what happened."

And he told the king the whole story, and then the king decreed upon his enemies, the Gentile and the uncircumcised, that they be delivered into the hands of the Jewish man, his aide, to do to them as he wished and wanted. And so it was, that they were delivered into his hand, and he killed them with an unnatural death, and gave them hard and bitter punishments. May all your enemies, O Lord, perish thus! And he alone returned to the king and he added high positions to his former position.

Behold, here is before you what they planned to do to that righteous Jewish man: to kill him, and to destroy him totally—and thus was done to them, and their efforts came back upon their head. May all your enemies, O Lord, perish thus! And it was the charity done by the aforementioned Jew in the time of the famine which stood by him, and his charity stands for ever.[12]

(R. Y'huda Birdogo, publ. by Meir
Benayahu, in Edoth 1:108-10)

[12] The story of the precious stone found in the fish duplicates that of the ring of Solomon found in a fish.

The Three Parts of Hospitality

This happened to a man in the land of Uz (Job 1:1), in the city of Stanbul [i.e., Constantinople], may our city [Jerusalem] be rebuilt, Amen. And he was exceedingly rich, and his house was wide open, for he brought in guests always, all the days. And because of our many sins, this event happened, that a conflagration fell in his courtyard and all his property was burned and nothing remained for him, so that he became wretchedly poor. And when all the people of his city saw what had happened to him, they were amazed, saying: "In exchange for having been hospitable and having kept his house wide open, now it has become the opposite, his house became burned and the riches turned to poverty? Astonishing!" And they had thoughts about the attributes of God, blessed be He, heaven forfend! Until, after a while, a rabbi came there and said to him:

"My son, tell me how did you behave in hospitality?"

He said to him: "By the life of my head, I gave them to eat and to drink with all the honor in the world!"

And the rabbi of blessed memory asked him: "Did you let them have your company on the day on which they went their way?"

And he said to him, "It never entered my mind to do that for them."

And the aforementioned rabbi said to him that this is what caused him the misfortune, that all his property was burned, because we find concerning our father Abraham, peace be upon him, who was always bringing in guests, that it is written, *He planted a tamarisk tree* (Gen. 21:33). And our masters of blessed memory explained that *eshel* [tamarisk] consists of the first letters of *akhila* [eating], *sh'tiyya* [drinking], and *l'vaya* [accompanying], and thereafter the Holy One, blessed be He, rewarded him, *For all His ways are justice* (Deut. 32:4). For since he fulfilled only *akhila* and *sh'tiyya*, whose first letters make up the word *esh* [fire], therefore all his property was burned in fire. But had he been careful to fulfill all the letters of *eshel,* which mean eating, drinking, and accompanying, he surely would have been saved, for this is one of the things whose fruits a man enjoys in This World, etc.

And from that day on the man returned to be careful about the *mitzva* of accompanying every wayfarer. And as a reward for it the Holy One, blessed be He, gave him riches and property and honor all the days of his life, until he died old and sated of days.

(R. Y'huda Birdogo, publ. by Meir
Benayahu, *Edoth* 1:111)

The Ugly Girl

Once there was a girl, the only child of her parents, who had the face of an animal. The girl was kept locked in alone in a room and never left it. Nobody ever saw her face, and the food was given to her through a little opening in the door. But the girl was very wise and there was nobody in the whole country greater in wisdom than she.

In another country there was a youth who studied Tora day and night. He wandered from place to place and heard Tora from the mouth of great rabbis and scholars. One day he came to the city in which was the wise girl locked in her room.

Once the rabbi put a question to his students and asked them to give him the answer in the afternoon. The question was difficult, and all the students were sad because they could not find the answer. When they returned to the House of Study, the youth found a note with the answer on his table. He asked the other students, "Who wrote this note?"

"The girl who never leaves her room," his colleagues explained. "She is very wise and can answer all questions and solve all problems for which we cannot find the solution."

"She is the one I shall marry," the youth resolved. But his

colleagues explained to him, "Her parents will not give her to you, because she is blemished."

The youth asked his friends that they try to persuade the parents of the girl, and they tried. But the parents would not hear of it, and explained to the youth that it was impossible for anybody to marry their poor daughter. The youth argued stubbornly: "I don't care. I shall marry only her."

Her parents had no choice, and gave their consent that the peculiar youth should marry their daughter.

On the night of the wedding, after the wedding, when the bridegroom saw the bride, he did not remain with her beyond the dawn of the next day. The bride wept all the time because of her blemish. In the morning the youth took off, leaving behind his ring and his Tallith.

In due course the woman gave birth to a son. The son grew up in the house of his grandparents. When he started to go to school, the children mocked him and said: "Your father is dead, and you have two mothers and a stepfather!"

The boy could not stand these hurts and insults, and one day he asked his grandmother: "Tell me, grandmother, are you really my mother, or do I have another mother?"

"I am your mother, my son!" said his grandmother, for she did not want to hurt her grandson.

But the child grew, and his grandmother could no longer hide the truth from him. After he found out, he went to his mother and asked: "My dear mother, where is my father?"

His mother answered him: "Your father will come back. Now he is far away."

The son waited a whole year, and when he saw that his father was not coming back, he resolved to go out into the world and find him.

His poor mother gave him the Tallith and the ring, and told him the whole bitter truth: "Your father lives in such and such a city. He fled from me and left me."

The son took his father's belongings and set out on his way.

Many months passed, and the boy was still searching for his father. After long wanderings he came to the city in which his father lived. He went directly to the synagogue, and there he met his other grandfather, his father's father. But of course they did not recognize each other and did not know about each other. The old man asked the boy: "From where are you? What are you doing here?"

"I came to find my father who had left my mother," said the boy, and he told the whole story to the old man who was his grandfather. He also showed the old man the Tallith and ring of his father, and the old man immediately recognized that they belonged to his son. Next day the old man asked his son, who was the boy's father: "Where is your Tallith, my son?"

"I left it in some place, father."

The father looked at his son's hand and asked: "And where is your ring, my son?"

"When I washed myself in one of the rivers, the ring sank into the deep water."

The grandfather asked his son: "Would you recognize your Tallith and your ring if I should find them?"

"Certainly."

The old man took out the Tallith and the ring which he had gotten from the boy, and showed them to his son. His son then knew that his secret had become known. The old man called his grandson and presented him to his father.

The son asked his father that he should return home, but the father did not want to. The son argued: "Come, father, return home! Mother is the most beautiful and wisest of women. Why don't you want her? Who forced you to marry her?"

The father understood that some miracle had occurred to his wife and said to his son: "My son, you return first, and I shall come after you."

The same day the son set out on the return journey. On his way he met an old man whom the boy had never seen in his life. The old man said to the boy: "I know how greatly you love your father and your mother. I therefore give you this bottle for your mother. When she will wash her face in its water, she will become very beautiful."

The boy thanked the old man, hastened his steps, and came home. Instantly he gave the bottle to his mother, and when she washed her face in its water, it became very beautiful.

The boy and his mother knew that the old man was none other than the prophet Elijah of blessed memory.

The father too returned home from afar. And he was very happy because of his beautiful wife and because of his wise son who brought peace into the house and happiness to his parents.

(Moroccan Jewish Folktale)

ANGELS AND DEMONS

The Pious Bride and the Angel of Death

It happened to a man who begot children, but they all died. He stood in prayer and said: "Master of the World! If You let me see a son who reads the Tora and let me prepare the *ḥuppa* [wedding canopy] for him, I shall invite to his wedding all the students and the poor and the orphans who will be in the city." And the Holy One, blessed be He, took pity on him, and fulfilled his request. A son was born to him, and he called his name Mattanya for he was a gift of God. He taught him much Tora, and when he reached the *ḥuppa* he invited to his wedding all the students and the poor and the orphans who were in the city, and filled six houses with scholars.

The Holy One, blessed be He, sent the Angel of Death. He disguised himself as a beggar and said to the bridegroom: "Be charitable to me and seat me among the students." The groom answered: "I have already invited all those whom I had to invite." The Angel of Death asked him three times, but he did not want to invite him. Thereupon the Angel of Death knocked on the door and entered the wedding chamber. The groom encountered him, and he appeared to him like a man dressed in filthy clothes. The groom said to him: "Is it not enough that you forced your way into the wedding chamber, you did so in filthy clothes!" The angel departed in shame. Thereafter the groom entered to rejoice in his *ḥuppa* with his bride.

While the poor were enjoying themselves, the angel knocked on the door. The groom arose and saw him and became angry and said to him: "How long will you continue insolent? Have I not chased you away from the feast, and now you come here? Begone!"

In that hour the Angel of Death went and stationed himself before the groom, before his bed, like a pillar of fire reaching from the earth until the firmament. The groom said: "Who are you?" He answered: "I am the Angel of Death, and I came to take your soul."

Then the bride spoke up and said: "Master of the World! Will You make Your Tora a fraud? You wrote in Your Tora, *When a man taketh a new wife he shall not go out in the army, neither shall he be charged with anything; he shall be free for his house one year, and shall cheer his wife whom he hath taken* (Deut. 24:5). And now, not even a month, not even a week or day [has passed]! Master of the World! Give me pregnancy from him so that I shall not go out like a harlot!"

In that hour the Holy One, blessed be He, listened to her prayer and rebuked the Angel of Death. Thus she saved her husband from death. And what were her [good] deeds? Her mother used to draw water every day and supply the children in school. She was an old woman, and the daughter would take the staff and put it in her mother's hand and support her, and carry the water. And she would say to her mother: "My mother, do not cease [this] *mitzva* [good deed] all your days. Should you be unable to do even this, I shall do it in your name." And thus she acted all her days. Because of this *mitzva* she was able to save her husband from death.

('Aseret haDibrot, BhM 1:83-84)

The Devoted Bride

It happened to R. R'uven the scribe, who all his life never tasted the taste of sin, that once he went to the synagogue in the morning and found a man sitting in his seat. He rebuked him and said: *Stand not in the place of great men* (Prov. 25:6). The man got up and sat down near the door of the synagogue and began to cry in his heart. And his tears reached the Throne of Glory. Instantly the Holy One, blessed be He, sent for the soul of R. R'uven's son. And that son had been granted to him only when he reached eighty. And when the Angel of Death came, R. R'uven recognized him and said to him: "Why did you come? Has perchance my time come to depart from the world?" The Angel of Death answered him: "No, but the Holy One, blessed be He, sent me to take the soul of your son." He asked him: "Why?" He said to him: "Because you rebuked that poor man." R. R'uven said to him: "If so, I am surely guilty. But give me thirty days to arrange the wedding of my son, and let him rejoice with his bride. And thereafter take his soul." The Angel of Death allowed him the thirty days. . . .

What did R. R'uven do? He stood and divided his money into three parts: one for the poor and indigent; the second part he used to make his son rejoice; . . . and the third part he set aside, to wait and see what would happen.

Twenty-nine days later, during which R. R'uven caused his son to rejoice, Elijah of blessed memory came and sat down at the door of the youth. The youth became frightened and asked: "Old man, why did you come?" He said to him: "My son, I am Elijah, and I came to announce something to you." The youth bowed down to him, and said: "What message do you have for me?" Elijah said: "The Angel of Death will take your soul tomorrow, my son." The youth said to him: "Old man, is it not that from the day on which the Holy One, blessed be He, created the world and until now, everyone dies when his day comes?" He said to him: "Yes." The youth said: "If so, I shall be one of them." Elijah said to him: "My son, you will not die as the children of man die." The youth asked: "How will it be?" He said to him: "The Angel of Death will come to you with four evil features which were aroused in On High." The youth asked: "What can I do to escape from his hand?" Elijah said: "Tomorrow, when your father goes up before the pulpit [to pray] and you stand on his left side, look around and you will see a beggar, dressed in filthy clothes and rags. Give him honor, for he is the Angel of Death, perchance he will have pity on you."

Next day, when the hour arrived, he saw that man. He went and greeted him, and said to him: "Rabbi, stand there in the place of the great men!" He answered him: "My son, yesterday [!] your father told me, *Stand not in the place of great men,* and now you are telling me to sit there?" The youth said: "But see, I have given you honor." The old man said: "He to whom honor is due have mercy on you!" Then he went out and sat at the door of the *huppa* [wedding chamber], and the youth sat down before him. He said to him: "My son, I want to ask you a question." He said: "Ask." He said: "There was a man who borrowed from his friend a crate full of straw. He took it, mixed it into clay, and built himself a big house. After a time the owner of the straw came and said to him, 'Return to me my straw!' What should he do?" The youth said: "He should give him other straw in its place." He said: "But what if he does not want it, but only his own straw? What should he do then?" The youth said: "Let him demolish the house and dissolve it in water and give him his straw." He said to him: "My son, you are the straw, and the spirit is the house. The Holy One, blessed be He, has sent me, He who is owner of the straw, to take his straw."

Even before he concluded to speak, the father came from

the synagogue with his hands over his head, crying and moaning over the fruit of his loins. And he threw himself before the Angel of Death and said to him: "I beseech you, take my soul instead of his!" Instantly the Angel of Death clothed himself in four garbs of cruelty: Wrath and anger, ire and great fury. And he armed himself against him like a warrior going forth into battle. He drew his sword from its sheath, and placed his foot on the father's neck and prepared to strike him. Instantly the 248 members in his body began to tremble, and he got up to flee from him, and said to him: "Go and take the soul of him to whom you were sent! For I am not able to endure that with which you have come against me!"

When his grandmother saw this, she fell down, and her hair, disheveled, dragged in the dust, and she said: "I beseech you, take my soul instead of the fruit of my womb!" And she moaned and cried. Instantly the Angel of Death clothed himself in four garbs of cruelty, wrath and anger and ire and great fury, and armed himself against her like a warrior going forth into battle, and drew his sword from its sheath, and placed his foot on her neck in order to smite her. Instantly she fled from him, and ran and locked the door behind her, and said: "Go and take the soul of him to whom you were sent! For I cannot endure that with which you have come against me!"

In that hour, when the bride of the youth saw this great sight, she descended from her wedding chamber and fell down before the Angel of Death, and said to him: "I beseech you, take my soul instead of this youth, and let him be so that he be sated with his days. . . ." Instantly the Angel of Death clothed himself in four garbs of cruelty, and drew his sword from its sheath, and placed his foot on her neck. She said: "Finish the work of the King of the kings of kings who sent you!" And he became confounded over her, once, twice, and a third time, but she repeated, "Finish the work of the King of the kings of kings!" Then the Angel of Death took pity on her, and a tear of mercy fell from his eye.

The Holy One, blessed be He, said: "This one, who is cruel and slays people, had pity on these. I, who wrote of Myself, *God, merciful and gracious* (Exod. 34:6), should have no mercy on them?"

(Gaster, *Sefer haMa'asiyyot*, Hebrew pt., 98-99)

The Story of the Jerusalemite Which Was Copied by R. Abraham the Son of Maimon

This is a story about a man who was a great merchant. He had only one son whom he taught Scripture, Mishna, and Gemara. And he took a wife for him, and the son had children during his lifetime. And when his time had come to die, he sent for all the elders of his city and said to them:

"Know that I have much property, and my wife has a marriage contract which stipulates that she get more than a hundred sela's of silver. All the rest of my fortune shall belong to my son if he keeps the commandments which I command him before you. But if he transgresses my last will, I consecrate it to heaven."

And he called his son and said to him in their presence:

"My son, know that I have much property, and silver and gold, and precious stones and pearls. I earned all of it in my travels which I undertook across the sea and on dry land. But many troubles befell me in the sea, and therefore I want you to swear a binding oath that you will not endanger yourself on the sea. I leave you much money which will be enough for you and your children and your children's children. But if you violate your oath, then, behold, I consecrate the whole fortune to heaven."

And the son swore before the elders of the city that he would never go on the sea. Then the man died, and the son sat and occupied himself with the Tora, and kept the oath he had rendered his father.

And it came to pass two years later that a ship came to the port of that city, and the men asked after that merchant, whether he was still alive. They were told that he had died and that his son was left in his place, and that he was very rich and a scholar.

The men of the ship said to them: "We beg of you, show us his house."

They went to his house and greeted him and said to him: "Are you the son of that great merchant who used to go with much merchandise to the ends of the world?"

He said to them: "I am his son."

They said to him: "If so, what did your father bequeath to you before he died of all that which he had overseas of property and trusts?"

He said to them: "He bequeathed me nothing of what he had overseas, but he made me swear and commanded me never to sail across the sea."

They said to him: "If so, if he did not bequeath to you what he had in trust or all that he had overseas, he was not of sound mind when he died. For know that everything in this ship, silver and gold and pearls, everything belongs to your father who entrusted it to us. And although he is dead, and did not bequeath it to you, God forbid that we deny our trust, for we are honest people, and we fear the Lord, the God of Heaven, and we do not desire the money of others, for, thank God, blessed be He, we have a great fortune of our own. And now, come with these your servants and take everything that is in the ship, for it is yours."

And the son of the merchant rejoiced in his heart, and went to the ship, and brought all that fortune to his house, and he invited the men of the ship, and gave them a feast and a holiday.

On the morrow the men of the ship said to him: "Let it be known to you that your father was a wise and clever man, but if he made you swear that you would not sail on the sea he was not in his sound mind when he died. And in truth, the oath which he made you take is void, for your father has much more property and trusts than that which we have brought to you, ten times as much. And how could he make you swear to lose all that fortune? He surely was out of his mind. And now if you will listen to us, obtain permission from the king and the sages, and come with us, and buy of the merchandise which is found in our country, and you will earn great profit from it, and you will bring back all the money which your father deposited in our country, and you will return in joy."

He said to them: "But my father made me swear that I shall never sail the sea. I shall not transgress the oath. And in that he did not bequeath that money to me, his intention was that I should not desire to transgress the oath he made me take."

They said to him: "Did he, then, love you more than he loved himself? Did he not sail the seas all his life, until he acquired great riches? He surely was out of his mind, and therefore that oath is void, for *Job speaketh without knowledge* (Job 34:35). Therefore it is better that you ask to be released of your oath and come with us."

And they importuned him until finally he gave in, and they made him change his mind, and he had to go with them to fetch the fortune. What did he do? He went and bought much merchandise, and boarded the ship with them, and they sailed together.

And when they were on the great sea, the wrath of God was kindled because he sailed and transgressed the oath and the command of his father. *And the Lord flung a great storm upon the sea, and there was a mighty tempest in the sea* (Jon. 1:4), and the ship was wrecked, and drowned were all those men who went with him and gave him advice, and caused him to change his mind to sail the sea and to trangress the oath and the command of his father. And the Lord, blessed be He, gave a sign to the celestial Prince of the Sea, and he cast that man up on the dry land, naked and barefoot, at the end of the world, in a place where there was no human habitation, so that he should suffer his punishment in his life for the sin he had committed.

And when he reached dry land and saw himself naked and barefoot, he recognized that the Holy One, blessed be He, was wroth with him, and that the day of his calamity had come upon him. Whereupon he lifted up his eyes to heaven and accepted the divine judgment. And he began to walk along the seashore, hoping to find a city, or something to eat and to cover himself with, for he was as naked as when he came out of his mother's womb. And when he had walked a full day, he found a tree with its branches overhanging the seashore, and he figured in his heart that this tree was certainly planted by people. And he went to find its roots, but did not find them until it became dark, for the tree was forty parasangs. When he saw that he could find nothing to eat or to wear, he went and covered himself with the branches of the tree to protect himself from the cold of the night.

And it came to pass at midnight that he heard the voice of a lion roaring, and saw it coming near to devour him. And he was sore afraid that the lion would eat him because he had transgressed the oath of his father. He lifted up his voice weeping, and prayed to the Lord, the God of Israel, that He save him, *and turn his anger away and stir not up His wrath* (Ps. 78:38), and punish him not by making him suffer an unusual death.

What did he do? He got hold of the branches of the tree and climbed up into its foliage, and when the lion came it did not find him, and turned and went away. And the man gave thanks to God, blessed be He, that he had saved him from the lion. And he thought that he would climb up higher on the tree, perhaps he would find something to eat, for he was very hungry. And when he climbed up, he found a big bird, Qipofa[13] is its name. And when the bird saw him, it opened its mouth to swallow him. But he tried to

---

[13] A kind of owl.

escape, and the Lord, blessed be He, put wisdom in his heart, and he mounted that bird. When he was riding it, the Qipofa was afraid, and did not move, nor did it rise from its place all night. And the youth was afraid and prayed to the Lord, blessed be He, that He save him, and with both hands held onto the feathers of the bird, and was unable to get off its back. And also the Qipofa was afraid for it did not know who was bestraddling it.

And when the pillar of dawn rose, the Qipofa looked at the man, and continued to be afraid of him, and it flew in fear and dread all day long, and took him across the sea, and carried him to the end of the world, until the evening. And while it was flying over the sea, he saw it beneath him and was afraid lest he fall, and he prayed to the Lord, blessed be He, that He rescue him. And at eventide the Qipofa passed over a country and came near the earth. And the man heard the voice of boys who were reading in the weekly portion of *These are the ordinances, If thou buyest a Hebrew slave* (Exod. 21:2). And when he heard this, he said in his heart: "Surely there are Jews in this country. I shall throw myself down here, perhaps they will have pity on me, or I shall sell myself to one of them as a Hebrew slave."

And so he did, and threw himself down, and he fell down at the door of the synagogue of that city, and the Qipofa flew on. And when the man fell down he could not get up for two hours, for he was almost broken in pieces by the force of the fall, and because he was weak from having had nothing to eat for two days.

And then he got on his feet, and tried the door of the synagogue, but found it locked. And he cried and said: "*Open for me, gates of righteousness!* (Ps. 118:19)."

A boy came out and said to him: "Who are you?"

He said to him: "*I am a Hebrew, and I fear the Lord of Heaven* (Jon. 1:9)."

The boy went and told his master, and he told him to open the door. And when he saw that he was naked, he asked him what had happened to him. And he *told him all that had happened to him* (Esth. 4:7), from beginning to end, and the many troubles that had befallen him.

The rabbi answered and said to him: "All that has happened to you is like nothing compared to what you will suffer now that you have come here."

The youth said to him: "Are you, then, not Jews? Are the Jews not merciful sons of merciful fathers? You will surely have pity on a man like me, poor and destitute, naked and barefoot."

The rabbi said to him: "Don't talk, for you cannot escape death."

The youth said to him: "*Wherefore speaketh my lord such words as these* (Gen. 44:7)?"

He said to him: "Because this country is not a country of the sons of man, but of demons, and these boys are the sons of demons. And now they all will gather in a minute to pray, and when they see you they will kill you."

And when the youth heard this he got very frightened, and fell down to kiss the feet of that rabbi, and cried and beseeched him that he give him an advice, to save him from death, for he was versed in the Tora and God-fearing, except that he had sinned by following the advice of those men who misled him to violate the command of his father and the oath.

And when the rabbi heard him, his compassion was aroused, and he said to him: "Since you are a learned man, and know the Book, and you have repented of what you had done, it is meet that one should have pity on you. And since you kissed my feet and fell down before me, I shall exert myself for you, and try to save you."

What did the rabbi do? He brought him in his house, gave him to eat and to drink, and had him sleep there with him, so that the others did not notice him all night. Next day the rabbi said to him: "Come with me to the synagogue and sit under the wing of my robe and say nothing until I speak to them about you."

And they went to the synagogue, and he sat under the

wing of the rabbi. And when the pillar of dawn rose the demons came to the synagogue like torches of fire, and he heard the sound of lightnings shaking the world, and the voice of thunder. And that man trembled, no spirit was left in him for fear. And they began to recite the Verses of Songs[14] as the Children of Israel do. And one demon stood near the rabbi and said to his fellow: "I smell the smell of a man!"

And the voice was heard among them, and they said: "Behold, he is next to the rabbi!"

And they did him no harm since he was under the wing of the rabbi, and they respected the rabbi.

And when the rabbi saw that the thing had become known, he waited until they completed the Verses of Songs, and then told the cantor: "Don't pray until I say what I have to say."

And the demons said to him: "Our master, *speak, for your servants are listening* (1 Sam. 3:10)."

He said to them: "I request of you that you harm not this man for he is *come under the shadow of my beam* (Gen. 19:8)."

And they said to him: "And what has one born of a woman to do among us? And why did he come here?"

And the rabbi related to them the whole story, from beginning to end.

They said to him: "How can we let live such a wicked man, who transgressed the command of his father and the oath of God? He must surely die."

The rabbi said to them: "He has already received his punishment in the multitude of troubles that befell him. And he is versed in the Tora, and he is worthy of being protected by his Tora. And if he deserved death, the Lord, blessed be He, would not have saved him from the lion, and from the sea, and from the Qipofa, and from the many other dangers."

The demons answered him: "He deserves death even

---

[14] The beginning of the morning prayers.

more so, for he knew and rebelled, and did not observe the command of his father, and also violated his oath, and the errors have become for him willful sins. And the Lord, blessed be He, saved him from all that has befallen him only in order that he suffer a painful death at our hands."

He said to them: "You cannot kill him except if he be sentenced according to the Tora, since he is versed in the Tora. And now listen to me, and let the cantor announce that no demon must harm him until after the prayer, and we shall take him before King Ashmodai, and let him sentence him to death or to life."

All of them answered and said: "*Good is the thing that you have spoken* (Deut. 1:14)."

Instantly he ordered the cantor of the synagogue that he announce that no demon must harm him until Ashmodai, the king of the demons, sentenced him. And after the prayer they took him before Ashmodai and said to him: "Our Lord king, this man sinned against God, and violated his oath, and did not keep the command of his father, and already this and this has happened to him, and we did not want to kill him until we brought him before you, because he is versed in the Tora."

And when the king heard this, he called his law court and said to them: "This man did so and so, and this and this has happened to him. *Execute justice in the morning* (Jer. 21:12), and investigate his case, for he is versed in the Tora. Therefore judge him according to the Tora of Moses."

The law court went and investigated his case, and sentenced him to die, for it is written, *Accursed is he who dishonoreth his father and his mother* (Deut. 27:16), and this man had dishonored his father. And since he violated the oath and the imprecation, he must die. From whence do we know this? From Jonathan, the son of Saul who violated the imprecation.

They came before King Ashmodai and told him that he had been sentenced to die because of the aforementioned considerations.

Ashmodai said to them: "Be moderate in judgment. Sleep over it, for it is said, The community shall judge, and the community shall save. And thus Moses their master held back the sentence of him who had gathered wood on the Sabbath because it had not been declared."[15]

They said to him: "We shall do as you have said, for you are our lord, and our eyes are toward you."

The king said to them: "Let the man come with me tonight, lest anybody harm him, until the sentence is confirmed." And he did so.

In that hour Ashmodai asked him whether he had studied the Bible and the Mishna, and commanded that they put before him the Tora, the Prophets, and the Writings, and the order of the Mishna, and the Gemara. And they tested him and found that he was learned and well versed in everything.

And when Ashmodai saw this he said to him: "Now I know that you are indeed a learned man, and you have found favor in my eyes. Swear to me that you will stay and teach my son what you know, and I shall save you from the hand of the demons. For I know that all of them will agree to kill you."

He swore to him about everything.

The king then said to him: "Come, I shall teach you arguments you can use tomorrow, for they will say that you must die. And you answer them that you are a judge and a sage, and that you want to see the sentence and to study their arguments. Then they will come before me, and I shall save you."

Next day the law court came before King Ashmodai and said to him: "We found nothing in his favor."

The youth answered and said to them: "I myself am a greater expert in the law than you, and I want to study my case."

They said to him: "No man finds himself guilty."

[15] Cf. Num. 15:34.

And they consulted among themselves and said: "The best thing for us to do is to follow the advice of King Ashmodai who always studies in the supernal yeshiva, and descends and studies in the yeshiva of below, and is knowledgeable in the laws of heaven and earth."

And they went and asked Ashmodai what should be with his sentence. He said to them: "This man is not guilty of a capital crime, for everything he did he did not in rebellion nor in treachery, but those men incited him and led him astray with their words, and he who is forced, the Merciful One absolves him. From whence do we know this? From *And unto the damsel thou shalt do nothing* (Deut. 22:26). And you know that God has already slain those men in the sea, but him He saved."

And when the law court heard this, they absolved him.

Then Ashmodai took him and brought him to his house, and set his son before him, and he taught him the Tora, Prophets, and Writings, and Mishna and Gemara. And Ashmodai gave him much honor. And at the end of three years the son of Ashmodai completed the study of the whole Tora.

One day a country rebelled against King Ashmodai, and he gathered his armies, and appointed that man over his house and over everything he had, and gave the keys of all his treasuries into his hand, and ordered all the men of his house not to do anything without his permission. And he showed him all his treasuries, and showed him one door which had no key. And he said to him: "You can dispose of all my treasuries, except this house."

Ashmodai went to besiege that country. One day that man passed that door of which Ashmodai had commanded him not to enter. He said in his heart: "What is in this house that the king commanded me not to enter it, alone of all his treasuries?"

He approached the door, and looked in, and saw the daughter of Ashmodai sitting on a golden throne, and seven maidens dancing and playing before her. And she was very beautiful of countenance and beautiful of appearance.

And when she saw him, she said to him: "Enter!"

He went in and stood before her. She said to him: "You fool of a man! You transgressed the command of your father, and transgressed the command of my father the king. What are you doing here among the women? Now you must know for sure that today you will die, for my father already knows that you came in here, and he is coming with his drawn sword in his hand to kill you."

And when the man heard this, he fell upon her feet and kissed them and cried, and implored her to save him from the hand of her father that he should not kill him, for he did not enter there for fornication, and did not intend anything evil.

And when the daughter of Ashmodai heard this, she said to him: "Since you are versed in the Tora, the modesty that is in you will save you from death. And now leave this room and when my father comes and says to you, 'Why did you disobey my command?' and will want to kill you, tell him, 'My lord, know that I entered because I love your daughter very much, and I ask you to give her to me to wife.' And I know that your words will please him, and he will give me to you, for from the day that you came to us he set his eyes on you that you should marry me, for you are versed in the Tora. But it is not good manners for the woman to ask the man, and it would be a shame for a great king like him to ask a man to take his daughter."

And when the man heard her words he rejoiced in his heart. And, behold, he was still saying to his heart that he should leave the room, when, behold, Ashmodai came, with his drawn sword in his hand, and said to him: "Why did you disobey my command? Now your day has come to be repaid for all you have done."

He said to him: "My lord king, God forbid, I entered here only because of my great desire for your daughter. Now I beg of you, give her to me to be my wife, for she is very pleasing to my eyes."

And when Ashmodai heard this, he rejoiced in his heart. He said: "I shall give her to you gladly. Wait until I return from the war." And he added: "From now on you have my permission to enter the house in which my daughter is, and to play with her, and stay with her as you wish."

Instantly Ashmodai returned, and he conquered that country and destroyed it. Then he said to his armies: "Come with me to the wedding of my daughter, whom I am giving to a man who is a great sage and versed in the Tora."

What did they do? They gathered all the animals and birds which they found in the desert, until they lost count of them, and brought them all to the feast. And King Ashmodai gave that man a huge fortune which was priceless and numberless, and they wrote out a marriage contract. And all his princes and servants were with him, and he gave them a great feast and presented them gifts with royal bounty.

At eventide the king gave his daughter to that man as is the custom of the whole earth, and both entered a room, and she said to him: "Do not think in your heart that you are a man and I am a she-demon, for everything that is found in a woman is found also in me, and I lack nothing. But beware: come not to me if you do not desire me."

He said: "I, too, love you like the light of my eye, and shall never leave you."

She said to him: "Swear me that it will be so."

And he swore to her, and wrote down the oath in a document and signed it. Then he went in unto her, and she bore him a son. And when the son was eight days old he circumcised him according to the law of the Tora, and called his name Solomon, after the name of King Solomon. And he dwelt there two years.

And one day the man was playing with his son Solomon, and his wife, the daughter of Ashmodai, was there. And the man sighed a great sigh. And his wife said to him: "Why are you sighing?"

And he said to her: "I am sighing because of my son and my wife whom I left in my country."

She said to him: "Do you miss here anything? Am I not beautiful in your eyes? Or do you lack money or honor? Tell me, and I shall fulfill your wish."

He said to her: "I lack nothing, but when I see my son Solomon, I remember my other children."

She said to him: "I told you that if my love is not engraved in your heart you should not marry me, and now you sigh for your first wife and remember her. Do not repeat this."

He said to her: "I shall refrain from so doing."

After days he again sighed. She said to him: "When will you cease sighing for your first wife and her children? But since it is so, I shall take you to them, but you must name me the time when you go and when you will return to me."

He said to her: "You name the time."

She said: "I shall give you one year to go and to come back to me."

He said to her: "So I shall do."

She said to him: "Swear to me!"

And he swore, and wrote down the oath and signed it, and gave it to her. And she kept all the oaths to be a witness for her.

What did she do? She invited all her servants and gave them a great feast. After they had eaten and drunk, she said to them: "My lord my husband wants to see his wife and children whom he has in a certain place. And now, who of you has the power to take him there?"

One of them answered: "I shall take him in twenty years."

The second said: "And I in ten years."

The third one said: "And I in one year."

Then one of her servants, who was a hunchback and blind in one eye, said: "I shall take him in one day."

She said to him: "May your strength be straight! But take

good care that you do him no harm, and do him nothing, and carry him gently, for he is your master, and he is versed in the Tora, and he has no strength to endure anything bad."

He said to her: "I shall do as you say, my mistress."

She went and said to her husband: "Take care not to make this one angry, for he is easy to anger, and it is because of his anger that he is half blind."

He said to her: "I shall not anger him with anything."

She said to him: "Go in peace. But remember your oath."

What did that servant do? He took him on his shoulder and brought him to his city, and set him down outside the city on top of a mountain, in peace. And it came to pass when dawn rose that the demon assumed a human form, and both of them entered the city. They met a Gentile who had known him. He said to him: "Are you not so-and-so who went overseas and whose ship sank?"

He said to him: "Yes."

The Gentile said to him: "I shall go and tell your wife, who has been sitting in widowhood for many years."

And he went and told them, and they rejoiced greatly. And his relatives and acquaintances came, and he told them all the troubles that had befallen him on the way, and how the Lord had saved him. And he gave a feast to all his relatives and acquaintances. When they had eaten and drunk, that man said to that blind demon who had brought him there at the command of Ashmodai's daughter: "Why are you blind?"

He said to him: "Is it not said, *He who keepeth his mouth and tongue, keepeth his soul from troubles* (Prov. 21:23)? Why do you shame me? Have the sages of blessed memory not said, 'He who shames his friend in public has no share in the World to Come (B. Bab.Metz. 59a)'?"

But he again angered him a second time and said to him: "Why are you a hunchback?"

He said to him: "It has already been said, *As a dog that returneth to his vomit, so is a fool who repeateth his folly* (Prov.

26:11). But I shall tell you: the truth is that I am blind in one of my eyes because I am easy to anger. One day I was quarreling with my friend, and he smote me with a knife and blinded my eye. And as for your question, why I am a hunchback, go ask the craftsman who made me."

He said to him: "I beg your pardon. Forgive me!"

He said to him: "I shall not forgive the insult for ever."

That man said to the people of his house: "Give him to eat and to drink."

He said to him: "I shall never eat nor drink of that which belongs to you. But tell them to recite the after-meal grace, and I shall return to my place."

After they said the grace, he said to him: "What do you want me to tell my mistress, your wife?"

He said to him: "Go and tell her that I shall never return to her, for she is not my wife and I am not her husband."

He said to him: "Do not say that, and don't violate your oath!"

He said to him: "I do not care for the oath which I have given her."

And he took his first wife, and embraced her and kissed her before him and said to him: "This is my wife, who is created in the image and likeness of God, and your mistress is a she-demon. Therefore tell her that I shall never return to her."

When the demon heard this, he left, and returned to his mistress, and told her everything that had enraged him.

And she said to him: "How is my lord, my husband?"

He said to her: "Why do you ask about a man who does not love you, who despises you, and who said that he would never return to you, and that you are not his wife and he is not your husband?"

She said to him: "I do not believe you and your words, for everything he did he did only so as to anger you, for I know that he is versed in the Tora and would not violate his oath. I shall wait until the appointed time, and then we shall see what will happen."

When the time came, she called that servant and said to him: "Go and fetch my lord, my husband!"

He said to her: "I have told you in his name that he told me that he would never return to you."

She said to him: "When he told you those things the time had not come yet. But now go and tell him that the time of his oath to return to me has arrived."

He went as she had commanded and said to him: "My mistress sends you her regards and reminds you to return to her, for the time of your oath has arrived."

That man answered and said to him: "Go and tell her that I don't want her regards and shall never return to her."

When he heard this, he returned to his mistress and told her the words of her husband.

She went and told the whole story to her father Ashmodai, and asked his advice what to do.

Her father answered her: "Is it perhaps because he quarreled with your blind servant that he does not want to come with him? Moreover, it may not be according to his honor to come with one who is blind and a hunchback. But do this: send to him respected envoys to warn him of his oath."

She did so, and they went and warned him.

And he said to them: "I shall never return to her."

They said to him: "But you are versed in the Tora. Why, then, do you transgress your oath, since the time you had given her has already passed, and you are in violation of the prohibition of *You shall not swear falsely in My name* (Lev. 19:12)? Moreover, you are also in violation of a positive commandment, for it is written, *He shall not diminish her food, her raiment, and her conjugal rights* (Exod. 21:10)."

But he answered them as he had the first time.

The envoys returned and told her his answer. She again sent more numerous and more honored envoys to warn him, for she thought in her heart: "Perhaps the first envoys did not please his eyes."

The envoys went and warned him, and he said to them:

"Do not continue to talk, for I shall never return to her."

They returned and told her: "Do not continue to send envoys, for he does not want you."

When she heard this she went and told her father and asked for his advice what she should do. Her father told her: "I shall gather all my armies and go to him. If he wants to return, good, and if not, I shall kill him and all the people of his city."

She said to him: "God forbid, my lord, that you yourself should go to him. Send with me some of your servants, those whom it pleases you, and I shall go to him. Perhaps he will respect me and come back with me."

And so he did. He sent with her his armies, and they went with her to his place. And she took along also their son Solomon. And they came there at midnight, and her armies wanted to enter the city to kill him and all the people of his place. But she did not let them enter the city and spill innocent blood.

She said to them: "It is nighttime now, and all of them are asleep. And you know that they entrust their souls to the hands of the Holy One, blessed be He, and we shall be unable to do them any harm as long as their souls are in His hands, blessed be He. But this is what we shall do with them, and we shall not sin: We shall wait until the light of the morning, and then we shall enter the city. If they will listen to us, good, and if not, we shall know what to do."

They said to her: "Our mistress, do as is good in your eyes."

She said to her son: "Solomon, go to your father and tell him that I have come to fetch him, and let him return with me and not violate his oath."

The boy went and found him asleep in his bed. He awakened him from his sleep, and stood trembling.

He said to him: "Who are you and why did you awaken me from my sleep?"

He said to him: "I am your son Solomon, the son of the daughter of King Ashmodai."

Instantly he got up in fear and dread, and embraced him and kissed him and said to him: "Why did you come here?"

He said to him: "Because my mother, your wife, has come here for the sake of your honor, that you return with her and fulfill your oath, and she sent me to warn you."

He said to him: "Tell her, please, that I shall never return to her, for she is not my wife and I am not her husband, for I am a man and she is of the demons, and the nature of the one is not like the nature of the other, and the two things do not mix properly."

His son answered him and said: "God forbid, upon your honor, for your words are not right. All the time you were with us they caused you no harm, and moreover, they gave you great honor for her sake. And also my mother honored you very much, and also my grandfather Ashmodai appointed you to be a prince and a great one over all the demons, and commanded them to do your bidding. And why do you kick her away, and why do you despise her? Don't you remember the kindness she did to you when she saved you from the hand of my grandfather Ashmodai? And he, too, was kind to you and saved you from the hand of the demons. And now, my lord, my father, listen to my voice and it will be well with you, and come back with my mother, and fear no harm or hurt."

His father answered him: "My son Solomon, do not continue talking to me about this, for I shall never return to her, for all those oaths were given under constraint, for fear lest they kill me, and they are not valid, for he who is forced, the Merciful One absolves him."

His son said to him: "I beg of you, do not destroy yourself willfully."

He said: "Get out, and stop talking things which have nothing real in them."

The boy returned and told his mother all these things. And her anger was kindled when she heard the words of her son Solomon, and she said: "I shall not kill him until I warn him before the congregation and hear what he answers, and what decision the law court and the congregation give me. If they hold a Tora court, good, and if not, I shall take vengeance on all of them."

And she went to the synagogue and said to the people of her army and all the princes: "Wait for me outside the synagogue, and I shall enter and hear what he answers."

She went in, and waited until the public finished the Verses of Songs. Then she said to the cantor: "Wait, don't pray until I say what I have to say."

And he said: "Speak."

She said to the congregation: "Know, my lords, that I am embittered because of this man, Dihon ben Shalmon. This man was delivered to us because of his sins, and my father was most kind to him and saved him from the demons who had sentenced him to die. And I, too, saved him from the hand of my father who wanted to kill him because he disobeyed his command. And my father gave me to him, and appointed him a great prince over all his armies. And he took me to wife according to the laws of Moses and Israel. And he wrote me a marriage contract for a large amount; and he swore to me that he would never leave me. And thereafter he wanted to come to see his first wife and his children, and he gave me a binding oath that he would return to me after twelve months. And, behold, his oaths are written with his own hand and signature. And now he wants to repay me evil for good, and he does not want to return with me. And now I want you to ask him why he did this, *execute justice in the morning*, and see these documents."

The judges said to her: "Stand here, you and your litigant."

And they both stood before the judges. They said to him: "Why do you violate your oath and do not return with her who has done so much good to you? And, moreover, you cannot render your oath null and void."

He said to them: "Know, my lords, that I gave all those oaths under constraint, for I knew that if I did not fulfill their wishes they would kill me. Therefore I have asked concerning those oaths and have obtained a release from all of them. And it is not of the way of nature that a man should marry a she-demon and beget demons on her. I want to remain with my wife who is human as I am, and be fruitful and multiply as it is written, *I will make him a helpmeet like unto him* (Gen. 2:18), and this one is not like unto me. And because of this I don't want to return with her. Let her go and take for herself one of the demons who is like unto her, and let them be like with like. And I shall stay here with my wife who is the wife of my youth."

She said to the judges: "Don't you agree that he who takes a wife must write her a letter of divorce, as it is said, *If he hates her let him send her away* (Mal. 2:16)?"

The judges said: "It is true and correct, for this is what the law says."

She said to them: "If so, let him write me a letter of divorce, and pay me what is stipulated in my marriage contract."

She produced her marriage contract, and they found in it a huge amount of money.

The judges said to him: "Either pay her the marriage settlement, or return with her."

He said to them: "Behold, all my fortune is delivered into your hands. And I shall give her a letter of divorce, and her marriage settlement, but shall never return with her."

The judges said to him: "Either you divorce her with a letter of divorce and pay the full amount of her marriage settlement, or we shall give her permission to do as she wishes."

He said to them: "I shall not pay more than is the custom among us."

They said to him: "You have already undertaken to do everything as written in her marriage contract."

She said to them: "Since you judged me according to the law and the Halakha, and have not played favorites, I do not demand that he return with me against his will, since he has rejected me. But I beg of you to give me permission to kiss him, and then I shall return to my place."

They said to him: "Do as she wishes, and let her kiss you, and she will set you free of all that which we have imposed on you."

Instantly she went and kissed him, and strangled him, and he died.

And she said to him: "This is your reward for having transgressed the command of your father, and for having violated three oaths, and for having wanted to leave me in widowhood with my husband alive. Now both I and your wife will be widows. As the master of proverbs said: 'He who wants to take my husband will die a peculiar death, and will see neither good nor joy, neither for me nor for his wife.' "

Then she said to the congregation: "If you do not want me to take revenge on you, take my son Solomon and marry him to the daughter of the greatest man of the generation, and put him over you as the head and the chief, for he is one of you, and let him dwell with you. For after I have killed his father I shall have no pleasure in seeing him dwell with me, for he will remind me of sin and cause me *a drooping of the soul* (Job 11:20). And I shall give him a great fortune so that he lack nothing. And you command that he receive his share in his father's inheritance."

And they did so, and the congregation took him and put him over them as the head and the chief, and he ruled over them. And she returned to her place, to the house of her father as in her youth.

Hence a man should keep the command of his father, and should not violate his oath, as it is said, *For the Lord will not hold him guiltless who taketh His name in vain* (Exod. 20:7).

(*Ma'ase Yerushalmi,* Yemenite manuscript, ed. J.L. Zlotnik)

The Angel of Death

A story about Ben Sever who strove to do charity all his life.

Once it became known to him that there was an orphan in a certain nearby country, who was nearing the age of marriage but had neither silver nor gold to wed a girl. What did Ben Sever do? He took everything he could find in his house and went and gave it to that orphan. And it came to pass as he was on his way back home, he came across a river which was four parasangs long, and there was there [i.e., in it] a dragon which devoured all the passersby. But when Ben Sever reached that dragon, it made itself into a kind of bridge, and Ben Sever crossed over it, and it did him no harm.

On the other side of the river, Ben Sever met a man who was exceedingly ugly, and who said to him: "Are you Ben Sever?" He said to him: "Yes." The man then asked him: "From where are you coming?" And Ben Sever told him all that had happened to him. The man then said to him: "Your ledger is with me, for your time has come to pass away from the world." In that hour the face of Ben Sever turned into greenness [from fright] and he lifted up his eyes toward heaven and said: "Master of the World! Should a man who has occupied himself with the Tora and with charity die at a young age? Is this the Tora and is this its reward? And has it been decreed that I should die far from my home like an animal, and the members of my family should not lay me out?" In that hour a heavenly voice went forth and said: "Behold, you are given time to go to your bed."

After he left behind the Angel of Death, Ben Sever came upon a city, and saw people coming out of it. He said to them: "Is there here a sage or a teacher? I want to go and pay my respects to him." They said to him: "There is here a great sage, and his name is Shefifon ben Layish ["Serpent, son of Lion"]." Ben Sever went to him, and when Shefifon saw him he rejoiced over him and bid him enter. And he saw that his face was greenish, and said to him: "What is the matter, Ben Sever? Do you perchance need some bread, or do you need anything else?" Ben Sever said to him: "I need neither bread nor anything else, for, behold, all the good things I have with me." Shefifon said to him: "If so, why is your face greenish?" And Ben Sever related to him all that happened to him on the way. Shefifon said to him: "Strengthen yourself! I am certain that the Holy One, blessed be He, will save you from death."

When five days had passed, a great cloud surrounded the house of Shefifon ben Layish. His disciples said to him: "Don't you see the great cloud which surrounds your house?" He said to them: "Go and see whether it surrounds the whole city or only this house." In that hour the Angel of Death came before Shefifon and said to him: "Give me the pledge which you hold in your hand!" Shefifon said to him: "What pledge do you have with me?" He said to him: "Your life and the life of Ben Sever." Shefifon said to him: "Go and do your work, you have nothing with me!" The Angel of Death went and brought the matter before the Shekhina, and said before Him: "Master of the World! Shefifon does not let me enter his house; he put a spell on me with Your Great Name." He said to him: "Go and tell Shefifon: 'I do not seek your life, Shefifon, only the life of Ben Sever.' " The Angel of Death went and said to him: "I do not seek your life, Shefifon, only the life of Ben Sever." But Shefifon answered him as he did the first time. In that hour a heavenly voice issued forth and said: "What can I do to these two pious men? For We decree a decree and it is not possible to carry it out. . . . For who rules over me so that if I decree a decree he can annul it? The Tzaddiq. And for his sake I annul it." And He said to them: "Go and add seventy years to the life of each of them."

(Ma'asiyyot, OM 2:334)

Sins and Repentance

A terrifying event took place in the holy community of Lvov [Lemberg] in the year 5439 [1679 C.E.]. When the Great Warner gave a sermon in the holy community of

Pozna, in its course he told this terrifying story.

A man became ill at the fair in the holy community of Lvov and was close to death, and was actually dying. And important people came to be there at the time of the departure of his soul. But the sick man suddenly regained his strength and cried out with a bitter voice, "Woe, woe!" like a man who awakens from his sleep. And he said: "Help me, my brothers and friends, multiply prayer over me!" And they said to him: "Of what are you terrified, and why have you been seized with pain like a woman in childbirth?" And he said: "Look, what has come to me: a man full of eyes, and his appearance was unlike all the creatures in the world, and many dogs followed him, and each one of them was different from the others in appearance, and they opened their mouths over me to swallow me, and each one said, 'This limb is mine, for it created me.' And thus they came in packs, and each of them said: 'You created me by such and such a sin which you committed.' And they opened their mouths wide to swallow me. And likewise several hundreds of satans came upon me, and said, 'I shall take the eye,' and so all the limbs. And the man ordered them that they should fulfill their desire, and that each should rule over his limb and his sinew and his love bone. And because of this I screamed, for I was terrified. Help me, I beg of you, my brothers and friends, save me from their hands."

And also the men who were watching his soul became terrified very much, and trembling and shaking seized them, and they read "O, with Your strength..."[16] and other prayers to save his soul from their hand. And at one point the aforementioned sick man cried: "My brothers and friends, be silent, for succor has come from heaven to have

---

[16] Hebrew: *Anna b'khoah.* Prayer hymn probably composed by 13th-century Spanish Kabbalists, but ascribed to the *tanna* R. N'ḥunya ben haKana. The initials of its words form a Kabbalistic holy name of God.

mercy upon me. Behold him who is come to me: a man dressed in linen and his appearance is like an angel of God, and he said to the man full of eyes: 'What are you doing here? Go your way with your host! I was sent by the Awesome and Fearsome to save this man from your hands, and I am a messenger from the Creator, may He be exalted, to prevent you from touching this man in any of his limbs. True, you are the works of this man's own hands, and it is he who gave you life with the many sins he committed, and he created you. But it is now ten years since God lighted up his spirit, and since he has regretted the previous acts he had committed, and he repented, for he had walked in darkness and had not known how great was the punishment of sin. But when he learned in books of morals, and in particular in the holy Sh'LaH,[17] and there he saw the greatness of the punishment, how much is the harm of the sin, he cried and asked mercy before the Holy One, blessed be He, and made repentance. But he has not yet completed his repentance, and since he has not completed the repentance he saw the hosts of the S.A.[18] so that he be terrified by seeing how much harm is caused by sins. But since he made repentance and resolved in his heart and in his soul to be all his days in repentance, you have no permission to touch him, for this is not your share. It is enough for you that you have frightened him. Had he completed his repentance, you would have been unable even to appear before him, but since he has not completed it, the fright he suffered is enough, for he has seen his sin."

And after these words more was there than what is written here, and he went his way, and he left life for all Israel, and related more such things about the might of the Lord. Therefore every one must put straight the transgres-

---

[17] Sh'LaH, initials of the title Sh'ne Luḥot haB'rit ("Two Tablets of the Covenant"), the major ethical work of the Kabbalist and communal leader R. Isaiah haLevi Horowitz (1565?-1630)

[18] S.A., initials of Sitra Aḥra ("Other Side"), i.e., Satan.

sion he committed, with everything possible, and we shall
be tranquil and peaceful and flourishing until the coming
of the Messiah. Amen.

(*Notzer T'ena,* by Shim'on Rabi of Tarnow,
pp. 13a-b)

ANIMAL TALES

The Ape and the Leopard

There was an ape who lived with two small apes upon a
rock near a bush. He loved the little one and hated the
older. A hungry leopard came forth from his lair, and the
ape trembled with fear for himself and the one he loved,
seeing that the feline leaped from the mountain of leopards
and approached with great ferocity, to destroy and devour,
and roared towards his prey, and beat a straight path in his
fury and wrath. And the ape said: "Let me be bereaved of
him whom I hate, I shall hide my face from him, and he
will serve as the leopard's food." And he took him and
flung him on his back, his intention being thus to expose
him first to the leopard. But the small one, upon whom he
took pity, he placed under his belly, as he ran to escape.
And when he saw that the leopard came nearer and nearer,
he wanted to throw off him whom he carried on his back,
but that one felt that this was his intention and held on
tight to the fringes of his hair, desperately trying to save his
own life. And when the ape saw that he was unable to get
rid of him, and the leopard had almost overtaken them, he
let go of the one whom he loved, and himself escaped with
the ape who was clinging to his back. And when the ape
saw that his intentions were frustrated, his reins and heart
turned to the ape he hated, and his hatred changed into
love, and he took pity on him as a man takes pity on the son
who serves him.

The lesson is that you should love your sons equally, for

if you love one of them more, and put your hope in him, suddenly a turn of the wheel can tear him away, so that you cast your eyes about and, behold, he is no more. And he whom you hated and kept at a distance becomes the restorer of your soul and your supporter in old age.

(Berekhya haNaqdan, *Mishle Shu'alim*, pp. 112-13)

The Grasshopper and the Ant

The grasshopper went to the ant and asked food of her, because she was short of provision, had neither wheat nor barley. But the ant turned her away from her for she herself had no covering for the winter, and scorned her request, and mocked her, and said: "Sorrow will be your end. Look here, than whom are you more deserving that you slept through the days of harvest, and made no effort to prepare food for yourself? How foolish would be the heart of him who would give you that which he laid by for himself! Know that I do not have enough to give you. What did you do at the time of the harvest, when the grass sprouted and the leaves could be seen, and all the creatures went out to glean and to prepare what is necessary for the winter? The sluggard says: 'There is a lion in the streets!' But he who wants to reap crops, must gather sheaves in his arms, like me who carried them on my shoulders and prepared my bread in the summer."

And the grasshopper answered: "Throughout the days of the ripening fruits, when the wagons are filled with sheaves, I learned to sing beautiful songs and acquired many friends. And all the worries fled from my heart, for I was delighted with my songs, and they told me that my voice was sweet. But now the drought consumes me, and the cold and the wind and the ice have become a burden unto me."

And the ant said: "Now neither the granary nor the winepress will succor you. You taught your voice songs and did not think of your food. But even if you nest in cedars, and even if your neck is adorned with chains, go try the house of a rich man, make fine music, sing many songs, and try to fill with them your soul when it is hungry. Lo, your words are an abomination for me, go away and leave me alone, for you trouble my thoughts. Although I am low of stature and have neither strength nor power, I filled my tent with good things. But if I was wise, I was wise for myself, while you will not find sustenance in songs, when the cruel ice comes. For slumber is clothed in rags, and sloth makes for deep sleep."

This parable is for him who is too slothful to lay by provisions for his house. Will others hear his cry? For at harvest he was fast asleep. Such a man is counted as guilty. And I intoned my parable and said:

My son, strive and work. Cross street and city in the heat of day. For autumn time gather garments and cattle and sheep, but all in honesty. And as for the fool, pierce his right eye, muzzle his mouth, and break his teeth.

(Berekhya haNaqdan, *Mishle Shu'alim*, p. 29)

Yadu'a, the Human Plant

There is an animal whose name is *Yadu'a* ["Known"]. Our master Rabbenu Shimshon wrote in the name of R. Meir bar Kalonimos that it is an animal whose name is Yadu'a, and a kind of big rope comes out of a root in the earth where this animal grows like cucumbers and gourds but the shape of the Yadu'a is like the shape of a man, both in the shape of its face and in the shape of its other limbs. And at its navel it is attached to that rope. And no creature can approach it as far as the rope reaches, for it tears to pieces and kills everything. And it grazes everything around it as far as the rope reaches. And when they come to hunt it, they shoot from a distance at the rope until it breaks, and then it instantly dies.

(Shabbatai Bass, *Sifte Ḥakhamim ad* Lev. 19:31)

The "Man of the Field"

There is an explanation of the verse, *Thou shalt be in league with the stones (avne) of the field* (Job 5:23). The spelling [in the Biblical text] is not *avne* but *adme* [which means "men of the field"]. What is *adme*? It happened to an old man that he stayed as a guest in a certain place in the house of a pious man, and his host honored him greatly. At noon the wife of the host said to her husband, "My lord, what shall we eat tonight in honor of our guest?" He said to her, "Our man (*adam*)." The old man heard it, understood it, and said to himself, "Perhaps in this place they eat one another. Just as they will eat that man in my honor, as my host said, so perhaps another guest will come after me and they will eat me in his honor." What did that old man do? He left that house and went to another house. When the time of the meal arrived, the first host went and asked all of his neighbors, "Have you seen the old man who came today to my house?" One of them said, "I saw him enter the house of so-and-so." He went there and found him at the table. He said to him: "My lord, why did you do this? Why did you leave my house? Come back with me!" He said to him, "I shall not go." And the host asked him twice and three times, and he did not listen. Finally the host left and after he was gone the second host said to him, "Why did you do this? Why did you shame this pious man, and he is a man of God?" He said to him, "I heard this and this, and I became troubled, and I fled out of fear and came here." That host began to laugh and said to him, "Have you not read the Book of Job?" He said to him, "I have." He said to him, "It is written there, *For thou shalt be in league with the stones of the field*, the spelling is *adme* [men of the field]. In our place here there is a kind of vegetable which grows out of the soil like all grasses, and it has the shape of a man, and it is rooted in the earth. And when it comes out of the earth its head comes out first, until the whole of it comes out of the earth...."

(Tanh. Buber 1, Introd., 63a)

The Pious Cow

Once there was a pious man who had a cow and he plowed with her every day, and when the Sabbath arrived he let her rest. After a time that righteous man became impoverished and had nothing left, and sold his cow to a Gentile. And the Gentile plowed with her six days and when the Sabbath arrived he took her out to plow with her. When she came out, she lay down under the yoke and did not want to do any work on the Sabbath. And he beat her, evil beatings, but it did not help. When he saw this he went to that righteous man and said to him: "Come, take your cow. For six days I worked with her and on the Sabbath I took her out to plow with her and she lay down under the yoke and did not want to do any work in the world. And I beat her, and it did not help at all."

The pious man understood why the cow did not work: because she had been accustomed to resting on the Sabbath. He said to him: "Come with me and I shall make her stand up and plow." When he came to the cow he whispered into her ear: "O cow, when you were in my hands you observed the Sabbath. But now that my sins caused me [to become poor] and I sold you to this man, I beg of you do as your master wishes."

When he spoke to her thus, the cow stood up and was ready to do her work. That man said: "Tell me, have you, perhaps, used some magic on her? I shall not let go of you until you tell me what you did to her, or what you whispered into her ear." The righteous man said to him: "Thus and thus did I speak to her."

When the Gentile heard it, he became frightened and he trembled and thought to himself: "If this animal which has no knowledge and no understanding recognized her Creator, I, whom God created in His image and likeness, and to whom He gave knowledge and understanding, does it not behove me to recognize my Creator?" Instantly he turned to the fear of heaven, and merited to learn Tora, and was called R. Hanina ben Torta ("son of the Cow").

('Aseret haDibrot, BhM 1:74-75)

The Fox and the Angel of Death

When the Holy One, blessed be He, created the Angel of Death, the latter saw the creatures, and said to Him: "Master of the World! Give me permission to slay them! . . ." The Holy One, blessed be He, said to him: "Cast into the sea one pair of each creature, and you will have authority over the rest." Instantly he did so, and began to cast into the sea one pair of every species, and caused them to sink into the sea.

When the fox saw this, what did he do? He promptly started to weep. The Angel of Death said to him: "Why are you crying?" He said: "Because of my companion whom you have cast into the sea!" The angel said to him: "And where is your companion?" The fox stepped to the edge of the water, and the Angel of Death saw the reflection of the fox in the sea and thought that he indeed had cast into the sea a pair other than him. So he said to the fox: "Begone!" Instantly the fox fled and escaped. He met the weasel, and told him what had happened and what had transpired. The weasel too went and did likewise and was saved. . . .

(Alfa Beta diBen Sira, ed. Steinschneider, p. 27b)

SATIRICAL TALES

Cast Thy Bread upon the Waters

There was a man who had a son, and he taught him every day: *Cast thy bread upon the waters, and after many days thou shalt find it* (Eccles. 11:1). After many days the man died, and that youth remembered what his father had commanded him, *Cast thy bread upon the waters*. And he would take every day bread and cast it into the sea. . . .

And there was a fish which would come to that place and eat the bread, and thus he did every day until he grew exceedingly, and he tormented his fellow fishes which were in that place, until all the fishes of the sea gathered and went to Leviathan and said to him:

"Our lord! There is here a fish which has become very big, and we have no life because of him, and in his strength he even eats twenty or more of us every day."

Instantly Leviathan sent for him. He sent a fish for him, but he ate the fish. He sent another messenger, but he ate him; until finally Leviathan himself went to him and said:

"In what place did you grow so big?"

And he answered: "Near the bank of the river."

Leviathan said to him: "These others who live in the midst of the sea did not grow so much, and you grew so big near the shore of the sea?"

He said to him: "Yes, because there is a man there who brings me bread every day, and I eat it in the morning and at noon, and I eat twenty fishes in the morning and thirty in the evening."

He said to him: "Why do you eat your fellow fishes?"

He answered: "Because they come to me, and I eat them, and of them it is said, *Hide not thyself from thine own flesh* (Isa. 58:7)."

He said to him: "Go and bring that man before me."

He said: "Tomorrow."

Thereupon that fish went and dug a hole in the place where that youth would come, and made a tunnel there, and put his mouth into it. Next day the youth came as was his wont, and wanted to stand on that spot, but fell into the water. The fish opened his mouth and swallowed him, and took him to Leviathan.

He said to him: "Vomit him out!"

He vomited him out, and he came out of the mouth of that fish and fell into the mouth of Leviathan.

He said to him: "My son, what did you intend in casting your bread into the water?"

He said to him: "Because my father had taught me since childhood, *Cast thy bread upon the water.*"

What did Leviathan do? He took him out of his mouth, and kissed him, and taught him seventy languages, and the whole Tora, and then hurled him three hundred parasangs from the sea to the dry land. And he fell down in a different place, where people did not walk. And when he fell down tired, he lifted up his eyes and saw two ravens flying over him. And one of them said to his father:

"My father, see whether this man is alive or dead."

And the father answered: "I do not know, my son."

He said: "I shall go down and eat his eyes, for I yearn to eat human eyes."

And the father said to him: "My son, do not go down, for perhaps he is alive."

But the son said: "I shall go down and eat his eyes."

Instantly he went down, and that man understood what they were saying to each other, and when the raven came down upon his forehead he quickly stretched forth his hands and grabbed him by his feet. Instantly the raven cried to his father and said: "My father, my father, know that the Lord has delivered me into his hands. I cannot get up."

When his father heard this, he wept and said: "Woe to me because of my son!"

And he cried and said: "You, man, let my son go! Be it the will of God that you understand my language! Get up and dig beneath you, and you will find there the treasure of Solomon king of Israel."

Instantly he let his son go, and dug beneath him, and found there the treasures of Solomon, precious stones and pearls, so that he and his children became exceedingly rich.

And of him did Ben Sira say, Spread out your bread and your table, and give to everyone who comes.

(Alfa Beta diBen Sira, OM 1:37)

The Herb of Life

There was a man who was going to the Land of Israel, and he lifted up his eyes and saw two ravens, father and son, between whom there fell a quarrel. And the father said to his son:

"Why don't you listen to my words which I have told you concerning the man who was lying in the field, when you told me that you yearn to eat his eyes, and I told you, don't go down to him and don't eat his eyes, for perhaps he is alive, and men are very cunning. And you said that he was dead, and you did not listen to me, and went down to him, and he grabbed you, and you cried to me a great cry, and I had pity on you, and because I saw you in great pain I showed him the treasure, as you saw. And likewise in other things you don't listen to me."

And the raven castigated his son because of this, but the son did not listen to him. And the father became very angry with him, and arose quickly against his son, in wrath, and killed him, and then his anger subsided. And once his anger had subsided, he repented of everything he had done to his son, and quickly flew away and brought an herb in his mouth, and put it on his son and brought him back to life, and the two of them went off together.

And that man saw all that the raven had done, and went and took that herb, and hid it, and continued on his way. And as he was walking on the road, he lifted up his eyes once more, and saw two birds quarreling, until one of them fell upon the other and killed it. Instantly the live bird arose and flew away, and that man remained sitting in his place to see what the live bird would do to its dead fellow, whether it would bring it back to life as did the raven to his son. And he waited about two hours, until he saw the live bird coming hurriedly with an herb in its mouth, and put it on the dead bird, and resuscitated it, and both of them flew off in the air, and went together in peace.

When the man saw what the bird did with the herb, he

said: "I shall go and take that herb, and see whether it is like the other herb which I took from the raven."

He went and took that herb, and saw that it was like the first one, and said: "Why am I standing here? Let me take this herb, since it has been proven twice, and I shall resurrect all the dead who are in the Land of Israel."

And it came to pass as he was walking on the road that he found a dead lion lying by the road. He said: "I shall now take of this herb, and put it on the lion, and see whether I shall resuscitate him or not."

Instantly he took of the herb and put it on the lion and resuscitated him. And the lion right away arose, and killed the man and ate him until he was well sated.

And those two ravens stood over that man and said: "Woe to you, woe to you, that you took the herb for your own misfortune."

And this is what Ben Sira said: "Do no good to the evil, and the evil will not overtake you."

(Alfa Beta diBen Sira, OM 1:38)

No Pity in Women

This is a story about King Solomon who said by the Holy Spirit: "*One man among a thousand I have found, but a woman among all those have I not found* (Eccles. 7:28)." When the people and the Sanhedrin heard this word, they were amazed. Solomon said: "If you wish, I shall show you." They all said: "Yes." He said to them: "Seek out a woman from among the best of the city, and also a man who should be the best of all." They investigated and found a man who had a good and beautiful wife. The king sent to call him, and they brought him before him. He said to him:

"Know that I want to honor you and to make you the prince of my palace."

He answered him and said: "I am your slave and shall be as one of your slaves."

King Solomon said to him: "If so, go and kill your wife and bring me her head tonight, and tomorrow I shall give you my daughter and shall make you commander over most of Israel."

The man said: "I shall do your will."

He went to his house, and his wife was pleasant and beautiful, and she had small children from him. It entered his heart, and he wept and mourned. When his wife saw that his face was dark and troubled, she approached him and said to him: "What is the matter, my lord, that I see that your face is troubled?" He said to her: "Leave me alone, for I have a worry in my heart." Instantly she brought before him food and drink, but he did not want to eat. He considered in his heart and said: "What shall I do? Shall I kill my wife, when I have small children from her?" He said to his wife: "Go and lie down with your children." When she lay down and sank in sleep, instantly he drew his sword to kill her. And he found her small son sleeping between her two breasts, and the other son was sleeping with his head on her shoulders. In that hour Satan entered into his heart to kill her. But he said: "What shall I do? If I kill her, these small children will die." Instantly he put back his sword, and said: "*The Lord rebuke thee, O Satan* (Zech. 3:2)." He returned a second time and said: "I shall kill her, and tomorrow the king will give me his daughter and all of his riches." Instantly he drew his sword against her, and saw her hair spread over the faces of the children. Instantly compassion entered his heart and he said: "If the king gives me his whole house and all his riches, I shall not kill this wife of mine!" Instantly he returned his sword in its hilt, and lay with his wife until the morning.

And behold, the emissaries of the king came for him and led him before him. The king said to him: "What did you do? Did you fulfill what you had said?"

He said: "May it be pleasing in the eyes of the king, let him not be angry with me because of this thing. I tried once and twice, and my heart did not allow me to do it."

Solomon said: "*Behold, one man among a thousand I have found!*"

He went out from before him, and they let him be thirty days. After thirty days the king sent in secret for his wife and had her brought before him. The king said to her: "Is your husband well?" She said to him: "Yes." He said to her:

"I have heard about your beauty and about the light which is in your face, and I would love you to take you to wife, and we shall make you rule over all the princesses and queens, and we shall clothe you in gold from your head to your feet."

She said to him: "Whatever you wish I shall do."

He said to her: "One thing will harm us, for I cannot do anything since you have a husband."

She said to him: "And what shall we do?"

He said to her: "Kill your husband, and then I shall take you to wife."

She said to him: "So let us do."

Solomon said in his heart: "If so, this woman will indeed kill her husband. Let us make some arrangement that he should not die." What did he do? He gave her a sword of tin. When she saw that it was shiny, he said: "With this sword kill him, for as soon as you put it on his neck it will be cut."

The woman returned home to her husband with the sword. Her husband came and she stood before him and embraced him and kissed him. She said to her husband: "Sit down, my lord, the crown of my head!" When he heard this, he rejoiced with a great joy. And he sat down, and there was no bad thought in his heart. Instantly she brought the table, and they ate and drank. Her husband said to her: "My wife, what is this affair of yours tonight?"

She said to him: "We seek to rejoice with you and to see you drunk tonight." He laughed before her with a good heart, and drank, and became drunk until he sank into sleep.

When she saw this, she arose and girded her loins, and

drew the sword which the king had given her, and began to cut the skin. Instantly her husband awoke from his sleep and saw and, behold, his wife stands over him to kill him. He said to her: "Tell me the matter, and who gave you this sword, and what happened. And if you do not tell me I shall cut your flesh into limbs and limbs."

She said to him: "This and this was the matter which King Solomon told me." He said to her: "Be not afraid!"

When he got up early in the morning, and behold the emissaries of the king came for them. Instantly he went with his wife to the king, and the Sanhedrin was sitting before him. When the king saw them he laughed. He said to them: "I beg of you, relate to me what happened." They said: "This and this happened. I woke up and found my wife standing over me to kill me. Had it not been of tin, I would by now be dead from the world. I had pity on her, but she did not pity me."

Solomon said: "I knew that there is no pity in women, therefore I gave her a tin sword."

And when the Sanhedrin heard this, they said:

"What the king said is true: *One man among a thousand I have found, but a woman among all those have I not found.*"

(M'shalim Shel Sh'lomo haMelekh, BhM 4:146-48)

The Girl Swallowed Up by the Stone

There was once a very rich man who had three daughters and three sons. One day the rich man was working in his farm, and he looked down at the earth. What did he see? A very long hair. He picked up the hair, and wound it around his hand, until the hair covered his whole hand. The rich man marveled at the length of the hair, and uttered an oath: "As God lives, I shall marry the girl who has such long hair, even if she is my own daughter Fatima."

The rich man sent his servants to search among all the

girls of the city, to find the one whose hair was that long. The servants matched the hair against the hair of all the girls of the city, but it was always longer than theirs. Finally they reached the house of the rich man himself. And, behold, they held the hair against the hair of his daughters, and found that it matched the hair of Fatima.

All the members of the family implored the father, and so did Fatima herself, that he should annul his oath, but it was of no avail. Preparations were made for the wedding, although everybody wept and mourned. Most of all the mother wept when she asked her daughter: "My dear daughter, will you become a rival wife of your own mother?"

And the daughter answered her with a proverb: "My dear mother, 'Before the meat is cooked, the Redeemer will come!' "

And verily, the Redeemer came, as the proverb had it.

One evening the little brother went out to the courtyard, to do what he had to do, and asked that his sister Fatima go with him.

Fatima rose and went with her brother as he had asked. But while she was waiting for him, she looked at one of the stones and said: "Stone, stone, how good would it be if you would open up and swallow me."

Suddenly the stone opened, and, in full view of her little brother, swallowed the girl. The boy fled back into the house, crying and shrieking, and told everybody about the miracle.

The unhappy mother went to the stone, burst into tears, and cried: "O my daughter, my daughter Fatima! Open up so I can see you!"

And, behold, the voice of Fatima could be heard: "Today you are my mother, tomorrow my rival wife, how, then, can I open my door for you?"

The sister came to the stone and cried: "O my sister, my sister Fatima! Open for me so I can see you!"

And again the voice of Fatima could be heard: "Today

you are my sister, tomorrow my daughter, how, then, can I open my door for you?"

The father came to the stone and cried: "O my daughter, my daughter Fatima! Open for me so I can see you!"

And, behold, the voice of Fatima's answer could be heard from the stone: "Today you are my father, tomorrow my husband, how, then, can I open my door for you?"

Thus all the members of the family implored her, but all their begging was of no avail.

At last the little brother came to the stone and said: "O my sister, my sister Fatima! Open for me so I can see you!"

Fatima's voice answered: "Only to you shall I open my door, for today you are my brother, and tomorrow as well!"

Suddenly the stone opened up, and the little boy was swallowed up in it.

(Dov Noy, *Jewish Folktales from Libya* [in Hebrew], pp. 139-40)

The Miser Who Swallowed His Pearls

It happened to a man who was totally wicked, and he was very rich and exceedingly stingy, and because of his great stinginess he never took a wife. And he had only one single servant. And it came to pass at the end of days that the man went to Jerusalem the holy city in order to merit burial in the Land of Israel. And in the course of days, *The Lord smote Nabal*[19] *so that he died* (1 Sam. 26:38). And before his death he called his servant and commanded him to slaughter a fatted hen and to cook it in much soup. And instantly the sick man took a box full of precious stones and pearls, and placed it before him, and began to swallow the pearls with the soup until none was left of the pearls. And he did all this so that no man should have any profit from him after his death. And a quarter of an hour passed and he died because his belly was swollen. And the men of his city

---

[19] The name Nabal means "wretch."

instantly occupied themselves with him and buried him.

Immediately after they buried him, the servant went and took a pickaxe and a spade, and he went to the land of his master's burial to dig and to take the dead out, to open the doors of his belly in order to take out what his master had swallowed. And it came to pass when he came to the grave and dug up the earth, that he saw and, behold, another man was buried there. And the man who was buried asked him: "What do you seek, O servant?" And he said: "I seek my master whom they buried here today." And he said to him: "My son, be it known to you that I am the *Ḥakham* [sage] N. N. from the city N. abroad, and today I passed away from the world, and they buried me at the border of my estate abroad, and from heaven they exchanged us: me they brought to the holy mountain Jerusalem, and your master who was buried here they took there to my grave which they dug me abroad."

And when the servant heard these words, he put back the dust to the earth as it had been, and he arose [and went] to the city which he had told him, and instantly asked about the grave of that *Ḥakham*. And they showed it to him. And in the dead of the night and in the darkness he dug up the grave, and found his master there, and instantly he opened the doors of his belly and found there all the fortune, and took it in his hand and went on his way.

(Yitzḥaq Farḥi, *Z'khut ha Rabbim*)

HEROIC TALES

The Mediterranean War

And it came to pass at the turn of the year in the seventy-second year after the descent of Israel into Egypt, after the death of Joseph, that Zepho the son of Eliphaz the son of Esau (Gen. 36:11) fled from Egypt, he and his men, and they went and came to Africa, which is the same as

Dinhabah (Gen. 36:32), to Angias king of Africa. And Angias received them with great honor and made Zepho the commander of his army. And Zepho found favor in the eyes of Angias and in the eyes of his people, and Zepho was the army commander of Angias king of Africa many days.

And Zepho incited Angias king of Africa to gather all his host to go to fight the Egyptians and the Children of Jacob and to avenge on them the vengeance of his brother Esau. But Angias did not want to listen to Zepho to do this thing for Angias knew the valor of the Children of Jacob and what they had done to his host in their war with the Children of Esau. And Zepho was very great in those days in the eyes of Angias and in the eyes of all his people, and he always incited them to fight Egypt, but they did not want to.

And it came to pass in those days that there was in the land of Kittim[20] a man in the city of Fozimna by the name of Uzo, who became a false god to the Children of Kittim. And the man died, and he had no son but a daughter whose name was Iania. And the girl was very beautiful, good of looks and wise; in the whole earth there was not seen like her beauty and like her wisdom. And the men of Angias saw her, and came and praised her to him. And Angias sent to the Children of Kittim and asked her to take her to be his wife, and the Children of Kittim were inclined to give her to him.

And it came to pass when the envoys of Angias left the land of Kittim to go their way, that, behold, envoys of Turanus[21] king of Vivento arrived in Kittim. For also Turanus king of Vivento sent his envoys to ask Iania to be his wife, for all his men had praised her to him as well, and therefore he sent his servants to her. And the servants of Turanus came to Kittim and asked Iania to let them take her to Turanus their king to be his wife.

[20] Kittim is usually taken to mean Crete.
[21] Tyrannus?

And the men of Kittim said to them: "We cannot give her, for Angias king of Africa asked her to be his wife before you came, and we promised her to him. And now we cannot do this thing, to remove the girl from the hand of Angias and to give her to Turanus. For we are very much afraid of Angias, lest he come against us in war and destroy us, and Turanus your lord could not save us from his hand."

And when the envoys of Turanus heard all the words of the Children of Kittim, they turned and went back to their lord and told him all the words of the Children of Kittim. And the Children of Kittim sent a writing to Angias saying: "Behold, Turanus sent for Iania to take her to wife, and this is what we replied to him. And we have heard that he has gathered all his host to go to war against you, and he put his face to go across Sardonia[22] to fight Lucus your brother, and thereafter he will come to fight you."

And Angias heard the words of the Children of Kittim which they had sent to him in a writing, and he became wroth. And he arose and gathered all his host and came to the islands of the sea across Sardonia to Lucus his brother, king of Sardonia. And Nivelus son of Lucus heard that Angias his uncle had come, and he went out with a heavy host to meet him and kissed him and embraced him. And Nivelus said to Angias: "When you greet my father, when he goes forth with you to fight Turanus, ask him to make me the commander of his army."

And Angias did so, and he came to his brother, and his brother came forth to meet him and greeted him. And Angias asked of Lucus his brother to put his son Nivelus to be commander of his army, and Lucus did so. And Angias and Lucus arose and went to meet Turanus in war, and a great host and many people were with them. And they came in ships and came to the district of Asturas. And behold, Turanus came to meet them, for he had gone forth to Sardonia and planned to destroy it, and thereafter to

---

[22] Sardinia?

cross over to Angias to fight him. And Angias and his brother Lucus met Turanus in the Plain of Canapia, and there was a very strong and great battle between them in that place. And the fighting became heavy against Lucus king of Sardonia, and all his host fell, and also his son Nivelus fell in that battle.

And his uncle Angias commanded his servants and they made a golden Golem[23] and put the body of Nivelus into it. And Angias continued to wage war against Turanus, and overpowered him and slayed him, and all his people fell to the mouth of the sword. And Angias avenged the death of his nephew Nivelus, and the death of the hosts of his brother Lucus. And it came to pass when Turanus died that the hand of all those who remained of his host became weak in the war, and they fled before Angias and before his brother Lucus. And Angias and his brother Lucus pursued them until the crossroads between Alpano[24] and Rome and slayed all the host of Turanus by the mouth of the sword.

And Lucus king of Sardonia commanded his servants, and they made a brazen casket and placed the body of his son Nivelus into it and buried him in that place. And they buried also Turanus king of Vivento there in that place together with Nivelus. And behold, at the crossroads between Alpano and Rome there is the tomb of Nivelus on one side, and the tomb of Turanus on the other, and a pavement is between them, to this day.

And it came to pass after Nivelus was buried that his father Lucus returned with his hosts to Sardonia. And his brother Angias, king of Africa, went with his host until the city of Vivento, which is the city of Turanus. And the inhabitants of Vivento heard the news and they were sore afraid of him, and went out to meet him with weeping and with supplications. And the inhabitants of Vivento entreated Angias that he slay them not and destroy not their city,

---

[23] Here evidently meaning a hollow statue.
[24] Albano?

and he did so. For Vivento was counted among the cities of the Children of Kittim in those days, therefore he did not destroy the city. But from that day on battalions of the king of Africa would go to Kittim to take booty and gather spoils. And whenever they went, Zepho, the army commander of Angias, would go with them.

And it came to pass thereafter that Angias with his host turned and came to the city of Fozimna, and there Angias took Iania the daughter of Uzo to wife, and brought her to Africa to his city.

And it came to pass at that time that Pharaoh king of Egypt commanded all his people to build him a strong palace in Egypt. And he commanded also all the Children of Jacob to help Egypt in the building. And the Egyptians made for Pharaoh a beautiful and pleasant palace for his house of kingdom, and he settled in it and renewed his rule, and he reigned in safety.

And Zebulun the son of Jacob died in that year, which was the seventy-fourth year since the descent of Israel into Egypt. And Zebulun died at the age of 114 years, and was placed in a casket and given in the hands of his sons. And in the year 75 his brother Simeon died, at the age of 120 years, and he too was put in a casket and given in the hand of his sons.

And Zepho the son of Eliphaz the son of Esau, the commander of the army of Angias king of Dinhabah, was still inciting Angias day after day to wage war and fight the Children of Jacob in Egypt. But Angias did not want to do this thing because his servants related to him all the valor of the Children of Jacob and what they did to them in their war with the Children of Esau. And Zepho incited Angias day after day to go to war against the Children of Jacob in those days. And it came to pass one day that Angias listened to the words of Zepho and decided to fight the Children of Jacob in Egypt. And Angias mustered all his people, a people as numerous as the sand which is on the shore of the sea, and he turned his face to go to Egypt to war.

And there was a youth among the servants of Angias, fifteen years old, and Balaam son of Beor was his name. And the youth was very wise and knew the art of divination. And Angias said to Balaam: "Perform divination so that we know who will prevail in this war to which we are going." And Balaam commanded that they bring him wax, and he made of it figures of a chariot and horesmen, the image of the army of Angias and of the army of Egypt. And he put them in divining water, which he had with him for this purpose, and took in his hand palm fronds, and he divined and conjured with them on the water. And there appeared to him in the water the image of the figures of the hosts of Angias falling before the image of the figures of Egypt and the Children of Jacob. And Balaam told this thing to Angias, and Angias despaired and did not gird himself to go down to Egypt to war, but remained in his city.

And when Zepho the son of Eliphaz saw that Angias became despondent of going out to fight Egypt, he fled from Angias from Africa, and went and came to Kittim. And all the people of Kittim received him with great honor, and they hired him to fight their wars all the days. And Zepho became very rich in those days, and the battalions of the king of Africa were still foraging in the land of Kittim in those days. And the Children of Kittim gathered and went to Mount Copatizia fleeing from the battalions of Angias king of Africa who were coming to them.

And it happened one day that a young bull of Zepho got lost, and he went to search for it, and he heard it lowing in the vicinity of that mountain. And Zepho went and saw, and behold, at the foot of that mountain was a large cave, and a huge rock was put at the mouth of the cave. And Zepho shattered the rock and went into the cave and saw, and behold, a big animal was eating the ox. Its upper half had the shape of a man, and its lower half the shape of an animal. And Zepho arose against that animal and killed it with his sword. And the inhabitants of Kittim heard this thing and rejoiced greatly, and said: "What shall we do to this man who killed this animal which devoured our cattle?" And they all decided to dedicate to him a day in the year as a feast day, and they called the name of that day Zepho, after his name. And they offered libations to him every year on that day and brought him presents.

In those days Iania the daughter of Uzo, the wife of King Angias, fell ill, and her illness grieved Angias and his princes very much. And Angias said to his wise men: "What shall I do to Iania and how shall I heal her illness?" And his wise men said to him: "Because the air of our country is not like the air of Kittim, and our water is not like their water; this is what caused Queen Iania to fall ill. For when the air and the water changed for her, she fell ill, and especially so since even in her country she used to drink only the water which came from Forma which her forefathers had brought up on bridges."

And Angias commanded his servants and they brought him vessels full of the waters of Forma from Kittim. And they weighed those waters against all the waters of Africa, and they found the waters of Forma lighter than the waters of Africa. And Angias saw this thing, and commanded all his princes to gather hewers of stone by the thousands and tens of thousands, and they hewed stones without number. And the builders came and built a huge bridge and they brought a conduit of water from the land of Kittim to Africa. And those waters were for Queen Iania and all those with her, to drink and to bake with them and to wash clothes and wash themselves in them. And also to slake with them every seed of which she ate and every fruit of the earth. And the king further commanded that they bring also of the soil of the land of Kittim, and they brought of it in many ships, and they also brought stones to build with them, and the builders built palaces for Queen Iania, and the queen recovered of her illness.

And it came to pass at the turn of the year that the

legions of Africa again went to the land of Kittim to take booty, again and again. And Zepho son of Eliphaz heard about it, and he went forth to meet them, and fought them, and they fled from before him, and he saved the land of Kittim from them. And the Children of Kittim saw the bravery of Zepho, and they took counsel and made Zepho king over them, and he became their king. And it came to pass while he reigned that they went to conquer the Children of Tubal and all the islands of the sea which were around them. And their king Zepho went forth at their head, and they fought the Children of Tubal and the islands and conquered them. And when they returned from the war, they renewed his kingship and built for him a very big palace to be his royal house and his seat. And they made for him a great throne, and Zepho ruled over all the land of Kittim and over all the land of Italy for fifty years.

(From *Sefer haYashar*, pp. 219-25)

Moses King of Ethiopia

And it came to pass in those days that there was a great war between the Children of Ethiopia and the Children of the East and Aram, who rebelled against the king of Ethiopia under whose hands they had been. And Kikanos king of Ethiopia went forth with all the Children of Ethiopia, with a great multitude like the sand of the sea, very many, and he went to wage war against Aram and the Children of the East to bring them back under his hand. And when Kikanos marched off, he left behind in the city Balaam the sorcerer, him and his two sons, to guard the city and the gate of the land. And Kikanos went forth and marched against Aram and the Children of the East, and fought them and beat them, and they all fell slain before Kikanos and his people. And he took captive of them a great captivity, and he subdued them under his hand as they had been at first, and he camped in their land to take tribute from them as was his due.

And Balaam son of Beor, after the king of Ethiopia had left him to guard the city and the gate of the city, arose and took counsel with the people of the land to rebel against King Kikanos and not to let him enter the city when he returned. And the people of the land listened to him, and they rendered an oath to him, and they made him king over them and made his two sons commanders of armies. And they arose and heightened the walls of the city on two sides, and built a very strong and huge building. And on the third side they dug many pits without number between the city and the river which surrounds the land of Ethiopia, and led there the water of the river. And for the fourth side they collected many snakes with their magic and sorcery. And thus they fortified the city and dwelt in it, and nobody went in or out before them.

And Kikanos fought Aram and the Children of the East and subdued them under his hand as at first, and they gave him taxes as was his due, and he went and returned to his country. And it came to pass when Kikanos king of Ethiopia approached his city, and all the commanders of the soldiers with him, that they lifted up their eyes and saw, behold, the walls of the city were built up and were very high. And the men were astonished at this, and they said to one another: "They saw that we tarried in the war, and were very much afraid for us, therefore did they this thing, and they heightened the walls of the city and fortified them, lest the kings of Canaan come to wage war against them."

And the king and the soldiers approached the gate of the city, and they saw, and behold, all the gates of the city were closed. And they called to the gatekeepers saying: "Open for us and let us enter the city!" But the gatekeepers refused to open for them as Balaam the sorcerer, their king, had commanded them, and they did not let them enter the city. And they waged war against them before the city at the gate, and on that day there fell of the army of Kikanos 130 men. And on the second day they continued to fight, and they fought beyond the river, and they tried to cross over but could not, and many of them sank into the pits and died. And the king commanded that they cut trees and make rafts to cross over on them, and they did so. But when they reached the place of the pits, the water whirled like millstones, and there drowned that day 200 men on ten rafts. And it came to pass on the third day that they tried to fight from the side of the snakes, but could not approach there. And the snakes killed 170 men of them, and they ceased to fight against Ethiopia. And they besieged Ethiopia for nine years, none came out and none went in.

At that time, when there was the war and siege of Ethiopia, Moses fled from before Pharaoh who wanted to kill him, because he had killed the Egyptian. And Moses was eighteen years old when he fled from Egypt from before Pharaoh, and he escaped and took refuge in the camp of Kikanos, whose army at that time was besieging Ethiopia. And Moses remained in the camp of Kikanos king of Ethiopia nine years, throughout the time that they besieged Ethiopia, and he came and went with them. And the king and the princes and all the warriors loved Moses, because he was great and dear, and his stature was like a powerful lion and his face like the sun, and the power of his strength like a strong lion, and he became a counselor to the king.

And it came to pass after nine years that Kikanos became ill of the illness of which he was to die, and his illness overpowered him, and he died on the seventh day. And his servants embalmed him and took him and buried him opposite the gate of the city which faced the land of Egypt. And they built a fine and huge and very high building over him, and they placed large stones on top of it. And the scribes of Kikanos engraved upon those stones all the heroic deeds of their king Kikanos and all his wars which he had waged; and, behold, they are written to this very day.

And it came to pass after the death of Kikanos king of Ethiopia that his men and his soldiers were hard pressed by the war. And they said to one another: "Come, give us advice, what is to be done at this time, now that we have dwelt in the desert, away from our houses, for nine years. If we should decide to fight the city, many of us will fall and we shall die; and if we stay put here in the siege, we shall die. Because now all the kings of Aram and the Children of the East will hear that our king died, and they will come upon us suddenly, to fight us, and they will wage war against us, and will leave no remnant of us. Therefore, let us set a king over us, and let us sit in siege until the city is delivered into our hands."

And they searched on that day in all the army of Kikanos for a man to be king, and they found no youth like Moses to be king over them. And they hurriedly took off their garments and threw them on the ground, and made a mound and seated Moses on it. And they arose and blew the horns and cried before him and said: "Long live the king! Long live the king!" And all the people and all the princes rendered an oath to him that they would give him the Ethiopian Queen Adonia, the widow of Kikanos, to wife, and they made Moses king over them on that day.

And all the people of Ethiopia let the voice pass on that day saying: "Every man must give to Moses of whatever is found in his hand." And they spread the garment upon the mound, and every man threw on it a golden nose ring, and every man a *q'sita* [coin], of whatever was in his hand. And also stones of onyx, bdellium, pearls, and marble did all the Children of Ethiopia throw to Moses on the mound, and also a very great quantity of silver and gold. And Moses took all the silver and the gold, and all the vessels and the bdellium and the onyx which all the Children of Ethiopia had given him, and he deposited it into his treasury. And on that day Moses became king over all the Children of Ethiopia in place of Kikanos king of Ethiopia. In the fifty-fifth year of Pharaoh king of Egypt, which was the 157th year since Israel had gone down to Egypt, Moses became king over Ethiopia. He was twenty-seven years old when he became king over Ethiopia, and he ruled forty years. And God made Moses liked and favored in the eyes of all the Children of Ethiopia, and the Children of Ethiopia loved him very much, and Moses was good with God and with men.

And it came to pass in the seventh day of his rule that all the Children of Ethiopia gathered together and assembled and came before Moses and bowed down before him to the earth. And all the Children of Ethiopia together spoke before the king and said: "Give us advice, and let us see what can be done to this city. For it is today nine years that we have been sitting in siege over this city, and we have not seen our children and our wives."

And the king answered them and said: "If you will listen to my voice in all that which I shall command you, God will give the city into our hands and we shall capture it. Because if you go on fighting in the manner of the first fight which we had fought prior to the death of Kikanos, then many victims will fall from among us as in the past. But now, behold the advice in this matter, if you listen to my voice, and the city will be given into our hands."

And all the soldiers answered the king saying: "Whatever our Lord will command so will your servants do."

And Moses said to them: "Go about and announce in all the camp to all the people saying: 'Thus speaks the king: Go to the forest, and each one of you bring back a young stork. And every man who disobeys the command of the king and does not bring back his fledgling bird, will die, and the king will take whatever belonged to him. And when you bring the storks, guard them well, and rear them until they grow up, and teach them to fly like hawks."

And the Children of Ethiopia heard the words of Moses, and arose and announced all over the camp, saying: "To you, all the Children of Ethiopia, by order of the king: Go all of you to the forest and catch young storks, every man his fledgling in his hand, and bring them back with you.

And every man who disobeys the command of the king will die, and the king will take all that is his."

And all the people did as told, and they went to the forest and climbed up the cypresses, and each man caught his fledgling in his hand, all the young storks, and brought them back in the evening. And they brought them up as commanded by the king, and they taught them to fly like hawks, everything that the king commanded the Children of Ethiopia obeyed.

And it came to pass that when the young storks grew up, the king ordered that they should be starved for three days, and all the people did it. And it came to pass on the third day that the king said to them: "Be strong and you will prevail! And let every man put on his fighting gear, and every man gird on his sword, and every man ride his horse, and let every man take his stork in his hand. And let us arise and fight the city from the place where there are the snakes."

And all the people did as the king commanded. And every man took his stork in his hand, and they went, and when they reached the place of the snakes the king said to them: "Let every man send his stork on the snakes." And each man sent his stork as the king commanded, and the storks ran to the snakes and ate them all, and eliminated them from that place. And the king and his servants saw that all the snakes were eliminated from that place, and all the people sent up a great cry of jubilation. And they drew near and fought the city and took it and captured it, and they entered the city. And on that day there died one thousand and one hundred men of the people of the city, all the inhabitants of the city, and of the people who besieged them not even one died. And all the Children of Ethiopia returned to their homes and to their wives and to their children and to all that they had.

And Balaam the sorcerer, when he saw that the city was captured and that the gate was opened, fled, together with his two sons and eight brothers, and returned to Egypt to

Pharaoh king of Egypt. They were the magicians and the warlocks mentioned in the book of the Tora who stood up against Moses when God brought the plagues upon Egypt.

And Moses captured the city with his wisdom, and the Children of Ethiopia placed him on the royal throne instead of Kikanos king of Ethiopia. And they put the royal crown on his head, and gave him the Ethiopian Queen Adonia, the wife of Kikanos, to wife. But Moses feared the Lord, the God of his fathers, and did not turn his eyes toward her. For Moses remembered that Abraham had made his servant Eliezer swear saying: "Do not take a wife for my son Isaac from the daughters of Canaan." And Isaac did likewise when Jacob fled from before his brother, and he commanded him saying: "Do not take a wife from the daughters of Canaan and do not intermarry with all the Children of Ham. For the Lord our God gave Ham son of Noah and his children and all his seed as slaves to the Children of Shem and to the Children of Japheth and to their seed after them forever." Therefore Moses did not turn his heart and his eyes to the wife of Kikanos all the days of his rule over Ethiopia.

And Moses feared the Lord his God all his days, and Moses walked before the Lord in truth with all his heart and all his soul. Moses never turned aside from the good way, all the days of his life he never deviated from the way in which had walked Abraham, Isaac and Jacob, neither to the right nor to the left. And Moses became strong in the kingdom of the Children of Ethiopia, and he led the Children of Ethiopia lawfully in his wisdom, and Moses succeeded in his rule.

And Aram and the Children of the East heard at that time that Kikanos king of Ethiopia had died, and they rebelled from under the hand of Ethiopia in those days. And Moses gathered all the Children of Ethiopia, a very heavy multitude, some thirty thousand men, and went forth to fight Aram and the Children of the East. And first they went to the Children of the East, and all the Children of the East heard the news and came forth against them and waged war with them. And the war was strong upon the Children of the East, and the Lord gave all the Children of the East into the hands of Moses, and some three hundred men of them fell slain. And all the Children of the East turned around and fled, and Moses and the Children of Ethiopia pursued them and subdued them under their hand, and imposed a tax upon them as due.

And from there Moses and all the people that was with him passed on to the land of Aram to wage war. And the men of Aram, too, came out against them, and fought them, and the Lord delivered them into the hands of Moses, and many of Aram fell slain. And Aram, too, submitted to Moses and to Ethiopia, and they too gave taxes as due. And Moses subdued Aram and the Children of the East under the hand of Ethiopia. Then Moses and all the people who were with him turned back and returned to the land of Ethiopia. And Moses became strong in his rule over the Children of Ethiopia. And the Lord was with him, and all the Children of Ethiopia feared him. And it came to pass at the end of fifteen years that Saul king of Edom died, and Baal Hanan son of Akhbor became king in his stead.

In the sixteenth year of the rule of Moses over Ethiopia, Baal Hanan son of Akhbor became king in the land of Edom over all the Children of Edom for thirty-eight years. In his days Moab rebelled from under the hand of Edom. Moab had been under the hand of Edom since the days of Haddad son of Baddad who had defeated them and Midian and subdued Moab under the hand of Edom. And it came to pass when Baal Hanan son of Akhbor became king over the Children of Edom that the Children of Moab rebelled from under the hand of Edom.

And Angias king of Africa died in those days, and his son Azdrubal [Hasdrubal] became king in his stead. And in those days Ianius king of the Children of Kittim died, and they buried him in his palace which he had built himself in the Plain of Campania as a royal seat, and Latianus became king in his place. In the twenty-second year of the rule of Moses over the Children of Ethiopia Latianus became king over the Children of Kittim for forty-five years. And he, too, built himself a great and mighty tower, and built in it a beautiful palace as his seat to lead his kingdom as was lawful.

In the third year of his rule he had a voice pass to all his wise men, and they made him many ships. And Latianus gathered all his army, and they boarded the ships and went to fight Azdrubal son of Angias king of Africa. And he came to Africa and waged war against Azdrubal and his army. And Latianus prevailed over Azdrubal, and he captured from Azdrubal the water channel which his father Angias had brought from the Children of Kittim when he took Iania daughter of Uzo to wife. And Latianus destroyed the bridge of that channel, and inflicted a very great defeat on all the army of Azdrubal. But the remaining warriors rallied, and their hearts became filled with zeal, and they wanted to die, and they waged another war against Latianus king of Kittim. And the battle became strong against all the men of Africa, and they all fell before Latianus and his people, and also Azdrubal the king fell in that battle.

And King Azdrubal had a very beautiful daughter and her name was Ospeziona. And all the men of Africa would embroider her picture on their clothes because of her great beauty. And the men of Latianus saw Ospeziona daughter of Azdrubal and they praised her to Latianus their king. And Latianus commanded, and they brought her to him, and he took her to wife, and turned back and went his way to Kittim.

And it came to pass after the death of Azdrubal son of Angias, when Latianus returned from the war to his country, that all the inhabitants of Africa arose and took Anibal [Hannibal] son of Angias, the younger brother of Azdrubal, and made him king instead of his brother over all the land of Africa. And when he became king he took counsel to go to Kittim to wage war against the Children of Kittim to avenge the death of his brother Azdrubal and to avenge the inhabitants of Africa, and so he did. And he made many ships and brought his army in them and went to Kittim.

And Anibal fought the Children of Kittim, and the Children of Kittim fell before Anibal and his army, and Anibal avenged the death of his brother. And Anibal fought the Children of Kittim eighteen years, and he dwelt in the land of Kittim and camped in it many days. And Anibal dealt a very great blow to the Children of Kittim, and killed their great men and their princes, and of the rest of the people he killed about eighty-thousand men.

And it came to pass after many days and years that Anibal turned back and returned to the land of Africa, and he ruled Africa securely. . . .

And Moses son of Amram was still king in the land of Ethiopia in those days, and he succeeded in his rule and led all the kingdom of the Children of Ethiopia in law, in justice, and in honesty. And all the children of Ethiopia loved Moses all the days of his kingship over them, and all the inhabitants of the land of Ethiopia feared him with a great fear.

And it came to pass in the fortieth year of the kingship of Moses over Ethiopia that Moses sat on the royal throne and Queen Adonia before him, and all the princes sat around him. And Queen Adonia said before the king and the princes:

"What is this thing that you have done, O all the Children of Ethiopia, for many days? As you well know, for forty years during which this man has ruled over Ethiopia, he has never come near me and he has not served the gods of the Children of Ethiopia! And now listen, O Children of Ethiopia, and let not this man who is not of your flesh continue to rule you. Behold, Menekris my oldest son, let him be king over you, for it is better for you to serve the son of your master than to serve a foreigner who was the slave of the king of Egypt."

And all the people and all the princes of the Children of Ethiopia heard all these words which Queen Adonia spoke in their ears. And all the people were ready until the evening, and they arose early in the morning and made Menekris son of Kikanos king of Ethiopia king over them.

But all the Children of Ethiopia were afraid to stretch forth their hand against Moses, for the Lord was with Moses, and because the Children of Ethiopia remembered the oath they had rendered to Moses. Therefore they did him no evil, but all the Children of Ethiopia gave Moses many presents, and sent him away from them in honor. And Moses left the land of Ethiopia and went on his way and ceased being king over Ethiopia. For the thing was from the Lord, for the end had come which was from the days of old to lead out Israel from the oppression of the Children of Ham. And Moses went to Midian, for he was afraid to return to Egypt because of Pharaoh....

(*Sefer haYashar*, pp. 249-58)

The Legend of B'ne Moshe

R. Yuda bar Simon said: Not to the place to which the ten tribes were exiled were the tribes of Judah and Benjamin exiled. The ten tribes were exiled beyond the River Sambatyon, and the tribes of Judah and Benjamin were exiled and dispersed in all the countries. And there are those who say that the Levites, the children of Moses, are encamped beyond the River Sambatyon.

Our masters said: In the hour in which Israel was exiled to Babylonia, they came to the Euphrates. The nations of the world said to the Levites: "Stand before our idols and sing a song as you used to sing in the Temple." The Levites said to them: "O you fools in the world! If we had sung a song for each miracle which the Holy One, blessed be He, performed for us, we would not have been exiled from our country. How can we sing before idols?"

Instantly the nations of the world rose up against them and slew of them great multitudes. And even though they slew many of them, great was the rejoicing that they did not serve idols. What did those Levites who remained do? They cut off their fingers so that they should be unable to play the harps. And when they were told, "Make music!" they showed their cut-off fingers and said to them, "*How can we sing?* (Ps. 137:4)"

When night fell, the cloud descended and covered them and their women and daughters and sons, and the Holy One, blessed be He, lighted up the way for them in a pillar of fire and led them all night until the dawn and left them on the shores of the sea. When the sun rose, the cloud and the pillar of fire departed, and the Holy One, blessed be He, made a river flow before them, and its name is Sambatyon. And the Holy One, blessed be He, locked them in so that no man should be able to cross over to them. And the river surrounded them by enclosing an area of three months' journey by three months' square. And the width of that river is two hundred cubits. And the river was full of sand and stones, and it churns sand and stones and makes a great noise which can be heard at night to a distance of half a day's walk. And it churns sand and stones all the six days of work and rests on the Sabbath. But then instantly fire rises from the Sabbath eve until the expiration of the Sabbath along the side of the valley, and the fire is ablaze and no man can approach the valley closer than a mile. And the fire consumes everything that grows around the river so that it sweeps the land clean.

And those Levites are of the Children of Moses, and they dwell beyond the valley. And there is no unclean animal among them, nor an unclean beast, nor any creeping thing of the earth; but have sheep and cattle. And they also have there six springs whose waters gather into one lake, and from this they irrigate their land. And that lake teems with all kinds of fish, and over the springs and the lakes fly all kinds of clean fowl. And they also have all kinds of fruit, and they sow and reap, they sow one measure and reap a hundred.

And they are strong in faith and knowledgeable in Tora, Mishna, and Agada. And they are wise, pious, and saintly, and they never swear falsely. And they live to be 120 years old, and no son of theirs dies in his father's lifetime, and they see three and four generations. And they themselves build houses, and plow and sow, for they have no slaves nor slave women, and they do not lock their houses at nighttime. And a small boy would go with his livestock to a distance of several days and would not be afraid of robbers, nor of wild beasts, nor of the things that creep on the ground, nor of demons, nor of any evil thing, for they are saintly, and still stand in the sanctity of our Master Moses, peace be upon him. This is why the Holy One, blessed be He, gave them all this, and chose them, and they see no man, nor does any man see them, except the four tribes of Dan and Naftali, Gad and Asher, who dwell beyond the River Kush.

How did they get there? Our Masters said: In the hour in which Jeroboam ben Nevat arose and made two golden calves and caused Israel to sin, and they split off from the kingdom of the House of David, he gathered ten tribes of Israel and said to them, "Go and fight Rehoboam and the inhabitants of Jerusalem." They said to him: "How can we fight our brothers, the sons of our Lord David, king of Israel and Judah?" The elders of Israel went up to Jeroboam and said to him: "In all Israel we have no brave warriors like the tribe of Dan. Command them to fight against Judah." Instantly Jeroboam said: "Sons of Dan, go forth and fight Judah and Benjamin." They said to him: "By the life of our father Dan, we shall not wage war against our brothers and shall not spill their blood in vain."

Instead, the Sons of Dan took swords and bows and arrows and lances and gave themselves up to wage war against Jeroboam, until God saved them from spilling the blood of their brothers and they announced in all the tribe of Dan and said: "Flee, O Sons of Dan, get yourselves out of the country, and let us go to Egypt!" And they took counsel to destroy Egypt and slay all its inhabitants, but their princes said to them: "Where are you going? Is it not written in the Tora, *Ye shall see them [the Egyptians] again no more for ever* (Exod. 14:13)?" And then they took counsel about Ammon, but they saw in the Tora that the Holy One, blessed be He, had prevented Israel from inheriting its boundaries. Then the Holy One, blessed be He, gave them a good spirit, and the Sons of Dan went up against the River Pishon, and they traveled on the camels and camped, until they reached the rivers of Kush. And they found the land fat, good, and wide, fields and vineyards, gardens and orchards. And the inhabitants of the land did not prevent the Sons of Dan from dwelling with them, and they made a covenant with them, and the Children of Kush paid them a tribute, and they dwelt with them many years until they were fruitful and multiplied exceedingly.

(Agadta diV'ne Moshe, BhM 6:15-17)

WISDOM STORIES

A Solomonic Judgment

This is the story of a man who lived in the days of David king of Israel, and he was a very rich man, and he had many male and female slaves and much property, and he had an only son. What did that man do? He bought much merchandise and gave it into the hand of his son. That son boarded a ship and sailed to Africa, and remained there many years, and during those years his father died, and left his property to a slave, the master of his treasury. And this slave began to oppress all members of the household with peculiar afflictions, until they left him and went their way and he alone remained with all that fortune which his master had left him, and he was eating and was joyful in his desire for the fortune.

After a time that young man returned from the cities of the sea and went to the house of his father and found that his father had passed to the house of his world. He began to enter his house. The slave came out to meet him and pushed him and said to him: "What do you want in my house, you good-for-nothing?" What did the young man do? He took the stick and began to beat him over his head and said to him: "You slave, you grabbed all my earnings and the earnings of father, my master, and are enjoying that fortune!" They made a great quarrel and there was nobody to separate them, until the son of the old man fled and went to complain against the slave to the king and said:

"May the king live forever! That certain man took all the fortune which my father, my master, had left to me, and he says to me, 'You are not the son of the old man, but I am.'"

The king said: "Do you have witnesses?" He said to him: "No." The king called that slave and said to him: "Do you have witnesses?" He said to him: "No." The king said to the slave: "Go in peace. You do not have to return anything."

When the son of the old man heard this, he began to weep and to cry before the king a second time, and a third. He cried to the king until the king shouted at him and said: "If you repeat, I shall send a hand against you. If you have witnesses, good, and if not, what shall I do for you?"

King Solomon[25] heard the thing, called him aside and said to him: "Cry again to the king, and if he becomes angry with you tell him, My lord the king, if you do not give me justice, put me into the hand of your son Solomon." He put him into the hand of his son Solomon that he should give him justice.

---

[25] Although Solomon evidently was not yet king, the storyteller is so used to the phrase "King Solomon" that he calls him "king" here and subsequently.

Solomon said to the young man: "Do you know in what place is your father buried?" He said to him: "No." He called again that slave and said to him: "Will you recognize the grave of your father?" He said to him: "Yes." The king said to him: "Go and bring me the arm of your father." And he cut off an arm of the old man and brought it to him. He said to them: "Let both of you let some blood, and let each of you receive his blood in his vessel." Then he said to the slave: "Dip the bone [of the arm] in your blood!" He dipped it and it did not become colored. He said to the son of the old man: "You, too, dip it in your blood!" And the bone became colored, and he showed it to all the people. He said to them: "See, this blood came from this bone."

Instantly all Israel were amazed, and he returned all the fortune to the young man, and as for the slave, he ruled over him against his will. This is why it is said that Solomon *was wiser than all men* (1 Kings 5:11).

(M'shalim Shel Sh'lomo haMelekh,
BhM 4:145-46)

Scholarship Is the Best Merchandise

This is a story about a scholar who was in a ship with many merchants. They said to that scholar: "Where is your merchandise?" He said to them: "My merchandise is greater than yours." They searched the ship but found nothing that belonged to him. They began to mock him. Pirates fell upon them, looted and took everything in the ship. They landed and entered the city, and they had no bread to eat and no clothes to wear. What did that scholar do? He went to the House of Study, sat down, and expounded. The people of the city came, and when they saw that he was very learned they treated him with great respect, and gave him a proper stipend, as it behoved, in greatness and in honor. The leaders of the community began to walk on his right and on his left and to accompany him. When the merchants saw this, they came to him, and entreated him and said to him: "We beg of you, do us a good deed and recommend us to the people of the city, for you know what we were and what we have lost in the ship. We beg of your, have pity on us, talk to them, even if only about a piece of bread that it be given us to eat, so that we live and die not of hunger." He said to them: "Did I not tell you that my merchandise was greater than yours? Yours is lost and mine remains!"

(Tanḥ. **Mishpatim**, par. 2)

The Wooden Sword

Shah Abbas was a ruler who loved justice and honesty. Every evening he would disguise himself and wander about in the streets of the city in order to learn about its citizens and to find out what was happening among them. Frequently he would disguise himself as a dervish, and visit the suburbs of the city in order to see with his own eyes how the poor people lived.

One evening as he walked about in a suburb he saw a faint light. He went toward it and saw a poor hovel, and in it a man sat and sang. Before him was a dish of simple food. He sat and ate, sang, and spent his time reciting praises and thanks. Shah Abbas entered and asked:

"Is a guest welcome?"

The man answered:

"A guest is the gift of God. Sit down and share my meal."

Shah Abbas sat down, and the man honored him with whatever he himself had. They spoke about this and that. Shah Abbas asked him:

"What is your work? How do you earn a living?"

The man answered:

"I am a cobbler. I repair shoes. I walk about all day long in the streets of the city and mend the shoes of the people.

In the evening I buy myself food with the pennies I earn."

Shah Abbas asked him:

"And what will you do tomorrow?"

The man answered:

"Blessed is the Lord day after day."

Shah Abbas sat with him a long time. Then he took his leave and said:

"I shall come back tomorrow."

Shah Abbas returned home, and next morning he issued a decree in the streets of the city which forbade the mending of shoes without a permit. The cobbler heard it, whereupon he went and drew water for several citizens and thus earned his wages for the day. In the evening he bought his usual portions of food. At night Shah Abbas came to visit him, and behold, he saw that the cobbler was seated as usual, was eating and drinking, singing and enjoying himself.

Shah Abbas asked him:

"Nu, what did you do today?"

The man told him:

"When I left my house I heard the decree which forbade the mending of shoes. I went, drew water for several citizens, and earned my wages for the day."

Shah Abbas said: "I was very worried about you when I heard that they forbade the mending of shoes. And what will you do if the king forbids the drawing of water?"

The cobbler answered:

"Blessed is the Lord day after day!"

Shah Abbas went home, and next morning he proclaimed a ban on drawing water.

The man heard it, went and cut wood for several citizens, and earned the wages of his day. In the evening he bought the usual portions of his food. At night Shah Abbas came to visit him, and behold, he saw that the cobbler was seated as usual, was eating and drinking, singing and enjoying himself. He greeted him and asked:

"What did you do today?"

He told him:

"I cut wood and earned my wages."

The shah asked him:

"What will be if tomorrow they will forbid the cutting of wood?"

The man answered:

"Blessed is the Lord day after day!"

The two sat as usual and spent the time pleasantly. When they parted, the shah promised to come back next day.

Next morning, early, the herald went out and proclaimed that all woodcutters were called up for guard duty. The cobbler, too, went to the palace, and there they gave him a sword and assigned him a place to guard. In the evening the man went to the store, gave the blade of the sword to the storekeeper, got his usual portion of food, and went home. In his house he took a length of board and shaped a blade of it and attached it to the hilt. He was still busy with this work when the disguised shah arrived. He asked him:

"What is this? Why is this day different from others?"

The man related to him:

"Today I guarded the palace, but I had no money, and I gave the blade as a pledge to the storekeeper. Now I am fitting a wooden blade into the hilt."

The shah asked him:

"And what will be if tomorrow they check the swords of the guards?"

The man answered:

"Blessed is the Lord day after day!"

The two of them sat as usual, and spent the time pleasantly.

Next day the captain of the guard called the cobbler, delivered a prisoner into his hands, and said:

"This prisoner has been sentenced to death. You must cut off his head."

The man said:

"In my whole life I never killed a man. I cannot kill a man."

The captain said to him:

"The order of the king is an order. Do as you are told!"

The man grabbed the sword hilt with one hand and the sheath with the other, and proclaimed before all the people who had gathered to see the execution:

"Mighty God! It is revealed and known before you that I am not a murderer. If this prisoner deserves to die, let my sword be a sword of steel. But if the prisoner is not guilty, I beseech You, change the steel blade into a blade of wood!"

And he drew his sword—and, behold, it was a wooden board! All the people who stood about saw it and were amazed. Shah Abbas called him to the palace, kissed him on his mouth, and made himself known to him, and appointed him as one of his councilors.

(Afghan Jewish Folktale)

A Jewish Virgil Legend

Before the beginnings of the Christian religion there lived Virgil, a man of many deeds and wonderful acts in the science of astronomy. He made a brazen fly which he set up in an open place, and it drove off all the flies to a distance of a bow shot. And if they approached it, they instantly died. It was he who made a brazen horse to heal all the ailments of horses, and it came to pass that when a horse fell sick and looked at the brazen horse, it instantly became well. He founded a great city on a marsh, and when the marsh was moved it shook the whole fort. And behold, the fly and the horse and the lion's cage which he made are all in the city of Nafes. It was he who cut off the fire in the city of Rome, because of Ceasar's daughter, and brought it back at will. It was he who made the great and wonderful bridge in the water, at which all the sages [who know] of wood and stone were amazed and wearied themselves to find its secret, but could not find its quality and on what it stood and where was its beginning and its end. It was he who made a garden, surrounded by air without a wall, and the air was as thick as a stone wall, so that nothing could get through it. In it two candles burn all the time and never go out, and when he died, one of them became extinguished and remained suspended in the air. It was he who made a metal head which spoke to him and answered questions and foretold the future.

One day he asked the head whether he should go on a journey. And the head answered that he should go as he wished, but that he should guard his head. And he did not understand and thought that it was the metal head he should guard. But the head did not speak of that, but of Virgil's own head. And it came to pass as the head had warned. For on the way the heat of the sun entered his brains and he fell mortally ill. And Virgil saw that he was about to die and commanded his disciples to take him away from Rome, and they took him and buried him in the land of Sazila [Sicily?], one mile from the sea. And his bones are still preserved from among all the others. And if his bones are touched and brought up, the sea becomes full of rage and falls [i.e., rises] upward as high as the bones were raised, until they are returned to their place, and then the sea subsides from its rage. For he was most wise of all men, and it was a splendid wisdom in an ugly vessel. For he was short of stature with a low head, and his spine was bent. And the wonders of his acts were many and could not be believed by the crowd. They were a subject of derision when they were recounted, for he who heard about him and did not know his essence and his quality would mock him, just as there are many of low mind who mock wisdom, and they would say that they were the acts of demons and spirits, and they did understand his word and did not understand that the hand of God did all of it....

(Matityahu Delacrut, *Tzel 'Olam*, pp. 24b-25a)

MIRACLE MEN

Rabbi Loew and the Golem

The Maharal[26] made a dream-question[27] about what power he could use in order to wage war against the priest, his adversary [Thaddeus, who plotted the destruction of the Jews by blood libels]. The answer came to him from heaven in alphabetic form [in Hebrew]: "Create a Golem, knead the clay, and thus you will destroy the plotters who want to tear Israel to pieces." Thereupon the Maharal said that those ten words [which he was given] contain a combination of names with whose power it is always possible to create a live Golem out of clay. And he summoned in secret me, Yitzḥaq ben Shimshon haKohen [Katz],[28] his son-in-law, and his great disciple, Ya'aqov ben Ḥayyim Sason haLevi, and showed us the reply from heaven which he had received to his dream-question. And he divulged to us the secret of the creation of a Golem from clay and dust of the earth. And he told us that he wanted to take us as his helpers, because for such a creation one needs the four powers of the four elements, fire, wind, water, dust. And of himself the Maharal said that he was born with the power of the wind element, and of me, that I was born with the power of the fire element, and of his disciple R. Ya'aqov Sason he said that he was born with the power of the water element. And therefore the three of us can accomplish and

---

26 Initials of the words Morenu Harav Rabbi Loew—Our Teacher the Master Rabbi Loew—by which R. Judah Loew ben Bezalel (c. 1525-1609) of Prague is usually referred to.

27 "Dream-question"—a Kabbalistic procedure to elicit an answer from heaven in a dream to a weighty question.

28 The title page of the book *Sefer Niflaot Maharal* ("Book of the Miracles of R. Loew"), Piotrkov, 1909, lists R. Yitzḥaq ben Shimshon haKohen (Katz, d. 1624) as the author. It is more likely that the book was written by Judah Rosenberg (1865-1935), who is mentioned on the title page as editor, possibly on the basis of older oral traditions.

complete the creation of the Golem. And he commanded us not to divulge this secret to anybody, and encouraged us with *tiqqunim*[29] and rules of conduct seven days in advance.

And on the twentieth of the month of Adar, in the year 5340 [1580 C.E.], all the three of us went at four after midnight behind the city of Prague, until the Moldava river. On the bank of the river we searched and found a place of clay and mud, and of the mud we made the form of a man, its length three cubits, and we shaped its face, and also his hands and feet, like a man lying on his back. Then all the three of us positioned ourselves at the feet of the Golem with our faces turned toward his face. And the Maharal first ordered me to walk seven times around the Golem, to begin from the right side and go around until his head, and from the head to the feet on the left side. And he gave me the combinations of letters which I had to recite as I was walking thus around the Golem. And so I did seven times. And when I finished the circumambulations, the body of the Golem became like glowing coals.

Then the Maharal ordered his disciple R. Ya'aqov Sason to perform seven such circumambulations, but he gave him other combinations of letters. And when he completed his circles the fire became extinguished, for water entered the body and mists began to issue from the body of the Golem, and also it became covered with a growth of hair like a thirty-year-old man, and also nails appeared on the tips of his fingers.

And then also the Maharal himself performed seven circumambulations, and at the end all the three of us together recited the verse, *And He breathed into his nostrils the breath of life, and the man became a living soul* (Gen. 2:7), for also in the air of the breath there must be found fire and water, for they give the word *Emesh* which is mentioned in

---

[29] *Tiqqunim* (sing. *tiqqun*) are Kabbalistic meditations for the purpose of strengthening the pure powers of the soul.

the Book of Creation.[30]

Then the Golem opened his eyes and looked at us like a man amazed. Then the Maharal cried out in an imperious voice: "Stand up on your feet!" Thereupon the Golem suddenly stood up. Then we put on him the clothes which we had brought with us, the kind of clothes which are suitable for a servant of a court of law. And we also put shoes on his feet. In brief, he became like an ordinary man. He could see, hear, and understand, but did not have the power of speech in his mouth. And at six in the morning, before it became light, we went home, four men.

On the way home the Maharal said to the Golem: "You must know that we created you out of the dust of the earth so that you protect the Jews from all evil and all the calamities which they suffer from their enemies. The name by which you will be called is Yosef. You will dwell with me, and stay in the chamber of my law court. Your work will be that of a servant of the court. You must obey everything I order you to do, even to enter into fire, or to immerse yourself in mighty waters, or to jump down from a tower, until you carry out my command exactly as I shall order you."

The Golem inclined his head at the words of the Maharal, like a man who signifies agreement with the words of his friend. To us the Maharal said that he gave the Golem the name Yosef because he put into him the spirit of Yosef Sheda who is mentioned in the Talmud, who was half man and half demon, and who served the sages of the Talmud and saved them many times from great calamities. And he also said concerning the Golem that even if he should enter into fire he would not be singed, and rivers could not sweep him away, nor could a sword kill him. And

[30] The Book of Creation (Hebrew *Sefer Yetzira*) is an old mystical treatise about the creation and structure of the metaphysical world, probably written between the third and the sixth centuries in Palestine or Babylonia. The word *Emesh* combines *Esh* ("fire") and *Mayim* ("water").

before the people of his house the Maharal said that when he went out early in the morning to the ritual bath, he found this poor mute man in the streets, and saw that he was totally witless, therefore he took pity on him and brought him back to his house. And the Maharal gave strict orders to the people of his house not to employ the Golem in the performance of any kind of housework.

And because the Golem always sat in the chamber of the law court, in a corner next to the edge of the table, with his head resting on his two hands, really like a lump of clay, bereft of all wisdom and understanding, and not thinking or worrying about anything in the world, therefore people called him "Yosele Golem," and some called him "the mute Yosele."

(Yitzḥaq Katz, *Sefer Niflaot Maharal*, pp. 12-14)

The End of the Golem

After King Rudolph issued his new law abolishing in his lands all legal proceedings of blood libels, and the Maharal saw that the land was quiet, and that another Passover had passed without any blood libel being heard in all the lands of the king, the Maharal summoned me, R. Yitzḥaq Katz, his son-in-law, and his disciple who adjudicated cases before him, R. Ya'aqov Sason haLevi, who had taken part in the creation of the Golem, and said to us that from now on there was no further need for the Golem. For no more proceedings of blood libel can take place in these lands. This thing happened on the night of the thirty-third day of the 'Omer in the year 5350 [1590 C.E.]. Then the Maharal commanded Yosele Golem not to go to sleep in his usual place which was in the chambers of the law court, but to take his couch up to the attic of the great synagogue, and there to lie down to sleep. And the Golem did as he was told. And this was close to midnight, and nobody saw or heard what was happening.

When two hours had passed after midnight, we went to the Maharal, I, his son-in-law, R. Yitzḥaq Katz, and his disciple the judge R. Yaʿaqov Sason haLevi. And the Maharal spread out on his table the question before us, whether or not a corpse like that of Yosele the Golem causes impurity like other corpses. The Maharal presented to us his opinion that even if after his death the Golem should remain flesh and bones, like unto all other men, even in that case no impurity would be pertinent to him. And how much more so since, as the Maharal knew in advance, the Golem after his death would become a lump of clay and dust, as he was prior to his creation. Therefore the Maharal took me with him to the attic, to assist at the death of the Golem, although I am a Kohen [who must not defile himself by approaching a dead body]. And this is how the end of the Golem came about:

All the three of us went up into the attic, and the Golem was asleep on his couch. The Maharal gave permission also to the old beadle R. Abraham Ḥayyim to follow us up into the attic, to hold two burning candles in his hands, but ordered him to stand at some distance. We took our places at the head of the Golem, and everything we did then was the reverse of what we had done at the creation of the Golem in order to make him alive. While then we had stationed ourselves at his feet with our faces toward his face, gone around him seven times, and begun to go around him on his right side, now we stood at his head with our faces turned toward his feet, and began to go around him on his left side, in order to remove from him the vitality of his soul and his spirit. The number of our circumambulations was seven this time too. The beginning of each circle was on the left side from his head toward his feet, and from his feet toward his head on the right side. Then we stopped and recited the combinations of letters as the Maharal instructed us. And thus we did at each of the seven circumambulations. The combinations of the letters which we now recited were the same as the ones in the hour of his creation, except that now we said them in reverse. And those who have knowledge in the practical Kabbala and know and understand thoroughly the Book of Creation will know the secret of the manner of creation, and understand the secret of the annulment of the manner of creation. After the seven circumabulations the Golem remained lying on his couch like a lump of hardened clay in the shape of a man.

The Maharal called the old beadle, R. Abraham Hayyim, to step closer. He took from his hands the two candles, and we disrobed the Golem and left only his shirt on him. And since there was no lack of old, unfit and torn Talliths there in the attic, R. Abraham Hayyim gathered up several such Talliths, and we wrapped the body of the Golem in two old Talliths, and tied them around him. Then we took the stiff body, and following the Maharal's instructions, we hid it under the big heap of old holy books which were there, until it was not at all visible that the Golem was hidden there. And the Maharal ordered R. Abraham Hayyim to carry down the couch and the clothes of the Golem from the attic of the synagogue, and to burn them by and by, so that nobody should notice it. Then we all came down from the attic, washed our hands in water, and went to sleep.

In the morning we let it be known that the servant Yosele Golem had become angry, and had run off in the night, and that it was not known where he went. And this is the belief that has persisted without fail among the people of the city of Prague. And only a few outstanding persons, those who were of a high degree, knew the truth.

In the second week after the absence of the Golem the Maharal issued orders that it be proclaimed that no man or woman should dare go up to the attic of the synagogue, and that the old and torn holy books should no longer be put there. And the reason he gave was that it could be feared that people would not be careful there with the fire, and it could easily happen that a great conflagration could break out there, and the whole synagogue could be consumed in the flames. But those who were intimate with the Maharal understood the real reason, which was to prevent that it become known that Yosele the Golem was resting there....

My teacher and father-in-law of blessed memory said that the spirit of the Golem would be resuscitated at the resurrection of the dead. But not in the first body of Yosef Sheda, and not in this second body of Yosele Golem, but in a third body which would arise from the coupling of a man and a woman, which will be brought to this world through a Righteous One, prior to the coming of the Messiah, in order to bring perfection to a very great and essential thing which is a deep secret. But it is possible that the power will be given him to resuscitate also his first two bodies. As it is written, *And He took of the spirit that was upon him* (Num. 11:25).

(Yitzḥaq Katz, *Sefer Niflaot Maharal*, pp. 69-70,73)

R. Ephraim al-Naqawa [31] Arrives in Tlemcen

On his way to Tlemcen many miracles occured to R. Ephraim al-Naqawa. Before he reached the city on the eve of the Sabbath, the sun set and he was, therefore, forced to spend the Sabbath in the desolate wilderness which was full of lions' and panthers' dens and snakes' and scorpions' holes, and all kinds of wild animals. Those who accompanied him left him and continued their way, but he did not want to desecrate the Sabbath and remained alone in this dreadful desert, without considering the great dangers which threatened his life.

When the sun set, heavy darkness covered the whole environs, and a terrible lion jumped out from its lair, and ran towards the rabbi to tear him to pieces. But as soon as it reached within four cubits of him, the lion became

---

[31] Born in Spain, R. Ephraim al-Naqawa came to North Africa after the Spanish exile of 1492. The same miraculous ride on a lion's back is attributed by another legend to Shabbatai Zevi.

transformed into a playful lamb, lay down before the rabbi like a dog which lies before its master, and all the wild animals which were round about withdrew from the rabbi because the fear of the lion befell them. Thus the lion protected the rabbi all night and during the day of the Sabbath. After the outgoing of the Sabbath the saint saw in the mouth of the lion a tortuous snake winding itself around its mane, like a halter in the mouth of a horse, as if motioning the rabbi that he should instantly get hold of the halter and ride on the lion's back, and he would take him to the goal of his journey. The saint instantly fulfilled the wish of the lion, rode on his back and held the tortuous snake like unto a rider who holds the bridle of his horse. And he rode on him until he came to the city of Tlemcen.

The Muslim inhabitants of the city who saw this miraculous and shattering sight instantly understood that it was a holy man of God who rode on the back of the king of beasts, and asked him to choose their city as his place of dwelling so that the Shekhina should rest upon it and the work of their hands be blessed through his merits.

The rabbi refused to fulfill their request because he did not want to live far from his brethren the Jews who at that time dwelt outside the walls of the city, and were exposed to the contempt and vilification of every passerby, and whose lives were in constant danger. But out of respect for the saint the rulers of the country allowed the Jews to settle in the city, and from that day on the Jews dwelt in Tlemcen.

(Abraham Elmaleh, in *Edoth* 2:205-6)

The Death of Abraham Azulai

It happened in Jerusalem to a Hasid, and he was a scholar of note and was a just and honest man, and he observed the commandments of the Tora in the most proper manner. And every Friday he made an immersion in honor of the Sabbath, even in the winter.

Once on Friday he, as was his wont, was going to immerse himself in the water, and a man came to him and said to him: "Do not submerge as yet." He said to him: "Why?" He said to him: "For the reason that there is here a dead man and we are nine, and you should complete with us the *minyan* [32] to say Kaddish.[33] Thereafter you can return here and immerse yourself."

And the Hasid went with him to the place of the House of the Worlds [i.e., cemetery], and there were nine men there, and he completed the *minyan,* and they buried the dead and said Kaddish. And he asked them what was the name of the dead man, and they said to him, R. Abraham Azulai,[34] and his home was not in Jerusalem but in a certain other city, "and he was meritorious and we brought him here to bury him in the Land of Israel."

And the Hasid was amazed at them for their speech and their shape was not like the shape of humans but like the shape of angels. And that Hasid scholar wrote down: "N. N. died on Friday, such and such a day of the month, in the year so and so of Creation." When he came to return to immerse himself, instantly the nine men disappeared from him. And the Hasid was very much amazed at this miracle. He went and submerged, and went to the synagogue to pray, and when he came to his house he was silent at his table and wondered about what he had seen.

And after the departure of the Sabbath he said: "I must investigate the miracle I saw. With the help of God I shall go and ask and see in his city how the matter stands." And he trod about from city to city, from place to place for a full year. He reached his city and asked: "Where is the house of R. Abraham Azulai?" They said to him: "In that place it is hidden." And he went there and saw people gathered to study Scripture, Zohar, and Mishna in honor of the

[32] The quorum of ten adult males required for public prayers.
[33] The prayer for the dead.
[34] Abraham Azulai (c. 1660-1741) was a Moroccan Kabbalist.

memory of his soul. He went and gave them peace, and said to them:

"What is this gathering and this studying which you are engaged in?"

They said to him: "Thus and thus is the matter."

Instantly he told them the story, etc., and said to them:

"Today it is one year [since I helped to bury him], and I have just arrived here. And if you do not believe me, behold here is this writing, and the date is from the past year."

When the people heard it they did not believe it, and he said to them: "Come and let us test the matter, let us dig up his grave and see whether he is there or not."

Next day they went to test the words of the Hasid, and opened his grave, and saw that he was not buried there, and then the words of the scholar Hasid were proven true. And they came to the house and made great honor to the scholar Hasid, and he sat among them and preached a fine sermon in honor of his soul. And the scholar Hasid returned to Jerusalem and told the scholars all these things.

(Hebrew manuscript by Y'aqov ben Mikhael)

The Miracle of the Sailing Ship

One year there were very high prices in the gates in the city of Jerusalem, and the sages decided to do something to help the poor, and they said: "Let us cast lots and send an emissary to Constantinople." And they made lots, and it fell on R. Yose, an old man who had never in his life gone out to any village but was sitting always in the House of Study, and in the evening would go home. And he did not know the shape of a coin. And thereafter some of the sages said: "Let us cast lots again, perhaps the lot will fall on another man who is strong and familiar with the villages and countries."

And this rabbi answered them: "It is not possible to change the lot. It is necessary that this one himself so should go." They said to him: "However, this one cannot entertain, he is meek, does not know language. Let us at least send with him a servant who is clever about roads, and who will be a master of language and he should know the language of Turkey, lest he return here with a broken soul."

And so they did, and they wrote for him an important document about the famine and the suffering of the poor. And R. Yose put it in his bosom. And several more Turks wrote letters to relatives and partners of theirs, and they noted down the date, month and day, and gave them into the hand of R. Yose. And they set out and went to the sea of Jaffa, from there to Kosta [Constantinople] it is by *fapor* [i.e., *vapeur,* steamer] of fire eight days, and by wind a hundred days, if there is wind. But it was caused by the Name, blessed be He, that they went from Jaffa to Kosta in six days in a ship of wind. While they were going in the ship, the sailor was amazed at this thing, and he knew that the ship was fleeing through a miracle. And R. Yose was constantly studying Tora by night and by day, and was not silent. And when they came off the ship, they went to the customs, and the Turks came and asked of them: "How many days were you on the sea until you arrived here?" And the servant said to them: "Six days." And they did not believe it, until they took out the letters which had the date of six days [earlier], and then they believed it. And they were greatly amazed with a great amazement, and they gathered around R. Yose and his servant because of this miracle which happened to them.

In that hour the *Padishah* [sultan] of Kosta came to the marketplace, and saw from afar the people gathered there, and asked what was there. And they told him the matter of the ship and the old R. Yose. And he came to the customs, and saw in the door the old man there, and saw that there was a pillar of fire over his head and its light went up to the firmament. And he was amazed with a great amazement over this miracle, and said to his aide: "Do you see the pillar of fire there?" He said to him: "If so, take the old man and his servant to my reception hall, and let him sit on a chair until I come." And the aide did so.

Thereafter the Padishah came to the house and came to the hall, and saw the old man, again with the pillar of fire over his head. And he prostrated himself before him. And they said to him: "You, why do you bow down before a Jew?" He said to them: "I see in him such a miracle." Instantly the Padishah asked mercy before the Lord, that just as he saw the pillar of fire they too should see that the cause was from the Name, blessed be He. Instantly they saw as the king saw the pillar of fire. And they came and kissed his hand and foot.

The king said to him: "Why have you come?" And the servant answered him: "Because of such and such a famine, etc." And the servant instantly took out the document and put it into the hand of the king. And he fetched the sages of Kosta and they read it before him. And the king was very sorry for the poor of Jerusalem. Then the king said: "Did you have no other man to send but the rabbi, such a great and old man?" The servant said to him: "Because of the lot, etc." And the king himself gave a money order to the sultan of Jerusalem,[35] how many golden denars he should give into the hand of old R. Yose, and he commanded his princes and his aides that they should give him their share, and they gave. And he sent him with his aide to the house of the rabbi that on the very same day he should take from every rich man[36] according to the reach of his hand. And they, too, made out a money order for Jerusalem and gave the document into the hands of old R. Yose. And he left Kosta and sat in the ship with his servant and reached Jerusalem. This time he arrived in eight days.

And when he came to the city, and they saw that R. Yose had come and it took him less than two weeks they thought

[35] Here we have a clear indication that the Turkish governor of Jerusalem is styled "sultan" by the storyteller.

[36] Meaning every rich Jew, over whom the Ḥakham Bashi (Chief Rabbi) of Constantinople had jurisdiction.

that he had turned back because he could not go on the mission. And they said to the rabbi: "How many times did we tell you, do not send this one, and you did not listen!" He said to them: "May God be merciful!"[37]

And when he reached the sages and took out the documents of money orders, they thought that it was their own document. And then they recognized the thing and they rejoiced with great rejoicing over these miracles which the Name, blessed be He, performed for R. Yose.

And all this why? Because of his Tora. And this is what is said: *When thou walkest, it shall lead thee* (Prov. 6:22). Ministering angels led and took the ship instantly to Kosta, for the sake of the merit of old R. Yose's Tora.

(Hebrew manuscript by Ya'aqov ben Mikhael)

The Jar of Tears

In a year of drought, when the situation was very bad, the rabbi called together all the people of the city to the synagogue. The people prayed day and night, but were not answered. They decreed a fast upon themselves, but were not answered. The rabbi made a dream fast[38] and requested that God answer him and let rain fall. But he was told from heaven: "Only if Raḥamim, who always sits in the corner of the synagogue, will pray, will God accept his prayer and make rain fall."

The rabbi called the *shammash* [sexton] and ordered him, "Bring Raḥamim here!"

The *shammash* said to the rabbi, "What do you want of him?"

The rabbi answered: "He must come to the reader's stand and pray."

The *shammash* was astonished: "But he is a complete

---

[37] A pious expression, meaning "What can we do!"
[38] Hebrew *ta'anit ḥalom*, a fast on account of a bad dream, or, as in the present context, on account of a public calamity.

ignoramus. He knows nothing. How can he come to the reader's desk and lead the prayers?"

"Nevertheless, call him," concluded the rabbi the conversation.

The *shammash* did as he was told, hurried to the house of Raḥamim, and invited him to the rabbi's house. Raḥamim did not know what it was about, but instantly fulfilled the rabbi's request. When he came there, the rabbi told him that he must ascend to the reader's stand and pray for rain.

Raḥamim declined, saying: "I don't know how to pray. There are better men than I."

The rabbi did not accept Raḥamim's refusal, and commanded him: "You must pray, be it as it may!"

Next day the rabbi invited the whole congregation to come to the synagogue. All the people of the city gathered, and the synagogue was crowded to overflowing. Everybody expected the rabbi to ascend to the reader's stand and lead the prayers. How great was their astonishment when they saw that the rabbi invited Raḥamim to the Holy Ark and asked him to pray before the congregation!

Raḥamim did as the rabbi told him, but said: "I beg of you, wait a few moments."

Thereupon Raḥamim left the synagogue and soon returned with a small earthenware jar in his hands. The jar had two spouts. Raḥamim went up with it to the reader's stand and asked the people to pray. When they opened the Holy Ark, all of them cried bitterly, and recited psalms. And Raḥamim stood all the time in front of the reader's stand, and held the small earthenware jar in his hands. He raised one of its spouts to his eye, and a moment later he inclined his ear to the other spout.

Before long, clouds covered the sky, and a torrential rain poured down upon the earth.

The rabbi asked Rahamim to come to him and said: "I want you to tell me why you brought along the earthenware jar, and what did you do with it?"

Raḥamim answered and related: "I am a poor man. I have

a large family, with small children in the house. I am a cobbler by trade, but I cannot manage to provide for my children. Every evening they cry for bread, and I have no bread to give them. My heart breaks. I would sit in a corner of the house, cry bitterly, and collect the tears in this jar. I instructed my wife to bury this jar with me when I die. When you asked me to come to pray before the congregation, I brought the jar with me, I looked into its spout and proclaimed: 'Master of the World! If You do not let rain fall, I shall break this jar in front of the whole congregation!' Then I bent my ear to the other spout of the jar, and heard a voice which said, 'Don't break it!' And instantly rain began to fall."

"This is the story of the jar," concluded Raḥamim his words. "And today it brought us help."

The rabbi said in his heart: "How true are the words of our masters. 'The gates of tears are not closed.'"

(Syrian Jewish Folktale)

The Butcher's Mitzva

There was once a rabbi who was a great sage and who served God and was full of His fear. One night he dreamed a dream in which they told him, "After your death you will have a share in the World to Come together with a butcher."

The Ḥakham awoke in the morning. He was full of wonderment, and he thought: "Why should my share in the World to Come be together with a butcher, when I am such a great sage?"

The Ḥakham prayed, and set out in order to find the butcher next to whom he would have his share in the World to Come. After a long search he found the butcher's shop, entered, and said: "My son, listen to me, what is your trade? What do you do? They told me in a dream that my share will be with your share in the World to Come."

The butcher said: "I have few mitzvot. But when I sell

meat I take care to give a full weight. I always add a little."

The Ḥakham answered: "That is not such a great *mitzva*. Anybody can do such a *mitzva*. Can that be the reason they told me that my share would be with your share? Perhaps you can remember something else? Think. Perhaps you remember and can tell me."

The butcher thought for a while. Did he have any other merits? He said: "I remember that once I did another *mitzva*."

The Ḥakham asked: "What did you do? Tell me!"

The butcher then related: "A Jewish girl child was captured, and there was nobody to save her. The girl cried in her captivity and wept, 'Who can save me, who can ransom me?' I paid the money, saved the girl, and took her to my house. I decided to marry her to my son. The boy agreed, and the girl, too, agreed, because I had ransomed her, although she had been engaged prior to that to another man."

The butcher continued the story, and the great sage heard how an engagement was arranged between the girl and the butcher's son, and how they made the preparations for the wedding. Many people came to attend the wedding of the poor girl. When everything was ready for the wedding benediction, just prior to the celebration under the *huppa* [the wedding canopy] and the reading of the *ketubba* [the marriage contract], the son of the butcher saw a young man sitting in a corner and crying.

He approached him and asked: "Why are you crying? All the invited guests came to rejoice at my wedding, and you with your crying disrupt the joy?"

The young man answered: "My heart is in pain because of this girl."

"What is the matter?" asked the bridegroom in surprise. "Why are you crying over my bride?"

The young man explained: "This girl, whom you are about to wed, was engaged to me. But after the outbreak of the war she was captured. Now I succeeded in getting together money to ransom her, and, behold, she is about to marry somebody else."

The bridegroom asked: "What marks of identification does she have?"

The youth named seven marks in his bride.

They took the bride into a separate room, examined her, and found in her all the marks mentioned by the young man. They brought her out of the room, and the butcher announced to his son: "My son, you cannot marry this girl!"

"Why?" asked the youth.

The butcher said: "Because she is engaged to somebody else. And what can we do?"

The bridegroom was silent and said nothing to his father. The father went up to the crying young man and said to him: "Go up in place of my son, and wed the girl."

The youth and the girl stepped up to the bench, and the rabbi pronounced the benediction over them instead of the girl and the butcher's son.

When the Ḥakham heard the story, he was deeply moved and said to the butcher: "The *mitzva* you performed was indeed a great *mitzva!*"

Because of this *mitzva* the butcher merited to sit next to the great sage in the World to Come.

(Georgian [Gruzinian] Jewish Folktale)

BIBLICAL AND OTHER HEROES

The Real Daughter of Noah

When God said to Noah the pious that he should build an ark of gopher wood, whose length should be three hundred cubits, width fifty cubits, and height thirty cubits, Noah could have finished the building of the ark in a very short time, but he spent a hundred years building it. And why? Because Noah hoped that the people would repent during that long time when they saw that the flood was coming upon the earth, and that the Holy One, blessed be He, would also repent of His intention to bring the flood.

And from where did Noah have the enormous sum of money which was needed to buy the materials: the wood, the nails, and the pitch?

Noah had an only daughter whose name was Naamah. And she was very beautiful of face and of appearance, and there was none like her among all the daughters of the East. When Noah bought the wood, and wanted to pay the storeowner for it, the latter refused and said: "I shall not accept money from you for the wood, but give me your daughter to wife!"

Noah had no choice but to agree, and he got the wood against his promise that he would let the storeowner have his daughter.

When he went to buy nails, the seller refused to accept money for his merchandise, and he, too, asked for the hand of Noah's daughter. Again, Noah had no choice but to agree. But from where would he take another daughter, when he had only a single one? Noah the pious lifted up his eyes to heaven and said:

"Master of the World! From where should I take a daughter for the owner of the nail store?"

In that hour a she-ass passed by, and, behold, she became transformed into a beautiful girl who was astoundingly like Noah's daughter. So he decided that he would give her to the nail seller.

When the building of the ark was finished, Noah went to the pitch seller, but he, too, refused to accept payment, just as the other two had done, and asked instead for the beautiful daughter of Noah.

Again Noah lifted up his eyes to the Holy One, blessed be He, in prayer. A bitch came to the place and was transformed into a beautiful girl who was astoundingly like Noah's daughter. And she was given to the pitch seller.

A short time prior to the flood Noah ordered his eldest son, Shem, who was very learned and a prophet, to bring his daughter into the ark. Shem went to look for his sister, and, behold, he found three girls who resembled one another like three drops of water, chatting among themselves. And he could not find out which of them was his true sister. However, wise Shem decided to test the three with questions, and to find out from their answers which one was his real sister. He asked the first one:

"How are you, my sister? Are you satisfied with your husband? Is there peace between you?"

The girl answered: "Our life is nice and pleasant. Only occasionally, when I bend down to lick the plate, this makes my husband angry."

Shem understood that this was the bitch which turned into a woman. He then asked the second girl: "And what is new with you, my sister? Are you satisfied with your husband? Does he behave properly?"

The girl answered: "My husband is good and behaves well. But occasionally, when I kick with my foot, he gets very angry, and then we quarrel."

Shem understood that this was the she-ass which turned into a woman.

Finally he addressed the third girl and asked her the same questions.

She answered: "Thank you, my brother. My husband is good and kind. He fears heaven and loves justice."

Instantly Shem took the third one and led her into the ark, for he knew that she was his real sister.

(Dov Noy, *Iraqi Jewish Folktales*, pp. 100-2)

Joshua and His Mother
(A MEDIEVAL OEDIPUS STORY)

The father of Joshua lived in Egypt and his wife was barren. And the Tzaddiq [i.e., Joshua's father] prayed to God for his wife and God listened to him. And when she became pregnant, the Tzaddiq mortified himself and wept day and night, without surcease. And this seemed wrong in the eyes of his wife, and she said to him: "You should rejoice that the Lord has heard your prayer!" And he did not answer her. And when she spoke to him day after day and importuned him with her words, he told her all his heart, that it was revealed to him from heaven on high that this son who will be born to him will cut off his head. And his wife believed him, for she knew that all his words were true.

And it came to pass when she gave birth that, behold, it was a son. And his mother took for him an ark and daubed it with slime and with pitch and she put her son into it and cast it into the Nile.[39] And the Lord prepared a great fish to swallow the ark.[40]

And it came to pass that one day the king made a feast unto all his princes and his servants (cf. Esth. 1:3). And they caught the fish which had swallowed the ark and brought it before the king, and they cut it open, and behold, a weeping child.[41] And the king and his princes marveled, and the king commanded that they bring a woman to suckle the child. And the boy grew up in the house of the king, and the king appointed him to be a guardsman.

And it came to pass after these things that that Tzaddiq, the father of Joshua, committed a transgression against the king of Egypt, and the king ordered the guardsman to cut off his head, and to take his wife and children and property for himself, as was their law in those days.

And it came to pass when he approached his mother in order to lie with her, that the whole bed became full of milk from her breasts. And Joshua was seized with great fear, and he took his spear to slay her for he thought she was a witch. But his mother remembered the words of his father the Tzaddiq, of blessed memory, and she stopped him

[39] Cf. Exod. 2:3.
[40] Cf. Jon. 2:1.
[41] Cf. Exod. 2:6.

saying: "This is no sorcery but the same milk which you sucked." And she told him all that had happened.

Joshua instantly separated himself from her, for he, too, remembered what was told about him, that he was found in a fish, although he did not know who was his father. And he repented.

This is why he was called Joshua son of Nun [i.e., "fish"], because he was found in a fish, and "fish" in Aramaic is Nun. And the spies [who went with him to the Land of Canaan] called him "Head cutter" because of what he had done to his father.

(Nissim ben Ya'qov ibn Shahin,
Ḥibbur MehaY'shu'a, OM, p. 209)

King Solomon and the Winds

Once King Solomon sat on his jewel-bedecked throne in the great hall of his cedar palace. A purple royal robe covered his body, the golden crown of the realm glittered on his head, and in his right hand he held his royal scepter. The sages of the people and the princes of Israel stood around him in a wide circle.

It was the hour when the king would command every day that the gates of his palace be opened so that the people who had requests or complaints should be able to come and speak face to face to the king. Before anybody else, however, his firstborn son, Absalom,[42] rushed into the hall. He was a boy of about twelve years of age, as yet not mature enough to understand the ways of the world, but already full of wonderment at the sight of all human and divine wisdom. He approached the throne and breathlessly addressed his father, his eyes gleaming with unconcealed anger:

[42] Absalom was the third son of David. According to the Bible, the son and heir of Solomon was Rehoboam, and Absalom was one of the older brothers of Solomon, cf. 2 Sam. 3:3. The Bible has no record of a son of Solomon by this name.

"My father, behold, I was walking along the streets of the city on my way home from the House of Study where my soul imbibed the wisdom of our God's commandments, when I saw a poor woman sitting on a stone at a corner. Her clothes showed that she was a widow, and as I approached her, since our Tora commands us to help the orphan and the widow within our walls, I saw that she held an empty wooden bowl in her hand, and flour was strewn all around her. The woman was crying, and I tried to comfort her. I told her to bring to the king her complaint against the evildoer who scattered her flour and robbed her of her food. She will soon be here, and I beg of you, lend me the tokens of your kingship and let me find the guilty one and punish him, and do justice to the widow. For this is what our Tora commands us, and the wrath of heaven visits the people, and blight, war, and pestilence come upon the city in whose streets widows cry."

When King Solomon heard the spirited words of his son, he rose from his royal throne, let Absalom sit in his place, wrapped the heavy royal robe around his tender narrow shoulders, put the scepter into his hand, and placed the crown upon his black locks. Thus he willingly gave him the tokens of his power. He retained only his ring which gave him power over the spirits of the earth, of the sea, and of the air. For only once was that ring removed from King Solomon's finger, when Ashmodai, king of the demons, outwitted him; and well did the king remember how he was punished and how he had to wander as a beggar in his own kingdom for forty years while nobody recognized him.

No sooner was Absalom seated on the royal throne, when the widow entered through the portals of the great hall, slowly approached the throne, and then stopped with her head bent low. She pointed to the empty bowl and was about to present her complaint. But Absalom anticipated her and said:

"I know of the evil act about which you wish to complain. Tell me the name of him who robbed you of your flour and scattered it, and rest assured that I shall punish him severely!"

And the widow answered and said:

"I know that the justice of our king is as great as his power, and his compassion for those who are persecuted is as great as his justice. Therefore the weak love him as much as the wrongdoers fear him. My lord, I was coming from the marketplace where I spent my last copper shekel on flour in order to knead it and bake myself a loaf of bread for tomorrow, the Sabbath, so as to be able to sanctify the day of rest as God commanded us. But as I was walking along the street, and I was near my hut, a great noise and whistling arose from heaven, a gust of wind swept through the street, got hold of my flour, spilled it on the ground, and scattered it in all directions, and I was left with the empty bowl in my hand. Now I shall have to hunger on the Sabbath of God, for it was my last coin for which I bought the flour in the market. This is, my lord, why I cried."

Thus spoke the widow and fell silent.

Perplexed, Absalom looked at his father, and a question was in his eyes. For although the crown and the scepter have given him power and dominion in the whole earth and over all men and animals living on it, the spirits of the water and the winds were subject only to him who wore the magic ring. Solomon understood his son's unspoken request, kissed the blue stone in the ring, and with a mighty silent gesture summoned the first of the winds, the West Wind.

And there was a movement and a rustle and a swish, and the West Wind flew in through the open windows of the great hall. His head was covered with long yellow hair, and the feathers of his wings were moist with the dew of the sea. Without heeding Absalom, who sat on the throne, the West Wind bowed down before the master of the ring. But Absalom turned to him angrily and addressed him in wrath:

"Speak and deny it not: Are you the one who spilled the

flour of this widow? Admit it, if you did it!"

And the West Wind answered and said:

"I was flying over the mountains of Cyprus, and saw the naked brown men who were cutting the green metal from the rocks. They were digging into the shoulder of the mountain day and night until they pried loose enough of the ore. Then they put it on burning coals and blew into the fire, and melted the ore until pure copper flowed out of the ashes like a fiery serpent. And I saw that the men hammered the glowing copper and fashioned it into plates to serve as covering for the roof of the Temple which you, Solomon, are building on Mount Zion in God's honor. But I have never seen this woman and have not touched her property."

Solomon dismissed the West Wind with a nod of his head, kissed the blue stone in his ring a second time, and with a silent, mighty gesture summoned the second of the winds, the East Wind. And there was a movement and a rustle and a swish like the beating of huge wings, and the East Wind flew in through the open windows of the great hall. His head was covered with red hair, and the feathers of his wings were yellow from the dust of the desert. Without heeding Absalom, who sat on the royal throne, the East Wind bowed down before the master of the ring. Absalom turned to him angrily and addressed him in wrath:

"Speak and deny it not: Are you the one who spilled the flour of this widow? Admit it, if you commited this evil deed!"

And the East Wind answered and said:

"I was flying in from over the desert and halted my wings above the dark mountains of Lebanon. I saw men in the depths of the forest with iron axes and metal hatchets. They raised their hands upon the thousand-year-old cedars in whose cool crowns I loved to rest when coming from the heat of the desert. They cut down the trees, trimmed their branches, and peeled the bark from the trunks. They smoothed the wood and fashioned beams to carry the roof of the Temple which you, Solomon, are building on Mount Zion in God's honor. But I have never seen this woman and have not touched her property."

Solomon dismissed the East Wind with a nod of his head, kissed the blue stone in his ring a third time, and with a silent, mighty gesture summoned the third of the winds, the North Wind.

And there was a movement and a rustle and a swish, like the beating of huge wings, and the North Wind flew in through the open windows of the great hall. His head was covered with white hair, and white were his long wings as the snow of the winter. Without heeding Absalom, who sat on the royal throne, the North Wind bowed down before the master of the ring. Absalom turned to him angrily and addressed him in wrath:

"Speak and deny it not: Are you the one who spilled the flour of this widow? Admit it, if you committed this evil deed!"

And the North Wind answered and said:

"I am coming from the marble quarries of Lydia. I let my cold breeze blow into the faces of the men who were cutting big white blocks from the bowels of the mountains. I looked and observed how they were driving their chisels deep into the boulders to break the marble loose from the rocks. And they shaped the mighty blocks into hewn stones, and smoothed them in order to make of them corner stones for the Temple which you, Solomon, are building on Mount Zion in God's honor. But I have never seen this woman and have not touched her property."

Solomon dismissed the North Wind with a nod of his head, kissed the blue stone in the ring a fourth time, and with a silent, mighty gesture summoned the fourth of the winds, the South Wind. And there was a movement and a rustle and a swish, like the beating of huge wings, and the South Wind flew in through the open windows of the great hall. His locks were brown and his wings red like the corals in the seas of the south. Without heeding Absalom, who sat on the royal throne, the South Wind bowed down before the master of the ring. But Absalom turned to him angrily and shouted at him full of wrath:

"Admit, you, that you robbed this widow of her flour. You are the culprit, you must be it, and if you try to deny it, it will be of no use. Your brothers are innocent of the crime. You are the one who grinds the face of the poor, who oppresses those who are without protection!"

And the South Wind answered and said:

"Yes. I am the one who did it."

He wanted to continue, but Absalom pointed the royal scepter at him in a threatening gesture, so as to cut him off. But Solomon, with a stern glance, silenced his son, and motioned the South Wind to continue.

"Yes, my lord, I did it. But see, O see, I was hovering over the sea along the shores of Araby, and the water below was blue and transparent. And suddenly I heard, across the silence, a sound rising up to me, like the voice of many men crying out in a moment of danger. I looked down, and behold, I saw an Egyptian ship sailing towards the Arabian coast. Three hundred people were on the ship, Egyptian peasants with their women and children, fleeing from their native land because of drought and famine, in order to find bread and shade in the oases of Araby. But the ship had sprung a leak and was about to sink. In great fear they directed it towards the shore, but they were still far from the land as the shot of an arrow from the bow, and already angry waves washed over the aft of the deck. And they all saw that death would overtake them in the sea so near the shore, in view of the land, and they all, men, women, and children, lifted up their voices in a great cry, and their clamor rose to heaven. And my compassion was kindled, and I descended, and lay myself upon the sea, and blew with all my strength over the water, until the waves of the sea rose and lifted their foamy head. And I pushed with all my strength against the sails of the sinking ship, and she jumped wildly ahead towards the land, and with a loud crash ran up the shore. The ship's keel and beams were splintered, but the people were saved. With loud words of thanks they climbed down from the wreckage of the ship, and with joy they stepped upon the good land. And, see, O my lord, at that moment, when I blew with all my strength to save the men, women, and children on the sinking ship, I also spilled the flour of this widow and scattered it all about."

The South Wind finished speaking and fell silent. And silent was also Absalom, and sunk in thoughts, he lowered his eyes.

And King Solomon dismissed the South Wind with a satisfied nod of his head, and ordered his treasurer to give a hundred gold shekels to the widow, and dismissed her too with kindness.

Quickly, and somewhat shamefacedly, Absalom took off the tokens of royalty. And King Solomon put back the royal crown on his anointed head, took the scepter in his strong hand, and threw the royal purple over his broad shoulders, and took his place on the throne of his father David.

(Sephardi Folktale, published
by Walter Schiller)

Elijah as Physician

A woman was badly scalded by boiling water. Her whole body was burned, and the best doctors gave her up. "No remedy can help her," they said.

The members of her family gathered around the bed of the dying woman in order to take leave of her. When it seemed that she had fallen asleep, they went out of the room and left her alone. Suddenly she opened her eyes, and saw an old man who had entered the room. The old man asked how she was feeling, passed his hand over her wounds, and said to her: "Get up!"

As soon as she heard these words, he disappeared as suddenly as he had come.

The woman moved her limbs, and, behold, she felt no pain. She rose from the bed, left the room, and called her children.

No one of those who were present, the doctors and the members of the family, could believe their eyes. Only when the woman told them everything did they understand that the old man was the prophet Elijah of blessed memory.

(Dov Noy, *Jewish Folktales from Tunisia* [in Hebrew], p. 175)

A Moroccan Jewish Midas Legend

Horns grew on the head of a king. The king was ashamed to have his hair cut, lest people find out his secret.

His hair grew like a forest. He wanted to have it shorn. He called the barber and made him swear that he would reveal to no man what his eyes saw.

And the barber could not contain the secret in himself. What did he do? He went into a cave and said:

"Cave, cave! The sultan has horns! The sultan has horns! The sultan has horns!"

Reeds and rushes grew at that cave. A goatherd passed by. He cut the reed and made a flute of it. The goatherd began to play the flute. A voice was heard from the flute: "The sultan has horns! The sultan has horns!" They heard the voice in the marketplace. They told it to the king. The king sent to call the barber. He said:

"Did I not tell you that you must not reveal my secret to anybody?"

The barber said: "I, forgive me, O king, my heart was swollen from the great secret. And I went to a cave and told it my secret."

The king said: "I forgive you."

Tell, O man, what is in your heart, even if to the wall, and suffer not.

(Told by an old Moroccan Jewish woman in Jerusalem and published by Zelda Shneursohn, in *Edoth* 1:40)

An Iraqi Jewish Legend about Alexander

[The same story is told by the Jews of Baghdad about Alexander the Great, who is called in the Koran "Alexander of the Horns".]

Two horns grew on the head of the king Alexander. He did not want to reveal his shame in public. What did he do? Every week he invited a barber to cut his hair. When the cutting was finished he killed the barber so that he should not reveal his secret in the city. In this manner all the barbers in the city were killed, until none was left except one Jewish barber.

The king said: "If I kill him, who will cut my hair in the days to come?" The king made the barber swear that he would not reveal the secret to any man, for on the day on which the matter was heard in the city he would surely be killed.

The barber carried in himself the secret until he became sick. His patience burst, he could not suffer longer. But he did not want to violate his oath which he rendered to the king. What did he do? Each time he shaved the king, he returned home, went down to the cellar of his house in which there was a spring of water, and shouted:

"Iskandar Abu Qarnayn! Iskandar Abu Qarnayn! Iskandar Abu Qarnayn!"[43]

And this gave him relief.

At that time there grew in the wall of the cellar, near that spring of water, a reed of rushes which absorbed the words of the barber. The barber cut down that reed and threw it outside his house. A shepherd passed by, took the reed and made a flute out of it. And it came to pass that when he played the flute, the voice was heard: Iskandar Abu

---

[43] Literally: "Alexander is a father of horns," i.e., has horns.

Qarnayn! Iskandar Abu Qarnayn! Iskandar Abu Qarnayn!

The thing was heard in the city and reached the ears of the king. The king called the barber, and rebuked him for having revealed his secret. The barber told the king all that had happened to him. The king believed the barber and forgave him.

(A. Ben-Ya'aqov, in *Edoth* 1:184-85)

7

HASIDISM

A very specially Jewish folktale type is the Hasidic story which originated, circulated, was given total credence, and considered sacred truth, among the followers of Hasidism in Eastern Europe, in the eighteenth and nineteenth centuries.

As I have stated elsewhere, "Hasidism is the Jewish religious and social movement, founded in Podolia and Volhynia by Israel Ba'al Shem Tov (1699?-1760), usually referred to by the acrostic BeShT. It taught that what God wanted of man was not asceticism and the mortification of the flesh as represented by Lurianic Kabbala [see Part 5], nor concentration on Halakhic study as demanded by Polish Talmudism, but devotion, or 'cleaving' (*d'vekut*) to Him. God, the BeShT taught, must be served with joy. One must surrender oneself to Him with enthusiasm (*hitlahavut*) so that one can give up the consciousness of separate existence and be joined to the eternal being of God. Since, however, most men cannot achieve this high state of spiritual union with God, they need the intermediacy of the Tzaddiq (the 'saintly' or 'pious one'), who is a manifestation of God and a connecting link between the Creator and Creation."[1]

The court of each Tzaddiq—that is, Hasidic rabbi— was a fertile breeding ground of innumerable stories

[1] Cf. R. Patai, *The Jewish Mind* (New York: Scribner's, 1977), pp. 181- 82.

about the wisdom, the insight, the spiritual grasp, and, last but not least, the manifest miracles of the saintly rabbi. These stories rapidly spread among the followers of the Tzaddiqim, were embellished and elaborated, and before long some of their devoted disciples felt impelled to collect them in writing and to publish them with a view to the greater glory of the saintly men. But the purpose of these collections of Hasidic legends was not only to praise the Tzaddiq and pay homage to his greatness (although several books have the explicit title "Praises of . . ." followed by the name of the Tzaddiq), but also to spread his doctrines and teachings, and thus to proselytize those Jews who were among the opponents (*Mitnagdim*) of Hasidism, and convert them into true believers in the Tzaddiq's miraculous powers and his divinely inspired insights which was considered a great *mitzva* (religious duty).

By the end of the nineteenth century many hundreds of books containing stories about the great masters of Hasidism had appeared in print, mostly in Hebrew, occasionally in Yiddish, or in a mixture of the two languages. One of the most popular of them is the *Shivḥe haBeShT,* or "Praises of the BeShT," which has been reissued in many editions. It is, however, surpassed in storytelling quality by the tales of R. Naḥman of Bratzlav (1772-1811), a great-grandson of the BeShT and one of the great Hasidic teachers. Despite the great abundance of printed Hasidic literature, the sources of Hasidic folklore are still far from being exhausted, and hitherto unpublished stories can still be recorded from the mouths of the believers or their descendants.

The artistry of R. Naḥman of Bratzlav was able to combine the miraculous with the allegorical. Both selections presented below from his pen (he wrote in Yiddish) abound in miracles, in elements of marvels and portents, but their ultimate purpose is to impart teaching in the form of allegories and parables. The heroine of "The Lost Princess" is, of course, none other than the People of Israel, or, to use the old Talmudic personification, the Community of Israel, who suffers in the Exile and waits and yearns for the Redemption. The story "How Satan Prevented the Coming of the Messiah" is a beautiful legendary presentation of the frequently discussed, but never satisfactorily solved, problem of why the Messiah has not come as yet.

Many of the typical Hasidic stories tell of a Tzaddiq performing an act or acts which are incomprehensible, puzzling, and strange in the eyes of those around him. At a critical juncture the meaning of the Tzaddiq's act or acts becomes clear, and the believers are thus supplied with an additional proof of his wisdom, piety, or miraculous powers. The two newly recorded tales from Lithuania, "The Gift of Elijah" and "The Bashful Bride," belong to this type.

The most ubiquitous characteristic of the Hasidic tale is its moral tone. It invariably contains the teaching that sin (or crime) is inevitably punished, if not in this world then in the next, and that, likewise, piety ultimately reaps its reward. Quite apart from the folkloristic value of the Hasidic tale, this literary genre must be recognized as the spiritual nourishment which sustained most of the East European Jews for three or four generations, until its gradual replacement by the new values of the Haskala, the Jewish Enlightenment.

ABOUT THE BA'AL SHEM TOV

(1699?-1760)

A Dream-Vision of the Ba'al Shem

On New Year's Day in 5507 [1746 C.E.], I performed, as is known to you, an adjuration for the ascent of my soul, and I

saw wondrous things in a vision, for Samael ascended to
accuse, with great joy, the like of which never existed, and
performed his acts—decrees of apostasy for many souls [i.e.,
people] who would be put to death in unnatural ways [i.e.,
tortured to death]. And a great fright seized me and I was
ready to give up my soul. And I asked my teacher and
master [i.e., the prophet Ahijah the Shilonite] that he
should come with me, for it is a great danger to go and
ascend to the supernal worlds, for ever since I could stand
on my own I never ascended ascents as great as this. And I
ascended step after step until I entered the hall of the
Messiah in which the Messiah studies the Tora with all the
Tannaites and the righteous, and also with the seven
shepherds.[2] And there I saw very great rejoicing, and I did
not know what that rejoicing was about, and I thought
that, heaven forfend, it was a rejoicing over my passing[3]
from this world. But they let me know subsequently that I
was not about to die as yet, for they took delight On High
when I engaged in *yihudim*[4] down below by means of their
holy teachings. But to this day I know not the reason of that
rejoicing. And I asked the mouth of the Messiah: "When
will the Master come?" And he replied: "When your
teaching will spread out over the whole world." And I
prayed there about what the Lord did in this manner, and
about *What meaneth the heat of this great anger* (Deut. 29:23),
that many souls from Israel were delivered to Samael to be
slain, and among them many who had become apostates
and then were killed. And they gave me permission to ask
the mouth of Samael himself, and I asked the mouth of
Samael why he did this and what was his intention in
making them abandon their faith, and thereafter being

[2] The reference is to Mic. 5:4.

[3] The Supernals would rejoice at seeing the soul of the Ba'al Shem
join them.

[4] Exercises of very intense emotional and mental concentration for
the purpose of bringing about the unification (*yihud*) of God the
King and His mate the Shekhina (or Matronit).

killed. And he answered me that his intention was to serve heaven, for had they remained alive after having abandoned their faith, then, when more evil decrees were issued, they would not sanctify the name of heaven, but all would abandon their faith in order to save their lives. Therefore he did things so that those who abandoned their faith should be killed thereafter, and because of this no son of Israel should abandon his faith but should sanctify the name of heaven.

(Bauminger, "Igrot R. Yisrael
Ba'al Shem Tov," pp. 164-66."

The Yom Kippur Flutist

There was once a villager who always used to come for the Days of Awe to pray in the House of Study of the Ba'al Shem Tov of blessed memory. He had a son who was very slow-witted and was unable to learn the shape of the letters or to recite any word of holiness. And his father would not take him along to the city on the Days of Awe because he knew nothing. But when he reached the age of Bar Mitzva, his father took him along on Yom Kippur so that he should be with him and that he should watch over him lest he eat something on that holy day because of his lack of knowledge and understanding.

And the boy had a flute he would always play while he was sitting in the field and watching the flock and the calves. And he took along the flute in his coat pocket, and his father did not know about it. The boy sat during the prayer in the House of Study and could not utter a word. During the *Musaf* prayer he said to his father: "Father, I have my flute with me, and I want very much to blow it." His father got very frightened and rebuked him and said to him: "Beware, and guard your soul from doing such a thing!" And the boy had to restrain himself.

At the time of the *Minha* prayer he again said: "Father, let me make a sound and play my flute!" The father cursed him with a strong curse and warned him with a great warning that he should not dare to do such a thing, but he could not take away the flute from the boy because it was forbidden to touch it on the holy day.

After the *Minha* prayer the boy again said to his father: "Whatever happens, let me play some notes on the flute!" And when the father saw that his desire was great and that his soul yearned very much to play the flute, he said to his son: "Where are you keeping the flute?" And the boy showed him, and he grabbed the flute in the pocket through the coat thus to prevent his son from taking it out. And thus he recited the *Neila* [closing] prayer, and with his hand he held the pocket of his son's coat with the flute.

In the midst of the prayer the boy tore the flute from his pocket and from the grasp of his father and let out a powerful note from the flute. And all the people who heard it were astounded. And the Ba'al Shem, contrary to his custom, finished his prayer quickly and said: "This boy with the voice of his flute lifted up all the prayers and eased my burden." And he said that since the boy could not utter a word of prayer, when throughout the holy day he saw and heard the fervent prayers of Israel, a holy spark was ignited in him and burned in him like fire. He who knows can clothe this burning holiness into words of prayer before Him, may He be blessed, but he knew nothing and found no way to slake his thirst except by playing the flute before Him, blessed be He. But his father prevented him, and the fire of his desire burned in him more and more strongly until it veritably consumed his soul, and because of the power of his yearning he played the flute with a true concentration of his heart, without any turning aside, in complete purity, for His name, blessed be He. And the Merciful One wants the heart. And the pure breath of his mouth was accepted with delight before Him, blessed be He, and thus he lifted up all the prayers.

(*Q'hal Ḥasidim heḤadash*, 11-12)

The Letter of the Ba'al Shem

It once happened that the Ba'al Shem Tov of blessed memory went on a voyage with his disciples, and he stayed overnight in the house of a tax collector who was one of his adherents, in a village at a distance of several miles from Brod, the capital. And the tax collector received him with great honor, as it was due to him, and gave a great banquet in his honor and for all those who had come with him. And it came to pass that before the Ba'al Shem took leave of him, he said to the tax collector: "Ask of me something that you need." And he answered him: "Thank God, He has favored me and I have everything and I have nothing to ask of the honor of your holiness." And the Ba'al Shem said to him: "If so, I shall ask of you a little thing, do not refuse it." And the tax collector answered him: "With my body and whole being I am ready to serve the honor of your holiness in everything my lord will order me to do! Heaven forfend that I should refuse your holy face!" And the Ba'al Shem sat down at the table and wrote a letter and folded it and signed it with his signature and wrote as the *addresse*: "To the Community of Brod, to the chiefs of the month,[5] the scholarly rabbi etc., and the scholarly rabbi etc." And he handed the letter to the tax collector and said to him: "I wish that you yourself take it to Brod." And the tax collector took the letter from his holy hand, and hid it in his upper pocket which was near his heart, and said: "So I shall do right away." And the Ba'al Shem said to him: "I too want to leave; come and accompany me." "So be it," said the tax collector, and quickly ran to take the horses' thongs and the ropes to tie his horses. And as the tax collector stood next to the box which was in the storehouse outside his house, the letter fell out of his pocket into the box, and

---

5 Hebrew: *Parn'se Ḥodesh*, officials whose term was one month.

he did not notice it. And he tied his horses and
accompanied the Ba'al Shem, and then returned home, and
completely forgot about the letter. And thereafter he again
was with the Ba'al Shem, and the Ba'al Shem asked nothing
of him about the letter.

   And it came to pass as the days lengthened, that the Holy
Ark became hidden, for our master the Ba'al Shem
ascended to heaven. Then the wheel turned over the tax
collector, and he went from his condition lower and lower,
until he became very poor. And he sold everything he had
in order to provide for his family. And these things
stretched out for many days, until seventeen years had
passed since the death of the holy Ba'al Shem. And one day
the tax collector went to the aforementioned box to see
whether perchance something was left in it to sell for the
sustenance of his soul, and he emptied the whole box, and
behold, at the bottom of the box lay the aforementioned
letter. And the tax collector was amazed when he saw it,
and his heart sank in him when he recognized the writing
of his holy hand, and said: "Now I know from whence
came upon me my misfortune, and why success has left
me." And with all this he did not dare to open the letter to
see what was in it. And he took counsel to go with it to
Brod, perhaps he could find the people named in the *addresse*
of the letter, and they would see whether there was still any
use in the letter. And he lifted up his heart and went, and
tramped about until he got to Brod, and he lodged in the
House of Study as is the wont of the poor. And he began to
search for the chiefs of the month who had been in Brod
about twenty years before. And an old man, to whom he
related the story of the letter, told him: "I clearly remember
that these men have never been in the office of chiefs of the
months in Brod from the time I became a man and until
this day." And he asked a second man, and a third one, and
all answered him in like manner. Meanwhile a man told
him: "Today is the drawing of lots for the new chiefs of the
month in the community house. Perhaps these men will be

drawn and become the new chiefs of the month." And they all laughed.

While they were still talking, behold, two boys came to the House of Study crying: *"Mazal Tov* [Good luck]! *Mazal Tov!"* in a jolly manner, saying that R. so-and-so and R. so-and-so became the chiefs of the month by the lot, and that the people of the community led them to the council house to seat them on their chairs. And when he asked and inquired again after their names, he saw that clearly they were the ones named in the *addresse.* And he consulted an old man about what to do, and he advised him that he should go and deliver the letter to them. And he went to the community house, and said to the new chiefs of the month, both of whom were young in days, about twenty or twenty-five years of age, and said to them: "Now, O blessed of the Lord, behold the letter sent to you by the holy Ba'al Shem." And the chiefs of the month filled their mouth with laughter and said: "From where did you come, you foolish man, who brought a letter from the holy Ba'al Shem who passed away seventeen years ago?" And he answered them: "Through the spirit of prophecy! I am from the village of so-and-so, and in my eyes, too, this is miraculous. But what had happened was this," and he told them everything. "And now, please, open the letter and see what is written in it. Perhaps there is some benefit in it. I am afraid to open it, for I can see that this is a miracle of the miracles of the Ba'al Shem who was perfect in knowledge!" And the chiefs of the month took the letter from the hands of the tax collector, and this was the text of the letter:

"To the scholarly rabbi so-and-so and to the scholarly rabbi so-and-so, chiefs of the month and leaders of the holy community of Brod. Behold, when he who presents this letter comes to you, make every effort for his sake, for he is a decent poor man, and all his days he had great riches, and the wheel turned over him and he lost his property. And now, please, make efforts for his benefit, for I, the Ba'al Shem Tov, ask you to do it. And if you do not believe me,

that I sent this letter, I am giving you a reliable sign:
Behold, your wives are pregnant, and behold, forthwith
people will tell you *Mazal Tov,* for the wife of so-and-so
will give birth to a son, and the wife of so-and-so will bear a
daughter. This will be the sign for you that I sent to you
him who presents this letter, so that you seek his welfare
with all your might. The words of Israel Ba'al Shem Tov."

And even before they finished reading the letter, behold,
messengers came from their houses saying that their wives
had given birth. And as it was written in the letter so it
happened. Instantly the whole city was abuzz, and all were
amazed at the greatness of the holiness and the miraculous
powers of our master the Ba'al Shem of blessed memory.
And that man became very rich, for all the people of the
city heaped benefits upon him, and especially the chiefs of
the months who sought his peace and wellbeing with all
their heart and soul.

(Rosenthal, *'Adat Tzaddiqim,* pp.8-10)

Three Mysterious Acts

In the holy community of Brod the Ba'al Shem sojourned in
the house of a rich and respected Jew [a *"g'vir"*] who was
one of his followers. And this man had a son-in-law who
was from the holy community of Pozna, a very eminent
and famous scholarly youth. One day the Ba'al Shem said to
the youth: "Do you wish to travel with me to the holy
community of Pozna? For I plan to go there." The youth
said: "Surely, that would be marvelous, for I have not seen
the face of my father and my mother for three years. But I
must ask permission from my father-in-law."

And he asked his father-in-law, who said: "How good
and how pleasant it will be for you to join the holy and
pure man on the road, and you will surely see miracles of
the Creator on the way, for his voyage is not without a
purpose."

And the youth went happily to the BeShT and said to

him: "Behold, I am ready to go." And he set out with the BeShT on Thursday, and he thought that they would arrive in Pozna within a few days, for it was a long way off. And the youth was joyful and had a happy heart.

When they left the city of Brod, the youth saw a miracle: the wagoner stood up and tied the reins to the wagon, and the horse went by itself as it wanted. And instantly the horse got off the highway, and went along a winding path. And the youth cried: "Our Master! We have lost our way!" But the BeShT smiled and said: "There is no need to shout. The horse will go as it will." And the wagoner fell asleep in the wagon, and the horse went where was not found even the foot of an animal or a bird. And the horse trotted unhurriedly, and nevertheless the wagon was carried along with enormous speed, beyond what was natural. (It was known that this was the wont of the BeShT in all his voyages.) And the youth saw all this and was amazed at the miraculous sight. And thus they traveled all Thursday until close to the *Minḥa* [afternoon] prayer, when they came to a place of high grasses like unto the height of a man. And the horse stopped of itself. And, behold, the BeShT was seized with an enormous enthusiasm, so that great fear fell upon the youth. And the BeShT awakened the driver and said: "Take the pail and search among the grasses, and you will find a well of water, and draw for us water to drink." And the Gentile driver went and searched among the grasses a long time until he found the well, and he drew water and gave it to the BeShT. And the BeShT recited the benediction with great devoutness, and drank, and gave also to the youth to drink, and said to him: "Recite the benediction with the greatest devotion." And he did so. And after that the BeShT said to the driver: "Lie down in your place!" And the wagoner lay down in the wagon, and immediately fell asleep. And the horse trotted on its own in a place which no man had ever crossed.

And, behold, the day was coming to an end, and the youth did not know where they were going, for all the way he saw no human settlement. And he thought that they would surely have to spend the Sabbath in the field, for the way to Pozna was long. And this caused the youth great distress, so much so that he asked the BeShT: "Our Master, in what place will we have our rest for the holy Sabbath?" The BeShT said to him: "Don't you know that we are going to Pozna? We will be there, God willing, for the Sabbath." The youth was greatly amazed: How can this be? For he was a native of Pozna, and the environs of the city were well known to him, all the villages and hamlets, for a distance of many miles. And even if they had been at a distance of twenty miles from Pozna, all the settlements would have been familiar to him. But, so far, not a single settlement could be seen. And the whole voyage became a vexation for him, for they would certainly have to spend the Sabbath in the fields, a thing he had never tried in his life, for he was the pampered son of a *g'vir,* and the son-in-law of another *g'vir.* And thus they drove on all through the night. And when the time for the morning prayer came, the horse stopped of itself. And after they concluded the prayer, the horse started out again of itself, and the wagoner was asleep all the time, for he was a Gentile, for this was the wont of the BeShT, to go on a trip with a Gentile precisely.

And next day, about midday, the youth asked the BeShT: "In what place will we rest? For the holy Sabbath approaches." The BeShT said to him: "Did I not tell you that we will be in Pozna?" The youth imagined in his mind that the BeShT was mocking him. And they traveled on, until not more than about two hours were left until the Sabbath, and still no human settlement could be seen. And the youth was greatly distressed because of this, until he actually despaired of his life.

But, behold, all of a sudden he espied a village in the distance, and he was filled with joy, for he thought that they would surely spend the Sabbath there, and not out in the open. And that moment they entered the village, and behold, the horse went on its own through the village and did not stop at any house. Again the youth became dispirited by this, for it seemed that they would not spend the Sabbath even in this village. And when the horse reached the end of the village, it stopped in front of a ruin. The youth thought that they would spend the Sabbath in this ruin, and became filled with joy, for it was better than being out in the field.

And the BeShT entered the ruin and the youth went after him. And, behold, in the ruined house lived an old man, a leper. From head to foot there was no hale spot in his body, he was so full of wounds and boils. And his wife and children walked about in torn and tattered garments. And when the BeShT opened the door, the old man became filled with joy, and ran up to the BeShT and said to him, "Peace be unto you, my Master and Teacher!" And he who saw not their joy has never seen joy in his life. And they went into a separate room, and talked there about half an hour. And then they took permission from each other, and parted from each other in fierce love, like unto the love of David and Jonathan. And then the BeShT got into the wagon, and the horse trotted along on its own, and the driver slept, and the youth no longer asked the BeShT in what place they would spend the Sabbath, for until the arrival of the Sabbath no more than a very short time still remained, and all around them no settlement could be seen. And the youth thought that surely they would immediately stop and take their Sabbath rest in the field. And all his thoughts were frightened and alarmed, and the branches of his heart were shaken, for never in his life had he experienced all this.

But behold, his soul and spirit returned to him, for the city of Pozna was revealed to him, and its walls, and also he saw the house of his father and his mother. The BeShT said to him: "You would not believe me when I told you that we would spend the Sabbath in Pozna. But it is not known to me whether you will be in your father's house for the Sabbath."

And the youth smiled and said: "Our Master! But I see my father's house not far. Why should I not be in his house for the Sabbath? Why should I go to another lodging?" And the BeShT remained silent.

And in the city there was a street which is called *Shuler Gass,* that is, there was the council house of the students who studied with the professors. And, behold, as they entered the city, the youth was filled with joy and delight, for he imagined to himself that the time had come for him to have the pleasure of seeing again the faces of his father and his mother. But, behold, suddenly great fright and deadly fear seized him, for he saw that the horse was going into the street of the students, and never since the city was founded had the horse of a Jew passed through that street, for once a Jew did pass through by mistake and the students stoned him with stones until his soul departed. And when he saw this sight, he said to the BeShT with fear and trembling: "My Lord, Our Master, we are in great danger, for the horse goes in this street, and in no time they will stone us with stones!"

But the BeShT smiled and said: "Until now we have not directed the horse, and now, too, there is no need to show him the way. Let him go as he wants, and the Good Name [God] will save us from the hands of the uncircumcised."

And when the students saw that Jews were driving in their street, they began to gather up big stones. And the youth saw all this and his heart melted in him, and he said: "Oh God, here the life of my youth is coming to an end!"

And one single Jew lived in that street, a tailor, whom the students needed to make them their clothes. And, behold, when the horse came to the house of the tailor, it stopped at the door. And at this sight the tailor and his workmen came out with great fear. And the BeShT said: "I want to spend the Sabbath with you!" The tailor said: "By all means, but how can my lord spend the Sabbath here, since he will be in great danger here from the uncircumcised?" And the BeShT said: "Do not worry at all. No evil thing will happen, God willing."

And he and the youth entered, and also the Gentile wagoner awoke, and brought his things into the house. And it was the time of *Minḥa.*

And the BeShT asked the tailor: "Is there a *minyan* [a quorum of ten adults] among your men?" And he said that he with his workers are only eight. And the BeShT said to the youth: "They are eight, and we are two; that is precisely a *minyan.*"

So, there were two reasons why it was not possible for the youth to see his father and his mother: he was afraid for his soul to go out into the street; and one just could not prevent a *minyan.* Immediately the BeShT stood before the *'Amud* [the prayer stand] with a voice so loud that the people of the house were astonished at this great sight. And also the youth was seized with trembling and shuddering from the noise and the devoutness of the BeShT, for even though he had seen him pray in the house of his father-in-law, he had never seen anything like this.

And behold, in the street there was confusion among the uncircumcised, for nothing like this had ever happened in their place. And all of them came running, flushed with anger, carrying big stones in their hands. And the BeShT concluded the prayer, and the uncircumcised surrounded the house cheek by jowl, and the tailor and the people of his house thought that, God forbid, the evil had overtaken them. And the tailor told the BeShT, and the BeShT went and stood in the door of the house and looked at them, and they were seized with fear and trembling until their spirit almost flew away out of their bodies, and all of them fell down to earth, and the stones dropped from their hands because of the great fear. And they arose and fled as one flees from the bear and the lion.

And they went to their great professor, and he saw that their faces, had changed like unto the faces of the dangerously ill, and he asked them, what is this? And they told him about the frightening sight. And the professor was wise and learned, in the Holy Language as well, and he had knowledge even of the Talmud, for there are among them scholars who study the Talmud, and he said: "I myself shall go and see this miraculous sight. It must be one of two things: either he is a great magician, or an awesome man of God."

And he went to the house of the tailor and found the BeShT receiving the Sabbath with a wonderful devoutness, singing with a loud voice. And he stood there during the whole reception of the Sabbath and the evening prayer. And after that the BeShT recited the sanctification of the cup (the *Qiddush*) with wonderful devoutness. And the professor stood there also during the entire meal and the after-meal grace. And he did not speak with BeShT even one word, and also the BeShT did not speak to him at all and did not look into his face.

And after the grace the professor asked the tailor that next morning, when the BeShT prepared to say the morning prayer, he should let him know. And the professor returned to his house. And in the morning the tailor sent for the professor, and he came immediately to the house of the tailor and found the BeShT at the beginning of the prayer, and he stood there throughout the prayer. And after the prayer the BeShT sat down to the morning meal, and the professor stood all through the meal and the after-meal grace, and did not say a word to the BeShT, only his eyes never left the face of the BeShT, but he looked at him with great depth. And this seemed miraculous in the eyes of all.

And after the after-meal grace the professor went away, and again asked the tailor that he should let him know the time of the *Minḥa*. And at the time of the *Minḥa* the tailor sent for the professor, and he came immediately, and stood there all through the *Minḥa* prayer. And thereafter the BeShT sat down to the Third Meal, and the professor stood and watched the face of the BeShT and marvelled at the sight. And during the meal the BeShT expounded before the youth a wonderful *d'rush* (homily), with extraordinary devotion, until all those who sat there were entranced. And the professor listened to the *d'rush* with great depth, for he was a great scholar and understood the Holy Language very thoroughly.

And after the after-meal grace the BeShT recited the evening prayer, again with wonderful devotion, and thereafter he performed the *Havdala* (separation of the Sabbath from the weekday) with a cup of wine with wonderful devotion. And the professor stood and heard and marveled. He spoke not a word to the BeShT, and the BeShT did not look at him at all. And after the *Havdala* the BeShT ordered the wagoner to hitch up the horse. And the professor returned to his house.

And the BeShT immediately set out on the return trip to Brod, and, as usual in his voyages, he leapt over the distance. And the youth sat wondering: what did he profit from this voyage? And, disheartened and disappointed, he said to the BeShT: "My Lord, Light of our eyes! Behold, you are a man of God who sees and understands that in this trip I wanted to enjoy human pleasures, in the company of my father and my mother and my brothers and my sisters. And the wheel turned around, and I saw with my eyes the house in which they dwell, but I was unable to enjoy their company. Thus a great pain was born in my heart, like unto thirst for water. I suffered from flame and dryness, and life-giving water almost reached my lips, but I could not lower my mouth to enjoy the drink of water and quench my thirst. Therefore the fruit of my thoughts departed from me. And now I request of my lord, *the chariot of Israel and its horsemen* (2 Kings 2:12): may the soul of your servant be dear in the eyes of my Master, and let this be my reward for the troubles of this voyage which was of no avail to me: let your honor reveal the meaning of these three things: the stopping of the horse among the grasses for the drinking of water, for it seems to me that it was not an empty move; and the second, the joy of the old leper the encounter with whom caused such joy to both of you; and the third, the staying of your honor for the Sabbath in Pozna was certainly not without design."

The BeShT said to him: "Two of these I shall reveal to you, and the third, what I did in Pozna, will become revealed to you after many days by itself. Behold, among those grasses are buried two Jews who had lost their way, and murderers had come upon them and killed them. And these many years their souls were unable to ascend, because it is a place where nobody passes, and had a Jew passed there he would have cleansed the air and they could have ascended. And as for what happened between me and the old man in the village, as it is known, there is a Messiah in every generation in This World, in reality, clothed in a body. And if the generation is worthy, he is ready to reveal himself; and if, God forbid, they are not worthy, he departs. And, behold, that old man was ready to be our True Messiah, and it was his desire to enjoy my company on the Sabbath. But I foresaw that he would depart at the Third Meal, and since I did not want to suffer pain on the Sabbath [I parted from him before the onset of the Sabbath]. And my intention in Pozna will become known to you after several years."

And on Monday they arrived in Brod, and the whole city was perplexed: how could they come and go in four days and traverse a distance so great?

And behold, that youth became an exceedingly great scholar who studied day and night with great diligence for many years. One day he said to his father-in-law: "I have conceived a desire to deal a little in commerce, for it is good to combine Tora with worldly affairs." His father-in-law said to him: "Very good, my mind agrees with you." And he gave him several thousands, and the youth traveled to the lands of Ashkenaz [Germany] to buy merchandise. One day he came on the Sabbath eve to a city and stayed there for the Sabbath. On the Sabbath he asked his landlord: "Is there in your community a famous rabbi?" The landlord said to him: "There is here a rabbi, a Gaon of the world and a saintly man, famous, and his name is Abraham the True Proselyte, for he is a proselyte." And the youth went to visit and to greet the rabbi. And when he came to his house, the youth marveled greatly at the sight of his splendor and radiance. And he spoke to him about Halakha, and he saw that the rabbi was truly a Gaon of the world, and their discussion lasted until the time of the *Minḥa*, and they prayed, and then the rabbi asked the youth to the Third Meal, and he ate with him.

And in the course of the meal the youth asked the rabbi that he should discourse on the Tora, and the rabbi did, and when he began to expound the youth was greatly amazed. The rabbi asked him: "Why are you so greatly amazed? Have you perhaps never heard such a *d'rush* [exposition]?" The youth said to him: "On the contrary, I am amazed because many years ago I heard this *d'rush* from the mouth of the holy BeShT in Pozna in the *Shuler* street in the house of the tailor." And the rabbi became frightened, and said to him: "And you, are you the young man who traveled with the BeShT?" The youth said: "I am he." And the rabbi said: "I shall reveal to you that I am the professor who stood before the BeShT throughout the Sabbath, and his whole voyage was for my sake, to elevate my soul from the depths of the husks, and to resuscitate my soul with the light of life and with the awesome prayer. Every word that issued from his holy mouth was a flame of fire in my heart, and consumed in me one power of the powers of uncleanness until they consumed all the powers of uncleanness that were in me. And after that, with his *d'rush*, he aroused in my heart the flames of holy fire so that immediately I fled to Ashkenaz and became a proselyte here. Therefore this *d'rush* is dear to me, very very much, for it was this *d'rush* which made me enter under the wings of the Shekhina. Therefore, when an honored guest comes to me, it is my wont to enjoy myself with it."

And this story was heard from the mouth of the holy prince of Israel, the rabbi of Rizon. The Name who creates souls, it is He who knows souls and sparks of holiness which He brought out from the depths of the husks. . . .

(Kadaner, *Sefer Sippurim Nora'im*, pp. 8b-11a)

How R. Dov-Ber [5a] Became a Disciple of the Ba'al Shem

I heard from a Hasid that when the Rabbi Dov-Ber of blessed memory heard of the great fame of the holy rabbi the Ba'al Shem and of all the people who were traveling to him and of the great and terrible things he did with his prayer, and behold the Rabbi Dov-Ber of blessed memory had a very acute mind and well versed in the Talmud and in all the decisions and had ten shares of knowledge in the wisdom of the Kabbala, and he wondered about the rumors about the greatness of the Ba'al Shem. And once he decided to travel to the Ba'al Shem in order to test him. And since the Rabbi Dov-Ber was always a great *matmid* [perseverer] in his studies, as soon as he was on his way a day or two and it was not possible for him to devote himself to his studies as at home, he began to regret that he had set out on the trip. And behold, thereafter, when he came to the Ba'al Shem of blessed memory, he thought that he would hear Tora from him, and the Ba'al Shem of blessed memory told him a story about how he had once traveled for several days and he had no more bread left to give to his uncircumcised, the carriage driver, and then he happened to meet a poor Gentile with a sack of bread and he bought the bread from him to supply his uncircumcised carriage driver, and more such stories. And then, on the second day, he again went to the Ba'al Shem, and he told him how, on a trip, he had no more fodder to give to the mare, and how he happened to meet, etc. And behold, all the stories which the Ba'al Shem of blessed memory related, there was in them so wonderful and great wisdom for those who understood. And behold, the Rabbi Dov-Ber, who did not understand it, returned to the house of lodging and said to his servant: "I would like

[5a] Dov Ber, the Maggid of Mezheritch (d. 1722), foremost disciple of the Ba'al Shem, and his successor in the leadership of the Hasidic movement.

to leave today, right away, to go home, but since the day is very advanced, therefore let us stay here until the light of the moon will shine and rise, and then we shall go our way." And behold, at midnight, when the Rabbi Dov-Ber prepared himself to go, then the Ba'al Shem sent to his servant to call him, and he went to the Ba'al Shem of blessed memory. And the Ba'al Shem asked him: "Can you study?" And he answered him, "Yes." And the Ba'al Shem said to him: "So I have heard that you can study." And the Ba'al Shem asked him: "Do you have knowledge in the wisdom of the Kabbala?" He said to him: "Yes." And the Ba'al Shem said to his servant: "Give me the book of *'Etz Ḥayyim.*" And the Ba'al Shem showed R. Dov-Ber a saying in the *'Etz Ḥayyim.* The Rabbi Dov-Ber said to him: "Let me study it and sit down." And then he told the Ba'al Shem of blessed memory the straight meaning (*p'shat*) of that saying. And the Ba'al Shem said to him: "You know nothing." And he reread it and said to the Ba'al Shem: "The correct meaning is as I told you, and if your honor knows another meaning, tell me and I shall hear who is right." And the Ba'al Shem said to him: "Stand up on your feet!" And he stood up, and, behold, in that saying there were several names of angels, and as soon as the Ba'al Shem uttered that saying the whole house became filled with light, and fire flared around it, and they saw with their senses the aforementioned angels. And he said to Rabbi Dov-Ber of blessed memory: "It is true that the simple meaning is as you said, but your learning was without a soul." And instantly the Rabbi Dov-Ber instructed his servant to go home and he remained there with the Ba'al Shem, and learned from him great and deep wisdoms. All this I heard from the mouth of the saint the Rabbi Dov-Ber of blessed memory.　　(Aharon of Apt, *Sefer Keter Shem Tov*, p. 35b)

The Forgotten Story

Before he passed away, the Ba'al Shem called all his disciples and instructed them how to conduct themselves .

and what would be the livelihood of each. And to some of them he revealed how time would treat them. And there was with him a disciple who was also his servant, and his name was R. Ya'aqov. And the Ba'al Shem called him and said to him: "You go to visit all the places where they know me and relate the stories of what you have seen me do, and from this you will have a livelihood." And R. Ya'aqov was pained and said: "What will be the purpose of this? To be a wanderer and to tell stories?" But the Ba'al Shem told him: "Don't worry, for this will make you rich, God willing."

And it came to pass when the Holy Ark became hidden[6] and went up to heaven and left life to us, that his disciples obeyed all he had told them, and R. Ya'aqov traveled to all the places and related stories about the Ba'al Shem, and from it made a comfortable living. And two and a half years after the death of the Ba'al Shem R. Ya'aqov heard that there was a *g'vir* in Italy who was giving a gold ducat for every story told to him about the Ba'al Shem. And R. Ya'aqov decided to go there and relate to him all the stories he knew about the Ba'al Shem, for then he would get a sum of several hundred ducats, and then he could rest from his wanderings for at least one year, if not longer.

And he bought himself a horse with a servant and prepared for the voyage, for it was very long. And on the way he tarried about seven months until he reached that place, for he stopped everywhere to collect some money for his traveling expenses. And when he came to the city in which the *g'vir* dwelt, he asked the people of the city about the *g'vir*, and they told him that he was wonderfully rich and that his court was like the court of the king, and that he behaved piously and was studying all day, and that he had trustees who took care of his business while he himself was studying and praying all day. And on the Sabbath, at each of the three meals, he would ask for stories about the Ba'al Shem, and after the Sabbath he would give a ducat for each

---

[6] I.e., when the Ba'al Shem died.

story. And R. Ya'aqov asked about the *g'vir*, what was his birthplace, and whether he had been living there for a long time, and they told him that he had arrived about ten years earlier, and had bought the court from the lord of the city who was a minister in Rome, and settled down there, and built a synagogue in his court, and the people of the city prayed there morning and evening, and on the Sabbath most of the people of the city ate at his table.

And R. Ya'aqov went to him and asked his attendants that they should tell the *g'vir* that the servant of the Ba'al Shem had come and that he would recount to him many stories about him, things which his own eyes had seen and which he had not heard from strangers. And the attendant went and told his master the *g'vir*, and the *g'vir* answered, "Let him wait until the Sabbath and then let him tell us." And he gave orders that in the meantime R. Ya'aqov should stay with him, and that they should give him a separate room upstairs, where he should stay until the Sabbath.

And behold, when the people of the city heard that he was the servant and disciple of the Ba'al Shem, they all gathered to hear stories from him, for they were accustomed, ever since the *g'vir* had come there, to hear stories about the Ba'al Shem every Sabbath. And when they sat down to the Sabbath meal, after the *z'mirot* [Sabbath songs], as customary, the *g'vir* asked R. Ya'aqov that he relate something about the Ba'al Shem. But, behold, R. Ya'aqov had completely forgotten all the stories, and could not remember even a single one. And he tried to conjure up the form of the Ba'al Shem in his mind, or the appearance of the town of Mezhibozh, or the shape of the companions, in order to be reminded thereby of a story. But he could not do even this, for he had totally forgotten everything that had happened to him. And he made great efforts to contemplate this, and to think of any place which would remind him of something from which he could branch out to a story about the Ba'al Shem. But he had forgotten everything, as if he had been born on that day. And however much he broke his brain to smithereens, he could remember nothing. And he was utterly confused, and all the people of the house of the *g'vir* and also the people of the city became very angry with him, for they thought that he had invented a lie when he told them that he had been with the Ba'al Shem, whom he surely had never seen in his life.

The *g'vir* himself smiled, and said to him: "Let us wait until tomorrow, perhaps you will remember something."

And R. Ya'aqov cried all night, and thought, and tried in his mind to draw the form of the companions, but nothing helped, for he had totally forgotten how to begin a story about the Ba'al Shem, just as if he had never seen him.

And at the Sabbath morning meal the *g'vir* asked him again, perhaps he remembered something of a story. But he did not know what to answer, and said to him: "It is clear to me that this is not a meaningless matter. Never before has anything like this happened to me." And the *g'vir* said to him: "Let us wait until the Third Meal, perhaps you will remember." But he did not, even at the Third Meal, and became exceedingly distraught about it.

Moreover, the people of the house of the *g'vir* wanted to show him contempt, saying, "How did he find it in his heart to mock the *g'vir* with words of a lie?" And all the people of the city became very angry, and they hurt him very much with their words. And the Tzaddiq, R. Ya'aqov, accepted everything with love, and was very much amazed by this, and exhausted himself to find some explanation which could enter his heart. It must be, he thought, that the Ba'al Shem is dissatisfied with him for not wishing to travel to places where the Ba'al Shem is known and for having instead gone to a foreign country where people are not worthy to hear such stories. And he thought many other such things. But no excuse entered his mind, and he was greatly amazed. And he suffered greatly, and prayed to God throughout the Sabbath.

And after the outgoing of the Sabbath the *g'vir* sent for him again, perhaps he remembered something he could tell him. And this thing oppressed R. Ya'aqov very much, that each time they asked him, "Did you remember? Do you know?" And R. Ya'aqov returned to his room and cried. And then he restrained himself and went out and said: "Perhaps they don't want it from Heaven that I should become rich, or that stories about the Ba'al Shem should be told in this place. I know it for sure that this is not a chance happening, God forbid. And now I shall return to my house."

And the *g'vir* sent to him again saying that he should wait until Tuesday, and if he remembered nothing then he should return home. And R. Ya'aqov tarried until Tuesday and nothing came into his mind, and he went to obtain from the *g'vir* permission to depart in peace. And the *g'vir* gave him a respectable donation, and he went to get on his carriage to drive off.

And as R. Ya'aqov sat in the carriage he remembered an awesome story about the Ba'al Shem. And he returned to the house of the *g'vir* and sent his servant to tell him that he remembered a precious story. And the *g'vir* sent for him and bade him enter his room, and said to him: "Tell the story!" And R. Ya'aqov related as follows:

Once before the Passover Holiday of the Christians, the Ba'al Shem was greatly preoccupied all the Sabbath, and was pacing up and down in his room. And after the Third Meal he right away ordered his horses to be tied, and he took with him three men, and I was one of them. And we sat in the wagon and drove all night, and none of us knew our destination. And at dawn we came to a big city of God, and the horses halted in front of a big house, and its doors and windows were closed. And the Ba'al Shem ordered that we knock on the door, and an old woman opened and screamed at us bitterly, "What do you want here at this time? All of you will be slaughtered, for today the Christians stab every Jew who goes out of the door of his house, for today is their holiday. And if they find no Jew in the street, then they cast lots and thus take a Jew on whom to avenge the death of their Messiah. And woe to him who is caught in their lots, for they drag him out of his house and torture him cruelly until he collapses from his wounds. And yesterday they cast the lots, and the son of the rabbi was caught, for the Christians knew that the Jews would not venture out into the streets today. And now if one of the Christians should see you, that Jews have come here from Poland, they will take and slaughter all of you, and to us too they will do terrible things because of you. Therefore hurry and flee out of the city!"

So the old woman screamed and wept and moaned, and her hands were on her head. But the Ba'al Shem paid no attention to her, and entered the house and went up to the big upper floor, and ordered that all the luggage be brought into the house. And the people of the house were all terror-stricken, lying along the walls of the house, and did not utter a word for fear. And the old woman entered the house screaming and shrieking, and she accosted the Ba'al Shem, who, however, did not answer her, but removed the curtain from one window and stood next to the window and looked out. And the old woman continued to scream, why did he remove the curtain, but he paid no attention to her.

And the Ba'al Shem saw that in the square of the city there stood a large raised platform and on it thirty steps, and a very great crowd gathered around the platform and they were waiting for the bishop. And in a little while one could hear the sound of many bells which announced the coming of the bishop.

And the Ba'al Shem stood by the window and looked. Suddenly he called me: "Ya'aqov, go and tell the bishop that he should come to me quickly!" And when the people of the house heard his words, they trembled, and no soul remained in them, and they raised their voices at him: "What are you doing, are you out of your senses to send a Jew to be slaughtered? The crowd will tear him to pieces, limb by limb!" And they cursed him in the bitterness of their hearts. But he paid no attention to them, and called out: "Ya'aqov! Go quickly! Be not afraid!" And I knew my sender, that he knows what he is doing, and I went without fear, out into the square, and I came to the platform, and nobody spoke to me, and I said to the bishop in the Jewish language, "The Ba'al Shem is here, and he asks you to come to him right away!" And the bishop answered me, "I know of his coming. Tell him that immediately after the sermon I shall come to him." And I returned and the people of the house saw from afar, through the windows. They were astonished that I could go to the platform, and speak to the bishop. They saw it, were astonished, and fell silent. And they asked forgiveness of the rabbi while I was coming back to the house. But he paid no attention to their first words, nor to their last words. And when I brought him the answer of the bishop, he shouted at me: "Go to him again and tell him that he must come right away, and should not be a fool!" And I returned to the platform and, behold, he had begun to preach, and I pulled his sleeve and told him the words of the Ba'al Shem. And the bishop said to the people, "Wait a little while, I shall come back to you." And he went after me and came with me to the Ba'al Shem. And the two of them withdrew into a separate room and closed the door after them, and remained there about two hours. And then the Ba'al Shem came out and ordered the horses to be tied, and drove off from there right away. And as to what was the matter with that bishop, I don't know, and even the name of the city is unknown to me to this day, and the Ba'al Shem did not tell me. This is how I remembered just now what had happened to me then, and all this took place about ten years ago."

And it came to pass when R. Ya'aqov finished speaking that the *g'vir* lifted up his hands and praised God and said to R. Ya'aqov: "I know that your words are true, and as soon as I saw you I recognized you, but I kept silent. And I shall tell you the rest of the story. Be it known to you that I am that bishop whom you called then. And before that I had been a Jew, and I fell into the depths of the husks, for I was a very learned man and I possessed a holy soul. And the Ba'al Shem in his graciousness brought me out of the depths of the husks, for the merits of my fathers stood by me, for my fathers were saints and they asked the Ba'al Shem to save me. And the Ba'al Shem spoke to me in my dreams, day after day, that I should return from my way, and that night I promised him that before dawn I would flee from the city, before the crowd gathered to listen to the sermon, for in my sermons I spoke evil against the people of God, until the hearts of the Christians became hot to kill a Jew. But on that day, when I got up before dawn, the husks overpowered me. But I saw that the Ba'al Shem had come there, and I was straddling the fence, until I saw the great crowd which gathered. And when I made one step out of my house all the bells lifted up their voices and announced my coming. Then my Inclination would not let me leave all that honor, and I went to preach. And when you came and called me, I wanted first to preach my sermon, for my Inclination overpowered me. But when you called me the second time, I changed into a different person and followed you. Then the Ba'al Shem gave me a restoration,[7] and I became a true penitent, and I distributed half of my possessions among the poor, for I was a very rich man, and a quarter I gave to the king that he allow me to go to another country—I gave him some excuse. And the Ba'al Shem ordered me what to do every year in order to atone for my sins, and told me, 'This is whereby you will know that your transgressions have been removed, and your sins atoned: When a man will come and will tell you your story.' Therefore as soon as I saw you, I became full of contrition. And when I saw that all the stories escaped your mind, I

---

[7] *Tiqqun* ("restoration"), a Kabbalistic procedure, consisting of prayers and concentrations, for the restoration of the spiritual lights which have fallen under the domination of the "husks" (*q'lippot*), the forces of evil.

understood that it was because of me, for the sin had not yet been atoned as it had to be, and I did what I did, and my prayer helped me, with the help of God, for you did remember the story. And now I know that, with the help of God, my sin has departed, and I have restored everything. And you no longer will have to walk off your feet to tell stories, for I shall give you many presents which will suffice for you all the days of your life, and may the merits of the Ba'al Shem stand by both of us so that we should be able to serve our Creator all the days of our lives, with a full heart and soul. Amen."

And now, O reader, see how great is the power of repentance. And understand that this story is true and clear like the sun. And the great moral lesson which this story teaches will make you understand by yourself, and your soul can grasp it, and may the merits of the Tzaddiqim protect you to guard you from all evil. Amen.

(*Adat Tzaddiqim*, no pagination)

The Death of the Ba'al Shem

On the seventh day of Passover, while praying, R. Pinḥas of Koretz[8] saw that it was decreed on the Ba'al Shem that he would soon pass away because of his great effort against the sect of Shabbatai Zevi.[9] And after Passover the Ba'al Shem suffered from diarrhea, but nevertheless he gathered enough strength to pray in front of the Holy Ark. But he said nothing to his disciples who were known to be powerful in their prayers, but sent them off to other places. . . .

On the eve of Shavuot his disciples gathered to spend the

[8] R. Pinḥas Shapiro of Koretz (d. 1791), a disciple of the Ba'al Shem.

[9] Shabbatai Zevi (1626-76), the false Messiah of Smyrna, converted to Islam in order to escape the death penalty. Despite this apostasy some of his followers continued to believe in him. A small Shabbataian sect still existed in days of the Ba'al Shem.

night in vigil according to the *tiqqun*[10] of the ARI[11] of blessed memory, and the Ba'al Shem said words of Tora before them about the weekly portion of the Bible and about the revelation of the Tora. In the morning he sent word to his disciples that they should all gather, and instructed R. Leib Kessler and another man whose name escapes me that they should take care of his burial. And he taught them about his body, and showed them signs on each limb how his soul was taking leave from this limb and then from another limb, so that they should understand the condition of the sick, for they were of the men of the *Ḥevra Qadisha*.[12] And he commanded that they should gather a *minyan*[13] to pray with him, and commanded that they give him the prayer book, and he said: "I shall very soon converse with the Name, blessed be He."

And after the prayer R. Naḥman of Horodenka[14] went to the House of Study to pray for him, but the Ba'al Shem said: "In vain does he storm heaven. Had he been able to enter that door through which I used to enter, he could have succeeded with his prayer."

At that time the soul of a dead man came to the Ba'al Shem to be redeemed by him. But he shouted at him and said: "Eighty years have you wandered, and you have not heard until today that I am in the world? Begone, you wicked one!" And immediately he said to the servant: "Hurry, run with a great cry and warn people to clear the

---

10 *Tiqqun*, or "restoration." Cf. footnote 7 above.

11 ARI. Initials of Ashkenazi Rabbi Yitzḥaq, better known as Yitzḥaq Luria (1534-72), foremost leader of the sixteenth-century Kabbalistic center of Safed, Palestine.

12 *Ḥevra Qadisha* (literally, "Holy Society") is the traditional Jewish organization whose main task was to take care of burials.

13 *Minyan* (literally, "count" or "number") is a quorum of ten adult Jewish males whose presence is required for public prayer, including the reading of the Tora.

14 Naḥman of Horodenka (d. 1780), a foremost disciple of the Ba'al Shem.

street, for I angered that spirit, lest he harm somebody."
And so it was: he harmed a virgin, the daughter of the
synagogue's beadle.

And the servant returned and heard the Ba'al Shem say:
"I forgive you those two hours, and do not torture me!"
The servant said to him: "With whom is the Master
speaking?" He said: "Do you not see the Angel of Death,
who would always flee from me, as people say, 'He banishes
him to the place where the black peppers grow.' But now
that permission has been given to him over me, his
shoulders became broad and a great joy is over him."

Thereafter all the people of the town came to see his face
on the holiday, and he said words of Tora before them. And
then, at the time of the meal, he commanded the servant to
put honey [i.e., mead] in a large flask, but the servant put it
into a small one. He said: "*There is no power on the day of
death* (Eccles. 8:8), even the attendant does not obey me."
Then he said: "Until now I have performed charity for you,
now you perform charity for me." And after that he went
to the house of honor [i.e., the toilet], and the servant
wanted to go after him, but he asked him: "Why is this day
different from other days that you want to come after me?
What have you seen in me?" And so the servant did not go
after him.

He also told them of a sign: when he will pass away, the
two clocks will stop. And when he returned, he washed his
hands, and the big clock stopped. And the people
surrounded it so that he should not notice that it stopped.
But he said to them: "I know that the clock stopped, and I
am not concerned about myself, because I know clearly that
I shall go out this door and instantly come back through the
other door." And he sat down on his bed and commanded
that they should stand about his bed, and he spoke to them
words of Tora about the pillar on which the pious go up
from the lower Garden of Eden to the Supernal Garden of
Eden, and about all the worlds, and how it was in the world
of the souls, and explained the order of sacrifices, and

commanded them to recite, *Let the graciousness of the Lord our God be upon us.* And he lay down and got up several times, and immersed himself in devotions, until they could not hear the words he pronounced. And he commanded that they cover him with a sheet, and he began to tremble and to shake, as he used to do when reciting the Eighteen Benedictions. And after that he gradually quieted down, and they say that the small clock stopped. And they waited a long time, and placed a feather on his nose, and saw that he had passed away.

(Miroz, *Shivḥe haBeShT*, pp. 160-61.)

The Drunkard Saint

In a small town a cruel decree was issued against the Jews. They hurried to the Ba'al Shem to ask him to annul the decree. The Ba'al Shem said to them:

"I am unable to help you in this matter. But in a certain small town there lives a man whose name is Hershele the Tzaddiq. Go to him and tell him that I, the Ba'al Shem Tov, request him that he should attempt to persuade those on high to help you."

A number of Jews gathered and traveled to the small town in which Hershele lived to ask him that he take action to annul the decree. The Jews of that place laughed and said:

"True, there lives here a man whose name is Hershele, but he is not a Tzaddiq. We call him Hershele the drunkard, because he is always in his cups."

But the visitors continued to ask: "And where does this Hershele live?"

They answered: "His place is in the tavern, there you will find him."

The emissaries went to the tavern and found there a Jew in torn and worn clothes, stretched out and drunk like Lot. They went over to him, shook him and asked: "Are you Hershele the Tzaddiq?"

Hershele laughed at them and said: "I am not Hershele the Tzaddiq, I am Hershele the drunkard."

The emissaries said to him: "Listen, Hershele! The Ba'al Shem Tov sent us to you that you do what you can to annul the cruel decree which has been issued against us!"

Hershele laughed bitterly and said: "Can't you see that I am drunk? I cannot pray now." And he stretched out on the floor and continued to sleep.

The visitors again shook him awake and again begged him: "Hershele, help us!"

But he insisted: "I cannot. I cannot."

When the emissaries did not let off, Hershele lifted up his two hands toward heaven, and said:

"God! These Jews are in great distress, help them!"

And he fell back on the floor as if he were a log of wood, and fell asleep.

When the emissaries saw that they would get nothing more out of Hershele, they rose, and returned to their town. When they reached the place, behold, rejoicing and happiness, it became known to them that the decree had been annulled. The Jews went to the Ba'al Shem Tov and told him in what condition they had found Hershele, that instead of finding Hershele the Tzaddiq, they found Hershele the drunkard. The Ba'al Shem Tov said to them:

"Although you saw Hershele when he was drunk, Hershele the drunkard is also Hershele the Tzaddiq. And if you want to know how that drunkard is a Tzaddiq, come to me at the outgoing of the Sabbath and I shall reveal it to you."

After the end of the Sabbath a crowd of Jews gathered in the house of the rabbi. Each one of them wanted to hear about Hershele. And the Ba'al Shem Tov recounted to them:

"Poor Hershele was orphaned in his childhood, so there was nobody who would have seen to his education. He never learned how to read and write, nor did he know how to pray. This is how he grew up, without the love of parents, without joy. He had to perform the hardest, most menial tasks in order to survive. His only joy was to drink a little liquor.

"One day he said to his fellows, stiff-necked Jews like himself: 'Jews, I want to have a little happiness in life, how does one do it?' His friends told him: 'If you should have five hundred rubles and take a trip to Petersburg, there you can spend them and make merry like a king in France.' Now Hershele worked even harder, saved a penny here, a penny there, until he managed to put aside five hundred rubles. He packed his few belongings in a bag and began to trek to Petersburg. After he had been walking a long way, he reached a forest near the outskirts of Petersburg. Suddenly his eyes perceived the bells of a carriage approaching. What did his eyes see? A great lord was driving in his carriage, and behind it, tied to the carriage by ropes, was dragged a Jewish family, father, mother, and eight children. Hershele cried: 'Master of the World! What do my eyes see! What is happening here?' And Hershele spread out his two arms, stood in front of the lord's carriage, and cried: 'I shall not let you move from here! Please, set these people free!' The lord said to him: 'Listen, man, what are you doing?' Hershele said to him: 'I know what I am doing, but tell me, what are you doing? Why are you dragging along these miserable people?' The lord said to him: 'I know very well what I am doing. This man owes me five hundred rubles, and I will drag them like this until they all perish.'

That instant Hershele put his hand into his pocket, took out the five hundred rubles which he had, and gave them to the lord. Thus he set the family free. Most of them were already dead; only the mother and two infants were left. The mother kissed Hershele's hand gratefully, and went her way, and Hershele returned to the town from which he had come, to his hard labor, to his sufferings. And, as you have seen, he drowns his sorrows in the cup. . . . And this Hershele, whatever he asks of the Holy One, blessed be He, is given to him, and all this because of the merit he acquired by saving those lives. But Hershele will never ask anything for himself. He is a Tzaddiq! A real saint!"

(Czechoslovakian Jewish Folktale)

R. LEIB SARAH'S (1730–1791)

Awesome Story About the Rabbi the Tzaddiq R. Leib Sarah's, or The Rabbi and the Emperor

I heard from an old man from Bunitz who went together with R. Leib Sarah's[15] to Vienna the capital. And behold, I shall spread it before the reader at length.

Behold, a small town near Mohilev of White Russia, and its name is Bunitz, and R. Leib Sarah's was there six months. For such was his way in holiness: all his days he would never abide for long in one place. And they did not yet know him in this town, and he lodged in the house of a *Nagid* [a leading Jew] who was the tenant of the *arenda* [lease] from the town. And when they got to know that he was a fearer of heaven and a Tzaddiq, all the people of the town honored him greatly. (And the business that had brought him to that city has remained unknown until now, and I, the writer, know what I was told by the pious of the generation, namely that his whole business was to provide for the hidden saints who are forbidden to reveal themselves all their days, for they are of the veiled world, and the aforementioned R. Leib knew of all of them and had an acquaintance with all of them, and he provided for

---

15 Arye Leib Sarah's (i.e., "son of Sarah"; 1730–91) was a semilegendary itinerant Tzaddiq. Popular legend relates that he came, while invisible, to Austrian Emperor Joseph II, to obtain the abrogation of certain measures in his *Toleranzpatent*, considered harmful to the Jews.

them all his days. And his way was to borrow some large amount from people who were near him, and he would give them a promissory note for it, and then would repay it when due. And several stories are known to me, the writer, about this, and God, blessed be He, willing, I shall bring them all out to light. And therefore I assume that this was his business also in Bunitz.)

And it came to pass on the eve of the holy Sabbath after midday after the rabbi had gone to the ritual bath, that he called the aforementioned *Nagid* and said to him: "I have a small request to your excellency: please, do not turn back my face! Behold, my way is on every Friday to drive out a little, to walk in the fields, and I have a reason for this. Therefore, your excellency, be so kind as to order your servant to harness for me the horse and drive with me a little to the free area."

And the *Nagid* instantly ordered his servant to drive with the old man to the place which he wanted. And it came to pass as they were driving outside the town that the rabbi asked the servant that he give him the ropes of the horses, and he sat next to him, and the servant gave them to him. And, behold, to the sight of the eyes of the servant there appeared town and village, town and village, and it seemed to him as if they were floating in the air. And thus they traveled two hours until they came to a very big city. And its people were all strange in the eyes of the servant. And the rabbi stopped the carriage in a street of the city and said to him: "Wait for me here, for I shall soon return and we shall drive back to our house." And the rabbi went away, and the servant stood there amazed, for he was afraid to say a word. And diverse and peculiar thoughts ran about in him, for he was afraid that he was, perhaps, crazed by the sight of his eyes, and that this place was a dwelling place of demons, for he did not know what to think of all this. And behold, a Jewish man passed by, and the servant recognized that it was a Jewish man, and asked him, saying: "By your kindness, tell me the name of this city!" And the man mocked him: "Are you a fool and an ignorant that you don't know that this is Vienna the capital? With whom did you come here?" The man asked him, and he answered: "With a merchant, and I travel with him always, and he did not tell me the name of this place." And the man went away, and the driver, the servant, remained amazed in his mind, standing like a silent stone, confused by the thoughts of his heart.

And behold, the rabbi returned to the carriage, and said to him: "Drive and let's go, for the day is turning." And the rabbi sat in the carriage until they got out of the city, and then he took the reins in his hands and drove fast, and the driver saw and was amazed by the sight of his eyes, by the towns and villages which flew past the sight of his eyes. And before long he saw also the town of Bunitz, and the horse came near the town slowly, as was his way, and the rabbi handed him back the reins of the horse, and they came to the town.

And the servant related to his master all that had happened to him, and he mocked him and thought him to be crazy and drunk. And the servant said: "If so, if the rabbi spends here the next Sabbath, for I heard from him, when he goes again to Vienna, give me money to buy something in Vienna, and I shall bring you the receipt of the shopkeeper from Vienna, and then you will believe me that I was in Vienna not in a dream but wide awake." And he said: "So we shall do as you said. And you keep quiet, lest the old man hear about it and refuse to take you along to drive with him." And so it was. On the next Friday the rabbi again asked the *Nagid* that he order his servant to drive with him. And the *Nagid* gave the servant money to buy him a small knife, and to bring back the *datte* [date] of the day on which he bought it. And when they came to Vienna, the servant right away went to a store and bought a small knife, and asked the storekeeper that he give him the *datte* of the day of the purchase, and he signed it. And the storekeeper did so.

And it came to pass when the servant returned with the rabbi from Vienna, and gave the knife with the date to his master, that he was very greatly amazed and he could not refrain from asking the rabbi: "Is it true what the servant said, that he was with your exalted honor in Vienna?" And he said to him then: "His words are true, for I know a short way to Vienna, and every Friday I go there on some business which must be taken care of." And the son-in-law of the *Nagid* said to him: "My soul yearns very much to be in Vienna. I beg of your exalted honor to take me along when he goes there next time." And the rabbi promised him. And on the third Friday all the three of them drove together, the rabbi, the son-in-law of the *Nagid*, and the servant. And the rabbi did as mentioned above, and when they arrived in Vienna he said to the son-in-law of *Nagid*: "Wait here, and I shall go for a short while to a place I have to go." And the young man nodded with his head, and in secret followed the rabbi to see what he would do there. And behold, the rabbi went to the court of the king, who at that time was the Emperor Joseph. And when they came to the court of the king the rabbi noticed that the young man was following him, and he turned his face back towards him, and shook his head and said: "How dare you walk in this dangerous place? And now hold onto my belt and don't let go of it, and walk next to me, behind me, and make sure not to let the belt slip out of your hand lest you cause your life to perish, God forbid!" And the young man held onto the belt and walked after him. And he saw that the rabbi went to the house of the king (and did there what he did, and all the children of our people know about it). And none of the guards of the king saw him. And the king was asleep at that time, and the rabbi waited for a long time, and said to the youth: "The day has already turned." Meanwhile the king woke up, and the rabbi spoke much with him. And the youth heard everything. And they returned home.

And that youth is the old man who related this to me, for

he himself was with the rabbi in Vienna, with the Emperor Joseph. And thereafter the rabbi remained in Bunitz six weeks, and also from there he went every Friday afternoon to Vienna, and this is known to everybody.

(*Sippure Tzaddiqim*, no pagination)

The Matchmaker

In the city of Lutsk there was a young man who asked R. Leib Sarah's several times that he should accept him as one of his adherents, but the rabbi refused. And this pained the young man very much and he asked his acquaintances that they should persuade the rabbi, for otherwise his life was not worth living. And they told the rabbi that it was truly a matter of life and death. And he said to them: "How much money does he have?" And they replied, "All his money is tied up in the *shnitt-ware* [dry goods] store which he owns." And the rabbi said: "I shall do as he wishes if he sells today all his merchandise and gives me the money as a loan for a full year; in that case he can become one of my adherents." And the man accepted, and went to the rabbi, and the rabbi said to him: "How much is the value of all your merchandise?" and he said: "Six hundred silver rubles." And the rabbi said to him: "No, what I am asking you is, how much can you get for it today if they have to pay you right away?" And the man answered: "I would certainly have to take a loss of a hundred rubles or even more." Then the rabbi said to him: "If you can bring me before the evening all the money you will get, I shall fulfill your wish." And the man agreed, and instantly the Hasidim went and removed all the merchandise from the store and sold it, and got for it 450 rubles, and he gave it to the rabbi. And the rabbi took the money and gave a promissory note to the young man for that amount. And the rabbi went his way and the young man remained naked and without a penny, but he did not want to sell the rabbi's note. And the man became destitute, and in addition to his calamity another one overtook him in that within a few days his wife died. And he remained deprived on all sides, but he found some comfort for his soul by sitting in the House of Study on the Tora and prayers, and his companions supported him by giving him just enough food. And thus passed a full year over him, until the rabbi returned to the city, and instantly gave the young man the 450 rubles, and said to him: "For a hundred rubles clothe yourself, and keep fifty rubles for expenses, and go to the city of Volkovisk, and take a room in the big inn which is there which is called so-and-so, and send for R. David the matchmaker, and give him a gold ducat for his trouble that he should go and tell the maiden daughter of the *g'vir* so-and-so that you want to marry her. And let him hear the answer from her mouth, and then see how she will react to you. But be careful and let nothing of what I told you fall to earth [i.e., remain undone]." And for the remaining two hundred rubles the rabbi gave him another note. And then the rabbi left.

And the young man hired a cart and went to Kovno, and there he outfitted himself for the hundred rubles, and traveled from there to Volkovisk. And he took lodgings in the inn as the rabbi had said to him. And he sent for R. David the matchmaker, and told him as mentioned. And the matchmaker said to him: "Are you making fun of me, or do I lack crazy people that you came to mock me? Let me tell you about that maiden lady. Her father was a certain *g'vir* who left behind him a great fortune, and she is his only daughter and inherited his entire estate. And she herself is accomplished to the highest degree and has many good qualities, and for this reason she cannot choose a match which would suit her, for she is, in addition, of the best of families. This is why she has reached maturity and does not want to marry until the Lord sends her the man who deserves her and who will be at least her equal in all the qualities. And now how can I go and suggest to her a match with somebody unknown whose family is unknown to me, and whom I have never seen before? Would I not be derided by all who would hear about this? My reward will be that they will curse me and drive me away from her house, as if I were a good-for-nothing. But, tell me, young man, who told you about her? If you came here only for this purpose, I am really astonished. Or did you see a dream and your spirit forced you to find its meaning? I shall tell you, don't try to fly after the stork in the sky lest you fall down to the nethermost underworld. Seek a woman according to your own value, and enjoy life with a woman whom you can love, from among your own people."

Thus the matchmaker redoubled and tripled his words, for he became angry, thinking that the young man had mocked him.

But the young man heard him out quietly to the end, and then took two gold ducats from his pocket and said to him: "It would seem that you are not a rich man. Here you have two gold pieces for your troubles. Go to the lady and tell her, 'Behold, yesterday a young man came here from Lutsk. I don't know him or his family, and he did not tell me who he was, but he gave me two gold pieces as my fee that I should come to you to tell you that he wanted to marry you.' If you will thus speak to her, no evil will befall you, for it will be a clear matter. And you will earn your fee by taking to her the message with which you were sent, namely to offer her a match. And hear what she answers and come and tell me."

And the matchmaker was astonished when he heard this and said to him: "I shall try to go and to tell her your words. But I cannot go to her house in the middle of the day, for she is busy with her business affairs, and many people come to her door early and late. Therefore I shall wait until the end of the holy Sabbath when there is nobody there, and she sits alone in the big house and then I shall tell her privately what you said and shall hear what reply is in her mouth, and shall bring it to you."

And it came to pass after the end of the holy Sabbath that the matchmaker went to the lady and appeased her lest she become angry with him because of what he was telling her, and he showed her the two gold ducats which the man from Lutsk who wanted to marry her had given him as his fee. And the lady answered him: "Return to him and write down his name and the name of his father, and come back to me on Tuesday and I shall give you my answer." And the matchmaker was amazed by these words, for he saw that they were not idle talk. And he instantly went to the young man and told him what had happened. And the man wrote down for him his name and the name of his father and gave it to him. And on Tuesday the matchmaker went to the lady and the slip of paper with the names was in his hand. And the lady said to him: "Behold, I see and sense that the matter is from the Lord, that a man from Lutsk should dare to come here and to say openly that he wants to marry me. Therefore it is God's will, and I cannot say anything about it. But in order to prevent tongues from wagging about my marriage to a poor man I shall put on him the mask of riches. Now this is what you do: Go and tell him to rent six new stores which are next to my stores, and I shall issue instructions that the merchandise which is being sent to me from Leipzig should be transferred to his name. And let him accept it and place the merchandise in those stores. Then, I know, the whole city will buzz, and they will say about him that he is richer than I, for the merchandise is very expensive and costs a fortune. And then it will be fitting for me to become bound to him in the covenant of marriage. But be careful in your spirit lest you divulge this thing to anybody."

And the matchmaker ran joyfully to take the message to him who had sent him, that the girl had accepted him and told him to do so. And the man instantly did as she had instructed him, and went and rented the stores. And the servants of the lady came and told her that a man from Lutsk had rented the stores next to hers from their owner, and therefore they wanted to cause him trouble. But the lady ordered them to restrain their spirits, and said to them, "What will that poor man put into those stores? And if, perchance, he is rich, he may deal in other types of merchandise and will not hurt me in any way."

A few days later all the merchandise arrived, and the servants of the lady saw that the merchandise which she needed was delivered to him, and that he arranged it in the stores in the proper order, for he had been a merchant before. And the servants got frightened when they saw this, and they all ran to tell the lady what they had seen. And the lady said: "I myself shall go to see this thing, whether what you say is true." And she went and saw him, and the picture of his beauty made her heart yearn. Then she said to her uncle who was keeping her accounts: "As I heard, this man is unmarried, for I heard that they offer him matches from here. And, having seen the riches he has, for the merchandise costs a fortune, it would seem right in my eyes to become married to him." And the thing appeared proper also in the eyes of her uncle, and then honorable people undertook steps, and with the help of God they were bound to each other in marriage, and instantly there was the wedding in accordance with the laws of Moses and Israel.

And about two years after the wedding the couple was seated in the big house after the end of the Sabbath, and they were drinking a warm drink, and a ring dropped from the hand of the woman on the floor and she took a candle and crouched down to look for it. And while she was searching, the rabbi, R. Leib Sarah's, entered in haste, and said to him: "Here is the money due to you, and tear up my promissory note." And instantly he left. And the man went to accompany him, but the rabbi said to him: "Go back to your house, for I do not want you to accompany me." And he returned to his house, but his wife said to him: "How could you leave the man alone, isn't he the Tzaddiq R. Leib

Sarah's?" And her husband said to her: "How do you know him?" Then she answered him: "You fool, do you think that when you sent to me the matchmaker, I was like a crazy woman to listen to him? I shall tell you what happened. This old man would come to me evening and morning and tell me, 'When a man comes from Lutsk, whose name will be so-and-so, get married to him.' But I did not turn to him, and my father and mother came to me in a dream, and said to me that that old man was a great Tzaddiq, and that he knew that this was the true mating for me. And I did not pay attention even to this, until I fell ill with a deadly disease. And then the old man came to me and said: "One of these two things: either you will die of this sickness and will lose the days of your youth, or you will marry the man about whom I was telling you.' Then I was forced against my will to agree, and I promised him that when you came here I would marry you. And you imagined that I was bereft of my senses that I accepted the words of the matchmaker. But now you tell me, from where do you know that old man, and what did he do to you?"

And he told her all that had happened to him, and then both of them understood that they had been in the hands of the rabbi like unto the clay in the hands of the potter, and that he had bent them as he wished.

(*Sippure Tzaddiqim*, no pagination)

The Rabbi's Promissory Note

Once the Rabbi R. Leib came to the city of Lutsk, and in that city he had many relatives, and they honored him. And it was his custom to repay loans to one, and to borrow from another. Once he borrowed three hundred rubles from a man and gave him a note. And that man was a shopkeeper, and in his shop he had a barrel of salt from which he would sell, and once as he went to measure out salt from the barrel the note fell out of his pocket into the salt barrel and sank into the salt. And it brought blessing to the barrel so that he was taking salt from it for a full year and the salt in the barrel did not diminish.

A year later, when the rabbi returned there, he wanted to repay the loan and asked the shopkeeper to return to him his note. The man looked everywhere, in all the nooks and crannies of his room, but he could not find it. And he went to the rabbi and told him, "I searched but cannot find it." And the rabbi asked him: "Did you buy salt this year?" And he said, "No." And the rabbi told him to look for it in the salt barrel, and so he did, and found it there. Then the rabbi said to him: "I don't have to repay you, because the note already repaid you by itself and even added to that which I received from you."

(*Sippure Tzaddiqim*, no pagination)

R. YITZHAQ,
THE "SEER" OF LUBLIN
(1745–1815)

*An Awesome and Wonderful Story About Our Master
the Tzaddiq, the Saint, the Exemplar of the
Generation, the Rabbi R. Yitzhaq of Lublin,*[16] *May
His Merits Protect Us*

The Tzaddiq of Lublin was an orphan, without father and mother, and grew up in the house of his grandfather, R. Koppel. And his grandfather sent him to the yeshiva to study, and he was the best of the students. And one day a very rich man came and wanted to choose him as a bridegroom for his daughter. But the saintly rabbi R.

---

[16] R. Ya'aqov Yitzhaq, the "Seer" of Lublin (1745–1815), was a Hasidic rabbi in Lancut, Rozwadow, and Lublin.

Yitzḥaq was unwilling, for he said that without his grandfather he could do nothing. And the head of the yeshiva sent for his grandfather, and his grandfather R. Koppel came, and the rich man named a large sum as the dowry, and R. Koppel agreed, and they concluded the arrangements for the match. And the rich man gave them expensive presents, and they set a date for the wedding.

And it came to pass when the time of the wedding arrived that both R. Koppel and the bridegroom came to the wedding, and prior to the ceremony his grandfather removed the bride's veil (*dektikh*) and said to the saintly rabbi, R. Yitzḥaq, that he should look at her because it is forbidden to wed a woman until he sees her. And it came to pass that when he looked at her she started to menstruate. Nevertheless they entered under the wedding canopy, but instantly after the wedding the groom fled to his grandfather. And after some weeks had passed, his father-in-law came to his grandfather and asked him that he should command him to return to his house, for what wrong did he find in him and his daughter? And his grandfather ordered him and he obeyed and drove back with his father-in-law.

And when he entered the house of his father-in-law, and she saw him, she again started to menstruate. And the thing was wondrous, and when he found out he returned to his grandfather, who became annoyed with him and said that it was not done to leave one's bride. And a short while later his father-in-law again came and took him back to his house, and when he entered it again happened as before that she began to menstruate, not at her right time. Then he saw that it was from heaven that they kept him away from her. And he fled, but this time he did not go to his grandfather, but roamed about in the world, and did not know where he went.

And it came to pass when he was on his way that he met some wagon drivers who were taking wheat to Lizhansk, and he asked them that they should take him along on the wagon, and they took him, and even gave him warm clothes to cover himself, for it was very cold. And they came to an inn and entered to eat and drink. And the holy rabbi R. Yitzḥaq sat down under the stove, and while he sat there the landlady saw him and she took a liking for him, and she gave him to eat, and then she solicited him. And he said to her that he had to go to the lavatory. And he entered the lavatory and she locked the door after him and entered her house. And he broke open the door and fled to another village. And when she saw that the youth had fled she entered to the wagoners and screamed aloud: "Behold, you brought that youth to mock me! Behold, he came to me and I cried for help and he fled and ran off." And when they heard this they said: "Behold, surely we shall find him on the way, and shall pay him back according to his deeds." And it came to pass while they drove that they found him walking on foot, and they caught him and gave him a thorough threshing, and said that they wanted to take him back to the inn to the aforementioned woman. And the holy rabbi answered, "Even if you kill me, I shall not return to that inn. But do this: take me to the holy rabbi R. Elimelekh[17] and ask him what should be done with me, and I shall accept willingly whatever he will say."

And when they heard his words, they ceased beating him, and made him get on the wagon to drive with him to Lizhensk. And when they approached the city, the holy Tzaddiq R. Elimelekh saw through the Holy Spirit that such a saintly Tzaddiq was about to arrive, and he said: "Come, let us go to greet Messiah the son of Joseph who is coming here." That day was Thursday, and the rabbi, the Tzaddiq R. Elimelekh, put on his Sabbath clothes, and his disciples did likewise and went outside the city, and all the men of the city after them. And it came to pass when they

---

[17] Elimelekh of Lizhensk (1717–87), Hasidic rabbi, was a teacher of R. Ya'aqov Yitzḥaq.

left the city behind, that from the distance the wagoners approached driving. When the wagoners saw the multitude, all dressed in their Sabbath clothes, they thought that they were going to a wedding, and they halted. And when they saw the rabbi, the Tzaddiq R. Elimelekh, they were afraid. And the holy rabbi approached them, and he helped down the rabbi, the Tzaddiq of Lublin, from the wagon, and kissed him on his forehead, and called him "Joseph the Tzaddiq." And the wagoners were frightened, and fell down upon the earth, for woe to them for having beaten him! And they went to the holy rabbi R. Elimelekh and entreated him that he give them a penance. And he gave them as penance that they should be fugitives and wanderers for two years, and he said to the one who beat him most that he be a fugitive and wanderer for three years. And also that they should take, at their own expense, the rabbi, the Tzaddiq of Lublin, to his grandfather, R. Koppel. And he gave them a letter to R. Koppel saying that he should hurriedly go to his father-in-law and give a letter of divorce to his daughter, and that R. Koppel should not object to this, for his grandson, the rabbi the Tzaddiq, knew what he was doing. And after he gave her the letter of divorce, the wagoners should bring him back to Lizhensk.

They accepted upon themselves everything, and also R. Koppel did according to the words of the holy rabbi of Lizhensk, and made all the arrangements for the letter of divorce, and his wife got the letter of divorce. And immediately after the divorce she changed her religion and was married to an uncircumcised lord, a *graf* [count]. And the holy rabbi of Lizhensk found for R. Yitzḥaq a wife and appointed him rabbi of Lancut. And he became the greatest of the disciples of the holy rabbi of Lizhensk. And he frequently came to Lizhensk, and he dwelt many years in Lancut. And after much time had passed, the holy rabbi, R. Elimelekh, said to him that he should leave that town and go to establish his dwelling in another place. And he did not specify the place, only told him: as the Lord had said to our father Abraham, peace be you upon him: *Get thee out of thy country . . . unto the land that I will show thee* (Gen. 12:1). And he took leave of him with a blessing of peace, and went to the House of Study.

And it came to pass at night that he saw in a dream our father Abraham, peace be upon him, and he gave him "peace," and the holy rabbi, R. Yitzhaq, asked him: "Who are you?" And he said: "I am he to whom the Holy One, blessed be He, said, *Get thee out of thy country*, etc., and I passed the test. And you, too, will pass the test."

And he instantly went to Poland, and behold, in the city of Lublin the rabbi passed away, and the leaders of the community went to the city of Lancut to take the rabbi, the Tzaddiq R. Yitzhaq, and to seat him on the chair of the rabbinate, and they did not find him at home. And they met him on the road, and took him with great honor, and seated him on the chair of the rabbinate in Lublin. May his merits protect us and all Israel!

(Sofer, *Sippure Ya'aqov*, 22a-23a)

The Wagoner's Gift

A Hasid told about a wonderful event which he had seen with his own eyes at the holy rabbi Yitzhaq, the Seer of Lublin. Once he drove in the company of many friends to Lublin with a wagoner. And it came to pass when they arrived in Lublin that the wagoner asked them: "Take this note of mine and give it to the holy rabbi for me." And they took it from him, and did so, and gave the note to the holy rabbi of blessed memory. And it came to pass when the rabbi saw the name of the wagoner on the note that he said: "The name of this man shines very much. Who is this man?" And the people were greatly amazed, and remained silent, for the wagoner was a very simple man; they had not seen anything of significance from him during the days that they had traveled with him.

And when the holy rabbi saw that the thing was wondrous in their eyes, he added a word saying: "Perhaps at this moment his soul is shining." And the aforementioned Hasidim, who knew their holy rabbi, that only truth was in his mouth, hurried to seek and find the wagoner in the marketplaces and the streets, to see what he was doing and what he did. And they came to a marketplace and heard the sound of laughter and merriment, and they turned in there and found the wagoner dancing and jumping and rejoicing to the sound of music instruments. And they asked him: "This merriment, what is it about?" And he answered them these words:

"Behold, I was walking about in search of a little joy, and when I got to this marketplace I heard the sound of music, the playing of violin and harp, and I turned in here and saw that it was the rejoicing of a wedding of an orphan youth and an orphan girl. And as I tarried a while, and behold a great quarrel broke out, for the girl was not able to give a Tallith to the bridegroom as she had bound herself to do. And then he was ready to tear up the betrothal document and the couple would have separated. Then my heart became very warm in me, and my heart was bitter for me over the shaming of the orphan girl who would not be married to the man as she had hoped for long, and I took the bundle of money which I had collected for the voyage, and gave it to her for the Tallith for the bridegroom, so that the match should not fall apart, God forbid. And the wedding was celebrated for good luck, and this is why I made my heart a little merry over this marriage."

And when the Hasidim heard the words of the wagoner, they understood the words of their holy rabbi, and saw how great was the power of one good deed (*mitzva*) to light up the soul of man, if he does it completely. May the Lord help us to fulfill *mitzvot* and good deeds for the sake of His blessed Name, may it be exalted. Amen.

(Bodeq, *Seder haDorot heHadash*, pp. 63-64)

R. NAḤMAN OF BRATZLAV (1772–1811)

The Lost Princess [18]

There was once a king. The king had six sons and one daughter. The daughter was very dear in his eyes, and he loved her very much, and often played with her. One day, when they were together, he became angry with her. A word escaped from his mouth: "The Evil One take you!"

At night the princess went to her room, but in the morning they could not find her. Her father was filled with sorrow, and went to look for her everywhere. Then the viceroy, seeing that the king was in great sorrow, approached him and asked that they give him a servant with a horse and money for expenses. And he went off to search for the princess. And he searched for a very long time, across deserts and fields and in forests, a very, very long time. And as he was walking in the desert he glimpsed a path, and he said to himself: "Since I have been searching for her such a long time in the deserts without finding her, I shall follow this path, perhaps I shall come to a place of human settlement." And he went for a long time, and finally he saw a castle and many soldiers standing around it. And the castle was very beautiful, and the soldiers stood around it in order, very neatly. And he was afraid of the soldiers: perhaps they will not let him enter. But he decided: "I shall try." And he left the horse behind, and approached the castle. They let him in. Nobody prevented him from entering. And he went from room to room without any hindrance. At last he came to a hall, and saw a king sitting there with a crown on his head, and many soldiers standing around him. And before the king were

---

[18] R. Naḥman of Bratzlav was a natural storyteller. His ability to spin a yarn comes through despite the peculiarities of his Yiddish style. In the following I purposely rendered his stories in a strictly literal translation in order to give the reader a taste of his original Yiddish style.

many musicians with instruments, and it was very pleasant and beautiful there. And neither the king nor anybody else asked him anything. And he saw there fine food, and he went and ate. Then he went and crouched down in a corner to see what would happen. And he saw that the king commanded that they bring the queen. They went to bring her, and there was a great commotion and great rejoicing, and the musicians were playing and singing as they brought in the queen. And they placed for her a chair and seated her next to the king. And, behold, she was the lost princess! And as soon as he saw her he recognized her. Then the queen looked around, and saw somebody crouching in the corner. She, too, recognized him, and got up from her chair, approached him, and touched him and asked him: "Do you recognize me?" And he answered her: "Yes, I recognize you. You are the princess who was lost." And he asked her: "How did you get here?" She answered: "Because that word escaped from the mouth of my father. For this is the place of the Evil One." Thereupon he told her that her father was very sad, and that he had been searching for her for many years. Then he asked her: "How can I get you away from here?" She answered him: "You cannot get me out of here except if you choose for yourself a place and dwell there for a year. And throughout the year you must yearn to free me. And on the last day of the year you must fast, and must not fall asleep for a full day."

And he went and did as she had said.

At the end of the year, on the last day, he fasted and did not sleep. Then he rose and went back to the castle. On the way he saw a tree on which very beautiful apples grew. And he desired them very much, and went and ate of them. And as soon as he ate the apple, he fell down and sleep snatched him away, and he slept for a very long time. And his servant tried to wake him, but could not arouse him from his sleep. Finally he awoke, and asked his servant: "Where in the world am I?" The servant told him the whole story: "You have been sleeping a very long time. It has been several years that you have slept, and I sustained myself from these fruits."

And the viceroy was in despair, but still he proceeded to the castle, and found there the princess. And she complained to him very much, and was full of sadness. She said: "Because of one day you have lost. For had you come on that day, you could have taken me away from here. But since fasting is a very difficult thing, especially on the last day—for then the Evil Inclination becomes very powerful—therefore return and choose for yourself another place and dwell there for a year, but on the last day you will be permitted to eat. However, do not sleep and do not drink wine, lest you fall asleep, for not to sleep is the main thing."

And he went and did as she had said.

On the last day, on his way to the castle, he saw a spring flowing, and its appearance was red, and the smell was that of wine. He asked the servant: "Do you see this spring? There should be water in it, but its appearance is red and its smell is that of wine." Still, he went and tasted of the spring. And instantly he fell asleep, and slept seventy years.

Many troops went by with their baggage train which traveled after them. And his servant hid for fear of the troops. Then a carriage came by, and in it sat the princess. She stopped near him, got off, and sat down next to him, and recognized him. And she shook him very strongly, but he did not awake. She began to lament over him: "You have made so many and so many efforts, and had troubles for so many years, and suffered so much toil so long in order to free me, and because of that one day on which you could have taken me away you lost." And she wept greatly, and said: "What a great pity for you and for me! I have been here for such a long time and cannot get out!" Then she took the kerchief from her head and wrote on it with her tears, and put it down next to him, and stood up and returned to her carriage and drove away.

When the viceroy awoke, he asked his servant: "Where in the world am I?" And the servant told him the whole story, and that many troops had passed by, and that a carriage stopped beside him, and that the princess wept over him and cried: "What a great pity for you and for me," as mentioned. And the viceroy looked around and saw the kerchief lying next to him, and asked: "From where did this come?" And his servant answered him: "She wrote on it with tears, and left it here." The viceroy took the kerchief and held it up against the sun, and saw the letters, and read what was written there, her complaints and cries, as mentioned, and that now she was no longer in that castle, but that he should search for a golden mountain with a castle of pearls: "There you will find me."

And he left his servant behind, and set out alone to search for her. And he went and searched for her for many years. And he thought to himself that certainly a golden mountain and a castle of pearls could not be found in an inhabited place. And since he was versed in maps, he decided: "I shall go to deserts to search there."

And after he had searched for her in the deserts for many, many years, he saw a very big man whose size was not at all human, and he was carrying a big tree the like of which in size cannot be found in an inhabited place. And that man asked him: "Who are you?" He said: "I am a man." The big man was amazed and said: "I have been in this desert for a long time and have never yet seen a man here." And the viceroy told him the whole story, as mentioned, and that he was looking for a golden mountain and a castle of pearls. The man said to him: "It certainly does not exist." And he put him off and said to him: "They deluded you with foolish things, for it surely does not exist." And the viceroy began to cry bitterly: "It surely exists, yes, it must exist somewhere." But the wild man put him off and repeated: "They deluded you with a foolish thing." But the viceroy said: "It surely exists somewhere." The wild man said to him: "To my mind it is nonsense. But since you insist, behold, I am in charge of all the animals, I shall do you a favor and shall call all the animals. They run about in the whole world. Perhaps one of them will know about the mountain with the aforementioned castle."

He called all the animals, from the smallest to the biggest, and asked them. All of them answered that they had not seen it. He said to him: "You see, they deluded you with nonsense. If you will listen to me, turn back, for surely you will not find it, since it does not exist in the world." But the viceroy insisted very much and said: "It surely must exist!"

Then the wild man said to him: "I have a brother, and he is in charge of all the birds. Perhaps they know, since they fly high in the air. Perhaps they saw the mountain with the castle. Go to him and tell him that I sent you."

And the viceroy went many, many years searching for him. Finally he found again a very big man, as mentioned, and he, too, carried a big tree, and he also asked him as did the first one. And the viceroy answered him, telling him the whole story, and that his brother had sent him to him. And he, too, put him off, saying that surely it did not exist. But the viceroy pressed also him very much: "It surely does exist." The man told him: "I am in charge of all the birds, I shall call them, perhaps they know." He called all the birds and asked them, from the smallest to the biggest. They answered him that they did not know of the mountain with the castle. The man said to him: "You see, it surely does not exist in the world. If you will listen to me you will turn back, for it surely does not exist." But the viceroy insisted very much and said: "Surely it exists in the world." The man said to him: "Farther in the desert lives my brother, who is in charge of all the winds. They run across the whole world. Perhaps they know."

The viceroy went for many, many years, searching. He found a big man, as mentioned, and he, too, carried a big tree. And the viceroy asked also him as mentioned. And told him the whole story as mentioned. And the man, too, put him off. But the viceroy begged him very much. Finally the man said to him that he would do him a favor and would call all the winds for his sake, and would ask them. He called them, and all the winds came, and he asked all of them. But none of them knew about a mountain with a castle. He said to him: "You see that they told you nonsense." The viceroy began to cry bitterly and said: "I know that it surely exists."

Just then he saw that one more wind came, and the man in charge was angry with him: "Why did you come so late? Did I not command that all the winds should come? Why did you not come with them?" The wind answered: "I came late because I had to carry a princess to a golden mountain with a castle of pearls." And the viceroy rejoiced greatly. And the man in charge of the winds asked the wind: "What is expensive there?" The wind answered: "All things are very expensive there." The man in charge of the winds then said to the viceroy: "Since you have been searching for such a long time, and had so many troubles, and now perhaps you will be hindered by lack of money, I therefore shall give you a jar into which you can dip your hand and you will always find money in it." And he commanded the wind to carry him there.

The storm wind came and carried him there, and set him down at the gate. And there stood soldiers who would not let him enter the city. And he dipped his hand into the jar and took out money and bribed them, and entered the city. And it was a beautiful city. And he went to a lord and made arrangements for meals, for he knew he would have to tarry there. For one needed much thought and wisdom to set the princess free. And how he set her free R. Naḥman did not relate. But in the end he did get her out. Amen. Selah.

(R. Naḥman of Bratzlav, *Sippure Maʿasiyyot*, pp. 11-15)

How Satan Prevented the Coming of the Messiah

This is a story about a man who had no children. After that he had an only son. And he brought him up, and got him married, and he sat on the upper story and studied, as is the wont of rich people. And he would study and pray always. Except that he felt in himself that he lacked something, and did not know what it was. And he found no interest in his study and in his prayer. And he told it to two young men, and they gave him advice that he should travel to that Tzaddiq. And that aforementioned son did a *mitzva*, through which he attained the rank of the Small Luminary.[19]

And that only son went and told his father that he felt no sense in his work, as mentioned, and that he lacked but did not know what it was, and that therefore he wanted to travel to that Tzaddiq. And his father answered him, "Why should you travel to him? Are you not a greater scholar than he? It does not befit you to travel to him. Turn away from this road." Until he prevented him from traveling. And he returned to his study, and again felt a great lack, as mentioned. And he again consulted those people as before, and they advised him as before to travel to the Tzaddiq. And he again went to his father, and his father turned him aside and prevented him as mentioned. And so it was several times. And the aforementioned son felt that he lacked, and he yearned very much to fill his lack, and did not know what it was, as mentioned. And he again went to his father and pressed him, until his father was forced to travel with him. For he did not want to let him travel alone, because he was an only son. And his father said to him: "Now see here, I shall go with you. And I shall show you that there is nothing real in him." And they hitched up the carriage and traveled. His father said to him: "This is how I shall make a test. If it will go smoothly, it is from heaven; and if not, it is not from heaven, and we shall return." And they traveled, and came to a little bridge. And one horse fell and the carriage turned over and they almost drowned.

[19] The second-highest rank in pious holiness according to Hasidic doctrine. The highest rank is that of Great Luminary.

The father said to the son: "See, it does not go smoothly, and the voyage is not from heaven." And they returned.

And the son returned to his study, and again saw the lack that he lacked and did not know. And he again pressed his father as before. And he was forced to travel with him a second time. And as they traveled his father set the test as at the first time, whether it would go smoothly. And it happened while they were traveling that the two rods which are called axles broke. And his father said to him: "See, that it does not go smoothly. For is this the way of nature that the two axles should break? And all the time that we traveled with this carriage, such a thing never happened." And they returned. And the aforementioned son returned, as was his wont (that is, to his study, etc., as mentioned). And again he felt the lack, as mentioned, and the men advised him to travel. And he returned to his father and pressed him, as mentioned, and was forced to travel with him again. And the son said to him, "We should not again set such a test, for this is the way of nature that a horse occasionally falls, or that the axles break, unless there will be something very strongly felt." And they traveled and came to a *kretchme* [inn] to stay overnight. And they found there a merchant, and began to talk to him as is the habit of the merchants, and they did not reveal to him that they were traveling there, for the rabbi was ashamed in himself to say that he was traveling to that Tzaddiq. And they were talking about affairs of the world, until in the round of the words they came to talk about Tzaddiqim, where are Tzaddiqim found. And he told them that there is found a Tzaddiq, and there, and there. And they began to speak about the Tzaddiq to whom they were traveling. He answered them: "This (in a language of surprise), is it not that he is a light one? For I am now coming from him and I was there, and saw that he committed a transgression." His father answered and said to his son: "Do you see, my son, what this merchant tells us innocently, and he is coming from there!" And they returned to their house.

And that son passed away, and he came in a dream to the aforementioned rabbi, his father. And he saw him that he was standing in great sorrow, and asked him, "Why are you in such sorrow?" And he answered him that he should travel to that aforementioned Tzaddiq (to whom he wanted to travel with him as mentioned), "and he will tell you why I am in sorrow." And he woke up, and said that it was a chance happening. Thereafter he again dreamt as before, and he said that this, too, was an empty dream. And so until three times, and he understood that it was a real thing.

And he traveled there and on the way he met the merchant whom he had met before when he was traveling with his son. And he recognized him and said to him, "You are he whom I saw in that *kretchme*." And he answered him, "Certainly, you have seen me." And he opened his mouth and said to him, "If you wish, I shall swallow you." He said to him, "What are you talking?" He answered him, "Remember, when you traveled with your son, and at first a horse fell on the bridge, and you turned back; then the axles broke; then you met me, and I told you that he is light. And after I removed him, your son, now you are permitted to travel. For he was in the rank of a Small Luminary, and the aforementioned Tzaddiq is of the rank of a Great Luminary, and had they been joined together the Messiah would have come. But now that I removed him you are permitted to travel." And in the middle of his words he disappeared. And the rabbi had nobody to talk with. And he traveled to the Tzaddiq and cried, "Woe, woe! Woe for those who are lost and found not! May the Name, blessed be He, bring back our dispersed soon, Amen."

And that merchant was Samael himself. . . .

(Naḥman of Bratzlav, *Sippure Ma'asiyyot*, pp. 46-49)

OTHER TZADDIQIM

The Holy Dance

When the Tzaddiq R. Zvi of Zhidachov[20] came to Sasov he heard that a letter had arrived from Berditchev saying that the holy rabbi of Berditchev[21] was very sick, and that the holy rabbi of Sasov should pray for him, and should always make mention of him, and that especially at the time of the dances on the holy Sabbath at night should he do so. And the rabbi, our master, prepared himself to see the dances and to observe how they were being performed. And it came to pass on the holy Sabbath in the evening that the holy rabbi R. Moshe Leib[22] took fine new shoes made of *saffian* [Morocco leather], and put them on and began to dance. And the rabbi, our master, related that the dances were supernal things, and each and every movement was an awesome and wondrous *yiḥud*,[23] until the whole house was filled with light, for almost all the Supernal Family danced with him—a matter which the mind cannot grasp at all.

(Bodeq, *Ma'ase Tzaddiqim*, 44)

Two Hasidim Visit Hell

I heard this from R. Zelig of the holy community of Letichev.... It happened to a man who was young in years, and he was a relative of R. Zelig, that he saw in a dream that he was walking in a field with two Hasidim. One of them said to the other: "Let us go and visit Gehenna and see what they are doing there."

They went and came to Gehenna, and they saw a large gate, and opened it, and saw that this was not Gehenna.

---

[20] R. Zvi Hirsh of Zhidachov (d. 1831).

[21] R. Levi Yitzḥaq, the Tzaddiq of Berditchev (d. 1809).

[22] R. Moshe Leib of Sasov (d. 1807).

[23] See note 4 on p. 670.

Meanwhile they saw that one of them had disappeared. They opened the second gate and saw that this too was a corridor, and the second Hasid disappeared, and the young man remained alone. And he debated with himself whether or not to enter, and settled in his mind, "Since I am here, I shall enter." He saw that this was Gehenna, and saw a man with a Tallith and Tefillin standing at the gate. The man asked him: "What are you doing here, and where are you from?" He said to him: "I am from the holy community of Bar, and I came to see Gehenna." And he saw bodies which were consumed by fire like *a brand plucked out of the fire* (Zech. 3:2), placed in great heaps like sheaves on the threshing floor.

The man said to him: "Since you are from the holy community of Bar, go to the other side of that heap and you will see a man young in years, also from the holy community of Bar, lying there." He felt greatly ashamed because that man was considered to be a decent person. And he returned to the gate and saw that the bodies were lying there quietly, and they were not being punished. He asked the man who was standing at the gate: "Why do they not punish the wicked today?"

The man answered him: "From your question I can tell that you did not say 'Arise and come' in the evening prayer, which shows that you forgot that today is the day of the New Moon."

Indeed so it was. After that he asked him to let him go out. He said: "I shall certainly not let you out." He asked him again and said: "Let me out for I am a decent man." He said to him: "What kind of decency is it that you went to collect alms and in the meantime had evil thoughts?" And he told him his thoughts. He said: "I had to obtain money to pay the tuition fee." The man began to smack his lips and said: "That is fine and good; nevertheless, I cannot let you go out." He began to beg and entreat him. He said to him: "I advise you to hide under my Tallith. Very soon the Prince of Gehenna will come here in a great storm, and they will open the gate, and you can slip through the gate, and go."

And when a great noise was heard from afar, from the Prince of Gehenna, the bodies began to tremble with great trembling, and he hid himself under the Tallith of the man. And when the Prince of Gehenna arrived, the man opened the gate, and the youth slipped through the gate and went out. But some of the wind of the storm entered him, and he began to cough in what is called the *veshet* [esophagus]. And because of the coughing he woke up from his sleep, and from that day on he suffered from coughing for a whole year, and he died of that disease. And that man from the holy community of Bar whom he saw in Gehenna lived for two more years after this event.

(Miroz, *Shivḥe haBeShT,* pp. 90-91)

The Lost Signet Ring

A parable. Once a king lost his signet ring. And this is a great loss, because he who would find it could stamp coins, and also because of the disgrace that the royal signet ring should be lying in the dust. And the king was much worried over the loss of his signet ring. And the princes of the realm were pained that the signet ring of the king was lost, and the sons of the king were pained that the signet ring of their father was lost, and they went to search for it. But because of their great zeal they passed by it and did not find it. And a villager went and found it. And that villager did not know the importance of the signet ring. And all had joy: the king over his signet ring, the princes of the kingdom over the king's signet ring that it was found, and the sons of the king over their father, as mentioned. And the villager rejoiced that he found the signet ring of the king. Even though he did not know what was the nature of the signet ring and what was its importance, nevertheless he had joy.... Likewise, my beloved, the reader, even if I do not understand the essence and purpose of the signet ring that was lost, nevertheless I found some dear things which were forgotten, as if they had been lost. And now, let those who understand rejoice in them!

> (R. Menahem Mendel of Vitebsk, *Sefer Liqqute Y'qarim*, as quoted in Mid. Ribash Tov, by Y'huda Lev Avraham, p. 13)

The Rabbi of Berditchev and the Tailor

When Yom Kippur ended R. Levi Yitzḥaq [of Berditchev] beckoned to a tailor and asked him to relate to the congregation the argument which he had that day with the Master of the World.

The tailor began in a trembling voice:

"I told the Master of the World: 'Today is the Day of Judgment. One must repent. But I did not sin much. I took a little leftover cloth from the rich. . . . And once I drank a small glass of brandy in the house of the *Poretz* [Squire] and took a bite of bread without washing my·hands. These are all my transgressions.

" 'But You, Master of the World, how many are Your transgressions! Why have You taken away small children who had not sinned? And from others You have taken the mothers of such children! But, Master of the World, I shall forgive You Your transgressions and may You forgive me mine, and let us drink *L'Ḥayyim*! [To Life!]' "

And as he related all this, the tailor drank *L'Ḥayyim* to the Master of the World.

The rabbi said after Yom Kippur:

"The tailor with his arguments saved the Jews. But a tailor remains a tailor. In exchange for a little leftover cloth he forgave the Master of the World such great sins! I, in that hour, would have asked another thing—that He should send us His Messiah to redeem the Jews. . . ."

> (Ashkenazi, *Otz'rot fun Idishen Humor*, p. 20)

Healing the Sick

It was told to me in the name of the old R. Leibush of Proskurov of blessed memory that he remembered that there was in the town of Yampol a decent man who lay sick, God forbid, for a long time, bereft of all sensation in hands and feet. And the saintly Tzaddiq R. Yosef of Yampol,[24] son of the Maggid of Zloczov,[25] had a strong love for the saintly and awesome Tzaddiq R. Barukh of Medzhibozh[26] of blessed memory, and both of them prayed for that sick man. And when they saw that no healing came to him, they decided that it was necessary to honor the rabbi of Neskhiz[27] with the task of healing that sick man. And that day was the day of a great rejoicing for the Maggid of Zloczov, whose seat of honor was in Yampol. And the old rabbi of Neskhiz came to the *Jahrzeit* [anniversary of the death] of his sainted master,[28] and he entered to R. Yosef of blessed memory, and R. Yosef importuned him about the healing of the sick man. And the matter seemed good in the eyes of the rabbi of Neskhiz, and he sent his servant to give the sick man a little of the leftover coffee which he had drunk at that time, and he gave him his staff, and told him: "Remain with the sick man until he recovers somewhat, and then give him the staff that he should come here with it." And the servant went to him, and gave him the coffee to taste little by little, and slowly his health returned. And he got up on his feet, and put on his clothes, and took the staff in his hand and went to the rabbi of Neskhiz. And the aforementioned R. Leibush remembered that the whole town gathered to see

[24] R. Yosef of Yampol (d. 1812).

[25] R. Y'ḥiel Mikhael, the Maggid of Zloczov (d. ca. 1786).

[26] R. Barukh of Medzhibozh (d. 1811) was a grandson of the Ba'al Shem Tov.

[27] R. Mord'khai of Neskhiz (d. 1800).

[28] R. Mord'khai of Neskhiz was a disciple of R. Y'ḥiel Mikhael of Zloczov.

this awesome miracle, and the whole town was in an uproar over this great sight, and they gave thanks to Him who performs great miracles.

(Landau, *Sefer Zikhron Tov*, p. 103)

The Stormwind

Our master of Mezheritch, of blessed memory, raised up souls of Israel from the depths and from the abysses of the sea. For at times there are great souls sunk in the depths of the husks because of sins and transgressions, and there are righteous men (Tzaddiqim) who are reached by acts like those of the wicked, as this is mentioned in the holy books. Behold, the aforementioned rabbi brought them out from the depths of the husks and gave them a perfection (*tiqqun*) according to the root of his soul. This matter has become famous due to several events. In a book there is mention of a wondrous story about a woman whose son went to change his religion, God forbid. And he already dwelt among priests in a house which was locked and bolted lest his relatives come and persuade him to return to the faith of Israel. And in truth that young man was very wonderful in his study. And his mother cried bitterly over him and went before the holy rabbi, the preacher (*maggid*) of blessed memory, and told him all that had happened, and begged him to save the soul of her son that it should not sink down, God forbid. And the rabbi commanded her to return to her house, and thereafter he gathered his disciples who were there and began to expound the verse *And if a soul sins* (Lev. 5:1), and the matter seemed strange in their eyes: what is this and for what is this? For this thing happened on the eve of the holy Sabbath. And so it was four times: he gathered them during the day, and expounded before them about the verse *And if a soul sins*, and also at night. During the night of the holy Sabbath, he preached to them three sermons about the verse *And if a soul sins*. And the matter was strange in the eyes of the disciples. And the seventh time when he said Tora, there arose a strong wind which shattered mountains and broke rocks, and in the midst of the quake there came that youth and told them all that had befallen him that day. For he did not know what was the matter, but suddenly, today, his heart turned to return to the faith of Israel. But he was not able to because the priests had locked him in. And he resolved in his mind that early next morning, when they would open his room, he would escape from there. But nevertheless his heart pounded in his chest, and he found no rest, until he became weary of his life. And he became very embittered, and cried in the bitterness of his soul about what he had done. But the door was locked, and although he tried with all his strength to break down the door, he could not. But then he resolved in his mind to throw himself down from the window, and resigned himself to giving up his life, for, [he thought,] if he should fall down and die, it would be an atonement for the great sin he had committed when he abandoned the living God. And so he did, and threw away his soul from himself and threw himself out the window. But by the mercy of God a wind of storm arose, and the wind remained until he stood up on his feet, so that his lifeblood was not spilled on the ground. And the disciples understood the words of their holy master and his great power to light up the darkness in which they had sat and their way in the thick darkness.

(Bodeq, *Seder haDorot HeḤadash*, pp. 26-27)

R. Eisik of Kalev

When he was three years old, Eisik lost his father. His mother remained destitute and could not afford to hire a teacher for him. She herself taught him to read, but he barely learned the prayers. He grew up wild, and when he was seven he had to go out to the field to lead the sheep to pasture.

To R. Leib Sarah's it became known that in Hungary there was a soul of a very high grade which had to be redeemed. He wandered the length and width of Hungary searching for it. Thus he came to Nyirbátor in the province of Szabolcs. Tired of the wandering, he lay down in the open in the shadow of a tree and rested. Suddenly he saw a shepherd boy surrounded by his flock. Soon he heard the voice of the boy: "Master of the World! Perhaps You have some sheep, I want to guard them for You. O God, sweet God, how I love You!"

Deeply touched, R. Leib arose, approached the boy, and said to him: "Yes, you will guard the lambs of God!" And he asked him: "Whose son are you?" Eisik told him the name of his mother and led him to her house. R. Leib asked the poor woman to entrust the boy to him; he would take care of him as if he were his own child, would teach him and bring him up to be a rabbi. The mother agreed.

R. Leib took the boy to R. Shmelke in Nikolsburg.

"Here," he said to R. Shmelke. "You have a soul from the uppermost hall of songs."

In the House of Study little Eisik was initiated into the mysteries of the Tora, and thus he grew to manhood.

After his marriage R. Eisik was invited to become the rabbi of Nagykálló.

It was his custom to wander about in the fields outside the town, where he would gaze at the green expanses and sink into deep thoughts.

Once he met a shepherd in the field. Surrounded by his flock the shepherd sang a Hungarian love song. The melody was full of sadness and yearning. Rabbi Eisik was seated on a haystack. But when he heard the melody he rose, went nearer and listened. The shepherd sang:

> *"Forest, forest, how big you are!*
> *Rose, rose, how far you are!*
> *Were the forest less big*
> *My Rose would not be so far!*

Who will lead me out of the forest
So I unite with my Rose?"

Hot tears ran down the cheeks of the rabbi. When the shepherd finished the song, he gave him a coin and asked: "Once more!" And while the shepherd sang, R. Eisik threw himself on the ground and one could hear him too sing a song in Hungarian:

"Galuth, galuth, how big you are!
Shekhina, Shekhina, how far you are!
Were the Galuth less big
The Shekhina would not be so far!
Who will lead me out of the Galuth,
So I unite with the Shekhina?"

"Sing it once more!" asked R. Eisik in great rapture, and gave another coin to the shepherd. This time the shepherd played the melody on his reed flute.

"Sing it once more!" said R. Eisik.

But, behold, the melody had escaped the shepherd. However hard he tried, he could not remember it. Now R. Eisik rose. He was full of joy and a glowing light surrounded him. He cried jubilantly: "I have redeemed it!"

Later he explained to his followers: "It was the melody to which the Jews sang their dirges at the waters of Babylon. It, too, was in exile for thousands of years, but now I have redeemed it!"

(Bloch, *Priester der Liebe*, pp. 182-84.)

The Sabbath Angels

The second wife of my grandfather, the rabbi R. Hershele of Tchortkov, was the sister of the high priest R. Ḥayyim Rappaport, the head of the court of the Jewish community of Lvov. And once the holy Gaon R. Ḥayyim Rappaport traveled through the town of Tchortkov, and he lodged in the house of another man. His sister the rebbetzen went to him with the request that he should stop over in her house and should not shame her husband the rabbi. And he answered that he [i.e., her husband] was walking in the way of the Hasidim and therefore he did not want to stop over in his house. And also, he had no time. And he went on from the town and the carriage broke, and a stormy pouring rain came, and he was forced to return to the town. And he lodged for the holy Sabbath in the house of the holy rabbi R. Hershele. And on the Sabbath eve, after the prayers, the rebbetzen set the table before the Gaon R. Hayyim, with wine and Sabbath loaves, so that he should not have to wait for her husband the rabbi R. Hershele. And he said that there was still time, for he had to study a certain matter. And while studying it, he became absorbed in the matter until about midnight, and then the holy rabbi, the rabbi R. Hershele, entered his room, wrapped in the Tallith. And the holy Gaon, R. Hayyim Rappaport, saw the light of his face. He stood up before him, and went to his sister and said: "Know, that I regret everything I told you, for I saw with my own eyes that he came from the House of Prayer with two Ministering Angels accompanying him."[29]

(Michelson, *Shemen haTov*, p. 107)

The Simpleton Makes Rain Fall

The old and venerable Hasid R. Dov Ber son of R. Lipa of blessed memory, of my city here, who is called R. Berl Lipeles, told me that once he spent the Sabbath with the rabbi, the Tzaddiq, the saintly R. Israel Abraham of Chernostraha, the son of our master R. Zusya of blessed memory. And there was there a respected man from the Holy Land, and he told before the holy rabbi, the aforementioned R. Israel Abraham, about the following event which is well known in the Holy Land:

[29] As it is stated in the Talmud, B. Shab. 119b.

This happened in the days of R. Yitzḥaq Luria of blessed memory. In one of the cities of the Land of the West [i.e., Morocco] there lived a simple and ignorant man. He was a *treger* [porter] in the market. And he went to the rabbi of that city, and asked him how to behave like a kosher Jew, for his heart impelled him to behave like a good Jew but he did not know how, for he was very ignorant. Therefore he came to ask the rabbi that he should show him the straight way of behavior in his work, like a good Jew. The rabbi asked him whether he could read. He answered him that he could not read at all; he could only recite the words of the prayer, stuttering and with difficulty. The rabbi cautioned him that he should, above all, avoid evil, that is, he should not steal, nor rob, heaven forfend! etc., and should pray every day, and recite some psalms.

The man observed the rabbi's instructions carefully in everything he commanded him. Within a short time the Holy One, blessed be He, made him succeed. Therefore he left his job, and bought himself a horse and became a water carrier. When he changed his occupation he went to his rabbi that he might teach him how to behave like a good Jew in his new work. The rabbi cautioned him in the matter according to his understanding, and he observed carefully the instructions of the rabbi in everything he commanded him. The Holy One, blessed be He, made him again successful. He left that work, too, and became a shopkeeper. He again went to the rabbi, to be taught the customs of Israel in this new work. And so he did: each time his job changed he went to the rabbi to ask him how to behave now. And the rabbi taught him according to the circumstances of that occupation; not to cheat anybody, and to give a good weight, and to measure well, etc. In brief, that man became a big merchant and a rich man. And he observed very carefully the instructions of the rabbi in everything he commanded him.

Once there was a drought there. The rabbi decreed a fast in that city, according to custom. And in the afternoon he sent a messenger to visit all the houses of the city and to see whether they observed the fast. The messenger came to the house of the aforementioned rich man, and saw that he was eating his midday meal with his family. The messenger went and told the rabbi that the rich man did not observe his decree to fast. The rabbi sent for him. He went to the rabbi. The rabbi asked him why he did not observe his decree and did not fast. The rich man excused himself before the rabbi saying that he did not know at all of the decree, and that had he known it, he certainly would have observed it. Then the rich man asked the rabbi why he had decreed the fast. The rabbi told him that such was the custom in Israel that in times of drought, heaven forfend, one must fast and ask for mercy from the Master of Mercy, that He should have compassion with His people, the House of Israel, etc.

The rich man heard everything the rabbi told him and spoke at length about it. Of course, he felt great compassion for Israel, and he went to the window in the house of the rabbi, and lifted up his eyes to heaven, and spoke in a language of request and supplication these words to God, blessed be He: "Master of the World! *Azoy vi ikh folg Dikh, beit ikh Dikh folg mikh oykh. Se zol gebn regin!* [As I follow You, I beg of You, You, too, should follow me. Let it rain!] As soon as he finished speaking, the sky became dark with clouds and rain began to fall as needed. The rabbi and all the people in his house saw it, and were amazed when they saw that his words bore fruit, and that his voice was heard in the Heights.... They began to search after his deeds, perchance he was one of the hidden saints, etc. Finally they asked him directly. And he admitted that it was true that he was totally ignorant, but that he observed most carefully whatever the rabbi had told him, fully and with an honest heart. And that each time he weighed something to sell it he saw on the tongue of his scales the Ineffable Name, blessed be He.

This is what the man from the Holy Land related before

the holy rabbi R. Israel Abraham of blessed memory.

(Sippure Tzaddiqim heHadash, pp. 20b-21a)

His Compassion Is All Over His Works

Once the Tzaddiq R. Zise[30] made the rounds to collect alms for the ransom of captives, and came to a lodging house, and the landlord was not at home, and the Tzaddiq saw there a bird cage, and [saw] how the birds were confined and their endeavor was to fly in the air of the world as is their nature, to be free birds. And he took pity on them and said, "I wear my feet down to obtain money for ransoming captives, and behold, there is no greater ransoming of captives than this: to free the birds from their captivity." And so he did, and opened the door of the cage, and the birds escaped.

And thereafter the landlord came back to his house, and saw that the cage was open and that the birds were gone, and he became exceedingly wroth, and said to the people of his house: "Who did to me this great evil?" And they said to him: "There is a man here who appears to be crazy. It was he who did this evil deed." The landlord said to the Tzaddiq: "You madman, how did you dare to do this evil thing, to let my birds out? You caused me great loss of money which I paid for them!" The Tzaddiq said to him: "It is written, *His compassion is all over His works* (Ps. 145:9), and my compassion was kindled to let them out of their cage." And the landlord gave the Tzaddiq a cruel beating. And then the Tzaddiq R. Zise said to the landlord: "Know that I go from town to town to collect money for ransoming captives, and, behold, your recompense will be paid in full by God, for you will be left hungry for bread."

And the Tzaddiq went his way, and when he arrived home, he told his brother, the great saintly rabbi, our

---

[30] R. M'shullam Zise (Zusya; d. 1880) was Tzaddiq of Annopol. His brother was R. Elimelekh of Lizhensk (1717–87).

master R. Elimelekh, what had happened. And many days later the two brothers Tzaddiqim sat at a meal, and the Tzaddiq R. Zise washed his hands before his brother the Tzaddiq R. Elimelekh, and at the moment R. Zise was drying his hands prior to reciting the benediction over the bread, a beggar came and stopped at the door. And R. Zise motioned to R. Elimelekh to look at the beggar and said to him: "This is the landlord of the lodging house who beat me so cruelly." And R. Zise asked the man: "It is known to me that you were a rich man, how did it come about that you have become a beggar?" And he told him, "Everything I had was consumed by fire and I remained destitute."

(Kadaner, *Sippurim Nora'im*, 34-35)

The Tzaddiq and the Child

Once on the eve of the holy day, the eve of Yom Kippur, when the entire holy people went to the House of Prayer, and also in the House of Prayer of the saint of blessed memory all the Hasidim who throng in his shadow were gathered, they were waiting for the righteous saint of blessed memory. And he did not come. But it was his way in holiness [to insist] that the supplicants should not wait for him, and therefore when he was late in coming they would pray without the rabbi. Thus they began to recite the Kol Nidre, and after it he arrived in the House of Prayer. And the Hasidim searched after the root of the matter [to find out] what it was. And it became known to them that while he was on his way to the House of Prayer he heard the voice of a child weeping and crying very much, and he ran to that place and he saw that there was nobody there, for the mother of the child had gone to the House of Prayer and had left the child weeping. And the saintly rabbi took pity on the child and spoke to it and jested with it, until sleep fell on the child, and then he went to recite the Kol Nidre.

(Bodeq, *Ma'ase Tzaddiqim*, p. 38)

The Love of Israel

The saintly rabbi said: "I learned to love Israel from a villager who was with a group of other villagers, and when his heart was merry with wine he said to his friend: "Do you love me or don't you?" And the other answered him: "I love you very much." And the villager said: "You say you love me, but you don't know what it is that I need. If you would really love me you would know what I need." And he fell silent and said nothing more. Learn from this that the true love of Israel is to feel all their needs and to suffer all their pains and feel their anguish.

(Bodeq, *Ma'ase Tzaddiqim*, p. 38)

The Tailor's Sleeve

I have heard from the rabbi R. David: Once there came to his holiness[31] an abandoned wife with her brother. The woman had been abandoned by her husband several years before, and they asked of his honor whether, perhaps, with the spirit of holiness, he could find the man so as to obtain from him a letter of divorce. The rabbi said to his attendant that he should bring him a vessel with water. He did so. The holy rabbi said to the woman: "Look into this water." She looked, and he said to her: "What do you see in the water?" And she said: "I see a big city and many houses." He said to her: "Look at the street in which there is the market." And she did so, and said: "I see the market." And he said to her again: "Look at the windows of the houses." And she looked, and suddenly she cried out: "There is my husband in one of the houses, and he is a tailor and he is sitting with many workers and sewing suits, and in his hands he holds a sleeve." And the rabbi said to her: "Snatch the sleeve from his hands!" And she put her hand into the water and pulled out the sleeve, and it was still warm from

[31] The reference is to R. Israel Hapstein of Kozenitz (d. 1814).

the hot iron. And the holy rabbi instructed the woman to keep the sleeve, and all saw this wonderful miracle with the sense of touch. And then the holy rabbi said to the woman and her brother: "Now go in peace, and soon you will obtain the letter of divorce from your husband." And they said to him: "Our holy rabbi, tell us which way should we go?" He said to them: "Wherever you want to." They said: "How can we get hold of a carriage? The driver will ask us where we want to go and we will not know what to answer him." He said to them: "Go, go in peace, and the good and merciful Lord will help you. God willing everything will be well."

And she left the honor of his holiness, and went along the street to find a cart and saw an uncircumcised driving his cart with two horses. They said to him: "Do you want to drive us?" He said to them: "Get into the cart!" And he did not ask them which way they wanted to go, nor did he mention the fare. And they sat and traveled about a half an hour when they reached a forest, and they did not know where they were going, but continued to go in full faith in the Tzaddiq. And suddenly sleep fell upon them, and the uncircumcised toppled over the cart, and they were spilled on the ground, and awoke from their sleep, and, behold, they were lying on the ground in the forest, and they could see neither the uncircumcised nor the cart. And they were filled with fear, for they were in their own eyes as a ship wrecked on high sea, for they did not know the way or where was the city which they needed to reach. And they went about half an hour until they reached the edge of the forest, and they saw a big city nearby. And when the woman saw it, she rejoiced greatly and said to her brother: "With the help of the Lord! The words of the holy Tzaddiq were true and faithful; behold, this is the city I saw in the water."

And when they entered the city the woman said: "Let us walk in the streets, perhaps God will make us chance upon the market which I saw in the water." And they walked for a short while, and instantly the woman noticed the market, and said to her brother: "With the help of God, this is the market I saw." And she walked in the market and looked at the windows until God made her chance upon the house in which was her husband. And when she saw her husband through a window her brother said to her: "Let us go to the rabbi and consult with him, for perhaps your husband will deny that he is your husband." And so they did, and went to the rabbi. And the rabbi asked them: "From where are you?" And they told him: "From Kozenitz." And the rabbi said to them: "That is very far, about eighty miles." And they said: "We left Kozenitz today." And the rabbi was greatly amazed at this miracle, and they related to him all that had happened, and they showed him the sleeve which she had pulled out of the water. And the rabbi was very greatly amazed at the miraculous story and said: "With the help of God who does not withhold His mercy from His people Israel, whose holy spirit inspires the Tzaddiqim of our times!" And the woman described to the rabbi the appearance of the house and the face of her husband. And the rabbi said: "I know him. He settled in this city several years ago, and he has here a wife and children. But do not worry, if God wills, everything will be well. But hold onto the sleeve."

And the rabbi put the woman and her brother in a room, and sent for the tailor. And the tailor instantly came to the house of the rabbi. And the rabbi asked him: "Do you have a wife?" The tailor said to the rabbi: "My lord, is it not known to your highness that I have a wife and children?" The rabbi said to him: "That is known to me, but I am asking you whether you have another wife from before you married this woman?" And the tailor denied it and said: "I never had another wife, for before I married this woman I was a bachelor at the time I came here."

The rabbi said to him: "What kind of suit have you been sewing today?" The tailor said to him: "My lord, my rabbi, let me tell your highness a miraculous thing that happened to me today. I sat at my table and also my workers sat at the table, and we were sewing suits, and in my hand there was a sleeve of the suit of a prince to press it with my hot iron. And behold, I was holding that sleeve in my hands, and behold, we all saw that the sleeve ran away from my hands, like a bird which flies off, and it disappeared. And we searched the whole house and could not find it. And behold, this in our eyes is a great miracle."

The rabbi said to him: "What will you give me if I return the sleeve to you?" The tailor said: "That is impossible!" The rabbi said: "Not at all!" And he went and opened the door and said to the woman: "Come here and give your husband his sleeve!" And the woman went and put the sleeve on the table.

And when the tailor saw the sleeve, he was greatly astonished, and said: "My lord, my rabbi, this indeed is my sleeve!" And in his great amazement he had not yet looked at the face of his wife. The rabbi said to him: "Truly this is your sleeve, but it seems to me that this woman is your first wife." And when the tailor looked into the face of the woman, he recognized her and fainted. And when he came to, the rabbi told him what had happened, and the tailor admitted everything and gave her a letter of divorce.

And R. David heard this miraculous story from the mouth of the woman and her brother and from people who were present when the woman pulled out the sleeve from the water.

(Kadaner, *Sippurim Nora'im*, pp. 36-38)

The Bashful Bride

Many Hasidim would come to the rabbi of Kozenitz, each with his request. Among them was a rich and good-hearted Hasid who always gave alms with an open hand. His request was that the rabbi bless him with sons, for many years had passed since he married, and without children he could not be happy.

But the rabbi each time rejected his request and said: "The time has not come yet."

The rich man returned home embittered. A year later he again came to the rabbi and with tears in his eyes asked him that he give him his blessing. This time the rabbi drew him near and said:

"I shall bless you on condition that you go to the city of Balta. There is a fair there which lasts three days. There you will meet the woman who was once your bride, to whom you returned the *t'naim* [terms of engagement]. Go, ask her forgiveness, and then you will be blessed with children."

"Rabbi," said the Hasid, "many years have passed since I last saw her. How shall I recognize her?"

"She will recognize you," said the rabbi. "But take money along!"

The Hasid returned home and told his wife that he must take a trip to Balta, for the rabbi had sent him there. He traveled to Balta and took a room in a lodging place. On the first day of the fair he walked about in the alleyways of the marketplace, and when he got tired, without meeting his bride, he returned to his lodgings. Next day the same thing happened. On the third day of the fair, in the afternoon, suddenly rain began to fall. There was thunder and lightning, and the Hasid entered a courtyard to seek cover from the rain until it passed. Suddenly he saw three girls on the other side of the yard. One of them said: "Look, this man was once engaged to me, and he returned the *t'naim* to me."

The Hasid went over to her, and the two other women disappeared. He told her that he had come to ask her for forgiveness, for the rabbi had sent him.

The girl said: "I shall forgive you on condition that you travel to such-and-such a city, and this is the address and the name. There you will find my brother, and give him ten thousand ducats. He has to arrange the wedding of his daughter, and does not have the money he promised as a dowry. Then I shall forgive you."

The Hasid told her that he would give her the money and let her take it to her brother. But she replied that she could not see her brother, and disappeared.

The Hasid had no choice but to travel to that place, and many days later he arrived there. Instantly he went to the address of her brother, and behold, there he saw a man walking to and fro in a room, with a face full of worry. He knocked on the door, entered, and greeted the man with "Peace be upon you!"

"From where does the Jew come?" asked the man.

The Hasid answered: "I have been sent here by your sister to give you ten thousand ducats so you can marry off your daughter."

The man got frightened and said: "Jew! Did you come to mock me and to strew salt on my wounds? My sister died many years ago because she was ashamed that her fiancé returned the *t'naim* and canceled the marriage."

The Hasid became very frightened, but remained undeterred. He took out the money and gave it to the brother of the bride, wished him *mazal tov* [good luck], and disappeared. In the house of the brother they thought that the prophet Elijah had brought the money.

The Hasid returned to the rabbi, tired and affrighted, and told him what had happened. The rabbi said to him: "Return home, and be assured that you will be blessed with sons and daughters!"

The blessing came true, and many children were born to him, and they live in comfort and happiness to this day.

(Lithuanian Jewish Folktale)

The Gift of Elijah

On the eve of the feast of Shavuot two Hasidim, who had lost all their property, went to their rabbi, on foot, and on the way they entered an inn to stay overnight. The innkeeper received them in a friendly manner, and when he learned that they were heading for the court of the rabbi, he gave them a small bottle of wine, a present to the rabbi.

In the evening, when the holiday began, the rabbi's table was full of good things, and there were many bottles of wine, but the rabbi drank only of that small bottle which the two Hasidim had brought him. And after each swallow the rabbi whispered: "The veritable taste of the Garden of Eden!" And he did the same also at the other meals of the holiday.

On their way back home the two Hasidim again stopped by at the same inn in order to buy some bottles of the same wine. But the innkeeper told them that he had had only one single bottle, and told them this story:

"Many years ago, when I was a young man I was a *shohet* [ritual slaughterer] and circumciser. Once, on the eve of Yom Kippur, I was busy early in the morning with slaughtering the *Kapparot*,[32] and there was a very long line of people waiting with their birds in their hands. And suddenly a village Jew drove up with his cart, and with tears in his eyes asked me to go with him to circumcise his son. I knew that the village in which he lived was far, but is it possible to leave a Jewish child uncircumcised? Without thinking much, I left all the slaughtering in the hands of the other *shohet* of the town, and set out on the trip. When I reached the house in the village, I found in it the woman in childbed all alone, for who would trouble himself on such a day, the eve of the holy Yom Kippur, to go to such a remote place? All the people had gone to the synagogue in the nearby small town, to recite the prayers and the supplications. The trouble was that there was no *sandaq*[33] in the village, and in the meanwhile time was passing and I

---

[32] *Kappara* (pl. *Kapparot*) is the ritual of symbolically transferring one's sins onto a cock (for a man) or a hen (for a woman) before Yom Kippur, after which the bird is slaughtered and eaten. Hence the bird itself is called *Kappara*.

[33] The *sandaq* (akin to "godfather") is the man who holds the child while the circumcision is being performed.

had to leave in order to get home in time for the Yom Kippur evening meal. But all of a sudden an old Jew appeared in the door of the house, and immediately agreed to be the *sandaq*. When the circumcision was finished, the old man disappeared, and the whole thing seemed miraculous in my eyes. The people of the house did not know the old man and had never seen him before. I left instructions with the mother and the father and hurried off, for I wanted to reach home in time. When I did, in fact, get home before it was too late, whom did I find there? The same old man who was the *sandaq*. I instantly invited him to the meal, but he refused, and took out of his pocket a small bottle of wine, gave it to me and said that this was my reward for the great *mitzva* which I fulfilled that day, in doing a good turn to a village Jew rather than earn money by slaughtering the *Kapparot*. And this is what he told me: 'You will enjoy the wine from this bottle on many joyous occasions, until you marry off your youngest grandson.' And, truly, the words of this blessing were fulfilled. Dozens of years have passed since, and I drank this wine at every happy event: at the wedding of my sons and daughters, and then at the weddings of my grandchildren, always from this little bottle which never emptied. And the taste of the wine was like that of the Garden of Eden. And on the day on which you came to my inn we celebrated the 'seven benedictions' at the wedding of my last grandson, and when you came and told me where you were heading, I saw in it a sign from heaven that I must send the bottle to the rabbi."

The two Hasidim looked at one another, and understood everything: that wine was the wine of the prophet Elijah. No wonder, therefore, that the rabbi tasted the taste of the Garden of Eden in it. . . .

(Lithuanian Jewish Folktale)

ABBREVIATIONS
AND ANNOTATED
BIBLIOGRAPHY

ABBA GURION, MID. ("The Mid. of Father Gurion"). Reprinted in
BhM 1:1-18. A Mid. on the Book of Esther, written in the
12th cent.

ABKIR, MID. A Mid. named after the initial letters of the formula
Amen B'Yamenu Ken Y'hi Ratzon ("Amen, in our days, so be it
the will [of God]"), which concludes each homily. No longer
extant, but many excerpts from it are preserved in the *Yalqut
Shim'oni.* It was probably written in the 11th cent.

ABOAB, ISAAC (end of 14th cent.), *Menorat haMoar* ("The Menorah
of Light"), Constantinople, 1514. Ethical religious treatise
which became the most popular work of religious edification
among the Jews in the Middle Ages.

'ADAT TZADDIQIM ("Community of Tzaddiqim"), by Michael Levi
Rodkinson-Frumkin, Lemberg, 1865. No pagination. A
collection of stories about Hasidim and Tzaddiqim.

ADDITIONS TO DANIEL. Apocryphal writings, including *Susannah* and
Bel and the Dragon, both written originally in Hebrew in the
3rd or 2nd cent. B.C.E.

AFGHAN JEWISH FOLKTALE. See Haifa Folklore Archives.

AGADAT B'RESHIT ("Legend of Genesis"). Ed. by Solomon Buber,
Cracow, 1903; repr. New York, 1959. Homiletic Mid.
compiled about the 10th cent.

AGADAT MASHIAH ("Legend of the Messiah"). Reprinted in BhM
3:141-43. Mid. fragment contained in the *Mid. Leqah Tov*
("Mid. of Good Teaching") of R. Tuvya ben Eliezer, 11th
cent.

AGADTA DI V'NE MOSHE ("Legend of the Sons of Moses"). Reprinted in BhM 6:15-18. Heroic Mid. about the lost tribes of Israel, identified with the "Sons of Moses." Written probably in the 9th or 10th cent.

AHARON OF APT, *Sefer Keter Shem Tov* ("Book of the Crown of Good Name"), Slavuta, no date. Stories about the Ba'al Shem Tov to whose name the title alludes.

ALFA BETA DI BEN SIRA ("Alphabet of Ben Sira"). First published in Constantinople, 1519; repr. in the OM of J.D. Eisenstain, pp. 35-50. Small treatise attributed to Jeshu'a ben Sira (2nd cent. B.C.E.), but actually the work of an 11th cent. C.E. author. Contains ethical teachings. Another edition was published by Steinschneider, Berlin, 1858.

ALFA BETA DI R. AKIBA ("Alphabet of R. Akiba"). Reprinted in BhM 3:12-64. Contains many mystical and eschatological discussions. Probably from the 8th or 9th cent.

AMORA, pl. *AMORAIM*. Talmudic sages of the 3rd to 5th cent. who lived either in Palestine or in Babylonia, and whose teachings are contained in the Y. and B. respectively.

APOC. OF BAR. I—Apocalypse of Baruch I, also called Baruch II. Printed in Charles. Pseudepigraphic composite work, attributed to the scribe of the prophet Jeremiah. Written in the 1st cent. C.E. Presents a systematic picture of Jewish eschatology of the period.

APOC. OF BAR. II—Apocalypse of Baruch II, also called Baruch III. Printed in Charles. Another pseudepigraphic book containing visions of the scribe of Jeremiah. Written in the 2nd cent. C.E. Extant in a Greek and a Slavonic version.

ARAMA, ISAAC (ca. 1420-1494), *'Aqedat Yitzhaq* ("The Binding of Isaac"), Salonica, 1522; Pressburg, 1849. Philosophical homilies and allegorical commentaries on the Pentateuch.

ARAMA, MEIR (1460-1545), *Sefer Meir T'hillot* ("The Book of Enlightening the Praises"), Venice, 1590. A commentary on the Book of Psalms.

'ASERET HA DIBROT, MID. ("Mid. of the Ten Commandments"). Printed in BhM 1:62-90. Contains a miscellany of cosmogonical descriptions and pious legends, appended to a commentary on the Ten Commandments. From the 11th cent.

ASHKENAZI, YITZHAQ, *Otzrot fun Idishen Humor* ("Treasuries of Jewish Humor"), New York: Tel Aviv Publishers, 1929. Jewish anecdotes in Yiddish.

AVOT DIR. NATHAN ("The Fathers According to R. Nathan"). Extra-canonical minor tractate of the Talmud, a commentary on the Mishna tractate *Avot.* Edited by R. Y'huda haNasi in the 2nd cent. C.E.

AVOT DIR. NATHAN A. A version of the preceding, published with critical apparatus by Solomon Schechter, Vienna, 1887; repr. New York, 1945.

AVRAHAM, Y'HUDA LEV, *Midrash Ribash Tov* ("Mid. of the Ba'al Shem Tov"), Kecskemét (Hungary), 1927. Legends about the Ba'al Shem.

AZULAI, HAYYIM YOSEF DAVID (1724-1806), *D'vash l'Fi* ("Honey For My Mouth"), Livorno, 1801. Treatise by a leading Kabbalist, rabbinical scholar and emissary, known by his acronym as Hida.

B. — *Babylonian Talmud.* After the Bible the most important source book of Jewish religion, and the main subject of study throughout Jewish history. Compiled in Babylonia about 500 C.E. In our source references the abbreviation B. is followed by an abbreviation of the name of the tractate and the folio numbers.

B.C.E. — Before the Common Era.

BACHARACH, NAFTALI HERZ, *'Emeq haMelekh* ("The Valley of the King"), Amsterdam, 1648. Kabbalistic treatise.

BAHYA BEN ASHER, *Bi'ur 'al haTora* ("Commentary on the Tora"), Naples, 1492, Venice, 1546. Commentary on the Pentateuch, written in 1291, by a leading Kabbalist and exegete.

BASS (or BASSISTA or M'SHORER), Shabbatai (1641-1718), *Sifte Hakhamim* ("The Lips of the Sages"), Frankfurt a. M., 1712. A popular commentary on the Bible, written in 1680, and often reprinted.

BAUMINGER, M. S., "Igrot R. Yisrael Ba'al Shem Tov" ("The Letters of R. Yisrael Ba'al Shem Tov"), in Yitzhaq Raphael (ed.), *Sefer Margaliot,* Jerusalem: Mosad haRav Kook, 1933, pp. 164-66.

BENAYAHU, MEIR, "The Death of Abraham Azulai" (Hebrew manuscript by Ya'aqov ben Mikhael of Persia, 19th cent.), and "The Miracle of the Sailing Ship" (Hebrew manuscript by the same author), *Edoth,* Jerusalem, 1947-48, 3:100-3.

BEN-YA'AQOV, A., "An Iraqi Jewish Legend About Alexander" (in Hebrew). *Edoth,* Jerusalem 1945-46, 1:184-85.

BEREKHIA HANAQDAN (early 13th cent.), *Mishle Shu'alim* ("Fox Fables"), ed. Lazarus Goldschmidt, Berlin: Erich Reiss, 1921.

BHM — *Bet haMidrash* ("House of Study"), ed. by Adolf Jellinek, 6 vols., 2nd ed., Jerusalem: Bamberger & Wahrmann, 1938. Invaluable collection of minor Midrashim in the original Hebrew or Aramaic, with introductions.

BIRDOGO, Y'HUDA, "The Reward of Charity," publ. (in Hebrew) by Meir Benayahu in *Edoth,* Jerusalem, 1945-46, 1:108-10.

————, "The Three Parts of Hospitality," same publisher, ibid., p. 111.

BLOCH, CHAJIM, *Priester der Liebe* ("Priests of Love"), Zurich-Leipzig-Wien: Amalthea Verlag, 1930. Hasidic stories in German rendering.

BODEQ, MENAHEM MENDEL (d. 1874), *Ma'ase Tzaddiqim* ("Story of Tzaddiqim"), Lemberg, 1864. A collection of stories about Hasidic rabbis.

————, *Seder haDorot heHadash* ("The New Order of the Generations"). Reprinted Jerusalem 1964-65. Hasidic stories.

CAN. RAB. — *Canticles Rabba* (in the original Hebrew: *Shir Hashirim Rabba*). Exegetical Mid. on the Song of Songs, the product of Palestinian Amoraim. Redacted not later than the 4th cent. C.E. Forms part of the standard editions of the *Mid. Rab.*

CARMILLY-WEINBERGER, MOSHE, *Censorship and Freedom of Expression in Jewish History,* New York: Sepher-Hermon Press, 1977. A study of internal Jewish censorship exercised by rabbinical authorities over Jewish books.

CHARLES, R. H., ED., *The Apocrypha and Pseudepigrapha,* 2 vols., Oxford, 1913. The most complete edition of the extra-canonical Jewish writings in English translation, with critical apparatus.

CORDOVERO, MOSES, *Pardes Rimmonim* ("Orchard of Pomegranates"), Cracow, 1592, Koretz, 1780. Major treatise of one of the leading Safed Kabbalists of the 16th cent.

CZECHOSLOVAKIAN JEWISH FOLKTALE. See Haifa Folklore Archives.

DAN. — *Daniel.* Late Biblical book, written partly in Hebrew and partly in Aramaic, and dating from about 164 B.C.E. Contains numerous apocalyptic visions.

DELACRUT, MATITYAHU (16th cent.), *Tzel 'Olam* ("Shadow of the World"), Jerusalem: Yoel Moshe Solomon, 1876. Hebrew translation of Gossuin de Metz (13th cent.), *Image du Monde,* a compilation from various Latin sources on the marvels of the world.

DEUT.—*Deuteronomy.* The fifth book of the Tora (Pentateuch). Contains a recapitulation of the desert wanderings of the Children of Israel, as well as laws, and ends with the death of Moses. Appears to be identical with "the book of the law" which was found in the days of King Josiah, in 621 B.C.E. (cf. 2 Kings 22 f.)

DEUT. RAB.—*Deuteronomy Rabba* (in the original Hebrew: *D'varim Rabba*). Agadic Mid. on the book of *Deut.,* compiled in the 8th cent. Forms part of the standard editions of the *Mid. Rab.*

DEUT. RAB. ed. Saul Lieberman, 2nd ed., Jerusalem: Wahrmann Books, 1964. Scholarly edition of the preceding.

DIVRE HAYAMIM SHEL MOSHE ("The Chronicles of Moses"). Reprinted in BhM 2:11. Epic Mid. about the life of Moses. Similar to the treatment of the subject in the *Sefer haYashar.* Redacted probably in the 9th cent.

D'MUT KISSE SHEL SH'LOMO ("The Shape of Solomon's Throne"). Reprinted in BhM 2:83-85. A fantastic account of the combination of miraculous and moralistic features in the structure and functioning of Solomon's throne. Written not later than the 13th cent.

ECCLES. RAB.—Ecclesiastes Rabba (in the Hebrew original: *Qohelet Rabba*). Exegetical Mid. on the *Book of Eccles.,* compiled in the 8th cent. Forms part of the standard editions of the *Mid. Rab.*

EDOTH ("COMMUNITIES"), A QUARTERLY FOR FOLKLORE AND ETHNOLOGY, ed. Raphael Patai, Jerusalem: The Palestine Institute of Folklore and Ethnology, Oct. 1945—July 1948. Three volumes of this pioneering journal appeared, mostly in Hebrew, partly in English.

ELE EZK'RA, MID. ("Mid. 'These I Remember' "). Printed in BhM 2:64-72. Legend of the ten martyr sages executed by the Romans after the defeat of Bar Kokhba (135 C.E.). Date of origin uncertain.

ELIYAHU KOHEN OF SMYRNA (d. 1729). Manuscript quoted by Azulai, *D'vash l'Fi.*

ELMALEH, ABRAHAM, "R. Ephraim al-Naqawa Arrives in Tlemcen," (in Hebrew). *Edoth,* Jerusalem, 1946-47, 2:201 ff. Story about the 15th-cent. miracle-working rabbi in Morocco.

1 ENOCH. Pseudepigraphic book, written in Hebrew or Aramaic, in the 2nd cent. B.C.E. It discusses the coming of the Messiah, resurrection, and other eschatological themes.

3 ENOCH. Cf. Odeberg.

ESTH. RAB.—*Esther Rabba.* Exegetical Mid. on the *Book of Esther.* Written in the 5th cent. C.E.

EXOD.—*Exodus.* The second book of the *Tora* (Pentateuch), containing the story of the Children of Israel from the slavery in Egypt to their wanderings in the desert, the Revelation on Mount Sinai, and the construction of the Tabernacles, as well as laws. The figure of Moses dominates the entire book. Composed, on the basis of much older sources, in early post-Exilic times.

EXOD. RAB.—*Exodus Rabba* (in the Hebrew original: *Sh'mot Rabba*). Partly exegetical and partly homiletical Mid., put in final shape in the 11th or 12th cent., but containing much older material. Forms part of the standard editions of the *Mid. Rab.*

EZEK.—*Ezekiel.* Biblical book, written in Babylonia by the prophet and priest Ezekiel, in 593-571 B.C.E., although it bears signs of some later editing.

4 EZRA. Also known as the *Second Book of Esdras.* Apocalyptic apocryphal book, purporting to record revelations vouchsafed to Ezra in Babylonia. It centers on the justification of the ways of God. Written, probably in Aramaic, in the 1st cent. C.E.

FARHI, YITZHAQ, *Z'KHUT HA RABBIM* ("The Merit of Many"), Constantinople, 1829. Reprinted by Meir Benayahu in *Edoth,* Jerusalem, 1947-48, 3:99-100.

Fragment (of a Mid.), printed in BhM 5:156. Mythical fragment about the translation of a pious girl into a constellation, which has its parallels in Indian, Persian, and Arabic traditions. From the Middle Ages.

GADOL UG'DOLA, MID. ("Mid. of Great (M.) and Great (F.)"). Printed in BhM 3:121-30. From the 14th cent. at the latest.

GAN 'EDEN W'GEHINNOM ("Paradise and Hell"). Printed in BhM 5:42-51. Compilation of legends from various sources, describing the Garden of Eden, Gehenna, the sufferings of the wicked, the rewards of the pious, etc. From different periods.

GASTER MOSES, *Sefer haMa'asiyyot* ("The Book of Stories"), Ramsgate, 1896. Collection of Hebrew legends.

GEN. — *Genesis.* The first book of the Bible, containing narrative material about the origins of the world, mankind, and the family of Abraham, until the death of Joseph in Egypt. Composed, with the utilization of old sources and traditions, in early post-Exilic times.

GEN. RAB. — *Genesis Rabba* (in the Hebrew original: *B'reshit Rabba*). Exegetical Agadic Mid. on the *Book of Gen.*, written partly in Hebrew and partly in Aramaic. Product of Palestinian Amoraim, 4th cent. C.E. Forms part of the standard edition of the *Mid. Rab.*

GEORGIAN (GRUZINIAN) JEWISH FOLKTALE. From the Caucasus. As told by Hakham Modgorshrili to Tamar Agmon. See Haifa Folklore Archives.

GINZBERG, LOUIS, *The Legends of the Jews,* 7 vols., Philadelphia: The Jewish Publication Society of America, 1909-46. The most valuable summary of the entire Mid. literature.

GOLIAT HAP'LISHTI, MID. ("Mid. of Goliath the Philistine"). Printed in BhM 4:140-41. Mid. fragment describing the attempt of the mother and brother of Goliath to kill David. The legend is similar to the one found in B. Sanh. 95a.

HAGADOL, MID. ("The Great Mid."), on *Exod.,* ed. by Mordecai Margalioth, Jerusalem, 1956. Late Mid. compiled by David ben 'Amram 'Adani, in Yemen, in the 13th cent.

HAI GAON, *Responsum.* Printed in Eliezer Ashkenazi, ed., *Ta 'am Z'qenim* ("The Meaning (or Taste) of the Elders"), Frankfurt a. M., 1854.

HAIFA FOLKLORE ARCHIVES. Stories supplied by Aliza Shenhar from the Folklore Archives of the University of Haifa.

HANE'ELAM, MID. ("The Hidden Midrash"). Part of the *Zohar.* Contains discussions on Creation, the World to Come, the soul, the nature of God, emanations, etc. Printed in separate columns parallel to the main text of the *Zohar,* and in the *Zohar Ḥadash.*

HEKHALOT TEXT, manuscript Munich 22d., publ. by G. Scholem, *Major Trends in Jewish Mysticism,* New York: Schocken Books, 1961, p. 367, n. 47 (in Hebrew).

HELLER BERNHARD, "Das jüdische Märchen" ("The Jewish Tale"), in Johannes Bolte and Georg Polivka, *Anmerkungen zu den Kinder- und Hausmärchen der Brüder Grimm,* Leipzig: Dieterich, 1930, 4:315-418.

ISA.—*Isaiah.* Biblical book containing in most of its first 39 chapters the prophecies of Isaiah who lived in the latter half of the 8th cent. B.C.E. in Jerusalem. Chapters 40-66 were written by one or more anonymous prophets who lived in the middle of the 6th cent. B.C.E. The unknown author(s) of these chapter is (are) often referred to as Deutero-Isaiah.

JER.—*Jeremiah.* Biblical book containing the prophecies of Jeremiah, whose activity fell into the last 40 years of the Kingdom of Judah (626—586 B.C.E.).

JOB. *The Book of Job* has as its frame Satan's vain contest with God for the soul of the pious Job, while its main content is the religious dialogue between Job, his friends, and God, on the problem of the suffering of the righteous. Written probably a little after 400 B.C.E.

JON.— *The Book of Jonah.* One of the twelve minor prophets. Tells of Jonah's attempt to escape from God who commanded him to preach repentance to sinful Nineveh. Written between 400 and 200 B.C.E.

JOSH.—*Joshua.* The first book of the so-called Early Prophets. It tells of the conquest of Canaan, and the division of the land, under the leadership of Joshua, successor to Moses. Put in final shape in the 7th cent. B.C.E.

JUB.— *Book of Jubilees.* Pseudepigraphic book, written in Hebrew, and containing a well developed angelology and demonology, with emphasis on the importance of the observance of the law. From the Maccabean period (2nd cent. B.C.E.).

JUDG.—*Judges.* Biblical book continuing the narrative where the *Book of Joshua* left off. A mixture of legends about, and history of, the struggles of the Tribes of Israel after their penetration into Canaan, and of their charismatic leaders called "Judges," in the 12th and 11th cent. B.C.E. Put in final shape in the 7th cent. B.C.E.

JUDITH. Apocryphal book about the heroism of a Jewish woman who kills the enemy general. Written in Hebrew or Aramaic, about 100 B.C.E.

KADANER, YA'AQOV, *Sefer Sippurim Noraim* ("Book of Terrible Stories"), Munkacs, 1912 (first published Lvov, 1875). Hasidic stories.

KATZ, YITZHAQ (d. 1624), *Sefer Niflaot Maharal* ("Book of Marvels of R. Löw"), Piotrkov, 1909. Stories about R. Y'huda Löw ben Bezalel (c. 1525–1609) of Prague, the legendary creator of the Golem.

KINGS. The two *Books of Kings,* which tell the story of the people of Israel and Judah from the old age of King David (ca. 960 B.C.E.) to the destruction of Jerusalem by Nebuchadnezzar (586 B.C.E.). They conclude with the release of King Jehoiachin from confinement (561 B.C.E.). Probably completed about 550 B.C.E.

KISSE W'IPPODROMIN SHEL SH'LOMO HAMELEKH ("King Solomon's Throne and Hippodrome"). Printed in BhM 5:34-39. Legendary description of the miraculous throne of Solomon and his race-course. Written in the Byzantine period.

KONEN, MID. ("Mid. 'He Established' "). Printed in BhM 2:23-29, and OM, p. 255. Mid. about Creation, Paradise, Hell, etc. Composed not earlier than the 11th cent.

LAM. RAB.—*Lamentations Rabba* (in the original Hebrew: *Ekha Rabbati*). Agadic Mid. on the *Book of Lamentations,* written in a mixture of Hebrew and Aramaic, and redacted in Palestine about the end of the 5th cent. C.E. Forms part of the standard editions of the *Mid. Rab.*

LANDAU, YITZHAQ, *Sefer Zikhron Tov* ("Book of Good Memory"), Piotrkov, 1892. Hasidic stories.

LEV. RAB.—*Leviticus Rabba* (in the original Hebrew: *WaYiqra Rabba*). Homiletical Mid. on the *Book of Leviticus,* written in Hebrew and Aramaic in Palestine, in the 5th cent. C.E. Forms part of the standard editions of the *Mid. Rab.*

L'HANUKKA, MID. ("Mid. For Hanukka"). Printed in BhM 1:132-36. Stories about the fight of the Hasmoneans against the Greeks, in which Judith is given a prominent role. Written not earlier than the 10th cent.

LITHUANIAN JEWISH FOLKTALE. See Haifa Folklore Archives.

M.—*Mishna.* The basic law code of Judaism, compiled by R. Y'huda haNasi in Palestine, ca. 200 C.E. Both the Babylonian Talmud (B.) and the Palestinian Talmud (Y.) are written in the form of extended commentaries to the M.

Ma'ase Avraham Avinu ("Story of Our Father Abraham"). Printed in BhM 1:25-34. Elaborate legend of the life of Abraham, his fight against idolatry, etc. Seems to have been written originally in Arabic and translated into Hebrew.

Ma'ase diR. Y'hoshu 'a ben Levi ("Story of R. Y'hoshu'a ben Levi"). Printed in BhM 2:48-51. A Mid. fragment of Essene origin, redacted probably in the 4th cent. C.E.

Ma'ase Yerushalmi. See Zlotnik.

Ma'asiyyot (Folktales). Collected and published in BhM and OM.

Ma'ayan Hokhma ("Source of Wisdom"). Printed in BhM 1:58-61. Mid. describing the encounter between Moses and the angels in heaven. Belongs to the *Hekhalot* ("Heavenly Halls") literature, and seems to have originated in the 12th cent.

Mass. (Massekhet) Gehinnom ("Tractate About Gehenna"). Printed in BhM 1:147-49. Fantastic description of Hell and the tortures of its inmates. From the early Middle Ages.

Mass. (Massekhet) Hekhalot ("Tractate About the Heavenly Halls"). Printed in BhM 2:40-47. Fantastic description of heavens, God's throne, the angels, etc. Related to the Enoch-literature, and derived from the *Ma'ase Merkava* ("Work of the Chariot") of the Essenes. Probably from the 4th cent. C.E.

Mass. (Massekhet) Hibbut haQever ("Tractate About the Sufferings in the Grave"). Printed in BhM 1:150-52. Description of the tribulations man experiences immediately before and after his death. From the Middle Ages.

Mass. (Massekhet) Kalla ("Tractate 'Bride' "). A minor tractate of the B., written probably by Yehudai Gaon in the 8th cent. Discusses betrothal, marriage, chastity, moral purity, etc.

Mass. (Massekhet) Sofrim ("Tractate of the Scribes"). A minor tractate of the B. Discusses the work of scribes, scrolls, and rules pertaining to religious writings. Dates from the 8th cent.

Menahem Mendel of Vitebsk, *Sefer Liqqute Y'qarim* ("Book of Precious Collectanea"), as quoted in *Mid. Ribash Tov,* by Y'huda Lev Avraham, Kecskemét, 1927.

Michelson, Abraham S.B., *Sefer Shemen haTov* ("The Book of Good Oil"), Piotrkov, 1905. Hasidic stories.

Mid.— *Midrash, pl. Midrashim.* General term denoting the extensive literature of legends, commentaries, homilies, ethical teachings, Biblical exegesis, sermons, proverbs, etc., produced by the Jewish sages and rabbis in Hebrew and Aramaic, from the 4th to the 14th centuries. The individual Midrashim are listed under the title which follows the word "Midrash."

MIROZ, BINYAMIN, *Shivḥe haBeShT* ("Praises of the Ba'al Shem Tov"), Tel Aviv: Talpiyot, 1961.

MOROCCAN JEWISH FOLKTALE. See Haifa Folklore Archives.

MOSES BEN SOLOMON OF BURGOS (1230/35—ca. 1300). Excerpts from his writings published by G. Scholem, in *Tarbiz,* Jerusalem, 1933, 4:208ff.

M'SHALIM SHEL SH'LOMO HAMELEKH ("Parables of King Solomon"). Printed in BhM 4:145-52. Stories glorifying the wisdom of King Solomon, some of which go back to the early Middle Ages.

NAHMAN OF BRATZLAV (1772—1811), *Sefer Sippure Ma'asiyyot* ("Book of Stories of Tales"). Most recent edition: Jerusalem: Bratzlav Hasidim, 1973. Hasidic stories by the great-grandson of R. Israel Ba'al Shem Tov, the founder of Bratzlav Hasidism.

NISSIM BEN YA'AQOV IBN SHAHIN (ca. 990—1062), *Ḥibbur mehaY'shu'a* ("Treatise on Salvation"), Ferrara, 1577. A collection of Hebrew stories and folktales from early sources by the leading North African rabbi of his age.

NOY, DOV, "The Real Daughter of Noah," in Noy's *Iraqi Jewish Folktales* (Orig. Hebrew title *HaNa'ara haY'fehfiyya* etc.), Tel Aviv: 'Am 'Oved, 1965, pp. 100-2.

————, *Jewish Folktales from Libya* (orig. Hebrew title *Shiv'im Sippurim w'Sippur miPi Y'hude Luv*), Jerusalem: BiT'futzot haGola, 1967.

————, *Jewish Folktales from Tunisia* (orig. Hebrew title *Shiv'im Sippurim w'Sippur miPi Y'hude Tunisia*), Jerusalem: BiT'futzot haGola, 1966.

NUM.—*Numbers.* The fourth book of the *Tora* (Pentateuch), telling the story of the Children of Israel from the Revelation at Mount Sinai to their arrival at the Plains of Moab. Composed, with the utilization of much older sources, in early post-Exilic times.

NUM. RAB.—*Numbers Rabba* (in the Hebrew original: *BaMidbar Rabba*). A combination of two different Midrashim on the *Book of Numbers,* both exegetical-homiletical, and both written in the 12th cent. Forms part of the standard editions of the *Mid. Rab.*

ODEBERG, HUGO, *3 Enoch or the Hebrew Book of Enoch,* Cambridge: At the University Press, 1928. Hebrew text, translation and commentary on the Hebrew *Book of Enoch,* which was composed in the 3rd cent. C.E.

OM — *Otzar Midrashim* ("Treasury of Midrashim"), ed. by J. D. Eisenstein, New York, 1915. Collection of 200 minor Midrashim in the original Hebrew and Aramaic, with introductory notes.

PATAI, RAPHAEL, *Adam waAdama* ("Man and Earth in Hebrew Custom, Belief and Legend"), Jerusalem: Hebrew University Press, 2 vols., 1942—43.

————, *The Hebrew Goddess,* 2nd ed., New York: Avon Books, 1978.

————, *The Jewish Mind,* New York: Scribners, 1977.

————, *Man and Temple in Ancient Jewish Myth and Ritual,* 2nd ed., New York: Ktav, 1967.

————, *Sex and Family in the Bible and the Middle East,* New York: Doubleday, 1959.

————, *Society, Culture and Change in the Middle East,* Philadelphia: University of Pennsylvania Press, 1971.

————, "What is Hebrew Mythology?" Transactions of the New York Academy of Sciences, ser. ii, vol. 27, Nov. 1964, pp. 73-81.

PES. DIR. KAHANA—*Pesiqta diR. K.* ("Chapter of R. K."), ed. Bernard Mandelbaum, New York: Jewish Theological Seminary of America, 1962, 2 vols. Homiletical Midrash on the festivals of the year, written in Palestine, probably in the 5th cent.

PES. RAB.— *Pesiqta Rabbati* ("Greater Chapter"), ed. M. Friedmann, Vienna, 1880; repr. Tel Aviv, 1963. Mid. on the festivals of the year, composed beginning with the year 845. In addition to the above edition, I also used the Sklov, 1806, edition.

PIRQE R. ELIEZER ("Chapters of R. E."). Many editions. I used the Warsaw, 1879, edition. Apocalyptic Mid., written in Palestine in the early 8th cent.

P'TIRAT MOSHE, MID. ("Mid. on the Death of Moses"). Repr. in BhM 1:115-29. Describes the last hours of Moses in a most touching manner. Redacted probably in the 9th cent. First printed in Constantinople, 1516.

Q'HAL ḤASIDIM HEḤADASH ("The New Community of Hasidim"), by Yitzḥaq Ber ben Z'vi Hirsh, Lemberg, 1902; repr. 1959–60. Collection of 200 Hasidic stories.

R.—Rabbi. Title of a sage, master, or teacher in Talmudic and later times.

R. YA'AQOV and R. YITZḤAQ, *Qabbalot* ("Mystical Traditions"), ed. G. Scholem in *Madda'e haYahadut,* Jerusalem, 1927, 2:257.

RA'AYA MEHEMNA ("The Faithful Shepherd"). Part of the *Zohar* dealing with the interpretation of the commandments. Written about 1300 by an unknown Kabbalist, in Aramaic. Included in the standard editions of the *Zohar.*

RAB., MID.—*Midrash Rabba* ("The Major Midrash"). The most important collection of Midrashim on the *Five Books of Moses* (the Pentateuch) and the Five Scrolls (*Song of Songs, Ruth, Lamentations, Ecclesiastes,* and *Esther*). Written from the 4th to the 12th cent. Frequently printed.

RABI, SHIM'ON, OF TARNOW, *Notzer T'ena* ("The Keeper of the Fig Tree"), Cracow, 1889. Stories about the acts of Hasidic rabbis.

RAPHAEL, YITZḤAQ, ED., *Sefer Margaliot,* Jerusalem: Mosad haRav Kook, 1933.

ROSENTHAL, SOLOMON GABRIEL, *'Adat Tzaddiqim* ("The Community of Tzaddiqim"), Lemberg, 1865; repr. Jerusalem, 1959. Stories about Hasidic rabbis.

SAM.—The two *Books of Samuel,* telling the story of the People of Israel from the birth of the prophet Samuel (ca. 1070 B.E.C.) to the close of David's reign (960 B.C.E.). Reached substantially its present form by 940–930 B.C.E., after which minor changes were made in the text until ca. 700 B.C.E.

SCHILLER, WALTER, "Das Mehl der Witwe" ("The Flour of the Widow"), *Anthropos,* Vienna, 1917–18, 12-13:513-16. Legend about King Solomon, recorded in 1912 in Dimotika, a small town south of Adrianople, from the mouth of an old Sephardi Jew.

SCHOLEM, G., "New Chapters About Ashmodai and Lilith" (in Hebrew), *Tarbiz,* 1948, 19:160-75.

School of the RaShBA (R. Sh'lomo ben Avraham Adret, ca. 1235–ca. 1310). Published by G. Scholem in *Tarbiz,* Jerusalem, 1948, 19:172. Kabbalistic comments.

SEDER ELIYAHU RABBA AND ZUTA ("The Great and the Small Treatise of Elijah"), ed. M. Friedmann, Vienna, 1904; repr. Jerusalem, 1960. Didactic, ethical Mid., compiled probably in the 8th cent.

SEDER GAN 'EDEN ("Treatise on Paradise"), printed in BhM 3:131-40. Fantastic, Kabbalistic description of the heavenly Paradise, its angels, the pious, etc., with strong Messianic overtones. Written probably in the 11th cent., with the utilization of older sources.

SEDER MAHANOT ("Treatise on the Heavenly Camps"), printed in BhM 5:182-90. Part of a Hebrew version of the Book of Enoch, also called Sefer Hekhalot ("Book of Heavenly Halls"). This text was used by Recanati in his Pentateuch commentary (Venice, 1545), and by others. Contains ancient material, although the time of its final redaction remains uncertain.

SEDER Y'TZIRAT HAW'LAD ("Treatise About the Formation of the Embryo"), printed in BhM 1:153-58. Based on Talmudic and Midrashic sources. Age uncertain.

SEFER HARAZIM ("The Book of Mysteries"), ed. Mordecai Margalioth, Tel Aviv: Y'di'ot Aharonot, 1967. Hebrew book of magic and incantations dating from the 3rd cent. C.E.

SEFER HAYASHAR ("Book of the Straight"), ed. Lazarus Goldschmidt, Berlin: Harz, 1923. Anonymous heroic Mid. written in Spain in the 11th cent., telling about the exploits of early Biblical heroes.

SEFER HEKHALOT ("Book of Heavenly Halls"), attributed to the Tanna R. Yishma'el the High Priest, Lemberg: Ch. Rosen, 1864. A Mid. discussing the heavenly halls as shown by Enoch-Metatron to R. Yishma'el. Probably written in the 4th cent. C.E.

SEFER TASHAQ by R. Yosef. Annotated edition by Jeremy Zwelling in preparation.

SHIR HASHIRIM ZUTA ("The Minor Song of Songs"), ed. S. Buber, 1894. Also known as Agadat Shir haShirim ("Agada of the Song of Songs"). Collection of excerpts from various Midrashim, some no longer extant. Redacted probably in the 10th cent.

SHIVHE HAARI ("Praises of R. Yitzhaq Luria"), Jerusalem: Israel Bach, 1864. A book devoted to the miraculous personality and deeds of R. Yitzhaq Luria, the foremost leader of the Kabbalists in 16th cent. Safed.

SHNEURSOHN, ZELDA, "A Moroccan Jewish Midas Legend" (in Hebrew), *Edoth,* 1945–46, 1:40.

SIPPURE TZADDIQIM ("Stories of Tzaddiqim"), by Michael Levi Rodkinson-Frumkin, Lemberg, 1864. Stories about Tzaddiqim.

SIPPURE TZADDIQIM HEḤADASH ("The New Stories of Tzaddiqim"), by Avraham Yitzḥaq Sobelman, Piotrkov, 1909. Collection of stories about Tzaddiqim.

SITRE TORA ("Secrets of the Tora"). Mainly allegorical explanations of the mysteries of the soul, printed in separate columns in the *Zohar,* paralleling some parts of the main text.

SOFER, YA‘AQOV, OF DOBROMIL, *Sippure Ya‘aqov* ("Stories of Jacob"), Husyatin, 1904. Stories about Tzaddiqim.

SPIRA, NATHAN NATA (d. 1662), *Tuv haAretz* ("The Goodness of the Land"), Venice, 1655; Zolkiev, 1781. Kabbalistic work on the excellencies of the Holy Land.

STORY OF DANIEL. Cf. Zotenberg.

SYRIAN JEWISH FOLKTALE. See Haifa Folklore Archives.

TANḤ. — *Midrash Tanhuma,* Warsaw: Levin-Epstein, N. D. Mid. on the *Five Books of Moses,* dating from the 9th–10th cent.

TANḤ. BUBER. A different version of the preceding, ed. by Solomon Buber, 1885; repr. New York, 1946. 2 vols.

TANNA, pl. TANNAIM, TANNAITES. Palestinian Jewish sages and teachers who lived from the 1st cent. B.C.E. to the end of the 2nd cent. C.E., and whose teachings are contained in the M., the Tosefta, the Talmuds and the Midrashim.

TARGUM. Aramaic translation-paraphrase of the Bible, dating from the 1st–3rd cent. C.E.

TEHILLIM — *Mid. Tehillim,* ed. S. Buber, Vilna, 1891. Agadic Mid. on the Psalms, also called *Shoḥer Tov* ("Good Friend"). Contains material from the 4th to the 12th cent.

TEMURA, MID. ("Mid. of Change"), repr. in BhM 1:106-14. Pseudepigraphic Mid. about contrasts and harmonies in the world. Written in the 12th cent. First printed in Livorno, 1786.

T'FILLAT R. SHIM‘ON BEN YOḤAI ("Prayer of R. S. b. Y."). Printed in BhM 4:117-26. Apocalyptic Mid. containing allusion to the Crusades. Dates from the 12th cent. at the earliest.

TOBIT. Apocryphal book, written probably in the 2nd cent. B.C.E.

It was very popular, and circulated in Hebrew, Aramaic, Syriac, Greek, and Latin versions.

TZIYONI, MENAHEM (14th–15th cent.). German Kabbalist whose major work, the *Sefer Tziyoni* ("Book of Tziyoni"), is a homiletical commentary on the Tora (Pentateuch). First printed in Cremona, 1559.

WAYOSHA', MID. ("Mid. 'And He saved' "). Printed in BhM 1:35-37. Late Agadic fragment on the Song of Moses at the Red Sea. Written in the late 11th cent.

Y.— *Yerushalmi.* The Jerusalem, or Palestinian Talmud. Written partly in Hebrew but mostly in Aramaic, and compiled in the late 4th cent. C.E. Considered less authoritative, and hence is much less studied, than the B. Quoted by tractate and folio of the Venice, 1523, edition.

YA'AQOV BEN MIKHAEL. See Benayahu.

YALQUT HAMAKHIRI ("The Makhiri Collection"), by Makhir ben Abba Mari of the 14th cent., ed. by Y'huda Z'ev Kahana Schapira, Berlin, 1892; repr. Jerusalem, 1964. Anthology of Agadic Midrashim.

YALQUT R'UVENI ("The R'uveni Collection"), by R'uven Katz (d. 1673), Warsaw: Levin-Epstein, 1889. Kabbalistic collection of legends and miscellaneous material based on the weekly portions of the Pentateuch. First printed in Wilmersdorf, 1681.

YALQUT SHIM'ONI ("The Shim'oni Collection"), by R. Shim'on haDarshan (13th cent.) of Frankfurt. The best known and most comprehensive Mid. collection.

YONA, MID. Late Agadic work on the *Book of Jonah.* Repr. in BhM 1:96-105. Written not earlier than the end of the 8th cent. First published in Prague, 1595.

ZECH.— *Zechariah.* Biblical book, one of the twelve minor prophets. Contains in chs. 1-8 the prophecies of Zechariah dated 520–518 B.C.E., to which are added in chs. 9-14 apocalyptic prophecies of anonymous authorship.

ZLOTNIK, JEHUDA L., *Ma'ase Yerushalmi* ("The Story of the Jerusalemite"). Jerusalem: Palestine Institute of Folklore and Ethnology, 1946. Story of a fateful involvement with a demon princess.

ZOHAR ("The Book of Splendor"). Quoted by volume and folio of the Vilna: Rom, 1894 edition (3 vols.). Written by R. Moses de Leon in Spain, from 1270 to 1300. The basic and most influential work of Kabbalism, written in an artificial Aramaic and attributed to the Tanna R. Shim'on ben Yoḥai and his son El'azar.

ZOHAR ḤADASH ("New Zohar"). Warsaw: Levin-Epstein, n.d. A collection of sayings and texts found in the manuscripts of the Safed Kabbalists after the printing of the Zohar, and assembled by Abraham ben Eliezer haLevi B'rukhim.

ZOTENBERG, HERMANN, "Geschichte Daniels" ("The Story of Daniel"), in Adalbert Merx, ed., *Archiv für wissenschaftliche Erforschung* I, Halle, 1870, pp. 385-427. A Persian Jewish apocalypse, written in 940.

ZUNZ, LEOPOLD, *Die gottesdienstlichen Vorträge der Juden,* Berlin: A. Ascher, 1932 (reprint).

INDEX

A

C

D

E

S

T

U

V